The Individual Investor's Guide to

The Top Mutual Funds®

The American Association of Individual Investors

2009 28th Edition

The American Association of Individual Investors is an independent, nonprofit corporation formed in 1978 for the purpose of assisting individuals in becoming effective managers of their own assets through programs of education, information, and research.

Previous editions were published under the titles "The Individual Investor's Guide to No-Load Mutual Funds" and "The Individual Investor's Guide to Low-Load Mutual Funds."

American Association of Individual Investors
625 North Michigan Avenue, Suite 1900
Chicago, Illinois 60611-3151
(312) 280-0170; (800) 428-2244
E-mail: members@aaii.com
Web site: www.aaii.com

ISBN 978-1-883328-25-2
ISSN: 1538-7070

Data in this guide was provided by Morningstar, Inc. and directly from the funds. While the material in this Guide cannot be guaranteed to be error free, it has been obtained from sources believed to be reliable.

AAII is not a registered investment adviser or a broker/dealer. Readers are advised that articles are provided solely for informational purposes and should not be construed as an offer to sell or the solicitation of an offer to buy securities. The opinions and analyses included herein are based on sources believed to be reliable and written in good faith, but no representation or warranty, expressed or implied, is made as to their accuracy, completeness, timeliness, or correctness. Neither we nor our information providers shall be liable for any errors or inaccuracies, regardless of cause, or the lack of timeliness of, or any delay or interruptions in, the transmission thereof to the users. All investment information contained herein should be independently verified.

Past performance is no guarantee of future results. Investment information provided may not be appropriate for all investors. Investment information is provided without consideration of your financial sophistication, financial situation, investing time horizon, or risk tolerance. Readers are urged to consult with their own independent financial advisers with respect to any investment.

Preface

The purpose of this *Guide* is to highlight the funds that would be of most interest to investors: funds open to new investors with historically superior returns in their classes, low expenses, no or low loads and that are directly available from the fund, no intermediary required. The funds are classified into useful categories of similar funds, the way investors approach fund selection, which makes comparison of fund alternatives more efficient and effective. This will allow you to dedicate more time to evaluating the better fund opportunities.

The *Guide* contains the information and performance statistics you will need to make well-informed decisions on your mutual fund investments. Our goal is to provide pertinent information, organized to minimize your time spent collecting and comparing data on the increasingly large universe of mutual funds.

AAII members who would like performance figures for no-load and low-load mutual funds that do not appear in this *Guide* can access this information on our Web site at www.aaii.com in the AAII Guides area.

New for 2009 is an inflation-protected bond category, which covers funds investing in TIPS (Treasury Inflation Protected Securities), on page 406. We have also divided international bond funds into general and emerging categories beginning on page 466.

Information for this *Guide* was gathered from direct contact with funds and from Morningstar, Inc. As always, our objective is full, accurate, and timely disclosure of investment information.

John Bajkowski oversaw the development of the fund analysis format and supervised the data collection and verification. Cara Scatizzi provided research assistance, Jean Henrich provided copy editing and Andrew Lautner designed the cover. Alyna Johnson served as project editor for the *Guide*.

Chicago
March 2009

John Markese, Ph.D.
President

Table of Contents

1

How to Use This Guide

Selecting a mutual fund, while less time-consuming than investing in individual securities, does require some homework. No one should put money into an investment that is not understood. This does not require a detailed investigation of the fund's investments, but it does require an understanding of the investment objectives and strategies and the possible risks and returns of a fund.

This *Guide* is designed to provide you with that understanding. We have kept the chapters brief and to the point, so that individuals new to mutual fund investing will not be overwhelmed with unnecessary details.

Chapters 2 through 10 deal with the basics of investing in mutual funds—diversification; loads; various categories of mutual funds and what they mean; how to read a mutual fund's prospectus and annual report, as well as any other material sent to you; how to evaluate the risk of a mutual fund; how to invest and redeem; common sense rules for mutual fund investors; practical answers to common questions; tie-breakers when choosing a mutual fund; and when to sell.

Chapter 11 describes how the mutual funds were chosen for inclusion in the *Guide*. Chapter 12 is a key to the terms used in the performance tables and the mutual fund data pages, and includes an explanation of how the returns were calculated and what the different risk measures mean.

Chapter 13 presents performance tables, which include the historical performance of funds along with corresponding benchmarks. While past performance is no indication of future performance, it may indicate the quality and consistency of fund management. From this section, you should pick out mutual funds that meet your investment objectives and risk tolerance. These funds can then be examined more closely in the individual mutual fund data pages that follow each performance category listing (Chapter 14).

The funds are grouped by category and listed alphabetically within each category; their ticker symbol and investment category are indicated at the top of the page after the fund's name. The data pages provide 10 years of per share data, performance statistics and risk measures, portfolio information, and shareholder services provided by the fund. Use the telephone numbers and Web addresses provided to contact the funds to request a copy of the prospectus and annual report. Make sure you read the prospectus carefully before investing in any mutual fund.

At the back of the *Guide* is a list of a special category of funds, index funds. And finally, there is an index of all funds that appear in the *Guide*.

2

Investing in Mutual Funds

A mutual fund is an investment company that pools investors' money to invest in securities. An open-end mutual fund continuously issues new shares when investors want to invest in the fund, and it redeems shares when investors want to sell. A mutual fund trades directly with its shareholders, and the share price of the fund represents the market value of the securities that the fund holds.

There are several advantages that mutual funds offer individual investors. They provide:

- Professional investment management usually at a low cost, even for small accounts;
- A diversified group of securities that only a large portfolio can provide;
- Information through prospectuses and annual reports that facilitates comparisons among funds;
- Special services such as check writing, dividend reinvestment plans, telephone switching, and periodic withdrawal and investment plans;
- Account statements that make it easy to track the value of your investment and that ease the paperwork at tax time.

Successful investing takes time and effort, and it requires special knowledge and relevant, up-to-date information. Investors must spend a considerable amount of energy searching for opportunities and monitoring each investment. Professional investment management is relatively cheap with mutual funds. The typical adviser charges about 0.5% annually for managing a fund's assets. For an individual making a $10,000 investment, that comes to only $50 a year.

Of course, mutual fund investing does not preclude investing in securities on your own. One useful strategy would be to invest in mutual funds and individual securities. The mutual funds would ensure your participation in overall market moves and lend diversification to your portfolio, while the individual securities would provide you with the opportunity to apply your specific investment analysis skills.

DIVERSIFICATION

If there is one ingredient to successful investing that is universally agreed upon, it is the benefit of diversification. This is a concept that is backed by a great deal of research, market experience, and common sense. Diversification reduces risk. Risk to investors is frequently defined as volatility of return—in other words, how much an investment's return might vary over a year. Investors prefer returns that are relatively predictable, and thus less volatile. On the other hand, they want returns that are high, but higher returns are accompanied by higher risks. Diversification eliminates some of the risk without reducing potential returns.

Mutual funds, because of their size and the laws governing their operation, provide investors with diversification that might be difficult for an individual to duplicate. This is true not only for common stock funds, but also for bond funds, municipal bond funds, international bond and stock funds—in fact, for almost all mutual funds. Even the sector funds that invest only within one industry offer diversification within that industry. The degree of diversification will vary among funds, but most will provide investors with some amount of diversification.

AVOIDING EXCESSIVE CHARGES

This book focuses on no-load and low-load mutual funds. Investors should realize that:

- A load is a sales commission that goes to the seller of the fund shares;
- A load does not go to anyone responsible for managing the fund's assets and does not serve as an incentive for the fund manager to perform better;
- Funds with loads, on average, consistently underperform no-load funds when the load is taken into consideration in performance calculations;
- For every high-performing load fund, there exists a similar no-load or low-load fund that can be purchased more cheaply;
- Loads understate the real commission charged because they reduce the total amount being invested: $10,000 invested in a 6% front-end load fund results in a $600 sales charge and only a $9,400 investment in the fund;
- If the money paid for the load had been working for you, as in

a no-load fund, it would have been compounding over your holding period.

The bottom line in any investment is how it performs for you, the investor, and that performance includes consideration of all loads, fees, and expenses. There may be some load funds that will do better even if you factor in the load, but you have no way of finding that fund in advance. The only guide you have is historical performance, which is not necessarily an indication of future performance. With a heavily loaded fund, you are starting your investment with a significant loss—the load. Avoid unnecessary charges whenever possible.

SORTING OUT CHARGES

It is best to stick with no-load or low-load funds, but they are becoming more difficult to distinguish from heavily loaded funds. The use of high front-end loads has declined, and funds are turning to other kinds of charges. Some mutual funds sold by brokerage firms, for example, have lowered their front-end loads, and others have introduced back-end loads (deferred sales charges), which are sales commissions paid when exiting the fund. In both instances, the load is often accompanied by annual charges.

On the other hand, some no-load funds have found that to compete, they must market themselves much more aggressively. To do so, they have introduced charges of their own.

The result has been the introduction of low loads, redemption fees, and annual charges. Low loads—up to 3%—are sometimes added instead of the annual charges. In addition, some funds have instituted a charge for investing or withdrawing money.

Redemption fees work like back-end loads: You pay a percentage of the value of your fund when you get out. Loads are on the amount you have invested, while redemption fees are calculated against the value of your fund assets. Some funds have sliding scale redemption fees, so that the longer you remain invested, the lower the charge when you leave. Some funds use redemption fees to discourage short-term trading, a policy that is designed to protect longer-term investors. These funds usually have redemption fees that disappear after six months.

Some funds, usually index funds, may charge a fee, 1% for example, on all new money invested in the fund. This charge defrays the cost of investing the new money. In effect, the new investment pays its way rather than having the transaction costs charged to investments already in the fund.

Probably the most confusing charge is the annual charge, the 12b-1 plan. The adoption of a 12b-1 plan by a fund permits the adviser to use fund assets to pay for distribution costs, including advertising, distribution of fund literature such as prospectuses and annual reports, and sales commissions paid to brokers. Some funds use 12b-1 plans as masked load charges: They levy very high rates on the fund and use the money to pay brokers to sell the fund. Since the charge is annual and based on the value of the investment, this can result in a total cost to a long-term investor that exceeds a high up-front sales load. A fee table (see Chapter 4: Understanding Mutual Fund Statements) is required in all fund prospectuses to clarify the impact of a 12b-1 plan and other charges.

The fee table makes the comparison of total expenses among funds easier. Selecting a fund based solely on expenses, including loads and charges, will not give you optimal results, but avoiding funds with high expenses and unnecessary charges is important for long-term performance.

3 Mutual Fund Categories

Mutual funds come in all shapes and sizes; there are thousands of mutual funds, each with its own characteristics. Many mutual funds, however, have shared investments that generally lead to other characteristics that are similar.

These shared characteristics allow us to divide mutual funds into categories. This chapter defines the mutual fund categories we used for this book. In this guide, the individual fund data pages appear alphabetically within each category; the fund's category is indicated beneath the fund's name.

The tables on pages 25 and 69 provide average returns and risk (see Chapter 12 for definitions of these terms) of funds by category, which illustrate some of the differences between these categories.

STOCK FUNDS

Portfolio managers of mutual funds that invest in common stocks can choose from the stocks of different industries, stocks at different stages of development, and even stocks of different countries and regions. Over the stock market cycles, large stocks behave differently from small stocks, domestic stocks do not move in unison with foreign or emerging market stocks, and stocks in different sectors or industries react differently to the same economic and business conditions.

For investors to make initial investment decisions on stock mutual funds and to compare and evaluate the ongoing performance of investments in stock mutual funds, grouping similar funds together into cohesive categories is a logical first step. The stock fund categories provided in this guide to facilitate your selection and monitoring of fund investments encompass domestic funds, sector funds, and international funds.

DOMESTIC STOCK FUNDS

In funds categorized by stock size, the "cap" stands for capitalization (market share price times number of shares of common stock

Fund Categories

Domestic Stock Funds
- Large-Cap Stock
- Mid-Cap Stock
- Small-Cap Stock

Sector Stock Funds
- Energy/Resources Sector Stock
- Financial/Banking Sector Stock
- Gold Sector Stock
- Health Sector Stock
- Real Estate Sector Stock
- Technology Sector Stock
- Telecommunications Sector Stock
- Utilities Sector Stock

International Stock Funds
- Global Stock
- Foreign Stock
- Regional/Country Stock
- Emerging Stock

Balanced Stock/Bond Funds
- Balanced: Domestic
- Balanced: Global
- Target Date: 2000–2014
- Target Date: 2015–2029
- Target Date: 2030+

Taxable Bond Funds
- Corporate High-Yield Bond
- Mortgage-Backed Bond
- Government: Short-Term Bond
- Government: Intermediate-Term Bond
- Government: Long-Term Bond
- Inflation-Protected Bond

outstanding).

Large-cap stocks are usually stocks of national or multinational firms with well-known products or services provided to consumers, other businesses, or governments. Most of the stocks in the Dow Jones industrial average, the S&P 500 and the NASDAQ 100 are, for example, large-cap stocks. While some large-cap stocks are more volatile than

General Bond: Short-Term
General Bond: Intermediate-Term
General Bond: Long-Term

Municipal Bond Funds

National Muni: Short-Term Bond
National Muni: Intermediate-Term Bond
National Muni: Long-Term Bond
National Muni: High-Yield Bond

State-Specific Bond Funds

Muni: Arizona Bond
Muni: California Bond
Muni: Colorado Bond
Muni: Connecticut Bond
Muni: Florida Bond
Muni: Georgia Bond
Muni: Hawaii Bond
Muni: Kentucky Bond
Muni: Maryland Bond
Muni: Massachusetts Bond
Muni: Michigan Bond
Muni: Minnesota Bond
Muni: New Jersey Bond
Muni: New York Bond
Muni: North Carolina Bond
Muni: Ohio Bond
Muni: Pennsylvania Bond
Muni: Tennessee Bond
Muni: Virginia Bond
Muni: West Virginia Bond
Muni: Wisconsin Bond

International Bond Funds

International: General
International: Emerging

others, a well-diversified mutual fund portfolio of large-cap stocks would perform similarly to most investors' conception of the stock market. Large-cap stocks, as a category, also tend to pay the highest cash dividends, although many large-cap stocks pay no dividends. Large-cap stock funds, in summary, tend to have the lowest volatility and highest dividend yield in the domestic common stock group.

Mid-cap stocks are, as their name implies, smaller than the largest domestic stocks. They are usually established firms in established industries with regional, national and sometimes international markets for their products and services. The S&P MidCap 400 index is a common benchmark for mid-cap stocks. These funds would tend to have lower dividend yields than large-cap funds and to have somewhat higher volatility.

Small-cap stocks are often emerging firms in sometimes emerging industries. But also, these small companies can be established firms with local, regional and sometimes even national and international markets. The benchmark for this group is the S&P SmallCap 600 index. These stocks must have liquid enough trading for mutual funds to invest and, although small, are still listed on the New York Stock Exchange, the American Stock Exchange or NASDAQ. These small-cap funds tend to be more volatile than large-cap and mid-cap funds, have very low dividend yields, and often do not move in tandem with large-cap and mid-cap funds.

The large-, mid- and small-cap categories capture a fund's predominant focus and are important because these size categories do not all behave alike in a market sense. The stocks do tend to move in somewhat different cycles and have pronounced differences in risk and return over time.

One other element can be superimposed over these stock size distinctions to better understand performance and risk in different market environments: the growth or value investment management style of the fund portfolio manager.

A small-cap growth fund will act differently than a small-cap value fund and a mid-cap growth fund is more likely to correlate with a small-cap growth fund than a mid-cap value fund. Portfolio managers of growth-managed funds seek out stocks that have either experienced rapid growth in sales or earnings or are expected to have rapid growth. Often these stocks have high price-earnings ratios (price per share divided by earnings per share) and are volatile when expectations for earnings or sales growth change even slightly. Few growth stocks pay any significant dividend, and they are often concentrated in industries such as technology, health, telecommunications and software.

The value style of investment management emphasizes low price to earnings, low price to sales (price per share divided by sales per share), and higher dividend yields. The trade-off relative to growth stocks is that value stocks have a lower expected growth rate in earnings and sales, but also less risk. Value stocks are often concentrated in insurance, banking, and electric and gas utilities, for example.

For purposes of diversification and risk, it pays to keep in mind the growth/value investment style mix of your stock mutual funds.

SECTOR STOCK FUNDS

Sector funds concentrate their stock holdings in just one industry or a few related industries. They are diversified within the sector, but are not broadly diversified. They may invest in the U.S. or internationally. They are still influenced and react to industry/sector factors as well as general stock market factors. Sector funds have greater risk than diversified common stock funds. While there are a substantial number of sectors represented by mutual funds, a handful of sector designations cover most of the sector fund offerings: energy/resources, financial/banking, gold, health, real estate, technology, telecommunications, and utilities. As is clear from this sector category list, some sectors are of greater risk than others—technology versus utilities, for example. By definition, a sector fund is a concentrated, not diversified, fund holding.

INTERNATIONAL STOCK FUNDS

International stock funds invest in the stocks of foreign firms. Some stock funds specialize in a single country, others in regions, such as the Pacific or Europe, and others invest in multiple foreign regions. In addition, some stock funds—usually termed "global funds"—invest in both foreign and U.S. securities. We have four classifications by type of investment for the international stock funds category—foreign stock funds, global stock funds, regional/country stock funds and emerging market stock funds.

International funds provide investors with added diversification. The most important factor when diversifying a portfolio is selecting investments whose returns are not highly correlated. Within the U.S., investors can diversify by selecting securities of firms in different industries. In the international realm, investors take the diversification process one step further by holding securities of firms in different countries. The more independently these foreign markets move in relation to the U.S. stock market, the greater the diversification benefit will be, and the lower the risk of the total portfolio.

In addition, international funds overcome some of the difficulties investors face in making foreign investments directly. For instance, individuals have to thoroughly understand the foreign brokerage process, be familiar with the various foreign marketplaces and their economies, be aware of currency fluctuation trends, and have access to reliable financial information in order to invest directly in foreign stocks. This can be a monumental task for the individual investor.

There are some risks unique to investing internationally. In addition to the risk inherent in investing in any security, there is an additional exchange rate risk. The return to a U.S. investor from a foreign security depends on both the security's return in its own currency and the rate at which that currency can be exchanged for U.S. dollars. Another uncertainty is political risk, which includes government restriction, taxation, or even total prohibition of the exchange of one currency into another. Of course, the more the mutual fund is diversified among various countries, the less the risk involved.

BALANCED STOCK/BOND FUNDS

In general, the portfolios of balanced funds consist of investments in common stocks and significant investments in bonds and convertible securities. The range as a percentage of the total portfolio of stocks and bonds is usually stated in the investment objective, and the portfolio manager has the option of allocating the proportions within the range. Some asset allocation funds—funds that have a wide latitude of portfolio composition change—can also be found in the balanced category. Some are also global balanced funds, allocating part of their portfolio to foreign investments.

Life cycle funds are also in this category and are designed to match a particular investment objective and risk/return profile. Target maturity balanced funds have year designations that investors can match to their planned retirement date. These funds decrease the allocation to stocks and increase the allocation to bonds as the maturity date nears. Risk declines and income increases as the maturity date approaches. Once the maturity date has passed, they become income funds. Life cycle funds are often composed of other funds from the same fund family.

A balanced fund is generally less volatile than a stock fund and provides a higher dividend yield.

BOND FUNDS

Bond mutual funds are attractive to investors because they provide diversification and liquidity, which is not as readily attainable in direct bond investments.

Bond funds have portfolios with a wide range of average maturities. Many funds use their names to characterize their maturity structure. Generally, short term means that the portfolio has a weighted average maturity of less than three years. Intermediate implies an average maturity of three to 10 years, and long term is over 10 years. The longer the maturity, the greater the change in fund value when interest rates change. Longer-term bond funds are riskier than shorter-term funds, and they usually offer higher yields.

TAXABLE BOND FUNDS

Bond funds are principally categorized by the types of bonds they hold.

Government bond funds invest in the bonds of the U.S. government and its agencies, while mortgage funds invest primarily in mortgage-backed bonds. General bond funds invest in a mix of government and agency bonds, corporate bonds (investment grade), and mortgage-backed bonds. Government and general bond funds are further categorized by maturity: short-term, intermediate-term and long-term.

A special category of inflation-protected bond funds hold Treasury Inflation Protected Securities (TIPS).

Corporate high-yield bond funds provide high income but invest generally in corporate bonds rated below investment grade, making them riskier.

MUNICIPAL BOND FUNDS

Tax-exempt municipal bond funds invest in bonds whose income is exempt from federal income tax. Some tax-exempt funds may invest in municipal bonds whose income is also exempt from the income tax of a specific state.

INTERNATIONAL BOND FUNDS

International bond funds allow mutual fund investors to hold a diversified portfolio of foreign corporate and government bonds.

These foreign bonds often offer higher yields, but carry additional risks beyond those of domestic bonds. As with foreign common stocks, currency risk can be as significant as the potential default of foreign government bonds—a particular risk with the debt of emerging countries. International bond funds are categorized as general or emerging.

INDEX FUNDS

One other fund type deserves a special mention—the index fund. An example of an index fund is the Vanguard 500 Index Fund, categorized as a large-cap stock fund. This fund is designed to match the Standard & Poor's 500 stock index and does so by investing in all 500 stocks in the S&P 500; the amounts invested in each stock are proportional to the firm's market capitalization representation in the S&P 500. Statistics on index funds are quite useful for comparison with other funds, since indexes represent a widely followed segment of the market. Index funds are available covering most major segments of the bond and stock markets—domestic and international. Because they are unmanaged, they make no research efforts to select particular stocks or bonds, nor do they make timing decisions. They are always 100% invested. This passive management approach makes the expenses and the cost of managing an index fund extremely low. Lists of index funds appear in the Appendix at the back of this *Guide*.

Understanding Mutual Fund Statements 4

One of the advantages of mutual fund investing is the wealth of information that mutual funds provide to fund investors and prospective investors. Taken together, the various reports provide investors with vital information concerning financial matters and how the fund is managed—both key elements in the selection process. In fact, mutual fund prospectuses, annual reports, and performance statistics are key sources of information most investors will need in the selection and monitoring process.

To new mutual fund investors, the information may seem overwhelming. However, regulations governing the industry have standardized the reports: Once you know where to look for information, the location will hold true for almost all funds.

There are basically five types of statements produced by the mutual fund: the prospectus; the statement of additional information; annual, semiannual, and quarterly reports; marketing brochures; and account statements. Actually, the second report—the statement of additional information—is part of the prospectus. However, mutual funds are allowed to simplify and streamline the prospectus, if they choose, by dividing it into two parts: a prospectus that all prospective investors must receive, and the statement of additional information—which the fund must send investors if they specifically request it. Some fund families also currently offer an abbreviated or "plain English" profile prospectus.

THE PROSPECTUS

The prospectus is the single most important document produced by the mutual fund, and it is a must-read for investors before investing. Current shareholders must be sent new prospectuses when they are updated, at least once every 14 months.

The prospectus is generally organized into sections, and it must cover specific topics. The front usually gives a quick synopsis of the fund: investment category, sales or redemption charges, minimum invest-

THE PROSPECTUS FEE TABLE: AN EXAMPLE

The following table describes the fees and expenses that may be incurred when you buy, hold or sell shares of the fund.

Shareholder Fees (paid by the investor directly)

Sales charge (load) on purchases and reinvested distributions.........None

Deferred sales charge (load) on redemptions ....None

Annual Operating Expenses (paid from fund assets)

Management fee..0.46%

Distribution and/or Service (12b-1) fees ....None

Other expenses..0.20%

Total annual fund operating expenses..0.66%

This **example** helps you compare the cost of investing in the fund with the cost of investing in other mutual funds.

Let's say, hypothetically, that the annual return for shares of the fund is 5% and that your shareholder fees and the annual operating expenses for shares of the fund are exactly as described in the fee table. This example illustrates the effect of fees and expenses, but is not meant to suggest actual or expected fees and expenses or returns, all of which may vary. For every $10,000 you invested, here's how much you would pay in total expenses if you sell all of your shares at the end of each time period indicated.

1 year	**$67**
3 years	**$211**
5 years	**$368**
10 years	**$822**

Source: Fidelity Equity-Income Fund prospectus, March 31, 2008.

FINANCIAL HIGHLIGHTS: AN EXAMPLE

500 Index Fund Investor Shares

	Year Ended December 31,				
	2007	2006	2005	2004	2003
Net Asset Value, Beginning of Period	**$130.59**	**$114.92**	**$111.64**	**$102.67**	**$81.15**
Investment Operations					
Net Investment Income	2.47	2.11	1.95	1.95[1]	1.44
Net Realized and Unrealized Gain (Loss) on Investments	4.58	15.70	3.31	8.97	21.51
Total from Investment Operations	7.05	17.81	5.26	10.92	22.95
Distributions					
Dividends from Net Investment Income	(2.49)	(2.14)	(1.98)	(1.95)	(1.43)
Distributions from Realized Capital Gains	—	—	—	—	—
Total Distributions	(2.49)	(2.14)	(1.98)	(1.95)	(1.43)
Net Asset Value, End of Period	**$135.15**	**$130.59**	**$114.92**	**$111.64**	**$102.67**
Total Return[2]	**5.39%**	**15.64%**	**4.77%**	**10.74%**	**28.50%**
Ratios/Supplemental Data					
Net Assets, End of Period (Millions)	$63,327	$72,013	$69,375	$84,167	$75,342
Ratio of Total Expenses to Average Net Assets	0.15%	0.18%	0.18%	0.18%	0.18%
Ratio of Net Investment Income to Average Net Assets	1.81%	1.74%	1.75%	1.86%[1]	1.61%
Turnover Rate[3]	5%	5%	6%	3%	1%

1 Net investment income per share and the ratio of net investment income to average net assets include $0.32 and 0.31%, respectively, resulting from a special dividend from Microsoft Corp. in November 2004.

2 Total returns do not include the account service fee that may be applicable to certain accounts with balances below $10,000.

3 Excludes the value of portfolio securities received or delivered as a result of in-kind purchases or redemption of the Fund's capital shares.

Source: Vanguard 500 Index Fund prospectus, April 29, 2008.

ment, retirement plans available, and address and telephone number. More detailed descriptions are in the body of the prospectus.

Fee Table

All mutual fund prospectuses must include a table near the front that delineates all fees and charges to the investor (see example at top left). The table contains three sections: The first section lists shareholder fees, including all front-end and back-end loads and redemption fees; the second section lists all annual fund operating expenses, including management fees and any 12b-1 charges, as a percentage of net assets; and the third section is an illustration of the total cost of these fees and charges to an investor over time. The illustration assumes an initial investment of $10,000 and a 5% growth rate for the fund, and states the total dollar cost to an investor if shares were redeemed at the end of one year, three years, five years, and 10 years.

Financial Highlights

One of the most important sections of the prospectus contains the financial highlights, which provide statistics on income and capital changes per share of the fund (see example at bottom left). The per share figures are given for the life of the fund or five years, whichever is less. Also included are important statistical summaries of investment activities throughout each period. These financial statements are also contained in the annual report.

This section summarizes the financial activity over the fund's fiscal year, which may or may not correspond to the calendar year, to arrive at the ending net asset value for the fund. The financial activity summarized includes increases in net asset value due to dividend and interest payments received and capital gains from investment activity. Decreases in net asset value are due to capital losses from investment activity, investment expenses, and payouts to fund shareholders in the form of distributions.

Potential investors may want to note the line items in this section.

Net investment income represents the dividends and interest earned by the fund during its fiscal year less expenses. Expenses reflect such fund costs as the management fee, legal fees, and transfer agent fees. These expenses are given in detail in the statement of operations section of the annual report. Net investment income is important for investors to note because it reflects the level and stability of net income over the time period. A high net investment income would most likely be found in funds that have income, rather than growth, as their investment category. Since net investment income must be distributed to shareholders to avoid direct taxation of the fund, a high net investment income has the potential of translating into a high tax liability for the investor.

Net realized and unrealized gain (loss) on investments is the change in the value of investments that have been sold (realized) during the period or that continue to be held (unrealized) by the fund.

Distributions to fund shareholders are also detailed. These distributions will include dividends from net investment income for the current fiscal period. Tax law requires that income earned must be distributed in the calendar year earned. Also included in distributions will be any realized net capital gains.

The *net asset value* at the end of the period reflects the value of one share of the fund. It is calculated by determining the total assets of the fund and dividing by the number of mutual fund shares outstanding. The figure will change for a variety of reasons, including changes in investment income, expenses, gains, losses, and distributions. Depending upon the source of change, a decline in net asset value may or may not be due to poor performance. For instance, a decline in net asset value may be due to a distribution of net realized gains on securities.

The financial ratios at the bottom of the financial highlights table are important indicators of fund performance and strategy. The *expense ratio (ratio of total expenses to average net assets)* relates expenses incurred by the fund to average net assets. These expenses include the investment advisory fee, legal and accounting fees, and 12b-1 charges to the fund; they do not include fund brokerage costs, loads, or redemption fees. A high expense ratio is difficult for a fund manager to overcome and detracts from your investment return. In general, common stock funds have higher expense ratios than bond funds, and smaller funds have higher expense ratios than larger funds. International funds also tend to have higher expense ratios than domestic funds. Index funds usually have the lowest expense ratios. The average expense ratio for common stock funds is 1.2%, international stock funds 1.3%, index stock funds 0.4%, and bond funds (taxable and non-taxable) about 0.7%.

The *ratio of net investment income to average net assets* is very similar to a dividend or bond yield. This, too, should reflect the investment category of the fund. Common stock funds with income as a significant part of their investment objective, such as large-cap value funds, would be expected to have the highest ratios and small-cap growth funds would normally have ratios close to 0%. Bond funds would normally have the highest ratios of all funds.

The portfolio *turnover rate* is the lower of purchases or sales divided by average net assets. It reflects how frequently securities are bought and sold by the fund. For purposes of determining the turnover rate for common stock funds, fixed-income securities with a maturity of less than a year are excluded, as are all government securities, short and long term. For bond funds, however, long-term U.S. government bonds are included.

Investors should take note of the portfolio turnover rate, because the higher the turnover, the greater the brokerage costs incurred by the fund. Brokerage costs are not reflected in the expense ratio but instead are directly reflected as a decrease in net asset value. In addition, mutual funds with high turnover rates generally have higher capital gains distributions—a potential tax liability. Small-cap growth stock funds are most likely to have high turnover rates. Some bond funds may also have very high portfolio turnover rates. A 100% portfolio turnover rate indicates that the value of the portfolio was completely turned over in a year; a 200% portfolio turnover indicates that the value of the portfolio was completely turned over twice in a year. The portfolio turnover rate for the average mutual fund is around 100% but varies with market conditions and investment category.

Investment Objective/Policy

The investment objective section of the prospectus describes the types of investments the fund will make—whether it is bonds, stocks, convertible securities, options, etc.—along with some general guidelines as to the proportions these securities will represent in the fund's portfolio. The investment objective statement usually indicates whether it will be oriented toward capital gains or income. In this section, the management will also briefly discuss its approach to market timing, risk assumption, and the anticipated level of portfolio turnover. Some prospectuses may indicate any investment restrictions they have placed on the fund, such as purchasing securities on margin, selling short, concentrating in firms or industries, trading foreign securities, and lending securities; this section may also state the allowable proportions in certain investment categories. The restrictions are usually given in more detail in the statement of additional information.

Fund Management

The fund management section names the investment adviser and gives the advisory fee schedule. Most advisers charge a management fee on a sliding scale that decreases as assets under management increase. Occasionally, some portion of the fund adviser's fees is subject to the fund's performance relative to the market.

Some prospectuses will describe the fund's officers and directors with a short biography of affiliations and relevant experience. For most funds, however, this information is provided in more detail in the statement of additional information. The fund shareholders elect the board of directors; the board of directors selects the fund adviser. The adviser is usually a firm operated by or affiliated with officers of the fund. Information on fund officers and directors is not critical to fund selection. The prospectus also names the portfolio manager of the fund. The portfolio manager is responsible for the day-to-day investment decisions of the fund and is employed by the fund adviser. Who the portfolio manager is and how long the manager has been in the position can be useful in judging historical performance.

Other Important Sections

There are several other sections in a mutual fund prospectus of which investors should be aware. They will appear under various headings, depending upon the prospectus, but they are not difficult to find.

Mutual funds that have 12b-1 plans must describe them in the prospectus. A description of these plans must be prominently and clearly placed in the prospectus, usually in a section titled "Distribution Plan." The distribution plan details the marketing aspects of the fund and how they relate to fund expenses. For instance, advertising, distribution of fund literature, and any arrangements with brokers would be included in the marketing plan; the 12b-1 plan pays for these distribution expenses. The distribution plan section specifies the maximum annual 12b-1 fee that can be charged. Funds often charge less than the maximum. The actual charge to the fund of a 12b-1 plan is listed at the front of the prospectus in the fee table.

The *capital stock* section, or *fund share characteristics* section, provides shareholders with a summary of their voting rights, participation in dividends and distributions, and the number of authorized and issued shares of the fund. Often, a separate section will discuss the tax treatment that will apply to fund distributions, which may include dividends, interest, and capital gains.

The *how-to-buy-shares* section gives the minimum initial investment and any subsequent minimums; it will also list load charges or fees. In addition, information on mail, wire, and telephone purchases is provided, along with distribution reinvestment options, automatic exchange, investment and withdrawal plans, and retirement options.

The *how-to-redeem-shares* section discusses telephone, written, and wire redemption options, including automatic withdrawal plans, with a special section on signature guarantees and other documents that may be needed. Also detailed are any fees for reinvestment or redemption. Shareholder services are usually outlined here, with emphasis on exchanges among funds in a family of funds. This will include any fees for exchanging, any limits on the number of exchanges allowed, and any other exchange restrictions.

STATEMENT OF ADDITIONAL INFORMATION

This document elaborates on the prospectus. The investment objectives section is more in-depth, with a list and description of investment restrictions. The management section gives brief biographies of directors and officers, and provides the number of fund shares owned beneficially by the officers and directors named. The investment adviser section, while reiterating the major points made in the prospectus, gives all the expense items and contract provisions of the agreement between the adviser and the fund. If the fund has a 12b-1 plan, further details will likely be in the statement of additional information.

Many times, the statement of additional information will include much more information on the tax consequences of mutual fund distributions and investment. Conditions under which withholding for federal income tax will take place are also provided. The fund's financial statements are incorporated by reference to the annual report to shareholders and generally do not appear in the statement of additional information. Finally, the independent auditors give their opinion on the accuracy of the fund's financial statements.

ANNUAL, SEMIANNUAL, AND QUARTERLY REPORTS

All funds must send their shareholders audited annual and semiannual reports. Mutual funds are allowed to combine their prospectus and annual report; some do this, but many do not.

The annual report describes the fund activities over the past year and provides a listing of all investments of the fund at market value as of the end of the fiscal year. Sometimes the cost basis of each investment is also given. Looking in-depth at the individual securities held by the fund is probably not the best use of time. However, it is helpful to be aware of the overall investment categories. For instance, investors should look at the percentage invested in common stocks, bonds, convertible bonds, and any other holdings. In addition, a look at the types of common stocks held and the percentage of fund assets by industry classification gives the investor some indication of how the portfolio will fare in various market environments.

The annual report will also have a balance sheet, listing all assets and liabilities of the fund by general category. This holds little interest for investors.

The statement of operations, similar to an income statement, is of interest only in that the fund expenses are broken down. For most funds, the management fee is by far the largest expense; the expense ratio in the prospectus conveys much more useful information. The statement of changes in net assets is very close to the financial information provided in the prospectus, but the information is not on a per share basis. Per share information will, however, frequently be detailed in the annual report in a separate section. Footnotes to the financial statements elaborate on the entries, but other than any pending litigation against the fund, they are most often routine.

The quarterly or semiannual reports are current accounts of the investment portfolio and provide more timely views of the fund's investments than does the annual report.

MARKETING BROCHURES AND ADVERTISEMENTS

These will generally provide a brief description of the fund. However, the most important bit of information is the telephone number to call and request the fund prospectus and annual report, if you have not received them already. These are also usually available on-line and at the fund's Web site.

The rules regarding mutual fund advertising have been tightened and standardized. All mutual funds that use performance figures in their ads must include one-, five-, and 10-year total return figures. Bond funds that quote yields must use a standardized method for computing yield, and they must include total return figures as well. Finally, any applicable sales commissions must be mentioned in the ad.

ACCOUNT STATEMENTS

Mutual funds send out periodic account statements detailing reinvestment of dividend and capital gains distributions, new purchases or redemptions, and any other account activity such as service fees. This statement provides a running account balance by date with share accumulations, an account value to date, and a total of distributions made to date. *These statements are invaluable for tax purposes and should be saved.* The fund will also send out, in January, a Form 1099-DIV for any distributions made in the previous year and a Form 1099-B if any mutual fund shares were sold.

5

Understanding Risk

Risk tolerance refers to the level of volatility of an investment that an investor finds acceptable. The anticipated holding period of an investment is important because it should affect the investor's risk tolerance. Time is a form of diversification; longer holding periods provide greater diversification across different market environments. Investors who anticipate longer holding periods can take on more risk.

The liquidity needs of an investor similarly help define the types of funds that the investor should consider. Liquidity implies preservation of capital, and if liquidity is important, then mutual funds with smaller variations in value should be considered. A liquid mutual fund is one in which withdrawals from the fund can be made at any time with a reasonable certainty that the per share value will not have dropped sharply. Highly volatile small-cap growth funds are the least liquid, and short-term bond funds are the most liquid. The table on page 25 lists the risk characteristics for different mutual fund categories.

A LOOK AT RISK

Risk is the most difficult concept for many investors to grasp, and yet much of the mutual fund investment decision depends on an understanding of risk. There are many different ways to categorize investment risk and numerous approaches to the measurement of risk. If we can assume that the volatility of the return on your mutual fund investment is the concern you grapple with when you think of risk, the task of making decisions about risk becomes easier.

Questions about how much value a mutual fund is likely to lose in a down market or how certain it is that a fund will be worth a given amount at the end of the year are the same concerns as volatility of return. Changes in the domestic and international economies, interest rates, exchange rates, corporate profits, consumer confidence, and general expectations all combine to move markets up and down, creating volatility, or risk.

Risk Characteristics for Different Mutual Fund Categories

Stock Funds	Total Risk	Standard Deviation (%)	Beta (X)	Average Maturity (Yrs)	Bull Market Return (%)	Bear Market Return (%)
Large-Cap Stock	av	17.2	1.06	na	109.4	-41.5
Mid-Cap Stock	abv av	19.9	1.18	na	143.7	-43.4
Small-Cap Stock	abv av	21.0	1.22	na	145.1	-43.5
Growth Style Average	abv av	20.0	1.19	na	129.9	-45.1
Value Style Average	av	17.1	1.03	na	123.1	-38.8
Energy/Resources Sector	high	33.3	1.35	na	270.3	-52.7
Financial/Banking Sector	abv av	20.9	1.11	na	88.2	-50.3
Gold Sector	high	43.5	1.28	na	276.7	-42.9
Health Sector	av	16.4	0.84	na	103.7	-27.7
Real Estate Sector	high	29.0	1.52	na	185.2	-51.6
Technology Sector	high	23.6	1.36	na	148.0	-50.9
Telecommunications Sector	high	22.8	1.31	na	190.1	-48.3
Utilities Sector	av	16.5	0.83	na	179.3	-33.8
Global Stock	abv av	19.6	1.11	na	171.5	-43.8
Foreign Stock	high	22.0	1.26	na	226.8	-49.6
Regional/Country Stock	high	27.2	1.43	na	319.8	-53.4
Emerging Stock	high	33.3	1.81	na	450.8	-62.3
Balanced Stock/Bond Funds						
Balanced: Domestic	blw av	11.0	0.66	7.3	77.3	-25.0
Balanced: Global	blw av	14.2	0.74	7.5	87.1	-29.6
Target Date: 2000-2014	blw av	8.8	0.55	6.2	53.9	-21.0
Target Date: 2015-2029	blw av	12.6	0.80	6.6	87.6	-31.7
Target Date: 2030+	av	16.4	0.99	6.6	114.7	-39.2
Bond Funds						
Corporate High-Yield Bond	blw av	10.8	0.62	6.1	51.3	-22.6
Mortgage-Backed Bond	low	3.3	0.03	7.3	16.8	2.7
Gov't: Short-Term Bond	low	1.8	-0.03	2.2	12.4	6.7
Gov't: Interm-Term Bond	low	4.1	-0.04	5.8	15.7	12.6
Gov't: Long-Term Bond	blw av	14.1	-0.16	19.3	21.6	37.5
Inflation-Protected Bond	blw av	8.2	0.18	9.1	22.3	0.7
General Bond: Short-Term	low	3.7	0.10	2.7	15.3	-6.6
General Bond: Interm-Term	low	5.0	0.14	6.8	20.8	-1.1
General Bond: Long-Term	low	8.0	0.23	15.5	26.1	-2.5
Nat'l Muni: Short-Term Bond	low	1.6	0.03	2.3	11.2	1.8
Nat'l Muni: Interm-Term Bond	low	4.0	0.10	7.6	15.1	-0.8
Nat'l Muni: Long-Term Bond	low	5.2	0.16	12.9	20.0	-4.8
Nat'l Muni: High-Yield Bond	low	7.9	0.33	17.3	25.7	-21.6
International Bond: General	low	6.9	0.13	7.8	28.8	0.7
International Bond: Emerging	blw av	13.3	0.65	9.9	82.8	-17.5

Total risk for a mutual fund measures variation in return from all sources. As an example, variation in return for common stocks is caused by factors unique to the firm, industry variables, and conditions affecting all stocks. Market risk refers to the variables such as interest rates, inflation, and the business cycle that affect all stocks to some degree. In well-diversified portfolios of common stock, the firm and industry risk of the various stocks in the portfolio offset each other; thus, these portfolios tend to have lower total risk, and this total risk is usually composed almost entirely of market risk. For less diversified portfolios, funds that hold very few stocks, or sector funds that concentrate investment in one industry, total risk is usually higher and is composed of firm and industry risk in addition to market risk.

Risk levels based upon total risk are given for all funds. The five categories (high, above average, average, below average, and low) serve as a way to compare the risk inherent in common stock funds, international funds, sector funds, bond funds, or any type of mutual fund. Shorter-term bond funds would be expected to have relatively low total risk while some of the concentrated, less-diversified, small-cap stock funds would likely be ranked in the high total risk category.

The total risk measure will enable you to construct a portfolio of funds that reflects your risk tolerance and the holding period you anticipate for your portfolio. Portfolios for individuals with low risk tolerance and short holding periods should be composed predominantly of funds that are less volatile, with lower total risk. Individuals with high risk tolerances and longer holding periods can form appropriate portfolios by combining mutual funds with higher total risk.

MEASURING TOTAL RISK: STANDARD DEVIATION

Total risk is measured by the standard deviation statistic, a numerical measure of how much the return on a mutual fund has varied, no matter what the cause, from the historical average return of the fund. Higher standard deviations indicate higher total risk. The category risk rank measures the total risk of a fund to the total risk for all funds in the same investment category. The rankings for category risk are high, above average, average, below average, and low. Funds ranked above average and high for category risk should produce returns above the average for the investment category.

The risk index indicates the magnitude of the standard deviation for a fund relative to the median standard deviation for funds in the category. A risk index of 1.2, for example, means that the standard deviation for a fund is 20% higher than the standard deviation for the category.

MEASURING MARKET RISK: BETA AND AVERAGE MATURITY

Market risk is a part of total risk, but measures only the sensitivity of the fund to movements in the general market. This is valuable information for the individual investor—particularly when combined with use of the total risk and category risk rank measures—to judge how a mutual fund will perform in different market situations. The market risk measure used for common stock funds is beta; for bond funds, average maturity is used.

Beta

Beta is a measure of the relative volatility inherent in a mutual fund investment. This volatility is compared to some measure of the market such as Standard & Poor's index of 500 common stocks. The market's beta is always 1.00 by definition, and a money market fund's beta is always 0. If you hold a mutual fund with a beta of 1.00, it will move, on average, in tandem with the market. If the market is up 10%, the fund will be up, on average, 10%, and if the market drops 10%, the fund will drop, on average, 10%. A mutual fund with a beta of 1.50 is 50% more volatile than the market: If the market is up 10%, the fund will be up, on average, 50% more, or 15%; conversely, if the market is down 10%, the fund, on average, will be down 15%. A negative beta, a rare occurrence, implies that the mutual fund moves in the opposite direction of the market's movement.

The higher the fund's beta, the greater the volatility of the investment in the fund and the less appropriate the fund would be for shorter holding periods or to meet liquidity needs. Remember that beta is a relative measure: A low beta only implies that the fund's movement is not volatile relative to the market. Its return, however, may be quite variable, resulting in high total risk. For instance, industry-specific sector fund moves may not be related to market volatility, but changes in the industry may cause these funds' returns to fluctuate widely. For a well-diversified stock fund, beta is a very useful measure of risk, but for concentrated funds, beta only captures a portion of the variability that the fund may experience. Betas for certain sector funds, for example, can be very misleading. Sector funds often have relatively low betas, but these funds are extremely volatile. In addition, the betas of sector funds sometimes change significantly from year to year.

Average Maturity

For all bond funds, the average maturity of the bonds in the portfolio is reported as a market risk measure, rather than beta. The volatility of a bond fund is determined by how the fund reacts primarily to changes in interest rates, although high-yield (junk) bond funds, inflation-protected bond funds and international bond funds can be affected significantly by factors other than interest rates. When interest rates rise, bond funds fall in value; and, conversely, when interest rates fall, bond mutual funds rise in value. The longer the average maturity of the bond fund, the greater will be the variation in the return on the bond fund when interest rates change. Bond mutual fund investors with less risk tolerance and shorter holding periods should seek shorter-maturity funds, and longer-term bond fund investors who are more risk tolerant will find funds with longer maturities a better match.

In the case where a bond fund holds mortgage-backed securities, average maturity may not capture the potential for decline in effective maturity when interest rates fall and mortgages are refinanced. Some mortgage funds also use derivatives, highly leveraged financial instruments that derive their value from movements in specific interest rates or indexes, which further complicate an analysis of their risk. Bond funds that hold corporate bonds and municipal bonds also face changing effective maturities when interest rates decline and bond issuers call bonds before maturity.

Investing & Redeeming: A Look at Fund Services 6

Mutual fund investors are usually most concerned with building and monitoring a portfolio that will deliver the best results, given their objectives. While total return and risk are crucial, services play an important role in facilitating the investment process.

A variety of useful shareholder options exist for investing and withdrawing money, both on an individual transaction and a systematic basis. By using services like those examined in this chapter, you may be able to manage your investments in a simpler, more efficient manner. This may even lead to improved results. Since our coverage is quite comprehensive, you may not find all the services discussed offered by the mutual funds you deal with. In addition, individual procedures can vary somewhat among funds.

MAKING INVESTMENTS

The traditional way of investing in a fund is simply to place a check in the mail. But it could take up to a week—or longer—for your money to arrive and be put to work. By letting a few days elapse you risk paying more per share for a volatile fund than you had expected. Of course, if you're lucky you might pay less.

It frequently makes sense to have a better idea about the price you will pay, especially if you're going to invest a fairly large sum in a more volatile fund. By taking action prior to 4 p.m. Eastern time, it's possible to buy at the price prevailing on the day you place your order. Of course, the price you'll pay is not the only consideration—putting the money to work sooner is beneficial to fixed-income investors who are placing a large amount—say $50,000 or more—into an account and don't want to wait to begin accruing dividends.

Buying at Today's Price

There are several ways to accomplish the purchase of shares at that day's net asset value:

- Transfer from a money fund. You can park your investment in the family's money market fund, wait until you're ready to invest, call the company before 4 p.m. Eastern time and request that the funds be transferred to the portfolio of your choice. Of course, you can usually also transfer from other bond and stock funds in the group. Most fund groups also support online purchase and sale of mutual funds through a secure Web site.

- Wire transfer from your bank. This is the quickest way to move money and is especially recommended for large sums. You will buy in at the day's net asset value if the wire arrives at your account prior to 4 p.m. Eastern time. Your fund company will provide the instructions that you need to convey to your bank. Banks generally charge for this service but mutual funds usually do not. (Incidentally, if you invest by wire you can redeem immediately if you need to—there is no clearing period before your funds will be released.)
- Telephone purchase. Some companies allow you to place a purchase order by phone, locking in that day's price if your order is entered before 4 p.m. Eastern time. You give your instructions to the telephone representative, then send a check or wire for the cost. The payment must reach the account in five to seven business days (depending on the requirements of the company), otherwise the order will be canceled with the investor assuming any resultant losses. Some funds will only accept wires for telephone purchases. There are special conditions that need to be satisfied when you place a telephone purchase order. These requirements, which vary by company, typically include investment minimums and maximums. Minimums may or may not be higher than the fund's usual investment minimum and could be $5,000 or $10,000. The maximum may be based on the total value of your existing accounts with the family. The details should be spelled out in the prospectus. It's best to verify the information with a shareholder representative before entering your order.
- Opening a new account by wire. A number of mutual funds allow you to establish an account by wire, provided you promptly send in a completed application and wire in the cost of your shares. If your wire arrives at your new account before 4 p.m. Eastern time you will buy at the current day's price. Again, there

are minimum investment requirements and other details which vary by fund. The first step is to phone for instructions.

Systematic Investments

The best way to build up your mutual fund assets is simply to put money to work on a regular basis. Modest, ongoing investments can be relatively painless and may eventually lead to significant wealth. For example, at 10% compounded annually, $100 invested at the beginning of each month would grow to $76,566 in 20 years; continuing the investments for just five additional years yields $133,780.

Systematic investment plans offer an ideal way to benefit from dollar-cost averaging. With fixed, periodic investments, you buy more shares when prices are low and fewer when they're high. This results in a lower average cost per share than a simple average of prices on your purchase dates. Dollar-cost averaging works especially well with more volatile portfolios.

There are several ways periodic investments can be made automatically, without sending in a check.

- Direct, systematic transfers. The systematic investment program, where money is taken either from your bank account or paycheck, transfers a predetermined, fixed amount at approximately the same date each month. In order for the payments to be routed directly from your bank account, your financial institution must be an Automated Clearing House (ACH) member, which most are. If you want the investment deducted directly from your paycheck, you need your employer's consent. In addition to the ACH periodic purchase you can make individual ACH purchases in varying amounts whenever you like by phoning your fund company. You would be purchasing your shares at the next business day's price if you call prior to the market's 4 p.m. closing. If you call after 4 p.m., you would buy at the price prevailing at the close of the second business day.
- Dividend transfers. By investing periodic distributions received from one mutual fund into shares of another in the same family, you can build a position in the latter. For example, the monthly dividends from a fixed-income fund could be moved into a small-cap portfolio. Although dividends from investment income are not fixed in amount like systematic purchases, they can be sufficiently stable. It wouldn't take an enormous investment in a fixed-income fund to generate $100 monthly in

dividends. Another example might be the transfer of quarterly income dividends and annual capital gains distributions from a large-cap fund into shares of a money market or short-term bond fund.

MAKING REDEMPTIONS

A variety of useful approaches are also available when you need to withdraw money from your mutual fund.

Mailing in a redemption letter is the old-fashioned way to withdraw money from a fund account. The letter must contain the necessary information—including name(s) of registered owner(s), fund name, account number and redemption amount—and be properly signed by the account owner(s). You may need a signature guarantee for your request to be processed.

There are several faster, simpler ways to redeem shares. Be sure to sign up for these additional services, if necessary.

- Requesting a check by phone. You may telephone your shareholder representative and request that a check be mailed to you or your bank. Of course, you lose interest during the mail transit time, an important consideration with larger redemptions.
- Drawing a check on a fixed-income fund. You can write a check on a money market or other fixed-income fund, perhaps on money just transferred in from another portfolio in the family. Funds generally place a minimum, commonly $100 or $500, on individual checks. If you draw your check on a fund with a fluctuating share price, it would give rise to a taxable event. Money market funds ordinarily maintain a stable $1 price, so you need not be concerned about taxable events when drawing checks on these funds.
- Wiring money from your fund. You can request your company to wire the proceeds to your bank account. This is the quickest way to make a direct transfer of money, and it is recommended for large sums. Your bank and fund will tell you about their fee policies.
- Making an ACH redemption. If you have established an Automated Clearing House linkage between your fund and bank, you can simply phone your company and request that the balance be transferred to your bank. However, it could take a few days for the money to reach your account.

- Many fund families allow you to request an electronic bank transfer and make an exchange with another fund on-line. Shareholders are normally subject to the same time-of-day limits imposed on telephone orders.

Systematic Withdrawal Plans

Systematic withdrawal plans are useful for retirees and others who want to receive regular monthly or quarterly checks. The payments could be sent to someone besides the account holder, such as a student in college or another dependent. A certain minimum account balance, such as $10,000, is required to establish the program. You can change your withdrawals or discontinue them at will. Most funds offer systematic withdrawal programs.

Three key variables you need to come to grips with in establishing a withdrawal plan are:

- Your fund's expected total return;
- The expected rate of inflation; and
- Your target withdrawal percentage.

For people who may be withdrawing money over a decade or longer, a conservative stock fund can lead to the best results. Stocks have generated significantly higher long-run total returns than bonds. In fact, it may be unwise to use a withdrawal plan with a fixed-income fund if you plan on making redemptions over an extended period. For longer-term bond fund investors it's better to only take the monthly dividend checks and not disturb the corpus, since doing so can significantly deplete your capital.

For example, an income-oriented stock fund is a good withdrawal plan candidate. Because your investment in an income-oriented stock fund may not yield sufficient dividends to meet your needs, you may need to dip into principal. But your capital can still grow if your withdrawal rate is not excessive.

The best way to plan your future withdrawal stream is to make some projections. You can get a good estimate of how long your capital will last under different assumptions using annual redemptions, even though you may want to redeem more frequently. The percentage of your initial capital withdrawn annually must be realistic; you don't want to deplete your nest egg too soon.

How Long Will Your Money Last?

If the rate at which you withdraw is too close to or exceeds your

Withdrawal Plans: How Long Will Your Capital Last?

Average Annual Growth[2] (%)	16%	15%	14%	13%	12%	11%	10%	9%	8%	7%	6%	5%
	If the Annual Withdrawal Rate of Your Initial Capital Is[1]:											
	The Number of Years Your Capital Will Last Is:											
1	6	6	7	7	8	9	10	11	13	15	18	22
2	6	7	7	8	9	9	11	12	14	16	19	25
3	6	7	7	8	9	10	11	13	15	18	22	29
4	7	7	8	8	9	10	12	14	16	20	26	37
5	7	7	8	9	10	11	13	15	18	23	32	62
6	7	8	8	9	10	12	14	17	21	28	49	*
7	7	8	9	10	11	13	15	19	25	40	*	*
8	8	8	9	10	12	14	17	22	33	*	*	*
9	8	9	10	11	13	16	20	28	*	*	*	*
10	8	9	10	12	14	18	25	*	*	*	*	*
11	9	10	11	13	16	22	45	*	*	*	*	*
12	9	11	12	15	19	32	*	*	*	*	*	*

[1]*Assumes withdrawals are made annually at the beginning of the year.*

[2]*Can be expressed either as a nominal total return or real (inflation-adjusted) rate.*

**Capital will last indefinitely.*

fund's total return (or growth rate), you will eventually deplete your capital. The table above shows approximately how long, in years, your principal will last given the return generated by your fund and your withdrawal rate on your starting investment amount. The numbers in the body of the table are conservative estimates since they assume withdrawals are made at the beginning of the year. Thus, the first annual redemption would occur immediately. When the portfolio's growth exceeds the withdrawal percentage by a sufficient amount, you could continue withdrawing for an indefinite period; asterisks appear in these instances.

The table can help you determine the best redemption rate. For example, if you assume your fund will grow at 9% per year in nominal terms, you could withdraw 10% of your initial investment amount annually for 20 years. If you trim your withdrawal rate back to 8%, or less, your capital would last indefinitely.

What about inflation? Suppose you expect the price level to increase by 4% per year, on average, and want to withdraw 10% in constant dollars. This means the amount you withdraw each year would need to increase by 4%. In this more realistic case, your capital would be growing at a real, or inflation-adjusted, rate of 5% (9% – 4%). You've simply reduced your 9% nominal return by the anticipated inflation percentage.

Now look in the 5% "average annual growth" row in the table. Your nest egg would last only 13 years, when inflation is factored in, with a 10% withdrawal rate. If you want the capital to last longer, you have to reduce your withdrawals. For instance, at an 8% redemption rate your capital would last 18 years; at 6% it would stretch for 32 years.

Taxes are another consideration. In addition to reducing an expected return for inflation, the careful planner can scale it back further based on an estimate of the impact of taxes on his or her results. Depending on your tax bracket and the fund you're using, your expected return after inflation and taxes could be as low as 2% to 1%, or less.

The table can also help you determine an appropriate withdrawal rate, based on how long your capital must last. Suppose your capital must last at least 20 years, during which you expect 4% inflation yearly. How much can you safely withdraw? If you estimate that your stock fund can return at least 9% annually in nominal terms (5% in real terms), you could withdraw up to 7%—in which case your principal should hold out for 23 years. It would be safer to withdraw a bit less than 7% to provide some margin for error. In fact, in a world with taxes and inflation you risk eventually depleting your capital with a withdrawal rate that exceeds 6% or so, especially if your returns don't live up to your expectations.

Comparing Fixed-Percentage and Fixed-Dollar Withdrawal Options

The most common withdrawal plan involves redeeming a fixed dollar amount over a year, often in monthly increments. The redemptions may be increased periodically for inflation. But if your withdrawal rate is too close to or exceeds the expected annual return after inflation, you would be redeeming an increasing percentage of your remaining balance each year.

Enter the fixed-percent option. As shown in the previous section, you might withdraw, say, 6% of your capital based on its value at the beginning of each year. Your annual dollar withdrawals would differ depending on the changing value of your principal. But if your withdrawal percentage is below the average total return the mutual fund generates, your dollar redemptions would gradually trend upward as your account grows. Naturally, there would be declines following years in which your fund had negative total returns. The fixed-percentage plan could be useful if you want to preserve your capital and perhaps even see it grow, but your withdrawals may not keep pace with inflation.

Fixed-Share Redemptions

Redeeming a constant number of fund shares can be advantageous for some people. Your dollar withdrawals will fluctuate with changes in the fund's share price, but fewer shares will be sold over the years to generate a given sum of withdrawals. Conversely, with a fixed-dollar withdrawal plan you sell more shares when prices are low and fewer when they are high.

The table below illustrates a fixed-share program where 2,000 shares are redeemed annually. The dollar amount withdrawn equals the net asset value multiplied by 2,000. In total, 6,000 shares are withdrawn over three years. Conversely, 6,167 shares would need to be redeemed to accommodate a $20,000 fixed yearly withdrawal. In both cases,

Fixed-Share Withdrawal vs. Fixed-Dollar Withdrawal

Fixed-Share Plan

Year	Price ($)	Shares (No.)	Redemption ($)
1	10	2,000	20,000
2	8	2,000	16,000
3	12	2,000	24,000
Total		6,000	60,000

Fixed-Dollar Plan

Year	Price ($)	Shares (No.)	Redemption ($)
1	10	2,000	20,000
2	8	2,500	20,000
3	12	1,667	20,000
Total		6,167	60,000

$60,000 is redeemed over three years.

The more volatile the fund's price, the fewer shares you would have to redeem to withdraw a given sum of money. But more volatility results in greater variations in monthly withdrawals.

In any case, if you can tolerate the fluctuations you might want to consider the fixed-share withdrawal plan.

Since a number of mutual funds do not formally offer a fixed-share withdrawal option, you could simply phone in periodically and request that the shares be sold and the money transferred to your money fund or sent to you by check.

Liquidation Over a Fixed Period

You could withdraw an increasing percentage of your account balance each year in order to liquidate it within a fixed period. For example, if you want the principal paid out over a four-year period to a child attending college, you could withdraw one-fourth of the account in the first year, one-third in the second, half in the third and the remainder in the fourth.

You may be required to use this approach when making withdrawals from an IRA or other tax-qualified retirement plan. Specifically, after age 70½ you must make your withdrawals over a maximum number of years based on an IRS life expectancy table or face a penalty tax for withdrawing less than your minimum required distribution.

Important Considerations

While withdrawal plans are a useful service, they can lead to certain problems. Here are some to ponder.

- Recordkeeping for tax purposes can be a headache, especially with more frequent redemptions. Each time you make a withdrawal you're selling shares, which results in a taxable event. You need to adopt a systematic procedure for calculating gains and losses on each withdrawal.
- Volatile stock and sector stock funds are generally poor candidates for withdrawal plans. These funds can plunge as fast as they can surge. Withdrawing money when the value of your account has taken a steep decline can lead to problems if it doesn't rebound quickly.
- It's best to be conservative. Too high a withdrawal rate can deplete your capital too soon. Be sure to compare your withdrawal rate with the rate at which you expect your fund to

compound, after inflation. If the former exceeds the latter by too many percentage points, your capital might not last as long as you'd like. The numbers in the table on page 34 are useful in this regard.

- Make sure you consider the impact of taxes on your investment earnings and withdrawals. Of course, the effect of taxes varies depending upon your circumstances, and tax rates are subject to change, but the tax factor is too important to overlook.
- It's a good idea to reevaluate your situation every year or so. Do some revised number crunching to see if you need to make any adjustments in your withdrawals.

What Every Investor Should Know About Mutual Funds 7

In mutual fund investing there are no immutable laws to guide us, as we have in physics. But the collective experience of fund investors can be distilled into a few general rules. Some of it has empirical evidence pointing its way. Most is simply common sense that investors often set aside or forget in the heat of making an investment decision.

TOP PERFORMANCE LISTS ARE DANGEROUS

Probably the single most potentially dangerous action a mutual fund investor can take is to glance at these ubiquitous lists. Funds make the top of the lists not because they are like all the rest of the funds, but because they are decidedly different in some important way. Risk is usually the first important difference. For stock funds, holding stocks that are more volatile than the average stock, holding fewer stocks, or concentrating on only a few industries, raises risk and puts a fund in position to have a greater chance at making the top of the list.

As an example, take sector funds. You can't beat the market by holding the market, which is why you can always find a sector fund of one kind or another at the top of most performance lists. Call it stock picking, or industry weighting, or both, but the net effect is increased risk, and less diversification than the overall stock market.

Picking the funds at the top of the performance lists assumes that either these same stocks, sectors or asset groups will continue to do well, or that the managers can continue to deftly take high risk and move money around better than all the rest.

For domestic bond funds, making the top of the list is a result of the maturity structure of the fund's portfolio. The longest maturity bond funds will be at the top of the performance lists when interest rates are falling, and at the bottom of the lists when interest rates rise. So, investing in bond funds that are at the top of the list is a forecast of interest rates—that they will stay constant or continue in the same direction, a prediction that even professional interest rate prognosticators have been woefully unsuccessful in getting right.

However, these top/bottom lists may hold a small glimmer of value. There is some empirical evidence that stock funds at the top of the heap one period have a greater likelihood to have this superior performance in the next period, on average—"hot hands" may stay hot. Why might a fund's superior performance persist? Probably because the stocks/sectors emphasized in the portfolio continue to have positive momentum into the next period. The shorter the time periods observed, the more likely this is to be true: quarter-to-quarter performance persistance is more likely than year-to-year. But be careful, this is based on performances of top funds on average, and investors don't invest in fund averages, but instead invest in individual funds.

What is more telling, however, is that bad funds tend to continue to be bad. But again, be careful. If an entire category of funds—small-stock value funds or emerging market funds, for example—do poorly, then making the bottom list is probably meaningless if your fund has a lot of peer companions. But if large-stock growth funds populate the top list or simply are not to be found in numbers on the bottom list, and your large-stock growth fund makes an appearance at the bottom of the pile, it isn't a good sign.

And, of course, being a knee-jerk contrarian and buying funds that make the bottom list on the theory that what falls must rise is probably a seriously flawed approach to fund selection.

SIZE MATTERS

The amount of money invested in a fund does matter, but whether larger is better than smaller depends on the investment objective of the fund. With a large-stock index fund, a U.S. government bond fund or a money market fund, the more dollars under management the better. This is because they all operate in very liquid segments of the market where large block transactions are less likely to impact prices—pushing prices up when purchasing and down when selling—and large-scale transactions might prove to be cheaper to accomplish. In addition, large amounts to manage in these funds will not interfere with their investment objective. And, since some fund expenses are fixed, spreading these expenses over more investment dollars should reduce expenses as a percentage of fund assets.

On the other hand, funds with investment objectives that cover less liquid market segments—small stocks or emerging markets—can be too large. That means that individual trades will tend to be larger, which may in turn lead to higher transaction costs tied to security pricing and a wide bid-ask spread on the stocks, making portfolio changes harder to accomplish. The classic response of funds that focus on small stocks is to migrate investments to mid-cap and large stocks when they start to achieve a large asset base.

Actively managed stock funds, when managers are picking stocks and industries and moving money around, can be flooded with new money and find themselves unable to deploy new money expeditiously or effectively. And a flood of new money usually comes after a performance that garners widespread attention and is often difficult to replicate, particularly with the surge of new investment in the fund. An index fund, passively managed and operating in a liquid segment of the market, would not be stumped by a large, sudden inflow of cash.

How large is large? When it comes to net assets, $100 billion may be just fine for an S&P 500 index fund, but $1 billion may choke an actively managed small-stock fund. And beware of funds that had extraordinary performance when they had $100 million or less, a relatively small amount in net assets. In order to invest larger amounts they may have to invest money in more stocks and industries, increasing diversification and decreasing risk, dulling performance.

FUND EXPENSES CAN BE COSTLY

Fund expenses count. And they count more for some investment categories than others. The general rule is that if you invest in a fund that has a significantly higher expense ratio than the average for its category, the long-term performance drag will be costly. Few active fund managers cover the cost of the increased expenses of active management compared to the rock-bottom cost of passively managing an index fund. And if a fund manager is saddled with a relatively high expense ratio due to a small net asset base or high management/research costs, or both, the task of providing above-average category performance is all the more difficult. Some managers, when faced with this dilemma, may boost the risk level of the fund to remain competitive.

Stock funds are more expensive to manage than bond funds, international funds are more expensive than domestic funds, and funds with large asset bases are cheaper than small funds. But if the expense ratio of a bond fund is approaching 1.00%, or a stock fund 1.50%, think twice before investing. And don't forget stock index funds often charge 0.25% or less.

LOADS ARE LOADS

Whether the sales charge, or load, is up front when you buy into the fund, at the end when you sell the fund, or is an as-you-go 12b-1 charge included in the expense ratio, it will cost you. As explained in Chapter 2, loads go to sales organizations and sales personnel; they are not used to secure better portfolio managers, better research or better anything. A load reduces your return dollar for dollar. So if you are not getting financial advice worth the load, buying a loaded fund will cost you, perhaps dearly. Load funds do not outperform on average similar objective funds with no loads, and in fact, they tend to underperform by the amount of the load. How could they, given what loads are used for? Want to invest with a hot manager in a fund that is loaded? Given the iffiness of historical performance as a predictor of future performance, find a no-load fund with a similar style, performance and risk, and save the load charge.

Don't forget that almost all fund performance data is reported without adjusting for front-end or back-end loads. However, performance data does adjust for the 12b-1 charge because it is included in the expense ratio, and fund performance net of the expense ratio is accounted for in performance statistics.

MARKET TIMING DOESN'T WORK

Wouldn't it be wonderful if either you or your fund manager could time the market? You'd make a mint, but it's only a dream. Nobody, but nobody, has consistently guessed the direction of the bond or stock market over any meaningful length of time, although many will make the claim. And remember that to be successful, timing requires two calls: When to get out, and when to get back in.

One reason beyond low expense ratios that index funds are tough to beat is that they are always 100% invested in the market—they have no cash holdings—when thc market takes off. Index funds always call bull markets correctly and they never miss a rally. Yet, they always fail to call a bear market or correction. However, being right on every bull market, as well as avoiding transaction costs and minimizing taxable distributions, is tough to beat.

Since returns on stock and bond funds have been distinctly positive on average annually since we have started keeping records, being ready for bull markets is more important than avoiding bear markets.

When investing in actively managed stock funds, you should hope for superior stock and industry selection, not market timing. If your actively managed portfolio is building up a large cash balance, in excess of 10% of the portfolio, your manager is either engaging in some subtle market timing or there has been a recent rush of cash into the fund. Either case may ultimately lead to poorer performance. For bond funds, when maturities are significantly shortened or lengthened, the impetus is usually market timing driven by an interest rate forecast.

GIVE NEW MANAGERS AND FUNDS TIME TO PROVE THEMSELVES BEFORE INVESTING WITH THEM

With the thousands of funds and fund managers in the investing universe that have track records of at least three years, why invest in an untried fund or manager? While finding funds that will be top performers in their category before the fact is daunting, avoiding disastrous fund investments is within reach. But it requires something upon which to base a judgment. At least a three-year performance history that can be compared to the performance of funds with similar investment objectives and assumed risk is indispensable to evaluate a fund manager or a fund. Consistently favorable performance relative to a peer group of funds over different market environments provides no guarantee of future performance, but it is infinitely better than nothing. You would be surprised how many new funds are quietly buried and new fund managers transferred after the first few disappointing years.

8 Practical Answers to Some Common Mutual Fund Questions

While you can easily call a mutual fund company with specific questions concerning the mechanics of your account and receive a prompt direct answer, the telephone representatives are unlikely to offer an answer to a general investment question, such as: "How many different funds should I own?"

This chapter provides practical answers to commonly asked mutual fund questions. While a series of often-asked questions and answers cannot substitute for a careful and thorough study of mutual funds, the more you know about how mutual funds operate and what contributes to performance, the better prepared you will be to make decisions when investing.

PORTFOLIO MANAGEMENT

How many different mutual funds should I own?

The number of funds suitable for an individual investor will vary depending on individual circumstances—there is no universal number that applies for everyone.

However, as a useful yardstick, consider the range of funds derived from the rationale that diversification should be one of every investor's goals. Simple but broad diversification would imply these funds: a domestic stock fund, a domestic bond fund, and an international stock fund. Dividing the domestic stock portion into these funds—one specializing in small stocks, one in mid-cap stocks, and the other in large-cap stocks—brings the count up to five. Splitting the international stock portion into funds specializing in developed economies and funds specializing in developing and emerging economies makes six. If you prefer a separate European fund and Far East fund, the total is up to seven. Building diversity in your domestic bonds by adding a junk bond fund stretches the number of funds to eight. For tax purposes, the addition of a tax-exempt bond fund would make nine funds. And if we include a money market fund, the number is 10.

The benefits of diversification are difficult to achieve with commitments of less than 10% of your portfolio to any one area, which sets the upper range at not much more than 10 funds. Thus, diversification implies a range of around four to nine funds—all unique in investment objective and security coverage.

Overdiversification results in fund investments that essentially duplicate each other; this adds nothing to performance, but it will add frustration as well as cost in keeping track of and monitoring so many funds.

Should I make sure to invest in more than one fund family, for diversification?

No—it is possible to stay within a fund family and be adequately diversified. However, there is a danger in remaining doggedly within one fund family solely for convenience—you could overlook a better-managed fund elsewhere. For instance, rather than seek out the best international fund, you may choose the one offered by the fund family you are in currently because it is most convenient.

What should I do when my fund closes to new investors?

Nothing. Many funds that close their doors to new investors will allow existing shareholders to continue to invest new money, although sometimes with limits, and most closed funds allow continuation of investments for existing IRA-type accounts.

In the long run, you may be better off if your fund closes and maintains its investment style and flexibility rather than outgrowing its past success.

Should I switch out of a fund if the portfolio manager changes?

No. The change of a portfolio manager is not reason, in and of itself, to leave a fund. Instead, monitor the fund closely to make sure the new manager is continuing the old manager's style, and that any changes won't significantly affect your investment. New portfolio managers have been known to take command of a fund and sell off securities, reflecting a change in style. A significant portfolio realignment might mean greater capital gains distributions, and therefore taxes, unless you hold the fund in a tax-sheltered account. On the other hand, if the fund is an index fund or less actively managed, the portfolio manager may not be all that important. Or the new portfolio manager may continue with the old style and perform just fine.

Switch to a fund with a similar investment objective only when the performance of your fund falls off against other funds with the same investment objective, or if your existing fund changes objectives so that it no longer reflects the objective you are seeking.

If a fund closes before I have a chance to invest and a clone is available, should I invest in the clone fund?

Most funds close to new investors because the portfolio manager feels a larger fund size will hamper his investment flexibility and style. Therefore, it is unlikely that any "clone" fund will in fact be a perfect clone of the original—what would be the point of closing the first one?

Clone funds—the Roman numeral II funds—often do not have the same portfolio manager or precisely the same investment strategy as the original. Any fund should be judged independently on its own financial merits.

PORTFOLIO EXPENSES AND CHARGES

If a fund offers class A, B, C, etc., shares, which one should I buy?

Many funds that have sales charges are offering investors a choice as to how the load will be paid. The different share classes reflect these various options, and generally the choices run somewhat like this: Class A shares have a front-end load, a sales commission on the money invested that is charged when the money is first invested; Class B shares have a back-end load, a sales charge levied on the value of the fund shares when they are sold, which sometimes decreases and eventually disappears; Class C shares might not have a front-end or back-end load, but instead contain an annual charge against your fund's value, a 12b-1 load. Other combinations of varying levels of these three loads may also be offered as an investment option.

If you intend to be invested in the fund for a long time, opt for the front-end or back-end load option, and avoid a high (greater than 0.25%) 12b-1 charge. If you intend to be in the fund only for a few years, select the fund class that does not charge a front-end or back-end load.

Of course, the best course of action is to avoid all loads, or at least high loads.

My fund just imposed a load. Should I bail out?

If your fund imposed a load, you may be grandfathered in and allowed to invest new funds without a load. But if they do charge a load on additional money you want to invest, you are faced with a dilemma. Don't sell on the news that the fund is going to impose a load, but certainly don't commit new money if you will be charged an unreasonable load.

Should I be concerned with fund expenses? After all, it's already reflected in the fund's performance numbers.

Fund expenses, including the management fee, reduce fund performance and all quoted return numbers reflect these costs. But the reason to examine past performance is to get an indication of the portfolio manager's skill. And while the performance numbers may provide some indication of the manager's past skill, the future performance of that manager remains uncertain. The only certainty about the fund's future is its expenses, which are assessed regardless of whether a fund's performance has been relatively good or bad.

Exceptionally high expenses are nearly impossible for portfolio managers to overcome relative to similar funds with average or low expenses. The lower the expenses, the better. Funds with low total assets under management, particularly if they are not part of a large family of funds, will have high expenses relative to assets under management. In addition, newly established funds have a high expense hurdle to overcome.

Should I pay any attention to mutual fund portfolio turnover rates?

The portfolio turnover rate (given in the prospectus) is the lower of purchases or sales of assets in the fund relative to the average assets in the fund for the year. A turnover ratio of 100% indicates that the dollar value of fund purchases or sales equaled the dollar value of total fund assets during the year. This doesn't mean that every single share was changed once during the year; perhaps only a small portion of the assets was transacted intensely. A portfolio turnover ratio of 200% indicates the portfolio, by value, was turned over twice during the year, and so on.

Is this important? Yes. The higher the portfolio turnover, the greater the transaction costs, which can hurt the performance of the fund; while these costs are reflected in the fund's net asset value and its performance figures, they are a concern for the future performance as noted in the question above.

Equally important for taxable investors, the higher the turnover, the more likely the fund is to make capital gains distributions; and taxes must be paid on these distributions.

What is high turnover and what is low? Stock funds average around 80% portfolio turnover, and bond funds are close to 100%.

Use portfolio turnover as a tie-breaker. If you find two funds in the same category that are equally appealing, lean toward the fund with a lower portfolio turnover.

Should I deal only with the fund family or go through some of the discount brokers that offer mutual funds?

Discount brokers such as Charles Schwab and Scottrade offer the convenience of buying different funds without going directly to each fund family and opening separate accounts. Only one brokerage account is necessary, and all mutual fund positions are consolidated in one report. Some of these transactions incur brokerage costs; others are essentially costless.

Not all funds or fund families participate, but if convenience is important and your mutual fund transaction sizes are reasonably large, these fund services offered by discount brokers may deserve a look.

9

Tie-Breakers: Key Points to Consider When It's a Close Call Between Funds

Even when you've done your research and narrowed down your choices for a particular type of fund, sometimes it's not a clear choice between the final two funds.

Flipping a coin is one approach. But a better strategy would be to zero in on a few key points that serve as tie-breakers. While no two funds are precisely alike, top-performing funds can share almost identical investment style and return profiles. This chapter reveals fund tie-breakers to consider and when they might be most important.

AFTERTAX RETURNS

Making tax avoidance your investment focus is a formula for investment disaster. But keeping your eye on aftertax returns is simply wise investing. For example, two funds have similar compound average annual five-year pretax returns. A five-year period is probably long enough to get a picture of how the funds have performed in different market environments, but still recent enough to be relevant.

However, one fund wins on a tax-adjusted return basis for the period, producing a higher aftertax return. Why? The fund might have a lower yield, defined as income divided by net asset value, or simply made less or no distributions of capital gains. Interest earned by the fund from non-tax-exempt sources is taxable at ordinary income tax rates. Municipal bond interest is usually not taxable at the federal level and may not be taxable at the state or local level, if the fund is a state-specific municipal bond fund. Qualified dividend income from stocks held by the fund is subject to the lower long-term capital gains rate. With long-term capital gains rates (on securities sold by the fund but held by the fund for longer than one year) significantly lower than short-term capital gains tax rates, the tax penalty on short-term capital gains is serious. And no capital gains distributions means no taxes, even at the lower capital gains rate. The tax-adjusted return assumes maximum tax rates, where the disparities between capital gains tax rates and income tax rates are the greatest. For investors in lower tax brackets, the tax-adjusted rate difference might not be great.

RISK

Risk is easy to ignore when funds are on the way up, but when markets fall, risk is suddenly right in your face. There are two useful quantitative measures of risk, both calculated based upon monthly fund returns for the last three years. Beta is a measure of a fund's return sensitivity to the returns of the overall stock market, and works well as a risk measure for diversified funds. The higher the beta, the higher the volatility, and therefore risk. Beta can range from very large negative numbers to very large positive numbers, theoretically, but most stock mutual fund betas cluster in the range of 0.50 to 1.50. A zero beta would imply no sensitivity to the stock market, and would more likely belong to a money market fund than a stock fund. A negative beta indicates that, on average, the fund and the market move in opposite directions—also an unlikely figure for any stock fund. The stock market's beta is by definition always 1.00; a fund with a beta of 1.50 is expected to be 50% more volatile than the market, and a fund with a beta of 0.50 would be only half as volatile. For instance, if the market rose 20%, a fund with a beta of 1.50 would be expected to be up 30% [20% + 0.50 (20%)] and if the market fell by 20%, the fund might drop 30%. When two stock funds with similar returns are considered, give a nod to the one with the lower beta.

A second measure of risk is standard deviation, a barometer of volatility from any source, rather than just the stock market. Numerically, standard deviation is less intuitive than beta, but the higher the standard deviation, the greater the risk. Beta assumes a diversified portfolio so that other factors—such as the risk unique to individual stocks and industries—is virtually eliminated, leaving only the risk of market moves. Standard deviation works for all portfolios, diversified or not, and captures the risk from all elements.

If the two funds have similar returns, but are not well diversified, you cannot count on beta. Pick the fund with the lower standard deviation. [For more on fund risk, see Chapter 5: Understanding Risk.]

FUND SIZE

What about total assets under management by the fund? Is bigger better or is smaller better? The answer, of course, is: It depends. A U.S. government bond fund or an index fund probably can't be 'too big,' since, in general, average costs decline and size doesn't get in the way of managing the assets. On the other hand, an aggressively managed fund, particularly one concentrating in mid-cap and small-cap stocks, can lose flexibility and be less nimble when assets grow too large. A fund that is growing too fast can also pose difficulties for the manager, who may have trouble simply getting the new money invested effectively and in a timely manner. Size and rapid growth often force funds to change their investment strategies. For actively managed mid- and small-cap stock funds, give the nod to the smaller asset size fund.

EXPENSE RATIOS

Expense ratios (fund expenses per share divided by net asset value per share) are often overlooked because expenses are netted out against income, and reported returns already include the impact of expenses. So, if the return is competitive, who cares about expenses? Well, two points are important. First, expense ratios are relatively unchangeable—they are easy to forecast, whereas returns are not. Second, the higher the expense of a fund, the greater the drag that a portfolio manager must overcome in the long run in order to be consistently better than other funds in the category. Also, high expense ratios are relatively easier to overcome in fund categories that produce higher returns on average, such as stock funds, than in fixed-income fund categories where expenses have a greater effect on returns. Two municipal bond funds share the same investment objectives and almost identical performance figures, but one is hard to beat on expenses. No contest. [For more on expense ratios, see Chapter 4: Understanding Mutual Fund Statements.]

PORTFOLIO MANAGER TENURE

What better way to judge a fund manager than by the performance of the fund? But the current fund portfolio manager may not have been running the fund when the performance numbers were inked. In an uncertain world, a manager's tenure and performance record provide useful information, at least valuable enough to break a tie.

LOADS

Sales commissions, also known as loads, are probably the clearest tie-breakers. Take the case of two international European stock funds. Both have comparable performance records and even similar risk, expense ratios, size, and manager profiles. They have identical investment objectives, focusing on European stocks, and they are offered by large fund families with a long menu of services. One charges a 3.0% front-end load and a 1.0% redemption fee for all money removed in less than 90 days. Neither front- and back-end loads nor redemption fees are reflected in performance figures. And while returns going forward are always uncertain, the load is charged with perfect certainty and reduces your performance dollar-for-dollar without any beneficial effect on fund performance. Choose the no-load fund. [For more on loads, see Chapter 2: Investing in Mutual Funds.]

10

The Sell Decision: Knowing When to Walk Away

Many people hop in and out of investments all too frequently. That's due in part to the fact that mutual fund advice and information are so freely available that individuals often are persuaded to switch from their more prosaic funds to those that have been delivering more exciting short-term returns. At the opposite extreme, others take the attitude that, once bought, mutual funds can practically be held for a lifetime. That can be true in some instances, but it's often not—you really must rethink your portfolio periodically.

This chapter analyzes legitimate reasons for selling funds, as well as several reasons for staying put.

LOUSY PERFORMANCE

Continuing poor performance of a fund relative to a relevant benchmark and its peers is the number one fund-related reason for selling a mutual fund. You should focus on a fund's returns over the past one, three, and five years. Longer periods can be misleading if there have been major changes in the fund or its management.

While quarterly returns can be monitored to alert you to signs of deteriorating performance, one-year returns are the shortest relevant performance span for long-term investors to examine. However, that doesn't mean you should automatically sell if one-year returns turn up poor. Deciding how much time to give a poor performer to rebound is not easy, but you should seriously start to think about selling a fund that has lagged its benchmark and peers for the past 18 months to two years.

How do you decide on a relevant benchmark? Different benchmarks are available for different market segments and investment styles. In this *Guide*, peer and index benchmarks are provided for each investment category and investment style.

A simple way to determine which benchmark to use is to check your fund's prospectus or annual report to find out what the fund compares its performance against. Another possibility is to compare your fund's performance with an index fund that has roughly the same portfolio composition. However, you're never going to find a perfect benchmark because each fund has its own unique portfolio.

Keep the following points in mind when comparing a fund's performance with its benchmark:

- Mutual funds hold some cash, which will affect their returns relative to a fully invested index.
- Mutual funds incur expenses and trading costs, which will result in some underperformance relative to an index.
- Each fund holds its own blend of stocks and sectors, which will cause its returns to deviate from an index or benchmark.
- A mutual fund may be more or less risky than its benchmark.

A fund that trails its benchmark may be considerably less risky than another in its category that beats the yardstick. For that reason, it's often more revealing to see how a fund performed relative to its peers. You can compare a fund with several of its most similar competitors or against an average for the category.

It's always important to prune out any genuine duds. Some people tenaciously hang onto unproductive investments because they hate to admit that they made a mistake, or they may hate to deal with the tax consequences, or they are loath to expend the effort to fill out the paperwork and move to a new fund or fund family. The problem is that these individuals face a high opportunity cost by clinging to losing or mediocre funds.

OTHER REASONS TO SELL

Don't sell solely because your fund's performance has been disappointing during the past year. Rather, view a single year of underperformance as a signal to take a closer look at the fund and how it fits with your objectives. You should examine the following factors that may impact a fund's performance or its suitability for your portfolio.

- ***A management change:*** Management's ability is crucial for stock funds. But a management change by itself is not always a reason to sell. Perhaps the manager who left was not exceptional. A good replacement for a skilled manager may be waiting in the wings at a large fund company. Conversely, if a star manager leaves a fund, an equal replacement may be hard to find. So take the exit of a star manager as a warning flag, but not an automatic sell. Finally, think seriously about selling if a fund has had more than its share of management turnover, because frequent changes are not healthy and constant shifting of a portfolio creates negative tax and transaction cost consequences.

- ***Rising expenses:*** Significantly higher expenses can hurt performance. Perhaps a 12b-1 fee has been added or management fees have increased. A money market fund may have lifted a fee waiver, causing its yield to drop significantly relative to other similar money market funds. An increase in costs is particularly hard on bond and money market funds because they earn lower gross returns than stock funds.

- ***A surge in assets:*** Performance could falter if a small-stock or micro-cap fund is flooded with investor money. And the fund could experience style drift if it is forced to start investing in bigger companies. Conversely, a surge in assets may be no problem for many other types of funds, particularly for high-grade bond and money market funds or index funds that could benefit from economies of scale.

- ***Shrinking assets:*** Watch out if a fund is rapidly losing assets because investors are jumping ship for some reason. Sizable redemptions can force management to dump good stocks to raise cash. If gains are realized, the fund could make an unusually high capital gains distribution, saddling those who hold shares in taxable accounts with a potentially large tax bill.

- ***A strategy change:*** Funds change strategies in various ways. A new portfolio manager might decide to fully hedge currency risk for a foreign stock fund that previously did not hedge. An active trader might take the helm of a fund that was noted for low turnover. Or a small-cap value fund might become a mid-cap growth fund. A strategy change will not necessarily hurt a fund's performance, but it might not help a laggard either. If the new strategy does not mesh with your objectives, it may be time to move on.

Even if your funds have compared favorably to their benchmarks and peers, there can be other, compelling reasons to sell. Conversely, you may not want to walk away from a laggard just yet. That's because personal factors often dominate in the decision-making process.

TAX CONSIDERATIONS

If selling seems warranted by the performance numbers and other factors, you also need to weigh any potential tax liability you would incur by taking a large gain. On the plus side, the tax consequences may be less painful with long-term capital gains taxed at lower rates. In addition, the long-term capital gains holding period is 12 months. Nevertheless, if you would be in for a hefty tax bill it may make sense to give a lazy performer more time. This obviously is not a concern if your fund is held in an individual retirement account or other tax-advantaged plan.

On the other hand, tax considerations may argue for a sale. Do you have a paper loss in a taxable account? Perhaps you hold a fund that has done poorly because it invests in a stock-market sector, country, or region that has experienced major problems. You might expect an eventual rebound, but in the meantime you could lock in your loss to offset other gains, thereby reducing your tax bill, and then reinvest in a peer fund that has better performance.

DUMPING EXCESS BAGGAGE

Individuals who own too many funds might consider paring their holdings down to a manageable number, perhaps to as few as five or six. Money-losing investments should be pruned along with unsuitable ones. Check for redundancy in your fund portfolio: Funds with different names may in fact share the same objectives and investing style. Your performance likely will improve, and your financial life will be a lot simpler. Plus, it will be much easier to track your asset allocation.

People often make purchases that they regret later. These could include a narrowly focused fund that makes you uncomfortable due to its risk, or any gimmicky fund that really doesn't add to your portfolio.

A broad-based asset allocation fund is unnecessary if you've allocated your assets properly in the first place.

Suppose you hold a fund invested in an asset class that has done poorly even though the manager has fared better than the benchmark. In this case, you need to decide whether you still want that asset class. This is often a difficult call. It depends on factors such as your age, time horizon, and investment outlook.

Generally, mutual funds are viewed as safe because you won't lose as much as you could with an individual stock. But narrowly focused funds such as sector funds can be dicey. If you have allocated too much to a focused fund that's on the skids, think about reducing or eliminating that position before the loss becomes unmanageable. If a volatile fund plunges 50%, it must rebound 100% just to recoup its loss. Consider selling when a speculative fund has fallen 15% to 20% below your cost. Even if you have a relatively minor position, you still may want to walk away.

ALLOCATION CHANGES

Other reasons to sell may arise in your periodic asset allocation review, which should be done at least annually. This entails checking your allocations to large-cap stocks, small-cap stocks, foreign equities, bonds, money market funds, and any subcategories. Recognize that your stock funds could plunge anywhere from 20% to more than 40% within a few months during a bear market. You might want to check and see how your funds and similar ones did during down periods to get a feel for what could happen during a bear market. If you feel uncomfortable with a decline of that magnitude you should rethink your asset allocation.

However, if selling would result in large capital gains, you may wish to consider the following alternatives:

- Sell stock funds held in tax-deferred retirement plans to restore your risk balance.
- Make a more gradual change in your asset allocation by investing any new money in the underweighted categories or reinvesting distributions from your overweighted funds into your underweighted holdings. This second alternative is particularly desirable if you feel there is a good chance your overweighted funds will continue to advance and you wish to make a more modest reallocation for the time being.

STAYING THE COURSE

It's generally unwise to make a big shift from stocks to cash because you fear a bear market. Trimming your stock allocation back a moderate amount—say, from 80% to 65% of your assets—can make sense if you are uncomfortable with the risk level of your fund portfolio, but drastically reducing it because you fear a plunge is basically market timing. The stock market will fluctuate, but you can't pinpoint when it will tumble or shoot up. If you have allocated your assets properly and have sufficient emergency money, you shouldn't need to worry.

Finally, don't panic and sell just after a big plunge. You could lock in a loss and miss any rebound. Panic-selling rarely makes sense because investors tend to overreact to recent bad news, hammering prices to unrealistic lows. But even if a bear market is long and painful, it's important to remember that stocks have a bullish bias and gain a lot more in the bullish phases than they lose on the downside—that's why the long-term trend of the market is up.

Of course, this assumes you have sufficient liquid assets in money market and short-term bond funds to meet emergencies and planned big-ticket expenditures over the next several years. The following is a good rule to keep in mind: Don't have money invested in stock funds that you will need within the next five years. By following the five-year rule, you greatly reduce the risk of having to sell shares after a market tumble.

11

Which Funds Were Included

The funds that appear in *The Individual Investor's Guide to the Top Mutual Funds* were selected from the universe of funds. Following are the various screens we used to arrive at the final selection.

HISTORICAL RECORD

Only those funds with three full years of data that are open to new investors (not closed) are included in the *Guide* so that there is a performance record of significant length and all performance measures can be calculated. Index funds with less than three full years may be included in the *Guide.*

SIZE

Funds must appear in the NASDAQ mutual fund listings and are generally required to have at least $50 million in assets to qualify for inclusion in the *Guide.*

LOADS

The decision as to what constitutes a significant load is difficult, but we took this approach in the *Guide*:

Funds with front-end loads, back-end loads, or redemption fees of 3% or less are included if the fund does not also have a 12b-1 charge. Funds with redemption fees that disappear after six months that also have 12b-1 charges appear in this *Guide.*

Funds with 12b-1 plans and no front- or back-end loads are included in the *Guide;* we note, however, if the fund has a 12b-1 plan and what the annual charge is. A 12b-1 fund fee greater than 0.25% is considered to be high. Investors should carefully assess these plans individually.

Funds that impose a load that exceeds 3% or increase an existing load above 3% are dropped from the *Guide.*

EXPENSES

Funds with significantly higher expense ratios than the average for their category are not included in this *Guide*.

PERFORMANCE

Funds that significantly underperformed the average performance of their category are not included in this *Guide*.

INTEREST AND AVAILABILITY

Only those funds of general interest to mutual fund investors and only those funds that are open (not closed to new investors) and available for investment by individual investors directly from the fund, without restrictions, are included in this *Guide*.

FUNDS NOT INCLUDED

AAII members who would like performance figures for no-load and low-load mutual funds that do not appear in this *Guide* can access this information on our Web site at www.aaii.com. Click on Top Mutual Funds Guide found under Publications in the left-hand menu for a complete downloadable file (covers 1,485 funds).

12

A Key to Terms and Statistics

Most of the information used in the mutual fund data pages and performance tables is provided by Morningstar Inc., but some may come from mutual fund reports (the prospectus and annual and quarterly reports) and solicitation of information directly from the fund. Any data source has the potential for error, however, and before investing in any mutual fund, the prospectus for the fund should be read and the annual report examined.

When *na* appears in the performance tables or on the mutual fund page, it indicates that the number was not available or does not apply in that particular instance. For example, the 10-year annual return figure would not be available for funds that have been operating for less than 10 years. We do not compile the bull and bear ratings for funds not operating during the entire bull or bear market period. Dashes (—) are used generally during years when the fund was not in operation or did not have a complete calendar year of operations. All numbers are truncated rather than rounded when necessary, unless noted otherwise in the following descriptions.

The following provides an explanation of the terms we have used in the performance tables and mutual fund data pages. The explanations are listed in the order in which the data and information appear on the mutual fund pages.

Fund Name: The funds are presented alphabetically by fund name within each category.

Ticker: The ticker symbol for each fund is given in parentheses for those investors who may want to access data with their computer or touch-tone phone. The ticker is four letters and is usually followed by an "X," indicating that it is a mutual fund. For example, the Brandywine Blue fund ticker symbol is BLUEX.

Investment Category: The fund's investment category is indicated at the top of the page below the fund's ticker symbol. After evaluating the information and statistics, we classified all mutual funds in exclusive categories by investment type. [For more complete definitions of the mutual fund investment categories used in the *Guide*, see Chapter 3: Mutual Fund Categories.]

Fund Telephone Number and Internet Address: The management company telephone number and Internet address (if applicable) that investors can call or access to have specific questions answered or to obtain a copy of the prospectus.

Fund Inception Date: The day the fund was made available to the public for purchase.

Performance

Return (%): Return percentages for the periods below.

3yr Annual: Assuming an investment on January 1, 2006, the annual total return if held through December 31, 2008.

5yr Annual: Assuming an investment on January 1, 2004, the annual total return if held through December 31, 2008.

10yr Annual: Assuming an investment on January 1, 1999, the annual total return if held through December 31, 2008.

Bull: This return reflects the fund's performance in the most recent bull market, starting March 1, 2003, and continuing through October 31, 2007.

Bear: This return reflects the fund's performance in the most recent bear market, from November 1, 2007, through December 31, 2008.

Differ From Category (+/–): The difference between the return for the fund and the average return for all funds in the same category for the *3yr Annual, 5yr Annual, 10yr Annual, Bull,* and *Bear* periods. When the difference from category is negative, the fund underperformed the average fund in its investment category for the period by the percent indicated. The rankings, with possibilities of high, above average, average, below average, and low, are relative to all other funds within the same investment category. A rank of high, for example, would indicate that the return is in the highest 20% for that time period of all funds in the investment category. (Note: State-specific muni fund averages are only calculated against other muni funds from the same state.)

Standard Deviation: A measure of total risk, expressed as an annual return, that indicates the degree of variation in return experienced relative to the average return for a fund as measured over the last 36 months. This monthly figure is then annualized to allow comparison to annual rates of return. The higher the standard deviation, the greater the total risk of the fund. Standard deviation of any fund can be compared to any other fund. Ranking possibilities are high, above average, average, below average, and low.

Category Risk Index: A numerical measure of relative category risk, the risk index is a ratio of the standard deviation of the fund to the average standard deviation of funds in the category as measured over the last three years. Ratios above 1.0 indicate higher than average risk and ratios below 1.0 indicate lower than average risk for the category. The ranking possibilities are high, above average, average, below average, and low.

Beta: A risk measure that relates the fund's volatility of returns to the market. The higher the beta of a fund, the higher the market risk of the fund. The figure is based on monthly returns for 36 months. A beta of 1.00 indicates that the fund's returns will, on average, be as volatile as the market and move in the same direction; a beta higher than 1.00 indicates that if the market rises or falls, the fund will rise or fall respectively but to a greater degree; a beta of less than 1.00 indicates that if the market rises or falls, the fund will rise or fall to a lesser degree. The S&P 500 index always has a beta of 1.00 because it is the measure we selected to represent the overall stock market. Beta is a meaningful figure of risk only for well-diversified common stock portfolios. For sector funds and other concentrated portfolios, beta is less useful than total risk as a measure of risk. Beta is not displayed for bond funds since they do not react in the same way to the factors that affect the stock market. For bond funds, the average maturity of the bond portfolio is more indicative of market risk, so it is used in place of beta.

Avg Mat: For bond funds, average maturity in years is an indication of market risk. When interest rates rise, bond prices fall, and when interest rates fall, bond prices rise. The longer the average maturity of the bonds held in the portfolio, the greater the fund's sensitivity to interest rate changes will be, and thus, the greater the risk. The refinancing of mortgages and the calling of outstanding bonds can affect average maturity when interest rates decline. An *na* indicates that the mutual fund did not provide an average maturity figure.

Return (%): This is a total return figure, expressed as a percentage. All distributions were assumed to have been reinvested. Rate of return is calculated on the basis of the calendar year. Return figures do not take into account front-end and back-end loads, redemption fees, or one-time or annual account charges, if any. The 12b-1 charge, as part of the expense ratio, is reflected in the return figure.

Differ From Category (+/–): The difference between the return for the fund and average return for all funds in the same investment category for the time period.

Return, Tax-Adjusted (%): Annual return after adjusting for the maximum federal tax on income, short-term capital gains and long-term capital gains distributions. Some funds may hold portions of their portfolio in investments that receive special tax treatment; adjustments for these tax differences have not been made in this *Guide.*

Per Share Data

Dividends, Net Income ($): Per share income distributions for the calendar year. The timing of net income distributions can be found in the prospectus.

Distrib'ns, Cap Gains ($): Per share distributions for the calendar year from realized capital gains after netting out realized losses. The timing of capital gains distributions can be found in the prospectus.

Net Asset Value ($): Calendar year-end net asset value is the sum of all securities held, based on their market value, divided by the number of mutual fund shares outstanding.

Expense Ratio (%): The sum of administrative fees plus adviser management fees and 12b-1 fees divided by the average net asset value of the fund, stated as a percentage. Brokerage costs incurred by the fund are not included in the expense ratio but are instead reflected directly in net asset value. Front-end loads, back-end loads, redemption fees, and account activity charges are not included in this ratio. Some funds are a "fund of funds" and their expense ratios will not reflect the expenses of funds held by the fund.

Yield (%): The per share annual income distribution made by the fund divided by the sum of the year-ending net asset value plus any capital gains distributions made during the year. This ratio is similar to a dividend yield and would be higher for income-oriented funds and lower for growth-oriented funds. The figure only reflects income; it is not total return. For some funds, the yield may be distorted if the fund reports short-term capital gains as income.

Portfolio Turnover (%): A measure of the trading activity of the fund, which is computed by dividing the lesser of purchases or sales for the year by the monthly average value of the securities owned by the fund during the year. Securities with maturities of less than one year are excluded from the calculation. The result is expressed as a percentage, with 100% implying a complete turnover within one year.

Total Assets (Millions $): Aggregate fund value in millions of dollars at the end of the calendar year.

Portfolio

Portfolio Manager: The name of the portfolio manager(s) and the year when the senior manager(s) began managing the fund are noted, providing additional information useful in evaluating past performance. (Senior managers are listed first.) Funds managed by a committee are so noted. For some funds, a recent change in the portfolio manager(s) may indicate that the long-term annual performance figures and other performance classifications are less meaningful.

Investment Style: For domestic stock funds investment style can be categorized by the size of firms the fund invests in as measured by market capitalization and the investment approach employed by the fund, either growth or value or both. The investment style attributed to the fund indicates that the historical performance of the fund most closely follows the style(s) checked (listed below). More than one size may be checked, indicating a mixture of size, and growth/value may be checked, indicating a blend of growth and value investment approaches. Style is *only* calculated for domestic stock funds.

Style Categories: Large Cap, Mid Cap, Small Cap, Growth, Grth/Val, Value ('Cap' denotes capitalization, which is market price per share for a firm's stock times the number of common stock shares outstanding).

Portfolio: The portfolio composition classifies investments by type and gives the percentage of the total portfolio invested in each. Some funds are a "fund of funds" and their portfolio holdings may be denoted by "100% other." Due to rounding of the percentages and the practice of leverage (borrowing) to buy securities, the portfolio total percentage may not equal 100.0%.

Number of Investments: Indicates the total number of stock, bond and other securities in a fund's portfolio. This figure can give insight into the fund's level of diversification. Generally, the higher the number of investments, the more diversified the fund.

Percent of Portfolio in Top 10 Investments: Investments, expressed as a percentage of the total portfolio assets, in the fund's top 10 portfolio holdings. The higher the percentage, the more concentrated the fund is in a few companies or issues, and the more the fund is susceptible to market fluctuations in these few holdings. Used in combination with number of investments, the percent of portfolio in top 10 investments figure can indicate how concentrated a fund is.

Shareholder Information

Minimum Investment and Minimum IRA Investment:

The minimum dollar amount initial and subsequent investments, by mail, in the fund are detailed. Minimum investment by telephone or by wire may be different. Often, funds will have a lower minimum IRA investment; this is also indicated.

Maximum Fees:

Load: The maximum load percentage is given, if any, and whether the load is front-end or back-end is indicated.

12b-1: If a fund has a 12b-1 plan, the percentage that the fund charges is given.

Other: Redemption fees are given along with the time period, if appropriate. "Maint fee for low bal" indicates that an annual fee may be levied on accounts below a certain threshold.

Services:

IRA: Notes whether the fund offers an individual retirement account option.

Keogh: Notes whether the fund offers a Keogh account option.

Telephone Exchange: Indicates whether telephone exchanges with other funds in the family are permitted.

Fund Performance Rankings and Information 13

When choosing among mutual funds, most investors start with performance statistics: How well have the various mutual funds performed in the past? If past performance alone could perfectly predict future performance, selection would be easy.

What past performance can tell you is how well the fund's management has handled different market environments, how consistent the fund has been, and how well the fund has done relative to its risk level, relative to other similar funds, and relative to the market.

We present performance statistics in several different forms. First, we provide an overall picture, with the average performance of each mutual fund category for the last five years, along with benchmarks for large, mid-cap and small-company domestic stocks; international stocks; bonds; and Treasury bills. The top 50 and bottom 50 mutual fund performers for the last year are given as a reference of recent performance. The list changes each year and reflects the cyclical nature of financial markets and the changing success of individual mutual fund managers. Lists of the top 50 mutual funds ranked by annual return over the last three years, five years, and 10 years are given for a long-term perspective on investment trends of performance.

Since the performance of a fund must be judged relative to similar funds, we have also classified the funds by investment category and ranked them according to their total return performance for the last year. These performance lists appear in Chapter 14 at the start of each category section. To make the comparison easier, we have also provided other data. The funds' annual returns for the last three years, five years, and 10 years give a longer-term perspective on the performance of the fund; category and total risk ranks are also given to judge performance. (To maintain ranking accuracy, funds are sorted by more decimal points of return than are shown in the *Guide*.)

Key to Fund Categories Used in Performance Tables

Domestic Stock Funds
Stk-LC, Large-Cap Stock
Stk-MC, Mid-Cap Stock
Stk-SC, Small-Cap Stock

Sector Stock Funds
Sec-E, Energy/Resources Sector Stock
Sec-F, Financial/Banking Sector Stock
Sec-G, Gold Sector Stock
Sec-H, Health Sector Stock
Sec-R, Real Estate Sector Stock
Sec-T, Technology Sector Stock
Sec-TC, Telecommunications Sector Stock
Sec-U, Utilities Sector Stock

International Stock Funds
IntS-Glb, Global Stock
IntS-F, Foreign Stock
IntS-R/C, Regional/Country Stock
IntS-E, Emerging Stock

Balanced Stock/Bond Funds
Bal, Balanced: Domestic
Bal-Glb, Balanced: Global
TD2000, Target Date 2000–2014
TD2015, Target Date 2015–2029
TD2030, Target Date 2030+

Taxable Bond Funds
B-CHY, Corporate High-Yield Bond
B-MB, Mortgage-Backed Bond
B-GvST, Government: Short-Term Bond
B-GvIT, Government: Intermediate-Term Bond
B-GvLT, Government: Long-Term Bond
B-IP, Inflation-Protected Bond
B-GenST, General Bond: Short-Term
B-GenIT, General Bond: Intermediate-Term
B-GenLT, General Bond: Long-Term

Municipal Bond Funds
B-MNST, National Muni: Short-Term Bond
B-MNIT, National Muni: Intermediate-Term Bond
B-MNLT, National Muni: Long-Term Bond
B-MHY, National Muni: High-Yield Bond

State-Specific Bond Funds
B-MS-AZ, Muni: Arizona Bond
B-MS-CA, Muni: California Bond
B-MS-CO, Muni: Colorado Bond
B-MS-CT, Muni: Connecticut Bond
B-MS-FL, Muni: Florida Bond
B-MS-GA, Muni: Georgia Bond
B-MS-HI, Muni: Hawaii Bond
B-MS-KY, Muni: Kentucky Bond
B-MS-MD, Muni: Maryland Bond
B-MS-MA, Muni: Massachusetts Bond
B-MS-MI, Muni: Michigan Bond
B-MS-MN, Muni: Minnesota Bond
B-MS-NJ, Muni: New Jersey Bond
B-MS-NY, Muni: New York Bond
B-MS-NC, Muni: North Carolina Bond
B-MS-OH, Muni: Ohio Bond
B-MS-PA, Muni: Pennsylvania Bond
B-MS-TN, Muni: Tennessee Bond
B-MS-VA, Muni: Virginia Bond
B-MS-WV, Muni: West Virginia Bond
B-MS-WI, Muni: Wisconsin Bond

International Bond Funds
IntB-Gen, International Bond: General
IntB-E, International Bond: Emerging

Total Risk and Return Performances for Different Mutual Fund Categories

	Annual Return (%)						Total Return (%)		Std Dev	Total
Stock Funds	**2008**	**2007**	**2006**	**2005**	**2004**	**5yr**	**Bull**	**Bear**	**(%)**	**Risk**
Large-Cap Stock	-38.6	8.5	13.0	6.5	11.6	-2.4	109.4	-41.5	17.2	av
Mid-Cap Stock	-40.3	10.0	13.2	10.2	16.4	-1.4	143.7	-43.4	19.9	abv av
Small-Cap Stock	-39.3	2.5	14.5	7.0	16.8	-2.4	145.1	-43.5	21.0	abv av
Growth Style	-42.3	14.3	9.8	8.1	12.1	-2.8	129.9	-45.1	20.0	abv av
Value Style	-35.0	0.3	17.3	6.6	16.5	-1.2	123.1	-38.8	17.1	av
Energy/Resources Sector	-53.1	40.9	13.6	38.3	29.8	6.4	270.3	-52.7	33.3	high
Financial/Banking Sector	-45.9	-10.1	15.1	6.7	13.5	-8.6	88.2	-50.3	20.9	abv av
Gold Sector	-37.4	23.7	33.1	33.3	-7.0	4.4	276.7	-42.9	43.5	high
Health Sector	-25.8	11.4	3.1	13.9	13.5	1.7	103.7	-27.7	16.4	av
Real Estate Sector	-44.2	-13.2	32.2	12.2	32.4	-1.7	185.2	-51.6	29.0	high
Technology Sector	-46.6	15.4	9.7	5.8	4.6	-5.8	148.0	-50.9	23.6	high
Telecommunications Sector	-44.4	15.5	20.9	7.0	19.2	-0.6	190.1	-48.3	22.8	high
Utilities Sector	-32.9	15.6	25.9	12.8	23.5	6.2	179.3	-33.8	16.5	av
Global Stock	-40.8	12.8	20.0	13.0	15.9	0.5	171.5	-43.8	19.6	abv av
Foreign Stock	-45.9	12.2	25.9	18.2	19.8	1.6	226.8	-49.6	22.0	high
Regional/Country Stock	-50.0	26.8	26.7	28.2	20.7	2.9	319.8	-53.4	27.2	high
Emerging Stock	-59.5	40.3	33.8	34.7	26.4	6.5	450.8	-62.3	33.3	high
Balanced Stock/Bond Funds										
Balanced: Domestic	-23.4	7.0	10.9	5.6	10.0	0.9	77.3	-25.0	11.0	blw av
Balanced: Global	-27.8	8.7	10.9	5.8	10.2	0.7	87.1	-29.6	14.2	blw av
Target Date: 2000-2014	-19.5	6.5	9.3	4.7	6.9	1.0	53.9	-21.0	8.8	blw av
Target Date: 2015-2029	-29.2	7.0	12.5	6.4	9.9	-0.5	87.6	-31.7	12.6	blw av
Target Date: 2030+	-36.1	7.6	14.8	7.9	12.2	-1.2	114.7	-39.2	16.4	av
Bond Funds										
Corporate High-Yield	-21.5	2.4	9.7	2.1	9.4	-0.7	51.3	-22.6	10.8	blw av
Mortgage-Backed	1.0	5.8	4.2	2.4	3.4	3.3	16.8	2.7	3.3	low
Gov't: Short-Term	4.9	6.3	3.8	1.6	1.1	3.4	12.4	6.7	1.8	low
Gov't: Interm-Term	9.6	7.8	3.4	2.1	3.2	5.1	15.7	12.6	4.1	low
Gov't: Long-Term	30.7	10.4	-0.1	8.5	9.0	10.8	21.6	37.5	14.1	blw av
Inflation-Protected	-2.7	10.7	0.1	2.3	8.1	3.6	22.3	0.7	8.2	blw av
General: Short-Term	-7.1	3.9	4.6	2.1	2.1	0.8	15.3	-6.6	3.7	low
General: Interm-Term	-2.4	5.2	4.5	2.1	4.3	2.6	20.8	-1.1	5.0	low
General: Long-Term	-3.7	5.1	4.3	2.5	6.3	2.8	26.1	-2.5	8.0	low
Nat'l Muni: Short-Term	1.1	3.1	3.1	1.7	1.4	2.3	11.2	1.8	1.6	low
Nat'l Muni: Interm-Term	-1.7	3.2	3.7	1.9	2.9	2.0	15.1	-0.8	4.0	low
Nat'l Muni: Long-Term	-5.4	2.3	4.7	3.4	4.5	1.7	20.0	-4.8	5.2	low
Nat'l Muni: High-Yield	-20.5	-1.0	6.9	5.5	5.8	-1.3	25.7	-21.6	7.9	low
Int'l Bond: General	-0.5	7.3	5.5	-3.3	7.9	3.4	28.8	0.7	6.9	low
Int'l Bond: Emerging	-16.7	6.0	11.4	12.8	13.2	4.3	82.8	-17.5	13.3	blw av
Index Comparisons										
DJ Industrial Average	-31.9	8.9	19.1	1.7	5.3	-1.1	54.5	-23.7	13.7	blw av
S&P 500	-37.0	5.5	15.8	4.9	10.9	-2.2	64.7	-41.4	15.3	av
S&P MidCap 400	-36.5	7.7	10.0	12.3	16.2	-0.3	103.2	-16.5	19.3	abv av
S&P SmallCap 600	-31.1	-0.3	15.1	7.7	22.7	0.9	121.2	-10.1	19.0	abv av
DJ Wilshire 5000	-37.3	5.7	15.9	6.3	12.6	-1.7	75.4	-42.0	16.0	av
MSCI EAFE	-43.1	11.6	26.9	14.0	20.7	2.1	134.7	-46.4	19.5	abv av
MSCI Europe	-46.1	14.4	34.3	9.9	21.4	2.0	134.8	-44.2	20.8	abv av
MSCI Far East	-32.3	0.3	8.9	24.1	16.7	1.4	125.5	-54.9	16.4	av
MSCI Pacific	-36.2	5.6	12.5	23.0	19.3	2.2	133.0	-50.6	18.0	av
ML High Yield Bond	-26.2	2.2	11.6	2.8	10.8	-0.8	43.8	7.1	13.5	blw av
BarCap GNMA	7.9	7.0	4.6	3.2	4.4	5.4	9.4	29.1	3.2	low
BarCap Govt 1-3 Yr	6.7	7.1	4.1	1.7	1.1	4.1	5.1	23.4	1.6	low
BarCap US Gov't Interm	10.4	8.5	3.8	1.7	2.3	5.3	5.2	30.3	3.3	low
BarCap US Gov't Long	22.7	9.7	2.1	6.6	8.0	9.6	8.7	40.0	10.4	blw av
BarCap Municipal	-2.5	3.4	4.9	3.5	4.5	2.7	12.8	26.4	5.0	low
Treasury Bills	2.0	5.0	4.8	3.1	1.3	3.3	6.9	11.5	0.5	low

The Top 50 Performers: 2008

Category	Fund (Ticker)	Annual Return (%) 2008	3yr	5yr	10yr	Category Risk	Total Risk
B-GvLT	Wasatch-Hoisington U.S. Treasury (WHOSX)	37.7	14.7	13.0	9.1	abv av	av
B-GvLT	American Century Target Mat 2025 Inv (BTTRX)	26.5	10.9	12.7	8.6	abv av	av
B-GvLT	Fidelity Spartan L/T Tr Bd Idx Inv (FLBIX)	24.1	11.4	na	na	low	blw av
B-GvLT	T. Rowe Price U.S. Treasury Long-Term (PRULX)	23.2	11.0	8.8	7.2	blw av	blw av
B-GvLT	Vanguard Long-Term U.S. Treasury (VUSTX)	22.5	10.8	9.2	7.8	low	blw av
B-GvLT	Dreyfus U.S. Treasury Long-Term (DRGBX)	21.5	10.7	8.3	6.7	blw av	blw av
B-GvIT	Fidelity Spartan Interm Tr Bd Idx Inv (FIBIX)	16.3	9.5	na	na	high	low
B-GvIT	T. Rowe Price U.S. Treasury Interm (PRTIX)	14.1	8.7	5.7	5.8	high	low
B-GvIT	Vanguard Interm-Term Treasury (VFITX)	13.3	8.7	6.3	6.5	high	low
B-GvIT	American Century Target Mat 2015 Inv (BTFTX)	12.7	8.2	7.7	7.1	high	low
B-GvIT	Dreyfus U.S. Treasury Intermediate Term (DRGIX)	11.1	7.4	5.0	5.3	av	low
B-GvIT	Fidelity Government Income (FGOVX)	11.0	7.4	5.6	5.7	abv av	low
IntB-Gen	Northern Global Fixed Income (NOIFX)	10.9	8.3	5.0	4.3	av	low
B-GvIT	Fidelity Intermediate Government (FSTGX)	10.0	7.1	5.0	5.5	low	low
B-GvIT	American Century Government Bond Inv (CPTNX)	9.5	7.0	5.2	5.4	av	low
B-GvST	Fidelity Spartan S/T Tr Bd Idx Inv (FSBIX)	8.7	6.6	na	na	high	low
B-GenLT	Vanguard Long-Term Bond Index (VBLTX)	8.6	5.9	6.3	6.6	high	blw av
B-MB	Payden GNMA (PYGNX)	7.6	6.1	5.0	na	high	low
B-MB	USAA GNMA (USGNX)	7.2	5.8	4.7	5.0	av	low
B-MB	Vanguard GNMA (VFIIX)	7.2	6.1	5.1	5.7	abv av	low
B-MB	Fidelity Ginnie Mae (FGMNX)	7.1	5.9	4.9	5.4	abv av	low
B-MB	American Century Ginnie Mae Inv (BGNMX)	7.0	5.8	4.6	5.0	abv av	low
B-GvST	Vanguard Short-Term Federal (VSGBX)	7.0	6.2	4.3	5.1	abv av	low
B-GvST	American Century Target Mat 2010 Inv (BTTNX)	6.9	6.0	4.6	5.6	high	low
B-GvST	Vanguard Short-Term Treasury (VFISX)	6.6	6.1	4.1	4.9	av	low
B-GvST	Dreyfus Short-Intermediate Government (DSIGX)	6.5	5.2	3.5	4.1	blw av	low
Bal	Hussman Strategic Total Return (HSTRX)	6.3	8.1	7.3	na	low	low
B-GenIT	Dreyfus Bond Market Index Basic (DBIRX)	5.8	5.6	4.6	5.4	blw av	low
B-MB	T. Rowe Price GNMA (PRGMX)	5.6	5.3	4.5	5.2	blw av	low
B-GenIT	T. Rowe Price U.S. Bond Index (PBDIX)	5.4	5.3	4.4	na	blw av	low
B-GenST	Vanguard Short-Term Bond Index (VBISX)	5.4	5.5	3.9	4.8	av	low
B-GenIT	Vanguard Total Bond Market Index (VBMFX)	5.0	5.4	4.5	5.3	blw av	low
B-GenIT	Vanguard Interm-Term Bond Index (VBIIX)	4.9	5.4	4.6	5.8	high	low
B-GvST	American Century Short-Term Govt Inv (TWUSX)	4.7	5.0	3.4	3.9	av	low
B-GenST	Janus Short-Term Bond (JASBX)	4.6	4.6	3.4	4.2	low	low
B-GenIT	PIMCO Total Return D (PTTDX)	4.4	5.6	4.8	5.8	av	low
B-GenIT	Fidelity U.S. Bond Index (FBIDX)	3.7	4.4	4.0	5.3	low	low
B-MNST	Vanguard Short-Term Tax-Ex (VWSTX)	3.7	3.7	2.7	3.1	blw av	low
B-GenLT	TCW Core Fixed-Income N (TGFNX)	3.6	4.7	3.8	na	low	low
B-MNIT	Fidelity Short-Intermediate Muni Income (FSTFX)	3.5	3.6	2.7	3.6	low	low
B-MS-MD	T. Rowe Price MD Short-Term Tax-Free (PRMDX)	3.3	3.3	2.3	3.0	blw av	low
B-MS-KY	Dupree KY Tax-Free Short-to-Medium (KYSMX)	3.1	3.2	2.4	3.3	av	low
B-MS-CA	Bernstein Short Duration CA Municipal (SDCMX)	3.0	3.1	2.2	2.8	low	low
B-MNST	T. Rowe Price Tax-Free Short-Interm (PRFSX)	3.0	3.3	2.5	3.5	high	low
B-MNST	Vanguard Ltd-Term Tax-Ex (VMLTX)	2.9	3.5	2.6	3.5	abv av	low
B-MS-NY	Bernstein Short Duration NY Municipal (SDNYX)	2.8	3.0	2.3	2.9	low	low
B-MNIT	Bernstein Diversified Municipal (SNDPX)	2.4	3.2	2.7	3.9	low	low
IntB-Gen	American Century International Bd Inv (BEGBX)	2.4	6.8	4.8	5.0	high	blw av
B-GenST	Weitz Short-Intermediate Income (WEFIX)	2.2	4.1	3.3	4.5	av	low
B-GenLT	Vanguard Long-Term Investment-Grade (VWESX)	2.2	2.9	4.5	5.6	high	blw av

The Bottom 50 Performers: 2008

Category	Fund (Ticker)	Annual Return (%) 2008	3yr	5yr	10yr	Category Risk	Total Risk
IntS-R/C	Metzler/Payden European Emerging Markets (MPYMX)	-66.6	-14.4	5.8	na	abv av	high
IntS-R/C	Matthews India (MINDX)	-62.4	-5.5	na	na	abv av	high
IntS-R/C	T. Rowe Price New Asia (PRASX)	-61.0	-4.1	5.7	8.6	abv av	high
IntS-E	Fidelity Emerging Markets (FEMKX)	-60.9	-8.9	6.1	7.5	abv av	high
IntS-E	T. Rowe Price Emerging Markets Stock (PRMSX)	-60.6	-9.4	5.5	9.4	high	high
IntS-R/C	T. Rowe Price Latin America (PRLAX)	-55.8	-0.1	17.1	14.9	high	high
IntS-R/C	Fidelity Latin America (FLATX)	-54.7	-2.1	15.5	12.5	high	high
IntS-R/C	Guinness Atkinson China & Hong Kong (ICHKX)	-54.5	1.6	4.6	7.9	abv av	high
IntS-E	Driehaus Emerging Markets Growth (DREGX)	-54.5	-2.9	9.5	14.6	blw av	high
IntS-E	Vanguard Emerging Mkts Stock Idx (VEIEX)	-52.9	-5.4	7.1	8.8	blw av	high
Sec-E	Fidelity Select Natural Resources (FNARX)	-52.4	-5.3	8.9	10.9	av	high
IntS-F	American Century Intl Discovery Inv (TWEGX)	-52.2	-7.9	3.6	7.1	high	high
IntS-R/C	Fidelity Southeast Asia (FSEAX)	-51.9	0.8	9.2	10.4	abv av	high
Sec-E	T. Rowe Price New Era (PRNEX)	-50.2	-6.4	6.7	9.2	blw av	high
Stk-MC	Janus Orion (JORNX)	-49.8	-7.6	1.8	na	high	high
Sec-TC	Fidelity Select Wireless (FWRLX)	-49.7	-11.3	3.1	na	abv av	high
Sec-F	Fidelity Select Brokerage & Investment (FSLBX)	-49.4	-15.1	-2.1	4.4	high	high
IntS-R/C	Matthews China (MCHFX)	-49.0	12.7	9.7	14.9	abv av	high
Stk-MC	American Century Vista Inv (TWCVX)	-48.7	-8.1	-0.5	5.6	high	high
Sec-TC	Fidelity Select Communications Equip (FSDCX)	-48.5	-16.7	-7.0	-4.7	high	high
Stk-LC	CGM Focus (CGMFX)	-48.2	2.3	8.5	17.6	high	high
IntS-Glb	Janus Contrarian (JSVAX)	-48.2	-7.8	2.2	na	high	high
IntS-E	Lazard Emerging Markets Equity Open (LZOEX)	-48.1	-3.7	10.4	10.2	low	high
Sec-TC	Fidelity Select Telecommunications (FSTCX)	-47.7	-10.5	-2.4	-5.2	abv av	high
Sec-E	Fidelity Select Materials (FSDPX)	-47.6	-6.9	0.9	6.5	low	high
IntS-F	Fidelity Overseas (FOSFX)	-47.4	-8.3	0.9	1.2	av	abv av
Stk-MC	Vanguard Mid-Cap Growth Index Inv (VMGIX)	-47.1	na	na	na	high	high
Sec-F	Fidelity Select Insurance (FSPCX)	-47.0	-17.4	-6.3	1.7	av	abv av
IntS-F	Artisan International Inv (ARTIX)	-47.0	-7.3	1.7	4.5	abv av	high
Sec-R	CGM Realty (CGMRX)	-46.9	-2.7	9.6	15.8	high	high
Stk-LC	Fidelity Growth Discovery (FDSVX)	-46.8	-8.4	-2.8	0.3	abv av	abv av
Stk-MC	Baron Partners (BPTRX)	-46.7	-10.3	3.2	na	high	high
Stk-MC	Rainier Mid Cap Equity (RIMMX)	-46.6	-6.3	na	na	high	high
Stk-MC	Fidelity Value (FDVLX)	-46.6	-14.4	-2.8	3.4	abv av	abv av
Sec-TC	T. Rowe Price Media & Telecommunications (PRMTX)	-46.5	-5.7	4.5	6.5	av	high
IntS-R/C	Fidelity Europe Capital Appreciation (FECAX)	-46.3	-5.9	2.4	2.9	blw av	abv av
Stk-MC	American Century Heritage Inv (TWHIX)	-46.2	-2.8	3.7	4.9	high	high
IntS-R/C	Matthews Pacific Tiger (MAPTX)	-46.2	-2.9	6.7	12.0	av	high
Sec-T	Baron iOpportunity (BIOPX)	-46.1	-9.9	-0.4	na	abv av	high
IntS-Glb	Janus Global Research (JARFX)	-45.5	-6.5	na	na	abv av	high
IntS-F	Masters' Select International (MSILX)	-45.5	-6.7	2.8	6.4	blw av	abv av
Stk-LC	Marsico 21st Century (MXXIX)	-45.3	-8.2	0.4	na	high	abv av
IntS-F	Vanguard International Growth (VWIGX)	-45.0	-7.1	1.9	1.3	av	abv av
Stk-SC	Fidelity Small Cap Growth (FCPGX)	-45.0	-10.1	na	na	abv av	abv av
IntS-F	T. Rowe Price Intl Gr & Inc (TRIGX)	-45.0	-8.1	2.0	2.5	blw av	abv av
IntS-F	HighMark International Opportunities M (HIOMX)	-44.9	-6.0	3.7	2.4	av	abv av
IntS-R/C	Fidelity China Region (FHKCX)	-44.9	1.5	5.9	8.4	av	high
IntS-R/C	Vanguard European Stock Index (VEURX)	-44.8	-5.7	2.0	0.7	blw av	abv av
Sec-R	Third Avenue Real Estate Value (TAREX)	-44.7	-13.0	-0.7	8.4	low	high
Stk-SC	Bridgeway Ultra-Small Company Market (BRSIX)	-44.7	-16.5	-6.1	8.4	blw av	abv av

The Top 50 Performers: 3 Years, 2006–2008

Category	Fund (Ticker)	Annual Return (%) 3yr	5yr	10yr	2008	Category Risk	Total Risk
B-GvLT	Wasatch-Hoisington U.S. Treasury (WHOSX)	14.7	13.0	9.1	37.7	abv av	av
IntS-R/C	Matthews China (MCHFX)	12.7	9.7	14.9	-49.0	abv av	high
B-GvLT	Fidelity Spartan L/T Tr Bd Idx Inv (FLBIX)	11.4	na	na	24.1	low	blw av
Sec-G	USAA Precious Metals and Minerals (USAGX)	11.1	11.2	19.3	-25.0	abv av	high
B-GvLT	T. Rowe Price U.S. Treasury Long-Term (PRULX)	11.0	8.8	7.2	23.2	blw av	blw av
B-GvLT	American Century Target Mat 2025 Inv (BTTRX)	10.9	12.7	8.6	26.5	abv av	av
B-GvLT	Vanguard Long-Term U.S. Treasury (VUSTX)	10.8	9.2	7.8	22.5	low	blw av
B-GvLT	Dreyfus U.S. Treasury Long-Term (DRGBX)	10.7	8.3	6.7	21.5	blw av	blw av
B-GvIT	Fidelity Spartan Interm Tr Bd Idx Inv (FIBIX)	9.5	na	na	16.3	high	low
B-GvIT	T. Rowe Price U.S. Treasury Interm (PRTIX)	8.7	5.7	5.8	14.1	high	low
B-GvIT	Vanguard Interm-Term Treasury (VFITX)	8.7	6.3	6.5	13.3	high	low
Sec-G	U.S. Gbl Inv Gold and Precious Metals (USERX)	8.6	9.7	13.8	-27.1	blw av	high
IntB-Gen	Northern Global Fixed Income (NOIFX)	8.3	5.0	4.3	10.9	av	low
B-GvIT	American Century Target Mat 2015 Inv (BTFTX)	8.2	7.7	7.1	12.7	high	low
Bal	Hussman Strategic Total Return (HSTRX)	8.1	7.3	na	6.3	low	low
Sec-G	Fidelity Select Gold (FSAGX)	7.6	9.6	14.3	-20.5	blw av	high
B-GvIT	Fidelity Government Income (FGOVX)	7.4	5.6	5.7	11.0	abv av	low
B-GvIT	Dreyfus U.S. Treasury Intermediate Term (DRGIX)	7.4	5.0	5.3	11.1	av	low
B-GvIT	Fidelity Intermediate Government (FSTGX)	7.1	5.0	5.5	10.0	low	low
B-GvIT	American Century Government Bond Inv (CPTNX)	7.0	5.2	5.4	9.5	av	low
IntB-Gen	American Century International Bd Inv (BEGBX)	6.8	4.8	5.0	2.4	high	blw av
B-GvST	Fidelity Spartan S/T Tr Bd Idx Inv (FSBIX)	6.6	na	na	8.7	high	low
IntB-Gen	T. Rowe Price International Bond (RPIBX)	6.4	4.2	4.3	1.7	abv av	blw av
B-GvST	Vanguard Short-Term Federal (VSGBX)	6.2	4.3	5.1	7.0	abv av	low
B-MB	Vanguard GNMA (VFIIX)	6.1	5.1	5.7	7.2	abv av	low
B-GvST	Vanguard Short-Term Treasury (VFISX)	6.1	4.1	4.9	6.6	av	low
B-MB	Payden GNMA (PYGNX)	6.1	5.0	na	7.6	high	low
B-GvST	American Century Target Mat 2010 Inv (BTTNX)	6.0	4.6	5.6	6.9	high	low
B-MB	Fidelity Ginnie Mae (FGMNX)	5.9	4.9	5.4	7.1	abv av	low
B-GenLT	Vanguard Long-Term Bond Index (VBLTX)	5.9	6.3	6.6	8.6	high	blw av
B-MB	USAA GNMA (USGNX)	5.8	4.7	5.0	7.2	av	low
B-MB	American Century Ginnie Mae Inv (BGNMX)	5.8	4.6	5.0	7.0	abv av	low
B-GenIT	Dreyfus Bond Market Index Basic (DBIRX)	5.6	4.6	5.4	5.8	blw av	low
B-GenIT	PIMCO Total Return D (PTTDX)	5.6	4.8	5.8	4.4	av	low
Sec-G	GAMCO Gold AAA (GOLDX)	5.5	6.9	16.4	-28.8	av	high
B-GenST	Vanguard Short-Term Bond Index (VBISX)	5.5	3.9	4.8	5.4	av	low
B-GenIT	Vanguard Interm-Term Bond Index (VBIIX)	5.4	4.6	5.8	4.9	high	low
Bal	Permanent Portfolio (PRPFX)	5.4	7.1	8.0	-8.4	av	blw av
B-GenIT	Vanguard Total Bond Market Index (VBMFX)	5.4	4.5	5.3	5.0	blw av	low
B-GenIT	T. Rowe Price U.S. Bond Index (PBDIX)	5.3	4.4	na	5.4	blw av	low
B-MB	T. Rowe Price GNMA (PRGMX)	5.3	4.5	5.2	5.6	blw av	low
Stk-MC	Gabelli ABC (GABCX)	5.3	4.5	5.2	-2.7	low	low
B-GvST	Dreyfus Short-Intermediate Government (DSIGX)	5.2	3.5	4.1	6.5	blw av	low
B-GvST	American Century Short-Term Govt Inv (TWUSX)	5.0	3.4	3.9	4.7	av	low
B-GenLT	TCW Core Fixed-Income N (TGFNX)	4.7	3.8	na	3.6	low	low
B-GenST	Janus Short-Term Bond (JASBX)	4.6	3.4	4.2	4.6	low	low
B-GenIT	Fidelity U.S. Bond Index (FBIDX)	4.4	4.0	5.3	3.7	low	low
Bal	FundX Flexible Income (INCMX)	4.3	4.0	na	-0.3	low	low
B-GenST	Weitz Short-Intermediate Income (WEFIX)	4.1	3.3	4.5	2.2	av	low
B-GenIT	Managers Fremont Bond (MBDFX)	3.9	4.0	5.5	4.1	abv av	low

The Top 50 Performers: 5 Years, 2004–2008

Category	Fund (Ticker)	Annual Return (%) 5yr	10yr	3yr	2008	Category Risk	Total Risk
IntS-R/C	T. Rowe Price Latin America (PRLAX)	17.1	14.9	-0.1	-55.8	high	high
IntS-R/C	Fidelity Latin America (FLATX)	15.5	12.5	-2.1	-54.7	high	high
Sec-E	ICON Energy (ICENX)	14.7	20.4	0.4	-33.4	low	high
Sec-E	Vanguard Energy (VGENX)	13.1	14.7	-2.2	-42.9	blw av	high
B-GvLT	Wasatch-Hoisington U.S. Treasury (WHOSX)	13.0	9.1	14.7	37.7	abv av	av
B-GvLT	American Century Target Mat 2025 Inv (BTTRX)	12.7	8.6	10.9	26.5	abv av	av
Sec-G	USAA Precious Metals and Minerals (USAGX)	11.2	19.3	11.1	-25.0	abv av	high
IntS-E	Lazard Emerging Markets Equity Open (LZOEX)	10.4	10.2	-3.7	-48.1	low	high
Sec-G	U.S. Gbl Inv Gold and Precious Metals (USERX)	9.7	13.8	8.6	-27.1	blw av	high
IntS-R/C	Matthews China (MCHFX)	9.7	14.9	12.7	-49.0	abv av	high
Sec-R	CGM Realty (CGMRX)	9.6	15.8	-2.7	-46.9	high	high
Sec-G	Fidelity Select Gold (FSAGX)	9.6	14.3	7.6	-20.5	blw av	high
IntS-E	Driehaus Emerging Markets Growth (DREGX)	9.5	14.6	-2.9	-54.5	blw av	high
IntS-R/C	Fidelity Southeast Asia (FSEAX)	9.2	10.4	0.8	-51.9	abv av	high
B-GvLT	Vanguard Long-Term U.S. Treasury (VUSTX)	9.2	7.8	10.8	22.5	low	blw av
Sec-E	Fidelity Select Natural Resources (FNARX)	8.9	10.9	-5.3	-52.4	av	high
B-GvLT	T. Rowe Price U.S. Treasury Long-Term (PRULX)	8.8	7.2	11.0	23.2	blw av	blw av
Stk-LC	CGM Focus (CGMFX)	8.5	17.6	2.3	-48.2	high	high
B-GvLT	Dreyfus U.S. Treasury Long-Term (DRGBX)	8.3	6.7	10.7	21.5	blw av	blw av
B-GvIT	American Century Target Mat 2015 Inv (BTFTX)	7.7	7.1	8.2	12.7	high	low
Sec-U	American Century Utilities Inv (BULIX)	7.5	1.6	0.4	-31.2	av	blw av
IntS-R/C	Matthews Asian Growth & Income (MACSX)	7.4	14.3	0.6	-32.1	low	av
Bal	Hussman Strategic Total Return (HSTRX)	7.3	na	8.1	6.3	low	low
Bal	Permanent Portfolio (PRPFX)	7.1	8.0	5.4	-8.4	av	blw av
IntS-E	Vanguard Emerging Mkts Stock Idx (VEIEX)	7.1	8.8	-5.4	-52.9	blw av	high
IntS-R/C	Fidelity Canada (FICDX)	7.1	11.3	-3.8	-42.7	av	high
Stk-SC	Pinnacle Value (PVFIX)	7.1	na	2.8	-16.9	low	blw av
Sec-G	GAMCO Gold AAA (GOLDX)	6.9	16.4	5.5	-28.8	av	high
Sec-E	T. Rowe Price New Era (PRNEX)	6.7	9.2	-6.4	-50.2	blw av	high
Sec-U	FBR Gas Utility Index (GASFX)	6.7	5.2	-0.3	-28.3	blw av	blw av
IntS-R/C	Matthews Pacific Tiger (MAPTX)	6.7	12.0	-2.9	-46.2	av	high
B-GvIT	Vanguard Interm-Term Treasury (VFITX)	6.3	6.5	8.7	13.3	high	low
IntS-F	Artisan International Value (ARTKX)	6.3	na	-2.3	-30.2	low	av
B-GenLT	Vanguard Long-Term Bond Index (VBLTX)	6.3	6.6	5.9	8.6	high	blw av
IntS-E	Fidelity Emerging Markets (FEMKX)	6.1	7.5	-8.9	-60.9	abv av	high
Stk-SC	Dreman Contrarian Small Cap Value R (DRSVX)	6.0	na	-1.3	-27.0	low	av
Sec-U	Fidelity Select Utilities Growth (FSUTX)	5.9	0.0	-0.6	-36.0	high	av
IntS-R/C	Fidelity China Region (FHKCX)	5.9	8.4	1.5	-44.9	av	high
Sec-H	Schwab Health Care (SWHFX)	5.9	na	-5.4	-25.0	av	blw av
IntS-F	Thomas White International (TWWDX)	5.8	3.7	-4.2	-43.5	av	abv av
IntS-R/C	Metzler/Payden European Emerging Markets (MPYMX)	5.8	na	-14.4	-66.6	abv av	high
IntS-R/C	T. Rowe Price New Asia (PRASX)	5.7	8.6	-4.1	-61.0	abv av	high
B-GvIT	T. Rowe Price U.S. Treasury Interm (PRTIX)	5.7	5.8	8.7	14.1	high	low
B-GvIT	Fidelity Government Income (FGOVX)	5.6	5.7	7.4	11.0	abv av	low
IntS-E	T. Rowe Price Emerging Markets Stock (PRMSX)	5.5	9.4	-9.4	-60.6	high	high
Stk-LC	Fairholme (FAIRX)	5.5	na	-2.7	-29.8	abv av	abv av
IntB-E	T. Rowe Price Emerging Markets Bond (PREMX)	5.5	10.8	-1.0	-17.8	abv av	blw av
IntS-F	Harbor International Inv (HIINX)	5.3	na	-2.9	-42.9	av	high
B-GvIT	American Century Government Bond Inv (CPTNX)	5.2	5.4	7.0	9.5	av	low
B-MB	Vanguard GNMA (VFIIX)	5.1	5.7	6.1	7.2	abv av	low

The Top 50 Performers: 10 Years, 1999–2008

Category	Fund (Ticker)	Annual Return (%) 10yr	5yr	3yr	2008	Category Risk	Total Risk
Sec-E	ICON Energy (ICENX)	20.4	14.7	0.4	-33.4	low	high
Sec-G	USAA Precious Metals and Minerals (USAGX)	19.3	11.2	11.1	-25.0	abv av	high
Stk-LC	CGM Focus (CGMFX)	17.6	8.5	2.3	-48.2	high	high
Sec-G	GAMCO Gold AAA (GOLDX)	16.4	6.9	5.5	-28.8	av	high
Sec-R	CGM Realty (CGMRX)	15.8	9.6	-2.7	-46.9	high	high
IntS-R/C	T. Rowe Price Latin America (PRLAX)	14.9	17.1	-0.1	-55.8	high	high
IntS-R/C	Matthews China (MCHFX)	14.9	9.7	12.7	-49.0	abv av	high
Sec-E	Vanguard Energy (VGENX)	14.7	13.1	-2.2	-42.9	blw av	high
IntS-E	Driehaus Emerging Markets Growth (DREGX)	14.6	9.5	-2.9	-54.5	blw av	high
IntS-R/C	Matthews Asian Growth & Income (MACSX)	14.3	7.4	0.6	-32.1	low	av
Sec-G	Fidelity Select Gold (FSAGX)	14.3	9.6	7.6	-20.5	blw av	high
Sec-G	U.S. Gbl Inv Gold and Precious Metals (USERX)	13.8	9.7	8.6	-27.1	blw av	high
IntS-R/C	Fidelity Latin America (FLATX)	12.5	15.5	-2.1	-54.7	high	high
Sec-G	American Century Global Gold Inv (BGEIX)	12.2	4.7	2.1	-27.3	abv av	high
IntS-R/C	Matthews Pacific Tiger (MAPTX)	12.0	6.7	-2.9	-46.2	av	high
IntS-R/C	Fidelity Canada (FICDX)	11.3	7.1	-3.8	-42.7	av	high
Stk-SC	Buffalo Small Cap (BUFSX)	10.9	1.1	-7.3	-29.9	av	abv av
Sec-E	Fidelity Select Natural Resources (FNARX)	10.9	8.9	-5.3	-52.4	av	high
IntB-E	T. Rowe Price Emerging Markets Bond (PREMX)	10.8	5.5	-1.0	-17.8	abv av	blw av
IntS-R/C	Fidelity Southeast Asia (FSEAX)	10.4	9.2	9.2	-51.9	abv av	high
IntS-E	Lazard Emerging Markets Equity Open (LZOEX)	10.2	10.4	-3.7	-48.1	low	high
Stk-MC	Janus Mid Cap Value Investor (JMCVX)	10.2	3.2	-3.5	-27.4	low	blw av
IntB-E	Payden Emerging Markets Bond (PYEMX)	10.1	5.1	0.5	-10.3	blw av	blw av
Stk-MC	Meridian Value (MVALX)	9.8	0.6	-4.6	-32.0	low	av
Sec-H	Fidelity Select Medical Equip/Systems (FSMEX)	9.5	3.4	-2.1	-23.4	abv av	av
IntS-E	T. Rowe Price Emerging Markets Stock (PRMSX)	9.4	5.5	-9.4	-60.6	high	high
Sec-E	T. Rowe Price New Era (PRNEX)	9.2	6.7	-6.4	-50.2	blw av	high
B-GvLT	Wasatch-Hoisington U.S. Treasury (WHOSX)	9.1	13.0	14.7	37.7	abv av	av
Stk-MC	Wells Fargo Advantage Mid Cap Dis Inv (SMCDX)	9.0	0.5	-7.7	-30.1	low	av
Stk-SC	Royce Low Priced Stock Svc (RYLPX)	8.9	-0.6	-8.0	-36.0	abv av	high
IntS-E	Vanguard Emerging Mkts Stock Idx (VEIEX)	8.8	7.1	-5.4	-52.9	blw av	high
Bal	Oakmark Equity & Income I (OAKBX)	8.6	4.5	1.3	-16.2	blw av	blw av
IntS-R/C	T. Rowe Price New Asia (PRASX)	8.6	5.7	-4.1	-61.0	abv av	high
B-GvLT	American Century Target Mat 2025 Inv (BTTRX)	8.6	12.7	10.9	26.5	abv av	av
Stk-SC	Bridgeway Ultra-Small Company Market (BRSIX)	8.4	-6.1	-16.5	-44.7	blw av	abv av
Sec-R	Cohen & Steers Realty Shares (CSRSX)	8.4	2.9	-10.1	-34.5	av	high
Sec-R	Third Avenue Real Estate Value (TAREX)	8.4	-0.7	-13.0	-44.7	low	high
IntS-R/C	Fidelity China Region (FHKCX)	8.4	5.9	1.5	-44.9	av	high
Stk-SC	T. Rowe Price Small-Cap Value (PRSVX)	8.4	2.5	-6.1	-28.7	low	av
Stk-SC	Royce Heritage Svc (RGFAX)	8.2	0.7	-7.5	-36.3	abv av	abv av
Stk-SC	Royce Special Equity Invt (RYSEX)	8.1	1.6	-1.4	-19.7	low	blw av
Bal	Permanent Portfolio (PRPFX)	8.0	7.1	5.4	-8.4	av	blw av
Stk-MC	Fidelity Low-Priced Stock (FLPSX)	7.9	0.5	-8.2	-36.2	blw av	abv av
IntS-R/C	Guinness Atkinson China & Hong Kong (ICHKX)	7.9	4.6	1.6	-54.5	abv av	high
Stk-SC	Heartland Value Plus (HRVIX)	7.8	2.9	-0.8	-17.9	low	av
Stk-MC	Delafield (DEFIX)	7.8	0.1	-7.7	-37.6	av	abv av
Sec-R	T. Rowe Price Real Estate (TRREX)	7.8	1.1	-12.3	-39.1	av	high
B-GvLT	Vanguard Long-Term U.S. Treasury (VUSTX)	7.8	9.2	10.8	22.5	low	blw av
Stk-SC	Stratton Small-Cap Value (STSCX)	7.7	2.9	-6.2	-25.8	low	av
Stk-SC	Value Line Emerging Opportunities (VLEOX)	7.7	-0.5	-8.1	-38.3	blw av	abv av

Individual Fund Listings

DOMESTIC STOCK FUNDS

Large-Cap Stock Funds
Category Performance Ranked by 2008 Returns

Fund (Ticker)	Annual Return (%) 2008	3Yr	5Yr	10Yr	Category Risk	Total Risk
American Century Equity Income Inv (TWEIX)	-20.1	-1.0	2.3	6.0	low	blw av
Parnassus Equity Income - Inv (PRBLX)	-23.0	0.2	2.5	6.1	low	blw av
Vanguard Dividend Growth (VDIGX)	-25.6	-1.7	1.9	0.1	low	blw av
FMI Large Cap (FMIHX)	-27.0	-3.9	2.6	na	low	blw av
Sequoia (SEQUX)	-27.1	-5.1	-0.7	2.0	low	blw av
Mairs & Power Growth (MPGFX)	-28.6	-6.2	0.3	5.4	low	blw av
Jensen J (JENSX)	-29.0	-4.6	-2.0	2.7	low	blw av
Fairholme (FAIRX)	-29.8	-2.7	5.5	na	abv av	abv av
Vanguard Equity-Income (VEIPX)	-31.0	-4.5	0.6	1.9	low	blw av
Wasatch-1st Source Income Equity (FMIEX)	-31.2	-2.5	3.6	6.4	blw av	blw av
Vanguard PRIMECAP Core (VPCCX)	-31.4	-6.2	na	na	blw av	av
Dreyfus Appreciation (DGAGX)	-32.4	-5.8	-1.7	-0.9	low	blw av
Oakmark I (OAKMX)	-32.7	-8.5	-3.3	0.7	av	av
Aston/Montag & Caldwell Growth N (MCGFX)	-32.7	-4.2	-0.7	-1.5	av	av
Fidelity Focused Stock (FTQGX)	-33.1	-6.3	2.3	-0.9	av	av
Schwab Core Equity (SWANX)	-33.3	-6.6	0.2	0.1	low	blw av
T. Rowe Price Dividend Growth (PRDGX)	-33.3	-6.0	-0.8	0.1	low	blw av
Sit Large Cap Growth (SNIGX)	-34.1	-6.3	0.3	-3.0	low	blw av
American Century Income & Growth Inv (BIGRX)	-34.7	-8.7	-2.1	-1.0	blw av	blw av
American Century Equity Growth Inv (BEQGX)	-34.8	-8.4	-1.2	-0.9	low	blw av
Vanguard U.S. Value (VUVLX)	-34.8	-9.7	-2.3	na	blw av	av
Gabelli Equity Income AAA (GABEX)	-35.0	-5.5	0.3	3.7	low	blw av
USAA Income Stock (USISX)	-35.6	-9.5	-2.6	-0.3	blw av	blw av
Sound Shore (SSHFX)	-35.6	-8.4	-1.1	2.3	av	av
T. Rowe Price Equity Income (PRFDX)	-35.8	-7.6	-1.1	2.1	low	blw av
Vanguard Value Index (VIVAX)	-36.0	-7.9	-0.7	0.6	low	blw av
Manning & Napier Equity (EXEYX)	-36.4	-7.3	0.3	na	av	av
Homestead Value (HOVLX)	-36.5	-8.3	-0.4	2.1	av	av
T. Rowe Price Growth & Income (PRGIX)	-36.6	-8.3	-2.6	-0.6	blw av	av
Vanguard Windsor II (VWNFX)	-36.8	-8.6	-0.7	1.0	blw av	av
Vanguard 500 Index (VFINX)	-37.1	-8.5	-2.3	-1.5	blw av	blw av
Vanguard Total Stock Mkt Idx (VTSMX)	-37.1	-8.5	-1.8	-0.7	blw av	av
Vanguard Large Cap Index (VLACX)	-37.1	-8.3	na	na	blw av	av
Fidelity Contrafund (FCNTX)	-37.2	-5.7	2.3	2.8	av	av

Large-Cap Stock Funds
Category Performance Ranked by 2008 Returns (cont.)

Fund (Ticker)	Annual Return (%) 2008	3Yr	5Yr	10Yr	Category Risk	Total Risk
Fidelity Spartan Total Market Index Inv (FSTMX)	-37.2	-8.5	-1.8	-0.8	blw av	av
American Century Growth Inv (TWCGX)	-37.9	-7.3	-1.7	-2.4	av	av
Schwab MarketTrack All Equity (SWEGX)	-38.1	-8.1	-1.1	0.0	av	av
Value Line Larger Companies (VALLX)	-38.2	-7.4	-1.0	-2.1	av	av
Vanguard Growth Index (VIGRX)	-38.4	-8.9	-3.2	-3.3	av	av
Stratton Multi Cap (STRGX)	-38.4	-9.7	0.8	3.5	abv av	abv av
American Beacon Lg Cap Value Plan (AAGPX)	-39.6	-9.7	-0.8	1.6	av	av
Fidelity Large Cap Value (FSLVX)	-39.8	-9.9	-0.9	na	av	av
T. Rowe Price Value (TRVLX)	-39.8	-10.1	-2.3	2.1	abv av	av
Fidelity Disciplined Equity (FDEQX)	-40.1	-8.8	-1.3	-0.2	av	av
Fidelity (FFIDX)	-40.4	-7.5	-1.7	-1.2	av	av
Vanguard Windsor (VWNDX)	-41.1	-12.1	-4.2	1.6	av	av
Fidelity Strategic Dividend & Income (FSDIX)	-41.2	-11.6	-2.8	na	abv av	av
Fidelity Equity-Income (FEQIX)	-41.7	-10.9	-3.6	-0.1	av	av
Rydex Nasdaq-100 Inv (RYOCX)	-41.9	-10.0	-4.2	-5.1	high	abv av
Brandywine Blue (BLUEX)	-43.9	-8.4	-0.2	3.2	high	abv av
Janus Research (JAMRX)	-44.4	-9.1	-2.3	-1.2	high	abv av
Fidelity Trend (FTRNX)	-44.5	-9.3	-2.4	0.2	high	abv av
Marsico 21st Century (MXXIX)	-45.3	-8.2	0.4	na	high	abv av
Fidelity Growth Discovery (FDSVX)	-46.8	-8.4	-2.8	0.3	abv av	abv av
CGM Focus (CGMFX)	-48.2	2.3	8.5	17.6	high	high
Large-Cap Stock Category Average	**-38.6**	**-9.3**	**-2.4**	**-0.4**	av	av

American Beacon Lg Cap Value Plan (AAGPX)

800-967-9009
www.americanbeaconfunds.com

Large-Cap Stock

PERFORMANCE — fund inception date: 8/1/94

	3yr Annual	5yr Annual	10yr Annual	Bull	Bear
Return (%)	-9.7	-0.8	1.6	140.8	-42.9
Differ From Category (+/-)	-0.4 av	1.6 abv av	2.0 abv av	31.4 high	-1.4 blw av

Standard Deviation	Category Risk Index	Beta
16.0%—av	0.93—av	1.04

	2008	2007	2006	2005	2004	2003	2002	2001	2000	1999
Return (%)	-39.6	2.9	18.7	9.6	19.1	35.3	-16.2	1.8	11.2	-5.0
Differ From Category (+/-)	-1.0	-5.6	5.7	3.1	7.5	4.6	5.1	12.0	12.7	-30.4
Return, Tax-Adjusted (%)	-39.9	2.2	18.0	8.8	18.9	35.0	-16.9	0.9	9.0	-9.2

PER SHARE DATA

	2008	2007	2006	2005	2004	2003	2002	2001	2000	1999
Dividends, Net Income ($)	0.40	0.36	0.28	0.25	0.23	0.23	0.25	0.25	0.55	0.43
Distrib'ns, Cap Gain ($)	0.00	0.71	0.61	0.76	0.00	0.00	0.00	0.17	0.49	3.05
Net Asset Value ($)	13.11	22.39	22.78	19.94	19.09	16.22	12.16	14.80	14.95	14.42
Expense Ratio (%)	na	0.83	0.85	0.86	0.94	0.95	0.93	0.93	0.84	0.90
Yield (%)	3.03	1.54	1.19	1.18	1.20	1.44	2.03	1.69	3.57	2.46
Portfolio Turnover (%)	na	20	26	25	29	27	34	34	33	33
Total Assets (Millions $)	3,288	5,034	3,057	785	113	24	17	13	13	15

PORTFOLIO (as of 10/31/08)

Portfolio Manager: Quinn/Crumpler/Posada - 1987

Investment Style

✔ Large Cap	Growth
Mid Cap	Grth/Val
Small Cap	✔ Value

Portfolio

81.2% U.S. stock	0.0% conv't
5.5% int'l stock	0.2% preferred
0.0% U.S. bonds	0.0% other
0.0% int'l bonds	13.1% cash

Number of Investments: 142
Percent of Portfolio in Top 10 Investments: 29%

SHAREHOLDER INFORMATION

Minimum Investment
Initial: $2,500 Subsequent: $50

Minimum IRA Investment
Initial: $2,500 Subsequent: $50

Maximum Fees
Load: none 12b-1: none
Other: none

Services
✔ IRA
✔ Keogh
✔ Telephone Exchange

American Century Equity Growth Inv (BEQGX)

800-345-2021
www.americancentury.com

Large-Cap Stock

PERFORMANCE — fund inception date: 5/9/91

	3yr Annual	5yr Annual	10yr Annual	Bull	Bear
Return (%)	-8.4	-1.2	-0.9	102.9	-37.5
Differ From Category (+/-)	0.9 abv av	1.2 abv av	-0.5 av	-6.5 av	4.0 abv av

Standard Deviation	Category Risk Index	Beta
15.0%—blw av	0.87—low	0.97

	2008	2007	2006	2005	2004	2003	2002	2001	2000	1999
Return (%)	-34.8	3.4	14.1	7.3	13.9	30.2	-20.4	-11.1	-11.0	18.4
Differ From Category (+/-)	3.8	-5.1	1.1	0.8	2.3	-0.5	0.9	-0.9	-9.5	-7.0
Return, Tax-Adjusted (%)	-35.0	2.0	13.4	7.0	13.7	30.1	-20.7	-11.3	-12.3	17.7

PER SHARE DATA

	2008	2007	2006	2005	2004	2003	2002	2001	2000	1999
Dividends, Net Income ($)	0.27	0.23	0.23	0.22	0.24	0.17	0.15	0.13	0.14	0.19
Distrib'ns, Cap Gain ($)	0.00	2.06	0.79	0.10	0.00	0.00	0.00	0.00	1.47	0.43
Net Asset Value ($)	15.56	24.19	25.64	23.37	22.08	19.60	15.19	19.24	21.77	26.23
Expense Ratio (%)	0.67	0.67	0.67	0.67	0.68	0.69	0.69	0.68	0.67	0.68
Yield (%)	1.73	0.88	0.86	0.91	1.09	0.85	0.98	0.67	0.58	0.70
Portfolio Turnover (%)	105	52	102	106	97	95	100	79	79	86
Total Assets (Millions $)	1,387	2,451	2,488	1,959	1,548	1,194	988	1,477	1,912	2,317

PORTFOLIO (as of 9/30/08)

Portfolio Manager: Martin/Vaiana - 1997

Investment Style

✔ Large Cap	Growth
Mid Cap	✔ Grth/Val
Small Cap	Value

Portfolio

98.0% U.S. stock	0.0% conv't
1.0% int'l stock	0.0% preferred
0.0% U.S. bonds	0.0% other
0.0% int'l bonds	1.0% cash

Number of Investments: 176

Percent of Portfolio in Top 10 Investments: 24%

SHAREHOLDER INFORMATION

Minimum Investment

Initial: $2,500 Subsequent: $50

Minimum IRA Investment

Initial: $2,500 Subsequent: $50

Maximum Fees

Load: none 12b-1: none

Other: none

Services

✔ IRA

✔ Keogh

✔ Telephone Exchange

American Century Equity Income Inv (TWEIX)

800-345-2021
www.americancentury.com

Large-Cap Stock

PERFORMANCE — fund inception date: 8/1/94

	3yr Annual	5yr Annual	10yr Annual	Bull	Bear
Return (%)	-1.0	2.3	6.0	91.6	-23.7
Differ From Category (+/-)	8.3 high	4.7 high	6.4 high	-17.8 blw av	17.8 high

Standard Deviation	Category Risk Index	Beta
11.2%—blw av	0.65—low	0.70

	2008	2007	2006	2005	2004	2003	2002	2001	2000	1999
Return (%)	-20.1	1.7	19.4	2.4	12.5	24.2	-5.0	11.3	21.9	-0.2
Differ From Category (+/-)	18.5	-6.8	6.4	-4.1	0.9	-6.5	16.3	21.5	23.4	-25.6
Return, Tax-Adjusted (%)	-20.6	0.1	18.0	1.5	11.3	23.5	-6.2	10.1	20.6	-3.1

PER SHARE DATA

	2008	2007	2006	2005	2004	2003	2002	2001	2000	1999
Dividends, Net Income ($)	0.24	0.21	0.20	0.17	0.20	0.19	0.16	0.17	0.18	0.22
Distrib'ns, Cap Gain ($)	0.00	0.73	0.55	0.32	0.42	0.12	0.10	0.04	0.00	0.48
Net Asset Value ($)	6.02	7.80	8.58	7.82	8.11	7.78	6.53	7.14	6.62	5.60
Expense Ratio (%)	0.97	0.97	0.98	0.99	1.00	1.00	1.00	1.00	1.00	1.00
Yield (%)	3.93	2.48	2.13	2.05	2.28	2.45	2.41	2.43	2.70	3.56
Portfolio Turnover (%)	165	160	150	174	91	120	139	169	141	180
Total Assets (Millions $)	3,070	4,316	4,621	3,820	2,919	2,105	1,241	832	385	328

PORTFOLIO (as of 9/30/08)

Portfolio Manager: Davidson/Toney/Liss - 1994

Investment Style

✔ Large Cap	Growth
✔ Mid Cap	Grth/Val
Small Cap	✔ Value

Portfolio

71.9%	U.S. stock	5.1%	conv't
6.1%	int'l stock	10.0%	preferred
6.6%	U.S. bonds	0.3%	other
0.0%	int'l bonds	0.0%	cash

Number of Investments: 87
Percent of Portfolio in Top 10 Investments: 38%

SHAREHOLDER INFORMATION

Minimum Investment
Initial: $2,500 Subsequent: $50

Minimum IRA Investment
Initial: $2,500 Subsequent: $0

Maximum Fees
Load: none 12b-1: none
Other: none

Services
✔ IRA
✔ Keogh
✔ Telephone Exchange

American Century Growth Inv (TWCGX)

800-345-2021
www.americancentury.com

Large-Cap Stock

PERFORMANCE — fund inception date: 6/30/71

	3yr Annual	5yr Annual	10yr Annual	Bull	Bear
Return (%)	-7.3	-1.7	-2.4	92.4	-38.6
Differ From Category (+/-)	2.0 abv av	0.7 abv av	-2.0 blw av	-17.0 blw av	2.9 abv av

Standard Deviation	Category Risk Index	Beta
16.6%—av	0.97—av	1.04

	2008	2007	2006	2005	2004	2003	2002	2001	2000	1999
Return (%)	-37.9	18.9	7.9	4.8	9.9	24.4	-26.2	-18.7	-14.8	34.6
Differ From Category (+/-)	0.7	10.4	-5.1	-1.7	-1.7	-6.3	-4.9	-8.5	-13.3	9.2
Return, Tax-Adjusted (%)	-37.9	18.9	7.9	4.7	9.9	24.4	-26.2	-18.7	-17.0	31.6

PER SHARE DATA

	2008	2007	2006	2005	2004	2003	2002	2001	2000	1999
Dividends, Net Income ($)	0.08	0.03	0.01	0.09	0.01	0.00	0.00	0.00	0.00	0.00
Distrib'ns, Cap Gain ($)	0.00	0.00	0.00	0.00	0.00	0.00	0.00	0.00	3.58	4.14
Net Asset Value ($)	16.31	26.38	22.20	20.58	19.71	17.94	14.42	19.52	24.00	32.28
Expense Ratio (%)	na	1.00	1.00	1.00	1.00	1.00	1.00	1.00	1.00	1.00
Yield (%)	0.51	0.12	0.06	0.41	0.03	0.00	0.00	0.00	0.00	0.00
Portfolio Turnover (%)	na	112	127	77	131	159	135	114	102	92
Total Assets (Millions $)	2,510	4,049	3,919	4,100	4,350	4,482	3,832	6,273	8,376	9,631

PORTFOLIO (as of 9/30/08)

Portfolio Manager: Woodhams/LeGard - 1997

Investment Style

✔ Large Cap	✔ Growth
Mid Cap	Grth/Val
Small Cap	Value

Portfolio

93.6%	U.S. stock	0.0%	conv't
4.3%	int'l stock	0.0%	preferred
0.0%	U.S. bonds	1.2%	other
0.0%	int'l bonds	0.8%	cash

Number of Investments: 87

Percent of Portfolio in Top 10 Investments: 25%

SHAREHOLDER INFORMATION

Minimum Investment

Initial: $2,500 — Subsequent: $50

Minimum IRA Investment

Initial: $2,500 — Subsequent: $50

Maximum Fees

Load: none — 12b-1: none

Other: none

Services

✔ IRA

✔ Keogh

✔ Telephone Exchange

American Century Income & Growth Inv (BIGRX)

800-345-2021
www.americancentury.com

Large-Cap Stock

PERFORMANCE

fund inception date: 12/17/90

	3yr Annual	5yr Annual	10yr Annual	Bull	Bear
Return (%)	-8.7	-2.1	-1.0	100.6	-39.0
Differ From Category (+/-)	0.6 av	0.3 av	-0.6 av	-8.8 av	2.5 abv av

Standard Deviation	Category Risk Index	Beta
15.1%—blw av	0.88—blw av	0.97

	2008	2007	2006	2005	2004	2003	2002	2001	2000	1999
Return (%)	-34.7	-0.3	17.1	4.7	12.9	29.6	-19.4	-8.4	-10.6	17.9
Differ From Category (+/-)	3.9	-8.8	4.1	-1.8	1.3	-1.1	1.9	1.8	-9.1	-7.5
Return, Tax-Adjusted (%)	-34.9	-2.3	16.1	3.9	12.6	29.3	-19.9	-8.8	-10.9	17.4

PER SHARE DATA

	2008	2007	2006	2005	2004	2003	2002	2001	2000	1999
Dividends, Net Income ($)	0.42	0.48	0.59	0.59	0.59	0.43	0.33	0.30	0.29	0.33
Distrib'ns, Cap Gain ($)	0.00	3.81	1.56	1.22	0.00	0.00	0.00	0.00	0.00	0.07
Net Asset Value ($)	18.51	28.88	33.30	30.33	30.67	27.70	21.74	27.35	30.19	34.05
Expense Ratio (%)	0.68	0.67	0.67	0.67	0.68	0.69	0.69	0.68	0.67	0.68
Yield (%)	2.28	1.46	1.69	1.87	1.91	1.54	1.50	1.11	0.95	0.97
Portfolio Turnover (%)	57	27	63	70	74	67	67	61	64	58
Total Assets (Millions $)	1,387	2,703	3,615	3,665	3,972	3,820	3,147	4,475	5,417	6,347

PORTFOLIO (as of 9/30/08)

Portfolio Manager: Borgwardt/Schniedwind/Zhang - 1990

Investment Style

✔ Large Cap	Growth
Mid Cap	Grth/Val
Small Cap	✔ Value

Portfolio

97.9% U.S. stock	0.0% conv't
1.7% int'l stock	0.0% preferred
0.0% U.S. bonds	0.0% other
0.0% int'l bonds	0.4% cash

Number of Investments: 191
Percent of Portfolio in Top 10 Investments: 25%

SHAREHOLDER INFORMATION

Minimum Investment
Initial: $2,500 Subsequent: $50

Minimum IRA Investment
Initial: $2,500 Subsequent: $50

Maximum Fees
Load: none 12b-1: none
Other: none

Services
✔ IRA
✔ Keogh
✔ Telephone Exchange

Aston/Montag & Caldwell Growth N (MCGFX)

800-992-8151
www.astonfunds.com

Large-Cap Stock

PERFORMANCE — fund inception date: 11/2/94

	3yr Annual	5yr Annual	10yr Annual	Bull	Bear
Return (%)	-4.2	-0.7	-1.5	78.2	-34.1
Differ From Category (+/-)	5.1 high	1.7 abv av	-1.1 blw av	-31.2 low	7.4 high

Standard Deviation	Category Risk Index	Beta
16.1%—av	0.94—av	0.97

	2008	2007	2006	2005	2004	2003	2002	2001	2000	1999
Return (%)	-32.7	21.0	8.0	5.3	4.0	17.2	-22.9	-13.4	-7.4	22.5
Differ From Category (+/-)	5.9	12.5	-5.0	-1.2	-7.5	-13.5	-1.6	-3.2	-5.9	-2.9
Return, Tax-Adjusted (%)	-33.1	18.6	7.9	5.3	4.0	17.2	-22.9	-13.4	-9.8	21.3

PER SHARE DATA

	2008	2007	2006	2005	2004	2003	2002	2001	2000	1999
Dividends, Net Income ($)	0.06	0.07	0.06	0.06	0.03	0.02	0.00	0.00	0.00	0.00
Distrib'ns, Cap Gain ($)	0.60	4.03	0.17	0.00	0.00	0.00	0.00	0.00	4.08	1.65
Net Asset Value ($)	17.35	26.76	25.49	23.80	22.65	21.79	18.60	24.12	27.83	34.64
Expense Ratio (%)	na	1.07	1.06	1.03	1.02	1.06	1.06	1.05	1.03	1.05
Yield (%)	0.31	0.24	0.21	0.27	0.14	0.07	0.00	0.00	0.00	0.00
Portfolio Turnover (%)	na	69	69	52	53	39	38	28	67	31
Total Assets (Millions $)	575	756	821	959	1,062	1,001	698	947	1,299	1,736

PORTFOLIO (as of 11/30/08)

Portfolio Manager: Canakaris - 1994

Investment Style

✔ Large Cap ✔ Growth
Mid Cap Grth/Val
Small Cap Value

Portfolio

97.6%	U.S. stock	0.0%	conv't
1.6%	int'l stock	0.0%	preferred
0.0%	U.S. bonds	0.0%	other
0.0%	int'l bonds	0.8%	cash

Number of Investments: 31
Percent of Portfolio in Top 10 Investments: 45%

SHAREHOLDER INFORMATION

Minimum Investment
Initial: $2,500 Subsequent: $50

Minimum IRA Investment
Initial: $500 Subsequent: $50

Maximum Fees
Load: none 12b-1: 0.25%
Other: none

Services
✔ IRA
Keogh
✔ Telephone Exchange

Brandywine Blue (BLUEX)

800-656-3017
www.brandywinefunds.com

Large-Cap Stock

PERFORMANCE — fund inception date: 1/10/91

	3yr Annual	5yr Annual	10yr Annual	Bull	Bear
Return (%)	-8.4	-0.2	3.2	137.8	-44.7
Differ From Category (+/-)	0.9 abv av	2.2 high	3.6 high	28.4 high	-3.2 blw av

Standard Deviation	Category Risk Index	Beta
19.2%—abv av	1.12—high	1.05

	2008	2007	2006	2005	2004	2003	2002	2001	2000	1999
Return (%)	-43.9	23.4	10.8	8.3	19.2	29.3	-13.5	-22.9	6.8	49.3
Differ From Category (+/-)	-5.3	14.9	-2.2	1.8	7.6	-1.4	7.8	-12.7	8.3	23.9
Return, Tax-Adjusted (%)	-43.9	21.6	10.3	7.7	19.2	29.3	-13.5	-22.9	0.9	47.6

PER SHARE DATA

	2008	2007	2006	2005	2004	2003	2002	2001	2000	1999
Dividends, Net Income ($)	0.00	0.00	0.00	0.00	0.00	0.00	0.00	0.00	0.00	0.00
Distrib'ns, Cap Gain ($)	0.00	3.87	1.10	1.14	0.00	0.00	0.00	0.00	10.71	2.18
Net Asset Value ($)	19.82	35.29	31.70	29.58	28.41	23.82	18.41	21.28	27.57	36.24
Expense Ratio (%)	1.13	1.12	1.10	1.12	1.13	1.14	1.13	1.09	1.07	1.08
Yield (%)	0.00	0.00	0.00	0.00	0.00	0.00	0.00	0.00	0.00	0.00
Portfolio Turnover (%)	267	184	207	181	247	300	311	274	245	228
Total Assets (Millions $)	2,864	3,732	2,131	1,352	663	379	240	257	388	399

PORTFOLIO (as of 9/30/08)

Portfolio Manager: D'Alonzo/Fenn/Ragard - 1991

Investment Style

✔ Large Cap ✔ Growth
✔ Mid Cap Grth/Val
Small Cap Value

Portfolio

86.8%	U.S. stock	0.0%	conv't
3.6%	int'l stock	0.0%	preferred
0.0%	U.S. bonds	0.0%	other
0.0%	int'l bonds	9.6%	cash

Number of Investments: 36
Percent of Portfolio in Top 10 Investments: 44%

SHAREHOLDER INFORMATION

Minimum Investment
Initial: $10,000 Subsequent: $1,000

Minimum IRA Investment
Initial: $10,000 Subsequent: $1,000

Maximum Fees
Load: none 12b-1: none
Other: none

Services
✔ IRA
✔ Keogh
✔ Telephone Exchange

CGM Focus
(CGMFX)

800-598-0778
www.cgmfunds.com

Large-Cap Stock

PERFORMANCE **fund inception date: 9/3/97**

	3yr Annual	5yr Annual	10yr Annual	Bull	Bear
Return (%)	2.3	8.5	17.6	420.1	-47.4
Differ From Category (+/-)	11.6 high	10.9 high	18.0 high	310.7 high	-5.9 low

Standard Deviation	Category Risk Index	Beta
32.3%—high	1.88—high	1.35

	2008	2007	2006	2005	2004	2003	2002	2001	2000	1999
Return (%)	-48.2	79.9	14.9	25.2	12.4	66.4	-17.8	47.6	53.9	8.4
Differ From Category (+/-)	-9.6	71.4	1.9	18.7	0.8	35.7	3.5	57.8	55.4	-17.0
Return, Tax-Adjusted (%)	-48.3	75.6	13.2	23.4	10.3	66.4	-17.8	45.8	52.5	8.3

PER SHARE DATA

	2008	2007	2006	2005	2004	2003	2002	2001	2000	1999
Dividends, Net Income ($)	0.22	0.05	0.81	0.44	0.04	0.00	0.00	0.01	0.36	0.03
Distrib'ns, Cap Gain ($)	0.00	9.91	2.92	3.12	4.07	0.00	0.00	1.44	0.00	0.00
Net Asset Value ($)	26.98	52.49	34.68	33.41	29.51	29.93	17.98	21.87	15.80	10.50
Expense Ratio (%)	na	1.27	1.02	1.07	1.12	1.18	1.20	1.20	1.21	1.21
Yield (%)	0.81	0.08	2.15	1.20	0.11	0.00	0.00	0.04	2.27	0.28
Portfolio Turnover (%)	na	384	333	282	327	204	155	254	551	288
Total Assets (Millions $)	4,161	5,460	2,276	1,636	925	774	385	250	79	69

PORTFOLIO (as of 9/30/08)

Portfolio Manager: Heebner - 1997

Investment Style

✔ Large Cap	Growth
✔ Mid Cap	✔ Grth/Val
✔ Small Cap	Value

Portfolio

62.7%	U.S. stock	0.0%	conv't
36.0%	int'l stock	0.0%	preferred
0.0%	U.S. bonds	0.0%	other
0.0%	int'l bonds	1.3%	cash

Number of Investments: 22

Percent of Portfolio in Top 10 Investments: 64%

SHAREHOLDER INFORMATION

Minimum Investment

Initial: $2,500 Subsequent: $50

Minimum IRA Investment

Initial: $1,000 Subsequent: $50

Maximum Fees

Load: none 12b-1: none

Other: none

Services

✔ IRA

✔ Keogh

✔ Telephone Exchange

Dreyfus Appreciation (DGAGX)

800-645-6561
www.dreyfus.com

Large-Cap Stock

PERFORMANCE — fund inception date: 1/18/84

	3yr Annual	5yr Annual	10yr Annual	Bull	Bear
Return (%)	-5.8	-1.7	-0.9	78.0	-34.0
Differ From Category (+/-)	3.5 high	0.7 abv av	-0.5 av	-31.4 low	7.5 high

Standard Deviation	Category Risk Index	Beta
13.3%—blw av	0.77—low	0.85

	2008	2007	2006	2005	2004	2003	2002	2001	2000	1999
Return (%)	-32.4	6.5	16.2	4.1	5.5	20.3	-17.2	-10.8	1.7	9.9
Differ From Category (+/-)	6.2	-2.0	3.2	-2.4	-6.1	-10.4	4.1	-0.6	3.3	-15.5
Return, Tax-Adjusted (%)	-33.1	5.8	15.3	3.9	5.3	20.1	-17.5	-11.1	0.1	9.6

PER SHARE DATA

	2008	2007	2006	2005	2004	2003	2002	2001	2000	1999
Dividends, Net Income ($)	0.72	0.64	0.62	0.54	0.52	0.41	0.30	0.31	0.29	0.23
Distrib'ns, Cap Gain ($)	1.23	1.30	1.79	0.00	0.00	0.00	0.02	0.00	3.22	0.31
Net Asset Value ($)	28.23	44.70	43.79	39.75	38.69	37.14	31.20	38.02	42.94	45.73
Expense Ratio (%)	na	0.95	0.95	0.92	0.95	0.96	0.97	0.91	0.88	0.88
Yield (%)	2.44	1.38	1.36	1.37	1.33	1.10	0.94	0.80	0.61	0.50
Portfolio Turnover (%)	na	7	1	7	8	5	1	5	4	11
Total Assets (Millions $)	2,482	4,391	4,398	4,472	4,436	3,994	338	230	220	232

PORTFOLIO (as of 10/31/08)

Portfolio Manager: Sarofim - 1984

Investment Style

✔ Large Cap	Growth
Mid Cap	✔ Grth/Val
Small Cap	Value

Portfolio

86.7% U.S. stock	0.0% conv't
13.4% int'l stock	0.0% preferred
0.0% U.S. bonds	0.0% other
0.0% int'l bonds	0.0% cash

Number of Investments: 62
Percent of Portfolio in Top 10 Investments: 45%

SHAREHOLDER INFORMATION

Minimum Investment
Initial: $2,500 Subsequent: $100

Minimum IRA Investment
Initial: $750 Subsequent: $0

Maximum Fees
Load: none 12b-1: none
Other: none

Services
✔ IRA
✔ Keogh
✔ Telephone Exchange

Fairholme

(FAIRX)

866-202-2263
www.fairholmefunds.com

Large-Cap Stock

PERFORMANCE **fund inception date: 12/29/99**

	3yr Annual	5yr Annual	10yr Annual	Bull	Bear
Return (%)	-2.7	5.5	na	167.7	-34.2
Differ From Category (+/-)	6.6 high	7.9 high	na	58.3 high	7.3 high

Standard Deviation	Category Risk Index	Beta
18.9%—abv av	1.10—abv av	1.08

	2008	2007	2006	2005	2004	2003	2002	2001	2000	1999
Return (%)	-29.8	12.3	16.7	13.7	24.9	23.9	-1.6	6.1	46.5	—
Differ From Category (+/-)	8.8	3.8	3.7	7.2	13.3	-6.8	19.7	16.3	48.0	—
Return, Tax-Adjusted (%)	-30.0	11.9	16.4	13.2	24.4	23.9	-1.8	5.9	45.9	—

PER SHARE DATA

	2008	2007	2006	2005	2004	2003	2002	2001	2000	1999
Dividends, Net Income ($)	0.11	0.21	0.24	0.23	0.06	0.00	0.03	0.03	0.04	—
Distrib'ns, Cap Gain ($)	0.43	0.48	0.17	0.48	0.53	0.01	0.10	0.09	0.25	—
Net Asset Value ($)	21.84	31.86	28.99	25.19	22.77	18.70	15.09	15.47	14.68	—
Expense Ratio (%)	na	1.00	1.00	1.00	1.00	1.00	1.00	1.00	1.00	—
Yield (%)	0.47	0.66	0.83	0.89	0.25	0.00	0.20	0.18	0.24	—
Portfolio Turnover (%)	na	14	20	37	23	13	48	29	39	—
Total Assets (Millions $)	7,247	6,690	3,839	1,578	264	93	49	26	17	—

PORTFOLIO (as of 8/31/08)

Portfolio Manager: Berkowitz/Trauner/Fernandez - 1999

Investment Style

✔ Large Cap	Growth
✔ Mid Cap	✔ Grth/Val
Small Cap	Value

Portfolio

70.2%	U.S. stock	0.0%	conv't
7.7%	int'l stock	0.0%	preferred
2.3%	U.S. bonds	5.0%	other
0.0%	int'l bonds	14.9%	cash

Number of Investments: 37
Percent of Portfolio in Top 10 Investments: 65%

SHAREHOLDER INFORMATION

Minimum Investment
Initial: $2,500 Subsequent: $1,000

Minimum IRA Investment
Initial: $2,500 Subsequent: $1,000

Maximum Fees
Load: 2.00% redemption 12b-1: none
Other: redemption fee applies for 60 days

Services
✔ IRA
Keogh
✔ Telephone Exchange

Fidelity
(FFIDX)
Large-Cap Stock

800-544-9797
www.fidelity.com

PERFORMANCE **fund inception date: 4/30/30**

	3yr Annual	5yr Annual	10yr Annual	Bull	Bear
Return (%)	-7.5	-1.7	-1.2	110.1	-42.1
Differ From Category (+/-)	1.8 abv av	0.7 abv av	-0.8 av	0.7 abv av	-0.6 av

Standard Deviation	Category Risk Index	Beta
16.8%—av	0.98—av	1.06

	2008	2007	2006	2005	2004	2003	2002	2001	2000	1999
Return (%)	-40.4	16.8	13.6	7.5	7.8	27.2	-22.3	-11.3	-11.0	24.2
Differ From Category (+/-)	-1.8	8.3	0.6	1.0	-3.8	-3.5	-1.0	-1.1	-9.5	-1.2
Return, Tax-Adjusted (%)	-40.9	15.9	13.5	7.3	7.6	27.1	-22.6	-11.5	-13.7	22.6

PER SHARE DATA

	2008	2007	2006	2005	2004	2003	2002	2001	2000	1999
Dividends, Net Income ($)	0.42	0.35	0.31	0.29	0.39	0.22	0.21	0.21	0.23	0.29
Distrib'ns, Cap Gain ($)	0.99	1.63	0.00	0.00	0.00	0.00	0.00	0.00	5.20	2.21
Net Asset Value ($)	22.76	39.85	35.84	31.82	29.88	28.08	22.26	28.88	32.77	42.61
Expense Ratio (%)	0.55	0.56	0.56	0.57	0.59	0.61	0.53	0.51	0.56	0.55
Yield (%)	1.75	0.84	0.86	0.91	1.30	0.78	0.94	0.72	0.60	0.64
Portfolio Turnover (%)	80	50	72	74	53	32	155	217	113	71
Total Assets (Millions $)	4,395	7,882	7,679	9,602	10,812	10,388	8,696	12,452	15,070	16,114

PORTFOLIO (as of 11/30/08)

Portfolio Manager: Avery - 2002

Investment Style

✔ Large Cap	Growth
✔ Mid Cap	✔ Grth/Val
Small Cap	Value

Portfolio

90.8%	U.S. stock	0.0%	conv't
5.0%	int'l stock	0.0%	preferred
0.0%	U.S. bonds	0.0%	other
0.0%	int'l bonds	4.2%	cash

Number of Investments: 136
Percent of Portfolio in Top 10 Investments: 27%

SHAREHOLDER INFORMATION

Minimum Investment
Initial: $2,500 Subsequent: $250

Minimum IRA Investment
Initial: $2,500 Subsequent: $200

Maximum Fees
Load: none 12b-1: none
Other: maint fee for low bal

Services
✔ IRA
✔ Keogh
✔ Telephone Exchange

Fidelity Contrafund (FCNTX)

800-544-9797
www.fidelity.com

Large-Cap Stock

PERFORMANCE — fund inception date: 5/17/67

	3yr Annual	5yr Annual	10yr Annual	Bull	Bear
Return (%)	-5.7	2.3	2.8	144.6	-38.6
Differ From Category (+/-)	3.6 high	4.7 high	3.2 high	35.2 high	2.9 abv av

Standard Deviation	Category Risk Index	Beta
16.2%—av	0.94—av	0.98

	2008	2007	2006	2005	2004	2003	2002	2001	2000	1999
Return (%)	-37.2	19.7	11.5	16.2	15.0	27.9	-9.7	-12.6	-6.9	25.0
Differ From Category (+/-)	1.4	11.2	-1.5	9.7	3.4	-2.8	11.6	-2.4	-5.3	-0.4
Return, Tax-Adjusted (%)	-37.4	18.6	9.9	15.9	15.0	27.9	-9.7	-12.8	-9.2	21.2

PER SHARE DATA

	2008	2007	2006	2005	2004	2003	2002	2001	2000	1999
Dividends, Net Income ($)	0.21	0.44	0.39	0.23	0.05	0.04	0.05	0.22	0.24	0.28
Distrib'ns, Cap Gain ($)	0.65	4.48	6.49	0.97	0.00	0.00	0.00	0.00	6.62	10.22
Net Asset Value ($)	45.26	73.11	65.21	64.76	56.74	49.35	38.60	42.77	49.18	60.02
Expense Ratio (%)	na	0.89	0.89	0.88	0.94	0.98	0.99	0.91	0.84	0.62
Yield (%)	0.45	0.56	0.54	0.34	0.07	0.08	0.12	0.51	0.43	0.39
Portfolio Turnover (%)	na	56	76	60	64	67	80	154	166	177
Total Assets (Millions $)	45,195	80,864	68,576	60,094	44,484	36,051	27,695	32,321	40,220	46,927

PORTFOLIO (as of 11/30/08)

Portfolio Manager: Danoff - 1990

Investment Style

✔ Large Cap	✔ Growth
✔ Mid Cap	Grth/Val
Small Cap	Value

Portfolio

76.9%	U.S. stock	0.0%	conv't
12.9%	int'l stock	0.0%	preferred
0.0%	U.S. bonds	0.6%	other
0.0%	int'l bonds	9.6%	cash

Number of Investments: 308

Percent of Portfolio in Top 10 Investments: 36%

SHAREHOLDER INFORMATION

Minimum Investment

Initial: $2,500 Subsequent: $250

Minimum IRA Investment

Initial: $500 Subsequent: $250

Maximum Fees

Load: none 12b-1: none

Other: maint fee for low bal

Services

✔ IRA
✔ Keogh
✔ Telephone Exchange

Fidelity Disciplined Equity (FDEQX)

800-544-6666
www.fidelity.com

Large-Cap Stock

PERFORMANCE — fund inception date: 12/28/88

	3yr Annual	5yr Annual	10yr Annual	Bull	Bear
Return (%)	-8.8	-1.3	-0.2	113.7	-42.2
Differ From Category (+/-)	0.5 av	1.1 abv av	0.2 av	4.3 abv av	-0.7 av

Standard Deviation	Category Risk Index	Beta
16.7%—av	0.97—av	1.07

	2008	2007	2006	2005	2004	2003	2002	2001	2000	1999
Return (%)	-40.1	10.8	14.5	10.2	12.0	27.1	-18.6	-14.3	-3.5	22.4
Differ From Category (+/-)	-1.5	2.3	1.5	3.7	0.4	-3.6	2.7	-4.1	-2.0	-3.0
Return, Tax-Adjusted (%)	-40.3	9.4	13.1	10.1	11.9	27.0	-18.7	-14.3	-6.1	18.7

PER SHARE DATA

	2008	2007	2006	2005	2004	2003	2002	2001	2000	1999
Dividends, Net Income ($)	0.26	0.26	0.19	0.18	0.18	0.11	0.03	0.05	0.16	0.27
Distrib'ns, Cap Gain ($)	0.00	2.43	2.49	0.00	0.00	0.00	0.00	0.00	3.57	4.90
Net Asset Value ($)	17.41	29.52	29.02	27.71	25.29	22.74	17.97	22.10	25.82	30.51
Expense Ratio (%)	0.87	0.90	0.91	0.87	0.90	0.90	1.00	0.84	0.79	0.62
Yield (%)	1.47	0.81	0.60	0.64	0.71	0.48	0.16	0.22	0.54	0.76
Portfolio Turnover (%)	186	152	98	80	64	64	68	101	118	113
Total Assets (Millions $)	9,080	12,112	8,143	6,104	4,951	3,987	2,752	2,992	3,393	3,614

PORTFOLIO (as of 11/30/08)

Portfolio Manager: Quinton - 2006

Investment Style

✔ Large Cap	Growth
✔ Mid Cap	✔ Grth/Val
Small Cap	Value

Portfolio

95.6%	U.S. stock	0.0%	conv't
2.1%	int'l stock	0.0%	preferred
0.0%	U.S. bonds	0.1%	other
0.0%	int'l bonds	2.2%	cash

Number of Investments: 126

Percent of Portfolio in Top 10 Investments: 31%

SHAREHOLDER INFORMATION

Minimum Investment

Initial: $2,500 Subsequent: $250

Minimum IRA Investment

Initial: $500 Subsequent: $100

Maximum Fees

Load: none 12b-1: none

Other: maint fee for low bal

Services

✔ IRA

✔ Keogh

✔ Telephone Exchange

Fidelity Equity-Income (FEQIX)

800-544-6666
www.fidelity.com

Large-Cap Stock

PERFORMANCE — fund inception date: 5/16/66

	3yr Annual	5yr Annual	10yr Annual	Bull	Bear
Return (%)	-10.9	-3.6	-0.1	110.3	-45.3
Differ From Category (+/-)	-1.6 blw av	-1.2 blw av	0.3 av	0.9 abv av	-3.8 blw av

Standard Deviation	Category Risk Index	Beta
16.7%—av	0.97—av	1.08

	2008	2007	2006	2005	2004	2003	2002	2001	2000	1999
Return (%)	-41.7	1.3	19.8	5.7	11.2	29.9	-17.2	-5.1	8.5	7.1
Differ From Category (+/-)	-3.1	-7.1	6.8	-0.8	-0.4	-0.8	4.1	5.1	10.0	-18.3
Return, Tax-Adjusted (%)	-42.2	0.3	18.5	4.8	10.5	29.3	-17.8	-6.1	6.6	4.7

PER SHARE DATA

	2008	2007	2006	2005	2004	2003	2002	2001	2000	1999
Dividends, Net Income ($)	0.96	1.02	0.94	0.84	0.81	0.71	0.68	0.76	0.87	0.81
Distrib'ns, Cap Gain ($)	0.85	3.20	3.50	2.13	1.66	0.93	0.14	1.18	3.32	5.14
Net Asset Value ($)	30.87	55.16	58.55	52.78	52.78	49.75	39.67	48.77	53.43	53.48
Expense Ratio (%)	0.66	0.67	0.67	0.69	0.70	0.71	0.67	0.67	0.67	0.67
Yield (%)	3.02	1.74	1.51	1.52	1.48	1.40	1.70	1.52	1.53	1.38
Portfolio Turnover (%)	23	24	19	19	25	23	23	25	26	30
Total Assets (Millions $)	17,311	30,460	30,629	26,058	26,372	23,520	17,734	21,832	22,353	22,829

PORTFOLIO (as of 11/30/08)

Portfolio Manager: Petersen - 1993

Investment Style

✔ Large Cap	Growth
Mid Cap	Grth/Val
Small Cap	✔ Value

Portfolio

88.5%	U.S. stock	0.4%	conv't
6.4%	int'l stock	1.1%	preferred
0.6%	U.S. bonds	0.5%	other
0.0%	int'l bonds	2.6%	cash

Number of Investments: 260

Percent of Portfolio in Top 10 Investments: 31%

SHAREHOLDER INFORMATION

Minimum Investment

Initial: $2,500 Subsequent: $250

Minimum IRA Investment

Initial: $500 Subsequent: $100

Maximum Fees

Load: none 12b-1: none

Other: maint fee for low bal

Services

✔ IRA

✔ Keogh

✔ Telephone Exchange

Fidelity Focused Stock (FTQGX)

800-544-6666
www.fidelity.com

Large-Cap Stock

PERFORMANCE — fund inception date: 11/12/96

	3yr Annual	5yr Annual	10yr Annual	Bull	Bear
Return (%)	-6.3	2.3	-0.9	125.6	-36.1
Differ From Category (+/-)	3.0 high	4.7 high	-0.5 av	16.2 high	5.4 high

Standard Deviation	Category Risk Index	Beta
16.5%—av	0.96—av	0.96

	2008	2007	2006	2005	2004	2003	2002	2001	2000	1999
Return (%)	-33.1	17.0	5.1	18.2	15.5	23.1	-39.3	-13.6	-6.1	34.7
Differ From Category (+/-)	5.5	8.5	-7.9	11.7	3.9	-7.6	-18.0	-3.4	-4.6	9.4
Return, Tax-Adjusted (%)	-33.2	15.4	5.1	18.1	15.4	23.0	-39.3	-13.6	-7.8	31.7

PER SHARE DATA

	2008	2007	2006	2005	2004	2003	2002	2001	2000	1999
Dividends, Net Income ($)	0.07	0.06	0.01	0.04	0.03	0.02	0.00	0.00	0.02	0.04
Distrib'ns, Cap Gain ($)	0.00	1.29	0.00	0.00	0.00	0.00	0.00	0.00	1.25	1.99
Net Asset Value ($)	8.83	13.29	12.50	11.90	10.10	8.77	7.14	11.76	13.61	15.82
Expense Ratio (%)	0.99	0.99	0.98	0.98	1.02	1.03	1.20	1.22	1.02	0.86
Yield (%)	0.79	0.41	0.07	0.33	0.29	0.22	0.00	0.00	0.13	0.22
Portfolio Turnover (%)	491	343	202	158	201	199	256	309	94	128
Total Assets (Millions $)	124	93	80	135	44	36	32	54	68	61

PORTFOLIO (as of 11/30/08)

Portfolio Manager: DuFour - 2007

Investment Style

✔ Large Cap	Growth
✔ Mid Cap	✔ Grth/Val
Small Cap	Value

Portfolio

80.2%	U.S. stock	0.0%	conv't
0.0%	int'l stock	0.0%	preferred
0.0%	U.S. bonds	0.0%	other
0.0%	int'l bonds	19.8%	cash

Number of Investments: 44

Percent of Portfolio in Top 10 Investments: 56%

SHAREHOLDER INFORMATION

Minimum Investment

Initial: $2,500 Subsequent: $250

Minimum IRA Investment

Initial: $500 Subsequent: $100

Maximum Fees

Load: none 12b-1: none

Other: maint fee for low bal

Services

✔ IRA

✔ Keogh

✔ Telephone Exchange

Fidelity Growth Discovery (FDSVX)

800-544-9797
www.fidelity.com

Large-Cap Stock

PERFORMANCE — fund inception date: 3/31/98

	3yr Annual	5yr Annual	10yr Annual	Bull	Bear
Return (%)	-8.4	-2.8	0.3	109.5	-48.8
Differ From Category (+/-)	0.9 abv av	-0.4 av	0.7 abv av	0.1 abv av	-7.3 low

Standard Deviation	Category Risk Index	Beta
18.9%—abv av	1.10—abv av	1.12

	2008	2007	2006	2005	2004	2003	2002	2001	2000	1999
Return (%)	-46.8	26.8	13.9	2.1	10.6	19.8	-16.0	-9.6	-8.4	42.5
Differ From Category (+/-)	-8.2	18.3	0.9	-4.4	-1.0	-10.9	5.3	0.6	-6.9	17.1
Return, Tax-Adjusted (%)	-46.8	26.7	13.7	1.9	10.4	19.7	-16.1	-9.8	-11.7	41.2

PER SHARE DATA

	2008	2007	2006	2005	2004	2003	2002	2001	2000	1999
Dividends, Net Income ($)	0.07	0.04	0.12	0.13	0.13	0.05	0.03	0.04	0.00	0.00
Distrib'ns, Cap Gain ($)	0.00	0.00	0.02	0.00	0.00	0.00	0.00	0.00	2.45	0.72
Net Asset Value ($)	8.61	16.26	12.85	11.41	11.30	10.34	8.67	10.35	11.49	14.91
Expense Ratio (%)	0.90	0.80	0.61	0.81	0.84	0.97	0.99	0.91	0.91	0.93
Yield (%)	0.84	0.21	0.93	1.13	1.15	0.48	0.34	0.38	0.00	0.00
Portfolio Turnover (%)	149	199	184	229	249	367	259	168	291	293
Total Assets (Millions $)	931	1,897	448	432	552	655	672	1,032	1,451	1,374

PORTFOLIO (as of 11/30/08)

Portfolio Manager: Weiner - 2007

Investment Style

✔ Large Cap	✔ Growth
Mid Cap	Grth/Val
Small Cap	Value

Portfolio

84.0%	U.S. stock	0.0%	conv't
9.9%	int'l stock	0.0%	preferred
0.0%	U.S. bonds	0.0%	other
0.0%	int'l bonds	6.1%	cash

Number of Investments: 90

Percent of Portfolio in Top 10 Investments: 44%

SHAREHOLDER INFORMATION

Minimum Investment

Initial: $2,500 Subsequent: $250

Minimum IRA Investment

Initial: $2,500 Subsequent: $200

Maximum Fees

Load: none 12b-1: none

Other: maint fee for low bal

Services

✔ IRA
✔ Keogh
✔ Telephone Exchange

Fidelity Large Cap Value (FSLVX)

800-544-6666
www.fidelity.com

Large-Cap Stock

PERFORMANCE — fund inception date: 11/15/01

	3yr Annual	5yr Annual	10yr Annual	Bull	Bear
Return (%)	-9.9	-0.9	na	124.9	-42.9
Differ From Category (+/-)	-0.6 blw av	1.5 abv av	na	15.5 abv av	-1.4 blw av

Standard Deviation	Category Risk Index	Beta
16.2%—av	0.94—av	1.05

	2008	2007	2006	2005	2004	2003	2002	2001	2000	1999
Return (%)	-39.8	3.7	17.1	11.2	17.7	25.9	-17.2	—	—	—
Differ From Category (+/-)	-1.2	-4.8	4.1	4.7	6.1	-4.8	4.1	—	—	—
Return, Tax-Adjusted (%)	-39.9	2.7	16.6	10.6	17.5	25.7	-17.5	—	—	—

PER SHARE DATA

	2008	2007	2006	2005	2004	2003	2002	2001	2000	1999
Dividends, Net Income ($)	0.19	0.13	0.13	0.11	0.05	0.09	0.08	—	—	—
Distrib'ns, Cap Gain ($)	0.00	0.87	0.26	0.34	0.11	0.00	0.00	—	—	—
Net Asset Value ($)	8.55	14.50	14.96	13.13	12.22	10.52	8.43	—	—	—
Expense Ratio (%)	0.85	0.89	0.84	1.06	1.18	1.19	1.20	—	—	—
Yield (%)	2.16	0.85	0.85	0.81	0.40	0.85	0.94	—	—	—
Portfolio Turnover (%)	204	164	175	170	72	95	81	—	—	—
Total Assets (Millions $)	1,017	1,626	1,307	516	162	24	16	—	—	—

PORTFOLIO (as of 11/30/08)

Portfolio Manager: Dirks - 2005

Investment Style

✔ Large Cap	Growth
Mid Cap	Grth/Val
Small Cap	✔ Value

Portfolio

100.0% U.S. stock	0.0% conv't
0.0% int'l stock	0.0% preferred
0.0% U.S. bonds	0.0% other
0.0% int'l bonds	0.0% cash

Number of Investments: 116

Percent of Portfolio in Top 10 Investments: 37%

SHAREHOLDER INFORMATION

Minimum Investment

Initial: $2,500 Subsequent: $250

Minimum IRA Investment

Initial: $500 Subsequent: $100

Maximum Fees

Load: none 12b-1: none

Other: maint fee for low bal

Services

✔ IRA

Keogh

✔ Telephone Exchange

Fidelity Spartan Total Market Index Inv (FSTMX)

800-544-9797
www.fidelity.com

Large-Cap Stock

PERFORMANCE — fund inception date: 11/5/97

	3yr Annual	5yr Annual	10yr Annual	Bull	Bear
Return (%)	-8.5	-1.8	-0.8	110.4	-40.3
Differ From Category (+/-)	0.8 abv av	0.6 abv av	-0.4 av	1.0 abv av	1.2 av

Standard Deviation	Category Risk Index	Beta
15.9%—av	0.92—blw av	1.04

	2008	2007	2006	2005	2004	2003	2002	2001	2000	1999
Return (%)	-37.2	5.5	15.7	6.4	12.1	31.2	-21.0	-10.8	-11.0	23.2
Differ From Category (+/-)	1.4	-3.0	2.7	-0.1	0.5	0.5	0.3	-0.6	-9.5	-2.2
Return, Tax-Adjusted (%)	-37.5	5.2	15.5	6.1	11.8	31.0	-21.5	-11.2	-11.4	22.7

PER SHARE DATA

	2008	2007	2006	2005	2004	2003	2002	2001	2000	1999
Dividends, Net Income ($)	0.64	0.65	0.52	0.51	0.47	0.32	0.32	0.32	0.30	0.29
Distrib'ns, Cap Gain ($)	0.00	0.24	0.00	0.00	0.00	0.00	0.00	0.00	0.18	0.19
Net Asset Value ($)	25.07	40.90	39.58	34.66	33.05	29.91	23.05	29.56	33.50	38.13
Expense Ratio (%)	0.10	0.10	0.10	0.17	0.25	0.25	0.25	0.25	0.25	0.27
Yield (%)	2.55	1.57	1.31	1.47	1.42	1.06	1.38	1.08	0.89	0.75
Portfolio Turnover (%)	4	4	6	6	3	3	7	16	11	4
Total Assets (Millions $)	3,933	4,855	3,666	1,955	2,774	1,970	1,033	1,103	1,028	756

PORTFOLIO (as of 11/30/08)

Portfolio Manager: Adams/Simon/ Waddell - 2005

Investment Style

✔ Large Cap	Growth
✔ Mid Cap	✔ Grth/Val
Small Cap	Value

Portfolio

97.1%	U.S. stock	0.0%	conv't
0.2%	int'l stock	0.0%	preferred
0.0%	U.S. bonds	0.0%	other
0.0%	int'l bonds	2.7%	cash

Number of Investments: 3,241
Percent of Portfolio in Top 10 Investments: 20%

SHAREHOLDER INFORMATION

Minimum Investment
Initial: $10,000 Subsequent: $1,000

Minimum IRA Investment
Initial: $0 Subsequent: $0

Maximum Fees
Load: 0.50% redemption 12b-1: none
Other: redemption fee applies for 90 days; maint fee for low bal

Services
✔ IRA
✔ Keogh
✔ Telephone Exchange

Fidelity Strategic Dividend & Income (FSDIX)

800-544-6666
www.fidelity.com

Large-Cap Stock

PERFORMANCE — fund inception date: 12/23/03

	3yr Annual	5yr Annual	10yr Annual	Bull	Bear
Return (%)	-11.6	-2.8	na	na	-45.1
Differ From Category (+/-)	-2.3 blw av	-0.4 av	na	na	-3.6 blw av

Standard Deviation	Category Risk Index	Beta
17.5%—av	1.02—abv av	1.10

	2008	2007	2006	2005	2004	2003	2002	2001	2000	1999
Return (%)	-41.2	3.1	13.9	9.7	14.7	—	—	—	—	—
Differ From Category (+/-)	-2.6	-5.4	0.9	3.2	3.1	—	—	—	—	—
Return, Tax-Adjusted (%)	-41.6	2.1	12.9	9.3	14.4	—	—	—	—	—

PER SHARE DATA

	2008	2007	2006	2005	2004	2003	2002	2001	2000	1999
Dividends, Net Income ($)	0.26	0.25	0.23	0.22	0.17	—	—	—	—	—
Distrib'ns, Cap Gain ($)	0.05	0.61	0.61	0.13	0.00	—	—	—	—	—
Net Asset Value ($)	7.16	12.57	13.01	12.16	11.40	—	—	—	—	—
Expense Ratio (%)	na	0.78	0.79	0.79	0.90	—	—	—	—	—
Yield (%)	3.67	1.88	1.69	1.74	1.53	—	—	—	—	—
Portfolio Turnover (%)	na	90	125	64	62	—	—	—	—	—
Total Assets (Millions $)	394	1,129	1,081	816	514	—	—	—	—	—

PORTFOLIO (as of 11/30/08)

Portfolio Manager: Young/Bewick - 2005

Investment Style

✔ Large Cap	Growth
Mid Cap	Grth/Val
Small Cap	✔ Value

Portfolio

70.1%	U.S. stock	0.0%	conv't
2.6%	int'l stock	21.7%	preferred
2.4%	U.S. bonds	0.7%	other
0.0%	int'l bonds	2.4%	cash

Number of Investments: 348

Percent of Portfolio in Top 10 Investments: 21%

SHAREHOLDER INFORMATION

Minimum Investment

Initial: $2,500 Subsequent: $250

Minimum IRA Investment

Initial: $500 Subsequent: $100

Maximum Fees

Load: none 12b-1: none

Other: maint fee for low bal

Services

✔ IRA

✔ Keogh

✔ Telephone Exchange

Fidelity Trend

800-544-5555
www.fidelity.com

(FTRNX)

Large-Cap Stock

PERFORMANCE					fund inception date: 6/16/58
	3yr Annual	5yr Annual	10yr Annual	Bull	Bear
Return (%)	-9.3	-2.4	0.2	121.6	-46.9
Differ From Category (+/-)	0.0 av	0.0 av	0.6 abv av	12.2 abv av	-5.4 low

Standard Deviation	Category Risk Index	Beta
19.3%—abv av	1.12—high	1.18

	2008	2007	2006	2005	2004	2003	2002	2001	2000	1999
Return (%)	-44.5	18.8	13.1	7.4	10.6	27.6	-20.9	-12.4	-7.2	40.7
Differ From Category (+/-)	-5.9	10.3	0.1	0.9	-1.0	-3.1	0.4	-2.2	-5.7	15.3
Return, Tax-Adjusted (%)	-44.5	17.5	12.9	7.3	10.4	27.5	-21.1	-12.7	-10.3	38.3

PER SHARE DATA

	2008	2007	2006	2005	2004	2003	2002	2001	2000	1999
Dividends, Net Income ($)	0.18	0.06	0.55	0.43	0.54	0.34	0.16	0.23	0.69	0.20
Distrib'ns, Cap Gain ($)	0.01	5.55	0.00	0.00	0.00	0.00	0.00	0.20	9.85	6.15
Net Asset Value ($)	39.09	70.72	64.18	57.22	53.66	48.98	38.64	49.04	56.42	71.72
Expense Ratio (%)	na	0.83	0.80	0.80	0.84	0.79	1.01	0.74	0.52	0.58
Yield (%)	0.46	0.07	0.85	0.74	1.00	0.69	0.40	0.46	1.04	0.25
Portfolio Turnover (%)	na	194	81	64	59	80	79	102	267	309
Total Assets (Millions $)	534	1,139	911	874	883	867	730	1,005	1,242	1,533

PORTFOLIO (as of 11/30/08)

Portfolio Manager: Feingold - 2007

Investment Style

✔ Large Cap ✔ Growth
✔ Mid Cap Grth/Val
✔ Small Cap Value

Portfolio

92.9% U.S. stock	0.0% conv't
5.1% int'l stock	0.0% preferred
0.0% U.S. bonds	0.3% other
0.0% int'l bonds	1.7% cash

Number of Investments: 167
Percent of Portfolio in Top 10 Investments: 25%

SHAREHOLDER INFORMATION

Minimum Investment
Initial: $2,500 Subsequent: $250

Minimum IRA Investment
Initial: $500 Subsequent: $250

Maximum Fees
Load: none 12b-1: none
Other: maint fee for low bal

Services
✔ IRA
✔ Keogh
✔ Telephone Exchange

FMI Large Cap (FMIHX)

800-811-5311
www.fiduciarymgt.com

Large-Cap Stock

PERFORMANCE — fund inception date: 12/31/01

	3yr Annual	5yr Annual	10yr Annual	Bull	Bear
Return (%)	-3.9	2.6	na	123.1	-29.7
Differ From Category (+/-)	5.4 high	5.0 high	na	13.7 abv av	11.8 high

Standard Deviation	Category Risk Index	Beta
12.2%—blw av	0.71—low	0.77

	2008	2007	2006	2005	2004	2003	2002	2001	2000	1999
Return (%)	-27.0	4.1	16.6	9.1	17.5	31.5	-15.0	—	—	—
Differ From Category (+/-)	11.6	-4.4	3.6	2.6	5.9	0.8	6.3	—	—	—
Return, Tax-Adjusted (%)	-27.1	3.5	16.2	8.6	17.1	31.2	-15.0	—	—	—

PER SHARE DATA

	2008	2007	2006	2005	2004	2003	2002	2001	2000	1999
Dividends, Net Income ($)	0.11	0.13	0.10	0.03	0.07	0.03	0.00	—	—	—
Distrib'ns, Cap Gain ($)	0.00	0.43	0.33	0.37	0.20	0.13	0.00	—	—	—
Net Asset Value ($)	11.04	15.26	15.19	13.39	12.66	11.02	8.50	—	—	—
Expense Ratio (%)	1.00	1.00	1.00	1.00	1.13	1.34	1.75	—	—	—
Yield (%)	1.03	0.85	0.63	0.24	0.56	0.24	0.00	—	—	—
Portfolio Turnover (%)	30	19	29	40	38	54	32	—	—	—
Total Assets (Millions $)	1,543	639	301	96	21	6	4	—	—	—

PORTFOLIO (as of 9/30/08)

Portfolio Manager: English/Kellner - 2001

Investment Style

✔ Large Cap	Growth
Mid Cap	✔ Grth/Val
Small Cap	Value

Portfolio

78.7%	U.S. stock	0.0%	conv't
10.4%	int'l stock	0.0%	preferred
0.0%	U.S. bonds	0.0%	other
0.0%	int'l bonds	10.9%	cash

Number of Investments: 29

Percent of Portfolio in Top 10 Investments: 44%

SHAREHOLDER INFORMATION

Minimum Investment

Initial: $1,000 Subsequent: $100

Minimum IRA Investment

Initial: $1,000 Subsequent: $100

Maximum Fees

Load: none 12b-1: none

Other: none

Services

✔ IRA

✔ Keogh

✔ Telephone Exchange

Gabelli Equity Income AAA (GABEX)

800-422-3554
www.gabelli.com

Large-Cap Stock

PERFORMANCE — fund inception date: 1/2/92

	3yr Annual	5yr Annual	10yr Annual	Bull	Bear
Return (%)	-5.5	0.3	3.7	114.4	-37.0
Differ From Category (+/-)	3.8 high	2.7 high	4.1 high	5.0 abv av	4.5 abv av

Standard Deviation	Category Risk Index	Beta
14.7%—blw av	0.85—low	0.95

	2008	2007	2006	2005	2004	2003	2002	2001	2000	1999
Return (%)	-35.0	8.9	19.2	6.3	13.0	28.2	-7.8	-0.9	11.3	9.3
Differ From Category (+/-)	3.6	0.4	6.2	-0.2	1.4	-2.5	13.5	9.3	12.8	-16.1
Return, Tax-Adjusted (%)	-35.3	8.3	18.5	5.8	12.3	27.9	-8.4	-1.8	7.4	6.1

PER SHARE DATA

	2008	2007	2006	2005	2004	2003	2002	2001	2000	1999
Dividends, Net Income ($)	0.36	0.33	0.39	0.36	0.35	0.27	0.25	0.24	0.48	0.23
Distrib'ns, Cap Gain ($)	0.00	0.40	0.45	0.19	0.31	0.00	0.00	0.16	2.08	2.14
Net Asset Value ($)	14.15	22.19	21.06	18.41	17.84	16.40	13.02	14.37	14.91	15.80
Expense Ratio (%)	1.43	1.42	1.46	1.46	1.49	2.09	1.50	1.55	1.66	1.32
Yield (%)	2.54	1.47	1.81	1.93	1.92	1.64	1.88	1.62	2.81	1.30
Portfolio Turnover (%)	22	12	14	11	12	27	12	41	33	39
Total Assets (Millions $)	860	1,226	886	647	396	301	197	152	94	89

PORTFOLIO (as of 9/30/08)

Portfolio Manager: Gabelli - 1992

Investment Style

✔ Large Cap	Growth
✔ Mid Cap	Grth/Val
Small Cap	✔ Value

Portfolio

83.3%	U.S. Stock	0.7%	conv't
14.1%	int'l stock	0.2%	preferred
0.2%	U.S. bonds	0.0%	other
0.0%	int'l bonds	1.5%	cash

Number of Investments: 391
Percent of Portfolio in Top 10 Investments: 19%

SHAREHOLDER INFORMATION

Minimum Investment
Initial: $1,000 Subsequent: $0

Minimum IRA Investment
Initial: $250 Subsequent: $0

Maximum Fees
Load: 2.00% redemption 12b-1: 0.25%
Other: redemption fee applies for 7 days

Services
✔ IRA
Keogh
✔ Telephone Exchange

Homestead Value (HOVLX)

800-258-3030
www.homesteadfunds.com

Large-Cap Stock

PERFORMANCE — fund inception date: 11/19/90

	3yr Annual	5yr Annual	10yr Annual	Bull	Bear
Return (%)	-8.3	-0.4	2.1	125.4	-40.0
Differ From Category (+/-)	1.0 abv av	2.0 abv av	2.5 high	16.0 abv av	1.5 abv av

Standard Deviation	Category Risk Index	Beta
16.4%—av	0.95—av	1.04

	2008	2007	2006	2005	2004	2003	2002	2001	2000	1999
Return (%)	-36.5	3.2	17.8	10.9	14.7	26.1	-11.6	5.9	9.6	-3.3
Differ From Category (+/-)	2.1	-5.3	4.8	4.4	3.1	-4.6	9.7	16.1	11.1	-28.7
Return, Tax-Adjusted (%)	-36.7	2.5	16.6	10.4	14.1	25.8	-12.1	4.5	8.9	-5.2

PER SHARE DATA

	2008	2007	2006	2005	2004	2003	2002	2001	2000	1999
Dividends, Net Income ($)	0.59	0.83	0.57	0.42	0.35	0.37	0.33	0.33	0.39	0.41
Distrib'ns, Cap Gain ($)	0.00	0.83	2.09	0.56	0.76	0.14	0.00	1.05	0.00	1.74
Net Asset Value ($)	22.03	35.48	35.94	32.78	30.44	27.52	22.24	25.50	25.38	23.53
Expense Ratio (%)	na	0.66	0.71	0.76	0.82	0.84	0.83	0.85	0.85	0.74
Yield (%)	2.70	2.29	1.49	1.24	1.12	1.32	1.47	1.24	1.52	1.63
Portfolio Turnover (%)	na	4	13	8	8	12	29	19	18	17
Total Assets (Millions $)	417	703	610	458	390	347	286	320	335	376

PORTFOLIO (as of 9/30/08)

Portfolio Manager: Morris/Teach/Ashton - 1990

Investment Style

✔ Large Cap — Growth
✔ Mid Cap — Grth/Val
Small Cap — ✔ Value

Portfolio

92.1%	U.S. stock	0.0%	conv't
3.8%	int'l stock	0.0%	preferred
0.0%	U.S. bonds	0.0%	other
0.0%	int'l bonds	4.1%	cash

Number of Investments: 51
Percent of Portfolio in Top 10 Investments: 33%

SHAREHOLDER INFORMATION

Minimum Investment
Initial: $500 — Subsequent: $0

Minimum IRA Investment
Initial: $200 — Subsequent: $0

Maximum Fees
Load: 2.00% redemption — 12b-1: none
Other: redemption fee applies for 30 days

Services
✔ IRA
Keogh
✔ Telephone Exchange

Janus Research

800-525-0020
www.janus.com

(JAMRX)

Large-Cap Stock

PERFORMANCE — fund inception date: 5/3/93

	3yr Annual	5yr Annual	10yr Annual	Bull	Bear
Return (%)	-9.1	-2.3	-1.2	125.6	-46.1
Differ From Category (+/-)	0.2 av	0.1 av	-0.8 blw av	16.2 high	-4.6 blw av

Standard Deviation	Category Risk Index	Beta
20.7%—abv av	1.20—high	1.30

	2008	2007	2006	2005	2004	2003	2002	2001	2000	1999
Return (%)	-44.4	24.5	8.6	6.8	10.7	32.1	-29.0	-29.8	-22.8	96.2
Differ From Category (+/-)	-5.8	16.0	-4.4	0.3	-0.9	1.4	-7.7	-19.6	-21.3	70.8
Return, Tax-Adjusted (%)	-44.4	24.5	8.6	6.7	10.7	32.1	-29.0	-29.9	-25.6	93.5

PER SHARE DATA

	2008	2007	2006	2005	2004	2003	2002	2001	2000	1999
Dividends, Net Income ($)	0.05	0.03	0.02	0.06	0.03	0.00	0.00	0.04	1.66	0.00
Distrib'ns, Cap Gain ($)	0.00	0.00	0.00	0.00	0.00	0.00	0.00	0.00	2.78	3.27
Net Asset Value ($)	17.22	31.04	24.95	22.98	21.57	19.50	14.76	20.79	29.67	43.81
Expense Ratio (%)	na	1.00	0.97	0.92	0.97	0.95	0.92	0.88	0.88	0.91
Yield (%)	0.27	0.08	0.07	0.26	0.13	0.00	0.00	0.21	5.12	0.00
Portfolio Turnover (%)	na	72	147	38	43	54	97	83	71	89
Total Assets (Millions $)	2,297	4,865	3,888	4,590	4,694	5,366	4,879	8,438	13,345	13,543

PORTFOLIO (as of 9/30/08)

Portfolio Manager: Goff - 2006

Investment Style

✔ Large Cap	✔ Growth
✔ Mid Cap	Grth/Val
Small Cap	Value

Portfolio

80.7%	U.S. stock	0.0%	conv't
19.3%	int'l stock	0.0%	preferred
0.0%	U.S. bonds	0.0%	other
0.0%	int'l bonds	0.0%	cash

Number of Investments: 106

Percent of Portfolio in Top 10 Investments: 19%

SHAREHOLDER INFORMATION

Minimum Investment

Initial: $2,500 Subsequent: $100

Minimum IRA Investment

Initial: $1,000 Subsequent: $100

Maximum Fees

Load: none 12b-1: none

Other: none

Services

✔ IRA

✔ Keogh

✔ Telephone Exchange

Jensen J
(JENSX)

800-992-4144
www.jenseninvestment.com

Large-Cap Stock

PERFORMANCE **fund inception date: 8/3/92**

	3yr Annual	5yr Annual	10yr Annual	Bull	Bear
Return (%)	-4.6	-2.0	2.7	63.3	-30.1
Differ From Category (+/-)	4.7 high	0.4 av	3.1 high	-46.1 low	11.4 high

Standard Deviation	Category Risk Index	Beta
13.2%—blw av	0.77—low	0.79

	2008	2007	2006	2005	2004	2003	2002	2001	2000	1999
Return (%)	-29.0	7.2	14.0	-1.4	6.0	16.0	-11.0	0.0	20.0	16.7
Differ From Category (+/-)	9.6	-1.3	1.0	-7.9	-5.6	-14.7	10.3	10.2	21.5	-8.7
Return, Tax-Adjusted (%)	-29.5	7.0	13.8	-1.6	5.9	15.9	-11.1	-0.2	17.0	16.6

PER SHARE DATA

	2008	2007	2006	2005	2004	2003	2002	2001	2000	1999
Dividends, Net Income ($)	0.30	0.25	0.21	0.19	0.16	0.15	0.07	0.08	0.08	0.05
Distrib'ns, Cap Gain ($)	0.65	0.21	0.00	0.00	0.00	0.00	0.00	0.00	3.07	0.00
Net Asset Value ($)	19.24	28.43	26.93	23.82	24.35	23.13	20.07	22.62	22.70	21.67
Expense Ratio (%)	0.85	0.85	0.85	0.85	0.88	0.90	1.00	0.95	0.94	0.96
Yield (%)	1.52	0.86	0.78	0.78	0.67	0.64	0.34	0.34	0.30	0.21
Portfolio Turnover (%)	8	14	10	9	5	7	1	4	32	14
Total Assets (Millions $)	1,449	1,888	1,833	2,275	2,547	1,718	1,051	118	40	27

PORTFOLIO (as of 9/30/08)

Portfolio Manager: Zagunis/Millen/Schoenstein - 1993

Investment Style

✔ Large Cap	✔ Growth
Mid Cap	Grth/Val
Small Cap	Value

Portfolio

98.3% U.S. stock	0.0% conv't
0.0% int'l stock	0.0% preferred
0.0% U.S. bonds	0.0% other
0.0% int'l bonds	1.7% cash

Number of Investments: 30
Percent of Portfolio in Top 10 Investments: 49%

SHAREHOLDER INFORMATION

Minimum Investment
Initial: $2,500 Subsequent: $100

Minimum IRA Investment
Initial: $2,500 Subsequent: $100

Maximum Fees
Load: none 12b-1: 0.25%
Other: none

Services
✔ IRA
✔ Keogh
✔ Telephone Exchange

Mairs & Power Growth (MPGFX)

800-304-7404
www.mairsandpower.com

Large-Cap Stock

PERFORMANCE — fund inception date: 11/7/58

	3yr Annual	5yr Annual	10yr Annual	Bull	Bear
Return (%)	-6.2	0.3	5.4	92.1	-30.6
Differ From Category (+/-)	3.1 high	2.7 high	5.8 high	-17.3 blw av	10.9 high

Standard Deviation	Category Risk Index	Beta
14.1%—blw av	0.82—low	0.85

	2008	2007	2006	2005	2004	2003	2002	2001	2000	1999
Return (%)	-28.6	4.9	10.2	4.3	17.9	26.3	-8.2	6.4	26.4	7.1
Differ From Category (+/-)	10.0	-3.6	-2.8	-2.2	6.3	-4.4	13.1	16.6	27.9	-18.3
Return, Tax-Adjusted (%)	-29.0	4.0	9.8	4.0	17.6	25.9	-8.6	5.3	23.9	5.5

PER SHARE DATA

	2008	2007	2006	2005	2004	2003	2002	2001	2000	1999
Dividends, Net Income ($)	1.22	1.04	0.93	0.78	0.68	0.53	0.45	0.51	0.55	0.47
Distrib'ns, Cap Gain ($)	0.86	3.59	0.99	0.93	0.82	0.77	0.24	2.00	4.82	2.74
Net Asset Value ($)	52.51	76.30	77.10	71.69	70.33	60.90	49.26	54.36	53.41	46.46
Expense Ratio (%)	na	0.68	0.69	0.70	0.73	0.75	0.78	0.76	0.78	0.79
Yield (%)	2.28	1.30	1.19	1.07	0.95	0.85	0.90	0.90	0.93	0.94
Portfolio Turnover (%)	na	4	4	3	3	2	1	8	15	5
Total Assets (Millions $)	1,683	2,614	2,694	2,523	2,056	1,307	772	677	582	547

PORTFOLIO (as of 6/30/08)

Portfolio Manager: Frels/Henneman - 1999

Investment Style

✔ Large Cap	Growth
✔ Mid Cap	✔ Grth/Val
Small Cap	Value

Portfolio

97.5% U.S. stock	0.0% conv't
0.0% int'l stock	0.0% preferred
0.0% U.S. bonds	0.0% other
0.0% int'l bonds	2.5% cash

Number of Investments: 46
Percent of Portfolio in Top 10 Investments: 42%

SHAREHOLDER INFORMATION

Minimum Investment
Initial: $2,500 — Subsequent: $100

Minimum IRA Investment
Initial: $1,000 — Subsequent: $100

Maximum Fees
Load: none — 12b-1: none
Other: none

Services
✔ IRA
Keogh
✔ Telephone Exchange

Manning & Napier Equity (EXEYX)

800-466-3863
www.manningnapier advisors.com

Large-Cap Stock

PERFORMANCE — fund inception date: 7/10/02

	3yr Annual	5yr Annual	10yr Annual	Bull	Bear
Return (%)	-7.3	0.3	na	125.4	-40.4
Differ From Category (+/-)	2.0 abv av	2.7 high	na	16.0 high	1.1 av

Standard Deviation	Category Risk Index	Beta
17.2%—av	1.00—av	1.06

	2008	2007	2006	2005	2004	2003	2002	2001	2000	1999
Return (%)	-36.4	3.7	20.5	10.5	15.8	27.3	—	—	—	—
Differ From Category (+/-)	2.2	-4.8	7.5	4.0	4.2	-3.3	—	—	—	—
Return, Tax-Adjusted (%)	-36.4	3.0	20.1	9.2	15.0	27.3	—	—	—	—

PER SHARE DATA

	2008	2007	2006	2005	2004	2003	2002	2001	2000	1999
Dividends, Net Income ($)	0.07	0.07	0.05	0.00	0.00	0.01	—	—	—	—
Distrib'ns, Cap Gain ($)	0.00	0.74	0.42	1.34	0.83	0.00	—	—	—	—
Net Asset Value ($)	12.17	19.22	19.32	16.41	16.06	14.58	—	—	—	—
Expense Ratio (%)	na	1.05	1.05	1.05	1.05	1.05	—	—	—	—
Yield (%)	0.54	0.36	0.25	0.00	0.00	0.04	—	—	—	—
Portfolio Turnover (%)	na	44	55	57	60	58	—	—	—	—
Total Assets (Millions $)	479	209	13	3	2	1	—	—	—	—

PORTFOLIO (as of 11/30/08)

Portfolio Manager: Coons/Herrmann/ Magiera/Tommasi - 2002

Investment Style

✔ Large Cap	Growth
Mid Cap	✔ Grth/Val
Small Cap	Value

Portfolio

98.6% U.S. stock	0.0% conv't
0.0% int'l stock	0.0% preferred
1.1% U.S. bonds	0.0% other
0.0% int'l bonds	0.3% cash

Number of Investments: 48
Percent of Portfolio in Top 10 Investments: 41%

SHAREHOLDER INFORMATION

Minimum Investment
Initial: $2,000 Subsequent: $0

Minimum IRA Investment
Initial: $2,000 Subsequent: $0

Maximum Fees
Load: none 12b-1: none
Other: none

Services
✔ IRA
✔ Keogh
✔ Telephone Exchange

Marsico 21st Century (MXXIX)

888-860-8686
www.marsicofunds.com

Large-Cap Stock

PERFORMANCE — fund inception date: 2/1/00

	3yr Annual	5yr Annual	10yr Annual	Bull	Bear
Return (%)	-8.2	0.4	na	201.9	-47.9
Differ From Category (+/-)	1.1 abv av	2.8 high	na	92.5 high	-6.4 low

Standard Deviation	Category Risk Index	Beta
19.9%—abv av	1.16—high	1.21

	2008	2007	2006	2005	2004	2003	2002	2001	2000	1999
Return (%)	-45.3	19.3	18.6	7.8	22.2	48.7	-10.5	-19.8	—	—
Differ From Category (+/-)	-6.7	10.8	5.6	1.3	10.7	18.0	10.8	-9.6	—	—
Return, Tax-Adjusted (%)	-45.3	18.6	18.4	7.8	22.2	48.7	-10.5	-19.8	—	—

PER SHARE DATA

	2008	2007	2006	2005	2004	2003	2002	2001	2000	1999
Dividends, Net Income ($)	0.03	0.00	0.13	0.00	0.00	0.00	0.00	0.00	—	—
Distrib'ns, Cap Gain ($)	0.00	0.74	0.00	0.00	0.00	0.00	0.00	0.00	—	—
Net Asset Value ($)	9.52	17.44	15.23	12.95	12.01	9.82	6.60	7.37	—	—
Expense Ratio (%)	1.29	1.31	1.33	1.39	1.50	1.55	1.60	1.50	—	—
Yield (%)	0.34	0.00	0.88	0.01	0.00	0.00	0.00	0.00	—	—
Portfolio Turnover (%)	143	105	136	175	191	236	388	399	—	—
Total Assets (Millions $)	1,209	2,716	1,276	442	323	162	54	69	—	—

PORTFOLIO (as of 11/30/08)

Portfolio Manager: Gilchrist - 2003

Investment Style

✔ Large Cap	✔ Growth
Mid Cap	Grth/Val
Small Cap	Value

Portfolio

76.6%	U.S. stock	0.0%	conv't
9.1%	int'l stock	0.0%	preferred
0.0%	U.S. bonds	0.0%	other
0.0%	int'l bonds	14.3%	cash

Number of Investments: 38

Percent of Portfolio in Top 10 Investments: 60%

SHAREHOLDER INFORMATION

Minimum Investment

Initial: $2,500 Subsequent: $100

Minimum IRA Investment

Initial: $1,000 Subsequent: $100

Maximum Fees

Load: 2.00% redemption 12b-1: 0.25%

Other: redemption fee applies for 30 days

Services

✔ IRA
✔ Keogh
✔ Telephone Exchange

Oakmark I
(OAKMX)
Large-Cap Stock

800-625-6275
www.oakmark.com

PERFORMANCE **fund inception date: 8/5/91**

	3yr Annual	5yr Annual	10yr Annual	Bull	Bear
Return (%)	-8.5	-3.3	0.7	78.2	-37.7
Differ From Category (+/-)	0.8 abv av	-0.9 blw av	1.1 abv av	-31.2 low	3.8 abv av

Standard Deviation	Category Risk Index	Beta
16.8%—av	0.98—av	1.04

	2008	2007	2006	2005	2004	2003	2002	2001	2000	1999
Return (%)	-32.7	-3.7	18.2	-1.4	11.7	25.2	-14.5	18.2	11.7	-10.5
Differ From Category (+/-)	5.9	-12.2	5.2	-7.9	0.1	-5.4	6.8	28.4	13.2	-35.9
Return, Tax-Adjusted (%)	-33.2	-5.0	17.3	-1.5	11.6	25.2	-14.6	18.0	11.2	-13.5

PER SHARE DATA

	2008	2007	2006	2005	2004	2003	2002	2001	2000	1999
Dividends, Net Income ($)	0.45	0.56	0.43	0.35	0.17	0.14	0.11	0.20	0.39	0.26
Distrib'ns, Cap Gain ($)	0.99	3.42	2.00	0.00	0.00	0.00	0.00	0.00	0.00	4.73
Net Asset Value ($)	25.75	40.37	45.92	40.88	41.77	37.54	30.08	35.27	29.99	27.20
Expense Ratio (%)	1.10	1.01	1.05	1.05	1.05	1.14	1.17	1.15	1.21	1.11
Yield (%)	1.68	1.26	0.90	0.84	0.40	0.37	0.37	0.55	1.29	0.82
Portfolio Turnover (%)	32	12	9	16	19	21	44	57	50	13
Total Assets (Millions $)	2,536	4,948	5,947	6,102	7,156	5,509	3,789	3,644	2,206	3,818

PORTFOLIO (as of 9/30/08)

Portfolio Manager: Grant/Nygren - 2000

Investment Style

✔ Large Cap	Growth
✔ Mid Cap	✔ Grth/Val
Small Cap	Value

Portfolio

89.2%	U.S. stock	0.0%	conv't
6.0%	int'l stock	0.0%	preferred
0.0%	U.S. bonds	0.0%	other
0.0%	int'l bonds	4.8%	cash

Number of Investments: 50
Percent of Portfolio in Top 10 Investments: 30%

SHAREHOLDER INFORMATION

Minimum Investment
Initial: $1,000 Subsequent: $100

Minimum IRA Investment
Initial: $1,000 Subsequent: $100

Maximum Fees
Load: 2.00% redemption 12b-1: none
Other: redemption fee applies for 90 days

Services
✔ IRA
✔ Keogh
✔ Telephone Exchange

Parnassus Equity Income - Inv

800-999-3505
www.parnassus.com

(PRBLX)

Large-Cap Stock

PERFORMANCE — fund inception date: 9/1/92

	3yr Annual	5yr Annual	10yr Annual	Bull	Bear
Return (%)	0.2	2.5	6.1	76.6	-24.2
Differ From Category (+/-)	9.5 high	4.9 high	6.5 high	-32.8 low	17.3 high

Standard Deviation	Category Risk Index	Beta
13.8%—blw av	0.80—low	0.87

	2008	2007	2006	2005	2004	2003	2002	2001	2000	1999
Return (%)	-23.0	14.1	14.6	2.6	9.3	15.6	-3.7	9.9	6.3	22.7
Differ From Category (+/-)	15.6	5.6	1.7	-3.9	-2.3	-15.1	17.6	20.1	7.8	-2.7
Return, Tax-Adjusted (%)	-23.2	12.3	13.0	1.6	8.5	15.3	-4.5	8.5	3.4	21.0

PER SHARE DATA

	2008	2007	2006	2005	2004	2003	2002	2001	2000	1999
Dividends, Net Income ($)	0.24	1.18	1.38	0.85	0.64	0.49	0.43	0.45	0.36	0.26
Distrib'ns, Cap Gain ($)	0.00	1.82	1.34	0.78	0.54	0.00	0.04	0.63	2.68	1.24
Net Asset Value ($)	19.29	25.31	24.83	24.02	25.00	24.00	21.20	22.50	21.48	23.13
Expense Ratio (%)	na	0.99	0.99	0.99	1.04	0.95	0.96	1.00	0.97	0.19
Yield (%)	1.25	4.33	5.28	3.40	2.50	2.02	2.00	1.94	1.48	1.06
Portfolio Turnover (%)	na	91	117	110	80	13	42	87	97	40
Total Assets (Millions $)	1,395	867	809	908	894	631	273	86	55	46

PORTFOLIO (as of 11/30/08)

Portfolio Manager: Ahlsten - 2001

Investment Style

✔ Large Cap	Growth
Mid Cap	✔ Grth/Val
Small Cap	Value

Portfolio

86.9% U.S. stock	0.0% conv't
3.9% int'l stock	0.0% preferred
0.0% U.S. bonds	0.0% other
0.0% int'l bonds	9.2% cash

Number of Investments: 45

Percent of Portfolio in Top 10 Investments: 48%

SHAREHOLDER INFORMATION

Minimum Investment

Initial: $2,000 Subsequent: $50

Minimum IRA Investment

Initial: $500 Subsequent: $50

Maximum Fees

Load: none 12b-1: none

Other: none

Services

✔ IRA

✔ Keogh

✔ Telephone Exchange

Rydex Nasdaq-100 Inv (RYOCX)

800-820-0888
www.rydexfunds.com

Large-Cap Stock

PERFORMANCE — fund inception date: 2/14/94

	3yr Annual	5yr Annual	10yr Annual	Bull	Bear
Return (%)	-10.0	-4.2	-5.1	114.3	-45.9
Differ From Category (+/-)	-0.7 blw av	-1.8 blw av	-4.7 low	4.9 abv av	-4.4 blw av

Standard Deviation	Category Risk Index	Beta
21.0%—abv av	1.22—high	1.26

	2008	2007	2006	2005	2004	2003	2002	2001	2000	1999
Return (%)	-41.9	18.0	6.2	1.3	9.6	46.2	-38.6	-34.7	-38.0	100.5
Differ From Category (+/-)	-3.3	9.5	-6.8	-5.2	-2.0	15.5	-17.3	-24.5	-36.5	75.1
Return, Tax-Adjusted (%)	-41.9	18.0	6.2	1.2	9.6	46.2	-38.6	-34.7	-38.1	100.3

PER SHARE DATA

	2008	2007	2006	2005	2004	2003	2002	2001	2000	1999
Dividends, Net Income ($)	0.00	0.00	0.00	0.04	0.00	0.00	0.00	0.00	0.00	0.00
Distrib'ns, Cap Gain ($)	0.00	0.00	0.00	0.00	0.00	0.00	0.00	0.00	0.17	0.16
Net Asset Value ($)	8.02	13.80	11.69	11.00	10.89	9.93	6.79	11.05	16.91	27.45
Expense Ratio (%)	1.28	1.22	1.20	1.20	1.22	1.27	1.08	1.16	1.15	1.15
Yield (%)	0.00	0.00	0.00	0.32	0.00	0.00	0.00	0.00	0.00	0.00
Portfolio Turnover (%)	57	72	122	132	139	180	109	228	385	773
Total Assets (Millions $)	377	738	673	975	1,035	940	443	926	1,743	3,010

PORTFOLIO (as of 12/31/08)

Portfolio Manager: Byrum/Dellapa/Harder/Holmes - 1997

Investment Style

✔ Large Cap ✔ Growth
✔ Mid Cap Grth/Val
✔ Small Cap Value

Portfolio

90.5%	U.S. stock	0.0%	conv't
6.3%	int'l stock	0.0%	preferred
0.0%	U.S. bonds	0.0%	other
0.0%	int'l bonds	3.2%	cash

Number of Investments: 103
Percent of Portfolio in Top 10 Investments: 44%

SHAREHOLDER INFORMATION

Minimum Investment
Initial: $2,500 Subsequent: $0

Minimum IRA Investment
Initial: $1,000 Subsequent: $0

Maximum Fees
Load: none 12b-1: none
Other: none

Services
✔ IRA
✔ Keogh
✔ Telephone Exchange

Schwab Core Equity (SWANX)

800-435-4000
www.schwab.com

Large-Cap Stock

PERFORMANCE — fund inception date: 7/1/96

	3yr Annual	5yr Annual	10yr Annual	Bull	Bear
Return (%)	-6.6	0.2	0.1	113.7	-36.0
Differ From Category (+/-)	2.7 high	2.6 high	0.5 av	4.3 abv av	5.5 high

Standard Deviation	Category Risk Index	Beta
14.8%—blw av	0.86—low	0.96

	2008	2007	2006	2005	2004	2003	2002	2001	2000	1999
Return (%)	-33.3	5.6	15.5	9.3	13.5	28.1	-19.3	-17.9	-7.8	27.7
Differ From Category (+/-)	5.3	-2.9	2.5	2.9	1.9	-2.6	2.0	-7.7	-6.3	2.3
Return, Tax-Adjusted (%)	-33.5	5.4	15.2	9.3	13.3	28.0	-19.5	-18.1	-9.4	25.8

PER SHARE DATA

	2008	2007	2006	2005	2004	2003	2002	2001	2000	1999
Dividends, Net Income ($)	0.22	0.18	0.10	0.09	0.16	0.11	0.07	0.08	0.07	0.04
Distrib'ns, Cap Gain ($)	0.00	0.05	0.32	0.00	0.00	0.00	0.00	0.00	1.44	1.47
Net Asset Value ($)	12.72	19.40	18.57	16.43	15.10	13.45	10.58	13.20	16.17	19.19
Expense Ratio (%)	na	0.75	0.75	0.75	0.75	0.75	0.75	0.75	0.75	0.75
Yield (%)	1.72	0.90	0.55	0.55	1.08	0.82	0.70	0.58	0.42	0.21
Portfolio Turnover (%)	na	18	42	48	86	73	114	106	96	99
Total Assets (Millions $)	1,415	2,032	1,298	643	293	256	180	218	325	361

PORTFOLIO (as of 7/31/08)

Portfolio Manager: Mano/Mortimer/Hsu/Davis - 2003

Investment Style

✔ Large Cap	Growth
Mid Cap	✔ Grth/Val
Small Cap	Value

Portfolio

99.7% U.S. stock	0.0% conv't
0.0% int'l stock	0.0% preferred
0.0% U.S. bonds	0.0% other
0.0% int'l bonds	0.3% cash

Number of Investments: 119

Percent of Portfolio in Top 10 Investments: 34%

SHAREHOLDER INFORMATION

Minimum Investment

Initial: $100 Subsequent: $0

Minimum IRA Investment

Initial: $0 Subsequent: $0

Maximum Fees

Load: 2.00% redemption 12b-1: none

Other: redemption fee applies for 30 days

Services

✔ IRA

✔ Keogh

✔ Telephone Exchange

Schwab MarketTrack All Equity (SWEGX)

800-435-4000
www.schwab.com

Large-Cap Stock

PERFORMANCE   fund inception date: 5/20/98

	3yr Annual	5yr Annual	10yr Annual	Bull	Bear
Return (%)	-8.1	-1.1	0.0	130.4	-41.5
Differ From Category (+/-)	1.2 abv av	1.3 abv av	0.4 av	21.0 high	0.0 av

Standard Deviation	Category Risk Index	Beta
17.0%—av	0.99—av	1.10

	2008	2007	2006	2005	2004	2003	2002	2001	2000	1999
Return (%)	-38.1	6.1	18.3	6.8	13.9	33.9	-20.5	-13.1	-9.0	25.0
Differ From Category (+/-)	0.5	-2.4	5.3	0.3	2.3	3.2	0.8	-2.9	-7.5	-0.4
Return, Tax-Adjusted (%)	-38.9	5.8	18.0	6.6	13.8	33.7	-20.9	-13.5	-9.7	24.6

PER SHARE DATA

	2008	2007	2006	2005	2004	2003	2002	2001	2000	1999
Dividends, Net Income ($)	0.23	0.22	0.27	0.13	0.12	0.09	0.09	0.05	0.22	0.05
Distrib'ns, Cap Gain ($)	0.52	0.01	0.00	0.00	0.00	0.00	0.02	0.14	0.01	0.10
Net Asset Value ($)	8.22	14.48	13.86	11.94	11.30	10.02	7.55	9.62	11.29	12.66
Expense Ratio (%)	na	0.50	0.50	0.50	0.50	0.50	0.50	0.50	0.56	0.54
Yield (%)	2.61	1.50	1.95	1.11	1.04	0.91	1.12	0.54	1.98	0.42
Portfolio Turnover (%)	na	10	8	49	7	10	15	5	12	6
Total Assets (Millions $)	375	646	548	478	488	458	356	446	438	251

PORTFOLIO (as of 7/31/08)

Portfolio Manager: Hung/Hastings/Mano/Lee/Kern - 2005

Investment Style

✔ Large Cap	Growth
Mid Cap	✔ Grth/Val
Small Cap	Value

Portfolio

67.9%	U.S. stock	0.0%	conv't
29.1%	int'l stock	0.0%	preferred
0.0%	U.S. bonds	0.2%	other
0.1%	int'l bonds	2.8%	cash

Number of Investments: 6
Percent of Portfolio in Top 10 Investments: 100%

SHAREHOLDER INFORMATION

Minimum Investment
Initial: $100   Subsequent: $0

Minimum IRA Investment
Initial: $0   Subsequent: $0

Maximum Fees
Load: 2.00% redemption   12b-1: none
Other: redemption fee applies for 30 days

Services
✔ IRA
✔ Keogh
✔ Telephone Exchange

Sequoia
(SEQUX)

800-686-6884
www.sequoiafund.com

Large-Cap Stock

PERFORMANCE **fund inception date: 7/15/70**

	3yr Annual	5yr Annual	10yr Annual	Bull	Bear
Return (%)	-5.1	-0.7	2.0	77.4	-29.6
Differ From Category (+/-)	4.2 high	1.7 abv av	2.4 high	-32.0 low	11.9 high

Standard Deviation	Category Risk Index	Beta
13.6%—blw av	0.79—low	0.77

	2008	2007	2006	2005	2004	2003	2002	2001	2000	1999
Return (%)	-27.1	8.3	8.3	7.7	4.6	17.1	-2.7	10.5	20.0	-16.6
Differ From Category (+/-)	11.5	-0.1	-4.7	1.2	-7.0	-13.6	18.6	20.7	21.5	-42.0
Return, Tax-Adjusted (%)	-27.8	5.6	6.8	6.7	4.6	17.0	-2.7	9.6	15.0	-17.6

PER SHARE DATA

	2008	2007	2006	2005	2004	2003	2002	2001	2000	1999
Dividends, Net Income ($)	0.42	0.45	0.00	0.00	0.00	0.00	0.01	0.96	1.66	0.86
Distrib'ns, Cap Gain ($)	6.72	27.12	15.60	10.64	0.21	0.61	0.16	3.38	28.51	6.59
Net Asset Value ($)	95.27	139.12	152.75	155.45	154.27	147.61	126.63	130.24	122.09	127.27
Expense Ratio (%)	na	1.00	1.00	1.00	1.00	1.00	1.00	1.00	1.00	1.00
Yield (%)	0.41	0.27	0.00	0.00	0.00	0.00	0.00	0.72	1.10	0.63
Portfolio Turnover (%)	na	13	14	8	6	3	8	7	36	12
Total Assets (Millions $)	3,113	3,513	3,600	3,761	3,772	3,975	3,905	4,230	3,944	3,898

PORTFOLIO (as of 9/30/08)

Portfolio Manager: Goldfarb/Poppe - 1998

Investment Style

✔ Large Cap   Growth
✔ Mid Cap   ✔ Grth/Val
Small Cap   Value

Portfolio

75.7%	U.S. stock	0.0%	conv't
9.0%	int'l stock	0.0%	preferred
0.0%	U.S. bonds	0.0%	other
0.0%	int'l bonds	15.4%	cash

Number of Investments: 26
Percent of Portfolio in Top 10 Investments: 81%

SHAREHOLDER INFORMATION

Minimum Investment
Initial: $5,000   Subsequent: $0

Minimum IRA Investment
Initial: $2,500   Subsequent: $0

Maximum Fees
Load: none   12b-1: none
Other: none

Services
IRA
✔ Keogh
✔ Telephone Exchange

Sit Large Cap Growth (SNIGX)

800-332-5580
www.sitfunds.com

Large-Cap Stock

PERFORMANCE — fund inception date: 9/2/82

	3yr Annual	5yr Annual	10yr Annual	Bull	Bear
Return (%)	-6.3	0.3	-3.0	107.9	-36.1
Differ From Category (+/-)	3.0 high	2.7 high	-2.6 low	-1.5 av	5.4 high

Standard Deviation	Category Risk Index	Beta
14.8%—blw av	0.86—low	0.94

	2008	2007	2006	2005	2004	2003	2002	2001	2000	1999
Return (%)	-34.1	14.1	9.5	9.5	12.7	26.3	-30.6	-27.8	-13.9	33.4
Differ From Category (+/-)	4.5	5.6	-3.5	3.0	1.1	-4.4	-9.3	-17.5	-12.4	8.0
Return, Tax-Adjusted (%)	-34.2	14.0	9.4	9.5	12.7	26.3	-30.6	-27.9	-15.5	32.0

PER SHARE DATA

	2008	2007	2006	2005	2004	2003	2002	2001	2000	1999
Dividends, Net Income ($)	0.22	0.13	0.28	0.07	0.12	0.02	0.00	0.00	0.00	0.00
Distrib'ns, Cap Gain ($)	0.00	0.00	0.00	0.00	0.00	0.00	0.00	0.34	5.03	3.41
Net Asset Value ($)	30.09	45.99	40.41	37.14	33.95	30.21	23.93	34.47	48.14	61.20
Expense Ratio (%)	1.00	1.00	1.00	1.00	1.00	1.00	1.00	1.00	1.00	1.00
Yield (%)	0.71	0.28	0.68	0.18	0.36	0.06	0.00	0.00	0.00	0.00
Portfolio Turnover (%)	22	28	24	23	30	33	35	45	48	70
Total Assets (Millions $)	236	224	107	82	65	62	55	95	149	164

PORTFOLIO (as of 9/30/08)

Portfolio Manager: Sit/Sit/Stellmacher - 1998

Investment Style

✔ Large Cap	✔ Growth
Mid Cap	Grth/Val
Small Cap	Value

Portfolio

89.1% U.S. stock	0.0% conv't
1.9% int'l stock	0.0% preferred
0.0% U.S. bonds	0.0% other
0.0% int'l bonds	9.0% cash

Number of Investments: 92

Percent of Portfolio in Top 10 Investments: 27%

SHAREHOLDER INFORMATION

Minimum Investment

Initial: $5,000 Subsequent: $100

Minimum IRA Investment

Initial: $2,000 Subsequent: $100

Maximum Fees

Load: 2.00% redemption 12b-1: none

Other: redemption fee applies for 30 days

Services

✔ IRA
✔ Keogh
✔ Telephone Exchange

Sound Shore

800-551-1980
www.soundshorefund.com

(SSHFX)

Large-Cap Stock

PERFORMANCE — fund inception date: 5/3/85

	3yr Annual	5yr Annual	10yr Annual	Bull	Bear
Return (%)	-8.4	-1.1	2.3	120.2	-38.8
Differ From Category (+/-)	0.9 abv av	1.3 abv av	2.7 high	10.8 abv av	2.7 abv av

Standard Deviation	Category Risk Index	Beta
16.6%—av	0.97—av	1.04

	2008	2007	2006	2005	2004	2003	2002	2001	2000	1999
Return (%)	-35.6	2.5	16.5	6.8	15.3	31.7	-15.5	-0.9	20.1	0.0
Differ From Category (+/-)	3.0	-6.0	3.5	0.3	3.7	1.0	5.8	9.3	21.6	-25.4
Return, Tax-Adjusted (%)	-35.8	0.8	15.1	5.7	14.4	31.4	-15.5	-2.6	18.9	-0.2

PER SHARE DATA

	2008	2007	2006	2005	2004	2003	2002	2001	2000	1999
Dividends, Net Income ($)	0.26	0.21	0.21	0.07	0.10	0.05	0.05	0.10	0.14	0.17
Distrib'ns, Cap Gain ($)	0.00	4.33	3.30	2.51	1.85	0.44	0.00	2.76	1.56	0.00
Net Asset Value ($)	22.76	35.68	39.19	36.63	36.70	33.51	25.81	30.58	33.70	29.47
Expense Ratio (%)	na	0.92	0.92	0.98	0.98	0.98	0.98	0.98	0.98	0.98
Yield (%)	1.12	0.52	0.48	0.17	0.26	0.14	0.19	0.30	0.40	0.57
Portfolio Turnover (%)	na	84	66	62	50	62	72	104	98	41
Total Assets (Millions $)	1,623	2,738	2,880	2,265	1,698	1,016	759	1,051	1,052	1,184

PORTFOLIO (as of 9/30/08)

Portfolio Manager: Burn III/Kane Jr./DeGulis - 1985

Investment Style

✔ Large Cap	Growth
✔ Mid Cap	Grth/Val
Small Cap	✔ Value

Portfolio

82.2%	U.S. stock	0.0%	conv't
13.1%	int'l stock	0.0%	preferred
0.0%	U.S. bonds	0.0%	other
0.0%	int'l bonds	4.7%	cash

Number of Investments: 41
Percent of Portfolio in Top 10 Investments: 35%

SHAREHOLDER INFORMATION

Minimum Investment
Initial: $10,000 Subsequent: $0

Minimum IRA Investment
Initial: $2,000 Subsequent: $0

Maximum Fees
Load: none 12b-1: none
Other: none

Services
✔ IRA
✔ Keogh
✔ Telephone Exchange

Stratton Multi Cap (STRGX)

800-472-4266
www.strattonmutualfunds.com

Large-Cap Stock

PERFORMANCE — fund inception date: 9/29/72

	3yr Annual	5yr Annual	10yr Annual	Bull	Bear
Return (%)	-9.7	0.8	3.5	156.1	-38.9
Differ From Category (+/-)	-0.4 av	3.2 high	3.9 high	46.7 high	2.6 abv av

Standard Deviation	Category Risk Index	Beta
18.8%—abv av	1.09—abv av	1.09

	2008	2007	2006	2005	2004	2003	2002	2001	2000	1999
Return (%)	-38.4	18.7	0.7	14.4	23.5	42.1	-21.4	10.1	22.0	-9.3
Differ From Category (+/-)	0.2	10.2	-12.3	7.9	11.9	11.4	-0.1	20.3	23.5	-34.7
Return, Tax-Adjusted (%)	-38.8	16.9	-0.3	13.6	22.6	41.3	-21.7	8.1	19.9	-10.6

PER SHARE DATA

	2008	2007	2006	2005	2004	2003	2002	2001	2000	1999
Dividends, Net Income ($)	0.14	0.19	0.21	0.07	0.04	0.09	0.15	0.26	0.33	0.41
Distrib'ns, Cap Gain ($)	1.16	4.73	2.67	2.07	1.99	1.32	0.23	2.75	2.44	1.33
Net Asset Value ($)	26.70	44.64	41.82	44.35	40.69	34.69	25.46	32.81	32.61	29.23
Expense Ratio (%)	na	1.06	1.06	1.08	1.15	1.28	1.28	1.21	1.24	1.13
Yield (%)	0.49	0.39	0.46	0.15	0.08	0.25	0.59	0.73	0.94	1.34
Portfolio Turnover (%)	na	26	31	29	44	38	41	14	49	39
Total Assets (Millions $)	75	101	100	173	110	57	38	49	47	44

PORTFOLIO (as of 9/30/08)

Portfolio Manager: Stratton - 1972

Investment Style

✔ Large Cap	Growth
✔ Mid Cap	✔ Grth/Val
Small Cap	Value

Portfolio

99.2%	U.S. stock	0.0%	conv't
0.8%	int'l stock	0.0%	preferred
0.0%	U.S. bonds	0.0%	other
0.0%	int'l bonds	0.0%	cash

Number of Investments: 50
Percent of Portfolio in Top 10 Investments: 33%

SHAREHOLDER INFORMATION

Minimum Investment
Initial: $2,000 Subsequent: $100

Minimum IRA Investment
Initial: $0 Subsequent: $0

Maximum Fees
Load: 1.50% redemption 12b-1: none
Other: redemption fee applies for 120 days

Services
✔ IRA
✔ Keogh
✔ Telephone Exchange

T. Rowe Price Dividend Growth (PRDGX)

800-638-5660
www.troweprice.com

Large-Cap Stock

PERFORMANCE — fund inception date: 12/31/92

	3yr Annual	5yr Annual	10yr Annual	Bull	Bear
Return (%)	-6.0	-0.8	0.1	98.0	-35.6
Differ From Category (+/-)	3.3 high	1.6 abv av	0.5 av	-11.4 blw av	5.9 high

Standard Deviation	Category Risk Index	Beta
14.8%—blw av	0.86—low	0.96

	2008	2007	2006	2005	2004	2003	2002	2001	2000	1999
Return (%)	-33.3	7.0	16.4	3.3	11.8	25.1	-18.5	-3.7	10.0	-2.9
Differ From Category (+/-)	5.3	-1.5	3.4	-3.2	0.3	-5.6	2.8	6.5	11.5	-28.3
Return, Tax-Adjusted (%)	-33.7	6.1	15.7	2.7	11.7	24.9	-18.9	-4.2	9.4	-4.3

PER SHARE DATA

	2008	2007	2006	2005	2004	2003	2002	2001	2000	1999
Dividends, Net Income ($)	0.35	0.38	0.35	0.26	0.25	0.23	0.20	0.28	0.29	0.45
Distrib'ns, Cap Gain ($)	0.30	1.25	0.77	0.65	0.00	0.00	0.00	0.00	0.05	0.72
Net Asset Value ($)	16.51	25.50	25.36	22.78	22.92	20.72	16.76	20.79	21.88	20.21
Expense Ratio (%)	na	0.69	0.72	0.75	0.78	0.83	0.83	0.82	0.81	0.77
Yield (%)	2.08	1.42	1.33	1.10	1.09	1.11	1.19	1.34	1.32	2.15
Portfolio Turnover (%)	na	16	20	23	17	18	20	35	35	38
Total Assets (Millions $)	641	884	871	773	755	695	531	692	751	1,028

PORTFOLIO (as of 9/30/08)

Portfolio Manager: Huber - 2000

Investment Style

✔ Large Cap	Growth
Mid Cap	✔ Grth/Val
Small Cap	Value

Portfolio

86.5%	U.S. stock	0.4%	conv't
7.5%	int'l stock	0.0%	preferred
0.0%	U.S. bonds	0.0%	other
0.0%	int'l bonds	5.6%	cash

Number of Investments: 110
Percent of Portfolio in Top 10 Investments: 21%

SHAREHOLDER INFORMATION

Minimum Investment
Initial: $2,500 — Subsequent: $100

Minimum IRA Investment
Initial: $1,000 — Subsequent: $50

Maximum Fees
Load: none — 12b-1: none
Other: none

Services
✔ IRA
✔ Keogh
✔ Telephone Exchange

T. Rowe Price Equity Income (PRFDX)

800-638-5660
www.troweprice.com

Large-Cap Stock

PERFORMANCE

fund inception date: 10/31/85

	3yr Annual	5yr Annual	10yr Annual	Bull	Bear
Return (%)	-7.6	-1.1	2.1	107.6	-38.7
Differ From Category (+/-)	1.7 abv av	1.3 abv av	2.5 high	-1.8 av	2.8 abv av

Standard Deviation	Category Risk Index	Beta
14.9%—blw av	0.87—low	0.96

	2008	2007	2006	2005	2004	2003	2002	2001	2000	1999
Return (%)	-35.8	3.2	19.1	4.2	15.0	25.7	-13.1	1.6	13.1	3.8
Differ From Category (+/-)	2.8	-5.2	6.1	-2.3	3.4	-5.0	8.2	11.8	14.6	-21.6
Return, Tax-Adjusted (%)	-36.5	2.0	18.3	3.2	14.3	25.2	-14.1	0.2	10.1	1.5

PER SHARE DATA

	2008	2007	2006	2005	2004	2003	2002	2001	2000	1999
Dividends, Net Income ($)	0.59	0.58	0.49	0.46	0.42	0.39	0.36	0.36	0.51	0.53
Distrib'ns, Cap Gain ($)	0.71	1.83	0.79	1.33	0.72	0.27	0.45	1.01	2.64	1.97
Net Asset Value ($)	17.08	28.10	29.55	25.92	26.59	24.16	19.79	23.65	24.67	24.81
Expense Ratio (%)	na	0.67	0.69	0.71	0.74	0.78	0.79	0.80	0.60	0.77
Yield (%)	3.31	1.93	1.61	1.68	1.53	1.59	1.77	1.45	1.86	1.97
Portfolio Turnover (%)	na	26	17	21	16	12	15	17	21	22
Total Assets (Millions $)	12,492	20,521	20,999	17,878	15,947	12,167	8,954	10,128	10,187	12,321

PORTFOLIO (as of 9/30/08)

Portfolio Manager: Rogers/Arricale/Finn/Giroux - 1985

Investment Style

✔ Large Cap	Growth
✔ Mid Cap	Grth/Val
Small Cap	✔ Value

Portfolio

91.1%	U.S. stock	0.0%	conv't
3.8%	int'l stock	0.0%	preferred
0.8%	U.S. bonds	0.0%	other
0.0%	int'l bonds	4.3%	cash

Number of Investments: 126
Percent of Portfolio in Top 10 Investments: 24%

SHAREHOLDER INFORMATION

Minimum Investment
Initial: $2,500 Subsequent: $100

Minimum IRA Investment
Initial: $1,000 Subsequent: $50

Maximum Fees
Load: none 12b-1: none
Other: none

Services
✔ IRA
✔ Keogh
✔ Telephone Exchange

T. Rowe Price Growth & Income (PRGIX)

800-638-5660
www.troweprice.com

Large-Cap Stock

PERFORMANCE — fund inception date: 12/21/82

	3yr Annual	5yr Annual	10yr Annual	Bull	Bear
Return (%)	-8.3	-2.6	-0.6	92.5	-39.0
Differ From Category (+/-)	1.0 abv av	-0.2 av	-0.2 av	-16.9 blw av	2.5 abv av

Standard Deviation	Category Risk Index	Beta
15.8%—av	0.92—blw av	1.02

	2008	2007	2006	2005	2004	2003	2002	2001	2000	1999
Return (%)	-36.6	6.2	14.4	2.5	10.8	28.2	-23.9	-2.2	8.9	3.7
Differ From Category (+/-)	2.0	-2.3	1.4	-3.9	-0.8	-2.5	-2.6	8.0	10.4	-21.7
Return, Tax-Adjusted (%)	-36.8	5.3	13.4	0.9	9.7	28.0	-24.3	-3.3	6.9	1.2

PER SHARE DATA

	2008	2007	2006	2005	2004	2003	2002	2001	2000	1999
Dividends, Net Income ($)	0.23	0.25	0.29	0.23	0.26	0.19	0.16	0.26	0.34	0.51
Distrib'ns, Cap Gain ($)	0.00	1.05	1.12	2.24	1.27	0.00	0.15	0.78	1.83	2.25
Net Asset Value ($)	13.88	22.19	22.14	20.62	22.51	21.72	17.11	22.82	24.44	24.44
Expense Ratio (%)	na	0.70	0.73	0.76	0.78	0.82	0.81	0.81	0.77	0.77
Yield (%)	1.65	1.07	1.24	1.00	1.09	0.87	0.92	1.10	1.29	1.91
Portfolio Turnover (%)	na	31	51	52	36	41	44	66	80	20
Total Assets (Millions $)	835	1,434	1,667	1,722	1,904	1,970	1,675	2,394	2,989	3,440

PORTFOLIO (as of 9/30/08)

Portfolio Manager: Huber - 2007

Investment Style

✔ Large Cap	Growth
Mid Cap	✔ Grth/Val
Small Cap	Value

Portfolio

91.0% U.S. stock	0.0% conv't
7.7% int'l stock	0.0% preferred
0.0% U.S. bonds	0.0% other
0.0% int'l bonds	1.3% cash

Number of Investments: 104

Percent of Portfolio in Top 10 Investments: 20%

SHAREHOLDER INFORMATION

Minimum Investment

Initial: $2,500 Subsequent: $100

Minimum IRA Investment

Initial: $1,000 Subsequent: $50

Maximum Fees

Load: none 12b-1: none

Other: none

Services

✔ IRA

✔ Keogh

✔ Telephone Exchange

T. Rowe Price Value (TRVLX)

800-638-5660
www.troweprice.com

Large-Cap Stock

PERFORMANCE — fund inception date: 9/30/94

	3yr Annual	5yr Annual	10yr Annual	Bull	Bear
Return (%)	-10.1	-2.3	2.1	121.7	-43.7
Differ From Category (+/-)	-0.8 blw av	0.1 av	2.5 high	12.3 abv av	-2.2 blw av

Standard Deviation	Category Risk Index	Beta
17.4%—av	1.01—abv av	1.12

	2008	2007	2006	2005	2004	2003	2002	2001	2000	1999
Return (%)	-39.8	0.7	19.7	6.3	15.3	30.0	-16.6	1.6	15.7	9.1
Differ From Category (+/-)	-1.2	-7.8	6.7	-0.2	3.7	-0.7	4.7	11.8	17.2	-16.3
Return, Tax-Adjusted (%)	-40.1	-0.1	19.1	5.6	15.2	29.7	-17.0	0.8	14.2	6.3

PER SHARE DATA

	2008	2007	2006	2005	2004	2003	2002	2001	2000	1999
Dividends, Net Income ($)	0.26	0.45	0.27	0.25	0.18	0.20	0.15	0.17	0.23	0.21
Distrib'ns, Cap Gain ($)	0.16	0.92	0.68	0.72	0.00	0.01	0.04	0.40	0.84	2.20
Net Asset Value ($)	15.15	25.87	27.05	23.38	22.90	20.01	15.56	18.88	19.15	17.50
Expense Ratio (%)	na	0.84	0.87	0.90	0.93	0.97	0.95	0.94	1.10	0.92
Yield (%)	1.69	1.67	0.97	1.03	0.78	0.99	0.96	0.88	1.15	1.06
Portfolio Turnover (%)	na	19	10	19	17	31	29	42	68	68
Total Assets (Millions $)	4,823	6,611	5,293	3,279	2,463	1,480	1,140	1,322	989	851

PORTFOLIO (as of 9/30/08)

Portfolio Manager: Linehan - 2003

Investment Style

✔ Large Cap — Growth
✔ Mid Cap — Grth/Val
Small Cap — ✔ Value

Portfolio

88.7%	U.S. stock	0.0%	conv't
6.3%	int'l stock	0.3%	preferred
1.2%	U.S. bonds	0.0%	other
0.0%	int'l bonds	3.5%	cash

Number of Investments: 130
Percent of Portfolio in Top 10 Investments: 19%

SHAREHOLDER INFORMATION

Minimum Investment
Initial: $2,500 — Subsequent: $100

Minimum IRA Investment
Initial: $1,000 — Subsequent: $50

Maximum Fees
Load: none — 12b-1: none
Other: none

Services
✔ IRA
✔ Keogh
✔ Telephone Exchange

USAA Income Stock (USISX)

800-531-8181
www.usaa.com

Large-Cap Stock

PERFORMANCE — fund inception date: 5/4/87

	3yr Annual	5yr Annual	10yr Annual	Bull	Bear
Return (%)	-9.5	-2.6	-0.3	93.0	-39.5
Differ From Category (+/-)	-0.2 av	-0.2 av	0.1 av	-16.4 blw av	2.0 abv av

Standard Deviation	Category Risk Index	Beta
15.2%—blw av	0.88—blw av	0.97

	2008	2007	2006	2005	2004	2003	2002	2001	2000	1999
Return (%)	-35.6	-3.4	19.0	5.8	12.0	25.7	-19.0	-4.2	10.8	2.4
Differ From Category (+/-)	3.0	-11.9	6.0	-0.7	0.4	-5.0	2.3	6.0	12.3	-23.0
Return, Tax-Adjusted (%)	-35.9	-4.7	17.8	3.6	11.5	25.4	-20.9	-5.7	9.0	-0.4

PER SHARE DATA

	2008	2007	2006	2005	2004	2003	2002	2001	2000	1999
Dividends, Net Income ($)	0.29	0.31	0.29	0.35	0.26	0.25	0.30	0.44	0.55	0.55
Distrib'ns, Cap Gain ($)	0.00	1.15	0.89	2.10	0.17	0.00	1.00	0.55	0.51	1.66
Net Asset Value ($)	9.35	14.89	16.88	15.20	16.66	15.27	12.37	16.83	18.63	17.83
Expense Ratio (%)	0.80	0.82	0.83	0.78	0.79	0.81	0.82	0.67	0.67	0.65
Yield (%)	3.09	1.92	1.63	1.99	1.52	1.63	2.23	2.50	2.87	2.82
Portfolio Turnover (%)	91	91	108	73	73	141	94	17	13	34
Total Assets (Millions $)	1,259	2,156	2,362	2,069	1,994	1,779	1,439	1,869	1,992	2,284

PORTFOLIO (as of 8/31/08)

Portfolio Manager: Schmidt/Wilderman - 2005

Investment Style

✔ Large Cap	Growth
Mid Cap	Grth/Val
Small Cap	✔ Value

Portfolio

100.0% U.S. stock	0.0% conv't
0.0% int'l stock	0.0% preferred
0.0% U.S. bonds	0.0% other
0.0% int'l bonds	0.0% cash

Number of Investments: 405

Percent of Portfolio in Top 10 Investments: 33%

SHAREHOLDER INFORMATION

Minimum Investment

Initial: $3,000 Subsequent: $50

Minimum IRA Investment

Initial: $250 Subsequent: $50

Maximum Fees

Load: none 12b-1: none

Other: none

Services

✔ IRA
✔ Keogh
✔ Telephone Exchange

Value Line Larger Companies (VALLX)

800-243-2729
www.valueline.com

Large-Cap Stock

PERFORMANCE — fund inception date: 3/20/72

	3yr Annual	5yr Annual	10yr Annual	Bull	Bear
Return (%)	-7.4	-1.0	-2.1	90.6	-39.9
Differ From Category (+/-)	1.9 abv av	1.4 abv av	-1.7 blw av	-18.8 blw av	1.6 abv av

Standard Deviation	Category Risk Index	Beta
17.0%—av	0.99—av	1.02

	2008	2007	2006	2005	2004	2003	2002	2001	2000	1999
Return (%)	-38.2	15.5	11.3	10.0	8.6	15.5	-27.0	-10.6	-14.0	30.9
Differ From Category (+/-)	0.4	7.0	-1.7	3.5	-3.0	-15.2	-5.7	-0.4	-12.5	5.5
Return, Tax-Adjusted (%)	-38.3	13.4	9.0	6.5	6.0	13.4	-27.2	-11.6	-15.5	28.8

PER SHARE DATA

	2008	2007	2006	2005	2004	2003	2002	2001	2000	1999
Dividends, Net Income ($)	0.03	0.08	0.00	0.00	0.00	0.00	0.00	0.00	0.00	0.00
Distrib'ns, Cap Gain ($)	0.17	2.92	3.40	5.96	4.84	3.99	0.39	2.37	4.34	5.20
Net Asset Value ($)	13.18	21.63	21.37	22.24	25.53	27.96	27.68	38.43	45.63	57.98
Expense Ratio (%)	na	0.88	1.08	1.16	1.16	1.15	1.14	1.09	0.95	0.82
Yield (%)	0.19	0.33	0.00	0.00	0.00	0.00	0.00	0.00	0.00	0.00
Portfolio Turnover (%)	na	112	203	218	200	110	28	50	28	27
Total Assets (Millions $)	192	304	299	301	319	342	335	496	602	762

PORTFOLIO (as of 9/30/08)

Portfolio Manager: Brooks - 2005

Investment Style

✔ Large Cap	✔ Growth
✔ Mid Cap	Grth/Val
Small Cap	Value

Portfolio

85.6%	U.S. stock	0.0%	conv't
9.8%	int'l stock	0.0%	preferred
0.0%	U.S. bonds	0.0%	other
0.0%	int'l bonds	4.5%	cash

Number of Investments: 101
Percent of Portfolio in Top 10 Investments: 15%

SHAREHOLDER INFORMATION

Minimum Investment
Initial: $1,000 Subsequent: $100

Minimum IRA Investment
Initial: $1,000 Subsequent: $100

Maximum Fees
Load: none 12b-1: 0.25%
Other: none

Services
✔ IRA
✔ Keogh
✔ Telephone Exchange

Vanguard 500 Index (VFINX)

800-662-7447
www.vanguard.com

Large-Cap Stock

PERFORMANCE — fund inception date: 8/31/76

	3yr Annual	5yr Annual	10yr Annual	Bull	Bear
Return (%)	-8.5	-2.3	-1.5	99.1	-40.0
Differ From Category (+/-)	0.8 abv av	0.1 av	-1.1 blw av	-10.3 av	1.5 abv av

Standard Deviation	Category Risk Index	Beta
15.2%—blw av	0.88—blw av	1.00

	2008	2007	2006	2005	2004	2003	2002	2001	2000	1999
Return (%)	-37.1	5.3	15.6	4.7	10.7	28.5	-22.2	-12.1	-9.1	21.0
Differ From Category (+/-)	1.5	-3.2	2.6	-1.8	-0.9	-2.2	-0.9	-1.9	-7.6	-4.4
Return, Tax-Adjusted (%)	-37.3	5.1	15.3	4.5	10.4	28.2	-22.7	-12.5	-9.5	20.4

PER SHARE DATA

	2008	2007	2006	2005	2004	2003	2002	2001	2000	1999
Dividends, Net Income ($)	2.51	2.49	2.14	1.98	1.95	1.43	1.36	1.28	1.30	1.41
Distrib'ns, Cap Gain ($)	0.00	0.00	0.00	0.00	0.00	0.00	0.00	0.00	0.00	1.00
Net Asset Value ($)	83.09	135.15	130.59	114.92	111.64	102.67	81.15	105.89	121.86	135.33
Expense Ratio (%)	na	0.15	0.18	0.18	0.18	0.18	0.18	0.18	0.18	0.18
Yield (%)	3.01	1.84	1.63	1.72	1.74	1.39	1.67	1.20	1.06	1.03
Portfolio Turnover (%)	na	5	5	7	3	2	7	4	9	6
Total Assets (Millions $)	38,778	63,327	72,013	69,375	84,167	75,342	56,224	73,151	88,240	104,652

PORTFOLIO (as of 9/30/08)

Portfolio Manager: Buek - 2005

Investment Style

✔ Large Cap	Growth
Mid Cap	✔ Grth/Val
Small Cap	Value

Portfolio

99.9% U.S. stock	0.0% conv't
0.1% int'l stock	0.0% preferred
0.0% U.S. bonds	0.0% other
0.0% int'l bonds	0.1% cash

Number of Investments: 513

Percent of Portfolio in Top 10 Investments: 21%

SHAREHOLDER INFORMATION

Minimum Investment

Initial: $3,000 — Subsequent: $100

Minimum IRA Investment

Initial: $3,000 — Subsequent: $100

Maximum Fees

Load: none — 12b-1: none

Other: none

Services

✔ IRA

✔ Keogh

✔ Telephone Exchange

Vanguard Dividend Growth (VDIGX)

800-662-6273
www.vanguard.com

Large-Cap Stock

PERFORMANCE — fund inception date: 5/15/92

	3yr Annual	5yr Annual	10yr Annual	Bull	Bear
Return (%)	-1.7	1.9	0.1	106.2	-27.3
Differ From Category (+/-)	7.6 high	4.3 high	0.5 abv av	-3.2 av	14.2 high

Standard Deviation	Category Risk Index	Beta
12.7%—blw av	0.74—low	0.81

	2008	2007	2006	2005	2004	2003	2002	2001	2000	1999
Return (%)	-25.6	7.0	19.5	4.2	11.0	29.2	-23.2	-19.5	18.7	-3.0
Differ From Category (+/-)	13.0	-1.5	6.5	-2.3	-0.6	-1.5	-1.9	-9.3	20.2	-28.4
Return, Tax-Adjusted (%)	-25.9	6.6	19.2	3.9	10.7	28.8	-24.4	-20.9	16.2	-5.7

PER SHARE DATA

	2008	2007	2006	2005	2004	2003	2002	2001	2000	1999
Dividends, Net Income ($)	0.26	0.28	0.26	0.24	0.22	0.19	0.38	0.37	0.53	0.51
Distrib'ns, Cap Gain ($)	0.00	0.10	0.00	0.00	0.00	0.00	0.00	0.41	0.73	1.20
Net Asset Value ($)	11.08	15.21	14.57	12.42	12.15	11.15	8.79	11.88	15.66	14.33
Expense Ratio (%)	0.32	0.38	0.37	0.37	0.40	0.34	0.34	0.37	0.40	0.38
Yield (%)	2.38	1.82	1.78	1.93	1.81	1.70	4.32	3.01	3.23	3.28
Portfolio Turnover (%)	36	41	16	20	23	104	24	48	47	55
Total Assets (Millions $)	1,778	1,371	1,217	984	984	783	555	706	954	841

PORTFOLIO (as of 9/30/08)

Portfolio Manager: Kilbride - 2006

Investment Style

✔ Large Cap	Growth
✔ Mid Cap	Grth/Val
Small Cap	✔ Value

Portfolio

89.0% U.S. stock	0.0% conv't
7.4% int'l stock	0.0% preferred
0.0% U.S. bonds	0.0% other
0.0% int'l bonds	3.6% cash

Number of Investments: 55

Percent of Portfolio in Top 10 Investments: 29%

SHAREHOLDER INFORMATION

Minimum Investment

Initial: $3,000 Subsequent: $100

Minimum IRA Investment

Initial: $3,000 Subsequent: $0

Maximum Fees

Load: none 12b-1: none

Other: none

Services

✔ IRA

✔ Keogh

✔ Telephone Exchange

Vanguard Equity-Income (VEIPX)

800-662-6273
www.vanguard.com

Large-Cap Stock

PERFORMANCE — fund inception date: 3/21/88

	3yr Annual	5yr Annual	10yr Annual	Bull	Bear
Return (%)	-4.5	0.6	1.9	107.4	-33.7
Differ From Category (+/-)	4.8 high	3.0 high	2.3 high	-2.0 av	7.8 high

Standard Deviation	Category Risk Index	Beta
12.9%—blw av	0.75—low	0.82

	2008	2007	2006	2005	2004	2003	2002	2001	2000	1999
Return (%)	-31.0	4.8	20.6	4.3	13.5	25.1	-15.7	-2.4	13.5	-0.2
Differ From Category (+/-)	7.6	-3.7	7.6	-2.2	1.9	-5.6	5.6	7.8	15.0	-25.6
Return, Tax-Adjusted (%)	-31.5	3.6	19.2	3.2	12.3	24.3	-16.5	-3.7	11.5	-2.0

PER SHARE DATA

	2008	2007	2006	2005	2004	2003	2002	2001	2000	1999
Dividends, Net Income ($)	0.73	0.74	0.71	0.68	0.60	0.57	0.48	0.51	0.61	0.65
Distrib'ns, Cap Gain ($)	0.11	1.36	1.42	1.05	1.17	0.42	0.00	0.60	1.14	0.87
Net Asset Value ($)	16.14	24.42	25.30	22.79	23.50	22.31	18.70	22.71	24.44	23.17
Expense Ratio (%)	0.30	0.29	0.31	0.32	0.32	0.45	0.46	0.47	0.43	0.41
Yield (%)	4.51	2.87	2.65	2.85	2.41	2.52	2.56	2.18	2.38	2.70
Portfolio Turnover (%)	55	51	26	42	36	55	21	31	36	18
Total Assets (Millions $)	2,218	3,237	3,306	2,818	3,162	2,590	1,931	2,250	2,561	2,874

PORTFOLIO (as of 9/30/08)

Portfolio Manager: Ryan/Stetler/Reckmeyer III - 2000

Investment Style

✔ Large Cap	Growth
Mid Cap	Grth/Val
Small Cap	✔ Value

Portfolio

92.3%	U.S. stock	0.0%	conv't
6.2%	int'l stock	0.0%	preferred
0.0%	U.S. bonds	0.0%	other
0.0%	int'l bonds	1.6%	cash

Number of Investments: 194
Percent of Portfolio in Top 10 Investments: 30%

SHAREHOLDER INFORMATION

Minimum Investment
Initial: $3,000 Subsequent: $100

Minimum IRA Investment
Initial: $3,000 Subsequent: $100

Maximum Fees
Load: none 12b-1: none
Other: none

Services
✔ IRA
✔ Keogh
✔ Telephone Exchange

Vanguard Growth Index (VIGRX)

800-662-7447
www.vanguard.com

Large-Cap Stock

PERFORMANCE — fund inception date: 11/2/92

	3yr Annual	5yr Annual	10yr Annual	Bull	Bear
Return (%)	-8.9	-3.2	-3.3	85.0	-40.2
Differ From Category (+/-)	0.4 av	-0.8 blw av	-2.9 low	-24.4 low	1.3 av

Standard Deviation	Category Risk Index	Beta
16.7%—av	0.97—av	1.06

	2008	2007	2006	2005	2004	2003	2002	2001	2000	1999
Return (%)	-38.4	12.5	9.0	5.0	7.1	25.9	-23.7	-13.0	-22.3	28.7
Differ From Category (+/-)	0.2	4.0	-4.0	-1.5	-4.4	-4.8	-2.4	-2.8	-20.8	3.3
Return, Tax-Adjusted (%)	-38.5	12.4	8.8	4.9	7.0	25.7	-24.1	-13.2	-22.4	27.8

PER SHARE DATA

	2008	2007	2006	2005	2004	2003	2002	2001	2000	1999
Dividends, Net Income ($)	0.26	0.27	0.24	0.20	0.29	0.18	0.23	0.19	0.13	0.23
Distrib'ns, Cap Gain ($)	0.00	0.00	0.00	0.00	0.00	0.00	0.00	0.00	0.00	1.04
Net Asset Value ($)	20.29	33.23	29.77	27.54	26.41	24.92	19.95	26.42	30.57	39.43
Expense Ratio (%)	na	0.22	0.22	0.22	0.22	0.23	0.23	0.22	0.22	0.22
Yield (%)	1.29	0.81	0.80	0.74	1.11	0.70	1.13	0.70	0.40	0.56
Portfolio Turnover (%)	na	23	28	23	24	44	23	31	33	33
Total Assets (Millions $)	4,279	6,992	6,707	6,761	7,711	7,586	6,094	8,445	11,162	15,232

PORTFOLIO (as of 9/30/08)

Portfolio Manager: O'Reilly - 1994

Investment Style

✔ Large Cap	✔ Growth
Mid Cap	Grth/Val
Small Cap	Value

Portfolio

99.8%	U.S. stock	0.0%	conv't
0.1%	int'l stock	0.0%	preferred
0.0%	U.S. bonds	0.0%	other
0.0%	int'l bonds	0.1%	cash

Number of Investments: 399

Percent of Portfolio in Top 10 Investments: 24%

SHAREHOLDER INFORMATION

Minimum Investment

Initial: $3,000 Subsequent: $100

Minimum IRA Investment

Initial: $3,000 Subsequent: $100

Maximum Fees

Load: none 12b-1: none

Other: none

Services

✔ IRA

✔ Keogh

✔ Telephone Exchange

Vanguard Large Cap Index (VLACX)

800-997-2798
www.vanguard.com

Large-Cap Stock

PERFORMANCE — fund inception date: 1/30/04

	3yr Annual	5yr Annual	10yr Annual	Bull	Bear
Return (%)	-8.3	na	na	na	-40.0
Differ From Category (+/-)	1.0 abv av	na	na	na	1.5 abv av

Standard Deviation	Category Risk Index	Beta
15.5%—av	0.90—blw av	1.01

	2008	2007	2006	2005	2004	2003	2002	2001	2000	1999
Return (%)	-37.1	6.2	15.4	6.1	—	—	—	—	—	—
Differ From Category (+/-)	1.5	-2.3	2.4	-0.4	—	—	—	—	—	—
Return, Tax-Adjusted (%)	-37.4	6.0	15.2	5.8	—	—	—	—	—	—

PER SHARE DATA

	2008	2007	2006	2005	2004	2003	2002	2001	2000	1999
Dividends, Net Income ($)	0.41	0.43	0.40	0.33	—	—	—	—	—	—
Distrib'ns, Cap Gain ($)	0.00	0.00	0.00	0.00	—	—	—	—	—	—
Net Asset Value ($)	16.41	26.59	25.42	22.38	—	—	—	—	—	—
Expense Ratio (%)	na	0.20	0.20	0.20	—	—	—	—	—	—
Yield (%)	2.46	1.60	1.56	1.46	—	—	—	—	—	—
Portfolio Turnover (%)	na	8	9	23	—	—	—	—	—	—
Total Assets (Millions $)	376	346	211	94	—	—	—	—	—	—

PORTFOLIO (as of 9/30/08)

Portfolio Manager: Ludt - 2004

Investment Style

✔ Large Cap	Growth
Mid Cap	✔ Grth/Val
Small Cap	Value

Portfolio

99.4%	U.S. stock	0.0%	conv't
0.2%	int'l stock	0.0%	preferred
0.0%	U.S. bonds	0.0%	other
0.0%	int'l bonds	0.4%	cash

Number of Investments: 745

Percent of Portfolio in Top 10 Investments: 19%

SHAREHOLDER INFORMATION

Minimum Investment

Initial: $3,000 — Subsequent: $100

Minimum IRA Investment

Initial: $3,000 — Subsequent: $100

Maximum Fees

Load: none — 12b-1: none

Other: none

Services

✔ IRA

✔ Keogh

✔ Telephone Exchange

Vanguard PRIMECAP Core (VPCCX)

800-662-6273
www.vanguard.com

Large-Cap Stock

PERFORMANCE — fund inception date: 12/9/04

	3yr Annual	5yr Annual	10yr Annual	Bull	Bear
Return (%)	-6.2	na	na	na	-34.5
Differ From Category (+/-)	3.1 high	na	na	na	7.0 high

Standard Deviation	Category Risk Index	Beta
15.3%—av	0.89—blw av	0.96

	2008	2007	2006	2005	2004	2003	2002	2001	2000	1999
Return (%)	-31.4	7.0	12.3	12.0	—	—	—	—	—	—
Differ From Category (+/-)	7.2	-1.5	-0.7	5.5	—	—	—	—	—	—
Return, Tax-Adjusted (%)	-31.5	6.6	12.0	11.9	—	—	—	—	—	—

PER SHARE DATA

	2008	2007	2006	2005	2004	2003	2002	2001	2000	1999
Dividends, Net Income ($)	0.12	0.14	0.09	0.05	—	—	—	—	—	—
Distrib'ns, Cap Gain ($)	0.00	0.20	0.11	0.03	—	—	—	—	—	—
Net Asset Value ($)	8.91	13.15	12.61	11.41	—	—	—	—	—	—
Expense Ratio (%)	0.50	0.55	0.60	0.75	—	—	—	—	—	—
Yield (%)	1.31	1.04	0.74	0.43	—	—	—	—	—	—
Portfolio Turnover (%)	9	10	5	6	—	—	—	—	—	—
Total Assets (Millions $)	2,681	3,270	2,556	1,220	—	—	—	—	—	—

PORTFOLIO (as of 9/30/08)

Portfolio Manager: Fried/Kolokotrones/Milias - 2004

Investment Style

✔ Large Cap ✔ Growth
Mid Cap Grth/Val
Small Cap Value

Portfolio

71.3%	U.S. stock	0.0%	conv't
15.4%	int'l stock	0.0%	preferred
0.0%	U.S. bonds	0.0%	other
0.0%	int'l bonds	13.3%	cash

Number of Investments: 136
Percent of Portfolio in Top 10 Investments: 38%

SHAREHOLDER INFORMATION

Minimum Investment
Initial: $10,000 Subsequent: $100

Minimum IRA Investment
Initial: $10,000 Subsequent: $100

Maximum Fees
Load: 1.00% redemption 12b-1: none
Other: redemption fee applies for 1 year

Services
✔ IRA
✔ Keogh
✔ Telephone Exchange

Vanguard Total Stock Mkt Idx (VTSMX)

800-997-2798
www.vanguard.com

Large-Cap Stock

PERFORMANCE — fund inception date: 4/27/92

	3yr Annual	5yr Annual	10yr Annual	Bull	Bear
Return (%)	-8.5	-1.8	-0.7	109.8	-40.2
Differ From Category (+/-)	0.8 abv av	0.6 abv av	-0.3 av	0.4 abv av	1.3 abv av

Standard Deviation	Category Risk Index	Beta
15.9%—av	0.92—blw av	1.04

	2008	2007	2006	2005	2004	2003	2002	2001	2000	1999
Return (%)	-37.1	5.4	15.5	5.9	12.5	31.3	-21.0	-11.0	-10.6	23.8
Differ From Category (+/-)	1.5	-3.1	2.5	-0.6	0.9	0.6	0.3	-0.8	-9.1	-1.6
Return, Tax-Adjusted (%)	-37.3	5.2	15.2	5.7	12.2	31.1	-21.4	-11.4	-11.1	23.1

PER SHARE DATA

	2008	2007	2006	2005	2004	2003	2002	2001	2000	1999
Dividends, Net Income ($)	0.59	0.60	0.52	0.47	0.44	0.33	0.29	0.30	0.34	0.33
Distrib'ns, Cap Gain ($)	0.00	0.00	0.00	0.00	0.00	0.00	0.00	0.00	0.14	0.32
Net Asset Value ($)	21.80	35.36	34.09	30.00	28.77	25.99	20.07	25.74	29.26	33.22
Expense Ratio (%)	na	0.15	0.19	0.19	0.19	0.20	0.20	0.20	0.20	0.20
Yield (%)	2.68	1.70	1.53	1.57	1.54	1.25	1.45	1.15	1.14	0.98
Portfolio Turnover (%)	na	4	4	12	4	11	4	7	7	3
Total Assets (Millions $)	39,440	50,183	39,095	29,785	31,718	24,059	14,254	15,781	16,856	18,133

PORTFOLIO (as of 9/30/08)

Portfolio Manager: O'Reilly - 1994

Investment Style

✔ Large Cap	Growth
✔ Mid Cap	✔ Grth/Val
Small Cap	Value

Portfolio

99.2%	U.S. stock	0.0%	conv't
0.3%	int'l stock	0.0%	preferred
0.0%	U.S. bonds	0.0%	other
0.0%	int'l bonds	0.4%	cash

Number of Investments: 3,502
Percent of Portfolio in Top 10 Investments: 17%

SHAREHOLDER INFORMATION

Minimum Investment
Initial: $3,000 Subsequent: $100

Minimum IRA Investment
Initial: $3,000 Subsequent: $100

Maximum Fees
Load: none 12b-1: none
Other: none

Services
✔ IRA
✔ Keogh
✔ Telephone Exchange

Vanguard U.S. Value (VUVLX)

800-662-6273
www.vanguard.com

Large-Cap Stock

PERFORMANCE — fund inception date: 6/29/00

	3yr Annual	5yr Annual	10yr Annual	Bull	Bear
Return (%)	-9.7	-2.3	na	100.3	-38.3
Differ From Category (+/-)	-0.4 av	0.1 av	na	-9.1 av	3.2 abv av

Standard Deviation	Category Risk Index	Beta
15.5%—av	0.90—blw av	1.00

	2008	2007	2006	2005	2004	2003	2002	2001	2000	1999
Return (%)	-34.8	-0.8	14.1	6.3	13.6	30.2	-15.3	2.9	—	—
Differ From Category (+/-)	3.8	-9.3	1.1	-0.2	2.1	-0.5	6.0	13.1	—	—
Return, Tax-Adjusted (%)	-35.2	-2.7	13.3	5.1	13.4	29.9	-15.9	2.5	—	—

PER SHARE DATA

	2008	2007	2006	2005	2004	2003	2002	2001	2000	1999
Dividends, Net Income ($)	0.30	0.35	0.24	0.28	0.20	0.18	0.16	0.10	—	—
Distrib'ns, Cap Gain ($)	0.00	1.51	0.40	0.88	0.00	0.00	0.00	0.00	—	—
Net Asset Value ($)	7.99	12.73	14.74	13.48	13.75	12.27	9.56	11.47	—	—
Expense Ratio (%)	0.37	0.33	0.39	0.39	0.49	0.63	0.54	0.51	—	—
Yield (%)	3.72	2.46	1.59	1.94	1.45	1.46	1.67	0.87	—	—
Portfolio Turnover (%)	86	114	57	52	56	50	46	54	—	—
Total Assets (Millions $)	527	1,080	1,512	1,013	881	534	451	436	—	—

PORTFOLIO (as of 9/30/08)

Portfolio Manager: Ricks/Stetler - 2007

Investment Style

✔ Large Cap	Growth
Mid Cap	Grth/Val
Small Cap	✔ Value

Portfolio

96.0%	U.S. stock	0.0%	conv't
0.3%	int'l stock	0.0%	preferred
0.3%	U.S. bonds	0.0%	other
0.0%	int'l bonds	3.5%	cash

Number of Investments: 511
Percent of Portfolio in Top 10 Investments: 32%

SHAREHOLDER INFORMATION

Minimum Investment
Initial: $3,000 Subsequent: $100

Minimum IRA Investment
Initial: $3,000 Subsequent: $100

Maximum Fees
Load: none 12b-1: none
Other: none

Services
✔ IRA
✔ Keogh
✔ Telephone Exchange

Vanguard Value Index

800-662-7447
www.vanguard.com

(VIVAX)

Large-Cap Stock

PERFORMANCE **fund inception date: 11/2/92**

	3yr Annual	5yr Annual	10yr Annual	Bull	Bear
Return (%)	-7.9	-0.7	0.6	125.3	-40.0
Differ From Category (+/-)	1.4 abv av	1.7 abv av	1.0 abv av	15.9 abv av	1.5 abv av

Standard Deviation	Category Risk Index	Beta
15.0%—blw av	0.87—low	0.96

	2008	2007	2006	2005	2004	2003	2002	2001	2000	1999
Return (%)	-36.0	0.0	22.1	7.0	15.2	32.2	-21.0	-11.9	6.0	12.5
Differ From Category (+/-)	-2.6	-8.5	9.1	0.5	3.6	1.5	0.3	-1.7	7.5	-12.9
Return, Tax-Adjusted (%)	-36.4	-0.3	21.7	6.7	14.9	31.8	-21.6	-13.3	4.6	10.1

PER SHARE DATA

	2008	2007	2006	2005	2004	2003	2002	2001	2000	1999
Dividends, Net Income ($)	0.66	0.68	0.59	0.56	0.46	0.37	0.31	0.32	0.36	0.36
Distrib'ns, Cap Gain ($)	0.00	0.00	0.00	0.00	0.00	0.00	0.00	0.98	0.98	1.96
Net Asset Value ($)	16.08	25.94	26.58	22.29	21.35	18.95	14.65	18.90	22.87	22.89
Expense Ratio (%)	na	0.20	0.21	0.21	0.21	0.23	0.23	0.22	0.22	0.22
Yield (%)	4.08	2.63	2.22	2.48	2.14	1.96	2.15	1.58	1.50	1.45
Portfolio Turnover (%)	na	20	20	21	18	47	26	38	37	41
Total Assets (Millions $)	2,618	4,310	4,417	3,376	3,592	2,921	2,197	3,018	3,450	3,378

PORTFOLIO (as of 9/30/08)

Portfolio Manager: O'Reilly - 1994

Investment Style

✔ Large Cap	Growth
Mid Cap	Grth/Val
Small Cap	✔ Value

Portfolio

99.6% U.S. stock	0.0% conv't
0.4% int'l stock	0.0% preferred
0.0% U.S. bonds	0.0% other
0.0% int'l bonds	0.1% cash

Number of Investments: 411
Percent of Portfolio in Top 10 Investments: 34%

SHAREHOLDER INFORMATION

Minimum Investment
Initial: $3,000 Subsequent: $100

Minimum IRA Investment
Initial: $3,000 Subsequent: $100

Maximum Fees
Load: none 12b-1: none
Other: none

Services
✔ IRA
✔ Keogh
✔ Telephone Exchange

Vanguard Windsor (VWNDX)

800-662-7447
www.vanguard.com

Large-Cap Stock

PERFORMANCE — fund inception date: 10/23/58

	3yr Annual	5yr Annual	10yr Annual	Bull	Bear
Return (%)	-12.1	-4.2	1.6	115.2	-46.0
Differ From Category (+/-)	-2.8 low	-1.8 blw av	2.0 abv av	5.8 abv av	-4.5 blw av

Standard Deviation	Category Risk Index	Beta
17.0%—av	0.99—av	1.08

	2008	2007	2006	2005	2004	2003	2002	2001	2000	1999
Return (%)	-41.1	-3.3	19.3	4.9	13.3	37.0	-22.3	5.7	15.8	11.5
Differ From Category (+/-)	-2.5	-11.8	6.3	-1.6	1.7	6.3	-1.0	15.9	17.3	-13.9
Return, Tax-Adjusted (%)	-41.4	-5.2	17.7	3.4	13.0	36.8	-22.7	4.8	12.7	8.4

PER SHARE DATA

	2008	2007	2006	2005	2004	2003	2002	2001	2000	1999
Dividends, Net Income ($)	0.27	0.29	0.28	0.26	0.26	0.17	0.17	0.20	0.27	0.27
Distrib'ns, Cap Gain ($)	0.00	2.02	1.53	1.56	0.09	0.00	0.00	0.31	1.85	1.90
Net Asset Value ($)	9.02	15.71	18.64	17.15	18.07	16.26	12.00	15.64	15.29	15.17
Expense Ratio (%)	0.30	0.30	0.35	0.36	0.43	0.48	0.45	0.41	0.31	0.28
Yield (%)	3.00	1.63	1.39	1.41	1.43	1.01	1.41	1.24	1.57	1.58
Portfolio Turnover (%)	55	40	38	32	28	23	30	33	41	56
Total Assets (Millions $)	6,643	12,885	14,699	13,362	16,385	14,681	10,999	16,027	16,615	16,700

PORTFOLIO (as of 9/30/08)

Portfolio Manager: Fedak/Mahedy/Mordy - 1999

Investment Style

✔ Large Cap	Growth
Mid Cap	Grth/Val
Small Cap	✔ Value

Portfolio

81.6%	U.S. stock	0.0%	conv't
15.2%	int'l stock	0.0%	preferred
0.2%	U.S. bonds	0.7%	other
0.0%	int'l bonds	2.3%	cash

Number of Investments: 159
Percent of Portfolio in Top 10 Investments: 24%

SHAREHOLDER INFORMATION

Minimum Investment
Initial: $3,000 — Subsequent: $100

Minimum IRA Investment
Initial: $3,000 — Subsequent: $100

Maximum Fees
Load: none — 12b-1: none
Other: none

Services
✔ IRA
✔ Keogh
✔ Telephone Exchange

Vanguard Windsor II (VWNFX)

800-997-2798
www.vanguard.com

Large-Cap Stock

PERFORMANCE — fund inception date: 6/24/85

	3yr Annual	5yr Annual	10yr Annual	Bull	Bear
Return (%)	-8.6	-0.7	1.0	122.9	-41.1
Differ From Category (+/-)	0.7 av	1.7 abv av	1.4 abv av	13.5 abv av	0.4 av

Standard Deviation	Category Risk Index	Beta
15.7%—av	0.91—blw av	1.00

	2008	2007	2006	2005	2004	2003	2002	2001	2000	1999
Return (%)	-36.8	2.2	18.2	7.0	18.3	30.0	-16.9	-3.5	16.8	-5.9
Differ From Category (+/-)	1.8	-6.3	5.2	0.5	6.7	-0.7	4.4	6.8	18.3	-31.3
Return, Tax-Adjusted (%)	-37.1	0.3	17.1	6.2	17.9	29.6	-17.7	-4.3	14.8	-8.4

PER SHARE DATA

	2008	2007	2006	2005	2004	2003	2002	2001	2000	1999
Dividends, Net Income ($)	0.76	0.81	0.80	0.67	0.58	0.53	0.51	0.55	0.61	0.68
Distrib'ns, Cap Gain ($)	0.00	3.45	1.44	0.88	0.00	0.00	0.00	0.15	1.24	2.50
Net Asset Value ($)	19.11	31.26	34.75	31.33	30.73	26.49	20.80	25.59	27.20	24.97
Expense Ratio (%)	na	0.32	0.33	0.35	0.36	0.43	0.42	0.40	0.37	0.37
Yield (%)	3.97	2.33	2.21	2.08	1.88	2.00	2.45	2.11	2.14	2.47
Portfolio Turnover (%)	na	51	34	28	22	29	41	33	26	26
Total Assets (Millions $)	18,229	30,925	31,569	29,064	29,016	22,766	17,739	22,429	25,083	26,902

PORTFOLIO (as of 9/30/08)

Portfolio Manager: Barrow/Davis/Lieberman/Shaw - 1985

Investment Style

✔ Large Cap	Growth
✔ Mid Cap	Grth/Val
Small Cap	✔ Value

Portfolio

90.6% U.S. stock	0.0% conv't
6.9% int'l stock	0.0% preferred
0.1% U.S. bonds	0.0% other
0.0% int'l bonds	2.5% cash

Number of Investments: 295
Percent of Portfolio in Top 10 Investments: 26%

SHAREHOLDER INFORMATION

Minimum Investment
Initial: $10,000 Subsequent: $100

Minimum IRA Investment
Initial: $10,000 Subsequent: $100

Maximum Fees
Load: none 12b-1: none
Other: none

Services
✔ IRA
✔ Keogh
✔ Telephone Exchange

Wasatch-1st Source Income Equity (FMIEX)

800-766-8938
www.wasatchfunds.com

Large-Cap Stock

PERFORMANCE — fund inception date: 9/25/96

	3yr Annual	5yr Annual	10yr Annual	Bull	Bear
Return (%)	-2.5	3.6	6.4	149.0	-33.1
Differ From Category (+/-)	6.8 high	6.0 high	6.8 high	39.6 high	8.4 high

Standard Deviation	Category Risk Index	Beta
15.1%—blw av	0.88—blw av	0.96

	2008	2007	2006	2005	2004	2003	2002	2001	2000	1999
Return (%)	-31.2	12.3	20.0	9.9	17.0	29.8	-11.3	3.3	16.7	12.3
Differ From Category (+/-)	7.4	3.8	7.0	3.4	5.4	-0.9	10.0	13.5	18.2	-13.1
Return, Tax-Adjusted (%)	-31.4	11.4	18.6	8.0	16.2	29.3	-12.0	1.9	14.1	9.3

PER SHARE DATA

	2008	2007	2006	2005	2004	2003	2002	2001	2000	1999
Dividends, Net Income ($)	0.24	0.21	0.21	0.16	0.14	0.17	0.18	0.17	0.23	0.23
Distrib'ns, Cap Gain ($)	0.00	0.67	1.01	1.56	0.47	0.11	0.09	0.45	0.91	1.16
Net Asset Value ($)	10.36	15.33	14.43	13.06	13.44	12.03	9.51	11.00	11.27	10.71
Expense Ratio (%)	1.04	1.15	1.19	1.19	1.21	1.22	1.20	1.20	1.81	1.21
Yield (%)	2.34	1.30	1.35	1.08	0.98	1.36	1.82	1.46	1.91	1.95
Portfolio Turnover (%)	5	26	37	44	24	18	32	42	47	34
Total Assets (Millions $)	745	349	143	115	99	74	53	53	47	49

PORTFOLIO (as of 9/30/08)

Portfolio Manager: Shive - 1996

Investment Style

✔ Large Cap	Growth
✔ Mid Cap	Grth/Val
Small Cap	✔ Value

Portfolio

75.5%	U.S. stock	0.0%	conv't
6.4%	int'l stock	0.0%	preferred
0.6%	U.S. bonds	0.0%	other
0.0%	int'l bonds	17.5%	cash

Number of Investments: 83

Percent of Portfolio in Top 10 Investments: 31%

SHAREHOLDER INFORMATION

Minimum Investment

Initial: $1,000 Subsequent: $25

Minimum IRA Investment

Initial: $1,000 Subsequent: $25

Maximum Fees

Load: none 12b-1: 0.25%

Other: none

Services

✔ IRA
✔ Keogh
✔ Telephone Exchange

Mid-Cap Stock Funds
Category Performance Ranked by 2008 Returns

Fund (Ticker)	Annual Return (%) 2008	3Yr	5Yr	10Yr	Category Risk	Total Risk
Gabelli ABC (GABCX)	-2.7	5.3	4.5	5.2	low	low
FMI Common Stock (FMIMX)	-20.5	-3.0	3.5	7.6	low	av
Ave Maria Rising Dividend (AVEDX)	-22.8	-3.3	na	na	low	blw av
American Century Mid Cap Value Inv (ACMVX)	-24.5	-3.8	na	na	low	av
Janus Mid Cap Value Investor (JMCVX)	-27.4	-3.5	3.2	10.2	low	blw av
Artisan Mid Cap Value (ARTQX)	-27.6	-5.7	4.1	na	av	abv av
FAM Value Inv (FAMVX)	-28.7	-8.4	-1.1	3.9	low	blw av
Osterweis (OSTFX)	-29.3	-6.3	1.1	7.2	low	blw av
Wells Fargo Advantage Mid Cap Dis Inv (SMCDX)	-30.1	-7.7	0.5	9.0	low	av
Meridian Growth (MERDX)	-30.4	-5.3	-0.5	7.0	low	av
Nicholas II I (NCTWX)	-30.8	-7.3	-1.1	-0.4	low	av
Heartland Select Value (HRSVX)	-31.3	-5.9	2.0	7.2	blw av	av
CRM Small/Mid Cap Value Inv (CRMAX)	-31.5	-4.1	na	na	blw av	av
Meridian Value (MVALX)	-32.0	-4.6	0.6	9.8	low	av
Westport Select Cap R (WPSRX)	-32.7	-7.0	-0.7	6.6	low	av
Hennessy Focus 30 (HFTFX)	-33.1	-7.3	3.8	na	high	high
PRIMECAP Odyssey Aggressive Growth (POAGX)	-34.6	-7.5	na	na	blw av	abv av
Vanguard Selected Value (VASVX)	-35.5	-8.5	0.4	5.0	low	av
Fidelity Low-Priced Stock (FLPSX)	-36.2	-8.2	0.5	7.9	blw av	abv av
Federated Mid-Cap Index (FMDCX)	-36.4	-9.1	-0.5	3.9	av	abv av
Dreyfus MidCap Index (PESPX)	-36.5	-9.1	-0.5	3.9	av	abv av
Madison Mosaic Mid-Cap (GTSGX)	-36.7	-7.2	-0.9	4.8	low	av
Vanguard Mid-Cap Value Index Inv (VMVIX)	-36.7	na	na	na	abv av	abv av
Marshall Mid-Cap Value Inv (MRVEX)	-37.2	-10.4	-2.1	5.1	blw av	av
Gabelli Asset AAA (GABAX)	-37.3	-5.1	0.8	3.8	low	av
Delafield (DEFIX)	-37.6	-7.7	0.1	7.8	av	abv av
Fidelity Spartan Extended Mkt Index Inv (FSEMX)	-38.5	-9.3	-0.6	1.4	av	abv av
T. Rowe Price Extended Equity Market Idx (PEXMX)	-38.5	-9.6	-0.8	1.4	av	abv av
Lazard U.S. Mid Cap Equity Open (LZMOX)	-38.6	-12.0	-1.7	3.7	blw av	av
Vanguard Extended Market Idx (VEXMX)	-38.8	-10.0	-0.9	1.6	av	abv av
Vanguard Mid Cap Growth (VMGRX)	-39.6	-8.0	-1.1	4.1	blw av	abv av
T. Rowe Price Mid-Cap Growth (RPMGX)	-39.7	-8.9	0.5	3.9	av	abv av
DWS Dreman Mid Cap Value S (MIDTX)	-39.8	-9.0	na	na	blw av	av
Value Line Premier Growth (VALSX)	-40.2	-7.8	0.6	3.5	blw av	abv av
Fidelity New Millennium (FMILX)	-40.3	-7.6	-2.0	4.8	av	abv av
Fidelity Mid Cap Value (FSMVX)	-40.6	-11.3	-0.7	na	av	abv av
TIAA-CREF Mid-Cap Value Retail (TCMVX)	-40.7	-8.9	1.1	na	blw av	av
Baron Asset (BARAX)	-40.8	-9.3	1.3	1.3	blw av	abv av
Neuberger Berman Mid Cap Growth Inv (NMANX)	-41.0	-6.4	1.6	-0.9	blw av	abv av
Vanguard Mid Capitalization Index (VIMSX)	-41.9	-11.2	-0.8	4.0	av	abv av
Aston/Optimum Mid Cap N (CHTTX)	-42.9	-8.0	-1.3	6.0	abv av	abv av

Mid-Cap Stock Funds
Category Performance Ranked by 2008 Returns (cont.)

Fund (Ticker)	Annual Return (%) 2008	3Yr	5Yr	10Yr	Category Risk	Total Risk
Janus Enterprise (JAENX)	-43.2	-7.8	1.0	-0.5	abv av	abv av
Brandywine (BRWIX)	-44.5	-9.2	-0.6	2.7	abv av	abv av
American Century Heritage Inv (TWHIX)	-46.2	-2.8	3.7	4.9	high	high
Fidelity Value (FDVLX)	-46.6	-14.4	-2.8	3.4	abv av	abv av
Rainier Mid Cap Equity (RIMMX)	-46.6	-6.3	na	na	high	high
Baron Partners (BPTRX)	-46.7	-10.3	3.2	na	high	high
Vanguard Mid-Cap Growth Index Inv (VMGIX)	-47.1	na	na	na	high	high
American Century Vista Inv (TWCVX)	-48.7	-8.1	-0.5	5.6	high	high
Janus Orion (JORNX)	-49.8	-7.6	1.8	na	high	high
Mid-Cap Stock Category Average	**-40.3**	**-9.8**	**-1.4**	**3.2**	**av**	**abv av**

American Century Heritage Inv (TWHIX)

800-345-8765
www.americancentury.com

Mid-Cap Stock

PERFORMANCE — fund inception date: 11/10/87

	3yr Annual	5yr Annual	10yr Annual	Bull	Bear
Return (%)	-2.8	3.7	4.9	187.0	-45.7
Differ From Category (+/-)	7.0 high	5.1 high	1.7 abv av	43.3 high	-2.3 blw av

Standard Deviation	Category Risk Index	Beta
22.7%—high	1.14—high	1.30

	2008	2007	2006	2005	2004	2003	2002	2001	2000	1999
Return (%)	-46.2	45.7	17.0	22.2	7.0	21.6	-16.0	-25.6	17.3	51.2
Differ From Category (+/-)	-5.9	35.7	3.8	12.0	-9.4	-16.7	2.7	-22.6	12.1	11.0
Return, Tax-Adjusted (%)	-46.3	44.7	15.9	22.1	7.0	21.6	-16.0	-25.6	12.7	48.5

PER SHARE DATA

	2008	2007	2006	2005	2004	2003	2002	2001	2000	1999
Dividends, Net Income ($)	0.13	0.00	0.00	0.00	0.00	0.00	0.00	0.00	0.00	0.04
Distrib'ns, Cap Gain ($)	0.00	1.06	1.07	0.09	0.00	0.00	0.00	0.00	3.64	1.48
Net Asset Value ($)	11.67	21.93	15.79	14.40	11.85	11.07	9.10	10.83	14.55	15.64
Expense Ratio (%)	na	1.00	1.00	1.00	1.00	1.00	1.00	1.00	1.00	1.00
Yield (%)	1.10	0.00	0.00	0.00	0.00	0.00	0.00	0.00	0.00	0.25
Portfolio Turnover (%)	na	128	230	236	264	129	128	152	119	134
Total Assets (Millions $)	1,090	2,548	1,104	883	1,234	1,259	1,002	1,281	1,860	1,349

PORTFOLIO (as of 9/30/08)

Portfolio Manager: Hollond/Walsh - 2007

Investment Style

Large Cap	✔ Growth
✔ Mid Cap	Grth/Val
✔ Small Cap	Value

Portfolio

84.0% U.S. stock	0.0% conv't
12.4% int'l stock	0.0% preferred
0.0% U.S. bonds	0.6% other
0.0% int'l bonds	3.1% cash

Number of Investments: 119
Percent of Portfolio in Top 10 Investments: 23%

SHAREHOLDER INFORMATION

Minimum Investment
Initial: $2,500 Subsequent: $50

Minimum IRA Investment
Initial: $2,500 Subsequent: $0

Maximum Fees
Load: none 12b-1: none
Other: none

Services
✔ IRA
✔ Keogh
✔ Telephone Exchange

American Century Mid Cap Value Inv (ACMVX)

800-345-2021
www.americancentury.com

Mid-Cap Stock

PERFORMANCE — fund inception date: 3/31/04

	3yr Annual	5yr Annual	10yr Annual	Bull	Bear
Return (%)	-3.8	na	na	na	-28.9
Differ From Category (+/-)	6.0 high	na	na	na	14.5 high

Standard Deviation	Category Risk Index	Beta
15.5%—av	0.78—low	0.93

	2008	2007	2006	2005	2004	2003	2002	2001	2000	1999
Return (%)	-24.5	-2.2	20.4	9.9	—	—	—	—	—	—
Differ From Category (+/-)	15.8	-12.2	7.2	-0.3	—	—	—	—	—	—
Return, Tax-Adjusted (%)	-24.8	-3.7	19.4	8.4	—	—	—	—	—	—

PER SHARE DATA

	2008	2007	2006	2005	2004	2003	2002	2001	2000	1999
Dividends, Net Income ($)	0.18	0.15	0.16	0.19	—	—	—	—	—	—
Distrib'ns, Cap Gain ($)	0.00	1.16	0.66	0.92	—	—	—	—	—	—
Net Asset Value ($)	8.38	11.31	12.87	11.37	—	—	—	—	—	—
Expense Ratio (%)	1.00	1.00	1.00	1.00	—	—	—	—	—	—
Yield (%)	2.19	1.19	1.15	1.54	—	—	—	—	—	—
Portfolio Turnover (%)	206	187	228	192	—	—	—	—	—	—
Total Assets (Millions $)	230	308	252	98	—	—	—	—	—	—

PORTFOLIO (as of 9/30/08)

Portfolio Manager: Davidson/Liss/Toney - 2004

Investment Style

Large Cap	Growth
✔ Mid Cap	Grth/Val
Small Cap	✔ Value

Portfolio

97.1% U.S. stock	0.0% conv't
1.5% int'l stock	0.0% preferred
0.0% U.S. bonds	0.0% other
0.0% int'l bonds	1.5% cash

Number of Investments: 121
Percent of Portfolio in Top 10 Investments: 24%

SHAREHOLDER INFORMATION

Minimum Investment
Initial: $2,500 Subsequent: $50

Minimum IRA Investment
Initial: $2,500 Subsequent: $0

Maximum Fees
Load: none 12b-1: none
Other: none

Services
✔ IRA
✔ Keogh
✔ Telephone Exchange

American Century Vista Inv (TWCVX)

800-345-8765
www.americancentury.com

Mid-Cap Stock

PERFORMANCE — fund inception date: 11/25/83

	3yr Annual	5yr Annual	10yr Annual	Bull	Bear
Return (%)	-8.1	-0.5	5.6	186.6	-49.7
Differ From Category (+/-)	1.7 abv av	0.9 abv av	2.4 abv av	42.9 high	-6.3 low

Standard Deviation	Category Risk Index	Beta
22.6%—high	1.14—high	1.24

	2008	2007	2006	2005	2004	2003	2002	2001	2000	1999
Return (%)	-48.7	38.7	9.0	8.8	15.7	42.8	-20.9	-27.6	-1.0	119.1
Differ From Category (+/-)	-8.4	28.7	-4.2	-1.4	-0.7	4.5	-2.2	-24.6	-6.2	78.9
Return, Tax-Adjusted (%)	-48.7	36.8	8.9	8.8	15.7	42.8	-20.9	-27.6	-6.7	117.3

PER SHARE DATA

	2008	2007	2006	2005	2004	2003	2002	2001	2000	1999
Dividends, Net Income ($)	0.00	0.00	0.00	0.00	0.00	0.00	0.00	0.00	0.00	0.00
Distrib'ns, Cap Gain ($)	0.00	2.09	0.13	0.00	0.00	0.00	0.00	0.00	6.33	0.95
Net Asset Value ($)	11.07	21.57	17.11	15.81	14.52	12.54	8.78	11.10	15.33	22.21
Expense Ratio (%)	na	1.00	1.00	1.00	1.00	1.00	1.00	1.00	1.00	1.00
Yield (%)	0.00	0.00	0.00	0.00	0.00	0.00	0.00	0.00	0.00	0.00
Portfolio Turnover (%)	na	121	234	284	255	280	293	290	135	187
Total Assets (Millions $)	1,602	2,887	2,031	1,992	1,568	1,295	907	1,251	2,081	1,800

PORTFOLIO (as of 9/30/08)

Portfolio Manager: Fogle/Eixmann - 1993

Investment Style

Large Cap	✔ Growth
✔ Mid Cap	Grth/Val
✔ Small Cap	Value

Portfolio

91.8% U.S. stock	0.0% conv't
5.0% int'l stock	0.0% preferred
0.0% U.S. bonds	0.0% other
0.0% int'l bonds	3.2% cash

Number of Investments: 109

Percent of Portfolio in Top 10 Investments: 26%

SHAREHOLDER INFORMATION

Minimum Investment

Initial: $2,500 Subsequent: $50

Minimum IRA Investment

Initial: $2,500 Subsequent: $50

Maximum Fees

Load: none 12b-1: none

Other: none

Services

✔ IRA

Keogh

✔ Telephone Exchange

Artisan Mid Cap Value (ARTQX)

800-344-1770
www.artisanfunds.com

Mid-Cap Stock

PERFORMANCE — fund inception date: 3/28/01

	3yr Annual	5yr Annual	10yr Annual	Bull	Bear
Return (%)	-5.7	4.1	na	148.4	-30.8
Differ From Category (+/-)	4.1 high	5.5 high	na	4.7 abv av	12.6 high

Standard Deviation	Category Risk Index	Beta
19.6%—abv av	0.98—av	1.14

	2008	2007	2006	2005	2004	2003	2002	2001	2000	1999
Return (%)	-27.6	1.6	14.1	15.4	26.2	36.8	-3.9	—	—	—
Differ From Category (+/-)	12.7	-8.4	1.0	5.2	9.8	-1.5	14.8	—	—	—
Return, Tax-Adjusted (%)	-27.7	-0.2	13.2	14.7	25.8	36.4	-3.9	—	—	—

PER SHARE DATA

	2008	2007	2006	2005	2004	2003	2002	2001	2000	1999
Dividends, Net Income ($)	0.02	0.08	0.06	0.01	0.00	0.00	0.00	—	—	—
Distrib'ns, Cap Gain ($)	0.12	2.33	1.18	0.82	0.30	0.24	0.00	—	—	—
Net Asset Value ($)	12.96	18.10	20.18	18.75	16.96	13.69	10.19	—	—	—
Expense Ratio (%)	1.21	1.20	1.20	1.22	1.39	1.59	1.95	—	—	—
Yield (%)	0.18	0.39	0.26	0.06	0.00	0.00	0.00	—	—	—
Portfolio Turnover (%)	70	0	52	52	54	12	168	—	—	—
Total Assets (Millions $)	2,283	3,034	2,819	2,706	720	100	36	—	—	—

PORTFOLIO (as of 9/30/08)

Portfolio Manager: Kieffer/Satterwhite/Sertl, Jr. - 2001

Investment Style

Large Cap	Growth
✔ Mid Cap	Grth/Val
Small Cap	✔ Value

Portfolio

94.1% U.S. stock	0.0% conv't
0.0% int'l stock	0.0% preferred
0.0% U.S. bonds	0.0% other
0.0% int'l bonds	5.9% cash

Number of Investments: 48
Percent of Portfolio in Top 10 Investments: 36%

SHAREHOLDER INFORMATION

Minimum Investment
Initial: $1,000 Subsequent: $50

Minimum IRA Investment
Initial: $1,000 Subsequent: $50

Maximum Fees
Load: none 12b-1: none
Other: none

Services
✔ IRA
✔ Keogh
✔ Telephone Exchange

Aston/Optimum Mid Cap N (CHTTX)

800-992-8151
www.astonfunds.com

Mid-Cap Stock

PERFORMANCE

fund inception date: 9/19/94

	3yr Annual	5yr Annual	10yr Annual	Bull	Bear
Return (%)	-8.0	-1.3	6.0	156.3	-46.0
Differ From Category (+/-)	1.8 abv av	0.1 av	2.8 high	12.6 abv av	-2.6 blw av

Standard Deviation	Category Risk Index	Beta
21.8%—abv av	1.10—abv av	1.30

	2008	2007	2006	2005	2004	2003	2002	2001	2000	1999
Return (%)	-42.9	12.9	20.9	1.3	18.8	41.4	-16.8	14.2	27.5	11.4
Differ From Category (+/-)	-2.6	2.9	7.7	-8.9	2.4	3.1	1.9	17.2	22.3	-28.8
Return, Tax-Adjusted (%)	-43.1	11.6	19.7	0.7	18.3	41.3	-16.8	13.9	23.2	11.2

PER SHARE DATA

	2008	2007	2006	2005	2004	2003	2002	2001	2000	1999
Dividends, Net Income ($)	0.14	0.00	0.00	0.00	0.00	0.00	0.00	0.00	0.00	0.00
Distrib'ns, Cap Gain ($)	0.29	2.19	1.83	0.91	0.74	0.07	0.00	0.25	3.31	0.15
Net Asset Value ($)	15.73	28.33	27.03	23.87	24.45	21.21	15.05	18.07	16.04	15.37
Expense Ratio (%)	na	1.15	1.16	1.23	1.29	1.34	1.30	1.30	1.30	1.30
Yield (%)	0.86	0.00	0.00	0.00	0.00	0.00	0.00	0.00	0.00	0.00
Portfolio Turnover (%)	na	26	31	27	27	59	45	44	109	101
Total Assets (Millions $)	480	795	628	570	449	192	101	51	30	19

PORTFOLIO (as of 11/30/08)

Portfolio Manager: Zerhusen - 1999

Investment Style

✔ Large Cap	Growth
✔ Mid Cap	✔ Grth/Val
Small Cap	Value

Portfolio

86.8% U.S. stock	0.0% conv't
9.7% int'l stock	0.0% preferred
0.0% U.S. bonds	0.0% other
0.0% int'l bonds	3.5% cash

Number of Investments: 41

Percent of Portfolio in Top 10 Investments: 39%

SHAREHOLDER INFORMATION

Minimum Investment

Initial: $2,500 Subsequent: $50

Minimum IRA Investment

Initial: $500 Subsequent: $50

Maximum Fees

Load: none 12b-1: 0.25%

Other: none

Services

✔ IRA

Keogh

✔ Telephone Exchange

Ave Maria Rising Dividend (AVEDX)

888-726-9331
www.schwartzinvest.com

Mid-Cap Stock

PERFORMANCE — fund inception date: 5/2/05

	3yr Annual	5yr Annual	10yr Annual	Bull	Bear
Return (%)	-3.3	na	na	na	-27.6
Differ From Category (+/-)	6.5 high	na	na	na	15.8 high

Standard Deviation	Category Risk Index	Beta
14.1%—blw av	0.71—low	0.86

	2008	2007	2006	2005	2004	2003	2002	2001	2000	1999
Return (%)	-22.8	-0.6	17.8	—	—	—	—	—	—	—
Differ From Category (+/-)	17.5	-10.6	4.6	—	—	—	—	—	—	—
Return, Tax-Adjusted (%)	-23.1	-1.2	17.3	—	—	—	—	—	—	—

PER SHARE DATA

	2008	2007	2006	2005	2004	2003	2002	2001	2000	1999
Dividends, Net Income ($)	0.15	0.16	0.14	—	—	—	—	—	—	—
Distrib'ns, Cap Gain ($)	0.08	0.32	0.26	—	—	—	—	—	—	—
Net Asset Value ($)	8.72	11.54	12.08	—	—	—	—	—	—	—
Expense Ratio (%)	na	1.14	1.25	—	—	—	—	—	—	—
Yield (%)	1.66	1.32	1.10	—	—	—	—	—	—	—
Portfolio Turnover (%)	na	41	65	—	—	—	—	—	—	—
Total Assets (Millions $)	67	83	35	—	—	—	—	—	—	—

PORTFOLIO (as of 11/30/08)

Portfolio Manager: Platte, Jr./Schwartz - 2005

Investment Style

Large Cap	Growth
✔ Mid Cap	Grth/Val
Small Cap	✔ Value

Portfolio

88.2%	U.S. stock	0.0%	conv't
0.0%	int'l stock	0.0%	preferred
0.0%	U.S. bonds	0.0%	other
0.0%	int'l bonds	11.8%	cash

Number of Investments: 46

Percent of Portfolio in Top 10 Investments: 33%

SHAREHOLDER INFORMATION

Minimum Investment

Initial: $1,000 — Subsequent: $0

Minimum IRA Investment

Initial: $0 — Subsequent: $0

Maximum Fees

Load: none — 12b-1: none

Other: none

Services

✔ IRA

Keogh

✔ Telephone Exchange

Baron Asset

(BARAX)

800-442-3814
www.baronfunds.com

Mid-Cap Stock

PERFORMANCE **fund inception date: 6/12/87**

	3yr Annual	5yr Annual	10yr Annual	Bull	Bear
Return (%)	-9.3	1.3	1.3	162.9	-43.6
Differ From Category (+/-)	0.5 av	2.7 high	-1.9 blw av	19.2 abv av	-0.2 av

Standard Deviation	Category Risk Index	Beta
18.8%—abv av	0.94—blw av	1.16

	2008	2007	2006	2005	2004	2003	2002	2001	2000	1999
Return (%)	-40.8	10.1	14.6	12.4	27.1	27.3	-20.0	-10.2	0.3	16.2
Differ From Category (+/-)	-0.5	0.1	1.4	2.2	10.7	-11.0	-1.3	-7.2	-4.9	-24.0
Return, Tax-Adjusted (%)	-41.3	9.6	13.3	11.6	26.1	27.3	-20.6	-11.7	-1.3	16.2

PER SHARE DATA

	2008	2007	2006	2005	2004	2003	2002	2001	2000	1999
Dividends, Net Income ($)	0.00	0.00	0.00	0.00	0.00	0.00	0.00	0.00	0.00	0.00
Distrib'ns, Cap Gain ($)	2.05	2.08	4.68	2.81	2.99	0.00	1.18	4.07	4.61	0.00
Net Asset Value ($)	35.63	63.77	59.80	56.29	52.52	43.83	34.42	44.46	54.39	58.77
Expense Ratio (%)	1.33	1.34	1.33	1.34	1.34	1.34	1.35	1.36	1.36	1.31
Yield (%)	0.00	0.00	0.00	0.00	0.00	0.00	0.00	0.00	0.00	0.00
Portfolio Turnover (%)	16	13	22	11	28	27	6	4	2	15
Total Assets (Millions $)	2,273	4,348	3,579	2,901	2,376	1,949	1,945	2,394	4,257	6,147

PORTFOLIO (as of 9/30/08)

Portfolio Manager: Peck - 2003

Investment Style

Large Cap	✔ Growth
✔ Mid Cap	Grth/Val
Small Cap	Value

Portfolio

91.5% U.S. stock	0.0% conv't
1.6% int'l stock	0.0% preferred
0.0% U.S. bonds	1.6% other
0.0% int'l bonds	5.3% cash

Number of Investments: 69
Percent of Portfolio in Top 10 Investments: 36%

SHAREHOLDER INFORMATION

Minimum Investment
Initial: $2,000 Subsequent: $0

Minimum IRA Investment
Initial: $2,000 Subsequent: $0

Maximum Fees
Load: none 12b-1: 0.25%
Other: none

Services
✔ IRA
Keogh
✔ Telephone Exchange

Baron Partners
(BPTRX)

800-442-3814
www.baronfunds.com

Mid-Cap Stock

PERFORMANCE

fund inception date: 4/30/03

	3yr Annual	5yr Annual	10yr Annual	Bull	Bear
Return (%)	-10.3	3.2	na	na	-51.4
Differ From Category (+/-)	-0.5 av	4.6 high	na	na	-8.0 low

Standard Deviation	Category Risk Index	Beta
22.4%—high	1.13—high	1.38

	2008	2007	2006	2005	2004	2003	2002	2001	2000	1999
Return (%)	-46.7	11.3	21.5	14.3	42.3	—	—	—	—	—
Differ From Category (+/-)	-6.4	1.3	8.3	4.1	25.9	—	—	—	—	—
Return, Tax-Adjusted (%)	-47.2	10.5	21.5	13.6	41.8	—	—	—	—	—

PER SHARE DATA

	2008	2007	2006	2005	2004	2003	2002	2001	2000	1999
Dividends, Net Income ($)	0.00	0.00	0.00	0.00	0.00	—	—	—	—	—
Distrib'ns, Cap Gain ($)	0.73	1.11	0.06	0.78	0.43	—	—	—	—	—
Net Asset Value ($)	12.20	23.76	22.34	18.43	16.85	—	—	—	—	—
Expense Ratio (%)	na	1.31	1.32	1.35	1.46	—	—	—	—	—
Yield (%)	0.00	0.00	0.00	0.00	0.00	—	—	—	—	—
Portfolio Turnover (%)	na	33	36	38	58	—	—	—	—	—
Total Assets (Millions $)	1,501	3,384	2,403	1,403	633	—	—	—	—	—

PORTFOLIO (as of 9/30/08)

Portfolio Manager: Baron - 2003

Investment Style

Large Cap	✔ Growth
✔ Mid Cap	Grth/Val
Small Cap	Value

Portfolio

96.8%	U.S. stock	0.0%	conv't
2.0%	int'l stock	0.0%	preferred
0.0%	U.S. bonds	1.3%	other
0.0%	int'l bonds	0.0%	cash

Number of Investments: 50
Percent of Portfolio in Top 10 Investments: 63%

SHAREHOLDER INFORMATION

Minimum Investment
Initial: $2,000 Subsequent: $0

Minimum IRA Investment
Initial: $2,000 Subsequent: $0

Maximum Fees
Load: none 12b-1: 0.25%
Other: none

Services
✔ IRA
Keogh
✔ Telephone Exchange

Brandywine (BRWIX)

800-656-3017
www.brandywinefunds.com

Mid-Cap Stock

PERFORMANCE — fund inception date: 12/12/85

	3yr Annual	5yr Annual	10yr Annual	Bull	Bear
Return (%)	-9.2	-0.6	2.7	145.2	-45.7
Differ From Category (+/-)	0.6 av	0.8 abv av	-0.5 av	1.5 av	-2.3 blw av

Standard Deviation	Category Risk Index	Beta
20.5%—abv av	1.03—abv av	1.21

	2008	2007	2006	2005	2004	2003	2002	2001	2000	1999
Return (%)	-44.5	21.7	11.0	14.3	13.1	31.4	-21.8	-20.6	7.0	53.5
Differ From Category (+/-)	-4.2	11.8	-2.2	4.1	-3.3	-6.9	-3.1	-17.6	1.9	13.3
Return, Tax-Adjusted (%)	-44.6	19.5	10.9	14.3	13.1	31.4	-21.8	-20.6	-0.5	51.4

PER SHARE DATA

	2008	2007	2006	2005	2004	2003	2002	2001	2000	1999
Dividends, Net Income ($)	0.00	0.00	0.00	0.00	0.00	0.00	0.00	0.00	0.00	0.00
Distrib'ns, Cap Gain ($)	0.11	5.22	0.25	0.00	0.00	0.00	0.00	0.00	16.11	3.12
Net Asset Value ($)	20.19	36.58	34.29	31.09	27.18	24.03	18.28	23.35	29.39	42.88
Expense Ratio (%)	1.08	1.08	1.08	1.08	1.09	1.09	1.08	1.06	1.04	1.05
Yield (%)	0.00	0.00	0.00	0.00	0.00	0.00	0.00	0.00	0.00	0.00
Portfolio Turnover (%)	210	162	200	183	279	279	273	284	244	208
Total Assets (Millions $)	2,423	4,864	4,230	3,954	3,731	3,796	2,997	4,265	5,771	5,515

PORTFOLIO (as of 9/30/08)

Portfolio Manager: D'Alonzo/Fenn/Ragard - 1985

Investment Style

Large Cap	✔ Growth
✔ Mid Cap	Grth/Val
✔ Small Cap	Value

Portfolio

91.0% U.S. stock	0.0% conv't
2.6% int'l stock	0.0% preferred
0.0% U.S. bonds	0.0% other
0.0% int'l bonds	6.4% cash

Number of Investments: 88
Percent of Portfolio in Top 10 Investments: 36%

SHAREHOLDER INFORMATION

Minimum Investment
Initial: $10,000 Subsequent: $1,000

Minimum IRA Investment
Initial: $10,000 Subsequent: $1,000

Maximum Fees
Load: none 12b-1: none
Other: none

Services
✔ IRA
Keogh
✔ Telephone Exchange

CRM Small/Mid Cap Value Inv (CRMAX)

800-876-2883
www.crmfunds.com

Mid-Cap Stock

PERFORMANCE

fund inception date: 9/1/04

	3yr Annual	5yr Annual	10yr Annual	Bull	Bear
Return (%)	-4.1	na	na	na	-34.8
Differ From Category (+/-)	5.7 high	na	na	na	8.6 high

Standard Deviation	Category Risk Index	Beta
17.6%—av	0.88—blw av	1.10

	2008	2007	2006	2005	2004	2003	2002	2001	2000	1999
Return (%)	-31.5	8.1	19.1	6.4	—	—	—	—	—	—
Differ From Category (+/-)	8.8	-1.9	5.9	-3.8	—	—	—	—	—	—
Return, Tax-Adjusted (%)	-31.6	7.1	18.1	6.2	—	—	—	—	—	—

PER SHARE DATA

	2008	2007	2006	2005	2004	2003	2002	2001	2000	1999
Dividends, Net Income ($)	0.05	0.01	0.00	0.01	—	—	—	—	—	—
Distrib'ns, Cap Gain ($)	0.00	0.91	0.85	0.10	—	—	—	—	—	—
Net Asset Value ($)	9.53	13.98	13.80	12.29	—	—	—	—	—	—
Expense Ratio (%)	1.23	1.42	1.47	1.20	—	—	—	—	—	—
Yield (%)	0.52	0.07	0.00	0.08	—	—	—	—	—	—
Portfolio Turnover (%)	78	94	109	71	—	—	—	—	—	—
Total Assets (Millions $)	72	74	30	26	—	—	—	—	—	—

PORTFOLIO (as of 6/30/08)

Portfolio Manager: Abramson/Rewey III - 2004

Investment Style

Large Cap	Growth
✔ Mid Cap	✔ Grth/Val
✔ Small Cap	Value

Portfolio

92.3%	U.S. stock	0.0%	conv't
0.0%	int'l stock	0.0%	preferred
0.0%	U.S. bonds	0.0%	other
0.0%	int'l bonds	7.7%	cash

Number of Investments: 64

Percent of Portfolio in Top 10 Investments: 28%

SHAREHOLDER INFORMATION

Minimum Investment

Initial: $2,500 Subsequent: $100

Minimum IRA Investment

Initial: $2,000 Subsequent: $100

Maximum Fees

Load: none 12b-1: none

Other: none

Services

✔ IRA
✔ Keogh
✔ Telephone Exchange

Delafield
(DEFIX)

800-221-3079
www.delafieldfund.com

Mid-Cap Stock

PERFORMANCE — fund inception date: 11/19/93

	3yr Annual	5yr Annual	10yr Annual	Bull	Bear
Return (%)	-7.7	0.1	7.8	149.7	-40.4
Differ From Category (+/-)	2.1 abv av	1.5 abv av	4.6 high	6.0 abv av	3.0 abv av

Standard Deviation	Category Risk Index	Beta
20.3%—abv av	1.02—av	1.22

	2008	2007	2006	2005	2004	2003	2002	2001	2000	1999
Return (%)	-37.6	4.8	20.3	6.0	20.8	40.1	-7.5	32.1	13.9	8.3
Differ From Category (+/-)	2.7	-5.2	7.1	-4.2	4.4	1.8	11.2	35.1	8.7	-31.8
Return, Tax-Adjusted (%)	-37.7	3.3	18.5	4.1	19.0	38.1	-7.5	30.6	13.5	8.1

PER SHARE DATA

	2008	2007	2006	2005	2004	2003	2002	2001	2000	1999
Dividends, Net Income ($)	0.07	0.15	0.19	0.03	0.00	0.00	0.00	0.06	0.07	0.09
Distrib'ns, Cap Gain ($)	0.00	2.42	2.63	3.07	2.78	2.38	0.00	1.13	0.16	0.00
Net Asset Value ($)	15.10	24.32	25.64	23.63	25.21	23.17	18.23	19.70	15.80	14.07
Expense Ratio (%)	na	1.23	1.32	1.33	1.32	1.32	1.20	1.25	1.28	1.25
Yield (%)	0.49	0.57	0.67	0.10	0.00	0.00	0.00	0.27	0.45	0.60
Portfolio Turnover (%)	na	61	72	71	55	78	79	98	99	105
Total Assets (Millions $)	373	699	531	372	345	247	144	199	99	86

PORTFOLIO (as of 9/30/08)

Portfolio Manager: Delafield/Sellecchia - 1993

Investment Style

Large Cap	Growth
✔ Mid Cap	Grth/Val
✔ Small Cap	✔ Value

Portfolio

75.2%	U.S. stock	0.0%	conv't
5.1%	int'l stock	0.0%	preferred
0.0%	U.S. bonds	0.0%	other
0.0%	int'l bonds	19.7%	cash

Number of Investments: 59

Percent of Portfolio in Top 10 Investments: 45%

SHAREHOLDER INFORMATION

Minimum Investment
Initial: $5,000 Subsequent: $0

Minimum IRA Investment
Initial: $250 Subsequent: $0

Maximum Fees
Load: 2.00% redemption 12b-1: 0.25%
Other: redemption fee applies for 90 days

Services
✔ IRA
✔ Keogh
✔ Telephone Exchange

Dreyfus MidCap Index (PESPX)

800-645-6561
www.dreyfus.com

Mid-Cap Stock

PERFORMANCE — fund inception date: 6/19/91

	3yr Annual	5yr Annual	10yr Annual	Bull	Bear
Return (%)	-9.1	-0.5	3.9	130.6	-39.7
Differ From Category (+/-)	0.7 av	0.9 abv av	0.7 av	-13.1 blw av	3.7 abv av

Standard Deviation	Category Risk Index	Beta
19.2%—abv av	0.96—av	1.19

	2008	2007	2006	2005	2004	2003	2002	2001	2000	1999
Return (%)	-36.5	7.5	9.8	12.0	15.9	34.9	-15.1	-1.1	16.7	14.0
Differ From Category (+/-)	3.8	-2.5	-3.4	1.8	-0.5	-3.4	3.6	1.9	11.5	-26.2
Return, Tax-Adjusted (%)	-37.2	5.9	9.0	11.2	15.3	34.7	-15.6	-1.9	13.2	9.8

PER SHARE DATA

	2008	2007	2006	2005	2004	2003	2002	2001	2000	1999
Dividends, Net Income ($)	0.32	0.35	0.28	0.26	0.16	0.12	0.12	0.15	0.21	0.20
Distrib'ns, Cap Gain ($)	0.93	2.78	1.18	1.15	0.73	0.09	0.32	0.58	3.38	4.47
Net Asset Value ($)	16.69	28.35	29.25	27.94	26.19	23.36	17.47	21.06	22.03	21.94
Expense Ratio (%)	na	0.50	0.50	0.50	0.50	0.51	0.50	0.50	0.50	0.50
Yield (%)	1.82	1.12	0.92	0.89	0.59	0.49	0.65	0.70	0.82	0.75
Portfolio Turnover (%)	na	23	16	20	14	12	19	28	45	50
Total Assets (Millions $)	1,422	2,328	2,285	2,200	1,709	1,228	735	633	493	323

PORTFOLIO (as of 10/31/08)

Portfolio Manager: Durante - 2000

Investment Style

Large Cap	Growth
✔ Mid Cap	✔ Grth/Val
Small Cap	Value

Portfolio

95.2% U.S. stock	0.0% conv't
0.0% int'l stock	0.0% preferred
0.0% U.S. bonds	0.2% other
0.0% int'l bonds	4.6% cash

Number of Investments: 407

Percent of Portfolio in Top 10 Investments: 17%

SHAREHOLDER INFORMATION

Minimum Investment

Initial: $2,500 Subsequent: $100

Minimum IRA Investment

Initial: $750 Subsequent: $0

Maximum Fees

Load: none 12b-1: none

Other: none

Services

✔ IRA

✔ Keogh

✔ Telephone Exchange

DWS Dreman Mid Cap Value S (MIDTX)

800-728-3337
www.dws-scudder.com

Mid-Cap Stock

PERFORMANCE — fund inception date: 8/1/05

	3yr Annual	5yr Annual	10yr Annual	Bull	Bear
Return (%)	-9.0	na	na	na	-42.7
Differ From Category (+/-)	0.8 av	na	na	na	0.7 abv av

Standard Deviation	Category Risk Index	Beta
18.4%—av	0.92—blw av	1.12

	2008	2007	2006	2005	2004	2003	2002	2001	2000	1999
Return (%)	-39.8	5.7	18.2	—	—	—	—	—	—	—
Differ From Category (+/-)	0.5	-4.3	5.0	—	—	—	—	—	—	—
Return, Tax-Adjusted (%)	-40.0	4.6	17.8	—	—	—	—	—	—	—

PER SHARE DATA

	2008	2007	2006	2005	2004	2003	2002	2001	2000	1999
Dividends, Net Income ($)	0.11	0.13	0.16	—	—	—	—	—	—	—
Distrib'ns, Cap Gain ($)	0.07	0.67	0.15	—	—	—	—	—	—	—
Net Asset Value ($)	6.85	11.64	11.78	—	—	—	—	—	—	—
Expense Ratio (%)	na	1.00	0.90	—	—	—	—	—	—	—
Yield (%)	1.59	1.09	1.31	—	—	—	—	—	—	—
Portfolio Turnover (%)	na	82	34	—	—	—	—	—	—	—
Total Assets (Millions $)	78	14	6	—	—	—	—	—	—	—

PORTFOLIO (as of 9/30/08)

Portfolio Manager: Dreman/Hutchinson/Roach - 2005

Investment Style

Large Cap	Growth
✔ Mid Cap	Grth/Val
Small Cap	✔ Value

Portfolio

88.5%	U.S. stock	0.0%	conv't
4.1%	int'l stock	0.0%	preferred
0.0%	U.S. bonds	0.0%	other
0.0%	int'l bonds	7.4%	cash

Number of Investments: 62
Percent of Portfolio in Top 10 Investments: 30%

SHAREHOLDER INFORMATION

Minimum Investment
Initial: $2,500 Subsequent: $50

Minimum IRA Investment
Initial: $1,000 Subsequent: $50

Maximum Fees
Load: 2.00% redemption 12b-1: none
Other: redemption fee applies for 15 days

Services
✔ IRA
✔ Keogh
✔ Telephone Exchange

FAM Value Inv
(FAMVX)

800-932-3271
www.famfunds.com

Mid-Cap Stock

PERFORMANCE — fund inception date: 1/2/87

	3yr Annual	5yr Annual	10yr Annual	Bull	Bear
Return (%)	-8.4	-1.1	3.9	85.4	-32.6
Differ From Category (+/-)	1.4 abv av	0.3 av	0.7 av	-58.3 low	10.8 high

Standard Deviation	Category Risk Index	Beta
14.8%—blw av	0.74—low	0.87

	2008	2007	2006	2005	2004	2003	2002	2001	2000	1999
Return (%)	-28.7	-0.8	8.7	5.5	16.8	24.9	-5.4	15.0	19.2	-4.9
Differ From Category (+/-)	-11.6	-10.8	-4.5	-4.7	0.4	-13.4	13.3	18.0	14.0	-45.1
Return, Tax-Adjusted (%)	-28.8	-2.0	7.9	5.1	16.3	24.5	-5.7	14.0	16.1	-5.9

PER SHARE DATA

	2008	2007	2006	2005	2004	2003	2002	2001	2000	1999
Dividends, Net Income ($)	0.17	0.25	0.31	0.37	0.07	0.09	0.11	0.17	0.36	0.29
Distrib'ns, Cap Gain ($)	0.00	3.57	2.24	0.87	1.36	0.87	0.44	1.30	4.03	1.09
Net Asset Value ($)	32.22	45.42	49.65	48.00	46.65	41.15	33.69	36.17	32.70	31.35
Expense Ratio (%)	na	1.18	1.18	1.18	1.20	1.24	1.21	1.21	1.26	1.23
Yield (%)	0.53	0.51	0.60	0.76	0.15	0.22	0.32	0.46	0.98	0.90
Portfolio Turnover (%)	na	9	18	14	10	9	17	10	9	16
Total Assets (Millions $)	568	873	1,049	1,097	920	580	470	501	367	373

PORTFOLIO (as of 9/30/08)

Portfolio Manager: Putnam/Fox - 1987

Investment Style

Large Cap	Growth
✔ Mid Cap	✔ Grth/Val
Small Cap	Value

Portfolio

82.3%	U.S. stock	0.0%	conv't
1.4%	int'l stock	0.0%	preferred
0.0%	U.S. bonds	0.0%	other
0.0%	int'l bonds	16.3%	cash

Number of Investments: 39

Percent of Portfolio in Top 10 Investments: 53%

SHAREHOLDER INFORMATION

Minimum Investment

Initial: $500 — Subsequent: $50

Minimum IRA Investment

Initial: $100 — Subsequent: $50

Maximum Fees

Load: none — 12b-1: none

Other: none

Services

✔ IRA

✔ Keogh

✔ Telephone Exchange

Federated Mid-Cap Index (FMDCX)

800-341-7400
www.federatedinvestors.com

Mid-Cap Stock

PERFORMANCE — fund inception date: 11/5/92

	3yr Annual	5yr Annual	10yr Annual	Bull	Bear
Return (%)	-9.1	-0.5	3.9	130.6	-39.7
Differ From Category (+/-)	0.7 av	0.9 abv av	0.7 av	-13.1 blw av	3.7 abv av

Standard Deviation	Category Risk Index	Beta
19.2%—abv av	0.96—av	1.19

	2008	2007	2006	2005	2004	2003	2002	2001	2000	1999
Return (%)	-36.4	7.5	9.8	12.0	15.8	34.9	-15.2	-1.3	16.7	13.8
Differ From Category (+/-)	3.9	-2.5	-3.4	1.8	-0.6	-3.4	3.5	1.7	11.5	-26.4
Return, Tax-Adjusted (%)	-37.1	5.7	8.9	11.0	15.1	34.7	-15.4	-1.9	13.6	10.9

PER SHARE DATA

	2008	2007	2006	2005	2004	2003	2002	2001	2000	1999
Dividends, Net Income ($)	0.25	0.31	0.32	0.24	0.14	0.10	0.10	0.13	0.16	0.16
Distrib'ns, Cap Gain ($)	0.81	2.48	1.06	1.16	0.77	0.14	0.00	0.25	2.33	2.22
Net Asset Value ($)	13.03	21.78	22.94	22.16	21.04	18.98	14.26	16.92	17.55	17.27
Expense Ratio (%)	na	0.49	0.49	0.49	0.49	0.49	0.50	0.58	0.57	0.60
Yield (%)	1.82	1.29	1.31	1.02	0.63	0.54	0.70	0.72	0.82	0.80
Portfolio Turnover (%)	na	17	13	14	16	11	40	30	38	40
Total Assets (Millions $)	587	1,126	1,215	945	794	613	381	376	222	127

PORTFOLIO (as of 9/30/08)

Portfolio Manager: Jelilian/Russo - 2003

Investment Style

Large Cap	Growth
✔ Mid Cap	✔ Grth/Val
Small Cap	Value

Portfolio

97.9% U.S. stock	0.0% conv't
0.0% int'l stock	0.0% preferred
0.0% U.S. bonds	0.0% other
0.0% int'l bonds	2.1% cash

Number of Investments: 404
Percent of Portfolio in Top 10 Investments: 7%

SHAREHOLDER INFORMATION

Minimum Investment
Initial: $25,000 Subsequent: $0

Minimum IRA Investment
Initial: $0 Subsequent: $0

Maximum Fees
Load: none 12b-1: none
Other: none

Services
✔ IRA
Keogh
✔ Telephone Exchange

Fidelity Low-Priced Stock (FLPSX)

800-544-9797
www.fidelity.com

Mid-Cap Stock

PERFORMANCE — fund inception date: 12/27/89

	3yr Annual	5yr Annual	10yr Annual	Bull	Bear
Return (%)	-8.2	0.5	7.9	155.6	-39.8
Differ From Category (+/-)	1.6 abv av	1.9 abv av	4.7 high	11.9 abv av	3.6 abv av

Standard Deviation	Category Risk Index	Beta
18.9%—abv av	0.95—blw av	1.16

	2008	2007	2006	2005	2004	2003	2002	2001	2000	1999
Return (%)	-36.2	3.1	17.7	8.6	22.2	40.8	-6.2	26.7	18.8	5.0
Differ From Category (+/-)	4.1	-6.9	4.5	-1.6	5.8	2.5	12.5	29.7	13.6	-35.2
Return, Tax-Adjusted (%)	-37.8	1.8	16.2	7.5	21.2	40.5	-6.7	25.1	15.5	3.7

PER SHARE DATA

	2008	2007	2006	2005	2004	2003	2002	2001	2000	1999
Dividends, Net Income ($)	0.17	0.57	0.33	0.26	0.12	0.02	0.03	0.16	0.16	0.15
Distrib'ns, Cap Gain ($)	4.11	3.18	3.78	2.62	2.09	0.44	0.54	1.54	3.43	1.19
Net Asset Value ($)	23.12	41.13	43.54	40.84	40.25	34.98	25.17	27.42	23.12	22.64
Expense Ratio (%)	0.98	0.96	0.87	0.95	0.97	1.01	0.97	1.00	0.81	1.08
Yield (%)	0.63	1.28	0.69	0.59	0.28	0.05	0.11	0.55	0.60	0.62
Portfolio Turnover (%)	36	11	26	24	28	23	26	44	15	24
Total Assets (Millions $)	18,351	35,231	39,340	36,721	35,976	26,725	15,104	12,429	6,834	6,646

PORTFOLIO (as of 10/31/08)

Portfolio Manager: Tillinghast - 1989

Investment Style

Large Cap	Growth
✔ Mid Cap	✔ Grth/Val
✔ Small Cap	Value

Portfolio

63.3%	U.S. stock	0.3%	conv't
23.5%	int'l stock	0.5%	preferred
0.0%	U.S. bonds	0.0%	other
0.0%	int'l bonds	12.5%	cash

Number of Investments: 783

Percent of Portfolio in Top 10 Investments: 29%

SHAREHOLDER INFORMATION

Minimum Investment

Initial: $2,500 Subsequent: $250

Minimum IRA Investment

Initial: $500 Subsequent: $250

Maximum Fees

Load: 1.50% redemption 12b-1: none

Other: redemption fee applies for 90 days; maint fee for low bal

Services

✔ IRA

✔ Keogh

✔ Telephone Exchange

Fidelity Mid Cap Value (FSMVX)

800-544-6666
www.fidelity.com

Mid-Cap Stock

PERFORMANCE — fund inception date: 11/15/01

	3yr Annual	5yr Annual	10yr Annual	Bull	Bear
Return (%)	-11.3	-0.7	na	139.0	-43.7
Differ From Category (+/-)	-1.5 blw av	0.7 abv av	na	-4.7 av	-0.3 av

Standard Deviation	Category Risk Index	Beta
19.3%—abv av	0.97—av	1.18

	2008	2007	2006	2005	2004	2003	2002	2001	2000	1999
Return (%)	-40.6	2.6	14.5	13.6	21.8	33.4	-13.6	—	—	—
Differ From Category (+/-)	-0.3	-7.4	1.3	3.4	5.4	-4.9	5.1	—	—	—
Return, Tax-Adjusted (%)	-40.7	1.9	13.9	12.3	21.4	33.4	-13.9	—	—	—

PER SHARE DATA

	2008	2007	2006	2005	2004	2003	2002	2001	2000	1999
Dividends, Net Income ($)	0.16	0.06	0.09	0.09	0.04	0.04	0.08	—	—	—
Distrib'ns, Cap Gain ($)	0.00	0.77	0.45	1.15	0.32	0.00	0.00	—	—	—
Net Asset Value ($)	9.51	16.28	16.67	15.05	14.35	12.08	9.08	—	—	—
Expense Ratio (%)	0.82	0.84	0.81	0.90	1.05	1.18	1.20	—	—	—
Yield (%)	1.65	0.35	0.52	0.58	0.27	0.33	0.88	—	—	—
Portfolio Turnover (%)	264	187	207	196	97	113	68	—	—	—
Total Assets (Millions $)	398	835	634	315	143	89	42	—	—	—

PORTFOLIO (as of 11/30/08)

Portfolio Manager: Dirks - 2005

Investment Style

Large Cap	Growth
✔ Mid Cap	Grth/Val
Small Cap	✔ Value

Portfolio

99.5%	U.S. stock	0.0%	conv't
0.5%	int'l stock	0.0%	preferred
0.0%	U.S. bonds	0.0%	other
0.0%	int'l bonds	0.0%	cash

Number of Investments: 111
Percent of Portfolio in Top 10 Investments: 17%

SHAREHOLDER INFORMATION

Minimum Investment
Initial: $2,500 Subsequent: $250

Minimum IRA Investment
Initial: $500 Subsequent: $100

Maximum Fees
Load: 0.75% redemption 12b-1: none
Other: redemption fee applies for 30 days; maint fee for low bal

Services
✔ IRA
Keogh
✔ Telephone Exchange

Fidelity New Millennium (FMILX)

800-544-6666
www.fidelity.com

Mid-Cap Stock

PERFORMANCE — fund inception date: 12/28/92

	3yr Annual	5yr Annual	10yr Annual	Bull	Bear
Return (%)	-7.6	-2.0	4.8	130.0	-43.1
Differ From Category (+/-)	2.2 abv av	-0.6 blw av	1.6 abv av	-13.7 blw av	0.3 av

Standard Deviation	Category Risk Index	Beta
19.8%—abv av	0.99—av	1.20

	2008	2007	2006	2005	2004	2003	2002	2001	2000	1999
Return (%)	-40.3	16.4	13.5	10.1	4.2	37.3	-19.9	-18.2	-6.1	108.7
Differ From Category (+/-)	0.0	6.4	0.3	-0.1	-12.2	-1.0	-1.2	-15.2	-11.3	68.5
Return, Tax-Adjusted (%)	-40.4	14.2	9.1	10.1	4.2	37.3	-19.9	-18.5	-10.3	103.9

PER SHARE DATA

	2008	2007	2006	2005	2004	2003	2002	2001	2000	1999
Dividends, Net Income ($)	0.09	0.02	0.00	0.00	0.00	0.01	0.00	0.00	0.00	0.00
Distrib'ns, Cap Gain ($)	0.10	4.37	10.30	0.00	0.00	0.00	0.00	0.53	10.11	6.37
Net Asset Value ($)	17.64	29.79	29.40	34.89	31.69	30.39	22.14	27.63	34.33	47.46
Expense Ratio (%)	na	0.93	0.91	0.80	0.92	0.76	1.02	0.98	0.89	0.93
Yield (%)	0.50	0.05	0.00	0.00	0.00	0.03	0.00	0.00	0.00	0.00
Portfolio Turnover (%)	na	87	147	120	96	97	91	85	97	116
Total Assets (Millions $)	1,190	2,300	2,360	3,478	3,618	3,656	2,616	2,939	3,572	3,772

PORTFOLIO (as of 11/30/08)

Portfolio Manager: Roth - 2006

Investment Style

Large Cap	✔ Growth
✔ Mid Cap	Grth/Val
Small Cap	Value

Portfolio

82.7% U.S. stock	0.2% conv't
13.0% int'l stock	0.3% preferred
0.0% U.S. bonds	0.7% other
0.0% int'l bonds	3.1% cash

Number of Investments: 241

Percent of Portfolio in Top 10 Investments: 21%

SHAREHOLDER INFORMATION

Minimum Investment

Initial: $2,500 Subsequent: $250

Minimum IRA Investment

Initial: $500 Subsequent: $250

Maximum Fees

Load: none 12b-1: none

Other: maint fee for low bal

Services

✔ IRA
✔ Keogh
✔ Telephone Exchange

Fidelity Spartan Extended Mkt Index Inv (FSEMX)

800-544-9797
www.fidelity.com

Mid-Cap Stock

PERFORMANCE — fund inception date: 11/5/97

	3yr Annual	5yr Annual	10yr Annual	Bull	Bear
Return (%)	-9.3	-0.6	1.4	151.7	-42.1
Differ From Category (+/-)	0.5 av	0.8 abv av	-1.8 blw av	8.0 abv av	1.3 abv av

Standard Deviation	Category Risk Index	Beta
19.1%—abv av	0.96—av	1.19

	2008	2007	2006	2005	2004	2003	2002	2001	2000	1999
Return (%)	-38.5	5.3	15.3	10.0	17.8	42.8	-18.1	-8.8	-16.0	33.1
Differ From Category (+/-)	1.8	-4.7	2.1	-0.2	1.4	4.5	0.6	-5.8	-21.2	-7.1
Return, Tax-Adjusted (%)	-39.0	4.4	14.6	9.8	17.7	42.7	-18.4	-9.5	-17.3	31.9

PER SHARE DATA

	2008	2007	2006	2005	2004	2003	2002	2001	2000	1999
Dividends, Net Income ($)	0.43	0.46	0.44	0.34	0.22	0.14	0.19	0.25	0.21	0.24
Distrib'ns, Cap Gain ($)	0.76	1.85	1.07	0.10	0.00	0.00	0.00	0.37	1.71	1.12
Net Asset Value ($)	22.55	38.32	38.53	34.74	31.98	27.32	19.23	23.70	26.72	33.96
Expense Ratio (%)	0.09	0.09	0.10	0.23	0.40	0.30	0.25	0.24	0.27	0.31
Yield (%)	1.84	1.14	1.11	0.97	0.68	0.51	0.98	1.03	0.73	0.68
Portfolio Turnover (%)	17	16	13	17	18	18	34	45	33	29
Total Assets (Millions $)	1,686	2,286	1,862	1,372	1,282	924	443	451	478	269

PORTFOLIO (as of 11/30/08)

Portfolio Manager: Adams/Simon/Waddell - 2005

Investment Style

Large Cap	Growth
✔ Mid Cap	✔ Grth/Val
✔ Small Cap	Value

Portfolio

95.1%	U.S. stock	0.0%	conv't
0.5%	int'l stock	0.0%	preferred
0.0%	U.S. bonds	0.2%	other
0.0%	int'l bonds	4.3%	cash

Number of Investments: 3,246
Percent of Portfolio in Top 10 Investments: 19%

SHAREHOLDER INFORMATION

Minimum Investment
Initial: $10,000 Subsequent: $1,000

Minimum IRA Investment
Initial: $0 Subsequent: $0

Maximum Fees
Load: 0.75% redemption 12b-1: none
Other: redemption fee applies for 90 days; maint fee for low bal

Services
✔ IRA
✔ Keogh
✔ Telephone Exchange

Fidelity Value
(FDVLX)

800-544-6666
www.fidelity.com

Mid-Cap Stock

PERFORMANCE — fund inception date: 12/1/78

	3yr Annual	5yr Annual	10yr Annual	Bull	Bear
Return (%)	-14.4	-2.8	3.4	149.9	-50.8
Differ From Category (+/-)	-4.6 low	-1.4 blw av	0.2 av	6.2 abv av	-7.4 low

Standard Deviation	Category Risk Index	Beta
21.2%—abv av	1.07—abv av	1.35

	2008	2007	2006	2005	2004	2003	2002	2001	2000	1999
Return (%)	-46.6	2.2	15.0	14.2	21.2	34.4	-9.3	12.2	8.1	8.5
Differ From Category (+/-)	-6.3	-7.8	1.8	4.0	4.8	-3.9	9.4	15.2	2.9	-31.7
Return, Tax-Adjusted (%)	-46.6	0.7	13.7	13.0	20.2	34.3	-9.6	11.8	7.2	5.5

PER SHARE DATA

	2008	2007	2006	2005	2004	2003	2002	2001	2000	1999
Dividends, Net Income ($)	0.23	0.56	0.56	0.43	0.16	0.23	0.36	0.51	0.95	0.73
Distrib'ns, Cap Gain ($)	0.00	7.09	6.09	5.14	3.71	0.05	0.00	0.00	0.00	5.62
Net Asset Value ($)	39.86	75.01	80.60	75.88	71.29	62.07	46.39	51.51	46.35	43.81
Expense Ratio (%)	0.76	0.69	0.66	0.72	0.93	0.98	0.95	0.77	0.48	0.54
Yield (%)	0.58	0.68	0.64	0.53	0.21	0.37	0.77	0.99	2.04	1.47
Portfolio Turnover (%)	50	44	36	29	40	40	42	49	48	50
Total Assets (Millions $)	8,696	20,399	18,254	14,328	10,279	6,984	5,092	5,238	3,522	4,383

PORTFOLIO (as of 11/30/08)

Portfolio Manager: Fentin - 1996

Investment Style

✔ Large Cap	Growth
✔ Mid Cap	Grth/Val
Small Cap	✔ Value

Portfolio

93.4%	U.S. stock	0.0%	conv't
4.8%	int'l stock	0.8%	preferred
0.3%	U.S. bonds	0.3%	other
0.0%	int'l bonds	0.3%	cash

Number of Investments: 298
Percent of Portfolio in Top 10 Investments: 13%

SHAREHOLDER INFORMATION

Minimum Investment
Initial: $2,500 Subsequent: $250

Minimum IRA Investment
Initial: $500 Subsequent: $100

Maximum Fees
Load: none 12b-1: none
Other: maint fee for low bal

Services
✔ IRA
✔ Keogh
✔ Telephone Exchange

FMI Common Stock (FMIMX)

800-811-5311
www.fiduciarymgt.com

Mid-Cap Stock

PERFORMANCE — fund inception date: 12/18/81

	3yr Annual	5yr Annual	10yr Annual	Bull	Bear
Return (%)	-3.0	3.5	7.6	111.5	-25.4
Differ From Category (+/-)	6.8 high	4.9 high	4.4 high	-32.2 low	18.0 high

Standard Deviation	Category Risk Index	Beta
17.3%—av	0.87—low	0.98

	2008	2007	2006	2005	2004	2003	2002	2001	2000	1999
Return (%)	-20.5	-2.0	17.1	9.4	18.7	24.0	-5.8	18.6	19.0	6.5
Differ From Category (+/-)	19.8	-12.0	3.9	-0.8	2.3	-14.3	12.9	21.6	13.8	-33.7
Return, Tax-Adjusted (%)	-21.2	-4.2	15.2	7.6	17.9	23.6	-5.8	15.8	17.8	5.9

PER SHARE DATA

	2008	2007	2006	2005	2004	2003	2002	2001	2000	1999
Dividends, Net Income ($)	0.06	0.08	0.07	0.02	0.71	0.00	0.00	0.00	0.00	0.00
Distrib'ns, Cap Gain ($)	0.97	3.66	2.97	2.95	0.50	0.48	0.00	2.68	1.07	0.43
Net Asset Value ($)	15.92	21.34	25.41	24.36	25.15	22.27	18.36	19.48	18.92	16.89
Expense Ratio (%)	1.22	1.20	1.21	1.21	1.23	1.25	1.10	1.20	1.20	1.30
Yield (%)	0.37	0.33	0.26	0.05	2.76	0.00	0.00	0.00	0.00	0.00
Portfolio Turnover (%)	40	50	38	34	34	34	29	46	46	75
Total Assets (Millions $)	429	421	486	446	435	328	111	64	50	41

PORTFOLIO (as of 9/30/08)

Portfolio Manager: Kellner/English - 1981

Investment Style

Large Cap	Growth
✔ Mid Cap	✔ Grth/Val
✔ Small Cap	Value

Portfolio

86.9%	U.S. stock	0.0%	conv't
0.0%	int'l stock	0.0%	preferred
0.0%	U.S. bonds	0.0%	other
0.0%	int'l bonds	13.1%	cash

Number of Investments: 46
Percent of Portfolio in Top 10 Investments: 33%

SHAREHOLDER INFORMATION

Minimum Investment
Initial: $1,000 Subsequent: $100

Minimum IRA Investment
Initial: $1,000 Subsequent: $100

Maximum Fees
Load: none 12b-1: none
Other: none

Services
✔ IRA
✔ Keogh
✔ Telephone Exchange

Gabelli ABC
(GABCX)
Mid-Cap Stock

800-422-3554
www.gabelli.com

PERFORMANCE **fund inception date: 5/14/93**

	3yr Annual	5yr Annual	10yr Annual	Bull	Bear
Return (%)	5.3	4.5	5.2	34.8	-3.0
Differ From Category (+/-)	15.1 high	5.9 high	2.0 abv av	-108.9 low	40.4 high

Standard Deviation	Category Risk Index	Beta
4.4%—low	0.22—low	0.25

	2008	2007	2006	2005	2004	2003	2002	2001	2000	1999
Return (%)	-2.7	7.0	11.9	4.9	1.9	4.9	0.8	4.5	10.7	9.1
Differ From Category (+/-)	37.6	-2.9	-1.3	-5.3	-14.5	-33.4	19.5	7.5	5.5	-31.1
Return, Tax-Adjusted (%)	-3.1	5.7	10.4	4.2	1.6	4.4	0.5	3.8	8.3	6.7

PER SHARE DATA

	2008	2007	2006	2005	2004	2003	2002	2001	2000	1999
Dividends, Net Income ($)	0.09	0.17	0.26	0.15	0.08	0.01	0.05	0.09	0.12	0.14
Distrib'ns, Cap Gain ($)	0.17	0.74	0.77	0.34	0.09	0.28	0.04	0.14	0.89	0.86
Net Asset Value ($)	9.28	9.80	10.00	9.85	9.85	9.83	9.64	9.65	9.45	9.45
Expense Ratio (%)	na	0.63	0.59	0.64	0.61	0.65	0.99	1.46	1.45	1.37
Yield (%)	0.98	1.58	2.41	1.47	0.76	0.10	0.52	0.91	1.16	1.40
Portfolio Turnover (%)	na	204	190	127	141	244	252	61	312	672
Total Assets (Millions $)	130	176	155	177	301	294	261	158	62	43

PORTFOLIO (as of 9/30/08)

Portfolio Manager: Gabelli - 1993

Investment Style

Large Cap	Growth
✔ Mid Cap	✔ Grth/Val
Small Cap	Value

Portfolio

68.8%	U.S. stock	0.0%	conv't
5.3%	int'l stock	0.0%	preferred
0.0%	U.S. bonds	0.0%	other
0.0%	int'l bonds	25.8%	cash

Number of Investments: 169

Percent of Portfolio in Top 10 Investments: 56%

SHAREHOLDER INFORMATION

Minimum Investment
Initial: $10,000 Subsequent: $0

Minimum IRA Investment
Initial: $10,000 Subsequent: $0

Maximum Fees
Load: 2.00% redemption 12b-1: none
Other: redemption fee applies for 7 days

Services
✔ IRA
Keogh
✔ Telephone Exchange

Gabelli Asset AAA (GABAX)

800-422-3554
www.gabelli.com

Mid-Cap Stock

PERFORMANCE — fund inception date: 3/3/86

	3yr Annual	5yr Annual	10yr Annual	Bull	Bear
Return (%)	-5.1	0.8	3.8	139.1	-39.5
Differ From Category (+/-)	4.7 high	2.2 high	0.6 av	-4.6 av	3.9 abv av

Standard Deviation	Category Risk Index	Beta
17.0%—av	0.85—low	1.08

	2008	2007	2006	2005	2004	2003	2002	2001	2000	1999
Return (%)	-37.3	11.8	21.8	4.4	16.4	30.5	-14.3	0.1	-2.4	28.4
Differ From Category (+/-)	3.0	1.8	8.6	-5.8	0.0	-7.8	4.4	3.1	-7.6	-11.8
Return, Tax-Adjusted (%)	-37.3	10.8	20.8	3.6	16.1	30.2	-14.3	-0.5	-5.4	25.8

PER SHARE DATA

	2008	2007	2006	2005	2004	2003	2002	2001	2000	1999
Dividends, Net Income ($)	0.23	0.15	0.31	0.12	0.03	0.03	0.01	0.00	0.31	0.00
Distrib'ns, Cap Gain ($)	0.03	3.04	2.44	2.04	0.76	0.59	0.00	0.98	5.57	4.63
Net Asset Value ($)	31.01	49.81	47.38	41.13	41.45	36.26	28.25	32.97	33.90	40.84
Expense Ratio (%)	na	1.36	1.36	1.37	1.38	1.38	1.38	1.36	1.36	1.37
Yield (%)	0.73	0.28	0.61	0.27	0.05	0.08	0.04	0.00	0.77	0.00
Portfolio Turnover (%)	na	9	7	6	7	7	8	15	48	32
Total Assets (Millions $)	1,722	2,952	2,519	2,254	2,218	1,960	1,503	1,911	1,909	1,994

PORTFOLIO (as of 9/30/08)

Portfolio Manager: Gabelli - 1986

Investment Style

✔ Large Cap	Growth
✔ Mid Cap	✔ Grth/Val
Small Cap	Value

Portfolio

82.8%	U.S. stock	0.1%	conv't
16.8%	int'l stock	0.0%	preferred
0.0%	U.S. bonds	0.0%	other
0.0%	int'l bonds	0.3%	cash

Number of Investments: 499
Percent of Portfolio in Top 10 Investments: 17%

SHAREHOLDER INFORMATION

Minimum Investment
Initial: $1,000 Subsequent: $0

Minimum IRA Investment
Initial: $250 Subsequent: $0

Maximum Fees
Load: 2.00% redemption 12b-1: 0.25%
Other: redemption fee applies for 7 days

Services
✔ IRA
Keogh
✔ Telephone Exchange

Heartland Select Value (HRSVX)

800-432-7856
www.heartlandfunds.com

Mid-Cap Stock

PERFORMANCE — fund inception date: 10/11/96

	3yr Annual	5yr Annual	10yr Annual	Bull	Bear
Return (%)	-5.9	2.0	7.2	147.0	-35.6
Differ From Category (+/-)	3.9 high	3.4 high	4.0 high	3.3 abv av	7.8 high

Standard Deviation	Category Risk Index	Beta
18.5%—av	0.93—blw av	1.13

	2008	2007	2006	2005	2004	2003	2002	2001	2000	1999
Return (%)	-31.3	4.0	16.6	13.4	17.0	35.6	-13.9	16.4	30.6	1.9
Differ From Category (+/-)	9.0	-6.0	3.4	3.2	0.6	-2.7	4.8	19.4	25.4	-38.3
Return, Tax-Adjusted (%)	-31.4	2.6	15.5	12.8	16.8	35.6	-14.0	16.1	29.9	0.9

PER SHARE DATA

	2008	2007	2006	2005	2004	2003	2002	2001	2000	1999
Dividends, Net Income ($)	0.13	0.17	0.14	0.06	0.01	0.01	0.03	0.02	0.14	0.17
Distrib'ns, Cap Gain ($)	0.00	2.42	1.76	0.91	0.21	0.00	0.00	0.16	0.14	0.25
Net Asset Value ($)	18.07	26.48	27.94	25.56	23.37	20.16	14.87	17.30	15.03	11.73
Expense Ratio (%)	na	1.24	1.25	1.27	1.33	1.47	1.46	1.48	1.22	0.74
Yield (%)	0.72	0.59	0.48	0.21	0.05	0.06	0.22	0.08	0.89	1.39
Portfolio Turnover (%)	na	63	51	42	72	47	39	108	120	160
Total Assets (Millions $)	263	332	290	155	110	76	56	29	10	7

PORTFOLIO (as of 9/30/08)

Portfolio Manager: Baszler/Denison/Fondrie - 2004

Investment Style

Large Cap	Growth
✔ Mid Cap	Grth/Val
Small Cap	✔ Value

Portfolio

76.6%	U.S. stock	0.0%	conv't
8.3%	int'l stock	0.0%	preferred
0.0%	U.S. bonds	0.0%	other
0.0%	int'l bonds	15.1%	cash

Number of Investments: 53
Percent of Portfolio in Top 10 Investments: 33%

SHAREHOLDER INFORMATION

Minimum Investment
Initial: $1,000 Subsequent: $100

Minimum IRA Investment
Initial: $500 Subsequent: $0

Maximum Fees
Load: 2.00% redemption 12b-1: 0.25%
Other: redemption fee applies for 10 days

Services
✔ IRA
✔ Keogh
✔ Telephone Exchange

Hennessy Focus 30 (HFTFX)

800-966-4354
www.hennessyfunds.com

Mid-Cap Stock

PERFORMANCE — fund inception date: 9/17/03

	3yr Annual	5yr Annual	10yr Annual	Bull	Bear
Return (%)	-7.3	3.8	na	na	-34.2
Differ From Category (+/-)	2.5 abv av	5.2 high	na	na	9.2 high

Standard Deviation	Category Risk Index	Beta
23.5%—high	1.18—high	1.16

	2008	2007	2006	2005	2004	2003	2002	2001	2000	1999
Return (%)	-33.1	6.6	11.9	32.7	14.1	—	—	—	—	—
Differ From Category (+/-)	7.2	-3.4	-1.3	22.5	-2.3	—	—	—	—	—
Return, Tax-Adjusted (%)	-33.1	4.2	11.7	30.2	14.1	—	—	—	—	—

PER SHARE DATA

	2008	2007	2006	2005	2004	2003	2002	2001	2000	1999
Dividends, Net Income ($)	0.00	0.00	0.00	0.00	0.00	—	—	—	—	—
Distrib'ns, Cap Gain ($)	0.00	2.02	0.10	1.61	0.00	—	—	—	—	—
Net Asset Value ($)	7.62	11.39	12.60	11.35	9.79	—	—	—	—	—
Expense Ratio (%)	na	1.23	1.21	1.35	1.41	—	—	—	—	—
Yield (%)	0.00	0.00	0.00	0.00	0.00	—	—	—	—	—
Portfolio Turnover (%)	na	112	124	136	357	—	—	—	—	—
Total Assets (Millions $)	152	209	209	151	59	—	—	—	—	—

PORTFOLIO (as of 9/30/08)

Portfolio Manager: Hennessy - 2003

Investment Style

Large Cap	Growth
✔ Mid Cap	✔ Grth/Val
Small Cap	Value

Portfolio

87.5% U.S. stock	0.0% conv't
0.0% int'l stock	0.0% preferred
0.0% U.S. bonds	0.0% other
0.0% int'l bonds	12.5% cash

Number of Investments: 34
Percent of Portfolio in Top 10 Investments: 37%

SHAREHOLDER INFORMATION

Minimum Investment
Initial: $2,500 Subsequent: $100

Minimum IRA Investment
Initial: $250 Subsequent: $100

Maximum Fees
Load: none 12b-1: none
Other: none

Services
✔ IRA
✔ Keogh
✔ Telephone Exchange

Janus Enterprise
(JAENX)

800-525-0020
www.janus.com

Mid-Cap Stock

PERFORMANCE — fund inception date: 9/1/92

	3yr Annual	5yr Annual	10yr Annual	Bull	Bear
Return (%)	-7.8	1.0	-0.5	163.8	-44.6
Differ From Category (+/-)	2.0 abv av	2.4 high	-3.7 low	20.1 high	-1.2 av

Standard Deviation	Category Risk Index	Beta
21.7%—abv av	1.09—abv av	1.35

	2008	2007	2006	2005	2004	2003	2002	2001	2000	1999
Return (%)	-43.2	21.8	13.2	11.3	20.6	35.8	-28.3	-40.0	-30.6	121.9
Differ From Category (+/-)	-2.9	11.8	0.0	1.2	4.2	-2.5	-9.6	-37.0	-35.8	81.7
Return, Tax-Adjusted (%)	-43.2	21.8	13.2	11.3	20.6	35.8	-28.3	-40.0	-30.6	120.0

PER SHARE DATA

	2008	2007	2006	2005	2004	2003	2002	2001	2000	1999
Dividends, Net Income ($)	0.00	0.00	0.00	0.00	0.00	0.00	0.00	0.00	0.00	0.00
Distrib'ns, Cap Gain ($)	0.00	0.00	0.00	0.00	0.00	0.00	0.00	0.00	0.00	3.33
Net Asset Value ($)	32.87	57.80	47.45	41.91	37.62	31.17	22.95	32.00	53.27	76.67
Expense Ratio (%)	na	0.93	0.99	0.95	1.03	0.89	0.90	0.90	0.88	0.95
Yield (%)	0.00	0.00	0.00	0.00	0.00	0.00	0.00	0.00	0.00	0.00
Portfolio Turnover (%)	na	32	40	28	27	22	64	85	80	98
Total Assets (Millions $)	1,220	2,184	1,776	1,792	1,835	1,884	1,626	3,209	6,267	4,435

PORTFOLIO (as of 9/30/08)

Portfolio Manager: Demain - 2007

Investment Style

Large Cap	✔ Growth
✔ Mid Cap	Grth/Val
✔ Small Cap	Value

Portfolio

85.2%	U.S. stock	0.0%	conv't
12.4%	int'l stock	0.0%	preferred
0.0%	U.S. bonds	0.0%	other
0.0%	int'l bonds	2.4%	cash

Number of Investments: 87

Percent of Portfolio in Top 10 Investments: 23%

SHAREHOLDER INFORMATION

Minimum Investment

Initial: $2,500 Subsequent: $100

Minimum IRA Investment

Initial: $1,000 Subsequent: $100

Maximum Fees

Load: none 12b-1: none

Other: none

Services

✔ IRA

✔ Keogh

✔ Telephone Exchange

Janus Mid Cap Value Investor (JMCVX)

800-525-0020
www.janus.com

Mid-Cap Stock

PERFORMANCE — fund inception date: 8/12/98

	3yr Annual	5yr Annual	10yr Annual	Bull	Bear
Return (%)	-3.5	3.2	10.2	141.6	-30.0
Differ From Category (+/-)	6.3 high	4.6 high	7.0 high	-2.1 av	13.4 high

Standard Deviation	Category Risk Index	Beta
15.1%—blw av	0.76—low	0.94

	2008	2007	2006	2005	2004	2003	2002	2001	2000	1999
Return (%)	-27.4	7.4	15.2	10.3	18.3	39.3	-13.1	20.5	27.3	21.5
Differ From Category (+/-)	12.9	-2.6	2.0	0.1	1.9	1.0	5.6	23.5	22.1	-18.7
Return, Tax-Adjusted (%)	-28.0	5.4	13.9	8.9	16.8	39.2	-13.2	19.9	24.8	19.2

PER SHARE DATA

	2008	2007	2006	2005	2004	2003	2002	2001	2000	1999
Dividends, Net Income ($)	0.19	1.00	0.74	0.87	0.08	0.10	0.03	0.03	0.10	0.04
Distrib'ns, Cap Gain ($)	0.79	2.12	1.19	1.20	1.93	0.00	0.00	0.35	1.36	1.24
Net Asset Value ($)	15.28	22.43	23.81	22.32	22.09	20.39	14.71	16.96	14.39	12.51
Expense Ratio (%)	na	0.85	0.93	0.92	0.94	1.08	1.15	1.22	1.59	1.62
Yield (%)	1.15	4.07	2.95	3.70	0.35	0.50	0.20	0.16	0.63	0.31
Portfolio Turnover (%)	na	95	95	86	91	97	39	116	129	154
Total Assets (Millions $)	4,980	5,610	5,373	4,496	3,453	1,747	948	265	51	25

PORTFOLIO (as of 9/30/08)

Portfolio Manager: Perkins/Kautz - 1998

Investment Style

Large Cap	Growth
✔ Mid Cap	Grth/Val
Small Cap	✔ Value

Portfolio

96.5% U.S. stock	0.0% conv't
3.5% int'l stock	0.0% preferred
0.0% U.S. bonds	0.0% other
0.0% int'l bonds	0.0% cash

Number of Investments: 150

Percent of Portfolio in Top 10 Investments: 16%

SHAREHOLDER INFORMATION

Minimum Investment

Initial: $2,500 Subsequent: $100

Minimum IRA Investment

Initial: $1,000 Subsequent: $100

Maximum Fees

Load: none 12b-1: none

Other: none

Services

✔ IRA

✔ Keogh

✔ Telephone Exchange

Janus Orion
(JORNX)

800-525-0020
www.janus.com

Mid-Cap Stock

PERFORMANCE — fund inception date: 6/30/00

	3yr Annual	5yr Annual	10yr Annual	Bull	Bear
Return (%)	-7.6	1.8	na	240.0	-51.6
Differ From Category (+/-)	2.2 abv av	3.2 high	na	96.3 high	-8.2 low

Standard Deviation	Category Risk Index	Beta
25.2%—high	1.27—high	1.51

	2008	2007	2006	2005	2004	2003	2002	2001	2000	1999
Return (%)	-49.8	32.3	18.6	20.9	14.8	43.8	-29.8	-14.7	—	—
Differ From Category (+/-)	-9.5	22.3	5.4	10.7	-1.5	5.5	-11.1	-11.7	—	—
Return, Tax-Adjusted (%)	-49.9	32.3	18.5	20.7	14.8	43.8	-29.8	-14.7	—	—

PER SHARE DATA

	2008	2007	2006	2005	2004	2003	2002	2001	2000	1999
Dividends, Net Income ($)	0.06	0.04	0.02	0.06	0.00	0.00	0.00	0.00	—	—
Distrib'ns, Cap Gain ($)	0.00	0.00	0.00	0.00	0.00	0.00	0.00	0.00	—	—
Net Asset Value ($)	6.47	13.01	9.86	8.33	6.94	6.04	4.20	5.98	—	—
Expense Ratio (%)	na	0.92	0.99	1.01	1.08	1.08	1.04	1.03	—	—
Yield (%)	0.92	0.32	0.23	0.75	0.00	0.00	0.00	0.00	—	—
Portfolio Turnover (%)	na	24	63	68	69	72	161	206	—	—
Total Assets (Millions $)	2,278	5,099	3,342	818	568	541	391	688	—	—

PORTFOLIO (as of 9/30/08)

Portfolio Manager: Eisinger - 2008

Investment Style

Large Cap	✔ Growth
✔ Mid Cap	Grth/Val
Small Cap	Value

Portfolio

63.1% U.S. stock	0.0% conv't
35.9% int'l stock	0.0% preferred
0.0% U.S. bonds	0.0% other
0.0% int'l bonds	1.0% cash

Number of Investments: 45
Percent of Portfolio in Top 10 Investments: 46%

SHAREHOLDER INFORMATION

Minimum Investment
Initial: $2,500 — Subsequent: $100

Minimum IRA Investment
Initial: $1,000 — Subsequent: $100

Maximum Fees
Load: none — 12b-1: none
Other: none

Services
✔ IRA
✔ Keogh
✔ Telephone Exchange

Lazard U.S. Mid Cap Equity Open (LZMOX)

800-986-3455
www.lazardnet.com

Mid-Cap Stock

PERFORMANCE

fund inception date: 11/3/97

	3yr Annual	5yr Annual	10yr Annual	Bull	Bear
Return (%)	-12.0	-1.7	3.7	119.5	-43.7
Differ From Category (+/-)	-2.2 blw av	-0.3 av	0.5 av	-24.2 blw av	-0.3 av

Standard Deviation	Category Risk Index	Beta
18.2%—av	0.91—blw av	1.13

	2008	2007	2006	2005	2004	2003	2002	2001	2000	1999
Return (%)	-38.6	-3.2	14.5	8.5	24.5	28.7	-14.8	12.5	22.0	3.9
Differ From Category (+/-)	1.7	-13.2	1.3	-1.7	8.1	-9.6	3.9	15.5	16.8	-36.3
Return, Tax-Adjusted (%)	-38.8	-4.8	13.7	7.2	23.1	28.7	-15.1	8.7	19.0	3.7

PER SHARE DATA

	2008	2007	2006	2005	2004	2003	2002	2001	2000	1999
Dividends, Net Income ($)	0.15	0.07	0.04	0.03	0.00	0.00	0.00	0.04	0.00	0.02
Distrib'ns, Cap Gain ($)	0.00	1.45	0.71	1.06	1.11	0.00	0.18	2.03	1.61	0.10
Net Asset Value ($)	7.40	12.29	14.23	13.07	13.06	11.38	8.84	10.57	11.30	10.74
Expense Ratio (%)	na	1.13	1.18	1.23	1.35	1.35	1.35	1.35	1.35	1.35
Yield (%)	1.99	0.51	0.26	0.22	0.00	0.00	0.00	0.31	0.01	0.14
Portfolio Turnover (%)	na	100	76	80	92	96	104	160	152	113
Total Assets (Millions $)	65	159	75	54	30	15	8	8	6	14

PORTFOLIO (as of 9/30/08)

Portfolio Manager: Lacey/Blake/Buesser/Failla - 2001

Investment Style

Large Cap	Growth
✔ Mid Cap	Grth/Val
Small Cap	✔ Value

Portfolio

94.9%	U.S. stock	0.0%	conv't
2.8%	int'l stock	0.0%	preferred
0.0%	U.S. bonds	0.0%	other
0.0%	int'l bonds	2.4%	cash

Number of Investments: 77

Percent of Portfolio in Top 10 Investments: 22%

SHAREHOLDER INFORMATION

Minimum Investment

Initial: $2,500 Subsequent: $50

Minimum IRA Investment

Initial: $0 Subsequent: $0

Maximum Fees

Load: 1.00% redemption 12b-1: 0.25%

Other: redemption fee applies for 30 days

Services

✔ IRA

✔ Keogh

✔ Telephone Exchange

Madison Mosaic Mid-Cap (GTSGX)

888-670-3600
www.mosaicfunds.com

Mid-Cap Stock

PERFORMANCE — fund inception date: 7/21/83

	3yr Annual	5yr Annual	10yr Annual	Bull	Bear
Return (%)	-7.2	-0.9	4.8	108.2	-38.5
Differ From Category (+/-)	2.6 abv av	0.5 av	1.6 abv av	-35.5 low	4.9 high

Standard Deviation	Category Risk Index	Beta
17.1%—av	0.86—low	1.07

	2008	2007	2006	2005	2004	2003	2002	2001	2000	1999
Return (%)	-36.7	8.6	16.3	0.5	18.8	28.5	-12.9	15.3	18.4	9.5
Differ From Category (+/-)	3.6	-1.4	3.1	-9.7	2.5	-9.8	5.8	18.3	13.2	-30.7
Return, Tax-Adjusted (%)	-37.2	7.1	15.1	-0.2	18.0	28.3	-13.0	13.7	14.2	9.5

PER SHARE DATA

	2008	2007	2006	2005	2004	2003	2002	2001	2000	1999
Dividends, Net Income ($)	0.00	0.00	0.00	0.00	0.00	0.00	0.00	0.01	0.04	0.00
Distrib'ns, Cap Gain ($)	0.46	1.30	0.91	0.60	0.63	0.11	0.06	0.72	1.95	0.00
Net Asset Value ($)	7.67	12.87	13.04	11.99	12.52	11.06	8.69	10.04	9.36	9.57
Expense Ratio (%)	na	1.25	1.25	1.25	1.25	1.25	1.24	1.25	1.25	1.25
Yield (%)	0.00	0.00	0.00	0.00	0.00	0.00	0.00	0.09	0.32	0.00
Portfolio Turnover (%)	na	43	47	46	38	25	35	47	75	65
Total Assets (Millions $)	88	148	147	146	115	55	26	13	9	9

PORTFOLIO (as of 11/30/08)

Portfolio Manager: Sekelsky/Eisinger - 1996

Investment Style

Large Cap	Growth
✔ Mid Cap	✔ Grth/Val
Small Cap	Value

Portfolio

93.8% U.S. stock	0.0% conv't
2.8% int'l stock	0.0% preferred
0.0% U.S. bonds	0.0% other
0.0% int'l bonds	3.4% cash

Number of Investments: 36
Percent of Portfolio in Top 10 Investments: 38%

SHAREHOLDER INFORMATION

Minimum Investment
Initial: $1,000 Subsequent: $50

Minimum IRA Investment
Initial: $500 Subsequent: $50

Maximum Fees
Load: none 12b-1: none
Other: none

Services
✔ IRA
✔ Keogh
✔ Telephone Exchange

Marshall Mid-Cap Value Inv (MRVEX)

800-236-3863
www.marshallfunds.com

Mid-Cap Stock

PERFORMANCE — fund inception date: 9/30/93

	3yr Annual	5yr Annual	10yr Annual	Bull	Bear
Return (%)	-10.4	-2.1	5.1	114.9	-40.1
Differ From Category (+/-)	-0.6 av	-0.7 blw av	1.9 abv av	-28.8 blw av	3.3 abv av

Standard Deviation	Category Risk Index	Beta
18.2%—av	0.91—blw av	1.13

	2008	2007	2006	2005	2004	2003	2002	2001	2000	1999
Return (%)	-37.2	0.7	13.8	7.1	16.6	35.8	-11.6	22.1	17.2	6.1
Differ From Category (+/-)	3.1	-9.3	0.6	-3.1	0.2	-2.5	7.1	25.1	12.1	-34.1
Return, Tax-Adjusted (%)	-37.9	-1.3	12.3	5.6	15.5	35.2	-11.7	19.0	15.6	3.3

PER SHARE DATA

	2008	2007	2006	2005	2004	2003	2002	2001	2000	1999
Dividends, Net Income ($)	0.02	0.06	0.07	0.05	0.06	0.01	0.01	0.01	0.08	0.08
Distrib'ns, Cap Gain ($)	0.55	1.99	1.38	1.50	0.96	0.45	0.00	1.68	0.70	1.38
Net Asset Value ($)	7.74	13.25	15.18	14.60	15.06	13.81	10.52	11.91	11.16	10.22
Expense Ratio (%)	1.24	1.21	1.19	1.20	1.22	1.27	1.26	1.30	1.33	1.25
Yield (%)	0.26	0.38	0.40	0.29	0.37	0.09	0.08	0.11	0.63	0.68
Portfolio Turnover (%)	41	62	63	37	33	39	44	104	94	90
Total Assets (Millions $)	107	459	619	651	544	347	210	190	115	116

PORTFOLIO (as of 11/30/08)

Portfolio Manager: Fahey - 1997

Investment Style

Large Cap	Growth
✔ Mid Cap	Grth/Val
Small Cap	✔ Value

Portfolio

93.3%	U.S. stock	0.0%	conv't
1.7%	int'l stock	0.0%	preferred
0.0%	U.S. bonds	0.0%	other
0.0%	int'l bonds	4.9%	cash

Number of Investments: 69

Percent of Portfolio in Top 10 Investments: 25%

SHAREHOLDER INFORMATION

Minimum Investment

Initial: $1,000 Subsequent: $50

Minimum IRA Investment

Initial: $0 Subsequent: $0

Maximum Fees

Load: 2.00% redemption 12b-1: none

Other: redemption fee applies for 30 days

Services

✔ IRA

✔ Keogh

✔ Telephone Exchange

Meridian Growth
(MERDX)
Mid-Cap Stock

800-446-6662
www.meridianfund.com

PERFORMANCE — fund inception date: 8/1/84

	3yr Annual	5yr Annual	10yr Annual	Bull	Bear
Return (%)	-5.3	-0.5	7.0	132.4	-34.8
Differ From Category (+/-)	4.5 high	0.9 abv av	3.8 high	-11.3 av	8.6 high

Standard Deviation	Category Risk Index	Beta
16.7%—av	0.84—low	1.04

	2008	2007	2006	2005	2004	2003	2002	2001	2000	1999
Return (%)	-30.4	5.4	15.8	0.3	14.4	47.9	-17.9	14.7	28.2	13.3
Differ From Category (+/-)	9.9	-4.6	2.6	-9.9	-2.0	9.6	0.8	17.7	23.0	-26.9
Return, Tax-Adjusted (%)	-30.9	4.0	14.5	0.0	14.2	47.3	-18.4	12.7	22.9	11.6

PER SHARE DATA

	2008	2007	2006	2005	2004	2003	2002	2001	2000	1999
Dividends, Net Income ($)	0.09	0.05	0.01	0.00	0.00	0.23	0.06	0.00	2.44	0.15
Distrib'ns, Cap Gain ($)	1.09	3.58	3.12	0.80	0.56	0.69	0.61	2.84	1.86	1.78
Net Asset Value ($)	25.07	37.72	39.24	36.57	37.24	33.03	22.98	28.79	28.06	25.40
Expense Ratio (%)	0.84	0.84	0.85	0.86	0.88	0.95	1.02	1.04	1.09	1.01
Yield (%)	0.34	0.13	0.02	0.00	0.00	0.68	0.24	0.00	8.14	0.55
Portfolio Turnover (%)	39	40	29	32	19	27	26	43	28	51
Total Assets (Millions $)	1,057	1,871	1,867	1,636	1,632	746	317	208	152	138

PORTFOLIO (as of 9/30/08)

Portfolio Manager: Aster Jr./Tao - 1984

Investment Style

Large Cap	✔ Growth
✔ Mid Cap	Grth/Val
✔ Small Cap	Value

Portfolio

93.4% U.S. stock	0.0% conv't
2.7% int'l stock	0.0% preferred
0.0% U.S. bonds	0.0% other
0.0% int'l bonds	3.9% cash

Number of Investments: 46
Percent of Portfolio in Top 10 Investments: 31%

SHAREHOLDER INFORMATION

Minimum Investment
Initial: $1,000 Subsequent: $50

Minimum IRA Investment
Initial: $0 Subsequent: $0

Maximum Fees
Load: 2.00% redemption 12b-1: none
Other: redemption fee applies for 60 days

Services
✔ IRA
✔ Keogh
✔ Telephone Exchange

Meridian Value
(MVALX)

800-446-6662
www.meridianfund.com

Mid-Cap Stock

PERFORMANCE **fund inception date: 2/10/94**

	3yr Annual	5yr Annual	10yr Annual	Bull	Bear
Return (%)	-4.6	0.6	9.8	115.0	-33.5
Differ From Category (+/-)	5.2 high	2.0 abv av	6.6 high	-28.7 blw av	9.9 high

Standard Deviation	Category Risk Index	Beta
15.3%—av	0.77—low	0.96

	2008	2007	2006	2005	2004	2003	2002	2001	2000	1999
Return (%)	-32.0	7.7	18.6	2.9	15.1	34.7	-13.4	11.6	37.1	38.2
Differ From Category (+/-)	8.3	-2.3	5.4	-7.3	-1.3	-3.6	5.3	14.7	31.9	-2.0
Return, Tax-Adjusted (%)	-32.6	5.0	16.2	1.1	12.9	34.7	-13.4	11.6	34.6	34.9

PER SHARE DATA

	2008	2007	2006	2005	2004	2003	2002	2001	2000	1999
Dividends, Net Income ($)	0.00	0.35	0.41	0.32	0.28	0.00	0.00	0.04	1.09	0.68
Distrib'ns, Cap Gain ($)	1.32	6.04	5.09	4.28	5.11	0.00	0.00	0.04	0.68	1.68
Net Asset Value ($)	20.40	31.92	35.60	34.63	38.09	37.84	28.09	32.42	29.11	22.69
Expense Ratio (%)	1.09	1.08	1.08	1.09	1.09	1.11	1.12	1.10	1.41	1.42
Yield (%)	0.00	0.91	0.99	0.81	0.65	0.00	0.00	0.11	3.66	2.80
Portfolio Turnover (%)	61	75	58	59	81	60	54	77	86	124
Total Assets (Millions $)	935	1,593	1,753	1,903	2,406	1,916	1,185	1,135	286	35

PORTFOLIO (as of 9/30/08)

Portfolio Manager: Aster Jr./England/ Cordisco - 1994

Investment Style

Large Cap	Growth
✔ Mid Cap	✔ Grth/Val
Small Cap	Value

Portfolio

88.4%	U.S. stock	0.0%	conv't
6.9%	int'l stock	0.0%	preferred
0.0%	U.S. bonds	0.0%	other
0.0%	int'l bonds	4.7%	cash

Number of Investments: 56
Percent of Portfolio in Top 10 Investments: 31%

SHAREHOLDER INFORMATION

Minimum Investment
Initial: $1,000 Subsequent: $50

Minimum IRA Investment
Initial: $0 Subsequent: $0

Maximum Fees
Load: 2.00% redemption 12b-1: none
Other: redemption fee applies for 60 days

Services
✔ IRA
✔ Keogh
✔ Telephone Exchange

Neuberger Berman Mid Cap Growth Inv (NMANX)

800-877-9700
www.nb.com

Mid-Cap Stock

PERFORMANCE — fund inception date: 3/1/79

	3yr Annual	5yr Annual	10yr Annual	Bull	Bear
Return (%)	-6.4	1.6	-0.9	161.7	-44.3
Differ From Category (+/-)	3.4 high	3.0 high	-4.1 low	18.0 abv av	-0.9 av

Standard Deviation	Category Risk Index	Beta
18.8%—abv av	0.94—blw av	1.12

	2008	2007	2006	2005	2004	2003	2002	2001	2000	1999
Return (%)	-41.0	21.5	14.5	13.3	16.2	30.5	-31.3	-29.7	-11.5	50.7
Differ From Category (+/-)	-0.7	11.5	1.3	3.1	-0.2	-7.8	-12.6	-26.7	-16.7	10.5
Return, Tax-Adjusted (%)	-41.0	21.5	14.5	13.3	16.2	30.5	-31.3	-29.8	-17.9	48.7

PER SHARE DATA

	2008	2007	2006	2005	2004	2003	2002	2001	2000	1999
Dividends, Net Income ($)	0.00	0.00	0.00	0.00	0.00	0.00	0.00	0.00	0.00	0.00
Distrib'ns, Cap Gain ($)	0.00	0.00	0.00	0.00	0.00	0.00	0.00	0.05	5.36	1.20
Net Asset Value ($)	6.48	10.98	9.03	7.88	6.95	5.98	4.58	6.66	9.54	16.69
Expense Ratio (%)	1.01	1.02	1.04	1.07	0.06	1.12	1.05	0.95	0.92	1.00
Yield (%)	0.00	0.00	0.00	0.00	0.00	0.00	0.00	0.00	0.00	0.00
Portfolio Turnover (%)	70	49	45	65	102	145	98	102	105	115
Total Assets (Millions $)	260	475	380	351	347	335	280	497	767	822

PORTFOLIO (as of 11/30/08)

Portfolio Manager: Turek - 2003

Investment Style

Large Cap	✔ Growth
✔ Mid Cap	Grth/Val
✔ Small Cap	Value

Portfolio

93.4% U.S. stock	0.0% conv't
1.4% int'l stock	0.0% preferred
0.0% U.S. bonds	0.0% other
0.0% int'l bonds	5.2% cash

Number of Investments: 102
Percent of Portfolio in Top 10 Investments: 22%

SHAREHOLDER INFORMATION

Minimum Investment
Initial: $1,000 Subsequent: $100

Minimum IRA Investment
Initial: $1,000 Subsequent: $0

Maximum Fees
Load: none 12b-1: none
Other: none

Services
✔ IRA
✔ Keogh
✔ Telephone Exchange

Nicholas II I (NCTWX)

800-544-6547
www.nicholasfunds.com

Mid-Cap Stock

PERFORMANCE — fund inception date: 10/17/83

	3yr Annual	5yr Annual	10yr Annual	Bull	Bear
Return (%)	-7.3	-1.1	-0.4	99.1	-34.1
Differ From Category (+/-)	2.5 abv av	0.3 av	-3.6 low	-44.6 low	9.3 high

Standard Deviation	Category Risk Index	Beta
16.0%—av	0.80—low	1.02

	2008	2007	2006	2005	2004	2003	2002	2001	2000	1999
Return (%)	-30.8	6.4	8.2	5.9	12.0	33.2	-20.4	-3.2	-2.1	1.1
Differ From Category (+/-)	9.5	-3.6	-5.0	-4.3	-4.4	-5.0	-1.7	-0.2	-7.3	-39.1
Return, Tax-Adjusted (%)	-31.7	4.6	7.4	4.5	11.3	33.2	-20.4	-3.7	-9.4	0.8

PER SHARE DATA

	2008	2007	2006	2005	2004	2003	2002	2001	2000	1999
Dividends, Net Income ($)	0.11	0.10	0.06	0.02	0.00	0.00	0.00	0.00	0.00	0.01
Distrib'ns, Cap Gain ($)	1.12	2.57	1.05	2.13	0.91	0.00	0.00	0.58	13.12	0.47
Net Asset Value ($)	13.77	21.74	22.93	22.20	22.98	21.34	16.01	20.09	21.34	35.96
Expense Ratio (%)	0.67	0.66	0.67	0.70	0.63	0.65	0.65	0.62	0.62	0.61
Yield (%)	0.71	0.40	0.26	0.08	0.00	0.00	0.00	0.00	0.00	0.02
Portfolio Turnover (%)	27	20	17	21	15	26	47	49	65	21
Total Assets (Millions $)	317	506	541	555	557	522	417	578	690	941

PORTFOLIO (as of 12/31/08)

Portfolio Manager: Nicholas - 1993

Investment Style

✔ Large Cap	✔ Growth
✔ Mid Cap	Grth/Val
Small Cap	Value

Portfolio

89.0% U.S. stock	0.0% conv't
5.4% int'l stock	0.0% preferred
0.0% U.S. bonds	0.0% other
0.0% int'l bonds	5.6% cash

Number of Investments: 84
Percent of Portfolio in Top 10 Investments: 26%

SHAREHOLDER INFORMATION

Minimum Investment
Initial: $100,000 — Subsequent: $100

Minimum IRA Investment
Initial: $0 — Subsequent: $0

Maximum Fees
Load: none — 12b-1: none
Other: none

Services
✔ IRA
✔ Keogh
✔ Telephone Exchange

Osterweis (OSTFX)

800-700-3316
www.osterweis.com

Mid-Cap Stock

PERFORMANCE — fund inception date: 10/1/93

	3yr Annual	5yr Annual	10yr Annual	Bull	Bear
Return (%)	-6.3	1.1	7.2	110.4	-32.0
Differ From Category (+/-)	3.5 high	2.5 high	4.0 high	-33.3 low	11.4 high

Standard Deviation	Category Risk Index	Beta
13.4%—blw av	0.67—low	0.83

	2008	2007	2006	2005	2004	2003	2002	2001	2000	1999
Return (%)	-29.3	4.6	11.3	9.0	17.6	33.1	-11.7	-9.9	7.3	67.4
Differ From Category (+/-)	11.0	-5.4	-1.9	-1.2	1.2	-5.2	7.0	-6.9	2.1	27.2
Return, Tax-Adjusted (%)	-29.5	4.1	9.9	8.2	16.8	32.9	-11.8	-10.2	3.6	64.9

PER SHARE DATA

	2008	2007	2006	2005	2004	2003	2002	2001	2000	1999
Dividends, Net Income ($)	0.04	0.32	0.20	0.15	0.34	0.23	0.05	0.05	0.01	0.00
Distrib'ns, Cap Gain ($)	0.32	0.53	2.22	1.18	0.94	0.00	0.00	0.21	4.53	1.98
Net Asset Value ($)	18.63	26.86	26.48	25.93	24.98	22.32	16.94	19.23	21.63	24.51
Expense Ratio (%)	1.18	1.21	1.26	1.32	1.36	1.41	1.43	1.45	1.57	1.75
Yield (%)	0.23	1.18	0.69	0.53	1.29	1.01	0.27	0.25	0.04	0.00
Portfolio Turnover (%)	56	50	30	38	58	34	49	32	39	31
Total Assets (Millions $)	334	356	301	230	155	111	72	57	50	42

PORTFOLIO (as of 9/30/08)

Portfolio Manager: Osterweis/Berler/Kovriga/Moore - 1993

Investment Style

Large Cap	Growth
✔ Mid Cap	✔ Grth/Val
Small Cap	Value

Portfolio

70.7%	U.S. stock	0.0%	conv't
8.1%	int'l stock	0.0%	preferred
3.2%	U.S. bonds	0.0%	other
0.0%	int'l bonds	18.1%	cash

Number of Investments: 35
Percent of Portfolio in Top 10 Investments: 50%

SHAREHOLDER INFORMATION

Minimum Investment
Initial: $5,000 Subsequent: $500

Minimum IRA Investment
Initial: $1,500 Subsequent: $500

Maximum Fees
Load: 2.00% redemption 12b-1: none
Other: redemption fee applies for 30 days

Services
✔ IRA
✔ Keogh
✔ Telephone Exchange

PRIMECAP Odyssey Aggressive Growth (POAGX)

800-729-2307
www.odysseyfunds.com

Mid-Cap Stock

PERFORMANCE — fund inception date: 11/1/04

	3yr Annual	5yr Annual	10yr Annual	Bull	Bear
Return (%)	-7.5	na	na	na	-41.6
Differ From Category (+/-)	2.3 abv av	na	na	na	1.8 abv av

Standard Deviation	Category Risk Index	Beta
18.9%—abv av	0.95—blw av	1.10

	2008	2007	2006	2005	2004	2003	2002	2001	2000	1999
Return (%)	-34.6	-0.2	21.5	7.9	—	—	—	—	—	—
Differ From Category (+/-)	5.7	-10.2	8.3	-2.3	—	—	—	—	—	—
Return, Tax-Adjusted (%)	-34.6	-0.3	21.3	7.9	—	—	—	—	—	—

PER SHARE DATA

	2008	2007	2006	2005	2004	2003	2002	2001	2000	1999
Dividends, Net Income ($)	0.00	0.00	0.00	0.00	—	—	—	—	—	—
Distrib'ns, Cap Gain ($)	0.00	0.09	0.20	0.00	—	—	—	—	—	—
Net Asset Value ($)	9.30	14.22	14.34	11.96	—	—	—	—	—	—
Expense Ratio (%)	na	0.78	0.99	1.25	—	—	—	—	—	—
Yield (%)	0.00	0.00	0.00	0.00	—	—	—	—	—	—
Portfolio Turnover (%)	na	6	12	7	—	—	—	—	—	—
Total Assets (Millions $)	219	331	159	32	—	—	—	—	—	—

PORTFOLIO (as of 9/30/08)

Portfolio Manager: Kolokotrones/Fried/Mordecai - 2004

Investment Style

Large Cap	✔ Growth
✔ Mid Cap	Grth/Val
Small Cap	Value

Portfolio

87.6%	U.S. stock	0.0%	conv't
6.5%	int'l stock	0.0%	preferred
0.0%	U.S. bonds	0.0%	other
0.0%	int'l bonds	5.9%	cash

Number of Investments: 78

Percent of Portfolio in Top 10 Investments: 37%

SHAREHOLDER INFORMATION

Minimum Investment

Initial: $2,000 Subsequent: $150

Minimum IRA Investment

Initial: $1,000 Subsequent: $150

Maximum Fees

Load: 2.00% redemption 12b-1: none

Other: redemption fee applies for 60 days

Services

✔ IRA

✔ Keogh

✔ Telephone Exchange

Rainier Mid Cap Equity (RIMMX)

800-248-6314
www.rainierfunds.com

Mid-Cap Stock

PERFORMANCE — fund inception date: 12/27/05

	3yr Annual	5yr Annual	10yr Annual	Bull	Bear
Return (%)	-6.3	na	na	na	-49.1
Differ From Category (+/-)	3.5 high	na	na	na	-5.7 blw av

Standard Deviation	Category Risk Index	Beta
23.3%—high	1.17—high	1.43

	2008	2007	2006	2005	2004	2003	2002	2001	2000	1999
Return (%)	-46.6	27.1	21.4	—	—	—	—	—	—	—
Differ From Category (+/-)	-6.3	17.1	8.2	—	—	—	—	—	—	—
Return, Tax-Adjusted (%)	-46.7	26.5	21.4	—	—	—	—	—	—	—

PER SHARE DATA

	2008	2007	2006	2005	2004	2003	2002	2001	2000	1999
Dividends, Net Income ($)	0.00	0.00	0.00	—	—	—	—	—	—	—
Distrib'ns, Cap Gain ($)	0.00	1.25	0.09	—	—	—	—	—	—	—
Net Asset Value ($)	23.61	44.22	35.81	—	—	—	—	—	—	—
Expense Ratio (%)	1.19	1.32	—	—	—	—	—	—	—	—
Yield (%)	0.00	0.00	0.00	—	—	—	—	—	—	—
Portfolio Turnover (%)	112	93	—	—	—	—	—	—	—	—
Total Assets (Millions $)	320	394	34	—	—	—	—	—	—	—

PORTFOLIO (as of 9/30/08)

Portfolio Manager: Brewer/Broughton/Dawson - 2005

Investment Style

Large Cap	✔ Growth
✔ Mid Cap	Grth/Val
Small Cap	Value

Portfolio

97.0%	U.S. stock	0.0%	conv't
3.0%	int'l stock	0.0%	preferred
0.0%	U.S. bonds	0.0%	other
0.0%	int'l bonds	0.0%	cash

Number of Investments: 115
Percent of Portfolio in Top 10 Investments: 21%

SHAREHOLDER INFORMATION

Minimum Investment
Initial: $25,000 Subsequent: $1,000

Minimum IRA Investment
Initial: $0 Subsequent: $0

Maximum Fees
Load: none 12b-1: 0.25%
Other: none

Services
✔ IRA
✔ Keogh
✔ Telephone Exchange

T. Rowe Price Extended Equity Market Idx (PEXMX)

800-638-5660
www.troweprice.com

Mid-Cap Stock

PERFORMANCE fund inception date: 1/30/98

	3yr Annual	5yr Annual	10yr Annual	Bull	Bear
Return (%)	-9.6	-0.8	1.4	151.0	-42.3
Differ From Category (+/-)	0.2 av	0.6 abv av	-1.8 blw av	7.3 abv av	1.1 abv av

Standard Deviation	Category Risk Index	Beta
19.6%—abv av	0.98—av	1.22

	2008	2007	2006	2005	2004	2003	2002	2001	2000	1999
Return (%)	-38.5	4.0	15.7	9.9	18.3	42.8	-18.2	-9.6	-15.6	33.7
Differ From Category (+/-)	1.8	-6.0	2.5	-0.3	1.9	4.5	0.5	-6.6	-20.8	-6.5
Return, Tax-Adjusted (%)	-38.8	3.0	15.4	9.8	18.2	42.7	-18.4	-10.3	-16.8	32.3

PER SHARE DATA

	2008	2007	2006	2005	2004	2003	2002	2001	2000	1999
Dividends, Net Income ($)	0.12	0.20	0.16	0.10	0.09	0.07	0.06	0.10	0.09	0.10
Distrib'ns, Cap Gain ($)	0.19	0.97	0.12	0.00	0.00	0.00	0.00	0.18	0.67	0.53
Net Asset Value ($)	9.47	15.95	16.47	14.47	13.25	11.27	7.94	9.77	11.12	14.05
Expense Ratio (%)	na	0.40	0.40	0.40	0.40	0.40	0.40	0.40	0.40	0.40
Yield (%)	1.24	1.18	0.96	0.69	0.67	0.62	0.75	1.00	0.76	0.68
Portfolio Turnover (%)	na	38	18	17	11	9	21	31	31	23
Total Assets (Millions $)	230	407	346	271	161	119	67	77	86	54

PORTFOLIO (as of 9/30/08)

Portfolio Manager: Bair/Uematsu - 2002

Investment Style

Large Cap	Growth
✔ Mid Cap	✔ Grth/Val
✔ Small Cap	Value

Portfolio

96.2% U.S. stock	0.0% conv't
0.2% int'l stock	0.0% preferred
0.0% U.S. bonds	0.0% other
0.0% int'l bonds	3.6% cash

Number of Investments: 2,002
Percent of Portfolio in Top 10 Investments: 15%

SHAREHOLDER INFORMATION

Minimum Investment
Initial: $2,500 Subsequent: $100

Minimum IRA Investment
Initial: $1,000 Subsequent: $50

Maximum Fees
Load: 0.50% redemption 12b-1: none
Other: redemption fee applies for 90 days

Services
✔ IRA
✔ Keogh
✔ Telephone Exchange

T. Rowe Price Mid-Cap Growth (RPMGX)

800-225-5132
www.troweprice.com

Mid-Cap Stock

PERFORMANCE — fund inception date: 6/30/92

	3yr Annual	5yr Annual	10yr Annual	Bull	Bear
Return (%)	-8.9	0.5	3.9	155.3	-42.2
Differ From Category (+/-)	0.9 abv av	1.9 abv av	0.7 av	11.6 abv av	1.2 abv av

Standard Deviation	Category Risk Index	Beta
19.8%—abv av	0.99—av	1.23

	2008	2007	2006	2005	2004	2003	2002	2001	2000	1999
Return (%)	-39.7	17.6	6.7	14.8	18.3	38.2	-21.3	-1.0	7.4	23.7
Differ From Category (+/-)	0.6	7.6	-6.5	4.6	1.9	-0.1	-2.6	2.0	2.2	-16.5
Return, Tax-Adjusted (%)	-40.3	16.1	5.6	13.8	18.0	38.2	-21.3	-1.0	5.8	22.6

PER SHARE DATA

	2008	2007	2006	2005	2004	2003	2002	2001	2000	1999
Dividends, Net Income ($)	0.00	0.06	0.08	0.00	0.00	0.00	0.00	0.00	0.00	0.00
Distrib'ns, Cap Gain ($)	1.99	5.33	4.07	3.15	0.90	0.00	0.00	0.00	3.27	1.88
Net Asset Value ($)	32.67	57.67	53.69	54.14	49.88	42.90	31.04	39.40	39.79	40.13
Expense Ratio (%)	na	0.77	0.80	0.80	0.83	0.87	0.88	0.85	0.86	0.87
Yield (%)	0.00	0.09	0.13	0.00	0.00	0.00	0.00	0.00	0.00	0.00
Portfolio Turnover (%)	na	35	34	29	30	30	36	53	54	53
Total Assets (Millions $)	8,936	16,902	14,629	15,187	12,651	9,869	5,713	6,739	6,589	5,243

PORTFOLIO (as of 9/30/08)

Portfolio Manager: Berghuis - 1992

Investment Style

Large Cap	✔ Growth
✔ Mid Cap	Grth/Val
Small Cap	Value

Portfolio

90.2%	U.S. stock	0.0%	conv't
4.8%	int'l stock	0.0%	preferred
0.0%	U.S. bonds	0.1%	other
0.0%	int'l bonds	5.0%	cash

Number of Investments: 143
Percent of Portfolio in Top 10 Investments: 20%

SHAREHOLDER INFORMATION

Minimum Investment
Initial: $2,500 Subsequent: $100

Minimum IRA Investment
Initial: $1,000 Subsequent: $50

Maximum Fees
Load: none 12b-1: none
Other: none

Services
✔ IRA
✔ Keogh
✔ Telephone Exchange

TIAA-CREF Mid-Cap Value Retail (TCMVX)

800-223-1200
www.tiaa-cref.org

Mid-Cap Stock

PERFORMANCE

fund inception date: 10/1/02

	3yr Annual	5yr Annual	10yr Annual	Bull	Bear
Return (%)	-8.9	1.1	na	182.5	-44.5
Differ From Category (+/-)	0.9 av	2.5 high	na	38.8 high	-1.1 av

Standard Deviation	Category Risk Index	Beta
18.7%—av	0.94—blw av	1.19

	2008	2007	2006	2005	2004	2003	2002	2001	2000	1999
Return (%)	-40.7	6.2	19.9	11.5	25.2	42.0	—	—	—	—
Differ From Category (+/-)	-0.4	-3.8	6.7	1.3	8.8	3.7	—	—	—	—
Return, Tax-Adjusted (%)	-40.9	5.1	18.2	10.4	24.4	41.1	—	—	—	—

PER SHARE DATA

	2008	2007	2006	2005	2004	2003	2002	2001	2000	1999
Dividends, Net Income ($)	0.21	0.01	0.00	0.00	0.02	0.04	—	—	—	—
Distrib'ns, Cap Gain ($)	0.03	1.28	1.91	1.09	0.71	0.59	—	—	—	—
Net Asset Value ($)	10.38	17.91	18.08	16.67	15.92	13.29	—	—	—	—
Expense Ratio (%)	0.62	0.78	0.63	0.44	0.44	0.47	—	—	—	—
Yield (%)	2.00	0.05	0.00	0.01	0.11	0.29	—	—	—	—
Portfolio Turnover (%)	41	90	131	110	173	215	—	—	—	—
Total Assets (Millions $)	105	185	146	105	60	18	—	—	—	—

PORTFOLIO (as of 9/30/08)

Portfolio Manager: Cutler/Kolefas - 2002

Investment Style

Large Cap	Growth
✔ Mid Cap	Grth/Val
Small Cap	✔ Value

Portfolio

90.9% U.S. stock	0.0% conv't
4.8% int'l stock	0.0% preferred
0.0% U.S. bonds	0.3% other
0.0% int'l bonds	4.0% cash

Number of Investments: 263

Percent of Portfolio in Top 10 Investments: 19%

SHAREHOLDER INFORMATION

Minimum Investment

Initial: $2,500 Subsequent: $100

Minimum IRA Investment

Initial: $2,000 Subsequent: $100

Maximum Fees

Load: none 12b-1: none

Other: none

Services

✔ IRA

Keogh

✔ Telephone Exchange

Value Line Premier Growth (VALSX)

800-243-2729
www.valueline.com

Mid-Cap Stock

PERFORMANCE — fund inception date: 5/30/56

	3yr Annual	5yr Annual	10yr Annual	Bull	Bear
Return (%)	-7.8	0.6	3.5	142.2	-42.7
Differ From Category (+/-)	2.0 abv av	2.0 high	0.3 av	-1.5 av	0.7 av

Standard Deviation	Category Risk Index	Beta
19.0%—abv av	0.95—blw av	1.18

	2008	2007	2006	2005	2004	2003	2002	2001	2000	1999
Return (%)	-40.2	18.2	10.6	11.4	18.4	29.6	-15.2	-17.7	-6.8	61.6
Differ From Category (+/-)	0.1	8.3	-2.6	1.2	2.0	-8.7	3.5	-14.7	-12.0	21.4
Return, Tax-Adjusted (%)	-40.6	17.1	9.6	10.5	18.1	29.6	-15.2	-18.1	-8.1	60.0

PER SHARE DATA

	2008	2007	2006	2005	2004	2003	2002	2001	2000	1999
Dividends, Net Income ($)	0.00	0.03	0.00	0.00	0.00	0.00	0.00	0.00	0.00	0.00
Distrib'ns, Cap Gain ($)	0.85	2.02	1.73	1.42	0.44	0.00	0.00	0.44	1.71	1.40
Net Asset Value ($)	16.69	29.38	26.61	25.60	24.23	20.84	16.08	18.95	23.55	27.09
Expense Ratio (%)	na	1.11	1.18	1.13	1.15	1.18	1.20	1.14	1.01	0.89
Yield (%)	0.00	0.10	0.00	0.00	0.00	0.00	0.00	0.00	0.00	0.00
Portfolio Turnover (%)	na	29	38	44	54	52	66	88	78	85
Total Assets (Millions $)	313	570	490	442	384	310	242	262	388	420

PORTFOLIO (as of 9/30/08)

Portfolio Manager: Grant - 1996

Investment Style

- Large Cap
- ✔ Mid Cap
- ✔ Small Cap
- ✔ Growth
- Grth/Val
- Value

Portfolio

78.4%	U.S. stock	0.0%	conv't
16.3%	int'l stock	0.0%	preferred
0.0%	U.S. bonds	0.0%	other
0.0%	int'l bonds	5.3%	cash

Number of Investments: 397

Percent of Portfolio in Top 10 Investments: 12%

SHAREHOLDER INFORMATION

Minimum Investment

Initial: $1,000 — Subsequent: $100

Minimum IRA Investment

Initial: $1,000 — Subsequent: $100

Maximum Fees

Load: none — 12b-1: 0.25%

Other: none

Services

- ✔ IRA
- ✔ Keogh
- ✔ Telephone Exchange

Vanguard Extended Market Idx (VEXMX)

800-662-7447
www.vanguard.com

Mid-Cap Stock

PERFORMANCE — fund inception date: 12/21/87

	3yr Annual	5yr Annual	10yr Annual	Bull	Bear
Return (%)	-10.0	-0.9	1.6	151.2	-42.6
Differ From Category (+/-)	-0.2 av	0.5 av	-1.6 blw av	7.5 abv av	0.8 abv av

Standard Deviation	Category Risk Index	Beta
19.8%—abv av	0.99—av	1.23

	2008	2007	2006	2005	2004	2003	2002	2001	2000	1999
Return (%)	-38.8	4.3	14.2	10.2	18.7	43.4	-18.1	-9.2	-15.6	36.2
Differ From Category (+/-)	1.5	-5.7	1.0	0.0	2.3	5.1	0.6	-6.2	-20.8	-4.0
Return, Tax-Adjusted (%)	-38.9	4.1	14.0	10.1	18.5	43.2	-18.4	-10.1	-18.2	33.4

PER SHARE DATA

	2008	2007	2006	2005	2004	2003	2002	2001	2000	1999
Dividends, Net Income ($)	0.41	0.46	0.47	0.33	0.28	0.21	0.18	0.21	0.26	0.32
Distrib'ns, Cap Gain ($)	0.00	0.00	0.00	0.00	0.00	0.00	0.00	0.81	4.43	3.64
Net Asset Value ($)	24.01	39.89	38.68	34.26	31.36	26.66	18.74	23.09	26.62	37.07
Expense Ratio (%)	na	0.24	0.25	0.25	0.25	0.26	0.26	0.25	0.25	0.25
Yield (%)	1.70	1.14	1.20	0.96	0.90	0.79	0.96	0.87	0.84	0.78
Portfolio Turnover (%)	na	14	16	27	17	8	17	20	33	26
Total Assets (Millions $)	3,080	5,254	6,172	5,441	5,484	4,259	2,629	3,115	3,881	4,221

PORTFOLIO (as of 9/30/08)

Portfolio Manager: Butler - 1997

Investment Style

Large Cap	Growth
✔ Mid Cap	✔ Grth/Val
✔ Small Cap	Value

Portfolio

99.6%	U.S. stock	0.0%	conv't
0.2%	int'l stock	0.0%	preferred
0.0%	U.S. bonds	0.0%	other
0.0%	int'l bonds	0.2%	cash

Number of Investments: 3,113
Percent of Portfolio in Top 10 Investments: 6%

SHAREHOLDER INFORMATION

Minimum Investment
Initial: $3,000 — Subsequent: $100

Minimum IRA Investment
Initial: $3,000 — Subsequent: $100

Maximum Fees
Load: none — 12b-1: none
Other: none

Services
✔ IRA
Keogh
✔ Telephone Exchange

Vanguard Mid Cap Growth (VMGRX)

800-997-2798
www.vanguard.com

Mid-Cap Stock

PERFORMANCE — fund inception date: 12/31/97

	3yr Annual	5yr Annual	10yr Annual	Bull	Bear
Return (%)	-8.0	-1.1	4.1	144.1	-43.4
Differ From Category (+/-)	1.8 abv av	0.3 av	0.9 abv av	0.4 av	0.0 av

Standard Deviation	Category Risk Index	Beta
18.8%—abv av	0.94—blw av	1.17

	2008	2007	2006	2005	2004	2003	2002	2001	2000	1999
Return (%)	-39.6	14.6	12.7	9.1	11.3	42.8	-28.6	-25.4	12.9	83.3
Differ From Category (+/-)	0.7	4.6	-0.5	-1.1	-5.1	4.5	-9.9	-22.4	7.7	43.1
Return, Tax-Adjusted (%)	-39.7	13.7	10.3	9.1	11.3	42.8	-28.6	-25.4	6.8	81.8

PER SHARE DATA

	2008	2007	2006	2005	2004	2003	2002	2001	2000	1999
Dividends, Net Income ($)	0.04	0.06	0.05	0.00	0.00	0.00	0.00	0.00	0.00	0.00
Distrib'ns, Cap Gain ($)	0.00	1.03	2.67	0.00	0.00	0.00	0.00	0.00	6.71	0.94
Net Asset Value ($)	11.11	18.46	17.07	17.51	16.05	14.41	10.09	14.12	18.92	22.09
Expense Ratio (%)	0.55	0.53	0.47	0.39	0.34	0.48	1.24	1.39	2.14	1.39
Yield (%)	0.36	0.31	0.22	0.02	0.00	0.00	0.00	0.00	0.00	0.00
Portfolio Turnover (%)	85	70	159	80	102	106	221	149	206	174
Total Assets (Millions $)	823	1,255	811	619	512	304	35	33	29	19

PORTFOLIO (as of 9/30/08)

Portfolio Manager: Antoian/Cunneen/Bundy - 2006

Investment Style

Large Cap	✔ Growth
✔ Mid Cap	Grth/Val
Small Cap	Value

Portfolio

89.2%	U.S. stock	0.0%	conv't
3.4%	int'l stock	0.0%	preferred
0.0%	U.S. bonds	0.0%	other
0.0%	int'l bonds	7.4%	cash

Number of Investments: 107
Percent of Portfolio in Top 10 Investments: 24%

SHAREHOLDER INFORMATION

Minimum Investment
Initial: $10,000 Subsequent: $100

Minimum IRA Investment
Initial: $3,000 Subsequent: $100

Maximum Fees
Load: none 12b-1: none
Other: none

Services
✔ IRA
✔ Keogh
✔ Telephone Exchange

Vanguard Mid Capitalization Index (VIMSX)

800-662-7447
www.vanguard.com

Mid-Cap Stock

PERFORMANCE — fund inception date: 5/21/98

	3yr Annual	5yr Annual	10yr Annual	Bull	Bear
Return (%)	-11.2	-0.8	4.0	146.3	-44.7
Differ From Category (+/-)	-1.4 blw av	0.6 av	0.8 abv av	2.6 abv av	-1.3 av

Standard Deviation	Category Risk Index	Beta
19.6%—abv av	0.98—av	1.23

	2008	2007	2006	2005	2004	2003	2002	2001	2000	1999
Return (%)	-41.9	6.0	13.6	13.9	20.3	34.1	-14.7	-0.5	18.1	15.3
Differ From Category (+/-)	-1.6	-4.0	0.4	3.7	3.9	-4.2	4.0	2.5	12.9	-24.9
Return, Tax-Adjusted (%)	-42.0	5.8	13.3	13.7	20.1	33.9	-15.2	-1.2	16.0	13.3

PER SHARE DATA

	2008	2007	2006	2005	2004	2003	2002	2001	2000	1999
Dividends, Net Income ($)	0.23	0.27	0.25	0.19	0.16	0.12	0.09	0.07	0.08	0.08
Distrib'ns, Cap Gain ($)	0.00	0.00	0.00	0.00	0.00	0.00	0.13	0.25	0.98	0.94
Net Asset Value ($)	11.80	20.70	19.78	17.63	15.64	13.13	9.88	11.81	12.21	11.30
Expense Ratio (%)	na	0.21	0.22	0.22	0.22	0.26	0.26	0.25	0.25	0.25
Yield (%)	1.94	1.28	1.24	1.08	1.02	0.92	0.92	0.58	0.59	0.62
Portfolio Turnover (%)	na	19	18	18	16	73	20	24	51	38
Total Assets (Millions $)	4,652	8,075	7,677	6,399	5,234	3,610	2,267	2,049	1,614	605

PORTFOLIO (as of 9/30/08)

Portfolio Manager: Butler - 1998

Investment Style

Large Cap	Growth
✔ Mid Cap	✔ Grth/Val
Small Cap	Value

Portfolio

98.9%	U.S. stock	0.0%	conv't
1.1%	int'l stock	0.0%	preferred
0.0%	U.S. bonds	0.0%	other
0.0%	int'l bonds	0.0%	cash

Number of Investments: 446

Percent of Portfolio in Top 10 Investments: 6%

SHAREHOLDER INFORMATION

Minimum Investment

Initial: $3,000 Subsequent: $100

Minimum IRA Investment

Initial: $3,000 Subsequent: $100

Maximum Fees

Load: none 12b-1: none

Other: none

Services

✔ IRA

✔ Keogh

✔ Telephone Exchange

Vanguard Mid-Cap Growth Index Inv (VMGIX)

800-662-7447
www.vanguard.com

Mid-Cap Stock

PERFORMANCE

fund inception date: 8/24/06

	3yr Annual	5yr Annual	10yr Annual	Bull	Bear
Return (%)	na	na	na	na	-48.4
Differ From Category (+/-)	na	na	na	na	-5.0 blw av

Standard Deviation	Category Risk Index	Beta
23.6%—high	1.19—high	1.29

	2008	2007	2006	2005	2004	2003	2002	2001	2000	1999
Return (%)	-47.1	17.2	—	—	—	—	—	—	—	—
Differ From Category (+/-)	-6.8	7.3	—	—	—	—	—	—	—	—
Return, Tax-Adjusted (%)	-47.2	17.2	—	—	—	—	—	—	—	—

PER SHARE DATA

	2008	2007	2006	2005	2004	2003	2002	2001	2000	1999
Dividends, Net Income ($)	0.06	0.05	—	—	—	—	—	—	—	—
Distrib'ns, Cap Gain ($)	0.00	0.00	—	—	—	—	—	—	—	—
Net Asset Value ($)	13.43	25.50	—	—	—	—	—	—	—	—
Expense Ratio (%)	na	0.24	—	—	—	—	—	—	—	—
Yield (%)	0.47	0.18	—	—	—	—	—	—	—	—
Portfolio Turnover (%)	na	56	—	—	—	—	—	—	—	—
Total Assets (Millions $)	275	389	—	—	—	—	—	—	—	—

PORTFOLIO (as of 9/30/08)

Portfolio Manager: O'Reilly - 2006

Investment Style

Large Cap	✔ Growth
✔ Mid Cap	Grth/Val
Small Cap	Value

Portfolio

99.1%	U.S. stock	0.0%	conv't
0.7%	int'l stock	0.0%	preferred
0.0%	U.S. bonds	0.0%	other
0.0%	int'l bonds	0.2%	cash

Number of Investments: 217

Percent of Portfolio in Top 10 Investments: 12%

SHAREHOLDER INFORMATION

Minimum Investment

Initial: $3,000 Subsequent: $100

Minimum IRA Investment

Initial: $3,000 Subsequent: $0

Maximum Fees

Load: none 12b-1: none

Other: none

Services

✔ IRA

Keogh

✔ Telephone Exchange

Vanguard Mid-Cap Value Index Inv (VMVIX)

800-662-7447
www.vanguard.com

Mid-Cap Stock

PERFORMANCE — fund inception date: 8/24/06

	3yr Annual	5yr Annual	10yr Annual	Bull	Bear
Return (%)	na	na	na	na	-41.3
Differ From Category (+/-)	na	na	na	na	2.1 abv av

Standard Deviation	Category Risk Index	Beta
20.6%—abv av	1.04—abv av	1.16

	2008	2007	2006	2005	2004	2003	2002	2001	2000	1999
Return (%)	-36.7	-4.4	—	—	—	—	—	—	—	—
Differ From Category (+/-)	3.6	-14.4	—	—	—	—	—	—	—	—
Return, Tax-Adjusted (%)	-36.9	-4.7	—	—	—	—	—	—	—	—

PER SHARE DATA

	2008	2007	2006	2005	2004	2003	2002	2001	2000	1999
Dividends, Net Income ($)	0.34	0.41	—	—	—	—	—	—	—	—
Distrib'ns, Cap Gain ($)	0.00	0.00	—	—	—	—	—	—	—	—
Net Asset Value ($)	12.92	20.95	—	—	—	—	—	—	—	—
Expense Ratio (%)	na	0.24	—	—	—	—	—	—	—	—
Yield (%)	2.63	1.95	—	—	—	—	—	—	—	—
Portfolio Turnover (%)	na	46	—	—	—	—	—	—	—	—
Total Assets (Millions $)	217	195	—	—	—	—	—	—	—	—

PORTFOLIO (as of 9/30/08)

Portfolio Manager: Butler - 2006

Investment Style

Large Cap	Growth
✔ Mid Cap	Grth/Val
Small Cap	✔ Value

Portfolio

98.7%	U.S. stock	0.0%	conv't
1.3%	int'l stock	0.0%	preferred
0.0%	U.S. bonds	0.0%	other
0.0%	int'l bonds	0.0%	cash

Number of Investments: 269

Percent of Portfolio in Top 10 Investments: 9%

SHAREHOLDER INFORMATION

Minimum Investment

Initial: $3,000 Subsequent: $100

Minimum IRA Investment

Initial: $3,000 Subsequent: $0

Maximum Fees

Load: none 12b-1: none

Other: none

Services

✔ IRA

Keogh

✔ Telephone Exchange

Vanguard Selected Value (VASVX)

800-997-2798
www.vanguard.com

Mid-Cap Stock

PERFORMANCE — fund inception date: 2/15/96

	3yr Annual	5yr Annual	10yr Annual	Bull	Bear
Return (%)	-8.5	0.4	5.0	138.4	-38.6
Differ From Category (+/-)	1.3 abv av	1.8 abv av	1.8 abv av	-5.3 av	4.8 abv av

Standard Deviation	Category Risk Index	Beta
16.8%—av	0.84—low	1.03

	2008	2007	2006	2005	2004	2003	2002	2001	2000	1999
Return (%)	-35.5	-0.3	19.1	10.6	20.3	35.2	-9.8	14.9	17.4	-2.8
Differ From Category (+/-)	4.8	-10.3	5.9	0.4	3.9	-3.1	8.9	17.9	12.2	-43.0
Return, Tax-Adjusted (%)	-35.9	-1.6	18.0	9.7	20.1	34.8	-10.6	14.4	16.4	-3.4

PER SHARE DATA

	2008	2007	2006	2005	2004	2003	2002	2001	2000	1999
Dividends, Net Income ($)	0.42	0.37	0.32	0.29	0.26	0.26	0.24	0.17	0.24	0.16
Distrib'ns, Cap Gain ($)	0.00	1.55	1.05	0.85	0.00	0.00	0.00	0.00	0.00	0.00
Net Asset Value ($)	11.88	19.09	21.09	18.86	18.07	15.23	11.46	12.97	11.43	9.94
Expense Ratio (%)	0.38	0.40	0.44	0.49	0.60	0.78	0.74	0.70	0.63	0.73
Yield (%)	3.51	1.79	1.44	1.47	1.43	1.70	2.09	1.31	2.09	1.60
Portfolio Turnover (%)	23	33	37	28	35	40	50	67	40	102
Total Assets (Millions $)	2,282	4,472	4,584	3,933	2,300	1,422	1,094	995	196	187

PORTFOLIO (as of 9/30/08)

Portfolio Manager: Barrow/Giambrone/Greenberg - 1999

Investment Style

✔ Large Cap	Growth
✔ Mid Cap	Grth/Val
Small Cap	✔ Value

Portfolio

80.0%	U.S. stock	0.0%	conv't
8.5%	int'l stock	0.0%	preferred
0.3%	U.S. bonds	0.0%	other
0.0%	int'l bonds	11.2%	cash

Number of Investments: 64
Percent of Portfolio in Top 10 Investments: 36%

SHAREHOLDER INFORMATION

Minimum Investment
Initial: $25,000 Subsequent: $100

Minimum IRA Investment
Initial: $25,000 Subsequent: $100

Maximum Fees
Load: 1.00% redemption 12b-1: none
Other: redemption fee applies for 1 year

Services
✔ IRA
✔ Keogh
✔ Telephone Exchange

Wells Fargo Advantage Mid Cap Dis Inv (SMCDX)

800-222-8222
www.wellsfargofunds.com

Mid-Cap Stock

PERFORMANCE — fund inception date: 12/31/98

	3yr Annual	5yr Annual	10yr Annual	Bull	Bear
Return (%)	-7.7	0.5	9.0	136.7	-34.6
Differ From Category (+/-)	2.1 abv av	1.9 abv av	5.8 high	-7.0 av	8.8 high

Standard Deviation	Category Risk Index	Beta
15.9%—av	0.80—low	0.95

	2008	2007	2006	2005	2004	2003	2002	2001	2000	1999
Return (%)	-30.1	-4.9	18.2	7.9	21.1	40.6	-11.8	12.4	22.7	35.2
Differ From Category (+/-)	10.2	-14.9	5.0	-2.3	4.7	2.3	6.9	15.4	17.6	-5.0
Return, Tax-Adjusted (%)	-30.2	-6.3	17.1	5.5	19.7	39.9	-12.4	12.4	21.1	35.2

PER SHARE DATA

	2008	2007	2006	2005	2004	2003	2002	2001	2000	1999
Dividends, Net Income ($)	0.12	0.17	0.12	0.00	0.05	0.02	0.00	0.00	0.06	0.00
Distrib'ns, Cap Gain ($)	0.00	1.88	1.41	3.59	1.80	0.72	0.52	0.00	0.96	0.00
Net Asset Value ($)	13.55	19.56	22.73	20.51	22.34	20.13	14.85	17.42	15.50	13.52
Expense Ratio (%)	na	1.31	1.31	1.34	1.30	1.50	1.50	1.50	1.50	—
Yield (%)	0.91	0.80	0.48	0.00	0.20	0.07	0.00	0.00	0.39	0.00
Portfolio Turnover (%)	na	113	125	94	62	252	431	648	301	—
Total Assets (Millions $)	362	705	860	545	675	315	155	92	18	6

PORTFOLIO (as of 10/31/08)

Portfolio Manager: Costomiris - 2001

Investment Style

Large Cap	Growth
✔ Mid Cap	Grth/Val
Small Cap	✔ Value

Portfolio

96.7% U.S. stock	0.0% conv't
3.1% int'l stock	0.0% preferred
0.0% U.S. bonds	0.0% other
0.0% int'l bonds	0.3% cash

Number of Investments: 78

Percent of Portfolio in Top 10 Investments: 32%

SHAREHOLDER INFORMATION

Minimum Investment

Initial: $2,500 Subsequent: $100

Minimum IRA Investment

Initial: $1,000 Subsequent: $100

Maximum Fees

Load: none 12b-1: none

Other: none

Services

✔ IRA
✔ Keogh
✔ Telephone Exchange

Westport Select Cap R (WPSRX)

888-593-7878
www.westportfunds.com

Mid-Cap Stock

PERFORMANCE — fund inception date: 12/31/97

	3yr Annual	5yr Annual	10yr Annual	Bull	Bear
Return (%)	-7.0	-0.7	6.6	119.9	-38.7
Differ From Category (+/-)	2.8 high	0.7 abv av	3.4 high	-23.8 blw av	4.7 abv av

Standard Deviation	Category Risk Index	Beta
17.2%—av	0.86—low	1.04

	2008	2007	2006	2005	2004	2003	2002	2001	2000	1999
Return (%)	-32.7	6.3	12.4	8.6	10.4	32.1	-15.3	8.2	13.6	42.7
Differ From Category (+/-)	7.6	-3.7	-0.8	-1.6	-6.0	-6.2	3.4	11.2	8.4	2.5
Return, Tax-Adjusted (%)	-32.7	4.6	10.7	7.3	10.4	32.1	-15.3	7.9	12.9	42.7

PER SHARE DATA

	2008	2007	2006	2005	2004	2003	2002	2001	2000	1999
Dividends, Net Income ($)	0.00	0.14	0.01	0.00	0.00	0.00	0.00	0.00	0.03	0.00
Distrib'ns, Cap Gain ($)	0.00	2.69	2.59	1.99	0.00	0.00	0.00	0.28	0.45	0.00
Net Asset Value ($)	15.70	23.31	24.56	24.16	24.06	21.79	16.49	19.45	18.23	16.47
Expense Ratio (%)	na	1.33	1.32	1.31	1.35	1.34	1.29	1.24	1.27	1.43
Yield (%)	0.00	0.52	0.04	0.00	0.00	0.00	0.00	0.00	0.17	0.00
Portfolio Turnover (%)	na	6	7	2	9	12	4	11	15	10
Total Assets (Millions $)	301	446	440	440	467	456	314	208	110	80

PORTFOLIO (as of 9/30/08)

Portfolio Manager: Knuth/Nicklin Jr. - 1997

Investment Style

Large Cap	Growth
✔ Mid Cap	✔ Grth/Val
Small Cap	Value

Portfolio

84.5%	U.S. stock	0.0%	conv't
1.6%	int'l stock	0.0%	preferred
0.0%	U.S. bonds	0.3%	other
0.0%	int'l bonds	13.7%	cash

Number of Investments: 50
Percent of Portfolio in Top 10 Investments: 52%

SHAREHOLDER INFORMATION

Minimum Investment
Initial: $5,000 Subsequent: $0

Minimum IRA Investment
Initial: $2,000 Subsequent: $0

Maximum Fees
Load: none 12b-1: none
Other: none

Services
✔ IRA
✔ Keogh
✔ Telephone Exchange

Small-Cap Stock Funds
Category Performance Ranked by 2008 Returns

Fund (Ticker)	Annual Return (%) 2008	3Yr	5Yr	10Yr	Category Risk	Total Risk
Pinnacle Value (PVFIX)	-16.9	2.8	7.1	na	low	blw av
Heartland Value Plus (HRVIX)	-17.9	-0.8	2.9	7.8	low	av
Royce Special Equity Invt (RYSEX)	-19.7	-1.4	1.6	8.1	low	blw av
Northern Small Cap Value (NOSGX)	-23.5	-5.7	2.1	6.6	low	av
Stratton Small-Cap Value (STSCX)	-25.8	-6.2	2.9	7.7	low	av
Dreman Contrarian Small Cap Value R (DRSVX)	-27.0	-1.3	6.0	na	low	av
Berwyn (BERWX)	-27.1	-9.2	0.6	6.1	low	av
FMA Small Company Inv (FMACX)	-28.5	-4.6	1.7	4.5	low	av
T. Rowe Price Small-Cap Value (PRSVX)	-28.7	-6.1	2.5	8.4	low	av
Buffalo Small Cap (BUFSX)	-29.9	-7.3	1.1	10.9	av	abv av
Nicholas Limited Edition I (NCLEX)	-30.3	-6.3	0.2	0.2	low	av
Fidelity Small Cap Value (FCPVX)	-30.3	-6.6	na	na	av	abv av
FMI Focus (FMIOX)	-30.5	-6.8	-1.9	7.4	low	av
CRM Small Cap Value Inv (CRMSX)	-30.7	-8.5	-0.1	7.2	low	av
Dreyfus Small Cap Stock Index (DISSX)	-30.8	-7.6	0.6	4.8	blw av	abv av
Vanguard Tax-Managed Small Cap Inv (VTMSX)	-30.9	-7.5	0.9	na	blw av	abv av
Gabelli Small Cap Growth AAA (GABSX)	-31.0	-4.1	2.6	7.0	low	av
Royce Total Return Invt (RYTRX)	-31.2	-6.9	0.5	6.2	low	av
Vanguard Small Cap Value Index (VISVX)	-32.1	-9.1	-0.3	5.2	blw av	abv av
American Beacon Small Cp Val Plan (AVPAX)	-32.2	-10.2	-1.2	na	blw av	abv av
TIAA-CREF Small-Cap Equity Retail (TCSEX)	-32.9	-9.5	-1.7	na	av	abv av
HighMark Cognitive Value M (HCLMX)	-33.1	-8.1	-0.9	na	low	av
Aston/TAMRO Small Cap N (ATASX)	-33.2	-5.1	-0.4	na	abv av	abv av
E*TRADE Russell 2000 Index (ETRUX)	-33.6	-8.4	-1.2	na	av	abv av
Westcore Small-Cap Value (WTSVX)	-33.6	-7.5	na	na	av	abv av
Northern Small Cap Index (NSIDX)	-34.1	-8.7	-1.4	na	av	abv av
Royce Value Svc (RYVFX)	-34.3	-7.3	4.1	na	high	high
Royce Pennsylvania Mutual Invt (PENNX)	-34.8	-8.4	0.7	7.0	blw av	abv av
Royce Low Priced Stock Svc (RYLPX)	-36.0	-8.0	-0.6	8.9	abv av	high
Vanguard Small Cap Index (NAESX)	-36.1	-9.3	-0.8	3.3	av	abv av
USAA Small Cap Stock (USCAX)	-36.1	-10.0	-1.3	na	blw av	abv av
Royce Heritage Svc (RGFAX)	-36.3	-7.5	0.7	8.2	abv av	abv av
Tamarack Enterprise S (TETSX)	-38.1	-11.3	-3.6	5.0	low	av
Value Line Emerging Opportunities (VLEOX)	-38.3	-8.1	-0.5	7.7	blw av	abv av
T. Rowe Price New Horizons (PRNHX)	-38.8	-11.3	-1.7	2.4	av	abv av
LKCM Small Cap Equity Instl (LKSCX)	-38.9	-11.4	-0.6	4.9	av	abv av
Baron Growth (BGRFX)	-39.2	-9.2	0.0	6.0	blw av	av
Tamarack Micro Cap Value S (TMVSX)	-39.4	-12.5	-2.4	5.3	blw av	abv av
Heartland Value (HRTVX)	-39.6	-9.9	-4.1	7.3	abv av	abv av
Vanguard Small Cap Growth Index (VISGX)	-40.0	-9.7	-1.5	3.0	abv av	abv av
UMB Scout Small Cap (UMBHX)	-40.2	-8.8	0.0	5.3	blw av	abv av

Small-Cap Stock Funds
Category Performance Ranked by 2008 Returns (cont.)

Fund (Ticker)	Annual Return (%) 2008	3Yr	5Yr	10Yr	Category Risk	Total Risk
Baron Small Cap (BSCFX)	-40.3	-9.3	-0.3	6.2	av	abv av
Kalmar Growth-with-Value Small Cap (KGSCX)	-40.4	-10.7	-3.3	2.2	blw av	abv av
Janus Triton (JATTX)	-40.6	-6.0	na	na	abv av	abv av
Royce Value Plus Svc (RYVPX)	-41.1	-10.2	1.0	na	abv av	high
Columbia Select Small Cap Z (UMLCX)	-41.5	-9.0	-1.0	4.1	av	abv av
Neuberger Berman Small Cap Growth Inv (NBMIX)	-42.3	-7.7	1.0	0.9	blw av	abv av
American Century New Opps Investor (TWNOX)	-42.5	-7.8	-2.3	2.4	av	abv av
Bridgeway Ultra-Small Company Market (BRSIX)	-44.7	-16.5	-6.1	8.4	blw av	abv av
Fidelity Small Cap Growth (FCPGX)	-45.0	-10.1	na	na	abv av	abv av
Small-Cap Stock Category Average	**-39.3**	**-10.8**	**-2.4**	**4.2**	**av**	**abv av**

American Beacon Small Cp Val Plan (AVPAX)

800-967-9009
www.americanbeaconfunds.com

Small-Cap Stock

PERFORMANCE — fund inception date: 3/1/99

	3yr Annual	5yr Annual	10yr Annual	Bull	Bear
Return (%)	-10.2	-1.2	na	146.3	-37.8
Differ From Category (+/-)	0.6 av	1.2 abv av	na	1.2 abv av	5.7 abv av

Standard Deviation	Category Risk Index	Beta
19.6%—abv av	0.93—blw av	1.18

	2008	2007	2006	2005	2004	2003	2002	2001	2000	1999
Return (%)	-32.2	-6.7	14.3	5.5	23.1	51.2	-7.0	27.2	19.0	—
Differ From Category (+/-)	7.1	-9.2	-0.2	-1.5	6.3	4.0	11.4	19.8	10.9	—
Return, Tax-Adjusted (%)	-32.3	-8.6	13.1	4.7	22.4	50.6	-7.8	25.5	17.8	—

PER SHARE DATA

	2008	2007	2006	2005	2004	2003	2002	2001	2000	1999
Dividends, Net Income ($)	0.16	0.16	0.13	0.09	0.06	0.03	0.12	0.08	0.18	—
Distrib'ns, Cap Gain ($)	0.00	2.47	1.56	0.89	0.77	0.44	0.28	0.77	0.17	—
Net Asset Value ($)	11.52	17.22	21.20	20.03	19.91	16.84	11.45	12.73	10.69	—
Expense Ratio (%)	na	1.05	1.06	1.10	1.15	1.16	1.11	1.17	—	—
Yield (%)	1.37	0.80	0.59	0.44	0.26	0.18	1.03	0.59	1.69	—
Portfolio Turnover (%)	na	52	48	47	35	75	81	93	—	—
Total Assets (Millions $)	652	1,158	1,364	1,384	756	86	35	1	0	—

PORTFOLIO (as of 10/31/08)

Portfolio Manager: Posada/Quinn/Crumpler - 1998

Investment Style

Large Cap	Growth
Mid Cap	Grth/Val
✔ Small Cap	✔ Value

Portfolio

87.4%	U.S. stock	0.0%	conv't
0.6%	int'l stock	0.0%	preferred
0.0%	U.S. bonds	0.0%	other
0.0%	int'l bonds	12.0%	cash

Number of Investments: 526
Percent of Portfolio in Top 10 Investments: 18%

SHAREHOLDER INFORMATION

Minimum Investment
Initial: $2,500 Subsequent: $50

Minimum IRA Investment
Initial: $2,500 Subsequent: $50

Maximum Fees
Load: none 12b-1: none
Other: none

Services
✔ IRA
✔ Keogh
✔ Telephone Exchange

American Century New Opps Investor (TWNOX)

800-345-8765
www.americancentury.com

Small-Cap Stock

PERFORMANCE — fund inception date: 12/26/96

	3yr Annual	5yr Annual	10yr Annual	Bull	Bear
Return (%)	-7.8	-2.3	2.4	125.7	-45.5
Differ From Category (+/-)	3.0 abv av	0.1 av	-1.8 blw av	-19.4 blw av	-2.0 blw av

Standard Deviation	Category Risk Index	Beta
20.7%—abv av	0.99—av	1.20

	2008	2007	2006	2005	2004	2003	2002	2001	2000	1999
Return (%)	-42.5	23.0	10.7	6.8	6.3	28.7	-22.7	-29.6	-18.3	147.9
Differ From Category (+/-)	-3.2	20.5	-3.8	-0.2	-10.5	-18.5	-4.3	-37.0	-26.3	113.8
Return, Tax-Adjusted (%)	-42.5	23.0	10.7	6.8	6.3	28.7	-22.7	-29.6	-23.7	144.1

PER SHARE DATA

	2008	2007	2006	2005	2004	2003	2002	2001	2000	1999
Dividends, Net Income ($)	0.00	0.00	0.00	0.00	0.00	0.00	0.00	0.00	0.00	0.00
Distrib'ns, Cap Gain ($)	0.00	0.00	0.00	0.00	0.00	0.00	0.00	0.00	3.65	1.14
Net Asset Value ($)	4.67	8.11	6.59	5.95	5.57	5.24	4.07	5.26	7.47	13.49
Expense Ratio (%)	na	1.50	1.50	1.50	1.49	1.50	1.50	1.50	1.50	1.50
Yield (%)	0.00	0.00	0.00	0.00	0.00	0.00	0.00	0.00	0.00	0.00
Portfolio Turnover (%)	na	201	298	260	269	217	175	189	112	156
Total Assets (Millions $)	120	253	245	249	287	324	285	413	621	747

PORTFOLIO (as of 9/30/08)

Portfolio Manager: Southwick/Ferretti - 2006

Investment Style

Large Cap	✔ Growth
Mid Cap	Grth/Val
✔ Small Cap	Value

Portfolio

93.3%	U.S. stock	0.0%	conv't
3.6%	int'l stock	0.0%	preferred
0.0%	U.S. bonds	0.7%	other
0.0%	int'l bonds	2.4%	cash

Number of Investments: 150
Percent of Portfolio in Top 10 Investments: 17%

SHAREHOLDER INFORMATION

Minimum Investment
Initial: $2,500 Subsequent: $50

Minimum IRA Investment
Initial: $2,500 Subsequent: $50

Maximum Fees
Load: 2.00% redemption 12b-1: none
Other: redemption fee applies for 180 days

Services
✔ IRA
✔ Keogh
✔ Telephone Exchange

Aston/TAMRO Small Cap N (ATASX)

800-992-8151
www.astonfunds.com

Small-Cap Stock

PERFORMANCE — fund inception date: 11/30/00

	3yr Annual	5yr Annual	10yr Annual	Bull	Bear
Return (%)	-5.1	-0.4	na	157.5	-37.6
Differ From Category (+/-)	5.7 high	2.0 abv av	na	12.4 abv av	5.9 abv av

Standard Deviation	Category Risk Index	Beta
21.7%—abv av	1.03—abv av	1.24

	2008	2007	2006	2005	2004	2003	2002	2001	2000	1999
Return (%)	-33.2	0.2	27.8	2.3	11.9	56.8	-11.1	13.5	—	—
Differ From Category (+/-)	6.1	-2.3	13.3	-4.7	-4.9	9.6	7.3	6.1	—	—
Return, Tax-Adjusted (%)	-33.2	-0.5	26.7	2.3	10.9	54.0	-11.1	13.2	—	—

PER SHARE DATA

	2008	2007	2006	2005	2004	2003	2002	2001	2000	1999
Dividends, Net Income ($)	0.00	0.00	0.00	0.00	0.00	0.00	0.00	0.04	—	—
Distrib'ns, Cap Gain ($)	0.00	0.97	1.14	0.00	1.00	2.03	0.00	0.08	—	—
Net Asset Value ($)	12.44	18.62	19.55	16.18	15.81	15.04	10.91	12.27	—	—
Expense Ratio (%)	na	1.30	1.30	1.30	1.30	1.30	1.30	1.30	—	—
Yield (%)	0.00	0.00	0.00	0.00	0.00	0.00	0.00	0.35	—	—
Portfolio Turnover (%)	na	59	58	56	103	115	267	175	—	—
Total Assets (Millions $)	140	213	211	126	143	66	41	6	—	—

PORTFOLIO (as of 9/30/08)

Portfolio Manager: Tasho - 2000

Investment Style

Large Cap	Growth
Mid Cap	✔ Grth/Val
✔ Small Cap	Value

Portfolio

91.8% U.S. stock	0.0% conv't
1.9% int'l stock	0.0% preferred
0.0% U.S. bonds	0.0% other
0.0% int'l bonds	6.4% cash

Number of Investments: 54

Percent of Portfolio in Top 10 Investments: 31%

SHAREHOLDER INFORMATION

Minimum Investment

Initial: $2,500 Subsequent: $50

Minimum IRA Investment

Initial: $500 Subsequent: $50

Maximum Fees

Load: none 12b-1: 0.25%

Other: none

Services

✔ IRA

Keogh

✔ Telephone Exchange

Baron Growth
(BGRFX)

800-442-3814
www.baronfunds.com

Small-Cap Stock

PERFORMANCE — fund inception date: 12/30/94

	3yr Annual	5yr Annual	10yr Annual	Bull	Bear
Return (%)	-9.2	0.0	6.0	141.3	-42.7
Differ From Category (+/-)	1.6 av	2.4 abv av	1.8 abv av	-3.8 av	0.8 av

Standard Deviation	Category Risk Index	Beta
18.7%—av	0.89—blw av	1.14

	2008	2007	2006	2005	2004	2003	2002	2001	2000	1999
Return (%)	-39.2	6.5	15.5	5.7	26.6	31.7	-12.3	12.6	-4.6	44.7
Differ From Category (+/-)	0.1	4.0	1.0	-1.3	9.8	-15.5	6.1	5.2	-12.7	10.6
Return, Tax-Adjusted (%)	-39.2	5.8	14.6	5.0	26.6	31.7	-12.3	11.5	-6.5	43.1

PER SHARE DATA

	2008	2007	2006	2005	2004	2003	2002	2001	2000	1999
Dividends, Net Income ($)	0.00	0.00	0.00	0.00	0.00	0.00	0.00	0.00	0.00	0.00
Distrib'ns, Cap Gain ($)	0.01	2.50	2.54	2.05	0.00	0.00	0.00	1.64	3.19	1.88
Net Asset Value ($)	30.81	50.67	49.88	45.40	44.87	35.44	26.90	30.67	28.82	33.68
Expense Ratio (%)	1.32	1.31	1.31	1.31	1.33	1.36	1.35	1.36	1.36	1.40
Yield (%)	0.00	0.00	0.00	0.00	0.00	0.00	0.00	0.00	0.00	0.00
Portfolio Turnover (%)	26	21	21	15	27	33	18	34	39	53
Total Assets (Millions $)	4,058	6,862	5,898	5,122	4,049	2,521	1,214	721	500	620

PORTFOLIO (as of 9/30/08)

Portfolio Manager: Baron - 1994

Investment Style

Large Cap	✔ Growth
✔ Mid Cap	Grth/Val
✔ Small Cap	Value

Portfolio

90.3% U.S. stock	0.0% conv't
2.1% int'l stock	0.0% preferred
0.0% U.S. bonds	1.6% other
0.0% int'l bonds	6.1% cash

Number of Investments: 113
Percent of Portfolio in Top 10 Investments: 26%

SHAREHOLDER INFORMATION

Minimum Investment
Initial: $2,000 Subsequent: $0

Minimum IRA Investment
Initial: $2,000 Subsequent: $0

Maximum Fees
Load: none 12b-1: 0.25%
Other: none

Services
✔ IRA
Keogh
✔ Telephone Exchange

Baron Small Cap (BSCFX)

800-442-3814
www.baronfunds.com

Small-Cap Stock

PERFORMANCE — fund inception date: 9/30/97

	3yr Annual	5yr Annual	10yr Annual	Bull	Bear
Return (%)	-9.3	-0.3	6.2	148.5	-43.2
Differ From Category (+/-)	1.5 av	2.1 abv av	2.0 abv av	3.4 abv av	0.3 av

Standard Deviation	Category Risk Index	Beta
20.0%—abv av	0.95—av	1.21

	2008	2007	2006	2005	2004	2003	2002	2001	2000	1999
Return (%)	-40.3	11.6	11.8	8.3	22.1	38.8	-9.7	5.1	-17.6	70.7
Differ From Category (+/-)	-1.0	9.1	-2.7	1.3	5.3	-8.4	8.7	-2.3	-25.7	36.6
Return, Tax-Adjusted (%)	-40.3	10.5	9.8	7.8	21.7	38.8	-10.2	5.1	-18.0	70.7

PER SHARE DATA

	2008	2007	2006	2005	2004	2003	2002	2001	2000	1999
Dividends, Net Income ($)	0.00	0.00	0.00	0.00	0.00	0.00	0.00	0.00	0.00	0.00
Distrib'ns, Cap Gain ($)	0.00	1.67	3.06	0.74	0.55	0.00	0.38	0.00	0.38	0.00
Net Asset Value ($)	14.24	23.83	22.83	23.17	22.08	18.56	13.37	15.21	14.46	18.00
Expense Ratio (%)	1.32	1.31	1.33	1.33	1.36	1.36	1.36	1.35	1.33	1.34
Yield (%)	0.00	0.00	0.00	0.00	0.00	0.00	0.00	0.00	0.00	0.00
Portfolio Turnover (%)	42	37	40	25	30	30	55	55	53	42
Total Assets (Millions $)	2,098	3,600	3,110	2,930	2,252	1,426	744	708	746	1,089

PORTFOLIO (as of 9/30/08)

Portfolio Manager: Greenberg - 1997

Investment Style

Large Cap	✔ Growth
Mid Cap	Grth/Val
✔ Small Cap	Value

Portfolio

85.5%	U.S. stock	0.0%	conv't
1.8%	int'l stock	0.0%	preferred
0.0%	U.S. bonds	2.4%	other
0.0%	int'l bonds	10.4%	cash

Number of Investments: 87
Percent of Portfolio in Top 10 Investments: 30%

SHAREHOLDER INFORMATION

Minimum Investment
Initial: $2,000 Subsequent: $0

Minimum IRA Investment
Initial: $2,000 Subsequent: $0

Maximum Fees
Load: none 12b-1: 0.25%
Other: none

Services
✔ IRA
✔ Keogh
✔ Telephone Exchange

Berwyn
(BERWX)

800-992-6757
www.berwynfunds.com

Small-Cap Stock

PERFORMANCE **fund inception date: 5/4/84**

	3yr Annual	5yr Annual	10yr Annual	Bull	Bear
Return (%)	-9.2	0.6	6.1	136.0	-31.5
Differ From Category (+/-)	1.6 av	3.0 high	1.9 abv av	-9.1 av	12.0 high

Standard Deviation	Category Risk Index	Beta
17.5%—av	0.83—low	1.01

	2008	2007	2006	2005	2004	2003	2002	2001	2000	1999
Return (%)	-27.1	-3.7	6.7	12.1	22.8	50.0	-6.9	28.9	2.0	-4.6
Differ From Category (+/-)	12.2	-6.2	-7.8	5.1	6.0	2.8	11.5	21.5	-6.0	-38.7
Return, Tax-Adjusted (%)	-27.2	-5.5	5.2	10.7	21.9	49.0	-8.4	27.1	2.0	-4.6

PER SHARE DATA

	2008	2007	2006	2005	2004	2003	2002	2001	2000	1999
Dividends, Net Income ($)	0.03	0.06	0.05	0.02	0.00	0.00	0.00	0.24	0.00	0.00
Distrib'ns, Cap Gain ($)	0.00	3.28	2.82	2.83	1.48	1.08	1.46	0.97	0.00	0.00
Net Asset Value ($)	17.78	24.42	28.81	29.67	28.96	24.78	17.23	20.07	16.52	16.18
Expense Ratio (%)	na	1.27	1.26	1.28	1.20	1.41	1.29	1.24	1.64	1.39
Yield (%)	0.14	0.23	0.15	0.05	0.00	0.00	0.00	1.12	0.00	0.00
Portfolio Turnover (%)	na	40	38	31	23	23	32	37	16	6
Total Assets (Millions $)	118	119	149	184	115	52	33	44	27	39

PORTFOLIO (as of 10/31/08)

Portfolio Manager: Killen/Killen/Grout/Cipolloni - 1984

Investment Style

Large Cap	Growth
Mid Cap	Grth/Val
✔ Small Cap	✔ Value

Portfolio

89.5%	U.S. stock	0.0%	conv't
0.0%	int'l stock	0.0%	preferred
0.0%	U.S. bonds	0.0%	other
0.0%	int'l bonds	10.5%	cash

Number of Investments: 45
Percent of Portfolio in Top 10 Investments: 35%

SHAREHOLDER INFORMATION

Minimum Investment
Initial: $3,000 Subsequent: $250

Minimum IRA Investment
Initial: $1,000 Subsequent: $250

Maximum Fees
Load: 1.00% redemption 12b-1: none
Other: redemption fee applies for 6 months

Services
✔ IRA
Keogh
✔ Telephone Exchange

Bridgeway Ultra-Small Company Market (BRSIX)

800-661-3550
www.bridgeway.com

Small-Cap Stock

PERFORMANCE — fund inception date: 7/31/97

	3yr Annual	5yr Annual	10yr Annual	Bull	Bear
Return (%)	-16.5	-6.1	8.4	161.0	-49.1
Differ From Category (+/-)	-5.7 low	-3.7 low	4.2 high	15.9 abv av	-5.6 blw av

Standard Deviation	Category Risk Index	Beta
18.8%—abv av	0.90—blw av	1.08

	2008	2007	2006	2005	2004	2003	2002	2001	2000	1999
Return (%)	-44.7	-5.5	11.4	4.0	20.1	79.4	4.9	23.9	0.6	31.4
Differ From Category (+/-)	-5.4	-7.9	-3.1	-3.0	3.3	32.2	23.3	16.5	-7.5	-2.7
Return, Tax-Adjusted (%)	-44.8	-6.0	11.0	3.6	19.9	79.3	4.9	23.9	0.4	31.4

PER SHARE DATA

	2008	2007	2006	2005	2004	2003	2002	2001	2000	1999
Dividends, Net Income ($)	0.21	0.04	0.08	0.03	0.03	0.00	0.00	0.01	0.04	0.00
Distrib'ns, Cap Gain ($)	0.00	0.65	0.37	0.53	0.15	0.04	0.00	0.00	0.00	0.00
Net Asset Value ($)	9.63	17.78	19.54	17.94	17.77	14.94	8.35	7.96	6.43	6.43
Expense Ratio (%)	0.66	0.67	0.65	0.73	0.67	0.75	0.75	0.75	0.75	0.75
Yield (%)	2.22	0.22	0.41	0.15	0.15	0.00	0.00	0.14	0.66	0.00
Portfolio Turnover (%)	29	34	26	13	19	18	56	215	40	48
Total Assets (Millions $)	324	981	1,176	758	806	752	100	39	64	69

PORTFOLIO (as of 9/30/08)

Portfolio Manager: Montgomery/Khoziaeva/Whipple - 1997

Investment Style

Large Cap	Growth
Mid Cap	✔ Grth/Val
✔ Small Cap	Value

Portfolio

97.3%	U.S. stock	0.0%	conv't
0.0%	int'l stock	0.0%	preferred
0.0%	U.S. bonds	0.0%	other
0.0%	int'l bonds	2.7%	cash

Number of Investments: 394
Percent of Portfolio in Top 10 Investments: 14%

SHAREHOLDER INFORMATION

Minimum Investment
Initial: $2,000 Subsequent: $500

Minimum IRA Investment
Initial: $2,000 Subsequent: $500

Maximum Fees
Load: 2.00% redemption 12b-1: none
Other: redemption fee applies for 6 months

Services
✔ IRA
✔ Keogh
✔ Telephone Exchange

Buffalo Small Cap (BUFSX)

800-492-8332
www.buffalofunds.com

Small-Cap Stock

PERFORMANCE — fund inception date: 4/14/98

	3yr Annual	5yr Annual	10yr Annual	Bull	Bear
Return (%)	-7.3	1.1	10.9	173.8	-36.3
Differ From Category (+/-)	3.5 abv av	3.5 high	6.7 high	28.7 high	7.2 high

Standard Deviation	Category Risk Index	Beta
20.3%—abv av	0.97—av	1.17

	2008	2007	2006	2005	2004	2003	2002	2001	2000	1999
Return (%)	-29.9	-0.4	13.9	3.2	28.8	51.2	-25.8	31.1	33.6	34.7
Differ From Category (+/-)	9.4	-2.9	-0.6	-3.8	12.0	4.0	-7.4	23.7	25.5	0.6
Return, Tax-Adjusted (%)	-30.4	-1.9	12.7	1.5	28.2	51.0	-25.8	31.1	31.0	34.3

PER SHARE DATA

	2008	2007	2006	2005	2004	2003	2002	2001	2000	1999
Dividends, Net Income ($)	0.00	0.00	0.00	0.00	0.02	0.00	0.00	0.00	0.00	0.00
Distrib'ns, Cap Gain ($)	0.76	2.66	2.04	3.11	0.88	0.20	0.03	0.03	1.67	0.21
Net Asset Value ($)	16.37	24.17	26.94	25.44	27.65	22.18	14.80	19.96	15.24	12.76
Expense Ratio (%)	1.00	1.01	1.01	1.01	1.01	1.02	1.01	1.04	1.12	—
Yield (%)	0.00	0.00	0.00	0.00	0.06	0.00	0.00	0.00	0.00	0.00
Portfolio Turnover (%)	37	15	27	35	22	23	6	31	42	—
Total Assets (Millions $)	1,191	2,043	2,019	1,867	1,971	1,418	770	1,027	49	24

PORTFOLIO (as of 9/30/08)

Portfolio Manager: Gasaway/Male/Sarris - 1998

Investment Style

Large Cap	✔ Growth
Mid Cap	Grth/Val
✔ Small Cap	Value

Portfolio

93.1%	U.S. stock	0.0%	conv't
2.9%	int'l stock	0.1%	preferred
0.0%	U.S. bonds	0.0%	other
0.0%	int'l bonds	3.9%	cash

Number of Investments: 58

Percent of Portfolio in Top 10 Investments: 35%

SHAREHOLDER INFORMATION

Minimum Investment
Initial: $2,500 Subsequent: $100

Minimum IRA Investment
Initial: $250 Subsequent: $0

Maximum Fees
Load: 2.00% redemption 12b-1: none
Other: redemption fee applies for 180 days

Services
✔ IRA
✔ Keogh
✔ Telephone Exchange

Columbia Select Small Cap Z (UMLCX)

800-345-6611
www.columbiafunds.com

Small-Cap Stock

PERFORMANCE — fund inception date: 12/31/92

	3yr Annual	5yr Annual	10yr Annual	Bull	Bear
Return (%)	-9.0	-1.0	4.1	189.5	-45.8
Differ From Category (+/-)	1.8 abv av	1.4 abv av	-0.1 av	44.4 high	-2.3 blw av

Standard Deviation	Category Risk Index	Beta
19.8%—abv av	0.94—av	1.19

	2008	2007	2006	2005	2004	2003	2002	2001	2000	1999
Return (%)	-41.5	10.8	16.3	2.6	22.6	48.7	-19.4	1.9	-1.0	29.7
Differ From Category (+/-)	-2.2	8.3	1.8	-4.4	5.8	1.5	-1.0	-5.5	-9.1	-4.4
Return, Tax-Adjusted (%)	-41.9	9.5	15.2	1.9	22.6	48.7	-19.4	1.8	-2.7	29.7

PER SHARE DATA

	2008	2007	2006	2005	2004	2003	2002	2001	2000	1999
Dividends, Net Income ($)	0.00	0.00	0.00	0.00	0.00	0.00	0.00	0.04	0.07	0.00
Distrib'ns, Cap Gain ($)	0.48	1.48	1.26	0.89	0.00	0.00	0.00	0.00	0.92	0.00
Net Asset Value ($)	10.52	18.52	18.05	16.59	17.00	13.86	9.32	11.56	11.38	12.53
Expense Ratio (%)	1.20	1.22	1.09	1.05	0.83	0.83	0.84	0.89	0.92	0.94
Yield (%)	0.00	0.00	0.00	0.00	0.00	0.00	0.00	0.32	0.55	0.00
Portfolio Turnover (%)	na	52	65	61	82	105	144	132	134	115
Total Assets (Millions $)	381	763	640	511	531	329	173	119	96	63

PORTFOLIO (as of 11/30/08)

Portfolio Manager: Pyle - 2001

Investment Style

Large Cap	✔ Growth
Mid Cap	Grth/Val
✔ Small Cap	Value

Portfolio

99.7%	U.S. stock	0.0%	conv't
0.0%	int'l stock	0.0%	preferred
0.0%	U.S. bonds	0.0%	other
0.0%	int'l bonds	0.3%	cash

Number of Investments: 41

Percent of Portfolio in Top 10 Investments: 41%

SHAREHOLDER INFORMATION

Minimum Investment

Initial: $2,500 Subsequent: $0

Minimum IRA Investment

Initial: $1,000 Subsequent: $0

Maximum Fees

Load: none 12b-1: none

Other: none

Services

✔ IRA

✔ Keogh

✔ Telephone Exchange

CRM Small Cap Value Inv (CRMSX)

800-276-2883
www.crmfunds.com

Small-Cap Stock

PERFORMANCE — fund inception date: 9/29/95

	3yr Annual	5yr Annual	10yr Annual	Bull	Bear
Return (%)	-8.5	-0.1	7.2	144.8	-34.3
Differ From Category (+/-)	2.3 abv av	2.3 abv av	3.0 abv av	-0.3 av	9.2 high

Standard Deviation	Category Risk Index	Beta
18.1%—av	0.86—low	1.06

	2008	2007	2006	2005	2004	2003	2002	2001	2000	1999
Return (%)	-30.7	-3.4	14.4	10.3	17.8	48.3	-17.9	26.3	18.0	10.9
Differ From Category (+/-)	8.6	-5.9	-0.1	3.3	1.0	1.1	0.5	18.9	9.9	-23.2
Return, Tax-Adjusted (%)	-30.7	-5.8	12.2	8.3	16.3	48.3	-18.5	24.4	16.9	10.9

PER SHARE DATA

	2008	2007	2006	2005	2004	2003	2002	2001	2000	1999
Dividends, Net Income ($)	0.07	0.05	0.03	0.00	0.00	0.00	0.02	0.10	0.02	0.00
Distrib'ns, Cap Gain ($)	0.00	3.88	3.79	3.52	2.36	0.00	0.62	1.47	0.81	0.00
Net Asset Value ($)	14.10	20.42	25.39	25.55	26.30	24.37	16.43	20.76	17.71	15.76
Expense Ratio (%)	1.11	1.12	1.14	1.22	1.22	1.27	1.26	1.28	1.42	1.42
Yield (%)	0.46	0.21	0.11	0.00	0.00	0.00	0.09	0.46	0.12	0.00
Portfolio Turnover (%)	79	84	80	84	77	74	61	90	96	64
Total Assets (Millions $)	120	194	288	291	296	254	155	116	84	80

PORTFOLIO (as of 6/30/08)

Portfolio Manager: Caputo/Chin - 2008

Investment Style

Large Cap	Growth
Mid Cap	Grth/Val
✔ Small Cap	✔ Value

Portfolio

93.1%	U.S. stock	0.0%	conv't
1.8%	int'l stock	0.0%	preferred
0.0%	U.S. bonds	0.0%	other
0.0%	int'l bonds	5.1%	cash

Number of Investments: 60
Percent of Portfolio in Top 10 Investments: 29%

SHAREHOLDER INFORMATION

Minimum Investment
Initial: $2,500 Subsequent: $100

Minimum IRA Investment
Initial: $2,000 Subsequent: $100

Maximum Fees
Load: none 12b-1: none
Other: none

Services
✔ IRA
✔ Keogh
✔ Telephone Exchange

Dreman Contrarian Small Cap Value R (DRSVX)

800-247-1014
www.dreman.com

Small-Cap Stock

PERFORMANCE

fund inception date: 12/31/03

	3yr Annual	5yr Annual	10yr Annual	Bull	Bear
Return (%)	-1.3	6.0	na	na	-30.4
Differ From Category (+/-)	9.5 high	8.4 high	na	na	13.1 high

Standard Deviation	Category Risk Index	Beta
18.2%—av	0.87—low	1.03

	2008	2007	2006	2005	2004	2003	2002	2001	2000	1999
Return (%)	-27.0	0.9	30.7	7.5	29.5	—	—	—	—	—
Differ From Category (+/-)	12.3	-1.6	16.2	0.5	12.7	—	—	—	—	—
Return, Tax-Adjusted (%)	-27.2	0.9	30.6	7.4	29.2	—	—	—	—	—

PER SHARE DATA

	2008	2007	2006	2005	2004	2003	2002	2001	2000	1999
Dividends, Net Income ($)	0.06	0.04	0.04	0.06	0.02	—	—	—	—	—
Distrib'ns, Cap Gain ($)	0.06	0.00	0.00	0.00	0.21	—	—	—	—	—
Net Asset Value ($)	12.95	17.91	17.77	13.63	12.73	—	—	—	—	—
Expense Ratio (%)	na	1.50	1.50	1.50	1.75	—	—	—	—	—
Yield (%)	0.44	0.19	0.25	0.42	0.18	—	—	—	—	—
Portfolio Turnover (%)	na	83	77	85	72	—	—	—	—	—
Total Assets (Millions $)	48	48	18	3	1	—	—	—	—	—

PORTFOLIO (as of 11/30/08)

Portfolio Manager: Dreman/Hoover/Roach - 2003

Investment Style

Large Cap	Growth
Mid Cap	✔ Grth/Val
✔ Small Cap	Value

Portfolio

92.2%	U.S. stock	0.0%	conv't
3.2%	int'l stock	0.0%	preferred
0.0%	U.S. bonds	0.0%	other
0.0%	int'l bonds	4.6%	cash

Number of Investments: 104
Percent of Portfolio in Top 10 Investments: 19%

SHAREHOLDER INFORMATION

Minimum Investment
Initial: $2,500 Subsequent: $1,000

Minimum IRA Investment
Initial: $0 Subsequent: $0

Maximum Fees
Load: 1.00% redemption 12b-1: 0.25%
Other: redemption fee applies for 1 year

Services
✔ IRA
Keogh
✔ Telephone Exchange

Dreyfus Small Cap Stock Index (DISSX)

800-645-6561
www.dreyfus.com

Small-Cap Stock

PERFORMANCE — fund inception date: 6/30/97

	3yr Annual	5yr Annual	10yr Annual	Bull	Bear
Return (%)	-7.6	0.6	4.8	139.9	-36.4
Differ From Category (+/-)	3.2 abv av	3.0 high	0.6 av	-5.2 av	7.1 high

Standard Deviation	Category Risk Index	Beta
18.8%—abv av	0.90—blw av	1.12

	2008	2007	2006	2005	2004	2003	2002	2001	2000	1999
Return (%)	-30.8	-0.7	14.6	7.3	22.2	37.7	-14.8	5.9	11.2	12.1
Differ From Category (+/-)	8.5	-3.2	0.1	0.3	5.4	-9.5	3.6	-1.5	3.1	-22.0
Return, Tax-Adjusted (%)	-31.7	-2.0	13.9	7.0	21.6	37.6	-14.9	5.6	9.1	11.1

PER SHARE DATA

	2008	2007	2006	2005	2004	2003	2002	2001	2000	1999
Dividends, Net Income ($)	0.23	0.15	0.12	0.11	0.10	0.05	0.04	0.04	0.03	0.04
Distrib'ns, Cap Gain ($)	1.04	1.96	0.95	0.25	0.54	0.00	0.03	0.09	1.46	0.59
Net Asset Value ($)	13.39	21.30	23.53	21.44	20.31	17.14	12.48	14.72	14.02	13.99
Expense Ratio (%)	0.50	0.50	0.50	0.50	0.50	0.50	0.50	0.50	0.50	0.50
Yield (%)	1.60	0.62	0.49	0.51	0.46	0.28	0.35	0.28	0.19	0.27
Portfolio Turnover (%)	32	25	25	14	16	14	12	42	37	42
Total Assets (Millions $)	699	956	922	768	569	324	172	103	61	44

PORTFOLIO (as of 10/31/08)

Portfolio Manager: Durante - 2000

Investment Style

Large Cap	Growth
Mid Cap	✔ Grth/Val
✔ Small Cap	Value

Portfolio

98.6% U.S. stock	0.0% conv't
0.3% int'l stock	0.1% preferred
0.0% U.S. bonds	0.0% other
0.0% int'l bonds	1.0% cash

Number of Investments: 606
Percent of Portfolio in Top 10 Investments: 8%

SHAREHOLDER INFORMATION

Minimum Investment
Initial: $2,500 — Subsequent: $100

Minimum IRA Investment
Initial: $750 — Subsequent: $0

Maximum Fees
Load: none — 12b-1: none
Other: none

Services
✔ IRA
✔ Keogh
✔ Telephone Exchange

E*TRADE Russell 2000 Index (ETRUX)

800-786-2575
www.etrade.com

Small-Cap Stock

PERFORMANCE — fund inception date: 12/29/00

	3yr Annual	5yr Annual	10yr Annual	Bull	Bear
Return (%)	-8.4	-1.2	na	136.1	-38.4
Differ From Category (+/-)	2.4 abv av	1.2 abv av	na	-9.0 av	5.1 abv av

Standard Deviation	Category Risk Index	Beta
20.0%—abv av	0.95—av	1.19

	2008	2007	2006	2005	2004	2003	2002	2001	2000	1999
Return (%)	-33.6	-1.8	18.0	4.2	17.2	45.3	-20.9	1.8	—	—
Differ From Category (+/-)	5.7	-4.3	3.5	-2.8	0.5	-1.9	-2.5	-5.6	—	—
Return, Tax-Adjusted (%)	-34.7	-3.0	16.7	3.4	16.5	45.2	-21.2	1.0	—	—

PER SHARE DATA

	2008	2007	2006	2005	2004	2003	2002	2001	2000	1999
Dividends, Net Income ($)	0.17	0.23	0.14	0.12	0.08	0.06	0.05	0.09	—	—
Distrib'ns, Cap Gain ($)	0.70	0.83	0.90	0.56	0.45	0.00	0.04	0.19	—	—
Net Asset Value ($)	7.30	12.34	13.61	12.41	12.55	11.17	7.74	9.89	—	—
Expense Ratio (%)	na	0.22	0.22	0.22	0.37	0.65	0.65	0.65	—	—
Yield (%)	2.18	1.76	0.98	0.89	0.64	0.55	0.65	0.86	—	—
Portfolio Turnover (%)	na	18	25	30	35	4	0	0	—	—
Total Assets (Millions $)	77	120	125	81	68	34	13	8	—	—

PORTFOLIO (as of 9/30/08)

Portfolio Manager: Schluchter, III/Yousif - 2003

Investment Style

Large Cap	Growth
Mid Cap	✔ Grth/Val
✔ Small Cap	Value

Portfolio

96.0%	U.S. stock	0.0%	conv't
0.7%	int'l stock	0.0%	preferred
0.0%	U.S. bonds	0.0%	other
0.0%	int'l bonds	3.3%	cash

Number of Investments: 1,961
Percent of Portfolio in Top 10 Investments: 8%

SHAREHOLDER INFORMATION

Minimum Investment
Initial: $5,000 Subsequent: $250

Minimum IRA Investment
Initial: $3,000 Subsequent: $250

Maximum Fees
Load: 1.00% redemption 12b-1: none
Other: redemption fee applies for 4 months

Services
✔ IRA
✔ Keogh
✔ Telephone Exchange

Fidelity Small Cap Growth (FCPGX)

800-544-5555
www.fidelity.com

Small-Cap Stock

PERFORMANCE — fund inception date: 11/3/04

	3yr Annual	5yr Annual	10yr Annual	Bull	Bear
Return (%)	-10.1	na	na	na	-47.5
Differ From Category (+/-)	0.7 av	na	na	na	-4.0 blw av

Standard Deviation	Category Risk Index	Beta
21.5%—abv av	1.02—abv av	1.28

	2008	2007	2006	2005	2004	2003	2002	2001	2000	1999
Return (%)	-45.0	16.8	13.1	14.2	—	—	—	—	—	—
Differ From Category (+/-)	-5.7	14.3	-1.3	7.2	—	—	—	—	—	—
Return, Tax-Adjusted (%)	-45.0	15.7	13.0	14.0	—	—	—	—	—	—

PER SHARE DATA

	2008	2007	2006	2005	2004	2003	2002	2001	2000	1999
Dividends, Net Income ($)	0.00	0.00	0.00	0.00	—	—	—	—	—	—
Distrib'ns, Cap Gain ($)	0.00	1.05	0.10	0.18	—	—	—	—	—	—
Net Asset Value ($)	8.69	15.78	14.45	12.86	—	—	—	—	—	—
Expense Ratio (%)	1.10	1.09	1.08	1.16	—	—	—	—	—	—
Yield (%)	0.00	0.00	0.00	0.00	—	—	—	—	—	—
Portfolio Turnover (%)	113	91	129	102	—	—	—	—	—	—
Total Assets (Millions $)	826	1,310	535	290	—	—	—	—	—	—

PORTFOLIO (as of 10/31/08)

Portfolio Manager: Harris - 2005

Investment Style

Large Cap	✔ Growth
Mid Cap	Grth/Val
✔ Small Cap	Value

Portfolio

84.3%	U.S. stock	0.0%	conv't
10.7%	int'l stock	0.0%	preferred
0.0%	U.S. bonds	0.0%	other
0.0%	int'l bonds	5.0%	cash

Number of Investments: 132
Percent of Portfolio in Top 10 Investments: 18%

SHAREHOLDER INFORMATION

Minimum Investment
Initial: $2,500 Subsequent: $250

Minimum IRA Investment
Initial: $2,500 Subsequent: $250

Maximum Fees
Load: 1.50% redemption 12b-1: none
Other: redemption fee applies for 90 days; maint fee for low bal

Services
✔ IRA
✔ Keogh
Telephone Exchange

Fidelity Small Cap Value (FCPVX)

800-544-5555
www.fidelity.com

Small-Cap Stock

PERFORMANCE — fund inception date: 11/3/04

	3yr Annual	5yr Annual	10yr Annual	Bull	Bear
Return (%)	-6.6	na	na	na	-35.7
Differ From Category (+/-)	4.2 high	na	na	na	7.8 high

Standard Deviation	Category Risk Index	Beta
19.9%—abv av	0.95—av	1.14

	2008	2007	2006	2005	2004	2003	2002	2001	2000	1999
Return (%)	-30.3	1.1	15.6	17.6	—	—	—	—	—	—
Differ From Category (+/-)	9.0	-1.4	1.1	10.6	—	—	—	—	—	—
Return, Tax-Adjusted (%)	-30.5	0.5	14.8	17.1	—	—	—	—	—	—

PER SHARE DATA

	2008	2007	2006	2005	2004	2003	2002	2001	2000	1999
Dividends, Net Income ($)	0.08	0.00	0.00	0.01	—	—	—	—	—	—
Distrib'ns, Cap Gain ($)	0.11	0.56	0.68	0.36	—	—	—	—	—	—
Net Asset Value ($)	9.32	13.60	14.00	12.75	—	—	—	—	—	—
Expense Ratio (%)	1.13	1.11	1.06	1.05	—	—	—	—	—	—
Yield (%)	0.79	0.00	0.00	0.08	—	—	—	—	—	—
Portfolio Turnover (%)	149	67	93	60	—	—	—	—	—	—
Total Assets (Millions $)	1,017	1,210	1,106	688	—	—	—	—	—	—

PORTFOLIO (as of 10/31/08)

Portfolio Manager: Myers - 2008

Investment Style

Large Cap	Growth
Mid Cap	Grth/Val
✔ Small Cap	✔ Value

Portfolio

90.6%	U.S. stock	0.0%	conv't
4.4%	int'l stock	2.2%	preferred
2.3%	U.S. bonds	0.0%	other
0.0%	int'l bonds	0.6%	cash

Number of Investments: 85
Percent of Portfolio in Top 10 Investments: 25%

SHAREHOLDER INFORMATION

Minimum Investment
Initial: $2,500 Subsequent: $250

Minimum IRA Investment
Initial: $2,500 Subsequent: $250

Maximum Fees
Load: 1.50% redemption 12b-1: none
Other: redemption fee applies for 90 days; maint fee for low bal

Services
✔ IRA
✔ Keogh
Telephone Exchange

FMA Small Company Inv (FMACX)

866-362-8333
www.fmausa.com

Small-Cap Stock

PERFORMANCE — fund inception date: 7/31/91

	3yr Annual	5yr Annual	10yr Annual	Bull	Bear
Return (%)	-4.6	1.7	4.5	127.3	-32.6
Differ From Category (+/-)	6.2 high	4.1 high	0.3 av	-17.8 blw av	10.9 high

Standard Deviation	Category Risk Index	Beta
17.2%—av	0.82—low	1.02

	2008	2007	2006	2005	2004	2003	2002	2001	2000	1999
Return (%)	-28.5	0.6	20.7	4.9	19.6	33.5	-12.4	4.6	27.7	-8.9
Differ From Category (+/-)	10.8	-1.9	6.2	-2.1	2.8	-13.7	6.0	-2.8	19.6	-43.0
Return, Tax-Adjusted (%)	-28.5	-1.4	18.8	2.4	16.9	33.5	-12.5	4.4	27.3	-9.1

PER SHARE DATA

	2008	2007	2006	2005	2004	2003	2002	2001	2000	1999
Dividends, Net Income ($)	0.03	0.00	0.01	0.01	0.01	0.00	0.04	0.08	0.15	0.07
Distrib'ns, Cap Gain ($)	0.00	2.75	2.50	3.55	3.86	0.00	0.00	0.00	0.00	0.00
Net Asset Value ($)	13.22	18.52	21.10	19.54	21.94	21.61	16.18	18.51	17.77	14.04
Expense Ratio (%)	na	1.25	1.24	1.20	1.20	1.20	1.14	1.14	1.02	1.03
Yield (%)	0.22	0.00	0.02	0.05	0.01	0.00	0.27	0.43	0.81	0.51
Portfolio Turnover (%)	na	132	135	169	145	107	99	99	108	121
Total Assets (Millions $)	95	183	223	165	224	183	143	158	128	122

PORTFOLIO (as of 12/31/08)

Portfolio Manager: Vorisek/Harmon - 1998

Investment Style

Large Cap	Growth
Mid Cap	✔ Grth/Val
✔ Small Cap	Value

Portfolio

97.3%	U.S. stock	0.0%	conv't
0.0%	int'l stock	0.0%	preferred
0.0%	U.S. bonds	0.0%	other
0.0%	int'l bonds	2.7%	cash

Number of Investments: 69

Percent of Portfolio in Top 10 Investments: 20%

SHAREHOLDER INFORMATION

Minimum Investment

Initial: $2,500 Subsequent: $100

Minimum IRA Investment

Initial: $500 Subsequent: $100

Maximum Fees

Load: none 12b-1: none

Other: none

Services

✔ IRA

Keogh

✔ Telephone Exchange

FMI Focus
(FMIOX)

800-811-5311
www.fiduciarymgt.com

Small-Cap Stock

PERFORMANCE — fund inception date: 12/16/96

	3yr Annual	5yr Annual	10yr Annual	Bull	Bear
Return (%)	-6.8	-1.9	7.4	116.1	-34.2
Differ From Category (+/-)	4.0 high	0.5 av	3.2 abv av	-29.0 low	9.3 high

Standard Deviation	Category Risk Index	Beta
18.1%—av	0.86—low	1.10

	2008	2007	2006	2005	2004	2003	2002	2001	2000	1999
Return (%)	-30.5	3.3	12.7	4.9	7.0	48.1	-22.3	2.5	23.4	54.1
Differ From Category (+/-)	8.8	0.8	-1.8	-2.1	-9.8	0.9	-3.9	-4.9	15.3	20.0
Return, Tax-Adjusted (%)	-32.9	2.2	10.7	3.3	6.3	48.1	-22.3	2.5	20.6	51.4

PER SHARE DATA

	2008	2007	2006	2005	2004	2003	2002	2001	2000	1999
Dividends, Net Income ($)	0.00	0.00	0.00	0.00	0.00	0.00	0.00	0.00	0.03	0.00
Distrib'ns, Cap Gain ($)	4.99	2.40	4.30	3.72	1.55	0.00	0.00	0.00	3.50	2.53
Net Asset Value ($)	16.73	31.07	32.29	32.50	34.75	34.02	22.97	29.54	28.81	26.12
Expense Ratio (%)	1.53	1.52	1.50	1.48	1.43	1.47	1.46	1.46	1.59	1.81
Yield (%)	0.00	0.00	0.00	0.00	0.00	0.00	0.00	0.00	0.08	0.00
Portfolio Turnover (%)	72	41	49	63	64	53	93	165	199	239
Total Assets (Millions $)	352	850	922	1,025	1,156	1,229	599	353	268	53

PORTFOLIO (as of 9/30/08)

Portfolio Manager: Lane/Primack - 1997

Investment Style

Large Cap	Growth
Mid Cap	✔ Grth/Val
✔ Small Cap	Value

Portfolio

86.3%	U.S. stock	0.0%	conv't
0.9%	int'l stock	0.0%	preferred
0.0%	U.S. bonds	0.0%	other
0.0%	int'l bonds	12.9%	cash

Number of Investments: 74

Percent of Portfolio in Top 10 Investments: 32%

SHAREHOLDER INFORMATION

Minimum Investment

Initial: $1,000 Subsequent: $100

Minimum IRA Investment

Initial: $1,000 Subsequent: $100

Maximum Fees

Load: none 12b-1: none

Other: none

Services

✔ IRA

✔ Keogh

✔ Telephone Exchange

Gabelli Small Cap Growth AAA (GABSX)

800-422-3554
www.gabelli.com

Small-Cap Stock

PERFORMANCE — fund inception date: 10/22/91

	3yr Annual	5yr Annual	10yr Annual	Bull	Bear
Return (%)	-4.1	2.6	7.0	152.1	-34.4
Differ From Category (+/-)	6.7 high	5.0 high	2.8 abv av	7.0 abv av	9.1 high

Standard Deviation	Category Risk Index	Beta
16.8%—av	0.80—low	1.03

	2008	2007	2006	2005	2004	2003	2002	2001	2000	1999
Return (%)	-31.0	7.2	19.1	5.9	21.6	37.5	-5.4	4.6	11.3	14.2
Differ From Category (+/-)	8.3	4.7	4.6	-1.1	4.8	-9.7	13.0	-2.8	3.2	-19.9
Return, Tax-Adjusted (%)	-31.7	6.5	17.8	4.8	20.9	37.4	-5.7	4.2	6.7	11.8

PER SHARE DATA

	2008	2007	2006	2005	2004	2003	2002	2001	2000	1999
Dividends, Net Income ($)	0.00	0.00	0.00	0.00	0.00	0.00	0.00	0.01	0.05	0.00
Distrib'ns, Cap Gain ($)	1.43	1.55	2.45	2.06	1.15	0.17	0.25	0.35	4.73	2.46
Net Asset Value ($)	20.53	31.92	31.20	28.25	28.62	24.49	17.93	19.21	18.71	21.43
Expense Ratio (%)	1.43	1.41	1.44	1.44	1.42	1.45	1.45	1.45	1.49	1.56
Yield (%)	0.00	0.00	0.00	0.00	0.00	0.00	0.01	0.07	0.23	0.00
Portfolio Turnover (%)	26	15	6	6	10	4	10	17	47	24
Total Assets (Millions $)	750	1,016	749	736	703	622	453	440	374	338

PORTFOLIO (as of 9/30/08)

Portfolio Manager: Gabelli - 1991

Investment Style

Large Cap	Growth
✔ Mid Cap	✔ Grth/Val
✔ Small Cap	Value

Portfolio

79.6%	U.S. stock	0.0%	conv't
7.8%	int'l stock	0.1%	preferred
0.0%	U.S. bonds	0.0%	other
0.0%	int'l bonds	12.5%	cash

Number of Investments: 580

Percent of Portfolio in Top 10 Investments: 18%

SHAREHOLDER INFORMATION

Minimum Investment

Initial: $1,000 Subsequent: $0

Minimum IRA Investment

Initial: $0 Subsequent: $0

Maximum Fees

Load: 2.00% redemption 12b-1: 0.25%

Other: redemption fee applies for 7 days

Services

✔ IRA

Keogh

✔ Telephone Exchange

Heartland Value (HRTVX)

800-432-7856
www.heartlandfunds.com

Small-Cap Stock

PERFORMANCE — fund inception date: 12/28/84

	3yr Annual	5yr Annual	10yr Annual	Bull	Bear
Return (%)	-9.9	-4.1	7.3	163.8	-44.4
Differ From Category (+/-)	0.9 av	-1.7 blw av	3.1 abv av	18.7 abv av	-0.9 av

Standard Deviation	Category Risk Index	Beta
21.8%—abv av	1.04—abv av	1.24

	2008	2007	2006	2005	2004	2003	2002	2001	2000	1999
Return (%)	-39.6	-5.6	28.0	1.9	9.1	70.1	-11.5	29.4	2.0	25.0
Differ From Category (+/-)	-0.3	-8.1	13.5	-5.1	-7.7	22.9	6.9	22.0	-6.1	-9.1
Return, Tax-Adjusted (%)	-39.6	-7.6	25.9	0.1	7.4	69.0	-12.4	26.2	-0.2	24.9

PER SHARE DATA

	2008	2007	2006	2005	2004	2003	2002	2001	2000	1999
Dividends, Net Income ($)	0.00	0.24	0.30	0.00	0.00	0.00	0.00	0.00	0.00	0.00
Distrib'ns, Cap Gain ($)	0.08	6.63	5.86	6.03	5.67	2.36	1.53	5.19	4.03	0.10
Net Asset Value ($)	25.04	41.50	51.22	44.80	49.81	51.14	31.46	37.25	32.98	36.50
Expense Ratio (%)	na	1.14	1.12	1.17	1.20	1.28	1.29	1.29	1.22	1.34
Yield (%)	0.00	0.49	0.52	0.00	0.00	0.00	0.00	0.00	0.00	0.00
Portfolio Turnover (%)	na	56	49	36	32	48	49	56	48	23
Total Assets (Millions $)	876	1,710	2,019	1,552	1,876	2,185	924	1,093	896	1,196

PORTFOLIO (as of 9/30/08)

Portfolio Manager: Nasgovitz/Evans/Denison - 1984

Investment Style

Large Cap	Growth
Mid Cap	Grth/Val
✔ Small Cap	✔ Value

Portfolio

82.2%	U.S. stock	0.0%	conv't
10.4%	int'l stock	0.0%	preferred
0.0%	U.S. bonds	0.0%	other
0.0%	int'l bonds	7.4%	cash

Number of Investments: 186

Percent of Portfolio in Top 10 Investments: 26%

SHAREHOLDER INFORMATION

Minimum Investment

Initial: $1,000 Subsequent: $100

Minimum IRA Investment

Initial: $500 Subsequent: $0

Maximum Fees

Load: 2.00% redemption 12b-1: 0.25%

Other: redemption fee applies for 10 days

Services

✔ IRA

✔ Keogh

✔ Telephone Exchange

Heartland Value Plus (HRVIX)

800-432-7856
www.heartlandfunds.com

Small-Cap Stock

PERFORMANCE — fund inception date: 10/26/93

	3yr Annual	5yr Annual	10yr Annual	Bull	Bear
Return (%)	-0.8	2.9	7.8	145.5	-22.6
Differ From Category (+/-)	10.0 high	5.3 high	3.6 high	0.4 av	20.9 high

Standard Deviation	Category Risk Index	Beta
16.9%—av	0.80—low	0.93

	2008	2007	2006	2005	2004	2003	2002	2001	2000	1999
Return (%)	-17.9	4.7	13.6	1.3	16.9	53.5	-3.8	34.7	-8.9	1.6
Differ From Category (+/-)	21.4	2.2	-0.9	-5.7	0.1	6.3	14.6	27.3	-17.0	-32.5
Return, Tax-Adjusted (%)	-18.0	1.7	12.1	0.5	16.5	53.5	-4.1	34.1	-9.7	0.4

PER SHARE DATA

	2008	2007	2006	2005	2004	2003	2002	2001	2000	1999
Dividends, Net Income ($)	0.10	0.42	0.20	0.16	0.07	0.05	0.12	0.18	0.29	0.44
Distrib'ns, Cap Gain ($)	0.00	4.89	2.41	1.20	0.65	0.00	0.00	0.00	0.00	0.00
Net Asset Value ($)	18.70	22.87	26.78	25.85	26.85	23.57	15.39	16.12	12.11	13.57
Expense Ratio (%)	na	1.21	1.26	1.25	1.23	1.34	1.44	1.48	1.36	1.39
Yield (%)	0.55	1.51	0.67	0.59	0.24	0.21	0.80	1.08	2.40	3.21
Portfolio Turnover (%)	na	107	45	36	57	68	65	80	121	82
Total Assets (Millions $)	672	239	240	275	417	219	58	60	44	87

PORTFOLIO (as of 9/30/08)

Portfolio Manager: Evans/Peck/Petroff - 2006

Investment Style

Large Cap	Growth
✔ Mid Cap	Grth/Val
✔ Small Cap	✔ Value

Portfolio

85.2%	U.S. stock	0.0%	conv't
0.0%	int'l stock	0.0%	preferred
0.0%	U.S. bonds	0.0%	other
0.0%	int'l bonds	14.8%	cash

Number of Investments: 57

Percent of Portfolio in Top 10 Investments: 41%

SHAREHOLDER INFORMATION

Minimum Investment

Initial: $1,000 Subsequent: $100

Minimum IRA Investment

Initial: $500 Subsequent: $0

Maximum Fees

Load: 2.00% redemption 12b-1: 0.25%

Other: redemption fee applies for 10 days

Services

✔ IRA
✔ Keogh
✔ Telephone Exchange

HighMark Cognitive Value M (HCLMX)

800-433-6884
www.highmarkfunds.com

Small-Cap Stock

PERFORMANCE — fund inception date: 5/29/01

	3yr Annual	5yr Annual	10yr Annual	Bull	Bear
Return (%)	-8.1	-0.9	na	133.2	-38.7
Differ From Category (+/-)	2.7 abv av	1.5 abv av	na	-11.9 blw av	4.8 abv av

Standard Deviation	Category Risk Index	Beta
18.5%—av	0.88—low	1.11

	2008	2007	2006	2005	2004	2003	2002	2001	2000	1999
Return (%)	-33.1	-5.0	22.1	5.7	16.6	39.8	-16.1	—	—	—
Differ From Category (+/-)	6.2	-7.5	7.6	-1.3	-0.2	-7.4	2.3	—	—	—
Return, Tax-Adjusted (%)	-33.2	-6.7	20.1	3.7	15.0	39.8	-16.1	—	—	—

PER SHARE DATA

	2008	2007	2006	2005	2004	2003	2002	2001	2000	1999
Dividends, Net Income ($)	0.09	0.10	0.06	0.03	0.03	0.00	0.01	—	—	—
Distrib'ns, Cap Gain ($)	0.00	1.38	1.49	1.75	1.28	0.00	0.01	—	—	—
Net Asset Value ($)	7.19	10.87	12.97	11.89	12.92	12.21	8.73	—	—	—
Expense Ratio (%)	1.01	0.94	1.00	1.09	1.14	1.60	1.57	—	—	—
Yield (%)	1.22	0.78	0.40	0.24	0.19	0.00	0.09	—	—	—
Portfolio Turnover (%)	109	103	76	59	76	65	51	—	—	—
Total Assets (Millions $)	64	95	101	85	83	82	57	—	—	—

PORTFOLIO (as of 11/30/08)

Portfolio Manager: Mudge III/Sokoloff - 2001

Investment Style

Large Cap	Growth
Mid Cap	Grth/Val
✔ Small Cap	✔ Value

Portfolio

98.7% U.S. stock	0.0% conv't
0.5% int'l stock	0.0% preferred
0.0% U.S. bonds	0.0% other
0.0% int'l bonds	0.8% cash

Number of Investments: 251

Percent of Portfolio in Top 10 Investments: 10%

SHAREHOLDER INFORMATION

Minimum Investment

Initial: $5,000 Subsequent: $100

Minimum IRA Investment

Initial: $0 Subsequent: $0

Maximum Fees

Load: 2.00% redemption 12b-1: none

Other: redemption fee applies for 30 days

Services

✔ IRA

Keogh

✔ Telephone Exchange

Janus Triton
(JATTX)

800-525-0020
www.janus.com

Small-Cap Stock

PERFORMANCE — fund inception date: 2/25/05

	3yr Annual	5yr Annual	10yr Annual	Bull	Bear
Return (%)	-6.0	na	na	na	-43.6
Differ From Category (+/-)	4.8 high	na	na	na	-0.1 av

Standard Deviation	Category Risk Index	Beta
21.3%—abv av	1.01—abv av	1.26

	2008	2007	2006	2005	2004	2003	2002	2001	2000	1999
Return (%)	-40.6	20.6	15.8	—	—	—	—	—	—	—
Differ From Category (+/-)	-1.3	18.1	1.3	—	—	—	—	—	—	—
Return, Tax-Adjusted (%)	-40.6	18.5	15.6	—	—	—	—	—	—	—

PER SHARE DATA

	2008	2007	2006	2005	2004	2003	2002	2001	2000	1999
Dividends, Net Income ($)	0.00	1.42	0.03	—	—	—	—	—	—	—
Distrib'ns, Cap Gain ($)	0.00	0.48	0.15	—	—	—	—	—	—	—
Net Asset Value ($)	8.50	14.30	13.46	—	—	—	—	—	—	—
Expense Ratio (%)	na	1.11	1.09	—	—	—	—	—	—	—
Yield (%)	0.04	9.60	0.19	—	—	—	—	—	—	—
Portfolio Turnover (%)	na	93	262	—	—	—	—	—	—	—
Total Assets (Millions $)	112	146	120	—	—	—	—	—	—	—

PORTFOLIO (as of 9/30/08)

Portfolio Manager: Meade/Schaub - 2006

Investment Style

Large Cap	✔ Growth
Mid Cap	Grth/Val
✔ Small Cap	Value

Portfolio

88.5% U.S. stock	0.0% conv't
6.7% int'l stock	0.0% preferred
0.0% U.S. bonds	0.1% other
0.0% int'l bonds	4.7% cash

Number of Investments: 85

Percent of Portfolio in Top 10 Investments: 23%

SHAREHOLDER INFORMATION

Minimum Investment

Initial: $2,500 — Subsequent: $100

Minimum IRA Investment

Initial: $1,000 — Subsequent: $100

Maximum Fees

Load: none — 12b-1: none

Other: none

Services

✔ IRA

✔ Keogh

✔ Telephone Exchange

Kalmar Growth-With-Value Small Cap (KGSCX)

800-282-2319
www.kalmarinvestments.com

Small-Cap Stock

PERFORMANCE — fund inception date: 4/11/97

	3yr Annual	5yr Annual	10yr Annual	Bull	Bear
Return (%)	-10.7	-3.3	2.2	126.5	-43.8
Differ From Category (+/-)	0.1 av	-0.9 blw av	-2.0 blw av	-18.6 blw av	-0.3 av

Standard Deviation	Category Risk Index	Beta
19.6%—abv av	0.93—blw av	1.18

	2008	2007	2006	2005	2004	2003	2002	2001	2000	1999
Return (%)	-40.4	12.6	6.1	5.2	12.8	43.5	-16.6	0.0	15.6	6.0
Differ From Category (+/-)	-1.1	10.1	-8.4	-1.8	-4.0	-3.7	1.8	-7.4	7.6	-28.1
Return, Tax-Adjusted (%)	-40.4	9.4	5.4	4.7	12.2	42.5	-16.6	0.0	11.8	6.0

PER SHARE DATA

	2008	2007	2006	2005	2004	2003	2002	2001	2000	1999
Dividends, Net Income ($)	0.00	0.00	0.00	0.00	0.00	0.00	0.00	0.00	0.00	0.00
Distrib'ns, Cap Gain ($)	0.00	3.66	0.75	0.49	0.53	0.72	0.00	0.00	2.59	0.00
Net Asset Value ($)	9.13	15.30	16.81	16.53	16.17	14.80	10.81	12.95	12.95	13.41
Expense Ratio (%)	na	1.34	1.32	1.29	1.27	1.26	1.23	1.23	1.22	1.25
Yield (%)	0.00	0.00	0.00	0.00	0.00	0.00	0.00	0.00	0.00	0.00
Portfolio Turnover (%)	na	38	31	30	23	46	40	46	63	52
Total Assets (Millions $)	214	358	435	415	372	270	171	208	214	195

PORTFOLIO (as of 10/31/08)

Portfolio Manager: Draper Jr./Hartley/Walker - 1997

Investment Style

Large Cap	✔ Growth
✔ Mid Cap	Grth/Val
✔ Small Cap	Value

Portfolio

82.0%	U.S. stock	0.0%	conv't
5.9%	int'l stock	0.0%	preferred
0.0%	U.S. bonds	0.0%	other
0.0%	int'l bonds	12.1%	cash

Number of Investments: 92

Percent of Portfolio in Top 10 Investments: 31%

SHAREHOLDER INFORMATION

Minimum Investment

Initial: $10,000 Subsequent: $1,000

Minimum IRA Investment

Initial: $1,000 Subsequent: $0

Maximum Fees

Load: 2.00% redemption 12b-1: none

Other: redemption fee applies for 90 days

Services

✔ IRA

Keogh

✔ Telephone Exchange

LKCM Small Cap Equity Instl (LKSCX)

800-688-5526
www.lkcm.com

Small-Cap Stock

PERFORMANCE

fund inception date: 7/14/94

	3yr Annual	5yr Annual	10yr Annual	Bull	Bear
Return (%)	-11.4	-0.6	4.9	149.4	-43.9
Differ From Category (+/-)	-0.6 blw av	1.8 abv av	0.7 av	4.3 abv av	-0.4 av

Standard Deviation	Category Risk Index	Beta
20.5%—abv av	0.98—av	1.20

	2008	2007	2006	2005	2004	2003	2002	2001	2000	1999
Return (%)	-38.9	-0.8	14.9	14.4	22.0	34.7	-11.8	7.5	11.3	16.8
Differ From Category (+/-)	0.4	-3.3	0.4	7.4	5.2	-12.5	6.6	0.1	3.2	-17.3
Return, Tax-Adjusted (%)	-38.9	-2.0	13.3	12.0	20.2	33.7	-11.9	6.2	7.8	16.4

PER SHARE DATA

	2008	2007	2006	2005	2004	2003	2002	2001	2000	1999
Dividends, Net Income ($)	0.00	0.00	0.00	0.00	0.00	0.00	0.00	0.07	0.05	0.03
Distrib'ns, Cap Gain ($)	0.01	1.79	2.32	3.46	2.40	1.00	0.01	0.92	3.10	0.25
Net Asset Value ($)	12.24	20.03	21.98	21.12	21.46	19.54	15.24	17.29	17.00	18.08
Expense Ratio (%)	na	0.94	0.96	0.99	0.96	0.97	0.94	0.92	0.93	0.90
Yield (%)	0.00	0.00	0.00	0.00	0.00	0.00	0.03	0.40	0.24	0.15
Portfolio Turnover (%)	na	60	56	56	53	43	52	62	79	48
Total Assets (Millions $)	386	595	607	370	344	267	207	221	211	230

PORTFOLIO (as of 9/30/08)

Portfolio Manager: King Jr./Purvis - 1994

Investment Style

Large Cap	Growth
Mid Cap	✔ Grth/Val
✔ Small Cap	Value

Portfolio

91.2% U.S. stock	0.0% conv't
0.0% int'l stock	0.0% preferred
0.0% U.S. bonds	2.7% other
0.0% int'l bonds	6.1% cash

Number of Investments: 91
Percent of Portfolio in Top 10 Investments: 18%

SHAREHOLDER INFORMATION

Minimum Investment
Initial: $10,000 Subsequent: $1,000

Minimum IRA Investment
Initial: $0 Subsequent: $0

Maximum Fees
Load: 1.00% redemption 12b-1: none
Other: redemption fee applies for 30 days

Services
✔ IRA
✔ Keogh
✔ Telephone Exchange

Neuberger Berman Small Cap Growth Inv (NBMIX)

800-877-9700
www.nb.com

Small-Cap Stock

PERFORMANCE — fund inception date: 10/20/98

	3yr Annual	5yr Annual	10yr Annual	Bull	Bear
Return (%)	-7.7	1.0	0.9	166.1	-44.7
Differ From Category (+/-)	3.1 abv av	3.4 high	-3.3 low	21.0 abv av	-1.2 blw av

Standard Deviation	Category Risk Index	Beta
19.5%—abv av	0.93—blw av	1.15

	2008	2007	2006	2005	2004	2003	2002	2001	2000	1999
Return (%)	-42.3	26.4	7.9	15.2	16.2	33.2	-44.5	-14.5	-28.7	130.4
Differ From Category (+/-)	-3.0	23.9	-6.6	8.2	-0.6	-14.0	-26.1	-21.9	-36.8	96.3
Return, Tax-Adjusted (%)	-42.3	26.4	7.9	15.2	16.2	33.2	-44.5	-14.5	-31.8	128.0

PER SHARE DATA

	2008	2007	2006	2005	2004	2003	2002	2001	2000	1999
Dividends, Net Income ($)	0.00	0.00	0.00	0.00	0.00	0.00	0.00	0.00	0.00	0.00
Distrib'ns, Cap Gain ($)	0.00	0.00	0.00	0.00	0.00	0.00	0.00	0.00	5.10	1.84
Net Asset Value ($)	12.05	20.87	16.51	15.29	13.27	11.42	8.57	15.43	18.04	32.87
Expense Ratio (%)	1.29	1.27	1.57	1.75	1.71	1.75	1.62	1.47	1.38	0.75
Yield (%)	0.00	0.00	0.00	0.00	0.00	0.00	0.00	0.00	0.00	0.00
Portfolio Turnover (%)	185	153	142	204	146	241	126	158	176	208
Total Assets (Millions $)	184	123	48	50	49	57	54	124	182	205

PORTFOLIO (as of 9/30/08)

Portfolio Manager: Burshtan - 2003

Investment Style

Large Cap	✔ Growth
Mid Cap	Grth/Val
✔ Small Cap	Value

Portfolio

94.4% U.S. stock	0.0% conv't
1.6% int'l stock	0.0% preferred
0.0% U.S. bonds	0.0% other
0.0% int'l bonds	4.0% cash

Number of Investments: 65

Percent of Portfolio in Top 10 Investments: 26%

SHAREHOLDER INFORMATION

Minimum Investment

Initial: $1,000 Subsequent: $100

Minimum IRA Investment

Initial: $1,000 Subsequent: $0

Maximum Fees

Load: none 12b-1: none

Other: none

Services

✔ IRA

✔ Keogh

✔ Telephone Exchange

Nicholas Limited Edition I (NCLEX)

800-544-6547
www.nicholasfunds.com

Small-Cap Stock

PERFORMANCE — fund inception date: 5/18/87

	3yr Annual	5yr Annual	10yr Annual	Bull	Bear
Return (%)	-6.3	0.2	0.2	126.1	-33.5
Differ From Category (+/-)	4.5 high	2.6 abv av	-4.0 low	-19.0 blw av	10.0 high

Standard Deviation	Category Risk Index	Beta
17.3%—av	0.82—low	1.04

	2008	2007	2006	2005	2004	2003	2002	2001	2000	1999
Return (%)	-30.3	11.1	6.3	7.7	13.9	39.5	-23.6	8.2	-8.7	-4.1
Differ From Category (+/-)	9.0	8.7	-8.2	0.7	-2.9	-7.7	-5.2	0.8	-16.8	-38.2
Return, Tax-Adjusted (%)	-30.4	9.8	5.7	6.3	13.7	39.5	-23.6	8.1	-13.8	-4.7

PER SHARE DATA

	2008	2007	2006	2005	2004	2003	2002	2001	2000	1999
Dividends, Net Income ($)	0.03	0.00	0.00	0.00	0.00	0.00	0.00	0.00	0.21	0.05
Distrib'ns, Cap Gain ($)	0.03	1.76	0.84	1.89	0.27	0.00	0.03	0.04	5.37	0.54
Net Asset Value ($)	13.93	20.07	19.62	19.23	19.59	17.43	12.49	16.37	15.16	22.61
Expense Ratio (%)	na	0.91	0.92	0.95	0.91	0.91	0.90	0.89	0.86	0.87
Yield (%)	0.21	0.00	0.00	0.00	0.00	0.00	0.00	0.00	1.02	0.23
Portfolio Turnover (%)	na	26	31	37	35	40	58	61	82	36
Total Assets (Millions $)	115	168	172	170	159	146	108	164	191	279

PORTFOLIO (as of 12/31/08)

Portfolio Manager: Nicholas - 1993

Investment Style

Large Cap	✔ Growth
✔ Mid Cap	Grth/Val
✔ Small Cap	Value

Portfolio

91.8%	U.S. stock	0.0%	conv't
1.1%	int'l stock	0.0%	preferred
0.0%	U.S. bonds	0.0%	other
0.0%	int'l bonds	7.1%	cash

Number of Investments: 95

Percent of Portfolio in Top 10 Investments: 28%

SHAREHOLDER INFORMATION

Minimum Investment

Initial: $100,000 Subsequent: $100

Minimum IRA Investment

Initial: $100,000 Subsequent: $100

Maximum Fees

Load: none 12b-1: none

Other: limited number of shares

Services

✔ IRA

✔ Keogh

✔ Telephone Exchange

Northern Small Cap Index (NSIDX)

800-595-9111
www.northernfunds.com

Small-Cap Stock

PERFORMANCE — fund inception date: 9/3/99

	3yr Annual	5yr Annual	10yr Annual	Bull	Bear
Return (%)	-8.7	-1.4	na	136.6	-38.8
Differ From Category (+/-)	2.1 abv av	1.0 av	na	-8.5 av	4.7 abv av

Standard Deviation	Category Risk Index	Beta
20.1%—abv av	0.96—av	1.20

	2008	2007	2006	2005	2004	2003	2002	2001	2000	1999
Return (%)	-34.1	-2.0	17.8	4.1	17.4	46.0	-21.0	1.6	-3.8	—
Differ From Category (+/-)	5.2	-4.5	3.3	-2.8	0.6	-1.2	-2.6	-5.8	-11.9	—
Return, Tax-Adjusted (%)	-35.4	-3.3	15.4	3.9	17.4	45.9	-21.3	1.4	-9.5	—

PER SHARE DATA

	2008	2007	2006	2005	2004	2003	2002	2001	2000	1999
Dividends, Net Income ($)	0.10	0.13	0.09	0.07	0.03	0.04	0.05	0.03	0.10	—
Distrib'ns, Cap Gain ($)	0.73	0.82	1.58	0.11	0.00	0.00	0.01	0.01	3.03	—
Net Asset Value ($)	5.44	9.55	10.72	10.52	10.27	8.77	6.03	7.71	7.63	—
Expense Ratio (%)	0.35	0.35	0.35	0.62	0.65	0.65	0.65	0.65	1.00	—
Yield (%)	1.61	1.28	0.72	0.70	0.30	0.43	0.80	0.40	0.98	—
Portfolio Turnover (%)	19	22	22	31	27	51	28	65	—	—
Total Assets (Millions $)	176	343	377	428	387	327	206	263	83	—

PORTFOLIO (as of 9/30/08)

Portfolio Manager: Rakvin/Reeder - 2005

Investment Style

Large Cap	Growth
Mid Cap	✔ Grth/Val
✔ Small Cap	Value

Portfolio

96.3% U.S. stock	0.0% conv't
0.6% int'l stock	0.0% preferred
0.0% U.S. bonds	0.1% other
0.0% int'l bonds	3.0% cash

Number of Investments: 1,912
Percent of Portfolio in Top 10 Investments: 7%

SHAREHOLDER INFORMATION

Minimum Investment
Initial: $2,500 Subsequent: $50

Minimum IRA Investment
Initial: $500 Subsequent: $50

Maximum Fees
Load: none 12b-1: none
Other: none

Services
✔ IRA
✔ Keogh
✔ Telephone Exchange

Northern Small Cap Value (NOSGX)

800-595-9111
www.northernfunds.com

Small-Cap Stock

PERFORMANCE — fund inception date: 3/31/94

	3yr Annual	5yr Annual	10yr Annual	Bull	Bear
Return (%)	-5.7	2.1	6.6	135.4	-29.0
Differ From Category (+/-)	5.1 high	4.5 high	2.4 abv av	-9.7 av	14.5 high

Standard Deviation	Category Risk Index	Beta
17.6%—av	0.84—low	1.00

	2008	2007	2006	2005	2004	2003	2002	2001	2000	1999
Return (%)	-23.5	-8.8	20.2	8.0	22.5	41.5	-6.3	5.8	8.4	12.1
Differ From Category (+/-)	15.8	-11.3	5.7	1.0	5.7	-5.7	12.1	-1.6	0.3	-22.0
Return, Tax-Adjusted (%)	-23.6	-9.9	18.3	6.8	21.5	41.4	-6.4	4.8	1.7	10.2

PER SHARE DATA

	2008	2007	2006	2005	2004	2003	2002	2001	2000	1999
Dividends, Net Income ($)	0.11	0.14	0.12	0.08	0.14	0.10	0.04	0.01	0.06	0.11
Distrib'ns, Cap Gain ($)	0.00	1.11	1.85	1.18	0.80	0.00	0.00	0.51	4.66	1.14
Net Asset Value ($)	10.52	13.89	16.60	15.45	15.46	13.40	9.54	10.22	10.15	14.10
Expense Ratio (%)	1.00	1.00	1.00	1.00	1.00	1.00	1.00	1.00	1.00	1.00
Yield (%)	1.06	0.91	0.62	0.46	0.88	0.77	0.45	0.11	0.37	0.73
Portfolio Turnover (%)	47	41	32	23	51	69	77	16	18	18
Total Assets (Millions $)	1,106	929	689	513	484	383	258	247	154	240

PORTFOLIO (as of 9/30/08)

Portfolio Manager: Bergson - 2001

Investment Style

Large Cap	Growth
Mid Cap	Grth/Val
✔ Small Cap	✔ Value

Portfolio

96.2% U.S. stock	0.0% conv't
0.2% int'l stock	0.0% preferred
0.0% U.S. bonds	0.0% other
0.0% int'l bonds	3.6% cash

Number of Investments: 620

Percent of Portfolio in Top 10 Investments: 13%

SHAREHOLDER INFORMATION

Minimum Investment

Initial: $2,500 — Subsequent: $50

Minimum IRA Investment

Initial: $500 — Subsequent: $50

Maximum Fees

Load: none — 12b-1: none

Other: none

Services

✔ IRA
✔ Keogh
✔ Telephone Exchange

Pinnacle Value (PVFIX)

877-369-3705
www.pinnaclevaluefund.com

Small-Cap Stock

PERFORMANCE — fund inception date: 4/1/03

	3yr Annual	5yr Annual	10yr Annual	Bull	Bear
Return (%)	2.8	7.1	na	na	-17.9
Differ From Category (+/-)	13.6 high	9.5 high	na	na	25.6 high

Standard Deviation	Category Risk Index	Beta
9.0%—blw av	0.43—low	0.46

	2008	2007	2006	2005	2004	2003	2002	2001	2000	1999
Return (%)	-16.9	15.4	13.2	8.5	19.7	—	—	—	—	—
Differ From Category (+/-)	22.4	12.9	-1.3	1.5	2.9	—	—	—	—	—
Return, Tax-Adjusted (%)	-18.3	15.0	12.0	7.5	18.8	—	—	—	—	—

PER SHARE DATA

	2008	2007	2006	2005	2004	2003	2002	2001	2000	1999
Dividends, Net Income ($)	0.14	0.17	0.21	0.09	0.64	—	—	—	—	—
Distrib'ns, Cap Gain ($)	1.33	0.18	0.81	0.75	0.00	—	—	—	—	—
Net Asset Value ($)	11.45	15.57	13.80	13.09	12.84	—	—	—	—	—
Expense Ratio (%)	na	1.49	1.49	1.49	0.00	—	—	—	—	—
Yield (%)	1.09	1.09	1.41	0.68	4.98	—	—	—	—	—
Portfolio Turnover (%)	na	27	29	28	72	—	—	—	—	—
Total Assets (Millions $)	57	64	30	17	—	—	—	—	—	—

PORTFOLIO (as of 9/30/08)

Portfolio Manager: Deysher - 2003

Investment Style

Large Cap Growth
Mid Cap Grth/Val
✔ Small Cap ✔ Value

Portfolio

40.2%	U.S. stock	0.0%	conv't
1.0%	int'l stock	0.6%	preferred
0.0%	U.S. bonds	0.0%	other
0.0%	int'l bonds	58.2%	cash

Number of Investments: 36
Percent of Portfolio in Top 10 Investments: 85%

SHAREHOLDER INFORMATION

Minimum Investment
Initial: $2,500 Subsequent: $100

Minimum IRA Investment
Initial: $1,500 Subsequent: $100

Maximum Fees
Load: 1.00% redemption 12b-1: none
Other: redemption fee applies for 1 year

Services
✔ IRA
Keogh
Telephone Exchange

Royce Heritage Svc (RGFAX)

800-221-4268
www.roycefunds.com

Small-Cap Stock

PERFORMANCE — fund inception date: 12/27/95

	3yr Annual	5yr Annual	10yr Annual	Bull	Bear
Return (%)	-7.5	0.7	8.2	153.4	-40.5
Differ From Category (+/-)	3.3 abv av	3.1 high	4.0 high	8.3 abv av	3.0 abv av

Standard Deviation	Category Risk Index	Beta
21.4%—abv av	1.02—abv av	1.29

	2008	2007	2006	2005	2004	2003	2002	2001	2000	1999
Return (%)	-36.3	1.2	22.6	8.7	20.3	38.0	-19.0	20.5	11.7	41.7
Differ From Category (+/-)	3.0	-1.3	8.1	1.7	3.5	-9.2	-0.6	13.1	3.6	7.6
Return, Tax-Adjusted (%)	-36.6	-0.4	21.1	6.8	18.3	37.6	-19.5	19.3	9.2	38.2

PER SHARE DATA

	2008	2007	2006	2005	2004	2003	2002	2001	2000	1999
Dividends, Net Income ($)	0.00	0.00	0.00	0.00	0.00	0.00	0.00	0.00	0.00	0.00
Distrib'ns, Cap Gain ($)	0.25	1.42	1.21	1.68	1.64	0.27	0.28	0.56	1.25	1.45
Net Asset Value ($)	7.95	12.88	14.09	12.47	13.00	12.19	9.03	11.47	9.99	10.10
Expense Ratio (%)	na	1.27	1.32	1.43	1.49	1.49	1.49	1.49	1.49	1.49
Yield (%)	0.00	0.00	0.00	0.00	0.00	0.00	0.00	0.00	0.00	0.00
Portfolio Turnover (%)	na	138	98	142	86	25	66	53	90	152
Total Assets (Millions $)	78	104	95	59	53	34	23	26	19	15

PORTFOLIO (as of 9/30/08)

Portfolio Manager: Royce/Harvey - 1995

Investment Style

Large Cap	Growth
Mid Cap	✔ Grth/Val
✔ Small Cap	Value

Portfolio

77.1%	U.S. stock	0.0%	conv't
11.8%	int'l stock	0.0%	preferred
0.0%	U.S. bonds	5.8%	other
0.0%	int'l bonds	5.3%	cash

Number of Investments: 175
Percent of Portfolio in Top 10 Investments: 21%

SHAREHOLDER INFORMATION

Minimum Investment
Initial: $2,000 Subsequent: $50

Minimum IRA Investment
Initial: $1,000 Subsequent: $100

Maximum Fees
Load: 1.00% redemption 12b-1: 0.25%
Other: redemption fee applies for 180 days

Services
✔ IRA
Keogh
✔ Telephone Exchange

Royce Low Priced Stock Svc (RYLPX)

800-221-4268
www.roycefunds.com

Small-Cap Stock

PERFORMANCE — fund inception date: 12/15/93

	3yr Annual	5yr Annual	10yr Annual	Bull	Bear
Return (%)	-8.0	-0.6	8.9	154.1	-40.1
Differ From Category (+/-)	2.8 abv av	1.8 abv av	4.7 high	9.0 abv av	3.4 abv av

Standard Deviation	Category Risk Index	Beta
22.4%—high	1.07—abv av	1.27

	2008	2007	2006	2005	2004	2003	2002	2001	2000	1999
Return (%)	-36.0	2.3	18.9	9.6	13.6	44.0	-16.3	25.0	23.9	29.7
Differ From Category (+/-)	3.3	-0.2	4.4	2.6	-3.2	-3.2	2.1	17.6	15.8	-4.4
Return, Tax-Adjusted (%)	-36.3	0.1	17.3	8.4	13.0	43.9	-16.4	25.0	22.1	27.5

PER SHARE DATA

	2008	2007	2006	2005	2004	2003	2002	2001	2000	1999
Dividends, Net Income ($)	0.00	0.42	0.13	0.00	0.00	0.00	0.00	0.00	0.00	0.00
Distrib'ns, Cap Gain ($)	0.27	2.05	1.53	1.28	0.55	0.06	0.02	0.02	0.74	0.79
Net Asset Value ($)	9.16	14.78	16.83	15.53	15.33	13.98	9.75	11.67	9.35	8.16
Expense Ratio (%)	na	1.49	1.46	1.49	1.49	1.49	1.49	1.49	1.49	1.49
Yield (%)	0.00	2.48	0.68	0.00	0.00	0.00	0.00	0.00	0.00	0.00
Portfolio Turnover (%)	na	30	27	21	26	42	29	31	56	103
Total Assets (Millions $)	1,869	3,337	4,067	3,932	4,770	3,044	1,789	1,016	130	24

PORTFOLIO (as of 9/30/08)

Portfolio Manager: George/Skinner, III - 2000

Investment Style

Large Cap	Growth
Mid Cap	✔ Grth/Val
✔ Small Cap	Value

Portfolio

65.5%	U.S. stock	0.0%	conv't
21.5%	int'l stock	0.0%	preferred
0.0%	U.S. bonds	2.8%	other
0.0%	int'l bonds	10.3%	cash

Number of Investments: 193

Percent of Portfolio in Top 10 Investments: 26%

SHAREHOLDER INFORMATION

Minimum Investment

Initial: $2,000 — Subsequent: $50

Minimum IRA Investment

Initial: $1,000 — Subsequent: $100

Maximum Fees

Load: 1.00% redemption — 12b-1: 0.25%

Other: redemption fee applies for 180 days

Services

✔ IRA

✔ Keogh

✔ Telephone Exchange

Royce Pennsylvania Mutual Invt (PENNX)

800-221-4268
www.roycefunds.com

Small-Cap Stock

PERFORMANCE — fund inception date: 12/12/62

	3yr Annual	5yr Annual	10yr Annual	Bull	Bear
Return (%)	-8.4	0.7	7.0	151.6	-38.7
Differ From Category (+/-)	2.4 abv av	3.1 high	2.8 abv av	6.5 abv av	4.8 abv av

Standard Deviation	Category Risk Index	Beta
19.5%—abv av	0.93—blw av	1.18

	2008	2007	2006	2005	2004	2003	2002	2001	2000	1999
Return (%)	-34.8	2.7	14.7	12.5	20.2	40.2	-9.3	18.3	18.3	5.9
Differ From Category (+/-)	4.5	0.2	0.2	5.5	3.4	-7.0	9.1	10.9	10.2	-28.2
Return, Tax-Adjusted (%)	-35.0	1.3	13.6	11.5	19.3	39.4	-9.6	16.2	13.7	4.5

PER SHARE DATA

	2008	2007	2006	2005	2004	2003	2002	2001	2000	1999
Dividends, Net Income ($)	0.01	0.08	0.04	0.00	0.00	0.00	0.00	0.02	0.05	0.04
Distrib'ns, Cap Gain ($)	0.10	1.01	0.77	0.63	0.53	0.36	0.12	0.70	1.59	0.45
Net Asset Value ($)	6.94	10.82	11.57	10.78	10.14	8.88	6.59	7.39	6.88	7.28
Expense Ratio (%)	na	0.88	0.87	0.90	0.89	0.93	0.94	0.99	1.03	1.04
Yield (%)	0.12	0.68	0.30	0.00	0.00	0.00	0.00	0.28	0.59	0.51
Portfolio Turnover (%)	na	43	38	26	32	30	33	39	45	21
Total Assets (Millions $)	2,303	3,158	2,866	1,850	1,242	839	462	445	370	371

PORTFOLIO (as of 9/30/08)

Portfolio Manager: Royce/Kaplan/Harvey/Romeo - 1973

Investment Style

Large Cap	Growth
✔ Mid Cap	✔ Grth/Val
✔ Small Cap	Value

Portfolio

85.6%	U.S. stock	0.0%	conv't
7.7%	int'l stock	0.0%	preferred
0.0%	U.S. bonds	2.7%	other
0.0%	int'l bonds	4.0%	cash

Number of Investments: 502
Percent of Portfolio in Top 10 Investments: 13%

SHAREHOLDER INFORMATION

Minimum Investment
Initial: $2,000 Subsequent: $50

Minimum IRA Investment
Initial: $1,000 Subsequent: $100

Maximum Fees
Load: 1.00% redemption 12b-1: none
Other: redemption fee applies for 180 days

Services
✔ IRA
✔ Keogh
✔ Telephone Exchange

Royce Special Equity Invt (RYSEX)

800-221-4268
www.roycefunds.com

Small-Cap Stock

PERFORMANCE — fund inception date: 5/1/98

	3yr Annual	5yr Annual	10yr Annual	Bull	Bear
Return (%)	-1.4	1.6	8.1	87.9	-21.9
Differ From Category (+/-)	9.4 high	4.0 high	3.9 high	-57.2 low	21.6 high

Standard Deviation	Category Risk Index	Beta
14.5%—blw av	0.69—low	0.78

	2008	2007	2006	2005	2004	2003	2002	2001	2000	1999
Return (%)	-19.7	4.7	14.0	-1.0	13.9	27.6	15.3	30.7	16.2	-9.7
Differ From Category (+/-)	19.6	2.2	-0.5	-8.0	-2.9	-19.6	33.7	23.3	8.2	-43.8
Return, Tax-Adjusted (%)	-20.5	2.8	12.6	-1.6	13.1	27.4	15.2	30.2	15.7	-10.1

PER SHARE DATA

	2008	2007	2006	2005	2004	2003	2002	2001	2000	1999
Dividends, Net Income ($)	0.21	0.12	0.11	0.22	0.18	0.05	0.03	0.11	0.11	0.09
Distrib'ns, Cap Gain ($)	0.75	2.32	1.51	0.50	0.67	0.15	0.00	0.00	0.00	0.00
Net Asset Value ($)	13.69	18.27	19.72	18.70	19.61	17.97	14.24	12.37	9.55	8.31
Expense Ratio (%)	na	1.11	1.13	1.14	1.15	1.19	1.20	1.49	1.49	1.49
Yield (%)	1.45	0.58	0.52	1.12	0.90	0.25	0.17	0.90	1.15	1.14
Portfolio Turnover (%)	na	29	16	22	17	22	41	124	61	57
Total Assets (Millions $)	316	386	438	524	857	748	394	6	3	3

PORTFOLIO (as of 9/30/08)

Portfolio Manager: Dreifus - 1998

Investment Style

Large Cap	Growth
Mid Cap	Grth/Val
✔ Small Cap	✔ Value

Portfolio

76.7%	U.S. stock	0.0%	conv't
0.0%	int'l stock	0.0%	preferred
0.0%	U.S. bonds	1.3%	other
0.0%	int'l bonds	22.0%	cash

Number of Investments: 63

Percent of Portfolio in Top 10 Investments: 52%

SHAREHOLDER INFORMATION

Minimum Investment

Initial: $2,000 Subsequent: $50

Minimum IRA Investment

Initial: $1,000 Subsequent: $100

Maximum Fees

Load: 1.00% redemption 12b-1: none

Other: redemption fee applies for 180 days

Services

✔ IRA
✔ Keogh
✔ Telephone Exchange

Royce Total Return Invt (RYTRX)

800-221-4268
www.roycefunds.com

Small-Cap Stock

PERFORMANCE — fund inception date: 12/15/93

	3yr Annual	5yr Annual	10yr Annual	Bull	Bear
Return (%)	-6.9	0.5	6.2	115.8	-34.9
Differ From Category (+/-)	3.9 abv av	2.9 abv av	2.0 abv av	-29.3 low	8.6 high

Standard Deviation	Category Risk Index	Beta
16.5%—av	0.79—low	1.02

	2008	2007	2006	2005	2004	2003	2002	2001	2000	1999
Return (%)	-31.2	2.3	14.5	8.2	17.5	29.9	-1.7	14.7	19.4	1.5
Differ From Category (+/-)	8.1	-0.2	0.0	1.2	0.7	-17.3	16.8	7.3	11.3	-32.6
Return, Tax-Adjusted (%)	-31.5	1.1	13.7	7.4	17.1	29.6	-2.0	13.7	17.0	-0.3

PER SHARE DATA

	2008	2007	2006	2005	2004	2003	2002	2001	2000	1999
Dividends, Net Income ($)	0.23	0.17	0.16	0.13	0.12	0.09	0.08	0.10	0.15	0.16
Distrib'ns, Cap Gain ($)	0.00	1.00	0.52	0.55	0.17	0.08	0.01	0.21	0.57	0.35
Net Asset Value ($)	8.70	12.93	13.75	12.60	12.26	10.69	8.37	8.59	7.77	7.15
Expense Ratio (%)	na	1.08	1.09	1.12	1.15	1.18	1.20	1.24	1.25	1.25
Yield (%)	2.62	1.25	1.09	0.95	0.95	0.86	0.89	1.19	1.79	2.13
Portfolio Turnover (%)	na	27	25	24	22	20	22	24	24	39
Total Assets (Millions $)	2,585	4,214	4,438	4,257	3,738	2,794	1,113	511	277	249

PORTFOLIO (as of 9/30/08)

Portfolio Manager: Royce/Kaplan/Necakov/Flynn - 1993

Investment Style

Large Cap	Growth
✔ Mid Cap	Grth/Val
✔ Small Cap	✔ Value

Portfolio

84.6% U.S. stock	0.4% conv't
4.9% int'l stock	0.4% preferred
0.2% U.S. bonds	4.7% other
0.1% int'l bonds	4.7% cash

Number of Investments: 433
Percent of Portfolio in Top 10 Investments: 14%

SHAREHOLDER INFORMATION

Minimum Investment
Initial: $2,000 Subsequent: $50

Minimum IRA Investment
Initial: $1,000 Subsequent: $100

Maximum Fees
Load: 1.00% redemption 12b-1: none
Other: redemption fee applies for 180 days

Services
✔ IRA
✔ Keogh
✔ Telephone Exchange

Royce Value Plus Svc (RYVPX)

800-221-4268
www.roycefunds.com

Small-Cap Stock

PERFORMANCE — fund inception date: 6/14/01

	3yr Annual	5yr Annual	10yr Annual	Bull	Bear
Return (%)	-10.2	1.0	na	263.7	-46.1
Differ From Category (+/-)	0.6 av	3.4 high	na	118.6 high	-2.6 blw av

Standard Deviation	Category Risk Index	Beta
22.0%—high	1.05—abv av	1.31

	2008	2007	2006	2005	2004	2003	2002	2001	2000	1999
Return (%)	-41.1	3.2	19.3	13.1	28.1	79.8	-14.8	—	—	—
Differ From Category (+/-)	-1.8	0.7	4.8	6.2	11.3	32.6	3.6	—	—	—
Return, Tax-Adjusted (%)	-41.3	2.4	19.0	12.7	28.1	78.8	-15.2	—	—	—

PER SHARE DATA

	2008	2007	2006	2005	2004	2003	2002	2001	2000	1999
Dividends, Net Income ($)	0.00	0.17	0.00	0.00	0.00	0.00	0.00	—	—	—
Distrib'ns, Cap Gain ($)	0.18	0.58	0.27	0.35	0.04	0.35	0.12	—	—	—
Net Asset Value ($)	7.95	13.81	14.09	12.03	10.94	8.57	4.97	—	—	—
Expense Ratio (%)	na	1.33	1.26	1.17	1.30	1.49	1.49	—	—	—
Yield (%)	0.00	1.17	0.02	0.00	0.00	0.00	0.00	—	—	—
Portfolio Turnover (%)	na	42	31	62	56	161	—	—	—	—
Total Assets (Millions $)	1,694	2,690	1,514	292	209	20	4	—	—	—

PORTFOLIO (as of 9/30/08)

Portfolio Manager: George/Skinner, III - 2001

Investment Style

Large Cap	✔ Growth
Mid Cap	Grth/Val
✔ Small Cap	Value

Portfolio

69.3%	U.S. stock	0.0%	conv't
17.4%	int'l stock	0.0%	preferred
0.0%	U.S. bonds	5.7%	other
0.0%	int'l bonds	7.7%	cash

Number of Investments: 136

Percent of Portfolio in Top 10 Investments: 24%

SHAREHOLDER INFORMATION

Minimum Investment

Initial: $2,000 Subsequent: $50

Minimum IRA Investment

Initial: $1,000 Subsequent: $100

Maximum Fees

Load: 1.00% redemption 12b-1: 0.25%

Other: redemption fee applies for 180 days

Services

✔ IRA

Keogh

✔ Telephone Exchange

Royce Value Svc (RYVFX)

800-221-4268
www.roycefunds.com

Small-Cap Stock

PERFORMANCE — fund inception date: 6/14/01

	3yr Annual	5yr Annual	10yr Annual	Bull	Bear
Return (%)	-7.3	4.1	na	211.1	-38.3
Differ From Category (+/-)	3.5 abv av	6.5 high	na	66.0 high	5.2 abv av

Standard Deviation	Category Risk Index	Beta
23.0%—high	1.10—high	1.29

	2008	2007	2006	2005	2004	2003	2002	2001	2000	1999
Return (%)	-34.3	3.7	16.7	17.2	30.9	54.3	-23.6	—	—	—
Differ From Category (+/-)	5.0	1.2	2.2	10.2	14.1	7.1	-5.2	—	—	—
Return, Tax-Adjusted (%)	-34.3	2.6	16.3	16.9	30.4	53.8	-24.1	—	—	—

PER SHARE DATA

	2008	2007	2006	2005	2004	2003	2002	2001	2000	1999
Dividends, Net Income ($)	0.00	0.16	0.02	0.00	0.00	0.00	0.00	—	—	—
Distrib'ns, Cap Gain ($)	0.00	0.69	0.22	0.16	0.19	0.15	0.16	—	—	—
Net Asset Value ($)	7.00	10.64	11.06	9.67	8.39	6.56	4.35	—	—	—
Expense Ratio (%)	na	1.36	1.31	1.28	1.49	1.49	1.49	—	—	—
Yield (%)	0.00	1.38	0.14	0.00	0.00	0.00	0.00	—	—	—
Portfolio Turnover (%)	na	67	41	44	83	181	—	—	—	—
Total Assets (Millions $)	702	664	452	113	38	4	1	—	—	—

PORTFOLIO (as of 9/30/08)

Portfolio Manager: George/Kaplan/Romeo - 2001

Investment Style

Large Cap	Growth
Mid Cap	✔ Grth/Val
✔ Small Cap	Value

Portfolio

73.3% U.S. stock	0.0% conv't
18.0% int'l stock	0.0% preferred
0.0% U.S. bonds	3.0% other
0.0% int'l bonds	5.7% cash

Number of Investments: 74

Percent of Portfolio in Top 10 Investments: 29%

SHAREHOLDER INFORMATION

Minimum Investment

Initial: $2,000 Subsequent: $50

Minimum IRA Investment

Initial: $1,000 Subsequent: $100

Maximum Fees

Load: 1.00% redemption 12b-1: 0.25%

Other: redemption fee applies for 180 days

Services

✔ IRA
✔ Keogh
✔ Telephone Exchange

Stratton Small-Cap Value (STSCX)

800-472-4266
www.strattonmutualfunds.com

Small-Cap Stock

PERFORMANCE — fund inception date: 4/12/93

	3yr Annual	5yr Annual	10yr Annual	Bull	Bear
Return (%)	-6.2	2.9	7.7	165.9	-31.7
Differ From Category (+/-)	4.6 high	5.3 high	3.5 high	20.8 abv av	11.8 high

Standard Deviation	Category Risk Index	Beta
17.4%—av	0.83—low	0.99

	2008	2007	2006	2005	2004	2003	2002	2001	2000	1999
Return (%)	-25.8	-2.3	13.8	10.8	26.4	49.6	-9.6	10.8	23.9	-2.0
Differ From Category (+/-)	13.5	-4.7	-0.7	3.8	9.6	2.4	8.8	3.4	15.8	-36.1
Return, Tax-Adjusted (%)	-25.8	-2.7	13.5	10.3	25.8	48.8	-9.6	10.4	22.9	-2.6

PER SHARE DATA

	2008	2007	2006	2005	2004	2003	2002	2001	2000	1999
Dividends, Net Income ($)	0.00	0.14	0.00	0.00	0.00	0.00	0.00	0.00	0.27	0.27
Distrib'ns, Cap Gain ($)	0.00	1.17	0.81	1.43	1.23	1.24	0.01	0.52	0.44	0.00
Net Asset Value ($)	34.25	46.14	48.43	43.28	40.33	32.96	22.88	25.30	23.32	19.44
Expense Ratio (%)	na	0.87	1.21	1.28	1.47	1.67	1.68	1.74	0.98	1.08
Yield (%)	0.00	0.29	0.00	0.00	0.00	0.00	0.00	0.00	1.13	1.38
Portfolio Turnover (%)	na	19	29	15	17	26	18	38	53	43
Total Assets (Millions $)	662	712	736	356	116	62	45	44	40	36

PORTFOLIO (as of 9/30/08)

Portfolio Manager: Van Horn - 2000

Investment Style

Large Cap	Growth
Mid Cap	Grth/Val
✔ Small Cap	✔ Value

Portfolio

99.7%	U.S. stock	0.0%	conv't
0.3%	int'l stock	0.0%	preferred
0.0%	U.S. bonds	0.0%	other
0.0%	int'l bonds	0.0%	cash

Number of Investments: 61

Percent of Portfolio in Top 10 Investments: 27%

SHAREHOLDER INFORMATION

Minimum Investment

Initial: $2,000 Subsequent: $100

Minimum IRA Investment

Initial: $0 Subsequent: $0

Maximum Fees

Load: 1.50% redemption 12b-1: none

Other: redemption fee applies for 120 days

Services

✔ IRA

✔ Keogh

✔ Telephone Exchange

T. Rowe Price New Horizons (PRNHX)

800-638-5660
www.troweprice.com

Small-Cap Stock

PERFORMANCE — fund inception date: 6/3/60

	3yr Annual	5yr Annual	10yr Annual	Bull	Bear
Return (%)	-11.3	-1.7	2.4	150.0	-42.5
Differ From Category (+/-)	-0.5 blw av	0.7 av	-1.8 blw av	4.9 abv av	1.0 av

Standard Deviation	Category Risk Index	Beta
20.1%—abv av	0.96—av	1.23

	2008	2007	2006	2005	2004	2003	2002	2001	2000	1999
Return (%)	-38.8	6.2	7.3	11.8	17.8	49.3	-26.7	-2.9	-1.9	32.5
Differ From Category (+/-)	0.5	3.7	-7.2	4.9	1.1	2.1	-8.2	-10.3	-10.0	-1.6
Return, Tax-Adjusted (%)	-39.2	4.5	6.5	11.3	17.8	49.3	-26.7	-3.4	-4.2	29.9

PER SHARE DATA

	2008	2007	2006	2005	2004	2003	2002	2001	2000	1999
Dividends, Net Income ($)	0.00	0.00	0.00	0.00	0.00	0.00	0.00	0.00	0.00	0.00
Distrib'ns, Cap Gain ($)	0.81	3.72	1.79	1.00	0.00	0.00	0.00	0.56	3.14	3.02
Net Asset Value ($)	17.79	30.51	32.29	31.74	29.24	24.80	16.61	22.63	23.89	27.53
Expense Ratio (%)	na	0.79	0.82	0.84	0.87	0.91	0.92	0.91	0.88	0.90
Yield (%)	0.00	0.00	0.00	0.00	0.00	0.00	0.00	0.00	0.00	0.00
Portfolio Turnover (%)	na	28	23	24	25	29	23	27	47	45
Total Assets (Millions $)	3,886	7,159	6,993	6,552	5,831	4,960	3,359	5,583	6,122	6,022

PORTFOLIO (as of 9/30/08)

Portfolio Manager: Laporte - 1987

Investment Style

Large Cap	✔ Growth
Mid Cap	Grth/Val
✔ Small Cap	Value

Portfolio

96.1%	U.S. stock	0.0%	conv't
1.3%	int'l stock	0.0%	preferred
0.0%	U.S. bonds	1.1%	other
0.0%	int'l bonds	1.6%	cash

Number of Investments: 271

Percent of Portfolio in Top 10 Investments: 19%

SHAREHOLDER INFORMATION

Minimum Investment

Initial: $2,500 Subsequent: $100

Minimum IRA Investment

Initial: $1,000 Subsequent: $50

Maximum Fees

Load: none 12b-1: none

Other: none

Services

✔ IRA

✔ Keogh

✔ Telephone Exchange

T. Rowe Price Small-Cap Value (PRSVX)

800-638-5660
www.troweprice.com

Small-Cap Stock

PERFORMANCE — fund inception date: 6/30/88

	3yr Annual	5yr Annual	10yr Annual	Bull	Bear
Return (%)	-6.1	2.5	8.4	146.9	-33.3
Differ From Category (+/-)	4.7 high	4.9 high	4.2 high	1.8 abv av	10.2 high

Standard Deviation	Category Risk Index	Beta
17.9%—av	0.85—low	1.04

	2008	2007	2006	2005	2004	2003	2002	2001	2000	1999
Return (%)	-28.7	-0.2	16.2	8.7	25.6	36.4	-1.8	21.9	19.7	1.1
Differ From Category (+/-)	10.6	-2.7	1.7	1.7	8.8	-10.8	16.6	14.5	11.6	-33.0
Return, Tax-Adjusted (%)	-29.5	-2.1	15.5	7.9	25.0	36.0	-2.2	21.0	17.4	-0.6

PER SHARE DATA

	2008	2007	2006	2005	2004	2003	2002	2001	2000	1999
Dividends, Net Income ($)	0.27	0.28	0.27	0.17	0.16	0.12	0.14	0.17	0.20	0.17
Distrib'ns, Cap Gain ($)	1.77	4.88	1.41	1.76	1.08	0.41	0.18	0.48	1.68	1.35
Net Asset Value ($)	23.50	35.92	41.21	36.91	35.68	29.39	21.94	22.66	19.14	17.62
Expense Ratio (%)	na	0.81	0.83	0.84	0.86	0.88	0.89	0.89	0.90	0.92
Yield (%)	1.06	0.68	0.63	0.43	0.43	0.40	0.63	0.73	0.96	0.89
Portfolio Turnover (%)	na	14	12	12	9	10	12	17	14	7
Total Assets (Millions $)	3,426	4,936	5,387	4,719	4,462	3,295	2,395	2,012	1,361	1,262

PORTFOLIO (as of 9/30/08)

Portfolio Manager: Athey - 1991

Investment Style

Large Cap	Growth
Mid Cap	Grth/Val
✔ Small Cap	✔ Value

Portfolio

87.7%	U.S. stock	0.2%	conv't
2.0%	int'l stock	0.6%	preferred
1.1%	U.S. bonds	0.9%	other
0.0%	int'l bonds	7.6%	cash

Number of Investments: 312
Percent of Portfolio in Top 10 Investments: 22%

SHAREHOLDER INFORMATION

Minimum Investment
Initial: $2,500 Subsequent: $100

Minimum IRA Investment
Initial: $1,000 Subsequent: $50

Maximum Fees
Load: 1.00% redemption 12b-1: none
Other: redemption fee applies for 90 days

Services
✔ IRA
✔ Keogh
✔ Telephone Exchange

Tamarack Enterprise S (TETSX)

800-422-2766
www.tamarackfunds.com

Small-Cap Stock

PERFORMANCE — fund inception date: 12/2/83

	3yr Annual	5yr Annual	10yr Annual	Bull	Bear
Return (%)	-11.3	-3.6	5.0	129.0	-43.2
Differ From Category (+/-)	-0.5 blw av	-1.2 blw av	0.8 av	-16.1 blw av	0.3 av

Standard Deviation	Category Risk Index	Beta
18.3%—av	0.87—low	1.08

	2008	2007	2006	2005	2004	2003	2002	2001	2000	1999
Return (%)	-38.1	-3.1	16.3	3.8	15.1	50.6	-3.5	29.5	12.3	-7.3
Differ From Category (+/-)	1.2	-5.6	1.8	-3.2	-1.7	3.4	14.9	22.1	4.2	-41.4
Return, Tax-Adjusted (%)	-39.2	-5.2	14.8	1.9	14.5	50.5	-3.5	28.8	10.4	-8.8

PER SHARE DATA

	2008	2007	2006	2005	2004	2003	2002	2001	2000	1999
Dividends, Net Income ($)	0.00	0.09	0.02	0.00	0.00	0.06	0.00	0.05	0.04	0.01
Distrib'ns, Cap Gain ($)	1.58	3.50	2.24	3.10	0.95	0.00	0.00	0.31	1.05	1.05
Net Asset Value ($)	10.96	20.41	24.75	23.24	25.38	22.87	15.23	15.77	12.47	12.11
Expense Ratio (%)	1.08	1.08	1.08	1.08	1.08	1.08	1.08	1.15	1.14	1.11
Yield (%)	0.00	0.37	0.08	0.00	0.00	0.24	0.00	0.33	0.29	0.11
Portfolio Turnover (%)	23	22	27	33	28	13	93	55	32	12
Total Assets (Millions $)	110	235	295	314	367	305	187	131	104	116

PORTFOLIO (as of 9/30/08)

Portfolio Manager: James/Prince - 1999

Investment Style

Large Cap	Growth
Mid Cap	✔ Grth/Val
✔ Small Cap	Value

Portfolio

97.4%	U.S. stock	0.0%	conv't
0.9%	int'l stock	0.0%	preferred
0.0%	U.S. bonds	0.0%	other
0.0%	int'l bonds	1.7%	cash

Number of Investments: 76
Percent of Portfolio in Top 10 Investments: 40%

SHAREHOLDER INFORMATION

Minimum Investment
Initial: $1,000 Subsequent: $100

Minimum IRA Investment
Initial: $250 Subsequent: $100

Maximum Fees
Load: 2.00% redemption 12b-1: none
Other: redemption fee applies for 30 days

Services
✔ IRA
✔ Keogh
✔ Telephone Exchange

Tamarack Micro Cap Value S (TMVSX)

800-422-2766
www.tamarackfunds.com

Small-Cap Stock

PERFORMANCE — fund inception date: 9/10/87

	3yr Annual	5yr Annual	10yr Annual	Bull	Bear
Return (%)	-12.5	-2.4	5.3	161.3	-44.9
Differ From Category (+/-)	-1.7 blw av	0.0 av	1.1 av	16.2 abv av	-1.4 blw av

Standard Deviation	Category Risk Index	Beta
19.5%—abv av	0.93—blw av	1.15

	2008	2007	2006	2005	2004	2003	2002	2001	2000	1999
Return (%)	-39.4	-9.2	21.6	7.3	23.7	50.0	-12.3	22.6	11.3	4.8
Differ From Category (+/-)	-0.1	-11.7	7.1	0.3	6.9	2.8	6.1	15.2	3.2	-29.3
Return, Tax-Adjusted (%)	-40.2	-10.3	20.5	5.9	22.9	49.5	-12.3	21.9	8.7	3.5

PER SHARE DATA

	2008	2007	2006	2005	2004	2003	2002	2001	2000	1999
Dividends, Net Income ($)	0.09	0.08	0.03	0.08	0.16	0.19	0.02	0.09	0.08	0.08
Distrib'ns, Cap Gain ($)	0.95	1.50	1.54	1.84	0.80	0.23	0.00	0.22	1.32	0.61
Net Asset Value ($)	10.46	19.07	22.77	20.02	20.43	17.29	11.86	13.54	11.31	11.46
Expense Ratio (%)	1.07	1.07	1.09	1.07	1.03	1.03	1.03	1.03	1.07	1.10
Yield (%)	0.80	0.40	0.14	0.35	0.75	1.08	0.20	0.68	0.63	0.65
Portfolio Turnover (%)	18	17	20	8	18	17	34	29	18	21
Total Assets (Millions $)	153	302	304	227	239	140	83	65	42	41

PORTFOLIO (as of 9/30/08)

Portfolio Manager: Scinto - 2006

Investment Style

Large Cap	Growth
Mid Cap	Grth/Val
✔ Small Cap	✔ Value

Portfolio

95.0%	U.S. stock	0.0%	conv't
1.7%	int'l stock	0.2%	preferred
0.0%	U.S. bonds	0.1%	other
0.0%	int'l bonds	3.0%	cash

Number of Investments: 498

Percent of Portfolio in Top 10 Investments: 11%

SHAREHOLDER INFORMATION

Minimum Investment

Initial: $1,000 Subsequent: $100

Minimum IRA Investment

Initial: $250 Subsequent: $100

Maximum Fees

Load: 2.00% redemption 12b-1: none

Other: redemption fee applies for 30 days

Services

✔ IRA

✔ Keogh

✔ Telephone Exchange

TIAA-CREF Small-Cap Equity Retail (TCSEX)

800-223-1200
www.tiaa-cref.org

Small-Cap Stock

PERFORMANCE — fund inception date: 10/1/02

	3yr Annual	5yr Annual	10yr Annual	Bull	Bear
Return (%)	-9.5	-1.7	na	131.7	-38.0
Differ From Category (+/-)	1.3 av	0.7 av	na	-13.4 blw av	5.5 abv av

Standard Deviation	Category Risk Index	Beta
19.7%—abv av	0.94—av	1.17

	2008	2007	2006	2005	2004	2003	2002	2001	2000	1999
Return (%)	-32.9	-6.3	17.7	3.2	20.4	47.1	—	—	—	—
Differ From Category (+/-)	6.4	-8.8	3.2	-3.8	3.6	-0.1	—	—	—	—
Return, Tax-Adjusted (%)	-33.0	-7.3	16.0	1.8	19.5	45.5	—	—	—	—

PER SHARE DATA

	2008	2007	2006	2005	2004	2003	2002	2001	2000	1999
Dividends, Net Income ($)	0.04	0.00	0.00	0.02	0.03	0.05	—	—	—	—
Distrib'ns, Cap Gain ($)	0.00	1.03	1.64	1.44	0.80	1.01	—	—	—	—
Net Asset Value ($)	8.90	13.33	15.33	14.42	15.35	13.43	—	—	—	—
Expense Ratio (%)	0.72	0.69	0.61	0.30	0.30	0.30	—	—	—	—
Yield (%)	0.48	0.01	0.00	0.12	0.16	0.33	—	—	—	—
Portfolio Turnover (%)	114	127	264	273	295	328	—	—	—	—
Total Assets (Millions $)	38	62	94	73	70	31	—	—	—	—

PORTFOLIO (as of 9/30/08)

Portfolio Manager: Shing/Cao - 2004

Investment Style

Large Cap	Growth
Mid Cap	✔ Grth/Val
✔ Small Cap	Value

Portfolio

98.4% U.S. stock	0.0% conv't
0.7% int'l stock	0.0% preferred
0.0% U.S. bonds	0.0% other
0.0% int'l bonds	0.9% cash

Number of Investments: 735

Percent of Portfolio in Top 10 Investments: 6%

SHAREHOLDER INFORMATION

Minimum Investment

Initial: $2,500 Subsequent: $100

Minimum IRA Investment

Initial: $2,000 Subsequent: $100

Maximum Fees

Load: 2.00% redemption 12b-1: none

Other: redemption fee applies for 60 days

Services

✔ IRA

Keogh

✔ Telephone Exchange

UMB Scout Small Cap (UMBHX)

800-996-2862
www.umb.com

Small-Cap Stock

PERFORMANCE — fund inception date: 11/17/86

	3yr Annual	5yr Annual	10yr Annual	Bull	Bear
Return (%)	-8.8	0.0	5.3	143.7	-42.5
Differ From Category (+/-)	2.0 abv av	2.4 abv av	1.1 av	-1.4 av	1.0 av

Standard Deviation	Category Risk Index	Beta
19.0%—abv av	0.90—blw av	1.11

	2008	2007	2006	2005	2004	2003	2002	2001	2000	1999
Return (%)	-40.2	13.3	12.0	5.5	24.7	38.1	-11.7	11.3	21.8	1.2
Differ From Category (+/-)	-0.9	10.8	-2.5	-1.4	7.9	-9.1	6.7	3.9	13.7	-32.9
Return, Tax-Adjusted (%)	-40.2	12.0	11.1	5.1	24.0	37.7	-12.0	7.7	20.6	-0.4

PER SHARE DATA

	2008	2007	2006	2005	2004	2003	2002	2001	2000	1999
Dividends, Net Income ($)	0.00	0.00	0.00	0.00	0.00	0.00	0.03	0.14	0.17	0.15
Distrib'ns, Cap Gain ($)	0.00	1.40	0.94	0.41	0.60	0.28	0.11	1.82	0.23	0.57
Net Asset Value ($)	10.55	17.64	16.83	15.85	15.39	12.83	9.49	10.89	11.59	9.87
Expense Ratio (%)	1.01	1.02	1.06	0.96	0.89	0.87	0.88	0.99	0.91	0.89
Yield (%)	0.00	0.00	0.00	0.00	0.00	0.00	0.27	1.07	1.47	1.42
Portfolio Turnover (%)	226	207	92	66	109	89	105	122	16	13
Total Assets (Millions $)	445	718	648	427	196	60	38	37	31	37

PORTFOLIO (as of 9/30/08)

Portfolio Manager: Votruba - 2002

Investment Style

Large Cap	✔ Growth
✔ Mid Cap	Grth/Val
✔ Small Cap	Value

Portfolio

90.1% U.S. stock	0.0% conv't
0.0% int'l stock	0.0% preferred
0.0% U.S. bonds	0.0% other
0.0% int'l bonds	9.9% cash

Number of Investments: 113
Percent of Portfolio in Top 10 Investments: 25%

SHAREHOLDER INFORMATION

Minimum Investment
Initial: $1,000 Subsequent: $100

Minimum IRA Investment
Initial: $100 Subsequent: $100

Maximum Fees
Load: 2.00% redemption 12b-1: none
Other: redemption fee applies for 2 months

Services
✔ IRA
✔ Keogh
✔ Telephone Exchange

USAA Small Cap Stock (USCAX)

800-531-8181
www.usaa.com

Small-Cap Stock

PERFORMANCE — fund inception date: 8/2/99

	3yr Annual	5yr Annual	10yr Annual	Bull	Bear
Return (%)	-10.0	-1.3	na	115.6	-41.4
Differ From Category (+/-)	0.8 av	1.1 av	na	-29.5 low	2.1 av

Standard Deviation	Category Risk Index	Beta
19.1%—abv av	0.91—blw av	1.16

	2008	2007	2006	2005	2004	2003	2002	2001	2000	1999
Return (%)	-36.1	-0.8	15.3	7.9	18.7	27.3	-11.0	-9.2	-14.0	—
Differ From Category (+/-)	3.2	-3.3	0.8	0.9	1.9	-19.9	7.4	-16.6	-22.1	—
Return, Tax-Adjusted (%)	-36.2	-2.4	14.3	6.8	18.3	27.3	-11.0	-9.2	-14.0	—

PER SHARE DATA

	2008	2007	2006	2005	2004	2003	2002	2001	2000	1999
Dividends, Net Income ($)	0.01	0.01	0.02	0.00	0.01	0.00	0.00	0.00	0.00	—
Distrib'ns, Cap Gain ($)	0.00	1.49	0.89	1.07	0.35	0.00	0.00	0.00	0.00	—
Net Asset Value ($)	8.40	13.16	14.76	13.59	13.57	11.73	9.21	10.34	11.38	—
Expense Ratio (%)	1.31	1.31	1.30	1.34	1.40	1.40	1.40	0.00	0.43	—
Yield (%)	0.11	0.08	0.13	0.00	0.03	0.00	0.00	0.00	0.00	—
Portfolio Turnover (%)	84	84	66	69	184	170	200	145	37	—
Total Assets (Millions $)	383	510	436	330	245	161	102	92	87	—

PORTFOLIO (as of 10/31/08)

Portfolio Manager: Ko/McCormack/Pedersen - 2003

Investment Style

Large Cap	Growth
Mid Cap	Grth/Val
✔ Small Cap	✔ Value

Portfolio

94.4% U.S. stock	0.0% conv't
2.0% int'l stock	0.0% preferred
0.0% U.S. bonds	0.0% other
0.0% int'l bonds	3.6% cash

Number of Investments: 245
Percent of Portfolio in Top 10 Investments: 15%

SHAREHOLDER INFORMATION

Minimum Investment
Initial: $3,000 Subsequent: $50

Minimum IRA Investment
Initial: $250 Subsequent: $50

Maximum Fees
Load: none 12b-1: none
Other: none

Services
✔ IRA
✔ Keogh
✔ Telephone Exchange

Value Line Emerging Opportunities (VLEOX)

800-243-2729
www.valueline.com

Small-Cap Stock

PERFORMANCE — fund inception date: 6/23/93

	3yr Annual	5yr Annual	10yr Annual	Bull	Bear
Return (%)	-8.1	-0.5	7.7	133.2	-41.9
Differ From Category (+/-)	2.7 abv av	1.9 abv av	3.5 high	-11.9 blw av	1.6 av

Standard Deviation	Category Risk Index	Beta
19.3%—abv av	0.92—blw av	1.18

	2008	2007	2006	2005	2004	2003	2002	2001	2000	1999
Return (%)	-38.3	12.3	11.9	8.0	16.6	33.6	-14.2	3.8	5.5	70.6
Differ From Category (+/-)	1.0	9.8	-2.6	1.0	-0.2	-13.6	4.2	-3.6	-2.6	36.5
Return, Tax-Adjusted (%)	-38.4	12.0	11.6	7.8	16.6	33.6	-14.4	3.7	2.7	69.8

PER SHARE DATA

	2008	2007	2006	2005	2004	2003	2002	2001	2000	1999
Dividends, Net Income ($)	0.00	0.00	0.00	0.00	0.00	0.00	0.00	0.00	0.00	0.00
Distrib'ns, Cap Gain ($)	0.21	0.71	0.48	0.39	0.00	0.00	0.16	0.10	2.99	0.50
Net Asset Value ($)	20.79	34.02	30.92	28.05	26.32	22.56	16.88	19.85	19.21	21.31
Expense Ratio (%)	1.12	1.15	1.10	1.14	1.19	1.35	1.48	1.46	1.34	1.34
Yield (%)	0.00	0.00	0.00	0.00	0.00	0.00	0.00	0.00	0.00	0.00
Portfolio Turnover (%)	26	24	40	44	55	79	130	111	104	203
Total Assets (Millions $)	551	995	750	534	372	214	110	58	50	40

PORTFOLIO (as of 9/30/08)

Portfolio Manager: Grant - 1998

Investment Style

Large Cap	✔ Growth
✔ Mid Cap	Grth/Val
✔ Small Cap	Value

Portfolio

91.5%	U.S. stock	0.0%	conv't
3.6%	int'l stock	0.0%	preferred
0.0%	U.S. bonds	0.0%	other
0.0%	int'l bonds	4.9%	cash

Number of Investments: 367

Percent of Portfolio in Top 10 Investments: 11%

SHAREHOLDER INFORMATION

Minimum Investment

Initial: $1,000 Subsequent: $100

Minimum IRA Investment

Initial: $1,000 Subsequent: $100

Maximum Fees

Load: none 12b-1: 0.25%

Other: none

Services

IRA

✔ Keogh

✔ Telephone Exchange

Vanguard Small Cap Growth Index (VISGX)

800-662-7447
www.vanguard.com

Small-Cap Stock

PERFORMANCE — fund inception date: 5/21/98

	3yr Annual	5yr Annual	10yr Annual	Bull	Bear
Return (%)	-9.7	-1.5	3.0	151.1	-44.1
Differ From Category (+/-)	1.1 av	0.9 av	-1.2 blw av	6.0 abv av	-0.6 av

Standard Deviation	Category Risk Index	Beta
21.8%—abv av	1.04—abv av	1.32

	2008	2007	2006	2005	2004	2003	2002	2001	2000	1999
Return (%)	-40.0	9.6	11.9	8.6	16.0	42.8	-15.5	-0.8	1.5	19.7
Differ From Category (+/-)	-0.7	7.1	-2.6	1.6	-0.8	-4.4	2.9	-8.2	-6.6	-14.3
Return, Tax-Adjusted (%)	-40.1	9.5	11.9	8.6	16.0	42.8	-15.5	-0.9	0.5	19.6

PER SHARE DATA

	2008	2007	2006	2005	2004	2003	2002	2001	2000	1999
Dividends, Net Income ($)	0.10	0.09	0.05	0.04	0.02	0.02	0.03	0.01	0.00	0.04
Distrib'ns, Cap Gain ($)	0.00	0.00	0.00	0.00	0.00	0.00	0.00	0.00	0.57	0.00
Net Asset Value ($)	11.90	20.01	18.34	16.43	15.16	13.08	9.17	10.87	10.97	11.38
Expense Ratio (%)	na	0.22	0.23	0.23	0.23	0.27	0.27	0.27	0.27	0.25
Yield (%)	0.84	0.46	0.29	0.24	0.13	0.16	0.27	0.13	0.02	0.30
Portfolio Turnover (%)	na	32	40	39	41	108	61	74	136	82
Total Assets (Millions $)	1,871	2,825	2,208	1,726	1,435	907	388	357	356	167

PORTFOLIO (as of 9/30/08)

Portfolio Manager: O'Reilly - 2004

Investment Style

Large Cap	✔ Growth
Mid Cap	Grth/Val
✔ Small Cap	Value

Portfolio

98.5% U.S. stock	0.0% conv't
1.3% int'l stock	0.0% preferred
0.0% U.S. bonds	0.1% other
0.0% int'l bonds	0.2% cash

Number of Investments: 941
Percent of Portfolio in Top 10 Investments: 5%

SHAREHOLDER INFORMATION

Minimum Investment
Initial: $3,000 Subsequent: $100

Minimum IRA Investment
Initial: $3,000 Subsequent: $100

Maximum Fees
Load: none 12b-1: none
Other: none

Services
✔ IRA
✔ Keogh
✔ Telephone Exchange

Vanguard Small Cap Index (NAESX)

800-662-7447
www.vanguard.com

Small-Cap Stock

PERFORMANCE — fund inception date: 10/3/60

	3yr Annual	5yr Annual	10yr Annual	Bull	Bear
Return (%)	-9.3	-0.8	3.3	151.2	-40.8
Differ From Category (+/-)	1.5 av	1.6 abv av	-0.9 blw av	6.1 abv av	2.7 abv av

Standard Deviation	Category Risk Index	Beta
20.1%—abv av	0.96—av	1.24

	2008	2007	2006	2005	2004	2003	2002	2001	2000	1999
Return (%)	-36.1	1.1	15.6	7.3	19.8	45.6	-20.1	3.0	-2.7	23.1
Differ From Category (+/-)	3.2	-1.4	1.1	0.3	3.1	-1.6	-1.7	-4.3	-10.8	-11.0
Return, Tax-Adjusted (%)	-36.3	0.9	15.4	7.1	19.7	45.4	-20.4	2.6	-5.7	20.6

PER SHARE DATA

	2008	2007	2006	2005	2004	2003	2002	2001	2000	1999
Dividends, Net Income ($)	0.40	0.41	0.36	0.29	0.26	0.20	0.19	0.22	0.26	0.27
Distrib'ns, Cap Gain ($)	0.00	0.00	0.00	0.00	0.00	0.00	0.00	0.00	3.03	2.08
Net Asset Value ($)	20.40	32.58	32.62	28.52	26.83	22.60	15.66	19.82	19.44	23.60
Expense Ratio (%)	na	0.22	0.23	0.23	0.23	0.27	0.27	0.27	0.27	0.25
Yield (%)	1.98	1.26	1.11	1.01	0.98	0.90	1.22	1.13	1.15	1.03
Portfolio Turnover (%)	na	16	24	18	19	39	32	39	49	42
Total Assets (Millions $)	4,050	6,214	6,808	5,902	6,247	4,871	2,943	3,545	3,577	3,553

PORTFOLIO (as of 9/30/08)

Portfolio Manager: Buek - 1991

Investment Style

Large Cap	Growth
Mid Cap	✔ Grth/Val
✔ Small Cap	Value

Portfolio

98.8% U.S. stock	0.0% conv't
0.9% int'l stock	0.0% preferred
0.0% U.S. bonds	0.0% other
0.0% int'l bonds	0.3% cash

Number of Investments: 1,739

Percent of Portfolio in Top 10 Investments: 3%

SHAREHOLDER INFORMATION

Minimum Investment

Initial: $3,000 Subsequent: $100

Minimum IRA Investment

Initial: $3,000 Subsequent: $100

Maximum Fees

Load: none 12b-1: none

Other: none

Services

✔ IRA

✔ Keogh

✔ Telephone Exchange

Vanguard Small Cap Value Index (VISVX)

800-662-7447
www.vanguard.com

Small-Cap Stock

PERFORMANCE — fund inception date: 5/21/98

	3yr Annual	5yr Annual	10yr Annual	Bull	Bear
Return (%)	-9.1	-0.3	5.2	134.5	-37.5
Differ From Category (+/-)	1.7 abv av	2.1 abv av	1.0 av	-10.6 av	6.0 abv av

Standard Deviation	Category Risk Index	Beta
19.2%—abv av	0.91—blw av	1.15

	2008	2007	2006	2005	2004	2003	2002	2001	2000	1999
Return (%)	-32.1	-7.1	19.2	6.0	23.5	37.1	-14.2	13.6	21.8	3.3
Differ From Category (+/-)	7.2	-9.6	4.7	-1.0	6.7	-10.1	4.2	6.3	13.7	-30.8
Return, Tax-Adjusted (%)	-32.4	-7.4	18.9	5.7	23.2	36.8	-15.1	12.3	20.3	1.9

PER SHARE DATA

	2008	2007	2006	2005	2004	2003	2002	2001	2000	1999
Dividends, Net Income ($)	0.30	0.35	0.31	0.26	0.22	0.20	0.09	0.06	0.08	0.07
Distrib'ns, Cap Gain ($)	0.00	0.00	0.00	0.00	0.00	0.00	0.28	0.55	0.50	0.50
Net Asset Value ($)	10.21	15.49	17.05	14.56	13.97	11.49	8.52	10.29	9.65	8.45
Expense Ratio (%)	na	0.22	0.23	0.23	0.23	0.27	0.27	0.27	0.27	0.25
Yield (%)	2.89	2.27	1.81	1.79	1.61	1.72	1.02	0.59	0.80	0.78
Portfolio Turnover (%)	na	34	25	28	30	109	57	59	82	80
Total Assets (Millions $)	2,435	3,678	4,314	3,446	2,947	1,730	1,176	802	317	204

PORTFOLIO (as of 9/30/08)

Portfolio Manager: Buek - 1999

Investment Style

Large Cap	Growth
Mid Cap	Grth/Val
✔ Small Cap	✔ Value

Portfolio

99.5% U.S. stock	0.0% conv't
0.5% int'l stock	0.0% preferred
0.0% U.S. bonds	0.0% other
0.0% int'l bonds	0.0% cash

Number of Investments: 986
Percent of Portfolio in Top 10 Investments: 5%

SHAREHOLDER INFORMATION

Minimum Investment
Initial: $3,000 Subsequent: $100

Minimum IRA Investment
Initial: $3,000 Subsequent: $100

Maximum Fees
Load: none 12b-1: none
Other: none

Services
✔ IRA
✔ Keogh
✔ Telephone Exchange

Vanguard Tax-Managed Small Cap Inv (VTMSX)

800-997-2798
www.vanguard.com

Small-Cap Stock

PERFORMANCE — fund inception date: 3/25/99

	3yr Annual	5yr Annual	10yr Annual	Bull	Bear
Return (%)	-7.5	0.9	na	144.1	-36.2
Differ From Category (+/-)	3.3 abv av	3.3 high	na	-1.0 av	7.3 high

Standard Deviation	Category Risk Index	Beta
18.8%—abv av	0.90—blw av	1.12

	2008	2007	2006	2005	2004	2003	2002	2001	2000	1999
Return (%)	-30.9	0.5	14.1	7.7	22.8	38.5	-14.5	5.4	13.4	—
Differ From Category (+/-)	8.4	-2.0	-0.4	0.7	6.0	-8.7	3.9	-2.0	5.3	—
Return, Tax-Adjusted (%)	-31.0	0.3	14.0	7.6	22.6	38.3	-14.7	5.2	13.2	—

PER SHARE DATA

	2008	2007	2006	2005	2004	2003	2002	2001	2000	1999
Dividends, Net Income ($)	0.27	0.23	0.20	0.20	0.17	0.11	0.09	0.09	0.07	—
Distrib'ns, Cap Gain ($)	0.00	0.00	0.00	0.00	0.00	0.00	0.00	0.00	0.00	—
Net Asset Value ($)	17.44	25.62	25.72	22.70	21.25	17.44	12.67	14.92	14.23	—
Expense Ratio (%)	na	0.12	0.14	0.14	0.14	0.17	0.17	0.20	0.20	—
Yield (%)	1.55	0.90	0.76	0.86	0.81	0.62	0.74	0.56	0.52	—
Portfolio Turnover (%)	na	53	42	20	19	21	21	25	64	—
Total Assets (Millions $)	1,258	1,793	1,756	1,458	1,282	929	601	568	368	—

PORTFOLIO (as of 9/30/08)

Portfolio Manager: Buek - 1999

Investment Style

Large Cap	Growth
Mid Cap	✔ Grth/Val
✔ Small Cap	Value

Portfolio

99.8% U.S. stock	0.0% conv't
0.2% int'l stock	0.0% preferred
0.0% U.S. bonds	0.0% other
0.0% int'l bonds	0.0% cash

Number of Investments: 604

Percent of Portfolio in Top 10 Investments: 7%

SHAREHOLDER INFORMATION

Minimum Investment

Initial: $10,000 Subsequent: $100

Minimum IRA Investment

Initial: $0 Subsequent: $0

Maximum Fees

Load: 1.00% redemption 12b-1: none

Other: redemption fee applies for 60 days

Services

✔ IRA
✔ Keogh
✔ Telephone Exchange

Westcore Small-Cap Value (WTSVX)

800-392-2673
www.westcore.com

Small-Cap Stock

PERFORMANCE

fund inception date: 12/13/04

	3yr Annual	5yr Annual	10yr Annual	Bull	Bear
Return (%)	-7.5	na	na	na	-39.3
Differ From Category (+/-)	3.3 abv av	na	na	na	4.2 abv av

Standard Deviation	Category Risk Index	Beta
20.3%—abv av	0.97—av	1.22

	2008	2007	2006	2005	2004	2003	2002	2001	2000	1999
Return (%)	-33.6	-3.4	23.5	4.4	—	—	—	—	—	—
Differ From Category (+/-)	5.7	-5.9	9.0	-2.6	—	—	—	—	—	—
Return, Tax-Adjusted (%)	-33.8	-3.7	23.3	4.1	—	—	—	—	—	—

PER SHARE DATA

	2008	2007	2006	2005	2004	2003	2002	2001	2000	1999
Dividends, Net Income ($)	0.13	0.12	0.09	0.11	—	—	—	—	—	—
Distrib'ns, Cap Gain ($)	0.00	0.09	0.00	0.07	—	—	—	—	—	—
Net Asset Value ($)	7.87	12.06	12.69	10.35	—	—	—	—	—	—
Expense Ratio (%)	na	1.30	1.30	1.30	—	—	—	—	—	—
Yield (%)	1.67	0.95	0.73	1.07	—	—	—	—	—	—
Portfolio Turnover (%)	na	35	43	27	—	—	—	—	—	—
Total Assets (Millions $)	145	157	58	24	—	—	—	—	—	—

PORTFOLIO (as of 11/30/08)

Portfolio Manager: Adelmann/Anguilm/Dayton - 2004

Investment Style

Large Cap	Growth
Mid Cap	Grth/Val
✔ Small Cap	✔ Value

Portfolio

95.0%	U.S. stock	0.0%	conv't
0.0%	int'l stock	0.0%	preferred
0.0%	U.S. bonds	0.0%	other
0.0%	int'l bonds	5.0%	cash

Number of Investments: 62
Percent of Portfolio in Top 10 Investments: 32%

SHAREHOLDER INFORMATION

Minimum Investment
Initial: $2,500 Subsequent: $100

Minimum IRA Investment
Initial: $1,000 Subsequent: $100

Maximum Fees
Load: 2.00% redemption 12b-1: none
Other: redemption fee applies for 90 days

Services
✔ IRA
✔ Keogh
✔ Telephone Exchange

Energy/Resources Sector Stock Funds
Category Performance Ranked by 2008 Returns

Fund (Ticker)	Annual Return (%) 2008	3Yr	5Yr	10Yr	Category Risk	Total Risk
ICON Energy (ICENX)	-33.4	0.4	14.7	20.4	low	high
Vanguard Energy (VGENX)	-42.9	-2.2	13.1	14.7	blw av	high
Fidelity Select Materials (FSDPX)	-47.6	-6.9	0.9	6.5	low	high
T. Rowe Price New Era (PRNEX)	-50.2	-6.4	6.7	9.2	blw av	high
Fidelity Select Natural Resources (FNARX)	-52.4	-5.3	8.9	10.9	av	high
Energy/Resources Sector Category Average	**-53.1**	**-8.8**	**6.4**	**9.8**	**av**	**high**

Fidelity Select Materials (FSDPX)

800-544-8544
www.fidelity.com

Energy/Resources Sector

PERFORMANCE — fund inception date: 9/29/86

	3yr Annual	5yr Annual	10yr Annual	Bull	Bear
Return (%)	-6.9	0.9	6.5	211.5	-49.0
Differ From Category (+/-)	1.9 av	-5.5 low	-3.3 blw av	-58.8 blw av	3.7 abv av

Standard Deviation	Category Risk Index	Beta
24.5%—high	0.74—low	1.36

	2008	2007	2006	2005	2004	2003	2002	2001	2000	1999
Return (%)	-47.6	29.2	19.4	14.3	13.0	50.3	1.0	7.7	-5.5	16.4
Differ From Category (+/-)	5.5	-11.7	5.8	-24.0	-16.8	18.6	7.7	18.8	-36.8	-15.6
Return, Tax-Adjusted (%)	-47.7	28.3	17.6	13.9	12.6	50.2	0.2	7.4	-5.7	16.4

PER SHARE DATA

	2008	2007	2006	2005	2004	2003	2002	2001	2000	1999
Dividends, Net Income ($)	0.20	0.36	0.48	0.25	0.12	0.12	0.46	0.20	0.11	0.03
Distrib'ns, Cap Gain ($)	0.00	2.21	4.79	0.93	0.74	0.00	0.00	0.00	0.00	0.00
Net Asset Value ($)	30.46	58.48	47.34	44.11	39.72	36.00	24.06	24.28	22.72	24.15
Expense Ratio (%)	0.89	0.96	1.01	1.06	1.17	1.42	1.49	1.78	1.92	2.04
Yield (%)	0.65	0.59	0.92	0.55	0.29	0.33	1.91	0.82	0.48	0.12
Portfolio Turnover (%)	77	185	124	89	175	226	230	141	257	82
Total Assets (Millions $)	140	389	175	149	128	172	27	18	26	23

PORTFOLIO (as of 11/30/08)

Portfolio Manager: Welo - 2008

Investment Style

Large Cap	Growth
Mid Cap	Grth/Val
Small Cap	Value

Portfolio

89.1% U.S. stock	0.0% conv't
6.0% int'l stock	0.0% preferred
0.0% U.S. bonds	0.0% other
0.0% int'l bonds	4.9% cash

Number of Investments: 48

Percent of Portfolio in Top 10 Investments: 57%

SHAREHOLDER INFORMATION

Minimum Investment

Initial: $2,500 Subsequent: $250

Minimum IRA Investment

Initial: $500 Subsequent: $100

Maximum Fees

Load: 0.75% redemption 12b-1: none

Other: redemption fee applies for 30 days

Services

✔ IRA

Keogh

✔ Telephone Exchange

Fidelity Select Natural Resources (FNARX)

800-544-8544
www.fidelity.com

Energy/Resources Sector

PERFORMANCE — fund inception date: 3/3/97

	3yr Annual	5yr Annual	10yr Annual	Bull	Bear
Return (%)	-5.3	8.9	10.9	307.5	-51.1
Differ From Category (+/-)	3.5 abv av	2.5 abv av	1.1 abv av	37.2 high	1.6 av

Standard Deviation	Category Risk Index	Beta
32.5%—high	0.98—av	1.46

	2008	2007	2006	2005	2004	2003	2002	2001	2000	1999
Return (%)	-52.4	50.0	19.1	46.0	23.5	29.4	-11.8	-11.4	30.4	38.7
Differ From Category (+/-)	0.7	9.1	5.5	7.7	-6.3	-2.3	-5.1	-0.3	-0.9	6.8
Return, Tax-Adjusted (%)	-52.6	49.2	18.4	45.1	23.1	29.4	-11.9	-12.0	28.7	38.7

PER SHARE DATA

	2008	2007	2006	2005	2004	2003	2002	2001	2000	1999
Dividends, Net Income ($)	0.01	0.03	0.07	0.04	0.07	0.00	0.02	0.01	0.01	0.00
Distrib'ns, Cap Gain ($)	0.48	1.50	0.95	0.95	0.28	0.00	0.00	0.40	0.99	0.00
Net Asset Value ($)	18.83	40.05	27.86	24.25	17.33	14.32	11.06	12.55	14.58	12.02
Expense Ratio (%)	0.85	0.92	0.93	1.04	1.59	1.72	1.56	1.67	1.85	2.47
Yield (%)	0.05	0.07	0.24	0.15	0.39	0.00	0.18	0.07	0.06	0.00
Portfolio Turnover (%)	44	116	119	101	32	70	115	138	164	155
Total Assets (Millions $)	1,005	2,336	1,233	683	179	54	27	25	22	18

PORTFOLIO (as of 11/30/08)

Portfolio Manager: Dowd - 2006

Investment Style

Large Cap	Growth
Mid Cap	Grth/Val
Small Cap	Value

Portfolio

79.9%	U.S. stock	0.0%	conv't
19.0%	int'l stock	0.0%	preferred
0.0%	U.S. bonds	0.0%	other
0.0%	int'l bonds	1.1%	cash

Number of Investments: 145

Percent of Portfolio in Top 10 Investments: 35%

SHAREHOLDER INFORMATION

Minimum Investment

Initial: $2,500 Subsequent: $250

Minimum IRA Investment

Initial: $500 Subsequent: $100

Maximum Fees

Load: 0.75% redemption 12b-1: none

Other: redemption fee applies for 30 days

Services

✔ IRA

✔ Keogh

✔ Telephone Exchange

ICON Energy (ICENX)

800-764-0442
www.iconfunds.com

Energy/Resources Sector

PERFORMANCE — fund inception date: 11/5/97

	3yr Annual	5yr Annual	10yr Annual	Bull	Bear
Return (%)	0.4	14.7	20.4	295.3	-31.2
Differ From Category (+/-)	9.2 high	8.3 high	10.6 high	25.0 abv av	21.5 high

Standard Deviation	Category Risk Index	Beta
27.2%—high	0.82—low	1.02

	2008	2007	2006	2005	2004	2003	2002	2001	2000	1999
Return (%)	-33.4	38.7	9.6	41.9	38.1	32.6	-5.8	-3.4	78.6	50.2
Differ From Category (+/-)	19.7	-2.2	-4.0	3.6	8.3	0.9	0.9	7.7	47.3	18.2
Return, Tax-Adjusted (%)	-37.0	34.1	8.0	41.3	38.1	32.6	-5.8	-3.4	75.5	50.2

PER SHARE DATA

	2008	2007	2006	2005	2004	2003	2002	2001	2000	1999
Dividends, Net Income ($)	0.12	0.11	0.00	0.08	0.00	0.00	0.00	0.02	0.09	0.00
Distrib'ns, Cap Gain ($)	7.82	9.67	3.36	0.85	0.00	0.00	0.00	0.00	1.12	0.00
Net Asset Value ($)	14.26	33.64	31.71	31.95	23.17	16.77	12.64	13.41	13.89	8.49
Expense Ratio (%)	1.16	1.17	1.17	1.21	1.35	1.40	1.35	1.39	1.36	1.45
Yield (%)	0.52	0.25	0.00	0.25	0.00	0.00	0.00	0.14	0.59	0.00
Portfolio Turnover (%)	120	55	23	28	13	43	27	135	124	34
Total Assets (Millions $)	371	793	730	893	426	81	97	57	45	18

PORTFOLIO (as of 9/30/08)

Portfolio Manager: Rollingson/Straus - 2007

Investment Style

Large Cap	Growth
Mid Cap	Grth/Val
Small Cap	Value

Portfolio

89.7%	U.S. stock	0.0%	conv't
4.0%	int'l stock	0.0%	preferred
0.0%	U.S. bonds	0.0%	other
0.0%	int'l bonds	6.4%	cash

Number of Investments: 30
Percent of Portfolio in Top 10 Investments: 71%

SHAREHOLDER INFORMATION

Minimum Investment
Initial: $1,000 Subsequent: $100

Minimum IRA Investment
Initial: $1,000 Subsequent: $100

Maximum Fees
Load: none 12b-1: none
Other: none

Services
✔ IRA
✔ Keogh
✔ Telephone Exchange

T. Rowe Price New Era (PRNEX)

800-638-5660
www.troweprice.com

Energy/Resources Sector

PERFORMANCE — fund inception date: 1/20/69

	3yr Annual	5yr Annual	10yr Annual	Bull	Bear
Return (%)	-6.4	6.7	9.2	275.7	-49.8
Differ From Category (+/-)	2.4 abv av	0.3 av	-0.6 av	5.4 av	2.9 av

Standard Deviation	Category Risk Index	Beta
28.7%—high	0.86—blw av	1.40

	2008	2007	2006	2005	2004	2003	2002	2001	2000	1999
Return (%)	-50.2	40.6	17.0	29.8	30.0	33.2	-6.4	-4.4	20.3	21.2
Differ From Category (+/-)	2.9	-0.3	3.4	-8.5	0.2	1.5	0.3	6.7	-11.0	-10.8
Return, Tax-Adjusted (%)	-50.4	39.5	16.2	28.6	29.1	33.0	-6.7	-5.4	18.4	18.7

PER SHARE DATA

	2008	2007	2006	2005	2004	2003	2002	2001	2000	1999
Dividends, Net Income ($)	0.49	0.54	0.57	0.37	0.23	0.25	0.20	0.27	0.29	0.30
Distrib'ns, Cap Gain ($)	0.39	2.84	1.55	2.32	1.46	0.00	0.00	0.68	1.51	1.82
Net Asset Value ($)	29.58	61.16	46.00	41.10	33.68	27.22	20.63	22.24	24.30	21.80
Expense Ratio (%)	na	0.63	0.66	0.68	0.69	0.72	0.72	0.72	0.72	0.74
Yield (%)	1.63	0.84	1.19	0.85	0.65	0.91	0.96	1.17	1.12	1.27
Portfolio Turnover (%)	na	18	16	36	19	18	11	18	28	33
Total Assets (Millions $)	3,306	6,921	4,438	3,763	2,161	1,334	985	1,070	1,195	1,082

PORTFOLIO (as of 9/30/08)

Portfolio Manager: Ober - 1997

Investment Style

Large Cap	Growth
Mid Cap	Grth/Val
Small Cap	Value

Portfolio

65.0% U.S. stock	0.0% conv't
32.0% int'l stock	0.0% preferred
0.0% U.S. bonds	0.0% other
0.0% int'l bonds	3.1% cash

Number of Investments: 103

Percent of Portfolio in Top 10 Investments: 31%

SHAREHOLDER INFORMATION

Minimum Investment
Initial: $2,500 Subsequent: $100

Minimum IRA Investment
Initial: $1,000 Subsequent: $50

Maximum Fees
Load: none 12b-1: none
Other: none

Services
✔ IRA
✔ Keogh
✔ Telephone Exchange

Vanguard Energy (VGENX)

800-662-6273
www.vanguard.com

Energy/Resources Sector

PERFORMANCE — fund inception date: 5/23/84

	3yr Annual	5yr Annual	10yr Annual	Bull	Bear
Return (%)	-2.2	13.1	14.7	323.3	-42.0
Differ From Category (+/-)	6.6 high	6.7 high	4.9 high	53.0 high	10.7 high

Standard Deviation	Category Risk Index	Beta
27.4%—high	0.82—blw av	1.24

	2008	2007	2006	2005	2004	2003	2002	2001	2000	1999
Return (%)	-42.9	37.0	19.6	44.5	36.6	33.7	-0.7	-2.6	36.4	20.9
Differ From Category (+/-)	10.2	-3.9	6.0	6.3	6.8	2.1	6.0	8.5	5.1	-11.1
Return, Tax-Adjusted (%)	-43.6	35.7	19.0	43.9	36.2	33.0	-2.5	-4.3	34.5	20.2

PER SHARE DATA

	2008	2007	2006	2005	2004	2003	2002	2001	2000	1999
Dividends, Net Income ($)	1.26	1.18	1.03	0.74	0.52	0.39	0.36	0.40	0.36	0.35
Distrib'ns, Cap Gain ($)	2.47	4.31	1.45	1.03	0.20	0.74	1.59	1.54	1.38	0.00
Net Asset Value ($)	44.13	82.39	64.63	56.05	40.00	29.85	23.20	25.29	28.07	21.92
Expense Ratio (%)	0.25	0.25	0.28	0.33	0.38	0.40	0.39	0.41	0.48	0.41
Yield (%)	2.71	1.35	1.55	1.29	1.30	1.27	1.45	1.49	1.22	1.61
Portfolio Turnover (%)	22	22	10	1	26	23	28	24	18	22
Total Assets (Millions $)	4,532	8,816	6,628	5,650	4,706	2,219	1,305	1,282	1,351	1,018

PORTFOLIO (as of 9/30/08)

Portfolio Manager: Bevilacqua/Bandtel/Troyer - 1998

Investment Style

Large Cap	Growth
Mid Cap	Grth/Val
Small Cap	Value

Portfolio

52.2%	U.S. stock	0.0%	conv't
43.5%	int'l stock	0.0%	preferred
0.0%	U.S. bonds	0.1%	other
0.0%	int'l bonds	4.2%	cash

Number of Investments: 105
Percent of Portfolio in Top 10 Investments: 39%

SHAREHOLDER INFORMATION

Minimum Investment
Initial: $25,000 Subsequent: $100

Minimum IRA Investment
Initial: $0 Subsequent: $0

Maximum Fees
Load: 1.00% redemption 12b-1: none
Other: redemption fee applies for 1 year

Services
✔ IRA
✔ Keogh
✔ Telephone Exchange

Financial/Banking Sector Stock Funds
Category Performance Ranked by 2008 Returns

Fund (Ticker)	Annual Return (%) 2008	3Yr	5Yr	10Yr	Category Risk	Total Risk
Fidelity Select Banking (FSRBX)	-37.5	-17.7	-9.1	-2.1	blw av	abv av
T. Rowe Price Financial Services (PRISX)	-40.1	-14.3	-5.6	2.0	low	abv av
Schwab Financial Services (SWFFX)	-44.2	-16.0	-4.9	na	blw av	abv av
Fidelity Select Insurance (FSPCX)	-47.0	-17.4	-6.3	1.7	av	abv av
Fidelity Select Brokerage & Investment (FSLBX)	-49.4	-15.1	-2.1	4.4	high	high
Financial/Banking Sector Category Average	**-45.9**	**-19.1**	**-8.6**	**0.1**	**av**	**abv av**

Fidelity Select Banking (FSRBX)

800-544-8544
www.fidelity.com

Financial/Banking Sector

PERFORMANCE — fund inception date: 6/30/86

	3yr Annual	5yr Annual	10yr Annual	Bull	Bear
Return (%)	-17.7	-9.1	-2.1	53.0	-45.4
Differ From Category (+/-)	1.4 av	-0.5 av	-2.2 blw av	-35.2 blw av	4.9 high

Standard Deviation	Category Risk Index	Beta
19.2%—abv av	0.92—blw av	0.70

	2008	2007	2006	2005	2004	2003	2002	2001	2000	1999
Return (%)	-37.5	-21.2	13.1	-0.2	11.7	32.2	-7.8	0.4	18.2	-10.1
Differ From Category (+/-)	8.4	-11.1	-2.0	-6.9	-1.8	-2.3	0.2	2.7	-18.1	-10.0
Return, Tax-Adjusted (%)	-37.9	-22.3	10.5	-1.7	10.1	31.8	-8.2	-0.2	15.9	-13.9

PER SHARE DATA

	2008	2007	2006	2005	2004	2003	2002	2001	2000	1999
Dividends, Net Income ($)	0.51	0.64	0.71	0.62	0.57	0.48	0.34	0.47	0.60	0.36
Distrib'ns, Cap Gain ($)	0.05	1.88	5.39	3.23	3.46	0.46	0.00	0.02	2.47	7.44
Net Asset Value ($)	14.76	24.48	34.03	35.65	39.60	39.11	30.31	33.21	33.56	31.50
Expense Ratio (%)	0.90	0.91	0.92	0.95	1.07	1.10	1.09	1.18	1.19	1.16
Yield (%)	3.44	2.42	1.80	1.59	1.32	1.21	1.12	1.41	1.66	0.92
Portfolio Turnover (%)	86	112	70	51	28	33	41	63	94	22
Total Assets (Millions $)	247	249	370	373	507	472	397	493	496	515

PORTFOLIO (as of 11/30/08)

Portfolio Manager: Montemaggiore - 2008

Investment Style

Large Cap	Growth
Mid Cap	Grth/Val
Small Cap	Value

Portfolio

95.6%	U.S. stock	0.0%	conv't
0.0%	int'l stock	2.0%	preferred
0.0%	U.S. bonds	0.0%	other
0.0%	int'l bonds	2.4%	cash

Number of Investments: 43
Percent of Portfolio in Top 10 Investments: 64%

SHAREHOLDER INFORMATION

Minimum Investment
Initial: $2,500 Subsequent: $250

Minimum IRA Investment
Initial: $500 Subsequent: $100

Maximum Fees
Load: 0.75% redemption 12b-1: none
Other: redemption fee applies for 30 days

Services
✔ IRA
Keogh
✔ Telephone Exchange

Fidelity Select Brokerage & Investment (FSLBX)

800-544-8544
www.fidelity.com

Financial/Banking Sector

PERFORMANCE — fund inception date: 7/29/85

	3yr Annual	5yr Annual	10yr Annual	Bull	Bear
Return (%)	-15.1	-2.1	4.4	183.5	-52.3
Differ From Category (+/-)	4.0 high	6.5 high	4.3 high	95.3 high	-2.0 av

Standard Deviation	Category Risk Index	Beta
24.2%—high	1.16—high	1.47

	2008	2007	2006	2005	2004	2003	2002	2001	2000	1999
Return (%)	-49.4	-0.2	21.2	29.8	12.9	36.4	-17.3	-9.1	28.0	30.6
Differ From Category (+/-)	-3.5	9.9	6.1	23.1	-0.6	1.9	-9.3	-6.8	-8.3	30.7
Return, Tax-Adjusted (%)	-50.1	-1.5	19.2	28.9	12.8	36.4	-17.5	-10.5	25.3	28.9

PER SHARE DATA

	2008	2007	2006	2005	2004	2003	2002	2001	2000	1999
Dividends, Net Income ($)	0.93	0.87	0.59	0.19	0.24	0.16	0.23	0.12	0.00	0.05
Distrib'ns, Cap Gain ($)	2.51	5.78	8.65	3.45	0.00	0.00	0.00	3.41	6.49	3.13
Net Asset Value ($)	31.74	67.30	74.08	68.95	55.87	49.68	36.54	44.42	53.14	46.83
Expense Ratio (%)	0.87	0.89	0.89	0.98	1.10	1.16	1.11	1.08	1.28	1.24
Yield (%)	2.71	1.19	0.71	0.26	0.42	0.32	0.62	0.25	0.00	0.10
Portfolio Turnover (%)	84	124	112	98	64	64	74	105	47	59
Total Assets (Millions $)	358	788	1,242	1,020	436	407	349	462	636	469

PORTFOLIO (as of 11/30/08)

Portfolio Manager: Hesse - 2007

Investment Style

Large Cap	Growth
Mid Cap	Grth/Val
Small Cap	Value

Portfolio

72.6% U.S. stock	0.0% conv't
24.7% int'l stock	0.1% preferred
0.0% U.S. bonds	0.0% other
0.0% int'l bonds	2.6% cash

Number of Investments: 74

Percent of Portfolio in Top 10 Investments: 50%

SHAREHOLDER INFORMATION

Minimum Investment

Initial: $2,500 Subsequent: $250

Minimum IRA Investment

Initial: $500 Subsequent: $100

Maximum Fees

Load: 0.75% redemption 12b-1: none

Other: redemption fee applies for 30 days

Services

✔ IRA

✔ Keogh

✔ Telephone Exchange

Fidelity Select Insurance (FSPCX)

800-544-8544
www.fidelity.com

Financial/Banking Sector

PERFORMANCE — fund inception date: 12/16/85

	3yr Annual	5yr Annual	10yr Annual	Bull	Bear
Return (%)	-17.4	-6.3	1.7	99.0	-49.6
Differ From Category (+/-)	1.7 abv av	2.3 abv av	1.6 abv av	10.8 abv av	0.7 abv av

Standard Deviation	Category Risk Index	Beta
20.1%—abv av	0.96—av	1.16

	2008	2007	2006	2005	2004	2003	2002	2001	2000	1999
Return (%)	-47.0	-4.4	11.3	13.7	12.7	27.4	-5.7	-5.0	53.2	-6.0
Differ From Category (+/-)	-1.1	5.7	-3.8	7.0	-0.8	-7.1	2.3	-2.7	16.9	-5.9
Return, Tax-Adjusted (%)	-47.2	-5.4	10.2	13.3	12.6	27.0	-6.4	-5.1	52.7	-9.0

PER SHARE DATA

	2008	2007	2006	2005	2004	2003	2002	2001	2000	1999
Dividends, Net Income ($)	0.54	0.30	0.40	0.60	0.10	0.08	0.09	0.03	0.12	0.00
Distrib'ns, Cap Gain ($)	0.02	4.56	4.64	1.26	0.59	1.29	1.55	0.30	0.65	6.60
Net Asset Value ($)	32.75	62.94	70.96	68.38	61.80	55.42	44.59	48.86	51.75	34.30
Expense Ratio (%)	0.93	0.98	1.02	1.05	1.23	1.24	1.17	1.16	1.36	1.31
Yield (%)	1.64	0.44	0.52	0.86	0.16	0.14	0.19	0.06	0.22	0.00
Portfolio Turnover (%)	60	58	44	50	59	95	104	175	107	72
Total Assets (Millions $)	87	179	210	208	171	109	107	115	211	46

PORTFOLIO (as of 11/30/08)

Portfolio Manager: Wilhelm - 2008

Investment Style

Large Cap	Growth
Mid Cap	Grth/Val
Small Cap	Value

Portfolio

92.5%	U.S. stock	0.0%	conv't
6.2%	int'l stock	0.0%	preferred
0.0%	U.S. bonds	0.0%	other
0.0%	int'l bonds	1.3%	cash

Number of Investments: 54
Percent of Portfolio in Top 10 Investments: 63%

SHAREHOLDER INFORMATION

Minimum Investment
Initial: $2,500 Subsequent: $250

Minimum IRA Investment
Initial: $500 Subsequent: $100

Maximum Fees
Load: 0.75% redemption 12b-1: none
Other: redemption fee applies for 30 days

Services
✔ IRA
✔ Keogh
✔ Telephone Exchange

Schwab Financial Services (SWFFX)

800-435-4000
www.schwab.com

Financial/Banking Sector

PERFORMANCE — fund inception date: 7/3/00

	3yr Annual	5yr Annual	10yr Annual	Bull	Bear
Return (%)	-16.0	-4.9	na	111.7	-47.8
Differ From Category (+/-)	3.1 abv av	3.7 high	na	23.5 high	2.5 abv av

Standard Deviation	Category Risk Index	Beta
19.4%—abv av	0.93—blw av	1.13

	2008	2007	2006	2005	2004	2003	2002	2001	2000	1999
Return (%)	-44.2	-7.4	14.7	12.1	17.3	35.5	-12.5	-8.0	—	—
Differ From Category (+/-)	1.7	2.7	-0.4	5.4	3.8	1.0	-4.5	-5.7	—	—
Return, Tax-Adjusted (%)	-44.4	-7.6	14.4	11.3	16.0	35.3	-13.0	-8.4	—	—

PER SHARE DATA

	2008	2007	2006	2005	2004	2003	2002	2001	2000	1999
Dividends, Net Income ($)	0.15	0.21	0.11	0.11	0.09	0.10	0.15	0.09	—	—
Distrib'ns, Cap Gain ($)	0.00	0.02	0.19	0.64	0.94	0.00	0.00	0.06	—	—
Net Asset Value ($)	7.99	14.61	16.02	14.23	13.34	12.27	9.13	10.59	—	—
Expense Ratio (%)	na	0.90	0.98	1.07	1.05	1.03	0.89	0.00	—	—
Yield (%)	1.89	1.42	0.68	0.71	0.65	0.81	1.61	0.84	—	—
Portfolio Turnover (%)	na	54	57	74	85	181	151	0	—	—
Total Assets (Millions $)	72	83	103	38	21	20	16	23	—	—

PORTFOLIO (as of 7/31/08)

Portfolio Manager: Mano/Mortimer/Hsu/Davis - 2000

Investment Style

Large Cap	Growth
Mid Cap	Grth/Val
Small Cap	Value

Portfolio

95.4%	U.S. stock	0.0%	conv't
0.0%	int'l stock	0.0%	preferred
0.0%	U.S. bonds	0.2%	other
0.0%	int'l bonds	4.3%	cash

Number of Investments: 71
Percent of Portfolio in Top 10 Investments: 37%

SHAREHOLDER INFORMATION

Minimum Investment
Initial: $100 Subsequent: $0

Minimum IRA Investment
Initial: $0 Subsequent: $0

Maximum Fees
Load: 2.00% redemption 12b-1: none
Other: redemption fee applies for 30 days

Services
✔ IRA
✔ Keogh
✔ Telephone Exchange

T. Rowe Price Financial Services (PRISX)

800-638-5660
www.troweprice.com

Financial/Banking Sector

PERFORMANCE — fund inception date: 9/30/96

	3yr Annual	5yr Annual	10yr Annual	Bull	Bear
Return (%)	-14.3	-5.6	2.0	100.2	-45.9
Differ From Category (+/-)	4.8 high	3.0 abv av	1.9 abv av	12.0 abv av	4.4 high

Standard Deviation	Category Risk Index	Beta
19.1%—abv av	0.91—low	1.13

	2008	2007	2006	2005	2004	2003	2002	2001	2000	1999
Return (%)	-40.1	-9.4	15.9	5.0	13.4	35.0	-10.2	-3.2	36.7	1.7
Differ From Category (+/-)	5.8	0.7	0.8	-1.6	-0.1	0.5	-2.1	-0.9	0.4	1.8
Return, Tax-Adjusted (%)	-40.3	-11.0	13.7	2.8	12.5	34.4	-10.5	-5.0	35.8	0.4

PER SHARE DATA

	2008	2007	2006	2005	2004	2003	2002	2001	2000	1999
Dividends, Net Income ($)	0.26	0.39	0.43	0.32	0.17	0.23	0.13	0.15	0.09	0.10
Distrib'ns, Cap Gain ($)	0.00	1.88	2.70	3.28	1.10	0.51	0.06	1.68	0.55	0.85
Net Asset Value ($)	9.96	17.10	21.38	21.14	23.50	21.86	16.75	18.84	21.38	16.12
Expense Ratio (%)	na	0.91	0.90	0.93	0.93	0.97	1.00	0.97	1.00	1.14
Yield (%)	2.61	2.05	1.78	1.31	0.69	1.02	0.77	0.73	0.41	0.58
Portfolio Turnover (%)	na	140	113	56	36	51	49	55	32	37
Total Assets (Millions $)	257	368	445	394	412	371	265	309	337	159

PORTFOLIO (as of 9/30/08)

Portfolio Manager: Arricale/Dopkin/Fortune/Ng - 2007

Investment Style

Large Cap	Growth
Mid Cap	Grth/Val
Small Cap	Value

Portfolio

77.5% U.S. stock	0.0% conv't
6.3% int'l stock	5.8% preferred
1.6% U.S. bonds	1.4% other
0.0% int'l bonds	7.4% cash

Number of Investments: 85
Percent of Portfolio in Top 10 Investments: 41%

SHAREHOLDER INFORMATION

Minimum Investment
Initial: $2,500 Subsequent: $100

Minimum IRA Investment
Initial: $1,000 Subsequent: $50

Maximum Fees
Load: none 12b-1: none
Other: none

Services
✔ IRA
✔ Keogh
✔ Telephone Exchange

Gold Sector Stock Funds
Category Performance Ranked by 2008 Returns

Fund (Ticker)	Annual Return (%) 2008	3Yr	5Yr	10Yr	Category Risk	Total Risk
Fidelity Select Gold (FSAGX)	-20.5	7.6	9.6	14.3	blw av	high
USAA Precious Metals and Minerals (USAGX)	-25.0	11.1	11.2	19.3	abv av	high
U.S. Gbl Inv Gold and Precious Metals (USERX)	-27.1	8.6	9.7	13.8	blw av	high
American Century Global Gold Inv (BGEIX)	-27.3	2.1	4.7	12.2	abv av	high
GAMCO Gold AAA (GOLDX)	-28.8	5.5	6.9	16.4	av	high
Gold Sector Category Average	**-37.4**	**0.3**	**4.4**	**12.8**	**av**	**high**

American Century Global Gold Inv (BGEIX)

800-345-2021
www.americancentury.com

Gold Sector

PERFORMANCE — fund inception date: 8/17/88

	3yr Annual	5yr Annual	10yr Annual	Bull	Bear
Return (%)	2.1	4.7	12.2	201.2	-33.8
Differ From Category (+/-)	1.8 av	0.3 abv av	-0.6 av	-75.5 low	9.1 abv av

Standard Deviation	Category Risk Index	Beta
43.6%—high	1.00—abv av	1.02

	2008	2007	2006	2005	2004	2003	2002	2001	2000	1999
Return (%)	-27.3	15.1	27.0	29.1	-8.2	46.7	73.0	34.0	-24.0	-3.2
Differ From Category (+/-)	10.1	-8.6	-6.1	-4.2	-1.2	-11.6	5.5	14.0	-3.9	-7.1
Return, Tax-Adjusted (%)	-28.6	14.9	26.9	29.1	-8.3	46.3	72.7	33.5	-24.2	-3.6

PER SHARE DATA

	2008	2007	2006	2005	2004	2003	2002	2001	2000	1999
Dividends, Net Income ($)	0.00	0.23	0.05	0.00	0.08	0.21	0.04	0.06	0.03	0.05
Distrib'ns, Cap Gain ($)	1.94	0.00	0.00	0.00	0.00	0.00	0.00	0.00	0.00	0.00
Net Asset Value ($)	14.23	22.34	19.63	15.50	12.00	13.17	9.13	5.30	4.00	5.29
Expense Ratio (%)	0.68	0.67	0.67	0.67	0.68	0.69	0.69	0.68	0.67	0.68
Yield (%)	0.00	1.03	0.23	0.00	0.64	1.56	0.39	1.08	0.64	0.97
Portfolio Turnover (%)	17	3	18	5	14	22	31	14	17	53
Total Assets (Millions $)	719	1,096	1,071	777	695	737	421	193	142	202

PORTFOLIO (as of 9/30/08)

Portfolio Manager: Martin/Sterling - 1992

Investment Style

Large Cap	Growth
Mid Cap	Grth/Val
Small Cap	Value

Portfolio

10.5%	U.S. stock	0.0%	conv't
88.5%	int'l stock	0.0%	preferred
0.0%	U.S. bonds	0.1%	other
0.0%	int'l bonds	0.9%	cash

Number of Investments: 79
Percent of Portfolio in Top 10 Investments: 62%

SHAREHOLDER INFORMATION

Minimum Investment
Initial: $2,500 Subsequent: $50

Minimum IRA Investment
Initial: $2,500 Subsequent: $0

Maximum Fees
Load: 1.00% redemption 12b-1: none
Other: redemption fee applies for 60 days

Services
✔ IRA
✔ Keogh
✔ Telephone Exchange

Fidelity Select Gold (FSAGX)

800-544-8544
www.fidelity.com

Gold Sector

PERFORMANCE — fund inception date: 12/16/85

	3yr Annual	5yr Annual	10yr Annual	Bull	Bear
Return (%)	7.6	9.6	14.3	202.3	-27.3
Differ From Category (+/-)	7.3 high	5.2 high	1.5 abv av	-74.4 blw av	15.6 high

Standard Deviation	Category Risk Index	Beta
40.7%—high	0.94—blw av	0.94

	2008	2007	2006	2005	2004	2003	2002	2001	2000	1999
Return (%)	-20.5	24.9	25.4	40.7	-9.8	32.0	64.2	24.9	-18.1	8.3
Differ From Category (+/-)	16.9	1.2	-7.7	7.4	-2.8	-26.3	-3.3	4.9	2.0	4.4
Return, Tax-Adjusted (%)	-20.6	22.7	23.1	38.5	-9.8	31.1	63.3	24.2	-18.3	8.3

PER SHARE DATA

	2008	2007	2006	2005	2004	2003	2002	2001	2000	1999
Dividends, Net Income ($)	0.00	0.18	0.02	0.02	0.00	1.42	0.36	0.22	0.07	0.00
Distrib'ns, Cap Gain ($)	0.17	5.03	5.10	3.84	0.00	0.00	0.00	0.00	0.00	0.00
Net Asset Value ($)	31.58	39.88	36.50	33.24	26.91	29.83	23.92	14.81	12.04	14.78
Expense Ratio (%)	0.81	0.87	0.82	0.89	1.04	1.11	1.24	1.43	1.41	1.54
Yield (%)	0.00	0.39	0.04	0.05	0.00	4.76	1.50	1.48	0.58	0.00
Portfolio Turnover (%)	55	85	108	79	41	44	49	23	71	59
Total Assets (Millions $)	1,689	1,715	1,537	1,044	690	847	697	305	240	200

PORTFOLIO (as of 11/30/08)

Portfolio Manager: Wickwire - 2007

Investment Style

Large Cap	Growth
Mid Cap	Grth/Val
Small Cap	Value

Portfolio

13.4%	U.S. stock	0.0%	conv't
84.7%	int'l stock	0.0%	preferred
0.0%	U.S. bonds	0.2%	other
0.0%	int'l bonds	1.6%	cash

Number of Investments: 62

Percent of Portfolio in Top 10 Investments: 71%

SHAREHOLDER INFORMATION

Minimum Investment

Initial: $2,500 Subsequent: $250

Minimum IRA Investment

Initial: $500 Subsequent: $100

Maximum Fees

Load: 0.75% redemption 12b-1: none

Other: redemption fee applies for 30 days

Services

✔ IRA
✔ Keogh
✔ Telephone Exchange

GAMCO Gold AAA (GOLDX)

800-422-3554
www.gabelli.com

Gold Sector

PERFORMANCE — fund inception date: 7/11/94

	3yr Annual	5yr Annual	10yr Annual	Bull	Bear
Return (%)	5.5	6.9	16.4	239.9	-35.8
Differ From Category (+/-)	5.2 abv av	2.5 abv av	3.6 high	-36.8 av	7.1 abv av

Standard Deviation	Category Risk Index	Beta
43.2%—high	0.99—av	1.19

	2008	2007	2006	2005	2004	2003	2002	2001	2000	1999
Return (%)	-28.8	24.7	32.3	33.6	-10.9	49.4	87.1	25.9	-15.6	10.0
Differ From Category (+/-)	8.6	1.0	-0.8	0.3	-3.9	-8.9	19.7	5.9	4.5	6.1
Return, Tax-Adjusted (%)	-28.8	22.9	30.5	33.0	-11.1	49.2	87.1	25.4	-15.6	10.0

PER SHARE DATA

	2008	2007	2006	2005	2004	2003	2002	2001	2000	1999
Dividends, Net Income ($)	0.00	0.74	0.49	0.11	0.20	0.17	0.00	0.06	0.00	0.00
Distrib'ns, Cap Gain ($)	0.00	2.27	2.04	0.46	0.00	0.00	0.00	0.00	0.00	0.00
Net Asset Value ($)	20.03	28.11	24.98	20.80	16.00	18.18	12.28	6.56	5.26	6.23
Expense Ratio (%)	na	1.46	1.44	1.50	1.54	1.55	1.67	2.46	2.40	—
Yield (%)	0.00	2.43	1.82	0.53	1.25	0.92	0.00	0.99	0.00	0.00
Portfolio Turnover (%)	na	12	12	4	11	12	53	37	21	52
Total Assets (Millions $)	367	483	419	334	279	352	138	15	13	14

PORTFOLIO (as of 9/30/08)

Portfolio Manager: Bryan - 1994

Investment Style

Large Cap — Growth
Mid Cap — Grth/Val
Small Cap — Value

Portfolio

10.1%	U.S. stock	0.0%	conv't
86.4%	int'l stock	0.0%	preferred
0.0%	U.S. bonds	1.4%	other
0.0%	int'l bonds	2.1%	cash

Number of Investments: 65
Percent of Portfolio in Top 10 Investments: 62%

SHAREHOLDER INFORMATION

Minimum Investment
Initial: $1,000 — Subsequent: $0

Minimum IRA Investment
Initial: $250 — Subsequent: $0

Maximum Fees
Load: 2.00% redemption — 12b-1: 0.25%
Other: redemption fee applies for 7 days

Services
✔ IRA
Keogh
✔ Telephone Exchange

U.S. Gbl Inv Gold and Precious Metals (USERX)

800-873-8637
www.usfunds.com

Gold Sector

PERFORMANCE — fund inception date: 7/1/74

	3yr Annual	5yr Annual	10yr Annual	Bull	Bear
Return (%)	8.6	9.7	13.8	309.2	-32.3
Differ From Category (+/-)	8.3 high	5.3 high	1.0 av	32.5 abv av	10.6 high

Standard Deviation	Category Risk Index	Beta
40.7%—high	0.94—blw av	1.02

	2008	2007	2006	2005	2004	2003	2002	2001	2000	1999
Return (%)	-27.1	16.9	50.1	32.7	-6.5	67.0	81.3	11.1	-29.9	-2.7
Differ From Category (+/-)	10.3	-6.8	17.0	-0.5	0.5	8.7	13.8	-8.9	-9.8	-6.6
Return, Tax-Adjusted (%)	-27.8	14.6	50.1	32.5	-6.6	67.0	81.3	11.1	-29.9	-2.7

PER SHARE DATA

	2008	2007	2006	2005	2004	2003	2002	2001	2000	1999
Dividends, Net Income ($)	0.00	1.63	0.00	0.12	0.05	0.03	0.00	0.00	0.00	0.00
Distrib'ns, Cap Gain ($)	0.73	0.80	0.00	0.00	0.00	0.00	0.00	0.00	0.00	0.00
Net Asset Value ($)	10.83	16.13	16.07	10.70	8.15	8.76	5.26	2.90	2.61	3.72
Expense Ratio (%)	1.27	1.28	1.47	1.97	1.93	2.64	3.57	5.79	5.74	5.24
Yield (%)	0.00	9.65	0.00	1.10	0.56	0.29	0.00	0.00	0.00	0.00
Portfolio Turnover (%)	93	72	78	66	85	138	164	95	82	388
Total Assets (Millions $)	154	197	241	95	76	86	48	23	22	34

PORTFOLIO (as of 9/30/08)

Portfolio Manager: Holmes/Aldis - 1999

Investment Style

Large Cap	Growth
Mid Cap	Grth/Val
Small Cap	Value

Portfolio

10.6%	U.S. stock	0.0%	conv't
65.0%	int'l stock	0.0%	preferred
0.0%	U.S. bonds	7.1%	other
0.0%	int'l bonds	17.4%	cash

Number of Investments: 92
Percent of Portfolio in Top 10 Investments: 56%

SHAREHOLDER INFORMATION

Minimum Investment
Initial: $5,000 Subsequent: $50

Minimum IRA Investment
Initial: $100 Subsequent: $50

Maximum Fees
Load: 0.50% redemption 12b-1: 0.25%
Other: redemption fee applies for 30 days

Services
✔ IRA
✔ Keogh
✔ Telephone Exchange

USAA Precious Metals and Minerals (USAGX)

800-531-8181
www.usaa.com

Gold Sector

PERFORMANCE

fund inception date: 8/15/84

	3yr Annual	5yr Annual	10yr Annual	Bull	Bear
Return (%)	11.1	11.2	19.3	344.8	-30.6
Differ From Category (+/-)	10.8 high	6.8 high	6.5 high	68.1 abv av	12.3 high

Standard Deviation	Category Risk Index	Beta
43.3%—high	1.00—abv av	1.20

	2008	2007	2006	2005	2004	2003	2002	2001	2000	1999
Return (%)	-25.0	27.6	43.1	39.2	-10.8	71.4	67.6	30.9	-15.0	7.1
Differ From Category (+/-)	12.4	3.9	10.0	5.9	-3.8	13.1	0.1	10.9	5.1	3.2
Return, Tax-Adjusted (%)	-26.2	26.1	41.3	39.0	-10.9	70.2	65.3	30.6	-15.2	7.1

PER SHARE DATA

	2008	2007	2006	2005	2004	2003	2002	2001	2000	1999
Dividends, Net Income ($)	0.01	0.59	0.76	0.00	0.00	0.86	0.38	0.05	0.02	0.00
Distrib'ns, Cap Gain ($)	2.58	2.26	1.78	0.16	0.15	0.00	0.00	0.00	0.00	0.00
Net Asset Value ($)	21.27	32.52	27.78	21.18	15.33	17.35	10.62	6.58	5.06	5.98
Expense Ratio (%)	1.19	1.21	1.21	1.23	1.26	1.47	1.56	1.68	1.58	1.52
Yield (%)	0.05	1.68	2.57	0.00	0.00	4.94	3.60	0.70	0.47	0.00
Portfolio Turnover (%)	28	12	29	27	27	31	41	52	27	33
Total Assets (Millions $)	879	1,002	696	394	325	331	144	78	69	88

PORTFOLIO (as of 8/31/08)

Portfolio Manager: Johnson/Denbow - 1994

Investment Style

Large Cap	Growth
Mid Cap	Grth/Val
Small Cap	Value

Portfolio

14.5%	U.S. stock	0.0%	conv't
81.7%	int'l stock	0.0%	preferred
0.0%	U.S. bonds	0.2%	other
0.0%	int'l bonds	3.6%	cash

Number of Investments: 52

Percent of Portfolio in Top 10 Investments: 54%

SHAREHOLDER INFORMATION

Minimum Investment

Initial: $3,000 Subsequent: $50

Minimum IRA Investment

Initial: $250 Subsequent: $50

Maximum Fees

Load: none 12b-1: none

Other: none

Services

✔ IRA

✔ Keogh

✔ Telephone Exchange

Health Sector Stock Funds
Category Performance Ranked by 2008 Returns

Fund (Ticker)	Annual Return (%) 2008	3Yr	5Yr	10Yr	Category Risk	Total Risk
Fidelity Select Biotechnology (FBIOX)	-11.4	-2.0	2.8	4.8	high	av
Fidelity Select Pharmaceuticals (FPHAX)	-22.8	-0.5	2.2	na	blw av	blw av
Fidelity Select Medical Equip/Systems (FSMEX)	-23.4	-2.1	3.4	9.5	abv av	av
Schwab Health Care (SWHFX)	-25.0	-5.4	5.9	na	av	blw av
T. Rowe Price Health Sciences (PRHSX)	-28.8	-2.5	4.0	6.4	abv av	av
Health Sector Category Average	**-25.8**	**-5.4**	**1.7**	**5.1**	**av**	**av**

Fidelity Select Biotechnology (FBIOX)

800-544-8544
www.fidelity.com

Health Sector

PERFORMANCE — fund inception date: 12/16/85

	3yr Annual	5yr Annual	10yr Annual	Bull	Bear
Return (%)	-2.0	2.8	4.8	90.5	-19.2
Differ From Category (+/-)	3.4 high	1.1 abv av	-0.3 av	-13.2 av	8.5 high

Standard Deviation	Category Risk Index	Beta
18.3%—av	1.12—high	0.69

	2008	2007	2006	2005	2004	2003	2002	2001	2000	1999
Return (%)	-11.4	2.6	3.5	8.7	11.9	32.9	-40.6	-25.0	32.7	77.7
Differ From Category (+/-)	14.4	-8.8	0.5	-5.2	-1.6	2.4	-17.4	-16.0	-14.9	55.8
Return, Tax-Adjusted (%)	-11.4	2.6	3.5	8.7	11.9	32.9	-40.6	-25.0	32.1	76.3

PER SHARE DATA

	2008	2007	2006	2005	2004	2003	2002	2001	2000	1999
Dividends, Net Income ($)	0.00	0.00	0.00	0.00	0.00	0.00	0.00	0.00	0.00	0.00
Distrib'ns, Cap Gain ($)	0.00	0.00	0.00	0.00	0.00	0.00	0.00	0.00	2.11	2.82
Net Asset Value ($)	59.11	66.68	64.96	62.70	57.65	51.48	38.73	65.12	86.80	67.13
Expense Ratio (%)	0.89	0.92	0.93	0.99	1.15	1.24	1.09	1.00	1.15	1.30
Yield (%)	0.00	0.00	0.00	0.00	0.00	0.00	0.00	0.00	0.00	0.00
Portfolio Turnover (%)	143	70	63	19	50	73	96	74	72	86
Total Assets (Millions $)	1,197	1,188	1,464	1,679	1,850	1,853	1,537	3,081	4,118	1,623

PORTFOLIO (as of 11/30/08)

Portfolio Manager: Kaul - 2005

Investment Style

Large Cap	Growth
Mid Cap	Grth/Val
Small Cap	Value

Portfolio

97.9%	U.S. stock	0.0%	conv't
1.1%	int'l stock	0.0%	preferred
0.0%	U.S. bonds	0.4%	other
0.0%	int'l bonds	0.6%	cash

Number of Investments: 68
Percent of Portfolio in Top 10 Investments: 77%

SHAREHOLDER INFORMATION

Minimum Investment
Initial: $2,500 Subsequent: $250

Minimum IRA Investment
Initial: $500 Subsequent: $100

Maximum Fees
Load: 0.75% redemption 12b-1: none
Other: redemption fee applies for 30 days

Services
✔ IRA
✔ Keogh
✔ Telephone Exchange

Fidelity Select Medical Equip/Systems (FSMEX)

800-544-8544
www.fidelity.com

Health Sector

PERFORMANCE — fund inception date: 4/28/98

	3yr Annual	5yr Annual	10yr Annual	Bull	Bear
Return (%)	-2.1	3.4	9.5	103.1	-23.1
Differ From Category (+/-)	3.3 high	1.7 abv av	4.4 high	-0.6 abv av	4.6 high

Standard Deviation	Category Risk Index	Beta
16.2%—av	0.99—abv av	0.85

	2008	2007	2006	2005	2004	2003	2002	2001	2000	1999
Return (%)	-23.4	17.8	4.0	7.4	17.4	33.3	-6.3	0.3	50.3	10.7
Differ From Category (+/-)	2.4	6.4	0.9	-6.5	3.9	2.8	16.9	9.3	2.7	-11.2
Return, Tax-Adjusted (%)	-23.9	16.4	2.6	6.9	17.3	32.8	-6.4	-0.1	46.8	10.0

PER SHARE DATA

	2008	2007	2006	2005	2004	2003	2002	2001	2000	1999
Dividends, Net Income ($)	0.00	0.00	0.00	0.00	0.00	0.00	0.00	0.00	0.00	0.00
Distrib'ns, Cap Gain ($)	0.77	2.18	2.25	0.84	0.11	0.53	0.11	0.34	2.31	0.42
Net Asset Value ($)	18.45	24.87	23.03	24.33	23.40	20.02	15.42	16.56	16.91	13.12
Expense Ratio (%)	0.88	0.92	0.92	0.98	1.15	1.29	1.23	1.23	1.65	2.38
Yield (%)	0.02	0.00	0.00	0.00	0.00	0.00	0.00	0.00	0.00	0.00
Portfolio Turnover (%)	129	71	99	28	33	82	87	64	101	85
Total Assets (Millions $)	1,117	953	801	1,185	866	440	145	148	155	39

PORTFOLIO (as of 11/30/08)

Portfolio Manager: Yoon - 2007

Investment Style

Large Cap	Growth
Mid Cap	Grth/Val
Small Cap	Value

Portfolio

92.6%	U.S. stock	0.0%	conv't
3.8%	int'l stock	0.0%	preferred
0.0%	U.S. bonds	0.0%	other
0.0%	int'l bonds	3.6%	cash

Number of Investments: 50

Percent of Portfolio in Top 10 Investments: 67%

SHAREHOLDER INFORMATION

Minimum Investment

Initial: $2,500 Subsequent: $250

Minimum IRA Investment

Initial: $500 Subsequent: $100

Maximum Fees

Load: 0.75% redemption 12b-1: none

Other: redemption fee applies for 30 days

Services

✔ IRA

✔ Keogh

✔ Telephone Exchange

Fidelity Select Pharmaceuticals (FPHAX)

800-544-8544
www.fidelity.com

Health Sector

PERFORMANCE — fund inception date: 6/18/01

	3yr Annual	5yr Annual	10yr Annual	Bull	Bear
Return (%)	-0.5	2.2	na	84.9	-24.3
Differ From Category (+/-)	4.9 high	0.5 abv av	na	-18.8 blw av	3.4 abv av

Standard Deviation	Category Risk Index	Beta
13.8%—blw av	0.84—blw av	0.74

	2008	2007	2006	2005	2004	2003	2002	2001	2000	1999
Return (%)	-22.8	13.3	12.4	9.7	3.3	20.3	-23.4	—	—	—
Differ From Category (+/-)	3.0	2.0	9.3	-4.2	-10.2	-10.2	-0.2	—	—	—
Return, Tax-Adjusted (%)	-23.0	12.5	11.9	9.7	3.3	20.3	-23.4	—	—	—

PER SHARE DATA

	2008	2007	2006	2005	2004	2003	2002	2001	2000	1999
Dividends, Net Income ($)	0.13	0.11	0.04	0.01	0.00	0.00	0.00	—	—	—
Distrib'ns, Cap Gain ($)	0.06	0.48	0.31	0.00	0.00	0.00	0.00	—	—	—
Net Asset Value ($)	8.81	11.64	10.79	9.92	9.05	8.76	7.28	—	—	—
Expense Ratio (%)	0.95	1.01	1.03	1.18	1.57	1.74	1.74	—	—	—
Yield (%)	1.46	0.90	0.36	0.15	0.00	0.00	0.00	—	—	—
Portfolio Turnover (%)	119	204	207	42	80	140	26	—	—	—
Total Assets (Millions $)	166	202	209	114	97	72	52	—	—	—

PORTFOLIO (as of 11/30/08)

Portfolio Manager: Oh - 2006

Investment Style

Large Cap	Growth
Mid Cap	Grth/Val
Small Cap	Value

Portfolio

93.0%	U.S. stock	0.0%	conv't
5.7%	int'l stock	0.0%	preferred
0.0%	U.S. bonds	0.0%	other
0.0%	int'l bonds	1.3%	cash

Number of Investments: 132

Percent of Portfolio in Top 10 Investments: 74%

SHAREHOLDER INFORMATION

Minimum Investment

Initial: $2,500 Subsequent: $250

Minimum IRA Investment

Initial: $500 Subsequent: $100

Maximum Fees

Load: 0.75% redemption 12b-1: none

Other: redemption fee applies for 30 days; maint fee for low bal

Services

✔ IRA
✔ Keogh
✔ Telephone Exchange

Schwab Health Care (SWHFX)

800-435-4000
www.schwab.com

Health Sector

PERFORMANCE — fund inception date: 7/3/00

	3yr Annual	5yr Annual	10yr Annual	Bull	Bear
Return (%)	-5.4	5.9	na	157.9	-26.8
Differ From Category (+/-)	0.0 av	4.2 high	na	54.2 high	0.9 av

Standard Deviation	Category Risk Index	Beta
14.4%—blw av	0.88—av	0.76

	2008	2007	2006	2005	2004	2003	2002	2001	2000	1999
Return (%)	-25.0	10.6	2.1	20.0	31.0	36.7	-24.4	-14.4	—	—
Differ From Category (+/-)	0.8	-0.8	-1.0	6.1	17.5	6.2	-1.2	-5.4	—	—
Return, Tax-Adjusted (%)	-25.1	10.5	1.9	20.0	31.0	36.7	-24.6	-14.5	—	—

PER SHARE DATA

	2008	2007	2006	2005	2004	2003	2002	2001	2000	1999
Dividends, Net Income ($)	0.09	0.05	0.00	0.00	0.00	0.00	0.03	0.01	—	—
Distrib'ns, Cap Gain ($)	0.00	0.10	0.13	0.00	0.00	0.00	0.00	0.00	—	—
Net Asset Value ($)	12.29	16.50	15.04	14.86	12.38	9.45	6.91	9.18	—	—
Expense Ratio (%)	na	0.82	0.84	0.89	1.04	1.04	0.89	—	—	—
Yield (%)	0.72	0.28	0.00	0.00	0.00	0.00	0.47	0.05	—	—
Portfolio Turnover (%)	na	34	76	42	105	200	99	92	—	—
Total Assets (Millions $)	523	828	595	499	77	29	20	33	—	—

PORTFOLIO (as of 7/31/08)

Portfolio Manager: Mano/Mortimer/Hsu/Davis - 2000

Investment Style

Large Cap	Growth
Mid Cap	Grth/Val
Small Cap	Value

Portfolio

99.2% U.S. stock	0.0% conv't
0.0% int'l stock	0.0% preferred
0.0% U.S. bonds	0.0% other
0.0% int'l bonds	0.8% cash

Number of Investments: 85
Percent of Portfolio in Top 10 Investments: 40%

SHAREHOLDER INFORMATION

Minimum Investment
Initial: $100 Subsequent: $0

Minimum IRA Investment
Initial: $0 Subsequent: $0

Maximum Fees
Load: 2.00% redemption 12b-1: none
Other: redemption fee applies for 30 days

Services
✔ IRA
✔ Keogh
✔ Telephone Exchange

T. Rowe Price Health Sciences (PRHSX)

800-638-5660
www.troweprice.com

Health Sector

PERFORMANCE — fund inception date: 12/29/95

	3yr Annual	5yr Annual	10yr Annual	Bull	Bear
Return (%)	-2.5	4.0	6.4	138.3	-29.1
Differ From Category (+/-)	2.9 abv av	2.3 high	1.3 high	34.6 high	-1.4 blw av

Standard Deviation	Category Risk Index	Beta
17.2%—av	1.05—abv av	0.96

	2008	2007	2006	2005	2004	2003	2002	2001	2000	1999
Return (%)	-28.8	18.7	9.5	13.5	15.8	37.4	-27.8	-6.0	52.1	7.9
Differ From Category (+/-)	-3.0	7.3	6.4	-0.4	2.3	6.9	-4.6	3.0	4.5	-14.0
Return, Tax-Adjusted (%)	-29.0	17.2	8.7	12.7	15.8	37.4	-27.8	-6.3	49.0	6.3

PER SHARE DATA

	2008	2007	2006	2005	2004	2003	2002	2001	2000	1999
Dividends, Net Income ($)	0.00	0.00	0.00	0.00	0.00	0.00	0.00	0.00	0.00	0.00
Distrib'ns, Cap Gain ($)	0.34	2.68	1.34	1.16	0.00	0.00	0.00	0.31	2.48	1.26
Net Asset Value ($)	19.80	28.32	26.13	25.07	23.11	19.95	14.51	20.08	21.70	15.93
Expense Ratio (%)	na	0.83	0.87	0.91	0.93	1.00	1.04	0.95	0.98	1.11
Yield (%)	0.00	0.00	0.00	0.00	0.00	0.00	0.00	0.00	0.00	0.00
Portfolio Turnover (%)	na	45	49	56	44	45	62	63	111	82
Total Assets (Millions $)	1,602	2,295	1,714	1,489	1,331	1,028	678	961	972	303

PORTFOLIO (as of 9/30/08)

Portfolio Manager: Jenner/Bussard/Laporte - 2000

Investment Style

Large Cap	Growth
Mid Cap	Grth/Val
Small Cap	Value

Portfolio

84.5%	U.S. stock	0.0%	conv't
12.2%	int'l stock	0.0%	preferred
0.0%	U.S. bonds	0.5%	other
0.0%	int'l bonds	2.8%	cash

Number of Investments: 178
Percent of Portfolio in Top 10 Investments: 27%

SHAREHOLDER INFORMATION

Minimum Investment
Initial: $2,500 Subsequent: $100

Minimum IRA Investment
Initial: $1,000 Subsequent: $50

Maximum Fees
Load: none 12b-1: none
Other: none

Services
✔ IRA
✔ Keogh
✔ Telephone Exchange

Real Estate Sector Stock Funds
Category Performance Ranked by 2008 Returns

Fund (Ticker)	Annual Return (%) 2008	3Yr	5Yr	10Yr	Category Risk	Total Risk
Cohen & Steers Realty Shares (CSRSX)	-34.5	-10.1	2.9	8.4	av	high
Vanguard REIT Index (VGSIX)	-37.1	-10.8	0.7	7.1	abv av	high
T. Rowe Price Real Estate (TRREX)	-39.1	-12.3	1.1	7.8	av	high
Third Avenue Real Estate Value (TAREX)	-44.7	-13.0	-0.7	8.4	low	high
CGM Realty (CGMRX)	-46.9	-2.7	9.6	15.8	high	high
Real Estate Sector Category Average	**-44.2**	**-14.4**	**-1.7**	**6.9**	**av**	**high**

CGM Realty (CGMRX)

800-343-5678
www.cgmfunds.com

Real Estate Sector

PERFORMANCE — fund inception date: 5/13/94

	3yr Annual	5yr Annual	10yr Annual	Bull	Bear
Return (%)	-2.7	9.6	15.8	485.8	-49.5
Differ From Category (+/-)	11.7 high	11.3 high	8.9 high	300.6 high	2.1 av

Standard Deviation	Category Risk Index	Beta
32.5%—high	1.12—high	1.75

	2008	2007	2006	2005	2004	2003	2002	2001	2000	1999
Return (%)	-46.9	34.4	29.0	26.9	35.5	89.7	3.4	5.1	29.1	2.6
Differ From Category (+/-)	-2.7	47.6	-3.2	14.7	3.1	46.2	-1.1	-5.5	2.5	4.5
Return, Tax-Adjusted (%)	-47.5	31.5	24.2	21.4	32.9	88.9	1.8	3.0	26.5	-0.2

PER SHARE DATA

	2008	2007	2006	2005	2004	2003	2002	2001	2000	1999
Dividends, Net Income ($)	0.61	0.25	0.50	0.46	0.18	0.07	0.58	0.71	0.73	0.81
Distrib'ns, Cap Gain ($)	0.00	4.69	7.45	9.85	3.75	0.53	0.00	0.00	0.00	0.00
Net Asset Value ($)	16.23	31.45	27.06	27.19	29.56	24.75	13.38	13.47	13.53	11.08
Expense Ratio (%)	na	0.86	0.88	0.92	0.96	1.02	1.03	1.00	1.02	1.06
Yield (%)	3.75	0.68	1.44	1.24	0.54	0.27	4.33	5.27	5.39	7.31
Portfolio Turnover (%)	na	200	160	136	43	68	173	131	78	49
Total Assets (Millions $)	1,033	1,991	1,474	1,030	785	645	340	384	500	372

PORTFOLIO (as of 9/30/08)

Portfolio Manager: Heebner - 1994

Investment Style

Large Cap	Growth
Mid Cap	Grth/Val
Small Cap	Value

Portfolio

90.8%	U.S. stock	0.0%	conv't
8.4%	int'l stock	0.0%	preferred
0.0%	U.S. bonds	0.0%	other
0.0%	int'l bonds	0.8%	cash

Number of Investments: 23

Percent of Portfolio in Top 10 Investments: 61%

SHAREHOLDER INFORMATION

Minimum Investment

Initial: $2,500 Subsequent: $50

Minimum IRA Investment

Initial: $1,000 Subsequent: $50

Maximum Fees

Load: none 12b-1: none

Other: none

Services

✔ IRA

✔ Keogh

✔ Telephone Exchange

Cohen & Steers Realty Shares (CSRSX)

800-437-9912
www.cohenandsteers.com

Real Estate Sector

PERFORMANCE — fund inception date: 7/2/91

	3yr Annual	5yr Annual	10yr Annual	Bull	Bear
Return (%)	-10.1	2.9	8.4	194.9	-44.8
Differ From Category (+/-)	4.3 high	4.6 high	1.5 high	9.7 high	6.8 high

Standard Deviation	Category Risk Index	Beta
28.6%—high	0.99—av	1.46

	2008	2007	2006	2005	2004	2003	2002	2001	2000	1999
Return (%)	-34.5	-19.2	37.1	14.8	38.4	38.0	2.7	5.6	26.6	2.6
Differ From Category (+/-)	9.7	-6.0	4.9	2.6	6.0	-5.5	-1.8	-4.9	0.0	4.5
Return, Tax-Adjusted (%)	-35.7	-22.0	34.5	12.6	35.8	35.4	0.7	3.6	24.2	0.6

PER SHARE DATA

	2008	2007	2006	2005	2004	2003	2002	2001	2000	1999
Dividends, Net Income ($)	2.02	1.95	2.36	2.24	2.24	2.77	2.38	2.27	2.24	1.98
Distrib'ns, Cap Gain ($)	0.00	11.77	7.22	5.04	4.67	1.04	0.00	0.00	0.00	0.00
Net Asset Value ($)	37.01	58.80	89.45	72.59	69.66	55.64	43.34	44.41	44.26	36.91
Expense Ratio (%)	na	0.95	0.96	0.97	1.01	1.07	1.08	1.09	1.07	1.06
Yield (%)	5.46	2.75	2.44	2.88	3.01	4.88	5.49	5.11	5.06	5.36
Portfolio Turnover (%)	na	58	31	28	29	37	37	45	33	21
Total Assets (Millions $)	2,329	2,295	3,602	2,466	2,300	1,681	1,258	1,388	1,312	1,467

PORTFOLIO (as of 9/30/08)

Portfolio Manager: Cohen/Steers/Harvey/Cheigh - 1991

Investment Style

Large Cap	Growth
Mid Cap	Grth/Val
Small Cap	Value

Portfolio

96.3% U.S. stock	0.0% conv't
0.4% int'l stock	0.0% preferred
0.0% U.S. bonds	0.0% other
0.0% int'l bonds	3.3% cash

Number of Investments: 55
Percent of Portfolio in Top 10 Investments: 54%

SHAREHOLDER INFORMATION

Minimum Investment
Initial: $10,000 Subsequent: $500

Minimum IRA Investment
Initial: $10,000 Subsequent: $500

Maximum Fees
Load: 2.00% redemption 12b-1: none
Other: redemption fee applies for 60 days

Services
IRA
Keogh
✔ Telephone Exchange

T. Rowe Price Real Estate (TRREX)

800-638-5660
www.troweprice.com

Real Estate Sector

PERFORMANCE — fund inception date: 10/31/97

	3yr Annual	5yr Annual	10yr Annual	Bull	Bear
Return (%)	-12.3	1.1	7.8	180.1	-48.6
Differ From Category (+/-)	2.1 abv av	2.8 high	0.9 abv av	-5.1 abv av	3.0 abv av

Standard Deviation	Category Risk Index	Beta
29.9%—high	1.03—av	1.53

	2008	2007	2006	2005	2004	2003	2002	2001	2000	1999
Return (%)	-39.1	-18.8	36.7	14.5	36.8	34.8	5.3	8.8	31.9	-1.3
Differ From Category (+/-)	-5.1	-5.6	4.5	2.3	4.4	-8.7	0.8	-1.8	5.3	0.6
Return, Tax-Adjusted (%)	-40.5	-20.3	35.1	12.9	35.2	32.8	3.5	6.8	29.6	-3.3

PER SHARE DATA

	2008	2007	2006	2005	2004	2003	2002	2001	2000	1999
Dividends, Net Income ($)	0.74	0.72	0.62	0.70	0.60	0.59	0.49	0.53	0.47	0.45
Distrib'ns, Cap Gain ($)	0.00	0.79	0.60	0.24	0.07	0.00	0.00	0.00	0.00	0.00
Net Asset Value ($)	11.13	19.18	25.33	19.49	17.90	13.65	10.62	10.54	10.19	8.11
Expense Ratio (%)	na	0.73	0.78	0.85	0.90	1.00	1.00	1.00	1.00	1.00
Yield (%)	6.64	3.60	2.39	3.54	3.33	4.32	4.61	5.02	4.61	5.54
Portfolio Turnover (%)	na	33	25	18	8	5	10	37	19	27
Total Assets (Millions $)	1,352	1,940	2,333	944	640	290	132	69	54	25

PORTFOLIO (as of 9/30/08)

Portfolio Manager: Lee - 1997

Investment Style

Large Cap	Growth
Mid Cap	Grth/Val
Small Cap	Value

Portfolio

90.3%	U.S. stock	0.0%	conv't
2.0%	int'l stock	0.0%	preferred
3.5%	U.S. bonds	0.0%	other
0.0%	int'l bonds	4.2%	cash

Number of Investments: 40

Percent of Portfolio in Top 10 Investments: 43%

SHAREHOLDER INFORMATION

Minimum Investment

Initial: $2,500 Subsequent: $100

Minimum IRA Investment

Initial: $1,000 Subsequent: $50

Maximum Fees

Load: 1.00% redemption 12b-1: none

Other: redemption fee applies for 90 days

Services

✔ IRA

✔ Keogh

✔ Telephone Exchange

Third Avenue Real Estate Value (TAREX)

800-443-1021
www.thirdavenuefunds.com

Real Estate Sector

PERFORMANCE — fund inception date: 9/17/98

	3yr Annual	5yr Annual	10yr Annual	Bull	Bear
Return (%)	-13.0	-0.7	8.4	173.8	-50.4
Differ From Category (+/-)	1.4 av	1.0 av	1.5 high	-11.4 abv av	1.2 av

Standard Deviation	Category Risk Index	Beta
23.7%—high	0.82—low	1.37

	2008	2007	2006	2005	2004	2003	2002	2001	2000	1999
Return (%)	-44.7	-8.4	30.1	14.3	28.1	37.3	4.2	18.2	30.9	5.1
Differ From Category (+/-)	-0.5	4.8	-2.1	2.1	-4.3	-6.2	-0.3	7.6	4.3	7.0
Return, Tax-Adjusted (%)	-45.3	-10.4	27.7	13.2	27.6	36.2	3.4	17.3	29.3	4.1

PER SHARE DATA

	2008	2007	2006	2005	2004	2003	2002	2001	2000	1999
Dividends, Net Income ($)	0.43	0.60	0.89	0.44	0.18	0.45	0.18	0.19	0.27	0.25
Distrib'ns, Cap Gain ($)	0.00	3.25	2.63	1.03	0.26	0.08	0.30	0.20	0.29	0.06
Net Asset Value ($)	14.95	27.83	34.64	29.36	26.96	21.38	15.96	15.78	13.68	10.89
Expense Ratio (%)	na	1.10	1.11	1.14	1.15	1.19	1.22	1.50	1.50	1.87
Yield (%)	2.85	1.91	2.39	1.46	0.66	2.10	1.08	1.17	1.93	2.30
Portfolio Turnover (%)	na	19	10	13	8	11	21	20	23	5
Total Assets (Millions $)	1,093	2,443	3,262	2,910	2,029	787	346	140	27	10

PORTFOLIO (as of 10/31/08)

Portfolio Manager: Winer - 1998

Investment Style

Large Cap	Growth
Mid Cap	Grth/Val
Small Cap	Value

Portfolio

25.8%	U.S. stock	1.9%	conv't
57.8%	int'l stock	0.7%	preferred
1.6%	U.S. bonds	0.9%	other
0.0%	int'l bonds	11.5%	cash

Number of Investments: 48

Percent of Portfolio in Top 10 Investments: 51%

SHAREHOLDER INFORMATION

Minimum Investment
Initial: $10,000 Subsequent: $1,000

Minimum IRA Investment
Initial: $2,500 Subsequent: $200

Maximum Fees
Load: 1.00% redemption 12b-1: none
Other: redemption fee applies for 1 year

Services
✔ IRA
✔ Keogh
✔ Telephone Exchange

Vanguard REIT Index (VGSIX)

800-662-6273
www.vanguard.com

Real Estate Sector

PERFORMANCE — fund inception date: 5/13/96

	3yr Annual	5yr Annual	10yr Annual	Bull	Bear
Return (%)	-10.8	0.7	7.1	162.9	-45.8
Differ From Category (+/-)	3.6 abv av	2.4 abv av	0.2 av	-22.3 av	5.8 high

Standard Deviation	Category Risk Index	Beta
30.2%—high	1.04—abv av	1.51

	2008	2007	2006	2005	2004	2003	2002	2001	2000	1999
Return (%)	-37.1	-16.5	35.0	11.8	30.7	35.6	3.7	12.3	26.3	-4.1
Differ From Category (+/-)	7.1	-3.3	2.8	-0.4	-1.7	-7.9	-0.8	1.7	-0.3	-2.2
Return, Tax-Adjusted (%)	-38.8	-17.9	33.3	9.9	28.6	33.3	1.3	9.6	23.4	-6.7

PER SHARE DATA

	2008	2007	2006	2005	2004	2003	2002	2001	2000	1999
Dividends, Net Income ($)	0.98	1.01	0.94	0.94	0.88	0.78	0.76	0.81	0.64	0.67
Distrib'ns, Cap Gain ($)	0.00	0.00	0.12	0.22	0.07	0.00	0.00	0.00	0.18	0.11
Net Asset Value ($)	12.13	20.45	25.58	19.80	18.79	15.18	11.84	12.13	11.56	9.85
Expense Ratio (%)	0.20	0.21	0.21	0.21	0.24	0.27	0.28	0.33	0.33	0.26
Yield (%)	8.06	4.93	3.65	4.69	4.67	5.13	6.41	6.67	5.48	6.73
Portfolio Turnover (%)	13	21	17	13	7	12	10	21	12	29
Total Assets (Millions $)	2,732	4,137	6,066	4,407	4,663	3,051	1,784	1,230	1,094	875

PORTFOLIO (as of 9/30/08)

Portfolio Manager: O'Reilly - 1996

Investment Style

Large Cap	Growth
Mid Cap	Grth/Val
Small Cap	Value

Portfolio

97.8% U.S. stock	0.0% conv't
0.0% int'l stock	0.0% preferred
0.0% U.S. bonds	0.0% other
0.0% int'l bonds	2.3% cash

Number of Investments: 98
Percent of Portfolio in Top 10 Investments: 42%

SHAREHOLDER INFORMATION

Minimum Investment
Initial: $3,000 Subsequent: $100

Minimum IRA Investment
Initial: $3,000 Subsequent: $0

Maximum Fees
Load: 1.00% redemption 12b-1: none
Other: redemption fee applies for 1 year

Services
✔ IRA
✔ Keogh
✔ Telephone Exchange

Technology Sector Stock Funds
Category Performance Ranked by 2008 Returns

Fund (Ticker)	Annual Return (%) 2008	3Yr	5Yr	10Yr	Category Risk	Total Risk
Fidelity Select Software & Comp (FSCSX)	-42.2	-3.7	-0.8	3.6	av	high
Janus Global Technology (JAGTX)	-43.3	-9.3	-3.4	-1.0	av	high
T. Rowe Price Science & Tech (PRSCX)	-43.8	-12.4	-6.9	-6.9	av	high
T. Rowe Price Global Technology (PRGTX)	-44.1	-11.3	-3.2	na	blw av	high
Baron iOpportunity (BIOPX)	-46.1	-9.9	-0.4	na	abv av	high
Technology Sector Category Average	**-46.6**	**-12.4**	**-5.8**	**-3.3**	**av**	**high**

Baron iOpportunity (BIOPX)

800-442-3814
www.baronfunds.com

Technology Sector

PERFORMANCE — fund inception date: 2/29/00

	3yr Annual	5yr Annual	10yr Annual	Bull	Bear
Return (%)	-9.9	-0.4	na	250.8	-49.8
Differ From Category (+/-)	2.5 high	5.4 high	na	102.8 high	1.1 av

Standard Deviation	Category Risk Index	Beta
24.1%—high	1.02—abv av	1.45

	2008	2007	2006	2005	2004	2003	2002	2001	2000	1999
Return (%)	-46.1	21.1	12.1	7.0	25.5	73.8	-29.1	-3.7	—	—
Differ From Category (+/-)	0.5	5.7	2.4	1.2	20.9	15.8	10.4	28.2	—	—
Return, Tax-Adjusted (%)	-46.1	21.1	12.1	7.0	25.5	73.8	-29.1	-3.7	—	—

PER SHARE DATA

	2008	2007	2006	2005	2004	2003	2002	2001	2000	1999
Dividends, Net Income ($)	0.00	0.00	0.00	0.00	0.00	0.00	0.00	0.00	—	—
Distrib'ns, Cap Gain ($)	0.00	0.00	0.00	0.00	0.00	0.00	0.00	0.00	—	—
Net Asset Value ($)	7.12	13.20	10.90	9.72	9.08	7.23	4.16	5.86	—	—
Expense Ratio (%)	1.42	1.42	1.45	1.50	1.50	1.50	1.50	—	—	—
Yield (%)	0.00	0.00	0.00	0.00	0.00	0.00	0.00	0.00	—	—
Portfolio Turnover (%)	61	46	67	84	86	90	96	123	—	—
Total Assets (Millions $)	101	211	156	161	168	167	63	101	—	—

PORTFOLIO (as of 9/30/08)

Portfolio Manager: Lippert - 2006

Investment Style

Large Cap	Growth
Mid Cap	Grth/Val
Small Cap	Value

Portfolio

88.7%	U.S. stock	0.0%	conv't
5.6%	int'l stock	0.0%	preferred
0.0%	U.S. bonds	1.3%	other
0.0%	int'l bonds	4.4%	cash

Number of Investments: 45

Percent of Portfolio in Top 10 Investments: 41%

SHAREHOLDER INFORMATION

Minimum Investment

Initial: $2,000 Subsequent: $0

Minimum IRA Investment

Initial: $2,000 Subsequent: $0

Maximum Fees

Load: 1.00% redemption 12b-1: 0.25%

Other: redemption fee applies for 6 months

Services

✔ IRA

Keogh

✔ Telephone Exchange

Fidelity Select Software & Comp (FSCSX)

800-544-8544
www.fidelity.com

Technology Sector

PERFORMANCE — fund inception date: 7/29/85

	3yr Annual	5yr Annual	10yr Annual	Bull	Bear
Return (%)	-3.7	-0.8	3.6	141.4	-44.6
Differ From Category (+/-)	8.7 high	5.0 high	6.9 high	-6.6 abv av	6.3 high

Standard Deviation	Category Risk Index	Beta
22.9%—high	0.97—av	1.28

	2008	2007	2006	2005	2004	2003	2002	2001	2000	1999
Return (%)	-42.2	23.8	24.9	0.0	7.6	35.0	-23.4	-7.0	-20.2	93.1
Differ From Category (+/-)	4.4	8.4	15.2	-5.8	3.0	-23.0	16.1	24.9	9.5	-32.6
Return, Tax-Adjusted (%)	-42.2	23.8	24.9	0.0	7.4	35.0	-23.4	-7.1	-26.7	90.8

PER SHARE DATA

	2008	2007	2006	2005	2004	2003	2002	2001	2000	1999
Dividends, Net Income ($)	0.00	0.00	0.00	0.00	0.51	0.00	0.00	0.00	0.00	0.00
Distrib'ns, Cap Gain ($)	0.00	0.00	0.00	0.00	0.00	0.00	0.00	0.24	31.32	6.33
Net Asset Value ($)	47.00	81.23	65.57	52.49	52.47	49.23	36.46	47.59	51.51	96.86
Expense Ratio (%)	0.86	0.91	0.91	0.92	1.06	1.05	1.05	0.99	1.11	1.27
Yield (%)	0.00	0.00	0.00	0.00	0.97	0.00	0.00	0.00	0.00	0.00
Portfolio Turnover (%)	38	139	59	94	81	198	325	272	59	72
Total Assets (Millions $)	506	978	926	629	826	823	648	964	1,042	1,413

PORTFOLIO (as of 11/30/08)

Portfolio Manager: Tandon - 2007

Investment Style

Large Cap	Growth
Mid Cap	Grth/Val
Small Cap	Value

Portfolio

87.5%	U.S. stock	0.0%	conv't
11.3%	int'l stock	0.0%	preferred
0.0%	U.S. bonds	0.0%	other
0.0%	int'l bonds	1.2%	cash

Number of Investments: 38

Percent of Portfolio in Top 10 Investments: 65%

SHAREHOLDER INFORMATION

Minimum Investment

Initial: $2,500 Subsequent: $250

Minimum IRA Investment

Initial: $500 Subsequent: $100

Maximum Fees

Load: 0.75% redemption 12b-1: none

Other: redemption fee applies for 30 days

Services

✔ IRA
✔ Keogh
✔ Telephone Exchange

Janus Global Technology (JAGTX)

800-525-0020
www.janus.com

Technology Sector

PERFORMANCE — fund inception date: 12/31/98

	3yr Annual	5yr Annual	10yr Annual	Bull	Bear
Return (%)	-9.3	-3.4	-1.0	135.8	-46.1
Differ From Category (+/-)	3.1 high	2.4 abv av	2.3 high	-12.2 av	4.8 high

Standard Deviation	Category Risk Index	Beta
23.8%—high	1.01—av	1.43

	2008	2007	2006	2005	2004	2003	2002	2001	2000	1999
Return (%)	-43.3	21.8	7.9	11.5	1.2	47.1	-41.0	-40.0	-33.7	211.5
Differ From Category (+/-)	3.3	6.4	-1.8	5.7	-3.4	-10.9	-1.5	-8.1	-4.0	85.8
Return, Tax-Adjusted (%)	-43.3	21.8	7.9	11.4	1.2	47.1	-41.0	-40.0	-34.1	211.1

PER SHARE DATA

	2008	2007	2006	2005	2004	2003	2002	2001	2000	1999
Dividends, Net Income ($)	0.00	0.06	0.00	0.01	0.00	0.00	0.00	0.00	0.33	0.02
Distrib'ns, Cap Gain ($)	0.00	0.00	0.00	0.00	0.00	0.00	0.00	0.00	0.00	0.18
Net Asset Value ($)	8.85	15.60	12.85	11.90	10.68	10.55	7.17	12.14	20.22	30.93
Expense Ratio (%)	na	1.03	1.11	1.03	1.06	1.07	0.94	0.90	0.90	1.02
Yield (%)	0.00	0.38	0.00	0.06	0.00	0.00	0.00	0.00	1.61	0.06
Portfolio Turnover (%)	na	57	85	31	24	48	66	60	47	31
Total Assets (Millions $)	475	970	913	1,044	1,289	1,615	1,183	2,518	5,309	7,409

PORTFOLIO (as of 9/30/08)

Portfolio Manager: Wilson - 2006

Investment Style

Large Cap	Growth
Mid Cap	Grth/Val
Small Cap	Value

Portfolio

62.1% U.S. stock	0.0% conv't
30.7% int'l stock	0.0% preferred
0.0% U.S. bonds	0.5% other
0.0% int'l bonds	6.8% cash

Number of Investments: 80

Percent of Portfolio in Top 10 Investments: 32%

SHAREHOLDER INFORMATION

Minimum Investment

Initial: $2,500 Subsequent: $100

Minimum IRA Investment

Initial: $1,000 Subsequent: $100

Maximum Fees

Load: 2.00% redemption 12b-1: none

Other: redemption fee applies for 90 days

Services

✔ IRA
✔ Keogh
✔ Telephone Exchange

T. Rowe Price Global Technology (PRGTX)

800-638-5660
www.troweprice.com

Technology Sector

PERFORMANCE — fund inception date: 9/29/00

	3yr Annual	5yr Annual	10yr Annual	Bull	Bear
Return (%)	-11.3	-3.2	na	158.2	-49.4
Differ From Category (+/-)	1.1 abv av	2.6 abv av	na	10.2 abv av	1.5 abv av

Standard Deviation	Category Risk Index	Beta
22.9%—high	0.97—blw av	1.35

	2008	2007	2006	2005	2004	2003	2002	2001	2000	1999
Return (%)	-44.1	13.4	10.0	10.9	10.2	49.8	-29.9	-36.1	—	—
Differ From Category (+/-)	2.5	-2.0	0.3	5.1	5.6	-8.2	9.6	-4.2	—	—
Return, Tax-Adjusted (%)	-44.1	13.4	10.0	10.9	10.2	49.8	-29.9	-36.1	—	—

PER SHARE DATA

	2008	2007	2006	2005	2004	2003	2002	2001	2000	1999
Dividends, Net Income ($)	0.00	0.00	0.00	0.00	0.00	0.00	0.00	0.00	—	—
Distrib'ns, Cap Gain ($)	0.00	0.00	0.00	0.00	0.00	0.00	0.00	0.00	—	—
Net Asset Value ($)	4.26	7.61	6.71	6.10	5.50	4.99	3.33	4.75	—	—
Expense Ratio (%)	na	1.19	1.28	1.50	1.50	1.50	1.50	1.50	—	—
Yield (%)	0.00	0.00	0.00	0.00	0.00	0.00	0.00	0.00	—	—
Portfolio Turnover (%)	na	107	125	96	137	151	211	189	—	—
Total Assets (Millions $)	89	190	138	122	92	85	55	84	—	—

PORTFOLIO (as of 9/30/08)

Portfolio Manager: Eiswert - 2008

Investment Style

Large Cap	Growth
Mid Cap	Grth/Val
Small Cap	Value

Portfolio

75.5%	U.S. stock	0.0%	conv't
19.8%	int'l stock	1.6%	preferred
0.0%	U.S. bonds	0.0%	other
0.0%	int'l bonds	3.2%	cash

Number of Investments: 58

Percent of Portfolio in Top 10 Investments: 43%

SHAREHOLDER INFORMATION

Minimum Investment

Initial: $2,500 Subsequent: $100

Minimum IRA Investment

Initial: $1,000 Subsequent: $50

Maximum Fees

Load: none 12b-1: none

Other: none

Services

✔ IRA

✔ Keogh

✔ Telephone Exchange

T. Rowe Price Science & Tech (PRSCX)

800-638-5660
www.troweprice.com

Technology Sector

PERFORMANCE — fund inception date: 9/30/87

	3yr Annual	5yr Annual	10yr Annual	Bull	Bear
Return (%)	-12.4	-6.9	-6.9	105.5	-49.0
Differ From Category (+/-)	0.0 av	-1.1 av	-3.6 low	-42.5 blw av	1.9 abv av

Standard Deviation	Category Risk Index	Beta
24.1%—high	1.02—av	1.42

	2008	2007	2006	2005	2004	2003	2002	2001	2000	1999
Return (%)	-43.8	11.8	7.0	2.4	1.6	51.2	-40.6	-41.2	-34.2	100.9
Differ From Category (+/-)	2.8	-3.6	-2.6	-3.4	-3.0	-6.8	-1.1	-9.3	-4.5	-24.8
Return, Tax-Adjusted (%)	-43.8	11.8	7.0	2.4	1.6	51.2	-40.6	-41.2	-36.5	95.2

PER SHARE DATA

	2008	2007	2006	2005	2004	2003	2002	2001	2000	1999
Dividends, Net Income ($)	0.00	0.00	0.00	0.00	0.00	0.00	0.00	0.00	0.00	0.00
Distrib'ns, Cap Gain ($)	0.00	0.00	0.00	0.00	0.00	0.00	0.00	0.00	7.28	10.72
Net Asset Value ($)	13.18	23.45	20.96	19.57	19.10	18.80	12.43	20.92	35.57	63.71
Expense Ratio (%)	na	0.93	0.97	1.00	1.01	1.09	1.11	1.00	1.09	0.87
Yield (%)	0.00	0.00	0.00	0.00	0.00	0.00	0.00	0.00	0.00	0.00
Portfolio Turnover (%)	na	80	101	59	55	48	60	144	134	128
Total Assets (Millions $)	1,325	2,674	2,735	3,228	3,911	4,391	2,839	5,209	8,892	12,271

PORTFOLIO (as of 9/30/08)

Portfolio Manager: Allen - 2009

Investment Style

Large Cap	Growth
Mid Cap	Grth/Val
Small Cap	Value

Portfolio

84.2%	U.S. stock	0.0%	conv't
10.3%	int'l stock	0.0%	preferred
0.4%	U.S. bonds	0.0%	other
0.0%	int'l bonds	5.1%	cash

Number of Investments: 63
Percent of Portfolio in Top 10 Investments: 47%

SHAREHOLDER INFORMATION

Minimum Investment
Initial: $2,500 Subsequent: $100

Minimum IRA Investment
Initial: $1,000 Subsequent: $50

Maximum Fees
Load: none 12b-1: none
Other: none

Services
✔ IRA
✔ Keogh
✔ Telephone Exchange

Telecommunications Sector Stock Funds
Category Performance Ranked by 2008 Returns

Fund (Ticker)	Annual Return (%) 2008	3Yr	5Yr	10Yr	Category Risk	Total Risk
T. Rowe Price Media & Telecommunications (PRMTX)	-46.5	-5.7	4.5	6.5	av	high
Fidelity Select Telecommunications (FSTCX)	-47.7	-10.5	-2.4	-5.2	abv av	high
Fidelity Select Communications Equip (FSDCX)	-48.5	-16.7	-7.0	-4.7	high	high
Fidelity Select Wireless (FWRLX)	-49.7	-11.3	3.1	na	abv av	high
Telecommunications Sector Category Average	**-44.4**	**-8.5**	**-0.6**	**-0.7**	**av**	**high**

Fidelity Select Communications Equip (FSDCX)

800-544-8544
www.fidelity.com

Telecommunications Sector

PERFORMANCE — fund inception date: 6/29/90

	3yr Annual	5yr Annual	10yr Annual	Bull	Bear
Return (%)	-16.7	-7.0	-4.7	158.2	-55.3
Differ From Category (+/-)	-8.2 low	-6.4 blw av	-4.0 av	-31.9 av	-7.0 low

Standard Deviation	Category Risk Index	Beta
27.5%—high	1.21—high	1.56

	2008	2007	2006	2005	2004	2003	2002	2001	2000	1999
Return (%)	-48.5	9.7	2.2	3.5	16.5	68.0	-47.8	-36.2	-28.8	122.5
Differ From Category (+/-)	-4.1	-5.8	-18.7	-3.5	-2.7	26.3	-11.0	-11.2	-4.4	28.6
Return, Tax-Adjusted (%)	-48.6	9.7	2.2	3.5	16.5	68.0	-47.8	-36.2	-33.7	120.4

PER SHARE DATA

	2008	2007	2006	2005	2004	2003	2002	2001	2000	1999
Dividends, Net Income ($)	0.05	0.00	0.00	0.00	0.00	0.00	0.00	0.00	0.00	0.00
Distrib'ns, Cap Gain ($)	0.00	0.00	0.00	0.00	0.00	0.00	0.00	0.00	15.45	3.07
Net Asset Value ($)	11.52	22.46	20.46	20.01	19.33	16.59	9.87	18.90	29.59	62.88
Expense Ratio (%)	0.93	1.00	0.94	0.89	1.23	1.58	1.22	0.98	1.11	1.34
Yield (%)	0.39	0.00	0.00	0.00	0.00	0.00	0.00	0.00	0.00	0.00
Portfolio Turnover (%)	39	122	167	226	205	111	198	368	112	299
Total Assets (Millions $)	127	291	348	438	782	606	321	788	1,677	2,261

PORTFOLIO (as of 11/30/08)

Portfolio Manager: Chai - 2003

Investment Style

Large Cap	Growth
Mid Cap	Grth/Val
Small Cap	Value

Portfolio

84.9% U.S. stock	0.3% conv't
10.1% int'l stock	0.0% preferred
0.0% U.S. bonds	0.0% other
0.0% int'l bonds	4.8% cash

Number of Investments: 65

Percent of Portfolio in Top 10 Investments: 72%

SHAREHOLDER INFORMATION

Minimum Investment

Initial: $2,500 Subsequent: $250

Minimum IRA Investment

Initial: $500 Subsequent: $100

Maximum Fees

Load: 0.75% redemption 12b-1: none

Other: redemption fee applies for 30 days

Services

✔ IRA
✔ Keogh
✔ Telephone Exchange

Fidelity Select Telecommunications (FSTCX)

800-544-8544
www.fidelity.com

Telecommunications Sector

PERFORMANCE — fund inception date: 7/29/85

	3yr Annual	5yr Annual	10yr Annual	Bull	Bear
Return (%)	-10.5	-2.4	-5.2	154.7	-52.6
Differ From Category (+/-)	-2.0 av	-1.8 av	-4.5 blw av	-35.4 av	-4.3 av

Standard Deviation	Category Risk Index	Beta
24.2%—high	1.06—abv av	1.42

	2008	2007	2006	2005	2004	2003	2002	2001	2000	1999
Return (%)	-47.7	8.1	26.7	5.1	17.5	25.5	-29.4	-28.0	-37.5	66.5
Differ From Category (+/-)	-3.3	-7.3	5.8	-1.9	-1.7	-16.2	7.4	-3.0	-13.1	-27.3
Return, Tax-Adjusted (%)	-47.9	8.0	26.5	5.0	17.3	25.4	-29.4	-28.0	-39.5	63.1

PER SHARE DATA

	2008	2007	2006	2005	2004	2003	2002	2001	2000	1999
Dividends, Net Income ($)	0.60	0.52	0.53	0.33	0.49	0.05	0.03	0.02	0.00	0.00
Distrib'ns, Cap Gain ($)	0.01	0.00	0.00	0.00	0.00	0.00	0.00	0.00	9.04	10.48
Net Asset Value ($)	26.66	52.04	48.57	38.75	37.17	32.04	25.57	36.22	50.31	88.70
Expense Ratio (%)	0.90	0.97	1.05	1.02	1.34	1.34	1.20	1.02	1.09	1.25
Yield (%)	2.23	0.99	1.09	0.85	1.31	0.15	0.11	0.05	0.00	0.00
Portfolio Turnover (%)	134	162	148	56	98	163	169	322	173	150
Total Assets (Millions $)	188	454	514	348	377	358	386	559	904	1,595

PORTFOLIO (as of 11/30/08)

Portfolio Manager: Baker - 2007

Investment Style

Large Cap	Growth
Mid Cap	Grth/Val
Small Cap	Value

Portfolio

81.0%	U.S. stock	0.0%	conv't
18.3%	int'l stock	0.0%	preferred
0.0%	U.S. bonds	0.0%	other
0.0%	int'l bonds	0.7%	cash

Number of Investments: 81

Percent of Portfolio in Top 10 Investments: 66%

SHAREHOLDER INFORMATION

Minimum Investment

Initial: $2,500 Subsequent: $250

Minimum IRA Investment

Initial: $500 Subsequent: $100

Maximum Fees

Load: 0.75% redemption 12b-1: none

Other: redemption fee applies for 30 days

Services

✔ IRA
✔ Keogh
✔ Telephone Exchange

Fidelity Select Wireless (FWRLX)

800-544-8544
www.fidelity.com

Telecommunications Sector

PERFORMANCE — fund inception date: 9/21/00

	3yr Annual	5yr Annual	10yr Annual	Bull	Bear
Return (%)	-11.3	3.1	na	337.6	-54.9
Differ From Category (+/-)	-2.8 blw av	3.7 abv av	na	147.5 high	-6.6 blw av

Standard Deviation	Category Risk Index	Beta
24.4%—high	1.07—abv av	1.47

	2008	2007	2006	2005	2004	2003	2002	2001	2000	1999
Return (%)	-49.7	27.4	8.7	17.3	42.5	68.3	-55.3	-34.8	—	—
Differ From Category (+/-)	-5.3	11.9	-12.2	10.3	23.3	26.6	-18.5	-9.8	—	—
Return, Tax-Adjusted (%)	-49.8	26.8	7.7	17.3	42.5	68.3	-55.3	-34.8	—	—

PER SHARE DATA

	2008	2007	2006	2005	2004	2003	2002	2001	2000	1999
Dividends, Net Income ($)	0.06	0.03	0.01	0.00	0.00	0.00	0.00	0.00	—	—
Distrib'ns, Cap Gain ($)	0.00	0.26	0.43	0.00	0.00	0.00	0.00	0.00	—	—
Net Asset Value ($)	4.29	8.64	7.00	6.84	5.83	4.09	2.43	5.43	—	—
Expense Ratio (%)	0.91	0.97	0.89	0.97	1.43	2.01	1.54	1.48	—	—
Yield (%)	1.39	0.33	0.13	0.00	0.00	0.00	0.00	0.00	—	—
Portfolio Turnover (%)	191	124	162	96	79	110	148	153	—	—
Total Assets (Millions $)	173	701	297	475	489	150	56	116	—	—

PORTFOLIO (as of 11/30/08)

Portfolio Manager: Baker - 2007

Investment Style

Large Cap	Growth
Mid Cap	Grth/Val
Small Cap	Value

Portfolio

45.0%	U.S. stock	0.0%	conv't
54.6%	int'l stock	0.0%	preferred
0.0%	U.S. bonds	0.0%	other
0.0%	int'l bonds	0.4%	cash

Number of Investments: 57

Percent of Portfolio in Top 10 Investments: 60%

SHAREHOLDER INFORMATION

Minimum Investment

Initial: $2,500 Subsequent: $250

Minimum IRA Investment

Initial: $500 Subsequent: $100

Maximum Fees

Load: 0.75% redemption 12b-1: none

Other: redemption fee applies for 30 days

Services

✔ IRA

✔ Keogh

✔ Telephone Exchange

T. Rowe Price Media & Telecommunications (PRMTX)

800-638-5660
www.troweprice.com

Telecommunications Sector

PERFORMANCE — fund inception date: 10/13/93

	3yr Annual	5yr Annual	10yr Annual	Bull	Bear
Return (%)	-5.7	4.5	6.5	302.8	-49.7
Differ From Category (+/-)	2.8 abv av	5.1 high	7.2 high	112.7 high	-1.4 av

Standard Deviation	Category Risk Index	Beta
24.0%—high	1.05—av	1.49

	2008	2007	2006	2005	2004	2003	2002	2001	2000	1999
Return (%)	-46.5	21.8	28.5	18.1	26.2	55.9	-28.4	-7.0	-25.2	93.0
Differ From Category (+/-)	-2.1	6.3	7.6	11.1	7.1	14.2	8.4	18.0	-0.8	-0.9
Return, Tax-Adjusted (%)	-46.9	20.4	28.5	18.1	26.2	55.9	-28.4	-7.0	-29.8	90.2

PER SHARE DATA

	2008	2007	2006	2005	2004	2003	2002	2001	2000	1999
Dividends, Net Income ($)	0.24	0.28	0.00	0.00	0.00	0.00	0.00	0.00	0.37	0.00
Distrib'ns, Cap Gain ($)	1.00	3.68	0.00	0.00	0.00	0.00	0.00	0.00	8.60	3.22
Net Asset Value ($)	24.65	48.47	43.18	33.59	28.43	22.51	14.43	20.15	21.65	39.99
Expense Ratio (%)	na	0.82	0.87	0.92	0.96	1.10	1.15	1.08	0.94	0.93
Yield (%)	0.93	0.53	0.00	0.00	0.00	0.00	0.00	0.00	1.22	0.00
Portfolio Turnover (%)	na	65	55	78	108	124	184	241	197	58
Total Assets (Millions $)	852	2,089	1,457	1,035	877	665	421	675	798	930

PORTFOLIO (as of 9/30/08)

Portfolio Manager: Ellenbogen/Bartolo/Adamson - 2005

Investment Style

Large Cap	Growth
Mid Cap	Grth/Val
Small Cap	Value

Portfolio

65.9%	U.S. stock	0.0%	conv't
27.8%	int'l stock	0.0%	preferred
0.0%	U.S. bonds	2.3%	other
0.0%	int'l bonds	4.1%	cash

Number of Investments: 69

Percent of Portfolio in Top 10 Investments: 47%

SHAREHOLDER INFORMATION

Minimum Investment

Initial: $2,500 Subsequent: $100

Minimum IRA Investment

Initial: $1,000 Subsequent: $50

Maximum Fees

Load: none 12b-1: none

Other: none

Services

✔ IRA
✔ Keogh
✔ Telephone Exchange

Utilities Sector Stock Funds
Category Performance Ranked by 2008 Returns

Fund (Ticker)	Annual Return (%) 2008	3Yr	5Yr	10Yr	Category Risk	Total Risk
FBR Gas Utility Index (GASFX)	-28.3	-0.3	6.7	5.2	blw av	blw av
American Century Utilities Inv (BULIX)	-31.2	0.4	7.5	1.6	av	blw av
Fidelity Utilities (FIUIX)	-34.6	-1.9	4.7	-0.5	abv av	av
Fidelity Select Utilities Growth (FSUTX)	-36.0	-0.6	5.9	0.0	high	av
Utilities Sector Category Average	**-32.9**	**-1.0**	**6.2**	**1.5**	**av**	**av**

American Century Utilities Inv (BULIX)

877-256-6083
www.americancentury.com

Utilities Sector

PERFORMANCE — fund inception date: 3/1/93

	3yr Annual	5yr Annual	10yr Annual	Bull	Bear
Return (%)	0.4	7.5	1.6	178.9	-32.7
Differ From Category (+/-)	1.4 high	1.3 high	0.1 high	-0.4 av	1.1 abv av

Standard Deviation	Category Risk Index	Beta
15.2%—blw av	0.92—av	0.80

	2008	2007	2006	2005	2004	2003	2002	2001	2000	1999
Return (%)	-31.2	17.8	24.9	14.3	23.8	23.9	-27.5	-21.1	3.9	11.4
Differ From Category (+/-)	1.7	2.2	-1.0	1.5	0.3	-0.6	-1.3	2.5	-3.8	-4.6
Return, Tax-Adjusted (%)	-31.5	17.4	24.5	13.8	23.3	23.5	-28.4	-21.7	0.5	9.4

PER SHARE DATA

	2008	2007	2006	2005	2004	2003	2002	2001	2000	1999
Dividends, Net Income ($)	0.45	0.36	0.40	0.40	0.29	0.25	0.27	0.25	0.98	0.35
Distrib'ns, Cap Gain ($)	0.00	0.00	0.00	0.00	0.00	0.00	0.00	0.01	0.83	0.93
Net Asset Value ($)	12.57	18.82	16.30	13.40	12.08	10.02	8.31	11.81	15.26	16.46
Expense Ratio (%)	0.68	0.67	0.68	0.67	0.68	0.69	0.69	0.68	0.67	0.68
Yield (%)	3.58	1.92	2.42	2.97	2.38	2.53	3.25	2.10	6.09	1.99
Portfolio Turnover (%)	19	20	45	21	31	34	26	10	32	50
Total Assets (Millions $)	250	496	337	293	194	144	119	200	296	319

PORTFOLIO (as of 9/30/08)

Portfolio Manager: Schniedwind/Sterling - 1997

Investment Style

Large Cap	Growth
Mid Cap	Grth/Val
Small Cap	Value

Portfolio

89.1%	U.S. stock	0.0%	conv't
10.1%	int'l stock	0.0%	preferred
0.0%	U.S. bonds	0.0%	other
0.0%	int'l bonds	0.8%	cash

Number of Investments: 61
Percent of Portfolio in Top 10 Investments: 35%

SHAREHOLDER INFORMATION

Minimum Investment
Initial: $2,500 Subsequent: $50

Minimum IRA Investment
Initial: $2,500 Subsequent: $0

Maximum Fees
Load: none 12b-1: none
Other: none

Services
✔ IRA
✔ Keogh
✔ Telephone Exchange

FBR Gas Utility Index (GASFX)

888-888-0025
www.fbrcapitalmarkets.com

Utilities Sector

PERFORMANCE — fund inception date: 5/10/89

	3yr Annual	5yr Annual	10yr Annual	Bull	Bear
Return (%)	-0.3	6.7	5.2	163.4	-28.9
Differ From Category (+/-)	0.7 av	0.5 abv av	3.7 high	-15.9 av	4.9 high

Standard Deviation	Category Risk Index	Beta
15.0%—blw av	0.91—blw av	0.77

	2008	2007	2006	2005	2004	2003	2002	2001	2000	1999
Return (%)	-28.3	14.0	21.2	13.5	23.0	23.4	-24.0	-14.8	55.8	-3.8
Differ From Category (+/-)	4.6	-1.6	-4.7	0.7	-0.5	-1.1	2.2	8.8	48.1	-19.8
Return, Tax-Adjusted (%)	-29.2	12.3	20.8	13.0	22.5	22.9	-25.1	-17.8	51.2	-6.5

PER SHARE DATA

	2008	2007	2006	2005	2004	2003	2002	2001	2000	1999
Dividends, Net Income ($)	0.48	0.48	0.50	0.53	0.40	0.37	0.44	0.51	0.52	0.51
Distrib'ns, Cap Gain ($)	0.74	1.75	0.00	0.00	0.00	0.00	0.00	2.03	2.51	1.42
Net Asset Value ($)	13.95	21.05	20.46	17.33	15.74	13.16	10.99	14.97	20.67	15.37
Expense Ratio (%)	na	0.75	0.80	0.80	0.85	0.85	0.85	0.85	0.85	0.85
Yield (%)	3.25	2.11	2.44	3.06	2.55	2.80	4.01	3.02	2.22	3.05
Portfolio Turnover (%)	na	22	16	20	34	39	29	38	16	10
Total Assets (Millions $)	186	278	285	281	238	212	159	229	318	184

PORTFOLIO (as of 9/30/08)

Portfolio Manager: Aylesworth - 2001

Investment Style

Large Cap	Growth
Mid Cap	Grth/Val
Small Cap	Value

Portfolio

76.2%	U.S. stock	0.0%	conv't
20.9%	int'l stock	0.0%	preferred
0.0%	U.S. bonds	0.0%	other
0.0%	int'l bonds	3.0%	cash

Number of Investments: 69
Percent of Portfolio in Top 10 Investments: 46%

SHAREHOLDER INFORMATION

Minimum Investment
Initial: $2,000 Subsequent: $0

Minimum IRA Investment
Initial: $1,000 Subsequent: $0

Maximum Fees
Load: 1.00% redemption 12b-1: none
Other: redemption fee applies for 90 days

Services
✔ IRA
✔ Keogh
✔ Telephone Exchange

Fidelity Select Utilities Growth (FSUTX)

800-544-8544
www.fidelity.com

Utilities Sector

PERFORMANCE — fund inception date: 12/10/81

	3yr Annual	5yr Annual	10yr Annual	Bull	Bear
Return (%)	-0.6	5.9	0.0	188.1	-36.6
Differ From Category (+/-)	0.4 av	-0.3 av	-1.5 av	8.8 high	-2.8 blw av

Standard Deviation	Category Risk Index	Beta
17.7%—av	1.07—high	0.79

	2008	2007	2006	2005	2004	2003	2002	2001	2000	1999
Return (%)	-36.0	18.1	30.0	9.3	24.2	26.4	-30.4	-21.9	-13.6	25.9
Differ From Category (+/-)	-3.1	2.5	4.1	-3.5	0.7	1.9	-4.2	1.7	-21.3	9.9
Return, Tax-Adjusted (%)	-36.2	17.8	29.8	9.0	23.9	26.1	-30.9	-22.5	-16.2	22.5

PER SHARE DATA

	2008	2007	2006	2005	2004	2003	2002	2001	2000	1999
Dividends, Net Income ($)	0.85	1.21	0.64	0.93	0.62	0.40	0.48	0.26	1.97	0.42
Distrib'ns, Cap Gain ($)	0.00	0.00	0.00	0.00	0.00	0.00	0.00	0.93	4.85	9.30
Net Asset Value ($)	40.26	64.27	55.41	43.10	40.26	32.94	26.40	38.59	50.80	66.10
Expense Ratio (%)	0.87	0.93	0.92	0.99	1.19	1.17	1.09	0.99	1.04	1.16
Yield (%)	2.11	1.88	1.15	2.15	1.53	1.21	1.81	0.65	3.53	0.55
Portfolio Turnover (%)	121	107	101	51	76	139	54	80	93	113
Total Assets (Millions $)	386	754	700	276	345	207	183	320	539	626

PORTFOLIO (as of 11/30/08)

Portfolio Manager: Simmons - 2006

Investment Style

Large Cap	Growth
Mid Cap	Grth/Val
Small Cap	Value

Portfolio

99.0% U.S. stock	0.0% conv't
0.0% int'l stock	0.0% preferred
0.0% U.S. bonds	0.0% other
0.0% int'l bonds	1.1% cash

Number of Investments: 41

Percent of Portfolio in Top 10 Investments: 61%

SHAREHOLDER INFORMATION

Minimum Investment

Initial: $2,500 Subsequent: $250

Minimum IRA Investment

Initial: $500 Subsequent: $100

Maximum Fees

Load: 0.75% redemption 12b-1: none

Other: redemption fee applies for 30 days

Services

✔ IRA

✔ Keogh

✔ Telephone Exchange

Fidelity Utilities (FIUIX)

800-544-6666
www.fidelity.com

Utilities Sector

PERFORMANCE — fund inception date: 11/27/87

	3yr Annual	5yr Annual	10yr Annual	Bull	Bear
Return (%)	-1.9	4.7	-0.5	154.5	-36.3
Differ From Category (+/-)	-0.9 blw av	-1.5 low	-2.0 blw av	-24.8 blw av	-2.5 av

Standard Deviation	Category Risk Index	Beta
16.8%—av	1.02—abv av	0.89

	2008	2007	2006	2005	2004	2003	2002	2001	2000	1999
Return (%)	-34.6	10.8	30.5	9.8	21.1	20.8	-26.7	-15.2	-20.5	26.7
Differ From Category (+/-)	-1.7	-4.8	4.6	-2.9	-2.4	-3.7	-0.5	8.4	-28.2	10.7
Return, Tax-Adjusted (%)	-34.9	10.5	30.2	9.6	20.7	20.5	-27.3	-15.6	-24.3	23.8

PER SHARE DATA

	2008	2007	2006	2005	2004	2003	2002	2001	2000	1999
Dividends, Net Income ($)	0.43	0.37	0.25	0.26	0.29	0.22	0.20	0.16	0.09	0.18
Distrib'ns, Cap Gain ($)	0.00	0.00	0.00	0.00	0.00	0.00	0.00	0.00	4.73	3.05
Net Asset Value ($)	13.07	20.55	18.87	14.67	13.59	11.48	9.70	13.49	16.09	25.77
Expense Ratio (%)	0.82	0.84	0.84	0.85	0.73	0.95	0.89	0.78	0.80	0.85
Yield (%)	3.28	1.80	1.32	1.77	2.13	1.91	2.06	1.18	0.43	0.62
Portfolio Turnover (%)	112	104	66	57	21	32	58	126	50	55
Total Assets (Millions $)	775	1,406	1,599	1,014	962	857	820	1,427	2,125	2,885

PORTFOLIO (as of 11/30/08)

Portfolio Manager: Simmons - 2005

Investment Style

Large Cap	Growth
Mid Cap	Grth/Val
Small Cap	Value

Portfolio

99.4%	U.S. stock	0.2%	conv't
0.0%	int'l stock	0.0%	preferred
0.0%	U.S. bonds	0.0%	other
0.0%	int'l bonds	0.4%	cash

Number of Investments: 46
Percent of Portfolio in Top 10 Investments: 70%

SHAREHOLDER INFORMATION

Minimum Investment
Initial: $2,500 Subsequent: $250

Minimum IRA Investment
Initial: $500 Subsequent: $100

Maximum Fees
Load: none 12b-1: none
Other: maint fee for low bal

Services
✔ IRA
✔ Keogh
✔ Telephone Exchange

Global Stock Funds
Category Performance Ranked by 2008 Returns

Fund (Ticker)	Annual Return (%) 2008	3Yr	5Yr	10Yr	Category Risk	Total Risk
USAA World Growth (USAWX)	-34.1	-3.7	2.6	1.5	low	blw av
Tweedy, Browne Global Value (TBGVX)	-38.4	-7.3	2.0	4.9	low	blw av
Oakmark Global I (OAKGX)	-38.8	-6.6	1.3	na	blw av	av
Fidelity Worldwide (FWWFX)	-40.3	-6.0	1.1	3.0	blw av	av
Janus Global Research (JARFX)	-45.5	-6.5	na	na	abv av	high
Janus Contrarian (JSVAX)	-48.2	-7.8	2.2	na	high	high
Global Stock Category Average	**-40.8**	**-7.5**	**0.5**	**2.8**	**av**	**abv av**

Fidelity Worldwide (FWWFX)

800-544-9797
www.fidelity.com

Global Stock

PERFORMANCE — fund inception date: 5/30/90

	3yr Annual	5yr Annual	10yr Annual	Bull	Bear
Return (%)	-6.0	1.1	3.0	174.1	-43.4
Differ From Category (+/-)	1.5 abv av	0.6 av	0.2 av	2.6 av	0.4 av

Standard Deviation	Category Risk Index	Beta
18.3%—av	0.93—blw av	1.11

	2008	2007	2006	2005	2004	2003	2002	2001	2000	1999
Return (%)	-40.3	18.4	17.4	13.5	12.2	38.4	-18.9	-6.3	-8.1	30.7
Differ From Category (+/-)	0.5	5.6	-2.6	0.5	-3.7	0.7	-2.0	3.6	-5.4	-7.4
Return, Tax-Adjusted (%)	-40.6	16.5	15.0	12.5	12.0	38.2	-18.9	-6.3	-11.1	28.7

PER SHARE DATA

	2008	2007	2006	2005	2004	2003	2002	2001	2000	1999
Dividends, Net Income ($)	0.17	0.12	0.17	0.10	0.10	0.07	0.02	0.00	0.40	0.10
Distrib'ns, Cap Gain ($)	0.00	2.38	2.66	1.04	0.02	0.00	0.00	0.00	2.25	1.52
Net Asset Value ($)	12.59	21.37	20.11	19.57	18.25	16.37	11.88	14.66	15.63	19.90
Expense Ratio (%)	na	1.02	1.02	1.01	1.19	1.28	1.20	1.05	1.04	1.07
Yield (%)	1.35	0.50	0.74	0.48	0.54	0.42	0.16	0.00	2.23	0.46
Portfolio Turnover (%)	na	128	205	93	95	106	120	152	235	164
Total Assets (Millions $)	875	1,697	1,377	1,278	1,169	957	642	807	928	1,125

PORTFOLIO (as of 11/30/08)

Portfolio Manager: Kennedy/DuFour - 2006

Investment Style

Large Cap	Growth
Mid Cap	Grth/Val
Small Cap	Value

Portfolio

42.8%	U.S. stock	0.0%	conv't
42.8%	int'l stock	0.5%	preferred
0.0%	U.S. bonds	0.0%	other
0.0%	int'l bonds	13.9%	cash

Number of Investments: 217

Percent of Portfolio in Top 10 Investments: 32%

SHAREHOLDER INFORMATION

Minimum Investment

Initial: $2,500 Subsequent: $250

Minimum IRA Investment

Initial: $500 Subsequent: $100

Maximum Fees

Load: 1.00% redemption 12b-1: none

Other: redemption fee applies for 30 days; maint fee for low bal

Services

✔ IRA
✔ Keogh
✔ Telephone Exchange

Janus Contrarian
(JSVAX)

800-525-0020
www.janus.com

Global Stock

PERFORMANCE — **fund inception date: 2/29/00**

	3yr Annual	5yr Annual	10yr Annual	Bull	Bear
Return (%)	-7.8	2.2	na	249.2	-50.0
Differ From Category (+/-)	-0.3 av	1.7 high	na	77.7 high	-6.2 low

Standard Deviation	Category Risk Index	Beta
22.5%—high	1.15—high	1.33

	2008	2007	2006	2005	2004	2003	2002	2001	2000	1999
Return (%)	-48.2	21.2	24.5	16.0	22.6	53.2	-23.8	-11.8	—	—
Differ From Category (+/-)	-7.4	8.4	4.5	3.0	6.7	15.5	-6.8	-1.9	—	—
Return, Tax-Adjusted (%)	-48.6	20.2	22.1	15.7	22.5	53.2	-23.8	-11.9	—	—

PER SHARE DATA

	2008	2007	2006	2005	2004	2003	2002	2001	2000	1999
Dividends, Net Income ($)	0.06	0.09	0.36	0.04	0.03	0.00	0.01	0.02	—	—
Distrib'ns, Cap Gain ($)	0.37	0.87	1.66	0.18	0.00	0.00	0.00	0.00	—	—
Net Asset Value ($)	9.63	19.44	16.83	15.14	13.24	10.82	7.06	9.26	—	—
Expense Ratio (%)	na	0.96	0.94	0.93	0.98	1.01	0.98	0.91	—	—
Yield (%)	0.59	0.42	1.92	0.24	0.19	0.00	0.08	0.26	—	—
Portfolio Turnover (%)	na	28	39	42	30	44	60	77	—	—
Total Assets (Millions $)	3,219	8,212	4,513	3,161	2,775	2,618	1,267	2,079	—	—

PORTFOLIO (as of 9/30/08)

Portfolio Manager: Decker - 2000

Investment Style

Large Cap	Growth
Mid Cap	Grth/Val
Small Cap	Value

Portfolio

71.0%	U.S. stock	0.0%	conv't
28.8%	int'l stock	0.0%	preferred
0.0%	U.S. bonds	0.0%	other
0.0%	int'l bonds	0.2%	cash

Number of Investments: 59

Percent of Portfolio in Top 10 Investments: 46%

SHAREHOLDER INFORMATION

Minimum Investment

Initial: $2,500 Subsequent: $100

Minimum IRA Investment

Initial: $1,000 Subsequent: $100

Maximum Fees

Load: none 12b-1: none

Other: none

Services

✔ IRA

✔ Keogh

✔ Telephone Exchange

Janus Global Research (JARFX)

800-525-0020
www.janus.com

Global Stock

PERFORMANCE — fund inception date: 2/25/05

	3yr Annual	5yr Annual	10yr Annual	Bull	Bear
Return (%)	-6.5	na	na	na	-47.8
Differ From Category (+/-)	1.0 abv av	na	na	na	-4.0 blw av

Standard Deviation	Category Risk Index	Beta
21.9%—high	1.12—abv av	1.35

	2008	2007	2006	2005	2004	2003	2002	2001	2000	1999
Return (%)	-45.5	26.7	18.3	—	—	—	—	—	—	—
Differ From Category (+/-)	-4.7	13.9	-1.6	—	—	—	—	—	—	—
Return, Tax-Adjusted (%)	-45.7	25.2	17.2	—	—	—	—	—	—	—

PER SHARE DATA

	2008	2007	2006	2005	2004	2003	2002	2001	2000	1999
Dividends, Net Income ($)	0.05	0.38	0.05	—	—	—	—	—	—	—
Distrib'ns, Cap Gain ($)	0.00	0.38	0.76	—	—	—	—	—	—	—
Net Asset Value ($)	8.45	15.60	12.92	—	—	—	—	—	—	—
Expense Ratio (%)	na	1.11	1.14	—	—	—	—	—	—	—
Yield (%)	0.60	2.39	0.34	—	—	—	—	—	—	—
Portfolio Turnover (%)	na	72	118	—	—	—	—	—	—	—
Total Assets (Millions $)	145	281	123	—	—	—	—	—	—	—

PORTFOLIO (as of 9/30/08)

Portfolio Manager: Goff - 2005

Investment Style

Large Cap	Growth
Mid Cap	Grth/Val
Small Cap	Value

Portfolio

56.1%	U.S. stock	0.0%	conv't
43.9%	int'l stock	0.0%	preferred
0.0%	U.S. bonds	0.0%	other
0.0%	int'l bonds	0.0%	cash

Number of Investments: 125

Percent of Portfolio in Top 10 Investments: 16%

SHAREHOLDER INFORMATION

Minimum Investment

Initial: $2,500 Subsequent: $100

Minimum IRA Investment

Initial: $1,000 Subsequent: $100

Maximum Fees

Load: 2.00% redemption 12b-1: none

Other: redemption fee applies for 90 days

Services

✔ IRA

✔ Keogh

✔ Telephone Exchange

Oakmark Global I (OAKGX)

800-625-6275
www.oakmark.com

Global Stock

PERFORMANCE — fund inception date: 8/4/99

	3yr Annual	5yr Annual	10yr Annual	Bull	Bear
Return (%)	-6.6	1.3	na	201.4	-41.5
Differ From Category (+/-)	0.9 abv av	0.8 abv av	na	29.9 high	2.3 abv av

Standard Deviation	Category Risk Index	Beta
17.0%—av	0.87—blw av	1.07

	2008	2007	2006	2005	2004	2003	2002	2001	2000	1999
Return (%)	-38.8	7.3	24.1	13.2	15.6	48.9	-2.2	20.0	15.8	—
Differ From Category (+/-)	2.0	-5.5	4.1	0.2	-0.3	11.2	14.7	29.9	18.5	—
Return, Tax-Adjusted (%)	-39.9	5.4	21.4	12.1	15.1	48.9	-2.2	19.5	15.0	—

PER SHARE DATA

	2008	2007	2006	2005	2004	2003	2002	2001	2000	1999
Dividends, Net Income ($)	0.70	0.04	0.31	0.26	0.10	0.00	0.00	0.00	0.17	—
Distrib'ns, Cap Gain ($)	0.03	3.04	3.54	0.97	0.37	0.05	0.00	0.29	0.05	—
Net Asset Value ($)	14.01	24.10	25.28	23.47	21.81	19.28	12.98	13.26	11.31	—
Expense Ratio (%)	1.16	1.13	1.18	1.20	1.26	1.28	1.55	1.75	1.75	—
Yield (%)	4.98	0.13	1.08	1.08	0.46	0.00	0.00	0.01	1.53	—
Portfolio Turnover (%)	41	35	41	17	16	42	86	114	147	—
Total Assets (Millions $)	1,346	2,826	2,548	1,957	1,535	1,168	231	76	28	—

PORTFOLIO (as of 9/30/08)

Portfolio Manager: McGregor/Taylor - 2003

Investment Style

Large Cap	Growth
Mid Cap	Grth/Val
Small Cap	Value

Portfolio

42.7%	U.S. stock	0.0%	conv't
51.7%	int'l stock	0.0%	preferred
0.0%	U.S. bonds	0.0%	other
0.0%	int'l bonds	5.6%	cash

Number of Investments: 38
Percent of Portfolio in Top 10 Investments: 41%

SHAREHOLDER INFORMATION

Minimum Investment
Initial: $1,000 Subsequent: $100

Minimum IRA Investment
Initial: $1,000 Subsequent: $100

Maximum Fees
Load: 2.00% redemption 12b-1: none
Other: redemption fee applies for 90 days

Services
✔ IRA
Keogh
✔ Telephone Exchange

Tweedy, Browne Global Value (TBGVX)

800-432-4789
www.tweedy.com

Global Stock

PERFORMANCE — fund inception date: 6/15/93

	3yr Annual	5yr Annual	10yr Annual	Bull	Bear
Return (%)	-7.3	2.0	4.9	152.8	-40.9
Differ From Category (+/-)	0.2 av	1.5 abv av	2.1 abv av	-18.7 blw av	2.9 abv av

Standard Deviation	Category Risk Index	Beta
15.2%—blw av	0.78—low	0.93

	2008	2007	2006	2005	2004	2003	2002	2001	2000	1999
Return (%)	-38.4	7.5	20.1	15.4	20.0	24.9	-12.2	-4.7	12.3	25.2
Differ From Category (+/-)	2.4	-5.3	0.1	2.4	4.1	-12.8	4.7	5.2	15.0	-13.0
Return, Tax-Adjusted (%)	-40.3	5.6	19.3	14.8	19.5	24.4	-12.9	-5.4	9.4	23.9

PER SHARE DATA

	2008	2007	2006	2005	2004	2003	2002	2001	2000	1999
Dividends, Net Income ($)	0.75	0.48	0.43	0.37	0.27	0.20	0.20	0.18	0.21	0.26
Distrib'ns, Cap Gain ($)	2.07	2.88	0.35	0.00	0.00	0.00	0.27	0.33	2.52	0.59
Net Asset Value ($)	15.62	29.91	30.93	26.40	23.19	19.55	15.81	18.53	19.98	20.21
Expense Ratio (%)	1.37	1.37	1.38	1.39	1.39	1.37	1.37	1.38	1.38	1.41
Yield (%)	4.25	1.45	1.38	1.38	1.16	1.02	1.24	0.97	0.91	1.24
Portfolio Turnover (%)	9	13	6	13	8	8	7	12	16	23
Total Assets (Millions $)	3,615	7,624	8,277	7,429	6,144	4,899	4,132	4,076	3,530	3,142

PORTFOLIO (as of 9/30/08)

Portfolio Manager: Browne/Browne/Spears/Shrager - 1993

Investment Style

Large Cap	Growth
Mid Cap	Grth/Val
Small Cap	Value

Portfolio

2.7%	U.S. stock	0.0%	conv't
86.1%	int'l stock	0.0%	preferred
0.0%	U.S. bonds	0.7%	other
0.0%	int'l bonds	10.5%	cash

Number of Investments: 146
Percent of Portfolio in Top 10 Investments: 41%

SHAREHOLDER INFORMATION

Minimum Investment
Initial: $2,500 Subsequent: $200

Minimum IRA Investment
Initial: $500 Subsequent: $200

Maximum Fees
Load: 2.00% redemption 12b-1: none
Other: redemption fee applies for 60 days

Services
✔ IRA
Keogh
✔ Telephone Exchange

USAA World Growth (USAWX)

800-531-8181
www.usaa.com

Global Stock

PERFORMANCE — fund inception date: 10/1/92

	3yr Annual	5yr Annual	10yr Annual	Bull	Bear
Return (%)	-3.7	2.6	1.5	143.8	-36.0
Differ From Category (+/-)	3.8 high	2.1 high	-1.3 av	-27.7 low	7.8 high

Standard Deviation	Category Risk Index	Beta
15.2%—blw av	0.78—low	0.95

	2008	2007	2006	2005	2004	2003	2002	2001	2000	1999
Return (%)	-34.1	9.3	23.9	7.7	18.3	27.7	-16.0	-17.5	-11.2	30.7
Differ From Category (+/-)	6.7	-3.5	3.9	-5.3	2.4	-10.0	0.9	-7.6	-8.5	-7.5
Return, Tax-Adjusted (%)	-34.7	7.9	21.6	6.3	17.8	27.6	-16.2	-17.7	-12.4	28.9

PER SHARE DATA

	2008	2007	2006	2005	2004	2003	2002	2001	2000	1999
Dividends, Net Income ($)	0.21	0.18	0.42	0.08	0.08	0.04	0.05	0.07	0.07	0.06
Distrib'ns, Cap Gain ($)	0.31	1.35	1.71	1.37	0.32	0.00	0.00	0.01	1.01	1.43
Net Asset Value ($)	12.86	20.31	19.96	17.83	17.90	15.47	12.14	14.51	17.69	20.96
Expense Ratio (%)	1.24	1.30	1.20	1.30	1.32	1.53	1.40	1.14	1.12	1.16
Yield (%)	1.63	0.82	1.93	0.42	0.45	0.23	0.43	0.49	0.38	0.27
Portfolio Turnover (%)	44	29	44	36	56	138	51	38	39	51
Total Assets (Millions $)	351	563	506	363	329	273	220	284	366	399

PORTFOLIO (as of 8/31/08)

Portfolio Manager: Mannheim/Todd - 2002

Investment Style

Large Cap	Growth
Mid Cap	Grth/Val
Small Cap	Value

Portfolio

35.4%	U.S. stock	0.0%	conv't
64.0%	int'l stock	0.0%	preferred
0.0%	U.S. bonds	0.0%	other
0.0%	int'l bonds	0.6%	cash

Number of Investments: 97

Percent of Portfolio in Top 10 Investments: 24%

SHAREHOLDER INFORMATION

Minimum Investment

Initial: $3,000 Subsequent: $50

Minimum IRA Investment

Initial: $250 Subsequent: $50

Maximum Fees

Load: none 12b-1: none

Other: none

Services

✔ IRA

✔ Keogh

✔ Telephone Exchange

Foreign Stock Funds
Category Performance Ranked by 2008 Returns

Fund (Ticker)	Annual Return (%) 2008	3Yr	5Yr	10Yr	Category Risk	Total Risk
Artisan International Value (ARTKX)	-30.2	-2.3	6.3	na	low	av
Tocqueville International Value (TIVFX)	-34.9	-8.3	2.6	5.3	low	av
UMB Scout International (UMBWX)	-38.1	-4.0	4.5	4.1	low	av
Oakmark International I (OAKIX)	-41.1	-8.6	0.8	6.9	low	av
Vanguard Tax-Managed Intl (VTMGX)	-41.3	-6.3	2.4	na	low	abv av
Fidelity Spartan International Index Inv (FSIIX)	-41.5	-6.5	2.2	1.0	blw av	abv av
SSgA International Stock Selection (SSAIX)	-41.5	-6.6	2.9	2.3	blw av	abv av
Vanguard Developed Markets Index (VDMIX)	-41.7	-6.5	2.1	na	blw av	abv av
Vanguard International Value (VTRIX)	-41.8	-5.8	3.3	3.4	blw av	abv av
Harbor International Inv (HIINX)	-42.9	-2.9	5.3	na	av	high
Thomas White International (TWWDX)	-43.5	-4.2	5.8	3.7	av	abv av
Vanguard Total Intl Stock Index (VGTSX)	-44.1	-6.5	2.6	1.7	blw av	abv av
Fidelity International Discovery (FIGRX)	-44.3	-6.3	3.0	5.0	blw av	abv av
HighMark International Opportunities M (HIOMX)	-44.9	-6.0	3.7	2.4	av	abv av
T. Rowe Price Intl Gr & Inc (TRIGX)	-45.0	-8.1	2.0	2.5	blw av	abv av
Vanguard International Growth (VWIGX)	-45.0	-7.1	1.9	1.3	av	abv av
Masters' Select International (MSILX)	-45.5	-6.7	2.8	6.4	blw av	abv av
Artisan International Inv (ARTIX)	-47.0	-7.3	1.7	4.5	abv av	high
Fidelity Overseas (FOSFX)	-47.4	-8.3	0.9	1.2	av	abv av
American Century Intl Discovery Inv (TWEGX)	-52.2	-7.9	3.6	7.1	high	high
Foreign Stock Category Average	**-45.9**	**-8.6**	**1.6**	**2.8**	**av**	**high**

American Century Intl Discovery Inv (TWEGX)

800-345-2021
www.americancentury.com

Foreign Stock

PERFORMANCE — fund inception date: 4/4/94

	3yr Annual	5yr Annual	10yr Annual	Bull	Bear
Return (%)	-7.9	3.6	7.1	330.7	-56.9
Differ From Category (+/-)	0.7 av	2.0 high	4.3 high	103.9 high	-7.3 low

Standard Deviation	Category Risk Index	Beta
26.7%—high	1.21—high	1.43

	2008	2007	2006	2005	2004	2003	2002	2001	2000	1999
Return (%)	-52.2	24.4	31.5	31.5	16.2	51.3	-12.9	-21.8	-14.3	88.5
Differ From Category (+/-)	-6.3	12.2	5.6	13.3	-3.6	9.1	0.6	-3.6	-2.4	41.5
Return, Tax-Adjusted (%)	-52.6	20.2	27.4	28.0	13.9	51.2	-12.9	-21.8	-16.2	86.8

PER SHARE DATA

	2008	2007	2006	2005	2004	2003	2002	2001	2000	1999
Dividends, Net Income ($)	0.01	0.05	0.00	0.13	0.00	0.03	0.02	0.00	0.00	0.00
Distrib'ns, Cap Gain ($)	0.33	4.21	3.92	2.82	2.09	0.00	0.00	0.00	1.64	0.81
Net Asset Value ($)	6.69	14.37	15.20	14.61	13.47	13.46	8.91	10.24	13.09	17.16
Expense Ratio (%)	na	1.36	1.41	1.47	1.49	1.57	1.53	1.45	1.36	1.55
Yield (%)	0.17	0.27	0.00	0.73	0.00	0.19	0.17	0.00	0.00	0.00
Portfolio Turnover (%)	na	162	148	145	201	215	224	180	113	110
Total Assets (Millions $)	748	1,730	1,495	1,236	1,105	1,077	794	1,016	1,576	1,723

PORTFOLIO (as of 9/30/08)

Portfolio Manager: Kopinski/Brady - 1997

Investment Style

Large Cap	Growth
Mid Cap	Grth/Val
Small Cap	Value

Portfolio

1.2%	U.S. stock	0.0%	conv't
97.6%	int'l stock	0.0%	preferred
0.0%	U.S. bonds	0.0%	other
0.0%	int'l bonds	1.2%	cash

Number of Investments: 123
Percent of Portfolio in Top 10 Investments: 21%

SHAREHOLDER INFORMATION

Minimum Investment
Initial: $10,000 Subsequent: $50

Minimum IRA Investment
Initial: $10,000 Subsequent: $0

Maximum Fees
Load: 2.00% redemption 12b-1: none
Other: redemption fee applies for 180 days

Services
✔ IRA
✔ Keogh
✔ Telephone Exchange

Artisan International Inv (ARTIX)

800-344-1770
www.artisanfunds.com

Foreign Stock

PERFORMANCE — fund inception date: 12/28/95

	3yr Annual	5yr Annual	10yr Annual	Bull	Bear
Return (%)	-7.3	1.7	4.5	218.0	-49.7
Differ From Category (+/-)	1.3 abv av	0.1 av	1.7 abv av	-8.8 av	-0.1 av

Standard Deviation	Category Risk Index	Beta
22.1%—high	1.00—abv av	1.29

	2008	2007	2006	2005	2004	2003	2002	2001	2000	1999
Return (%)	-47.0	19.7	25.5	16.2	17.7	29.1	-18.9	-15.9	-10.6	81.2
Differ From Category (+/-)	-1.1	7.5	-0.4	-2.0	-2.1	-13.1	-5.4	2.3	1.3	34.2
Return, Tax-Adjusted (%)	-47.6	17.1	23.5	15.6	17.5	28.7	-19.2	-16.0	-13.1	80.5

PER SHARE DATA

	2008	2007	2006	2005	2004	2003	2002	2001	2000	1999
Dividends, Net Income ($)	0.19	0.20	0.43	0.41	0.12	0.18	0.10	0.07	0.00	0.02
Distrib'ns, Cap Gain ($)	0.70	4.47	2.33	0.00	0.00	0.00	0.00	0.00	3.55	0.54
Net Asset Value ($)	14.96	29.88	28.99	25.31	22.14	18.91	14.79	18.36	21.90	28.50
Expense Ratio (%)	1.22	1.21	1.20	1.19	1.22	1.20	1.21	1.22	1.27	1.38
Yield (%)	1.19	0.59	1.38	1.62	0.55	0.92	0.67	0.35	0.00	0.08
Portfolio Turnover (%)	54	66	58	56	55	37	51	72	99	79
Total Assets (Millions $)	5,941	13,039	10,821	12,075	7,130	9,591	7,207	5,693	4,927	2,240

PORTFOLIO (as of 9/30/08)

Portfolio Manager: Yockey - 1995

Investment Style

Large Cap	Growth
Mid Cap	Grth/Val
Small Cap	Value

Portfolio

0.0% U.S. stock	0.0% conv't
93.4% int'l stock	0.0% preferred
0.0% U.S. bonds	0.8% other
0.0% int'l bonds	5.8% cash

Number of Investments: 80
Percent of Portfolio in Top 10 Investments: 32%

SHAREHOLDER INFORMATION

Minimum Investment
Initial: $1,000 Subsequent: $50

Minimum IRA Investment
Initial: $1,000 Subsequent: $50

Maximum Fees
Load: 2.00% redemption 12b-1: none
Other: redemption fee applies for 90 days

Services
✔ IRA
✔ Keogh
✔ Telephone Exchange

Artisan International Value (ARTKX)

800-399-1770
www.artisanfunds.com

Foreign Stock

PERFORMANCE — fund inception date: 9/23/02

	3yr Annual	5yr Annual	10yr Annual	Bull	Bear
Return (%)	-2.3	6.3	na	235.7	-34.6
Differ From Category (+/-)	6.3 high	4.7 high	na	8.9 abv av	15.0 high

Standard Deviation	Category Risk Index	Beta
15.8%—av	0.72—low	0.93

	2008	2007	2006	2005	2004	2003	2002	2001	2000	1999
Return (%)	-30.2	-0.7	34.4	10.0	32.2	56.5	—	—	—	—
Differ From Category (+/-)	15.7	-12.9	8.5	-8.2	12.4	14.3	—	—	—	—
Return, Tax-Adjusted (%)	-30.4	-2.3	32.8	8.8	31.8	55.8	—	—	—	—

PER SHARE DATA

	2008	2007	2006	2005	2004	2003	2002	2001	2000	1999
Dividends, Net Income ($)	0.21	0.51	0.44	0.47	0.11	0.09	—	—	—	—
Distrib'ns, Cap Gain ($)	0.00	1.67	1.28	0.60	0.21	0.30	—	—	—	—
Net Asset Value ($)	17.63	25.52	27.93	22.06	21.06	16.18	—	—	—	—
Expense Ratio (%)	1.23	1.23	1.25	1.31	1.56	2.45	—	—	—	—
Yield (%)	1.19	1.87	1.51	2.08	0.51	0.54	—	—	—	—
Portfolio Turnover (%)	45	46	43	53	15	9	—	—	—	—
Total Assets (Millions $)	813	1,404	1,654	657	458	45	—	—	—	—

PORTFOLIO (as of 9/30/08)

Portfolio Manager: Samra/OKeefe - 2002

Investment Style

Large Cap	Growth
Mid Cap	Grth/Val
Small Cap	Value

Portfolio

8.9%	U.S. stock	0.0%	conv't
85.2%	int'l stock	0.0%	preferred
0.0%	U.S. bonds	0.6%	other
0.0%	int'l bonds	5.3%	cash

Number of Investments: 44

Percent of Portfolio in Top 10 Investments: 45%

SHAREHOLDER INFORMATION

Minimum Investment

Initial: $1,000 Subsequent: $50

Minimum IRA Investment

Initial: $1,000 Subsequent: $50

Maximum Fees

Load: 2.00% redemption 12b-1: none

Other: redemption fee applies for 90 days

Services

✔ IRA

✔ Keogh

✔ Telephone Exchange

Fidelity International Discovery (FIGRX)

800-544-9797
www.fidelity.com

Foreign Stock

PERFORMANCE **fund inception date: 12/31/86**

	3yr Annual	5yr Annual	10yr Annual	Bull	Bear
Return (%)	-6.3	3.0	5.0	237.4	-47.2
Differ From Category (+/-)	2.3 high	1.4 abv av	2.2 abv av	10.6 abv av	2.4 abv av

Standard Deviation	Category Risk Index	Beta
20.5%—abv av	0.93—blw av	1.19

	2008	2007	2006	2005	2004	2003	2002	2001	2000	1999
Return (%)	-44.3	18.9	24.2	18.5	19.0	43.3	-9.9	-17.5	-14.1	53.7
Differ From Category (+/-)	1.6	6.7	-1.7	0.3	-0.8	1.1	3.6	0.7	-2.2	6.7
Return, Tax-Adjusted (%)	-44.6	17.9	23.3	17.4	18.7	42.9	-10.1	-17.5	-16.5	51.6

PER SHARE DATA

	2008	2007	2006	2005	2004	2003	2002	2001	2000	1999
Dividends, Net Income ($)	0.34	0.41	0.38	0.31	0.15	0.18	0.09	0.00	0.51	0.33
Distrib'ns, Cap Gain ($)	0.00	1.67	0.98	1.40	0.12	0.00	0.00	0.00	2.66	1.50
Net Asset Value ($)	23.63	43.08	37.92	31.66	28.20	23.92	16.82	18.76	22.72	30.10
Expense Ratio (%)	na	1.00	1.03	1.01	1.06	1.11	1.12	1.09	1.05	1.10
Yield (%)	1.42	0.92	0.96	0.92	0.52	0.75	0.53	0.00	2.00	1.04
Portfolio Turnover (%)	na	56	56	75	87	81	63	81	104	94
Total Assets (Millions $)	6,651	13,925	8,974	4,657	2,504	1,498	907	941	1,183	1,395

PORTFOLIO (as of 11/30/08)

Portfolio Manager: Kennedy - 2004

Investment Style

Large Cap Growth
Mid Cap Grth/Val
Small Cap Value

Portfolio

1.9% U.S. stock	0.0% conv't
89.9% int'l stock	1.0% preferred
0.0% U.S. bonds	0.0% other
0.0% int'l bonds	7.2% cash

Number of Investments: 176
Percent of Portfolio in Top 10 Investments: 26%

SHAREHOLDER INFORMATION

Minimum Investment
Initial: $2,500 Subsequent: $250

Minimum IRA Investment
Initial: $500 Subsequent: $100

Maximum Fees
Load: 1.00% redemption 12b-1: none
Other: redemption fee applies for 30 days; maint fee for low bal

Services
✔ IRA
Keogh
✔ Telephone Exchange

Fidelity Overseas (FOSFX)

800-544-9797
www.fidelity.com

Foreign Stock

PERFORMANCE — fund inception date: 12/4/84

	3yr Annual	5yr Annual	10yr Annual	Bull	Bear
Return (%)	-8.3	0.9	1.2	227.7	-50.7
Differ From Category (+/-)	0.3 av	-0.7 blw av	-1.6 blw av	0.9 abv av	-1.1 av

Standard Deviation	Category Risk Index	Beta
21.6%—abv av	0.98—av	1.28

	2008	2007	2006	2005	2004	2003	2002	2001	2000	1999
Return (%)	-47.4	21.8	20.4	19.2	13.5	44.2	-19.5	-20.3	-18.4	42.8
Differ From Category (+/-)	-1.5	9.6	-5.5	1.0	-6.3	2.1	-6.0	-2.1	-6.5	-4.2
Return, Tax-Adjusted (%)	-47.6	19.4	18.3	18.8	13.2	43.8	-19.6	-20.3	-20.8	40.9

PER SHARE DATA

	2008	2007	2006	2005	2004	2003	2002	2001	2000	1999
Dividends, Net Income ($)	0.37	0.57	0.55	0.41	0.19	0.30	0.09	0.00	0.86	0.44
Distrib'ns, Cap Gain ($)	0.00	5.75	4.64	0.16	0.11	0.00	0.00	0.00	4.12	2.64
Net Asset Value ($)	25.08	48.39	44.80	41.61	35.38	31.43	22.00	27.42	34.37	48.01
Expense Ratio (%)	na	0.91	0.90	0.86	1.00	1.00	1.16	1.12	1.16	1.23
Yield (%)	1.47	1.05	1.11	0.98	0.53	0.95	0.40	0.00	2.23	0.86
Portfolio Turnover (%)	na	87	132	87	79	104	72	95	132	85
Total Assets (Millions $)	5,445	9,106	7,714	5,371	4,687	3,961	2,843	3,481	4,653	5,404

PORTFOLIO (as of 11/30/08)

Portfolio Manager: Hart - 2006

Investment Style

Large Cap	Growth
Mid Cap	Grth/Val
Small Cap	Value

Portfolio

4.3%	U.S. stock	0.0%	conv't
89.0%	int'l stock	0.0%	preferred
0.0%	U.S. bonds	0.8%	other
0.0%	int'l bonds	5.9%	cash

Number of Investments: 130
Percent of Portfolio in Top 10 Investments: 29%

SHAREHOLDER INFORMATION

Minimum Investment
Initial: $2,500 Subsequent: $250

Minimum IRA Investment
Initial: $500 Subsequent: $100

Maximum Fees
Load: 1.00% redemption 12b-1: none
Other: redemption fee applies for 30 days; maint fee for low bal

Services
✔ IRA
✔ Keogh
✔ Telephone Exchange

Fidelity Spartan International Index Inv (FSIIX)

800-544-9797
www.fidelity.com

Foreign Stock

PERFORMANCE — fund inception date: 11/5/97

	3yr Annual	5yr Annual	10yr Annual	Bull	Bear
Return (%)	-6.5	2.2	1.0	199.0	-45.0
Differ From Category (+/-)	2.1 abv av	0.6 abv av	-1.8 blw av	-27.8 blw av	4.6 high

Standard Deviation	Category Risk Index	Beta
19.5%—abv av	0.89—blw av	1.17

	2008	2007	2006	2005	2004	2003	2002	2001	2000	1999
Return (%)	-41.5	10.7	26.1	13.7	19.8	38.3	-16.0	-21.9	-14.9	29.0
Differ From Category (+/-)	4.4	-1.5	0.2	-4.5	0.0	-3.9	-2.5	-3.7	-3.0	-18.0
Return, Tax-Adjusted (%)	-42.2	9.6	25.3	13.0	19.1	37.3	-16.7	-22.3	-15.3	28.5

PER SHARE DATA

	2008	2007	2006	2005	2004	2003	2002	2001	2000	1999
Dividends, Net Income ($)	0.94	1.19	0.83	0.60	0.55	0.55	0.39	0.32	0.29	0.38
Distrib'ns, Cap Gain ($)	0.00	0.36	0.08	0.07	0.07	0.00	0.00	0.00	0.08	0.00
Net Asset Value ($)	26.74	47.30	44.14	35.73	32.02	27.26	20.14	24.44	31.69	37.67
Expense Ratio (%)	0.10	0.10	0.10	0.20	0.47	0.39	0.35	0.35	0.35	0.36
Yield (%)	3.51	2.49	1.87	1.67	1.71	2.01	1.93	1.30	0.91	1.00
Portfolio Turnover (%)	4	2	2	6	31	19	12	4	3	2
Total Assets (Millions $)	3,332	4,811	2,833	1,251	955	455	346	319	349	186

PORTFOLIO (as of 11/30/08)

Portfolio Manager: Adams/Simon/Waddell - 2005

Investment Style

Large Cap	Growth
Mid Cap	Grth/Val
Small Cap	Value

Portfolio

0.7%	U.S. stock	0.0%	conv't
91.4%	int'l stock	0.1%	preferred
0.0%	U.S. bonds	1.0%	other
0.0%	int'l bonds	6.8%	cash

Number of Investments: 1,031
Percent of Portfolio in Top 10 Investments: 16%

SHAREHOLDER INFORMATION

Minimum Investment
Initial: $10,000 Subsequent: $1,000

Minimum IRA Investment
Initial: $0 Subsequent: $0

Maximum Fees
Load: 1.00% redemption 12b-1: none
Other: redemption fee applies for 90 days; maint fee for low bal

Services
✔ IRA
✔ Keogh
✔ Telephone Exchange

Harbor International Inv (HIINX)

800-422-1050
www.harborfunds.com

Foreign Stock

PERFORMANCE — fund inception date: 11/1/02

	3yr Annual	5yr Annual	10yr Annual	Bull	Bear
Return (%)	-2.9	5.3	na	257.8	-45.6
Differ From Category (+/-)	5.7 high	3.7 high	na	31.0 abv av	4.0 abv av

Standard Deviation	Category Risk Index	Beta
21.9%—high	1.00—av	1.29

	2008	2007	2006	2005	2004	2003	2002	2001	2000	1999
Return (%)	-42.9	21.3	32.1	20.3	17.4	40.3	—	—	—	—
Differ From Category (+/-)	3.0	9.1	6.2	2.1	-2.4	-1.9	—	—	—	—
Return, Tax-Adjusted (%)	-43.2	20.1	30.6	19.1	17.0	39.4	—	—	—	—

PER SHARE DATA

	2008	2007	2006	2005	2004	2003	2002	2001	2000	1999
Dividends, Net Income ($)	0.59	0.85	1.29	0.88	0.43	0.45	—	—	—	—
Distrib'ns, Cap Gain ($)	0.00	3.02	1.88	1.22	0.15	0.56	—	—	—	—
Net Asset Value ($)	39.81	70.73	61.58	49.03	42.52	36.68	—	—	—	—
Expense Ratio (%)	na	1.19	1.24	1.30	1.29	1.32	—	—	—	—
Yield (%)	1.47	1.15	2.02	1.74	1.00	1.21	—	—	—	—
Portfolio Turnover (%)	na	13	12	13	12	21	—	—	—	—
Total Assets (Millions $)	2,063	2,432	1,047	445	227	86	—	—	—	—

PORTFOLIO (as of 9/30/08)

Portfolio Manager: Castegren - 1987

Investment Style

Large Cap	Growth
Mid Cap	Grth/Val
Small Cap	Value

Portfolio

0.0%	U.S. stock	0.0%	conv't
91.0%	int'l stock	2.0%	preferred
0.0%	U.S. bonds	0.0%	other
0.0%	int'l bonds	7.0%	cash

Number of Investments: 105

Percent of Portfolio in Top 10 Investments: 24%

SHAREHOLDER INFORMATION

Minimum Investment

Initial: $2,500 Subsequent: $0

Minimum IRA Investment

Initial: $1,000 Subsequent: $0

Maximum Fees

Load: 2.00% redemption 12b-1: 0.25%

Other: redemption fee applies for 60 days

Services

✔ IRA

Keogh

✔ Telephone Exchange

HighMark International Opportunities M (HIOMX)

800-433-6884
www.highmarkfunds.com

Foreign Stock

PERFORMANCE — fund inception date: 9/4/79

	3yr Annual	5yr Annual	10yr Annual	Bull	Bear
Return (%)	-6.0	3.7	2.4	251.7	-48.7
Differ From Category (+/-)	2.6 high	2.1 high	-0.4 av	24.9 abv av	0.9 av

Standard Deviation	Category Risk Index	Beta
21.6%—abv av	0.98—av	1.25

	2008	2007	2006	2005	2004	2003	2002	2001	2000	1999
Return (%)	-44.9	18.7	27.2	20.6	19.7	43.8	-12.7	-21.5	-19.3	32.4
Differ From Category (+/-)	1.0	6.5	1.3	2.4	-0.1	1.6	0.8	-3.3	-7.4	-14.6
Return, Tax-Adjusted (%)	-45.6	17.4	25.0	19.4	19.3	43.4	-12.9	-21.5	-20.9	30.2

PER SHARE DATA

	2008	2007	2006	2005	2004	2003	2002	2001	2000	1999
Dividends, Net Income ($)	0.12	0.16	0.13	0.15	0.05	0.05	0.02	0.00	0.01	0.02
Distrib'ns, Cap Gain ($)	0.15	0.36	0.83	0.19	0.00	0.00	0.00	0.00	0.60	0.65
Net Asset Value ($)	5.16	9.85	8.74	7.63	6.60	5.56	3.90	4.49	5.72	7.84
Expense Ratio (%)	1.23	1.17	1.25	1.45	1.35	1.37	1.34	1.44	1.37	1.49
Yield (%)	2.18	1.57	1.34	1.86	0.80	0.86	0.49	0.00	0.14	0.21
Portfolio Turnover (%)	86	32	48	74	69	39	69	90	101	85
Total Assets (Millions $)	129	284	239	176	194	159	92	99	138	173

PORTFOLIO (as of 11/30/08)

Portfolio Manager: Hill/Craddock/Leve - 2006

Investment Style

Large Cap Growth
Mid Cap Grth/Val
Small Cap Value

Portfolio

0.0%	U.S. stock	0.0%	conv't
96.8%	int'l stock	0.2%	preferred
0.0%	U.S. bonds	0.2%	other
0.0%	int'l bonds	2.8%	cash

Number of Investments: 284
Percent of Portfolio in Top 10 Investments: 18%

SHAREHOLDER INFORMATION

Minimum Investment
Initial: $5,000 Subsequent: $100

Minimum IRA Investment
Initial: $0 Subsequent: $0

Maximum Fees
Load: 2.00% redemption 12b-1: none
Other: redemption fee applies for 30 days

Services
✔ IRA
Keogh
✔ Telephone Exchange

Masters' Select International (MSILX)

800-960-0188
www.mastersselect.com

Foreign Stock

PERFORMANCE — fund inception date: 12/1/97

	3yr Annual	5yr Annual	10yr Annual	Bull	Bear
Return (%)	-6.7	2.8	6.4	255.9	-50.0
Differ From Category (+/-)	1.9 abv av	1.2 abv av	3.6 high	29.1 abv av	-0.4 av

Standard Deviation	Category Risk Index	Beta
20.5%—abv av	0.93—blw av	1.20

	2008	2007	2006	2005	2004	2003	2002	2001	2000	1999
Return (%)	-45.5	20.7	23.6	23.7	14.3	38.8	-14.4	-18.0	-5.1	75.0
Differ From Category (+/-)	0.4	8.5	-2.3	5.5	-5.5	-3.4	-0.9	0.2	6.8	28.0
Return, Tax-Adjusted (%)	-46.5	17.2	20.7	20.4	14.2	38.7	-14.5	-18.1	-7.7	74.1

PER SHARE DATA

	2008	2007	2006	2005	2004	2003	2002	2001	2000	1999
Dividends, Net Income ($)	0.39	0.20	0.41	0.29	0.07	0.03	0.03	0.03	0.05	0.03
Distrib'ns, Cap Gain ($)	0.37	3.87	2.38	2.92	0.00	0.00	0.00	0.00	2.34	0.38
Net Asset Value ($)	9.47	18.68	18.74	17.48	16.89	14.83	10.70	12.53	15.31	18.67
Expense Ratio (%)	na	1.03	1.06	1.08	1.09	1.10	1.13	1.19	1.18	1.29
Yield (%)	3.95	0.90	1.93	1.43	0.41	0.18	0.31	0.26	0.25	0.17
Portfolio Turnover (%)	na	93	98	160	88	110	141	174	149	100
Total Assets (Millions $)	896	2,069	1,725	1,429	1,137	732	336	278	276	218

PORTFOLIO (as of 9/30/08)

Portfolio Manager: DeGroot/Gregory/Herro/Tyson - 1997

Investment Style

Large Cap	Growth
Mid Cap	Grth/Val
Small Cap	Value

Portfolio

1.3%	U.S. stock	0.0%	conv't
92.1%	int'l stock	0.0%	preferred
0.0%	U.S. bonds	0.0%	other
0.0%	int'l bonds	6.5%	cash

Number of Investments: 87
Percent of Portfolio in Top 10 Investments: 29%

SHAREHOLDER INFORMATION

Minimum Investment
Initial: $5,000 Subsequent: $250

Minimum IRA Investment
Initial: $1,000 Subsequent: $100

Maximum Fees
Load: 2.00% redemption 12b-1: none
Other: redemption fee applies for 180 days

Services
✔ IRA
✔ Keogh
✔ Telephone Exchange

Oakmark International I (OAKIX)

800-625-6275
www.oakmark.com

Foreign Stock

PERFORMANCE — fund inception date: 9/30/92

	3yr Annual	5yr Annual	10yr Annual	Bull	Bear
Return (%)	-8.6	0.8	6.9	187.3	-44.7
Differ From Category (+/-)	0.0 av	-0.8 blw av	4.1 high	-39.5 blw av	4.9 high

Standard Deviation	Category Risk Index	Beta
18.0%—av	0.82—low	1.10

	2008	2007	2006	2005	2004	2003	2002	2001	2000	1999
Return (%)	-41.1	-0.6	30.6	14.1	19.0	38.0	-8.5	-5.2	12.5	39.4
Differ From Category (+/-)	4.8	-12.8	4.7	-4.1	-0.8	-4.2	5.0	13.0	24.4	-7.6
Return, Tax-Adjusted (%)	-43.5	-3.3	27.5	12.4	18.5	37.7	-8.8	-5.6	10.4	37.7

PER SHARE DATA

	2008	2007	2006	2005	2004	2003	2002	2001	2000	1999
Dividends, Net Income ($)	1.39	0.17	0.44	0.59	0.27	0.11	0.13	0.16	0.51	0.49
Distrib'ns, Cap Gain ($)	0.10	4.25	3.48	1.00	0.05	0.00	0.00	0.00	0.50	0.00
Net Asset Value ($)	10.85	20.95	25.45	22.52	21.13	18.02	13.14	14.49	15.46	14.70
Expense Ratio (%)	1.10	1.05	1.10	1.11	1.20	1.25	1.31	1.30	1.30	1.29
Yield (%)	12.70	0.68	1.53	2.52	1.25	0.60	0.95	1.13	3.17	3.30
Portfolio Turnover (%)	41	50	37	14	21	34	24	58	64	54
Total Assets (Millions $)	2,592	7,300	8,005	5,816	4,677	3,509	1,721	964	818	785

PORTFOLIO (as of 9/30/08)

Portfolio Manager: Herro - 1992

Investment Style

Large Cap	Growth
Mid Cap	Grth/Val
Small Cap	Value

Portfolio

0.3%	U.S. stock	0.0%	conv't
97.9%	int'l stock	0.0%	preferred
0.0%	U.S. bonds	0.0%	other
0.0%	int'l bonds	1.9%	cash

Number of Investments: 47

Percent of Portfolio in Top 10 Investments: 35%

SHAREHOLDER INFORMATION

Minimum Investment

Initial: $1,000 Subsequent: $100

Minimum IRA Investment

Initial: $1,000 Subsequent: $100

Maximum Fees

Load: 2.00% redemption 12b-1: none

Other: redemption fee applies for 90 days

Services

✔ IRA

✔ Keogh

✔ Telephone Exchange

SSgA International Stock Selection (SSAIX)

800-647-7327
www.ssgafunds.com

Foreign Stock

PERFORMANCE

fund inception date: 3/7/95

	3yr Annual	5yr Annual	10yr Annual	Bull	Bear
Return (%)	-6.6	2.9	2.3	226.0	-46.5
Differ From Category (+/-)	2.0 abv av	1.3 abv av	-0.5 av	-0.8 abv av	3.1 abv av

Standard Deviation	Category Risk Index	Beta
19.9%—abv av	0.90—blw av	1.16

	2008	2007	2006	2005	2004	2003	2002	2001	2000	1999
Return (%)	-41.5	6.9	30.5	17.0	21.0	42.8	-13.7	-20.5	-16.4	32.5
Differ From Category (+/-)	4.4	-5.3	4.6	-1.2	1.2	0.6	-0.2	-2.3	-4.5	-14.5
Return, Tax-Adjusted (%)	-42.1	5.7	29.4	16.0	20.2	42.1	-14.1	-20.7	-18.5	31.9

PER SHARE DATA

	2008	2007	2006	2005	2004	2003	2002	2001	2000	1999
Dividends, Net Income ($)	0.22	0.32	0.19	0.15	0.19	0.13	0.07	0.04	0.00	0.13
Distrib'ns, Cap Gain ($)	0.00	0.35	0.35	0.33	0.00	0.00	0.00	0.00	1.26	0.00
Net Asset Value ($)	8.04	14.12	13.81	11.03	9.87	8.33	5.93	6.95	8.79	12.06
Expense Ratio (%)	1.00	1.00	1.00	1.00	1.00	1.00	1.00	1.00	1.00	1.00
Yield (%)	2.73	2.18	1.34	1.31	1.91	1.52	1.13	0.57	0.00	1.04
Portfolio Turnover (%)	75	54	60	59	78	70	50	85	64	62
Total Assets (Millions $)	1,211	3,200	1,609	394	156	123	82	72	93	120

PORTFOLIO (as of 11/30/08)

Portfolio Manager: Mallik/Rosenfeld - 2007

Investment Style

Large Cap	Growth
Mid Cap	Grth/Val
Small Cap	Value

Portfolio

0.0% U.S. stock	0.0% conv't
97.2% int'l stock	0.0% preferred
0.0% U.S. bonds	0.1% other
0.0% int'l bonds	2.7% cash

Number of Investments: 137

Percent of Portfolio in Top 10 Investments: 23%

SHAREHOLDER INFORMATION

Minimum Investment

Initial: $1,000 Subsequent: $100

Minimum IRA Investment

Initial: $250 Subsequent: $100

Maximum Fees

Load: none 12b-1: 0.22%

Other: none

Services

✔ IRA

Keogh

✔ Telephone Exchange

T. Rowe Price Intl Gr & Inc (TRIGX)

800-638-5660
www.troweprice.com

Foreign Stock

PERFORMANCE — fund inception date: 12/21/98

	3yr Annual	5yr Annual	10yr Annual	Bull	Bear
Return (%)	-8.1	2.0	2.5	218.6	-48.3
Differ From Category (+/-)	0.5 av	0.4 av	-0.3 av	-8.2 av	1.3 av

Standard Deviation	Category Risk Index	Beta
20.8%—abv av	0.95—blw av	1.25

	2008	2007	2006	2005	2004	2003	2002	2001	2000	1999
Return (%)	-45.0	8.7	29.9	15.7	23.1	39.4	-11.7	-17.6	-4.4	19.6
Differ From Category (+/-)	0.9	-3.5	4.0	-2.5	3.3	-2.8	1.8	0.6	7.5	-27.4
Return, Tax-Adjusted (%)	-45.8	7.1	28.7	14.9	22.7	39.2	-12.1	-18.0	-5.9	18.4

PER SHARE DATA

	2008	2007	2006	2005	2004	2003	2002	2001	2000	1999
Dividends, Net Income ($)	0.41	0.36	0.27	0.21	0.11	0.04	0.08	0.10	0.13	0.19
Distrib'ns, Cap Gain ($)	0.00	0.96	0.49	0.15	0.01	0.00	0.01	0.00	0.64	0.23
Net Asset Value ($)	9.39	17.78	17.60	14.14	12.53	10.28	7.40	8.48	10.41	11.71
Expense Ratio (%)	na	0.88	0.91	0.99	1.25	1.25	1.44	1.25	1.25	1.25
Yield (%)	4.36	1.92	1.49	1.46	0.87	0.38	1.07	1.17	1.17	1.59
Portfolio Turnover (%)	na	33	37	27	46	53	25	9	32	36
Total Assets (Millions $)	1,620	2,558	2,065	1,036	552	144	12	10	10	11

PORTFOLIO (as of 9/30/08)

Portfolio Manager: Mills - 2003

Investment Style

Large Cap	Growth
Mid Cap	Grth/Val
Small Cap	Value

Portfolio

0.4%	U.S. stock	0.0%	conv't
97.0%	int'l stock	0.6%	preferred
0.0%	U.S. bonds	0.0%	other
0.0%	int'l bonds	2.0%	cash

Number of Investments: 152
Percent of Portfolio in Top 10 Investments: 21%

SHAREHOLDER INFORMATION

Minimum Investment
Initial: $2,500 Subsequent: $100

Minimum IRA Investment
Initial: $1,000 Subsequent: $50

Maximum Fees
Load: 2.00% redemption 12b-1: none
Other: redemption fee applies for 90 days

Services
✔ IRA
✔ Keogh
✔ Telephone Exchange

Thomas White International (TWWDX)

800-811-0535
www.thomaswhite.com

Foreign Stock

PERFORMANCE — fund inception date: 6/28/94

	3yr Annual	5yr Annual	10yr Annual	Bull	Bear
Return (%)	-4.2	5.8	3.7	265.6	-46.6
Differ From Category (+/-)	4.4 high	4.2 high	0.9 abv av	38.8 high	3.0 abv av

Standard Deviation	Category Risk Index	Beta
21.4%—abv av	0.97—av	1.25

	2008	2007	2006	2005	2004	2003	2002	2001	2000	1999
Return (%)	-43.5	17.9	31.7	25.5	20.4	36.2	-11.4	-16.8	-14.7	26.3
Differ From Category (+/-)	2.4	5.7	5.9	7.3	0.6	-5.9	2.1	1.4	-2.8	-20.7
Return, Tax-Adjusted (%)	-43.9	16.0	30.3	23.9	19.9	35.7	-11.7	-17.0	-15.5	22.5

PER SHARE DATA

	2008	2007	2006	2005	2004	2003	2002	2001	2000	1999
Dividends, Net Income ($)	0.25	0.33	0.18	0.18	0.15	0.13	0.07	0.06	0.01	0.07
Distrib'ns, Cap Gain ($)	0.00	1.65	1.07	1.07	0.00	0.00	0.00	0.00	0.55	2.49
Net Asset Value ($)	11.76	21.25	19.62	15.92	13.79	11.59	8.61	9.79	11.84	14.54
Expense Ratio (%)	na	1.42	1.44	1.50	1.50	1.50	1.50	1.50	1.50	1.44
Yield (%)	2.10	1.45	0.89	1.05	1.09	1.12	0.79	0.65	0.05	0.38
Portfolio Turnover (%)	na	46	39	36	46	26	50	35	38	67
Total Assets (Millions $)	244	262	170	86	54	43	26	29	34	48

PORTFOLIO (as of 9/30/08)

Portfolio Manager: White Jr. - 1994

Investment Style

Large Cap	Growth
Mid Cap	Grth/Val
Small Cap	Value

Portfolio

0.0%	U.S. stock	0.0%	conv't
92.0%	int'l stock	1.1%	preferred
0.0%	U.S. bonds	0.0%	other
0.0%	int'l bonds	6.9%	cash

Number of Investments: 132

Percent of Portfolio in Top 10 Investments: 23%

SHAREHOLDER INFORMATION

Minimum Investment

Initial: $2,500 Subsequent: $100

Minimum IRA Investment

Initial: $1,000 Subsequent: $100

Maximum Fees

Load: 2.00% redemption 12b-1: none

Other: redemption fee applies for 60 days

Services

✔ IRA
Keogh
✔ Telephone Exchange

Tocqueville International Value (TIVFX)

800-697-3863
www.tocquevillefunds.com

Foreign Stock

PERFORMANCE — fund inception date: 8/1/94

	3yr Annual	5yr Annual	10yr Annual	Bull	Bear
Return (%)	-8.3	2.6	5.3	203.8	-38.6
Differ From Category (+/-)	0.3 av	1.0 abv av	2.5 abv av	-23.0 av	11.0 high

Standard Deviation	Category Risk Index	Beta
16.4%—av	0.75—low	0.95

	2008	2007	2006	2005	2004	2003	2002	2001	2000	1999
Return (%)	-34.9	1.4	16.9	21.0	21.7	53.7	1.5	-9.9	-19.8	31.0
Differ From Category (+/-)	11.0	-10.8	-9.0	2.8	1.9	11.5	15.0	8.3	-7.8	-16.0
Return, Tax-Adjusted (%)	-36.0	-0.7	14.0	18.9	21.5	53.5	1.5	-9.9	-19.9	28.1

PER SHARE DATA

	2008	2007	2006	2005	2004	2003	2002	2001	2000	1999
Dividends, Net Income ($)	0.20	0.10	0.27	0.05	0.08	0.04	0.01	0.00	0.03	0.05
Distrib'ns, Cap Gain ($)	0.51	1.93	2.30	1.86	0.00	0.00	0.00	0.00	0.00	1.22
Net Asset Value ($)	8.11	13.52	15.31	15.31	14.26	11.78	7.69	7.58	8.41	10.51
Expense Ratio (%)	na	1.59	1.61	1.66	1.71	1.77	1.73	1.77	1.72	1.67
Yield (%)	2.29	0.67	1.53	0.30	0.54	0.33	0.10	0.00	0.35	0.42
Portfolio Turnover (%)	na	49	39	35	43	55	61	54	45	78
Total Assets (Millions $)	111	202	236	238	210	144	84	70	84	100

PORTFOLIO (as of 9/30/08)

Portfolio Manager: Hunt/Sicart - 2001

Investment Style

Large Cap	Growth
Mid Cap	Grth/Val
Small Cap	Value

Portfolio

6.3%	U.S. stock	0.0%	conv't
86.3%	int'l stock	0.0%	preferred
0.0%	U.S. bonds	0.0%	other
0.0%	int'l bonds	7.4%	cash

Number of Investments: 64

Percent of Portfolio in Top 10 Investments: 30%

SHAREHOLDER INFORMATION

Minimum Investment

Initial: $1,000 Subsequent: $100

Minimum IRA Investment

Initial: $0 Subsequent: $0

Maximum Fees

Load: 2.00% redemption 12b-1: 0.25%

Other: redemption fee applies for 120 days

Services

✔ IRA

✔ Keogh

✔ Telephone Exchange

UMB Scout International (UMBWX)

800-996-2862
www.umb.com

Foreign Stock

PERFORMANCE — fund inception date: 9/14/93

	3yr Annual	5yr Annual	10yr Annual	Bull	Bear
Return (%)	-4.0	4.5	4.1	190.4	-40.0
Differ From Category (+/-)	4.6 high	2.9 high	1.3 abv av	-36.4 blw av	9.6 high

Standard Deviation	Category Risk Index	Beta
18.4%—av	0.84—low	1.08

	2008	2007	2006	2005	2004	2003	2002	2001	2000	1999
Return (%)	-38.1	17.7	21.5	19.5	18.0	33.0	-15.9	-11.0	-8.2	31.4
Differ From Category (+/-)	7.8	5.6	-4.4	1.3	-1.8	-9.1	-2.4	7.2	3.7	-15.6
Return, Tax-Adjusted (%)	-38.9	17.0	20.4	19.0	17.7	32.7	-16.2	-11.5	-8.8	30.5

PER SHARE DATA

	2008	2007	2006	2005	2004	2003	2002	2001	2000	1999
Dividends, Net Income ($)	0.46	0.46	0.33	0.23	0.17	0.14	0.14	0.23	0.05	0.21
Distrib'ns, Cap Gain ($)	0.98	0.60	1.30	0.30	0.00	0.00	0.00	0.01	0.56	0.36
Net Asset Value ($)	21.79	37.38	32.66	28.26	24.10	20.58	15.58	18.67	21.24	23.77
Expense Ratio (%)	0.96	0.97	1.03	1.04	1.10	1.14	1.12	0.91	0.91	0.86
Yield (%)	2.03	1.21	0.96	0.79	0.70	0.66	0.87	1.22	0.22	0.88
Portfolio Turnover (%)	17	19	23	19	12	12	13	10	8	8
Total Assets (Millions $)	2,747	3,692	3,019	1,820	1,023	593	354	358	307	268

PORTFOLIO (as of 9/30/08)

Portfolio Manager: Moffett/Anderson - 1993

Investment Style

Large Cap	Growth
Mid Cap	Grth/Val
Small Cap	Value

Portfolio

3.1% U.S. stock	0.0% conv't
86.2% int'l stock	0.0% preferred
0.0% U.S. bonds	1.6% other
0.0% int'l bonds	9.1% cash

Number of Investments: 93

Percent of Portfolio in Top 10 Investments: 23%

SHAREHOLDER INFORMATION

Minimum Investment

Initial: $1,000 Subsequent: $100

Minimum IRA Investment

Initial: $100 Subsequent: $100

Maximum Fees

Load: 2.00% redemption 12b-1: none

Other: redemption fee applies for 2 months

Services

✔ IRA
✔ Keogh
✔ Telephone Exchange

Vanguard Developed Markets Index (VDMIX)

800-997-2798
www.vanguard.com

Foreign Stock

PERFORMANCE — fund inception date: 5/8/00

	3yr Annual	5yr Annual	10yr Annual	Bull	Bear
Return (%)	-6.5	2.1	na	201.4	-45.3
Differ From Category (+/-)	2.1 abv av	0.5 av	na	-25.4 av	4.3 abv av

Standard Deviation	Category Risk Index	Beta
19.4%—abv av	0.88—blw av	1.17

	2008	2007	2006	2005	2004	2003	2002	2001	2000	1999
Return (%)	-41.7	10.9	26.1	13.3	20.2	38.6	-15.7	-22.1	—	—
Differ From Category (+/-)	4.2	-1.3	0.2	-4.9	0.4	-3.6	-2.2	-3.9	—	—
Return, Tax-Adjusted (%)	-42.7	9.9	25.1	12.5	19.3	37.7	-16.4	-22.6	—	—

PER SHARE DATA

	2008	2007	2006	2005	2004	2003	2002	2001	2000	1999
Dividends, Net Income ($)	0.40	0.39	0.30	0.22	0.19	0.14	0.12	0.12	—	—
Distrib'ns, Cap Gain ($)	0.00	0.00	0.00	0.00	0.00	0.00	0.00	0.00	—	—
Net Asset Value ($)	7.52	13.57	12.58	10.21	9.20	7.81	5.74	6.95	—	—
Expense Ratio (%)	na	0.00	0.00	0.00	0.00	0.00	0.00	0.00	—	—
Yield (%)	5.29	2.85	2.37	2.14	2.06	1.83	2.02	1.72	—	—
Portfolio Turnover (%)	na	7	9	10	4	7	5	3	—	—
Total Assets (Millions $)	2,328	3,864	2,856	1,780	1,198	734	399	189	—	—

PORTFOLIO (as of 9/30/08)

Portfolio Manager: No Manager - 2000

Investment Style

Large Cap	Growth
Mid Cap	Grth/Val
Small Cap	Value

Portfolio

0.0% U.S. stock	0.0% conv't
97.8% int'l stock	0.2% preferred
0.1% U.S. bonds	1.1% other
0.0% int'l bonds	0.9% cash

Number of Investments: 3
Percent of Portfolio in Top 10 Investments: 100%

SHAREHOLDER INFORMATION

Minimum Investment
Initial: $3,000 Subsequent: $100

Minimum IRA Investment
Initial: $3,000 Subsequent: $100

Maximum Fees
Load: 2.00% redemption 12b-1: none
Other: redemption fee applies for 2 months

Services
✔ IRA
Keogh
✔ Telephone Exchange

Vanguard International Growth (VWIGX)

800-997-2798
www.vanguard.com

Foreign Stock

PERFORMANCE — fund inception date: 9/30/81

	3yr Annual	5yr Annual	10yr Annual	Bull	Bear
Return (%)	-7.1	1.9	1.3	203.2	-47.8
Differ From Category (+/-)	1.5 abv av	0.3 av	-1.5 blw av	-23.6 av	1.8 abv av

Standard Deviation	Category Risk Index	Beta
21.2%—abv av	0.96—av	1.28

	2008	2007	2006	2005	2004	2003	2002	2001	2000	1999
Return (%)	-45.0	15.9	25.9	15.0	18.9	34.4	-17.8	-19.0	-8.7	26.3
Differ From Category (+/-)	0.9	3.7	0.0	-3.2	-0.9	-7.8	-4.3	-0.8	3.3	-20.7
Return, Tax-Adjusted (%)	-46.3	13.8	23.5	14.0	18.2	33.8	-18.3	-19.5	-10.3	24.8

PER SHARE DATA

	2008	2007	2006	2005	2004	2003	2002	2001	2000	1999
Dividends, Net Income ($)	0.56	0.53	0.53	0.37	0.31	0.21	0.18	0.24	0.22	0.26
Distrib'ns, Cap Gain ($)	0.90	2.21	2.04	0.31	0.00	0.00	0.00	0.04	1.42	0.90
Net Asset Value ($)	12.20	24.82	23.86	21.01	18.86	16.13	12.16	15.01	18.87	22.49
Expense Ratio (%)	0.47	0.51	0.55	0.58	0.63	0.69	0.67	0.61	0.53	0.58
Yield (%)	4.28	1.95	2.04	1.73	1.67	1.30	1.48	1.59	1.08	1.11
Portfolio Turnover (%)	55	41	45	48	45	59	40	48	48	37
Total Assets (Millions $)	7,732	14,296	11,800	8,871	8,097	6,424	4,768	6,088	8,900	9,681

PORTFOLIO (as of 9/30/08)

Portfolio Manager: Anderson/Dobbs/Maisoneuve - 2003

Investment Style

Large Cap	Growth
Mid Cap	Grth/Val
Small Cap	Value

Portfolio

0.0% U.S. stock	0.0% conv't
95.0% int'l stock	0.7% preferred
0.6% U.S. bonds	0.6% other
0.0% int'l bonds	3.1% cash

Number of Investments: 173
Percent of Portfolio in Top 10 Investments: 20%

SHAREHOLDER INFORMATION

Minimum Investment
Initial: $3,000 Subsequent: $100

Minimum IRA Investment
Initial: $3,000 Subsequent: $100

Maximum Fees
Load: 2.00% redemption 12b-1: none
Other: redemption fee applies for 2 months

Services
✔ IRA
✔ Keogh
✔ Telephone Exchange

Vanguard International Value (VTRIX)

800-997-2798
www.vanguard.com

Foreign Stock

PERFORMANCE — fund inception date: 5/16/83

	3yr Annual	5yr Annual	10yr Annual	Bull	Bear
Return (%)	-5.8	3.3	3.4	227.6	-45.2
Differ From Category (+/-)	2.8 high	1.7 high	0.6 abv av	0.8 abv av	4.4 high

Standard Deviation	Category Risk Index	Beta
19.9%—abv av	0.90—blw av	1.18

	2008	2007	2006	2005	2004	2003	2002	2001	2000	1999
Return (%)	-41.8	12.6	27.3	17.9	19.7	41.9	-13.4	-14.1	-7.5	21.7
Differ From Category (+/-)	4.1	0.4	1.4	-0.3	-0.1	-0.3	0.1	4.1	4.4	-25.3
Return, Tax-Adjusted (%)	-42.6	10.9	25.1	16.7	19.1	41.0	-13.9	-14.6	-8.6	20.1

PER SHARE DATA

	2008	2007	2006	2005	2004	2003	2002	2001	2000	1999
Dividends, Net Income ($)	0.99	0.94	0.88	0.56	0.48	0.46	0.29	0.30	0.73	0.66
Distrib'ns, Cap Gain ($)	0.00	2.42	3.09	1.10	0.00	0.00	0.00	0.00	0.19	0.73
Net Asset Value ($)	23.43	41.98	40.34	34.82	30.93	26.24	18.83	22.07	26.03	29.12
Expense Ratio (%)	0.42	0.40	0.45	0.50	0.56	0.62	0.65	0.64	0.53	0.59
Yield (%)	4.22	2.11	2.02	1.55	1.55	1.75	1.54	1.35	2.78	2.21
Portfolio Turnover (%)	59	38	36	32	74	27	26	37	78	41
Total Assets (Millions $)	5,250	9,695	7,681	4,127	2,663	1,704	1,104	895	835	1,045

PORTFOLIO (as of 9/30/08)

Portfolio Manager: Foong/Holt/D'Auria/Simms/Boyle - 2000

Investment Style

Large Cap	Growth
Mid Cap	Grth/Val
Small Cap	Value

Portfolio

0.3% U.S. stock	0.0% conv't
91.2% int'l stock	0.3% preferred
0.5% U.S. bonds	0.7% other
0.0% int'l bonds	7.0% cash

Number of Investments: 226
Percent of Portfolio in Top 10 Investments: 25%

SHAREHOLDER INFORMATION

Minimum Investment
Initial: $3,000 Subsequent: $100

Minimum IRA Investment
Initial: $3,000 Subsequent: $100

Maximum Fees
Load: 2.00% redemption 12b-1: none
Other: redemption fee applies for 2 months

Services
✔ IRA
✔ Keogh
✔ Telephone Exchange

Vanguard Tax-Managed Intl (VTMGX)

800-997-2798
www.vanguard.com

Foreign Stock

PERFORMANCE — fund inception date: 8/17/99

	3yr Annual	5yr Annual	10yr Annual	Bull	Bear
Return (%)	-6.3	2.4	na	203.0	-44.9
Differ From Category (+/-)	2.3 high	0.8 abv av	na	-23.8 av	4.7 high

Standard Deviation	Category Risk Index	Beta
19.4%—abv av	0.88—low	1.16

	2008	2007	2006	2005	2004	2003	2002	2001	2000	1999
Return (%)	-41.3	11.1	26.2	13.6	20.2	38.6	-15.7	-22.0	-14.3	—
Differ From Category (+/-)	-4.6	-1.1	0.3	-4.6	0.4	-3.6	-2.2	-3.8	-2.4	—
Return, Tax-Adjusted (%)	-42.0	10.3	25.2	12.7	19.4	37.8	-16.4	-22.5	-14.7	—

PER SHARE DATA

	2008	2007	2006	2005	2004	2003	2002	2001	2000	1999
Dividends, Net Income ($)	0.29	0.34	0.34	0.26	0.20	0.15	0.14	0.13	0.11	—
Distrib'ns, Cap Gain ($)	0.00	0.00	0.00	0.00	0.00	0.00	0.00	0.00	0.00	—
Net Asset Value ($)	8.74	15.40	14.16	11.48	10.33	8.76	6.43	7.79	10.14	—
Expense Ratio (%)	na	0.15	0.20	0.20	0.23	0.28	0.31	0.35	0.35	—
Yield (%)	3.30	2.18	2.37	2.23	1.95	1.74	2.17	1.60	1.08	—
Portfolio Turnover (%)	na	6	4	5	5	9	7	20	5	—
Total Assets (Millions $)	1,131	1,915	1,621	1,119	825	514	334	327	241	—

PORTFOLIO (as of 9/30/08)

Portfolio Manager: Kelly/Butler - 1999

Investment Style

Large Cap	Growth
Mid Cap	Grth/Val
Small Cap	Value

Portfolio

0.0% U.S. stock	0.0% conv't
97.5% int'l stock	0.3% preferred
0.0% U.S. bonds	2.2% other
0.0% int'l bonds	0.0% cash

Number of Investments: 996

Percent of Portfolio in Top 10 Investments: 14%

SHAREHOLDER INFORMATION

Minimum Investment

Initial: $10,000 Subsequent: $100

Minimum IRA Investment

Initial: $0 Subsequent: $0

Maximum Fees

Load: 1.00% redemption 12b-1: none

Other: redemption fee applies for 60 days

Services

✔ IRA
✔ Keogh
✔ Telephone Exchange

Vanguard Total Intl Stock Index (VGTSX)

800-997-2798
www.vanguard.com

Foreign Stock

PERFORMANCE — fund inception date: 4/29/96

	3yr Annual	5yr Annual	10yr Annual	Bull	Bear
Return (%)	-6.5	2.6	1.7	227.4	-47.8
Differ From Category (+/-)	2.1 abv av	1.0 abv av	-1.1 av	0.6 abv av	1.8 abv av

Standard Deviation	Category Risk Index	Beta
20.9%—abv av	0.95—blw av	1.24

	2008	2007	2006	2005	2004	2003	2002	2001	2000	1999
Return (%)	-44.1	15.5	26.6	15.5	20.8	40.3	-15.1	-20.2	-15.7	29.9
Differ From Category (+/-)	1.8	3.3	0.7	-2.7	1.0	-1.9	-1.6	-2.0	-3.8	-17.1
Return, Tax-Adjusted (%)	-44.7	14.4	25.6	14.7	20.0	39.4	-15.8	-20.7	-16.3	29.1

PER SHARE DATA

	2008	2007	2006	2005	2004	2003	2002	2001	2000	1999
Dividends, Net Income ($)	0.32	0.52	0.40	0.29	0.25	0.19	0.16	0.17	0.20	0.21
Distrib'ns, Cap Gain ($)	0.00	0.00	0.00	0.00	0.00	0.00	0.00	0.00	0.05	0.01
Net Asset Value ($)	10.79	19.89	17.67	14.27	12.60	10.64	7.72	9.28	11.83	14.31
Expense Ratio (%)	na	0.00	0.00	0.00	0.00	0.00	0.00	0.00	0.00	0.00
Yield (%)	3.01	2.62	2.27	2.06	2.02	1.78	2.03	1.77	1.68	1.46
Portfolio Turnover (%)	na	2	2	3	3	2	5	2	3	1
Total Assets (Millions $)	17,746	28,652	20,070	12,696	8,516	5,279	2,994	2,900	2,920	2,570

PORTFOLIO (as of 9/30/08)

Portfolio Manager: Kelly/Perre - 2008

Investment Style

Large Cap	Growth
Mid Cap	Grth/Val
Small Cap	Value

Portfolio

0.1%	U.S. stock	0.0%	conv't
96.8%	int'l stock	0.3%	preferred
0.0%	U.S. bonds	2.5%	other
0.0%	int'l bonds	0.4%	cash

Number of Investments: 1,851
Percent of Portfolio in Top 10 Investments: 53%

SHAREHOLDER INFORMATION

Minimum Investment
Initial: $3,000 Subsequent: $100

Minimum IRA Investment
Initial: $3,000 Subsequent: $100

Maximum Fees
Load: 2.00% redemption 12b-1: none
Other: redemption fee applies for 2 months

Services
✔ IRA
✔ Keogh
✔ Telephone Exchange

Regional/Country Stock Funds
Category Performance Ranked by 2008 Returns

Fund (Ticker)	Annual Return (%) 2008	3Yr	5Yr	10Yr	Category Risk	Total Risk
Matthews Asian Growth & Income (MACSX)	-32.1	0.6	7.4	14.3	low	av
Vanguard Pacific Stock Index (VPACX)	-34.4	-8.4	2.3	1.9	low	av
Matthews Asia Pacific (MPACX)	-37.5	-6.4	3.6	na	blw av	abv av
Fidelity Canada (FICDX)	-42.7	-3.8	7.1	11.3	av	high
T. Rowe Price European Stock (PRESX)	-43.4	-5.0	1.7	0.7	blw av	abv av
Fidelity Europe (FIEUX)	-44.1	-6.6	4.4	2.1	blw av	abv av
Vanguard European Stock Index (VEURX)	-44.8	-5.7	2.0	0.7	blw av	abv av
Fidelity China Region (FHKCX)	-44.9	1.5	5.9	8.4	av	high
Matthews Pacific Tiger (MAPTX)	-46.2	-2.9	6.7	12.0	av	high
Fidelity Europe Capital Appreciation (FECAX)	-46.3	-5.9	2.4	2.9	blw av	abv av
Matthews China (MCHFX)	-49.0	12.7	9.7	14.9	abv av	high
Fidelity Southeast Asia (FSEAX)	-51.9	0.8	9.2	10.4	abv av	high
Guinness Atkinson China & Hong Kong (ICHKX)	-54.5	1.6	4.6	7.9	abv av	high
Fidelity Latin America (FLATX)	-54.7	-2.1	15.5	12.5	high	high
T. Rowe Price Latin America (PRLAX)	-55.8	-0.1	17.1	14.9	high	high
T. Rowe Price New Asia (PRASX)	-61.0	-4.1	5.7	8.6	abv av	high
Matthews India (MINDX)	-62.4	-5.5	na	na	abv av	high
Metzler/Payden European Emerging Markets (MPYMX)	-66.6	-14.4	5.8	na	abv av	high
Regional/Country Stock Category Average	**-50.0**	**-8.4**	**2.9**	**6.3**	**av**	**high**

Fidelity Canada
(FICDX)
Regional/Country Stock

800-544-9797
www.fidelity.com

PERFORMANCE **fund inception date: 11/17/87**

	3yr Annual	5yr Annual	10yr Annual	Bull	Bear
Return (%)	-3.8	7.1	11.3	285.0	-46.8
Differ From Category (+/-)	4.6 abv av	4.2 high	5.0 abv av	-34.8 av	6.6 abv av

Standard Deviation	Category Risk Index	Beta
24.4%—high	0.90—av	1.36

	2008	2007	2006	2005	2004	2003	2002	2001	2000	1999
Return (%)	-42.7	35.0	15.0	27.8	23.9	51.9	-4.3	-9.7	12.2	40.5
Differ From Category (+/-)	7.3	8.2	-11.7	-0.4	3.2	2.2	5.8	2.3	33.6	-29.5
Return, Tax-Adjusted (%)	-42.8	33.7	14.3	27.7	23.8	51.6	-4.4	-9.7	10.1	40.4

PER SHARE DATA

	2008	2007	2006	2005	2004	2003	2002	2001	2000	1999
Dividends, Net Income ($)	0.14	0.40	0.36	0.16	0.08	0.13	0.04	0.03	1.04	0.03
Distrib'ns, Cap Gain ($)	0.00	3.27	1.03	0.01	0.00	0.00	0.00	0.00	0.00	0.00
Net Asset Value ($)	35.06	61.40	48.24	43.13	33.86	27.39	18.12	18.97	21.02	19.63
Expense Ratio (%)	na	0.94	0.97	1.04	1.15	1.42	1.46	1.20	1.06	1.06
Yield (%)	0.40	0.62	0.73	0.37	0.23	0.47	0.22	0.15	4.94	0.15
Portfolio Turnover (%)	na	42	50	24	47	52	98	93	1	286
Total Assets (Millions $)	2,438	4,649	3,118	2,106	646	226	78	86	150	58

PORTFOLIO (as of 11/30/08)

Portfolio Manager: Lober - 2008

Investment Style

Large Cap	Growth
Mid Cap	Grth/Val
Small Cap	Value

Portfolio

5.8%	U.S. stock	0.0%	conv't
87.8%	int'l stock	0.0%	preferred
0.0%	U.S. bonds	0.0%	other
0.0%	int'l bonds	6.5%	cash

Number of Investments: 78
Percent of Portfolio in Top 10 Investments: 45%

SHAREHOLDER INFORMATION

Minimum Investment
Initial: $2,500 Subsequent: $250

Minimum IRA Investment
Initial: $500 Subsequent: $100

Maximum Fees
Load: 1.50% redemption 12b-1: none
Other: redemption fee applies for 90 days

Services
IRA
Keogh
✔ Telephone Exchange

Fidelity China Region

800-544-9797
www.fidelity.com

(FHKCX)

Regional/Country Stock

PERFORMANCE **fund inception date: 11/1/95**

	3yr Annual	5yr Annual	10yr Annual	Bull	Bear
Return (%)	1.5	5.9	8.4	315.9	-52.3
Differ From Category (+/-)	9.9 high	3.0 abv av	2.1 abv av	-3.9 av	1.1 av

Standard Deviation	Category Risk Index	Beta
26.4%—high	0.97—av	1.29

	2008	2007	2006	2005	2004	2003	2002	2001	2000	1999
Return (%)	-44.9	46.2	29.6	14.4	11.5	45.4	-15.1	-10.5	-17.6	84.9
Differ From Category (+/-)	5.1	19.4	2.9	-13.8	-9.2	-4.3	-5.0	1.5	3.8	14.9
Return, Tax-Adjusted (%)	-45.1	43.0	28.9	14.0	10.9	44.6	-15.7	-11.0	-18.8	84.2

PER SHARE DATA

	2008	2007	2006	2005	2004	2003	2002	2001	2000	1999
Dividends, Net Income ($)	0.17	0.32	0.29	0.22	0.26	0.26	0.19	0.16	0.56	0.17
Distrib'ns, Cap Gain ($)	0.00	4.53	0.20	0.00	0.00	0.00	0.00	0.00	0.00	0.00
Net Asset Value ($)	17.01	31.17	24.52	19.30	17.06	15.53	10.86	13.00	14.70	18.51
Expense Ratio (%)	na	0.92	1.08	1.12	1.22	1.30	1.31	1.30	1.21	1.32
Yield (%)	1.00	0.89	1.17	1.13	1.52	1.67	1.74	1.23	3.80	0.91
Portfolio Turnover (%)	na	173	36	44	101	39	53	75	103	84
Total Assets (Millions $)	768	1,758	909	443	335	274	110	137	175	274

PORTFOLIO (as of 11/30/08)

Portfolio Manager: Wong - 2007

Investment Style

Large Cap	Growth
Mid Cap	Grth/Val
Small Cap	Value

Portfolio

0.0% U.S. stock	0.0% conv't
95.0% int'l stock	0.0% preferred
0.0% U.S. bonds	0.0% other
0.0% int'l bonds	5.1% cash

Number of Investments: 61
Percent of Portfolio in Top 10 Investments: 52%

SHAREHOLDER INFORMATION

Minimum Investment
Initial: $2,500 Subsequent: $250

Minimum IRA Investment
Initial: $500 Subsequent: $100

Maximum Fees
Load: 1.50% redemption 12b-1: none
Other: redemption fee applies for 90 days; maint fee for low bal

Services
✔ IRA
✔ Keogh
✔ Telephone Exchange

Fidelity Europe (FIEUX)

800-544-9797
www.fidelity.com

Regional/Country Stock

PERFORMANCE — fund inception date: 10/1/86

	3yr Annual	5yr Annual	10yr Annual	Bull	Bear
Return (%)	-6.6	4.4	2.1	272.4	-45.9
Differ From Category (+/-)	1.8 av	1.5 abv av	-4.2 blw av	-47.4 av	7.5 abv av

Standard Deviation	Category Risk Index	Beta
20.6%—abv av	0.76—blw av	1.18

	2008	2007	2006	2005	2004	2003	2002	2001	2000	1999
Return (%)	-44.1	16.4	25.1	18.1	28.9	46.9	-25.5	-16.1	-9.2	18.6
Differ From Category (+/-)	5.9	-10.4	-1.6	-10.1	8.2	-2.8	-15.4	-4.1	12.2	-51.4
Return, Tax-Adjusted (%)	-44.7	14.6	22.6	16.1	28.7	46.3	-25.7	-16.4	-11.5	17.3

PER SHARE DATA

	2008	2007	2006	2005	2004	2003	2002	2001	2000	1999
Dividends, Net Income ($)	0.73	0.65	0.46	0.30	0.09	0.29	0.14	0.24	0.12	0.18
Distrib'ns, Cap Gain ($)	0.00	3.08	5.07	3.97	0.08	0.00	0.00	0.00	4.09	1.94
Net Asset Value ($)	22.78	42.16	39.36	35.97	34.15	26.62	18.32	24.76	29.77	37.47
Expense Ratio (%)	na	1.01	1.05	1.07	1.05	0.98	1.13	0.99	1.06	0.89
Yield (%)	3.20	1.43	1.03	0.75	0.26	1.08	0.76	0.96	0.35	0.45
Portfolio Turnover (%)	na	100	127	99	106	162	127	123	144	106
Total Assets (Millions $)	2,685	5,282	4,388	2,766	2,208	1,476	896	1,153	1,407	1,478

PORTFOLIO (as of 11/30/08)

Portfolio Manager: Toraasen - 2006

Investment Style

Large Cap	Growth
Mid Cap	Grth/Val
Small Cap	Value

Portfolio

2.8%	U.S. stock	0.0%	conv't
96.0%	int'l stock	0.0%	preferred
0.0%	U.S. bonds	0.1%	other
0.0%	int'l bonds	1.1%	cash

Number of Investments: 116

Percent of Portfolio in Top 10 Investments: 28%

SHAREHOLDER INFORMATION

Minimum Investment

Initial: $2,500 Subsequent: $250

Minimum IRA Investment

Initial: $500 Subsequent: $100

Maximum Fees

Load: 1.00% redemption 12b-1: none

Other: redemption fee applies for 30 days; maint fee for low bal

Services

✔ IRA
✔ Keogh
✔ Telephone Exchange

Fidelity Europe Capital Appreciation (FECAX)

800-544-9797
www.fidelity.com

Regional/Country Stock

PERFORMANCE — fund inception date: 12/21/93

	3yr Annual	5yr Annual	10yr Annual	Bull	Bear
Return (%)	-5.9	2.4	2.9	229.4	-48.4
Differ From Category (+/-)	2.5 av	-0.5 av	-3.4 blw av	-90.4 blw av	5.0 abv av

Standard Deviation	Category Risk Index	Beta
21.9%—abv av	0.81—blw av	1.27

	2008	2007	2006	2005	2004	2003	2002	2001	2000	1999
Return (%)	-46.3	14.7	35.4	16.2	16.4	36.8	-15.1	-13.2	-5.8	23.7
Differ From Category (+/-)	3.7	-12.1	8.7	-12.0	-4.3	-12.9	-5.0	-1.2	15.6	-46.3
Return, Tax-Adjusted (%)	-47.0	11.7	33.5	13.8	16.0	36.3	-15.5	-13.5	-6.8	22.9

PER SHARE DATA

	2008	2007	2006	2005	2004	2003	2002	2001	2000	1999
Dividends, Net Income ($)	0.56	0.56	0.22	0.30	0.17	0.22	0.19	0.17	0.11	0.13
Distrib'ns, Cap Gain ($)	0.00	4.22	2.25	2.62	0.06	0.00	0.00	0.00	0.87	0.47
Net Asset Value ($)	13.67	26.61	27.29	22.02	21.53	18.70	13.83	16.50	19.19	21.46
Expense Ratio (%)	na	1.01	0.99	0.84	1.15	1.32	1.32	1.21	1.04	0.97
Yield (%)	4.09	1.81	0.74	1.21	0.78	1.17	1.37	1.03	0.54	0.59
Portfolio Turnover (%)	na	161	143	133	119	184	121	67	156	150
Total Assets (Millions $)	469	1,249	1,332	504	457	419	398	434	611	711

PORTFOLIO (as of 11/30/08)

Portfolio Manager: Reilly - 2007

Investment Style

Large Cap	Growth
Mid Cap	Grth/Val
Small Cap	Value

Portfolio

2.6%	U.S. stock	0.0%	conv't
91.8%	int'l stock	0.0%	preferred
0.0%	U.S. bonds	0.3%	other
0.0%	int'l bonds	5.3%	cash

Number of Investments: 118

Percent of Portfolio in Top 10 Investments: 30%

SHAREHOLDER INFORMATION

Minimum Investment

Initial: $2,500 Subsequent: $250

Minimum IRA Investment

Initial: $500 Subsequent: $100

Maximum Fees

Load: 1.00% redemption 12b-1: none

Other: redemption fee applies for 30 days; maint fee for low bal

Services

✔ IRA

✔ Keogh

✔ Telephone Exchange

Fidelity Latin America (FLATX)

800-544-9797
www.fidelity.com

Regional/Country Stock

PERFORMANCE — fund inception date: 4/19/93

	3yr Annual	5yr Annual	10yr Annual	Bull	Bear
Return (%)	-2.1	15.5	12.5	753.8	-57.0
Differ From Category (+/-)	6.3 high	12.6 high	6.2 high	434.0 high	-3.6 av

Standard Deviation	Category Risk Index	Beta
34.2%—high	1.26—high	1.84

	2008	2007	2006	2005	2004	2003	2002	2001	2000	1999
Return (%)	-54.7	43.7	44.3	55.1	41.1	65.7	-20.9	-6.1	-17.5	54.9
Differ From Category (+/-)	-4.7	16.9	17.6	26.9	20.4	16.0	-10.8	5.9	3.9	-15.1
Return, Tax-Adjusted (%)	-54.9	42.6	43.3	54.1	40.4	64.9	-21.4	-6.8	-17.7	54.3

PER SHARE DATA

	2008	2007	2006	2005	2004	2003	2002	2001	2000	1999
Dividends, Net Income ($)	0.46	0.65	0.61	0.46	0.30	0.23	0.17	0.25	0.07	0.14
Distrib'ns, Cap Gain ($)	0.00	1.72	0.77	0.38	0.00	0.00	0.00	0.00	0.00	0.00
Net Asset Value ($)	27.62	62.01	44.73	31.98	21.15	15.22	9.33	12.01	13.06	15.91
Expense Ratio (%)	na	0.98	1.02	1.04	1.16	1.31	1.41	1.35	1.23	1.30
Yield (%)	1.66	1.01	1.34	1.42	1.41	1.51	1.82	2.08	0.53	0.87
Portfolio Turnover (%)	na	52	60	40	25	28	128	96	51	49
Total Assets (Millions $)	2,091	5,831	3,666	1,851	501	270	149	210	268	410

PORTFOLIO (as of 11/30/08)

Portfolio Manager: Bottamini - 2005

Investment Style

Large Cap	Growth
Mid Cap	Grth/Val
Small Cap	Value

Portfolio

0.2%	U.S. stock	0.0%	conv't
97.0%	int'l stock	0.0%	preferred
0.0%	U.S. bonds	0.0%	other
0.0%	int'l bonds	2.8%	cash

Number of Investments: 89

Percent of Portfolio in Top 10 Investments: 45%

SHAREHOLDER INFORMATION

Minimum Investment

Initial: $2,500 Subsequent: $250

Minimum IRA Investment

Initial: $500 Subsequent: $100

Maximum Fees

Load: 1.50% redemption 12b-1: none

Other: redemption fee applies for 90 days; maint fee for low bal

Services

✔ IRA
✔ Keogh
✔ Telephone Exchange

Fidelity Southeast Asia (FSEAX)

800-544-9797
www.fidelity.com

Regional/Country Stock

PERFORMANCE — fund inception date: 4/19/93

	3yr Annual	5yr Annual	10yr Annual	Bull	Bear
Return (%)	0.8	9.2	10.4	493.4	-58.3
Differ From Category (+/-)	9.2 high	6.3 high	4.1 abv av	173.6 high	-4.9 blw av

Standard Deviation	Category Risk Index	Beta
27.8%—high	1.02—abv av	1.42

	2008	2007	2006	2005	2004	2003	2002	2001	2000	1999
Return (%)	-51.9	55.3	37.1	33.5	13.5	52.3	-11.4	-3.7	-30.5	91.5
Differ From Category (+/-)	-1.9	28.5	10.4	5.3	-7.2	2.6	-1.3	8.3	-9.1	21.5
Return, Tax-Adjusted (%)	-52.1	53.4	35.8	32.6	13.2	51.8	-11.7	-3.8	-30.5	91.4

PER SHARE DATA

	2008	2007	2006	2005	2004	2003	2002	2001	2000	1999
Dividends, Net Income ($)	0.19	0.28	0.23	0.26	0.14	0.13	0.08	0.03	0.00	0.02
Distrib'ns, Cap Gain ($)	0.00	2.89	1.29	0.43	0.00	0.00	0.00	0.00	0.00	0.00
Net Asset Value ($)	18.87	39.66	27.50	21.21	16.42	14.58	9.66	10.98	11.43	16.43
Expense Ratio (%)	na	0.98	1.04	1.09	1.20	1.32	1.50	1.52	1.35	1.43
Yield (%)	1.03	0.65	0.79	1.20	0.85	0.89	0.82	0.27	0.00	0.12
Portfolio Turnover (%)	na	72	100	109	131	115	131	91	88	93
Total Assets (Millions $)	1,597	5,369	2,010	975	519	438	238	258	279	502

PORTFOLIO (as of 11/30/08)

Portfolio Manager: Tan - 2007

Investment Style

Large Cap	Growth
Mid Cap	Grth/Val
Small Cap	Value

Portfolio

0.0%	U.S. stock	0.0%	conv't
85.3%	int'l stock	0.3%	preferred
0.0%	U.S. bonds	0.0%	other
0.9%	int'l bonds	13.5%	cash

Number of Investments: 79
Percent of Portfolio in Top 10 Investments: 46%

SHAREHOLDER INFORMATION

Minimum Investment
Initial: $2,500 Subsequent: $250

Minimum IRA Investment
Initial: $500 Subsequent: $100

Maximum Fees
Load: 1.50% redemption 12b-1: none
Other: redemption fee applies for 90 days; maint fee for low bal

Services
✔ IRA
✔ Keogh
✔ Telephone Exchange

Guinness Atkinson China & Hong Kong (ICHKX)

800-915-6566
www.gafunds.com

Regional/Country Stock

PERFORMANCE — fund inception date: 6/30/94

	3yr Annual	5yr Annual	10yr Annual	Bull	Bear
Return (%)	1.6	4.6	7.9	429.3	-61.8
Differ From Category (+/-)	10.0 high	1.7 abv av	1.6 abv av	109.5 abv av	-8.4 blw av

Standard Deviation	Category Risk Index	Beta
32.0%—high	1.18—abv av	1.67

	2008	2007	2006	2005	2004	2003	2002	2001	2000	1999
Return (%)	-54.5	65.0	39.6	6.6	12.1	65.2	-12.9	-23.5	-7.0	66.2
Differ From Category (+/-)	-4.5	38.2	12.9	-21.6	-8.6	15.5	-2.8	-11.5	14.4	-3.8
Return, Tax-Adjusted (%)	-55.0	64.2	39.6	5.0	11.5	65.2	-12.9	-24.0	-8.5	65.3

PER SHARE DATA

	2008	2007	2006	2005	2004	2003	2002	2001	2000	1999
Dividends, Net Income ($)	0.53	0.59	0.01	0.83	0.27	0.00	0.00	0.00	0.67	0.26
Distrib'ns, Cap Gain ($)	0.08	0.10	0.00	0.00	0.00	0.00	0.00	0.38	0.00	0.00
Net Asset Value ($)	18.98	43.02	26.48	18.97	18.57	16.81	10.17	11.67	15.75	17.65
Expense Ratio (%)	na	1.44	1.59	1.63	1.67	1.81	2.02	1.85	1.89	1.86
Yield (%)	2.75	1.36	0.03	4.36	1.46	0.00	0.00	0.00	4.24	1.46
Portfolio Turnover (%)	na	10	65	13	15	29	60	32	38	29
Total Assets (Millions $)	123	293	143	111	112	117	57	77	114	161

PORTFOLIO (as of 9/30/08)

Portfolio Manager: Harriss/Guinness - 1998

Investment Style

Large Cap	Growth
Mid Cap	Grth/Val
Small Cap	Value

Portfolio

0.0% U.S. stock	0.0% conv't
99.8% int'l stock	0.0% preferred
0.0% U.S. bonds	0.2% other
0.0% int'l bonds	0.0% cash

Number of Investments: 43

Percent of Portfolio in Top 10 Investments: 47%

SHAREHOLDER INFORMATION

Minimum Investment

Initial: $5,000 Subsequent: $250

Minimum IRA Investment

Initial: $1,000 Subsequent: $250

Maximum Fees

Load: 2.00% redemption 12b-1: none

Other: redemption fee applies for 30 days

Services

✔ IRA

Keogh

✔ Telephone Exchange

Matthews Asia Pacific (MPACX)

800-789-2742
www.matthewsfunds.com

Regional/Country Stock

PERFORMANCE — fund inception date: 10/31/03

	3yr Annual	5yr Annual	10yr Annual	Bull	Bear
Return (%)	-6.4	3.6	na	na	-42.7
Differ From Category (+/-)	2.0 av	0.7 abv av	na	na	10.7 abv av

Standard Deviation	Category Risk Index	Beta
19.8%—abv av	0.73—blw av	1.07

	2008	2007	2006	2005	2004	2003	2002	2001	2000	1999
Return (%)	-37.5	11.9	17.3	18.8	22.3	—	—	—	—	—
Differ From Category (+/-)	12.5	-14.9	-9.4	-9.4	1.6	—	—	—	—	—
Return, Tax-Adjusted (%)	-38.1	10.2	16.7	18.6	22.2	—	—	—	—	—

PER SHARE DATA

	2008	2007	2006	2005	2004	2003	2002	2001	2000	1999
Dividends, Net Income ($)	0.00	0.09	0.07	0.06	0.02	—	—	—	—	—
Distrib'ns, Cap Gain ($)	0.76	1.66	0.48	0.00	0.02	—	—	—	—	—
Net Asset Value ($)	10.03	17.29	16.92	14.89	12.58	—	—	—	—	—
Expense Ratio (%)	na	1.20	1.24	1.34	1.66	—	—	—	—	—
Yield (%)	0.00	0.49	0.41	0.38	0.18	—	—	—	—	—
Portfolio Turnover (%)	na	40	40	16	11	—	—	—	—	—
Total Assets (Millions $)	168	471	450	285	112	—	—	—	—	—

PORTFOLIO (as of 9/30/08)

Portfolio Manager: Ishida/Shroff - 2007

Investment Style

Large Cap	Growth
Mid Cap	Grth/Val
Small Cap	Value

Portfolio

0.0% U.S. stock	0.0% conv't
100.0% int'l stock	0.0% preferred
0.0% U.S. bonds	0.0% other
0.0% int'l bonds	0.0% cash

Number of Investments: 72

Percent of Portfolio in Top 10 Investments: 28%

SHAREHOLDER INFORMATION

Minimum Investment
Initial: $2,500 Subsequent: $100

Minimum IRA Investment
Initial: $500 Subsequent: $50

Maximum Fees
Load: 2.00% redemption 12b-1: none
Other: redemption fee applies for 90 days

Services
✔ IRA
Keogh
✔ Telephone Exchange

Matthews Asian Growth & Income (MACSX)

800-789-2742
www.matthewsfunds.com

Regional/Country Stock

PERFORMANCE **fund inception date: 9/12/94**

	3yr Annual	5yr Annual	10yr Annual	Bull	Bear
Return (%)	0.6	7.4	14.3	193.6	-32.9
Differ From Category (+/-)	9.0 high	4.5 high	8.0 high	-126.2 blw av	20.5 high

Standard Deviation	Category Risk Index	Beta
17.8%—av	0.65—low	1.00

	2008	2007	2006	2005	2004	2003	2002	2001	2000	1999
Return (%)	-32.1	21.5	23.3	15.7	21.4	38.6	9.0	14.2	3.7	48.8
Differ From Category (+/-)	17.9	-5.3	-3.4	-12.5	0.7	-11.1	19.1	26.2	25.1	-21.2
Return, Tax-Adjusted (%)	-34.1	18.2	20.5	14.1	19.6	37.5	8.1	12.2	-0.4	45.4

PER SHARE DATA

	2008	2007	2006	2005	2004	2003	2002	2001	2000	1999
Dividends, Net Income ($)	0.41	0.90	0.62	0.43	0.54	0.22	0.14	0.47	0.60	0.62
Distrib'ns, Cap Gain ($)	1.67	2.00	1.77	0.72	0.38	0.20	0.15	0.00	0.88	0.00
Net Asset Value ($)	11.49	19.78	18.68	17.14	15.82	13.82	10.31	9.72	8.93	10.04
Expense Ratio (%)	na	1.15	1.19	1.27	1.45	1.69	1.77	1.90	1.90	1.90
Yield (%)	3.15	4.15	3.01	2.38	3.32	1.60	1.33	4.83	6.08	6.19
Portfolio Turnover (%)	na	28	28	20	18	13	32	34	62	35
Total Assets (Millions $)	1,085	2,273	2,021	1,677	1,236	926	176	32	12	12

PORTFOLIO (as of 9/30/08)

Portfolio Manager: Foster/Matthews - 2005

Investment Style

Large Cap	Growth
Mid Cap	Grth/Val
Small Cap	Value

Portfolio

0.0%	U.S. stock	25.8%	conv't
72.0%	int'l stock	2.1%	preferred
0.0%	U.S. bonds	0.0%	other
0.0%	int'l bonds	0.0%	cash

Number of Investments: 74

Percent of Portfolio in Top 10 Investments: 28%

SHAREHOLDER INFORMATION

Minimum Investment

Initial: $2,500 Subsequent: $100

Minimum IRA Investment

Initial: $500 Subsequent: $50

Maximum Fees

Load: 2.00% redemption 12b-1: none

Other: redemption fee applies for 90 days

Services

✔ IRA

Keogh

✔ Telephone Exchange

Matthews China (MCHFX)

800-789-2742
www.matthewsfunds.com

Regional/Country Stock

PERFORMANCE — fund inception date: 2/19/98

	3yr Annual	5yr Annual	10yr Annual	Bull	Bear
Return (%)	12.7	9.7	14.9	465.1	-55.5
Differ From Category (+/-)	21.1 high	6.8 high	8.6 high	145.3 high	-2.1 av

Standard Deviation	Category Risk Index	Beta
31.2%—high	1.15—abv av	1.63

	2008	2007	2006	2005	2004	2003	2002	2001	2000	1999
Return (%)	-49.0	70.1	64.8	6.9	3.8	65.0	-7.6	20.9	-6.7	47.1
Differ From Category (+/-)	1.0	43.3	38.1	-21.3	-16.9	15.3	2.5	32.9	14.7	-22.9
Return, Tax-Adjusted (%)	-51.4	69.1	64.4	6.3	2.9	64.7	-8.2	20.1	-8.0	46.3

PER SHARE DATA

	2008	2007	2006	2005	2004	2003	2002	2001	2000	1999
Dividends, Net Income ($)	0.33	0.11	0.15	0.22	0.14	0.07	0.14	0.15	0.15	0.12
Distrib'ns, Cap Gain ($)	5.62	1.37	0.00	0.00	0.52	0.00	0.00	0.00	0.28	0.00
Net Asset Value ($)	14.34	39.73	24.16	14.76	14.01	14.12	8.60	9.45	7.94	8.97
Expense Ratio (%)	na	1.17	1.26	1.30	1.43	1.79	1.97	2.00	2.00	—
Yield (%)	1.63	0.26	0.63	1.47	0.97	0.47	1.65	1.60	1.80	1.33
Portfolio Turnover (%)	na	22	12	12	29	19	44	61	81	—
Total Assets (Millions $)	781	2,335	967	389	380	289	34	25	8	9

PORTFOLIO (as of 9/30/08)

Portfolio Manager: Gao/Headley/Foster - 1999

Investment Style

Large Cap	Growth
Mid Cap	Grth/Val
Small Cap	Value

Portfolio

3.3%	U.S. stock	0.0%	conv't
96.7%	int'l stock	0.0%	preferred
0.0%	U.S. bonds	0.0%	other
0.0%	int'l bonds	0.0%	cash

Number of Investments: 64
Percent of Portfolio in Top 10 Investments: 29%

SHAREHOLDER INFORMATION

Minimum Investment
Initial: $2,500 Subsequent: $100

Minimum IRA Investment
Initial: $500 Subsequent: $50

Maximum Fees
Load: 2.00% redemption 12b-1: none
Other: redemption fee applies for 90 days

Services
✔ IRA
Keogh
✔ Telephone Exchange

Matthews India (MINDX)

800-789-2742
www.matthewsfunds.com

Regional/Country Stock

PERFORMANCE — fund inception date: 10/31/05

	3yr Annual	5yr Annual	10yr Annual	Bull	Bear
Return (%)	-5.5	na	na	na	-58.8
Differ From Category (+/-)	2.9 abv av	na	na	na	-5.4 blw av

Standard Deviation	Category Risk Index	Beta
33.8%—high	1.24—abv av	1.88

	2008	2007	2006	2005	2004	2003	2002	2001	2000	1999
Return (%)	-62.4	64.1	36.4	—	—	—	—	—	—	—
Differ From Category (+/-)	-12.4	37.3	9.7	—	—	—	—	—	—	—
Return, Tax-Adjusted (%)	-62.9	63.0	36.4	—	—	—	—	—	—	—

PER SHARE DATA

	2008	2007	2006	2005	2004	2003	2002	2001	2000	1999
Dividends, Net Income ($)	0.11	0.21	0.00	—	—	—	—	—	—	—
Distrib'ns, Cap Gain ($)	0.69	0.68	0.00	—	—	—	—	—	—	—
Net Asset Value ($)	8.37	24.44	15.45	—	—	—	—	—	—	—
Expense Ratio (%)	na	1.28	1.41	—	—	—	—	—	—	—
Yield (%)	1.16	0.82	0.00	—	—	—	—	—	—	—
Portfolio Turnover (%)	na	26	22	—	—	—	—	—	—	—
Total Assets (Millions $)	317	1,311	670	—	—	—	—	—	—	—

PORTFOLIO (as of 9/30/08)

Portfolio Manager: Foster/Shroff - 2005

Investment Style

Large Cap	Growth
Mid Cap	Grth/Val
Small Cap	Value

Portfolio

0.0%	U.S. stock	0.0%	conv't
98.4%	int'l stock	0.0%	preferred
0.0%	U.S. bonds	1.6%	other
0.0%	int'l bonds	0.0%	cash

Number of Investments: 54

Percent of Portfolio in Top 10 Investments: 40%

SHAREHOLDER INFORMATION

Minimum Investment

Initial: $2,500 Subsequent: $100

Minimum IRA Investment

Initial: $500 Subsequent: $50

Maximum Fees

Load: 2.00% redemption 12b-1: none

Other: redemption fee applies for 90 days

Services

✔ IRA
✔ Keogh
✔ Telephone Exchange

Matthews Pacific Tiger (MAPTX)

800-789-2742
www.matthewsfunds.com

Regional/Country Stock

PERFORMANCE — fund inception date: 9/12/94

	3yr Annual	5yr Annual	10yr Annual	Bull	Bear
Return (%)	-2.9	6.7	12.0	359.0	-50.1
Differ From Category (+/-)	5.5 abv av	3.8 high	5.7 high	39.2 abv av	3.3 av

Standard Deviation	Category Risk Index	Beta
25.8%—high	0.95—av	1.45

	2008	2007	2006	2005	2004	2003	2002	2001	2000	1999
Return (%)	-46.2	33.6	27.2	22.5	23.3	60.1	-6.5	7.9	-24.0	83.0
Differ From Category (+/-)	3.8	6.8	0.5	-5.7	2.6	10.4	3.6	19.9	-2.6	13.0
Return, Tax-Adjusted (%)	-48.4	30.9	26.3	22.1	22.8	59.9	-6.5	7.7	-26.7	81.9

PER SHARE DATA

	2008	2007	2006	2005	2004	2003	2002	2001	2000	1999
Dividends, Net Income ($)	0.30	0.31	0.23	0.12	0.10	0.04	0.00	0.01	0.41	0.19
Distrib'ns, Cap Gain ($)	3.44	3.63	0.56	0.09	0.21	0.00	0.00	0.03	0.84	0.00
Net Asset Value ($)	11.05	27.86	23.71	19.27	15.90	13.15	8.24	8.81	8.20	12.32
Expense Ratio (%)	na	1.10	1.16	1.31	1.50	1.75	1.79	1.90	1.81	1.90
Yield (%)	2.05	1.00	0.94	0.62	0.59	0.33	0.00	0.12	4.53	1.53
Portfolio Turnover (%)	na	24	19	3	15	28	57	63	52	98
Total Assets (Millions $)	1,203	3,807	3,304	2,032	855	456	107	87	71	119

PORTFOLIO (as of 9/30/08)

Portfolio Manager: Gao/Shroff/Headley - 2006

Investment Style

Large Cap	Growth
Mid Cap	Grth/Val
Small Cap	Value

Portfolio

0.0% U.S. stock	0.0% conv't
100.0% int'l stock	0.0% preferred
0.0% U.S. bonds	0.0% other
0.0% int'l bonds	0.0% cash

Number of Investments: 74
Percent of Portfolio in Top 10 Investments: 26%

SHAREHOLDER INFORMATION

Minimum Investment
Initial: $2,500 Subsequent: $100

Minimum IRA Investment
Initial: $500 Subsequent: $50

Maximum Fees
Load: 2.00% redemption 12b-1: none
Other: redemption fee applies for 90 days

Services
✔ IRA
Keogh
✔ Telephone Exchange

Metzler/Payden European Emerging Markets (MPYMX)

800-572-9336
www.metzlerpayden.com

Regional/Country Stock

PERFORMANCE

fund inception date: 12/30/02

	3yr Annual	5yr Annual	10yr Annual	Bull	Bear
Return (%)	-14.4	5.8	na	511.7	-67.1
Differ From Category (+/-)	-6.0 low	2.9 abv av	na	191.9 high	-13.7 low

Standard Deviation	Category Risk Index	Beta
33.3%—high	1.22—abv av	1.74

	2008	2007	2006	2005	2004	2003	2002	2001	2000	1999
Return (%)	-66.6	28.4	46.2	37.9	53.2	44.7	—	—	—	—
Differ From Category (+/-)	-16.6	1.6	19.5	9.7	32.5	-5.0	—	—	—	—
Return, Tax-Adjusted (%)	-66.6	26.6	45.2	35.8	51.7	42.5	—	—	—	—

PER SHARE DATA

	2008	2007	2006	2005	2004	2003	2002	2001	2000	1999
Dividends, Net Income ($)	0.00	0.17	0.00	0.10	0.02	0.04	—	—	—	—
Distrib'ns, Cap Gain ($)	0.00	3.52	1.54	2.47	1.21	1.35	—	—	—	—
Net Asset Value ($)	12.67	37.87	32.42	23.24	18.71	13.07	—	—	—	—
Expense Ratio (%)	na	1.40	1.24	1.20	1.16	0.95	—	—	—	—
Yield (%)	0.00	0.41	0.00	0.38	0.11	0.26	—	—	—	—
Portfolio Turnover (%)	na	122	128	176	89	141	—	—	—	—
Total Assets (Millions $)	122	614	257	41	7	2	—	—	—	—

PORTFOLIO (as of 10/31/08)

Portfolio Manager: Brueck/Beer - 2002

Investment Style

Large Cap	Growth
Mid Cap	Grth/Val
Small Cap	Value

Portfolio

0.8%	U.S. stock	0.0%	conv't
98.9%	int'l stock	0.0%	preferred
0.0%	U.S. bonds	0.3%	other
0.0%	int'l bonds	0.0%	cash

Number of Investments: 73

Percent of Portfolio in Top 10 Investments: 54%

SHAREHOLDER INFORMATION

Minimum Investment

Initial: $5,000 Subsequent: $250

Minimum IRA Investment

Initial: $2,000 Subsequent: $250

Maximum Fees

Load: 2.00% redemption 12b-1: none

Other: redemption fee applies for 30 days

Services

✔ IRA
✔ Keogh
✔ Telephone Exchange

T. Rowe Price European Stock (PRESX)

800-638-5660
www.troweprice.com

Regional/Country Stock

PERFORMANCE — fund inception date: 2/28/90

	3yr Annual	5yr Annual	10yr Annual	Bull	Bear
Return (%)	-5.0	1.7	0.7	197.9	-45.7
Differ From Category (+/-)	3.4 abv av	-1.2 blw av	-5.6 low	-121.9 blw av	7.7 abv av

Standard Deviation	Category Risk Index	Beta
21.5%—abv av	0.79—blw av	1.27

	2008	2007	2006	2005	2004	2003	2002	2001	2000	1999
Return (%)	-43.4	15.3	31.5	8.9	16.4	36.5	-18.7	-20.7	-6.7	19.7
Differ From Category (+/-)	6.6	-11.5	4.8	-19.3	-4.3	-13.2	-8.6	-8.7	14.7	-50.3
Return, Tax-Adjusted (%)	-44.1	12.4	29.2	5.2	15.8	35.9	-19.0	-21.4	-8.2	17.6

PER SHARE DATA

	2008	2007	2006	2005	2004	2003	2002	2001	2000	1999
Dividends, Net Income ($)	0.39	0.32	0.26	0.32	0.27	0.22	0.14	0.36	0.16	0.14
Distrib'ns, Cap Gain ($)	0.00	3.13	2.09	4.16	0.01	0.02	0.00	0.00	1.42	1.90
Net Asset Value ($)	10.82	19.79	20.21	17.16	19.90	17.34	12.88	16.01	20.64	23.86
Expense Ratio (%)	na	0.98	1.03	1.06	1.07	1.12	1.11	1.09	1.02	1.05
Yield (%)	3.60	1.39	1.16	1.50	1.35	1.26	1.08	2.24	0.72	0.54
Portfolio Turnover (%)	na	88	84	82	22	23	16	6	24	15
Total Assets (Millions $)	533	1,149	1,011	812	852	889	641	847	1,232	1,587

PORTFOLIO (as of 9/30/08)

Portfolio Manager: Tenerelli - 2005

Investment Style

Large Cap	Growth
Mid Cap	Grth/Val
Small Cap	Value

Portfolio

1.1%	U.S. stock	0.0%	conv't
93.1%	int'l stock	1.7%	preferred
0.0%	U.S. bonds	0.0%	other
0.0%	int'l bonds	4.2%	cash

Number of Investments: 65
Percent of Portfolio in Top 10 Investments: 28%

SHAREHOLDER INFORMATION

Minimum Investment
Initial: $2,500 Subsequent: $100

Minimum IRA Investment
Initial: $1,000 Subsequent: $50

Maximum Fees
Load: 2.00% redemption 12b-1: none
Other: redemption fee applies for 90 days

Services
✔ IRA
✔ Keogh
✔ Telephone Exchange

T. Rowe Price Latin America (PRLAX)

800-638-5660
www.troweprice.com

Regional/Country Stock

PERFORMANCE — fund inception date: 12/29/93

	3yr Annual	5yr Annual	10yr Annual	Bull	Bear
Return (%)	-0.1	17.1	14.9	812.4	-58.3
Differ From Category (+/-)	8.3 high	14.2 high	8.6 high	492.6 high	-4.9 blw av

Standard Deviation	Category Risk Index	Beta
35.2%—high	1.29—high	1.90

	2008	2007	2006	2005	2004	2003	2002	2001	2000	1999
Return (%)	-55.8	48.9	51.2	60.0	38.3	57.9	-18.2	-0.3	-11.2	59.3
Differ From Category (+/-)	-5.8	22.1	24.5	31.8	17.6	8.2	-8.0	11.7	10.2	-10.7
Return, Tax-Adjusted (%)	-56.2	47.8	50.6	59.6	37.7	57.1	-18.2	-1.3	-11.4	59.1

PER SHARE DATA

	2008	2007	2006	2005	2004	2003	2002	2001	2000	1999
Dividends, Net Income ($)	0.32	0.40	0.31	0.20	0.21	0.16	0.00	0.15	0.04	0.04
Distrib'ns, Cap Gain ($)	0.87	1.85	0.23	-0.01	0.00	0.00	0.00	0.20	0.00	0.00
Net Asset Value ($)	22.73	53.89	37.74	25.32	15.95	11.69	7.51	9.17	9.56	10.81
Expense Ratio (%)	na	1.20	1.24	1.29	1.41	1.55	1.53	1.49	1.46	1.62
Yield (%)	1.35	0.71	0.81	0.78	1.31	1.36	0.00	1.60	0.41	0.37
Portfolio Turnover (%)	na	23	35	18	35	27	21	30	27	43
Total Assets (Millions $)	1,249	3,733	2,227	1,085	310	201	129	177	207	268

PORTFOLIO (as of 9/30/08)

Portfolio Manager: Buck - 2008

Investment Style

Large Cap	Growth
Mid Cap	Grth/Val
Small Cap	Value

Portfolio

1.8%	U.S. stock	0.0%	conv't
97.8%	int'l stock	0.0%	preferred
0.0%	U.S. bonds	0.0%	other
0.0%	int'l bonds	0.4%	cash

Number of Investments: 44

Percent of Portfolio in Top 10 Investments: 67%

SHAREHOLDER INFORMATION

Minimum Investment

Initial: $2,500 Subsequent: $100

Minimum IRA Investment

Initial: $1,000 Subsequent: $50

Maximum Fees

Load: 2.00% redemption 12b-1: none

Other: redemption fee applies for 90 days

Services

✔ IRA

✔ Keogh

✔ Telephone Exchange

T. Rowe Price New Asia (PRASX)

800-638-5660
www.troweprice.com

Regional/Country Stock

PERFORMANCE — fund inception date: 9/28/90

	3yr Annual	5yr Annual	10yr Annual	Bull	Bear
Return (%)	-4.1	5.7	8.6	471.2	-63.3
Differ From Category (+/-)	4.3 abv av	2.8 abv av	2.3 abv av	151.4 high	-9.9 low

Standard Deviation	Category Risk Index	Beta
33.1%—high	1.22—abv av	1.81

	2008	2007	2006	2005	2004	2003	2002	2001	2000	1999
Return (%)	-61.0	66.3	36.1	26.4	18.6	53.5	-9.4	-10.0	-30.8	99.8
Differ From Category (+/-)	-11.0	39.5	9.4	-1.8	-2.1	3.8	0.7	2.0	-9.4	29.8
Return, Tax-Adjusted (%)	-61.7	64.0	33.4	24.9	18.5	53.1	-9.7	-10.0	-30.8	99.5

PER SHARE DATA

	2008	2007	2006	2005	2004	2003	2002	2001	2000	1999
Dividends, Net Income ($)	0.40	0.19	0.21	0.12	0.00	0.06	0.04	0.00	0.00	0.04
Distrib'ns, Cap Gain ($)	0.00	1.75	1.59	0.72	0.05	0.01	0.00	0.00	0.00	0.00
Net Asset Value ($)	8.02	21.58	14.21	11.83	10.04	8.51	5.59	6.21	6.90	9.97
Expense Ratio (%)	na	0.93	1.05	1.05	1.09	1.17	1.17	1.22	1.08	1.21
Yield (%)	4.98	0.81	1.32	0.95	0.00	0.70	0.71	0.00	0.00	0.40
Portfolio Turnover (%)	na	53	76	56	72	72	72	49	52	69
Total Assets (Millions $)	1,660	5,567	2,255	1,442	997	885	543	639	800	1,375

PORTFOLIO (as of 9/30/08)

Portfolio Manager: Dydasco - 1996

Investment Style

Large Cap	Growth
Mid Cap	Grth/Val
Small Cap	Value

Portfolio

1.1%	U.S. stock	0.0%	conv't
91.3%	int'l stock	0.0%	preferred
0.0%	U.S. bonds	1.9%	other
0.0%	int'l bonds	5.7%	cash

Number of Investments: 91

Percent of Portfolio in Top 10 Investments: 29%

SHAREHOLDER INFORMATION

Minimum Investment

Initial: $2,500 Subsequent: $100

Minimum IRA Investment

Initial: $1,000 Subsequent: $50

Maximum Fees

Load: 2.00% redemption 12b-1: none

Other: redemption fee applies for 90 days

Services

✔ IRA
✔ Keogh
✔ Telephone Exchange

Vanguard European Stock Index (VEURX)

800-662-6273
www.vanguard.com

Regional/Country Stock

PERFORMANCE — fund inception date: 6/18/90

	3yr Annual	5yr Annual	10yr Annual	Bull	Bear
Return (%)	-5.7	2.0	0.7	219.5	-47.8
Differ From Category (+/-)	2.7 av	-0.9 av	-5.6 low	-100.3 blw av	5.6 abv av

Standard Deviation	Category Risk Index	Beta
20.6%—abv av	0.76—blw av	1.26

	2008	2007	2006	2005	2004	2003	2002	2001	2000	1999
Return (%)	-44.8	13.8	33.4	9.2	20.8	38.7	-18.0	-20.3	-8.3	16.6
Differ From Category (+/-)	5.2	-13.0	6.7	-19.0	0.1	-11.0	-7.9	-8.3	13.1	-53.4
Return, Tax-Adjusted (%)	-46.1	12.6	32.2	8.3	19.9	37.7	-18.8	-21.0	-8.9	15.7

PER SHARE DATA

	2008	2007	2006	2005	2004	2003	2002	2001	2000	1999
Dividends, Net Income ($)	1.50	1.22	0.92	0.70	0.58	0.46	0.40	0.45	0.42	0.50
Distrib'ns, Cap Gain ($)	0.00	0.00	0.00	0.00	0.00	0.00	0.00	0.00	0.05	0.15
Net Asset Value ($)	20.41	39.78	36.03	27.70	25.99	22.00	16.21	20.25	25.99	28.83
Expense Ratio (%)	na	0.22	0.27	0.27	0.27	0.32	0.33	0.30	0.29	0.29
Yield (%)	7.33	3.05	2.56	2.52	2.23	2.09	2.46	2.22	1.62	1.72
Portfolio Turnover (%)	na	9	6	5	5	6	15	3	8	7
Total Assets (Millions $)	10,342	25,212	18,461	11,580	9,220	6,252	3,998	4,405	5,611	6,106

PORTFOLIO (as of 9/30/08)

Portfolio Manager: Kelly/O'Reilly - 1992

Investment Style

Large Cap	Growth
Mid Cap	Grth/Val
Small Cap	Value

Portfolio

0.0%	U.S. stock	0.0%	conv't
97.9%	int'l stock	0.4%	preferred
0.1%	U.S. bonds	1.5%	other
0.0%	int'l bonds	0.0%	cash

Number of Investments: 529

Percent of Portfolio in Top 10 Investments: 19%

SHAREHOLDER INFORMATION

Minimum Investment

Initial: $3,000 Subsequent: $100

Minimum IRA Investment

Initial: $3,000 Subsequent: $100

Maximum Fees

Load: 2.00% redemption 12b-1: none

Other: redemption fee applies for 2 months

Services

✔ IRA

✔ Keogh

✔ Telephone Exchange

Vanguard Pacific Stock Index (VPACX)

800-662-6273
www.vanguard.com

Regional/Country Stock

PERFORMANCE — fund inception date: 6/18/90

	3yr Annual	5yr Annual	10yr Annual	Bull	Bear
Return (%)	-8.4	2.3	1.9	165.0	-39.7
Differ From Category (+/-)	0.0 av	-0.6 av	-4.4 blw av	-154.8 blw av	13.7 high

Standard Deviation	Category Risk Index	Beta
17.8%—av	0.65—low	0.96

	2008	2007	2006	2005	2004	2003	2002	2001	2000	1999
Return (%)	-34.4	4.7	11.9	22.5	18.8	38.4	-9.4	-26.4	-25.8	57.0
Differ From Category (+/-)	15.6	-22.1	-14.8	-5.7	-1.9	-11.3	0.7	-14.4	-4.4	-13.0
Return, Tax-Adjusted (%)	-34.8	3.9	11.1	21.9	18.1	37.7	-9.8	-26.5	-26.2	56.5

PER SHARE DATA

	2008	2007	2006	2005	2004	2003	2002	2001	2000	1999
Dividends, Net Income ($)	0.14	0.30	0.27	0.16	0.16	0.10	0.07	0.03	0.13	0.09
Distrib'ns, Cap Gain ($)	0.00	0.00	0.00	0.00	0.00	0.00	0.00	0.00	0.00	0.00
Net Asset Value ($)	8.20	12.72	12.43	11.34	9.38	8.03	5.88	6.56	8.95	12.22
Expense Ratio (%)	na	0.22	0.27	0.32	0.34	0.30	0.40	0.37	0.38	0.37
Yield (%)	1.70	2.38	2.14	1.41	1.67	1.30	1.13	0.48	1.39	0.73
Portfolio Turnover (%)	na	3	2	7	3	3	20	2	6	6
Total Assets (Millions $)	5,340	10,708	8,408	6,031	3,945	2,469	1,432	1,327	1,924	2,526

PORTFOLIO (as of 9/30/08)

Portfolio Manager: Buek - 1997

Investment Style

Large Cap	Growth
Mid Cap	Grth/Val
Small Cap	Value

Portfolio

0.0%	U.S. stock	0.0%	conv't
99.7%	int'l stock	0.0%	preferred
0.2%	U.S. bonds	0.1%	other
0.0%	int'l bonds	0.0%	cash

Number of Investments: 514
Percent of Portfolio in Top 10 Investments: 19%

SHAREHOLDER INFORMATION

Minimum Investment
Initial: $3,000 Subsequent: $100

Minimum IRA Investment
Initial: $3,000 Subsequent: $100

Maximum Fees
Load: 2.00% redemption 12b-1: none
Other: redemption fee applies for 2 months

Services
✔ IRA
✔ Keogh
✔ Telephone Exchange

Emerging Stock Funds
Category Performance Ranked by 2008 Returns

Fund (Ticker)	Annual Return (%) 2008	3Yr	5Yr	10Yr	Category Risk	Total Risk
Lazard Emerging Markets Equity Open (LZOEX)	-48.1	-3.7	10.4	10.2	low	high
Vanguard Emerging Mkts Stock Idx (VEIEX)	-52.9	-5.4	7.1	8.8	blw av	high
Driehaus Emerging Markets Growth (DREGX)	-54.5	-2.9	9.5	14.6	blw av	high
T. Rowe Price Emerging Markets Stock (PRMSX)	-60.6	-9.4	5.5	9.4	high	high
Fidelity Emerging Markets (FEMKX)	-60.9	-8.9	6.1	7.5	abv av	high
Emerging Stock Category Average	**-59.5**	**-9.1**	**6.5**	**9.4**	**av**	**high**

Driehaus Emerging Markets Growth (DREGX)

800-560-6111
www.driehaus.com

Emerging Stock

PERFORMANCE

fund inception date: 12/31/97

	3yr Annual	5yr Annual	10yr Annual	Bull	Bear
Return (%)	-2.9	9.5	14.6	513.9	-56.8
Differ From Category (+/-)	6.2 high	3.0 high	5.2 high	63.1 high	5.5 high

Standard Deviation	Category Risk Index	Beta
27.5%—high	0.83—blw av	1.43

	2008	2007	2006	2005	2004	2003	2002	2001	2000	1999
Return (%)	-54.5	42.3	41.2	38.9	24.1	65.5	-7.7	-2.0	-22.8	114.1
Differ From Category (+/-)	5.0	2.0	7.4	4.2	-2.3	5.8	-1.8	1.0	5.3	41.6
Return, Tax-Adjusted (%)	-55.4	37.9	40.7	36.5	22.5	65.5	-7.7	-2.0	-24.1	113.1

PER SHARE DATA

	2008	2007	2006	2005	2004	2003	2002	2001	2000	1999
Dividends, Net Income ($)	0.00	0.00	0.00	0.08	0.04	0.00	0.00	0.03	0.58	0.16
Distrib'ns, Cap Gain ($)	2.65	11.56	0.84	3.51	2.00	0.00	0.00	0.00	0.03	0.12
Net Asset Value ($)	17.19	43.45	39.09	28.29	23.00	20.29	12.26	13.27	13.56	18.36
Expense Ratio (%)	na	1.69	1.78	2.07	2.03	2.34	2.16	2.49	2.50	2.58
Yield (%)	0.00	0.00	0.00	0.24	0.17	0.00	0.00	0.22	4.26	0.87
Portfolio Turnover (%)	na	165	181	350	357	432	355	506	375	367
Total Assets (Millions $)	263	958	785	241	144	100	36	22	24	11

PORTFOLIO (as of 10/31/08)

Portfolio Manager: Schwab/Cleaver - 2008

Investment Style

Large Cap	Growth
Mid Cap	Grth/Val
Small Cap	Value

Portfolio

5.1%	U.S. stock	0.0%	conv't
91.3%	int'l stock	0.0%	preferred
0.0%	U.S. bonds	2.5%	other
0.0%	int'l bonds	1.2%	cash

Number of Investments: 73

Percent of Portfolio in Top 10 Investments: 30%

SHAREHOLDER INFORMATION

Minimum Investment

Initial: $10,000 Subsequent: $2,000

Minimum IRA Investment

Initial: $2,000 Subsequent: $500

Maximum Fees

Load: 2.00% redemption 12b-1: none

Other: redemption fee applies for 60 days

Services

✔ IRA

Keogh

✔ Telephone Exchange

Fidelity Emerging Markets (FEMKX)

800-544-9797
www.fidelity.com

Emerging Stock

PERFORMANCE — fund inception date: 11/1/90

	3yr Annual	5yr Annual	10yr Annual	Bull	Bear
Return (%)	-8.9	6.1	7.5	467.3	-63.0
Differ From Category (+/-)	0.2 blw av	-0.4 av	-1.9 blw av	16.5 abv av	-0.7 blw av

Standard Deviation	Category Risk Index	Beta
32.2%—high	0.97—abv av	1.76

	2008	2007	2006	2005	2004	2003	2002	2001	2000	1999
Return (%)	-60.9	45.0	33.3	44.3	22.9	48.7	-7.0	-2.5	-33.0	70.5
Differ From Category (+/-)	-1.4	4.7	-0.5	9.6	-3.5	-10.9	-1.1	0.5	-4.9	-2.0
Return, Tax-Adjusted (%)	-61.1	43.9	33.0	43.7	22.5	48.2	-7.2	-2.7	-33.1	70.5

PER SHARE DATA

	2008	2007	2006	2005	2004	2003	2002	2001	2000	1999
Dividends, Net Income ($)	0.24	0.19	0.20	0.21	0.10	0.12	0.05	0.03	0.03	0.00
Distrib'ns, Cap Gain ($)	0.00	1.37	0.00	0.00	0.00	0.00	0.00	0.00	0.00	0.00
Net Asset Value ($)	12.99	33.85	24.39	18.44	12.93	10.61	7.21	7.80	8.03	12.02
Expense Ratio (%)	na	0.99	1.01	1.07	1.18	1.36	1.39	1.45	1.35	1.42
Yield (%)	1.84	0.53	0.82	1.13	0.81	1.08	0.69	0.38	0.37	0.00
Portfolio Turnover (%)	na	52	66	68	12	105	120	113	100	94
Total Assets (Millions $)	1,937	6,438	3,525	1,990	760	484	265	243	270	555

PORTFOLIO (as of 11/30/08)

Portfolio Manager: von Rekowsky - 2004

Investment Style

Large Cap	Growth
Mid Cap	Grth/Val
Small Cap	Value

Portfolio

1.3%	U.S. stock	0.0%	conv't
92.8%	int'l stock	0.0%	preferred
0.0%	U.S. bonds	0.0%	other
0.0%	int'l bonds	6.0%	cash

Number of Investments: 199

Percent of Portfolio in Top 10 Investments: 28%

SHAREHOLDER INFORMATION

Minimum Investment

Initial: $2,500 Subsequent: $250

Minimum IRA Investment

Initial: $500 Subsequent: $100

Maximum Fees

Load: 1.50% redemption 12b-1: none

Other: redemption fee applies for 90 days; maint fee for low bal

Services

✔ IRA
✔ Keogh
✔ Telephone Exchange

Lazard Emerging Markets Equity Open (LZOEX)

800-986-3455
www.lazardnet.com

Emerging Stock

PERFORMANCE — fund inception date: 1/8/97

	3yr Annual	5yr Annual	10yr Annual	Bull	Bear
Return (%)	-3.7	10.4	10.2	443.5	-50.1
Differ From Category (+/-)	5.4 high	3.9 high	0.8 abv av	-7.3 av	12.2 high

Standard Deviation	Category Risk Index	Beta
26.9%—high	0.81—low	1.56

	2008	2007	2006	2005	2004	2003	2002	2001	2000	1999
Return (%)	-48.1	32.7	29.9	41.3	30.1	54.5	-0.7	-3.6	-29.8	55.2
Differ From Category (+/-)	11.4	-7.6	-3.9	6.6	3.7	-5.2	5.2	-0.6	-1.7	-17.3
Return, Tax-Adjusted (%)	-49.6	30.0	27.6	39.1	29.8	53.9	-1.0	-3.8	-29.8	54.8

PER SHARE DATA

	2008	2007	2006	2005	2004	2003	2002	2001	2000	1999
Dividends, Net Income ($)	0.43	0.22	0.18	0.14	0.10	0.14	0.06	0.03	0.00	0.08
Distrib'ns, Cap Gain ($)	1.34	3.20	2.28	1.67	0.00	0.00	0.00	0.00	0.00	0.00
Net Asset Value ($)	11.05	24.17	20.82	17.99	14.06	10.88	7.13	7.24	7.54	10.74
Expense Ratio (%)	na	1.47	1.54	1.59	1.60	1.60	1.60	1.60	1.60	1.60
Yield (%)	3.45	0.80	0.78	0.69	0.71	1.24	0.88	0.45	0.00	0.71
Portfolio Turnover (%)	na	53	46	48	43	29	31	43	72	46
Total Assets (Millions $)	1,135	1,469	440	196	31	19	9	7	5	10

PORTFOLIO (as of 9/30/08)

Portfolio Manager: Donald/Reinsberg/Chopra/McKee - 2001

Investment Style

Large Cap	Growth
Mid Cap	Grth/Val
Small Cap	Value

Portfolio

0.0%	U.S. stock	0.0%	conv't
98.8%	int'l stock	0.0%	preferred
0.0%	U.S. bonds	1.2%	other
0.0%	int'l bonds	0.0%	cash

Number of Investments: 83

Percent of Portfolio in Top 10 Investments: 27%

SHAREHOLDER INFORMATION

Minimum Investment

Initial: $2,500 Subsequent: $50

Minimum IRA Investment

Initial: $0 Subsequent: $0

Maximum Fees

Load: 1.00% redemption 12b-1: 0.25%

Other: redemption fee applies for 30 days

Services

✔ IRA
✔ Keogh
✔ Telephone Exchange

T. Rowe Price Emerging Markets Stock (PRMSX)

800-638-5660
www.troweprice.com

Emerging Stock

PERFORMANCE

fund inception date: 3/31/95

	3yr Annual	5yr Annual	10yr Annual	Bull	Bear
Return (%)	-9.4	5.5	9.4	461.8	-62.6
Differ From Category (+/-)	-0.3 blw av	-1.0 blw av	0.0 av	11.0 av	-0.3 blw av

Standard Deviation	Category Risk Index	Beta
32.3%—high	0.97—high	1.79

	2008	2007	2006	2005	2004	2003	2002	2001	2000	1999
Return (%)	-60.6	42.9	32.0	38.7	26.9	52.2	-5.0	-5.7	-26.4	87.4
Differ From Category (+/-)	-1.1	2.6	-1.8	4.0	0.5	-7.4	0.9	-2.7	1.7	14.9
Return, Tax-Adjusted (%)	-61.1	41.2	30.9	37.6	26.7	51.9	-5.0	-5.8	-26.4	87.4

PER SHARE DATA

	2008	2007	2006	2005	2004	2003	2002	2001	2000	1999
Dividends, Net Income ($)	0.61	0.30	0.24	0.18	0.04	0.09	0.02	0.01	0.00	0.00
Distrib'ns, Cap Gain ($)	0.00	2.95	1.20	1.05	0.18	0.00	0.00	0.00	0.00	0.00
Net Asset Value ($)	16.34	42.92	32.41	25.68	19.41	15.47	10.22	10.77	11.43	15.52
Expense Ratio (%)	na	1.20	1.25	1.27	1.33	1.43	1.51	1.58	1.50	1.75
Yield (%)	3.73	0.65	0.71	0.67	0.20	0.58	0.19	0.09	0.00	0.00
Portfolio Turnover (%)	na	44	49	53	70	66	70	70	56	59
Total Assets (Millions $)	2,184	4,761	2,627	1,554	753	439	170	155	152	162

PORTFOLIO (as of 9/30/08)

Portfolio Manager: Alderson/Pangaro - 1995

Investment Style

Large Cap	Growth
Mid Cap	Grth/Val
Small Cap	Value

Portfolio

1.4%	U.S. stock	0.0%	conv't
97.1%	int'l stock	0.0%	preferred
0.0%	U.S. bonds	0.3%	other
0.0%	int'l bonds	1.1%	cash

Number of Investments: 135

Percent of Portfolio in Top 10 Investments: 23%

SHAREHOLDER INFORMATION

Minimum Investment

Initial: $2,500 Subsequent: $100

Minimum IRA Investment

Initial: $1,000 Subsequent: $50

Maximum Fees

Load: 2.00% redemption 12b-1: none

Other: redemption fee applies for 90 days

Services

✔ IRA

✔ Keogh

✔ Telephone Exchange

Vanguard Emerging Mkts Stock Idx (VEIEX)

800-662-6273
www.vanguard.com

Emerging Stock

PERFORMANCE

fund inception date: 5/4/94

	3yr Annual	5yr Annual	10yr Annual	Bull	Bear
Return (%)	-5.4	7.1	8.8	434.4	-56.7
Differ From Category (+/-)	3.7 high	0.6 abv av	-0.6 av	-16.4 av	5.6 high

Standard Deviation	Category Risk Index	Beta
28.8%—high	0.86—blw av	1.58

	2008	2007	2006	2005	2004	2003	2002	2001	2000	1999
Return (%)	-52.9	38.9	29.3	32.0	26.1	57.6	-7.5	-2.9	-27.6	61.5
Differ From Category (+/-)	6.6	-1.4	-4.5	-2.7	-0.3	-2.1	-1.6	0.1	0.5	-11.0
Return, Tax-Adjusted (%)	-53.6	38.0	28.6	31.2	25.3	56.8	-8.0	-3.9	-28.3	60.2

PER SHARE DATA

	2008	2007	2006	2005	2004	2003	2002	2001	2000	1999
Dividends, Net Income ($)	0.70	0.59	0.40	0.31	0.26	0.17	0.12	0.21	0.22	0.27
Distrib'ns, Cap Gain ($)	0.00	0.00	0.00	0.00	0.00	0.00	0.00	0.00	0.00	0.00
Net Asset Value ($)	14.90	33.12	24.27	19.07	14.68	11.85	7.63	8.37	8.84	12.50
Expense Ratio (%)	na	0.37	0.42	0.45	0.48	0.53	0.57	0.60	0.59	0.58
Yield (%)	4.69	1.77	1.63	1.65	1.76	1.45	1.59	2.50	2.46	2.16
Portfolio Turnover (%)	na	9	26	15	11	16	65	23	40	22
Total Assets (Millions $)	5,143	13,313	8,109	6,018	3,140	1,873	896	801	913	1,138

PORTFOLIO (as of 9/30/08)

Portfolio Manager: Kelly/Perre - 1994

Investment Style

Large Cap	Growth
Mid Cap	Grth/Val
Small Cap	Value

Portfolio

0.5%	U.S. stock	0.0%	conv't
93.7%	int'l stock	0.3%	preferred
0.0%	U.S. bonds	5.3%	other
0.0%	int'l bonds	0.1%	cash

Number of Investments: 837

Percent of Portfolio in Top 10 Investments: 17%

SHAREHOLDER INFORMATION

Minimum Investment

Initial: $3,000 Subsequent: $100

Minimum IRA Investment

Initial: $3,000 Subsequent: $100

Maximum Fees

Load: 0.25% redemption 12b-1: none

Other: none

Services

✔ IRA
✔ Keogh
✔ Telephone Exchange

BALANCED STOCK/BOND FUNDS

Balanced: Domestic Funds
Category Performance Ranked by 2008 Returns

Fund (Ticker)	Annual Return (%) 2008	3Yr	5Yr	10Yr	Category Risk	Total Risk
Hussman Strategic Total Return (HSTRX)	6.3	8.1	7.3	na	low	low
FundX Flexible Income (INCMX)	-0.3	4.3	4.0	na	low	low
Manning & Napier Pro-Blend Cnsrv Term S (EXDAX)	-5.1	3.1	3.9	5.2	low	low
American Century One Choice: Very Con (AONIX)	-6.7	2.0	na	na	low	low
Permanent Portfolio (PRPFX)	-8.4	5.4	7.1	8.0	av	blw av
Vanguard Wellesley Income (VWINX)	-9.9	1.9	3.3	4.9	low	low
Berwyn Income (BERIX)	-10.2	1.4	2.7	5.9	low	low
Vanguard LifeStrategy Income (VASIX)	-10.6	1.0	2.4	3.7	low	low
Greenspring (GRSPX)	-11.8	1.4	3.8	6.9	av	blw av
Fidelity Asset Manager 20% (FASIX)	-14.2	-1.2	1.7	3.2	low	low
Janus Balanced (JABAX)	-15.3	1.0	3.8	3.9	blw av	blw av
American Century One Choice: Con (AOCIX)	-16.1	-0.4	na	na	low	low
Oakmark Equity & Income I (OAKBX)	-16.2	1.3	4.5	8.6	blw av	blw av
Schwab MarketTrack Conservative (SWCGX)	-18.4	-2.2	1.0	2.5	low	low
Manning & Napier Pro-Blend Mod Term S (EXBAX)	-18.5	-0.4	3.0	4.7	blw av	blw av
Vanguard LifeStrategy Conservative Gr (VSCGX)	-19.6	-1.7	1.4	2.8	low	blw av
T. Rowe Price Personal Strat Income (PRSIX)	-20.4	-2.2	1.6	3.4	blw av	blw av
FPA Crescent (FPACX)	-20.6	-1.6	3.1	7.2	av	blw av
Value Line Income & Growth (VALIX)	-21.6	-2.1	3.4	4.2	av	blw av
Vanguard Balanced Index (VBINX)	-22.3	-2.9	0.9	2.0	blw av	blw av
Vanguard Wellington (VWELX)	-22.3	-1.1	2.8	4.4	av	blw av
Manning & Napier Pro-Blend Extnd Term S (MNBAX)	-25.4	-2.2	2.6	5.1	abv av	blw av
Vanguard LifeStrategy Moderate Growth (VSMGX)	-26.5	-3.7	0.8	1.9	av	blw av
Leuthold Core Investment (LCORX)	-27.5	-1.1	3.7	7.4	high	blw av
Vanguard LifeStrategy Growth (VASGX)	-34.4	-6.5	-0.3	0.7	high	blw av
Balanced: Domestic Category Average	**-23.4**	**-3.2**	**0.9**	**3.1**	**av**	**blw av**

American Century One Choice: Con (AOCIX)

800-345-2021
www.americancentury.com

Balanced: Domestic

PERFORMANCE — fund inception date: 9/30/04

	3yr Annual	5yr Annual	10yr Annual	Bull	Bear
Return (%)	-0.4	na	na	na	-17.0
Differ From Category (+/-)	2.8 high	na	na	na	8.0 high

Standard Deviation	Category Risk Index	Beta
7.8%—low	0.71—low	0.49

	2008	2007	2006	2005	2004	2003	2002	2001	2000	1999
Return (%)	-16.1	7.0	10.0	3.7	—	—	—	—	—	—
Differ From Category (+/-)	-7.3	0.0	-0.9	-1.9	—	—	—	—	—	—
Return, Tax-Adjusted (%)	-17.4	5.6	8.8	2.7	—	—	—	—	—	—

PER SHARE DATA

	2008	2007	2006	2005	2004	2003	2002	2001	2000	1999
Dividends, Net Income ($)	0.35	0.41	0.34	0.30	—	—	—	—	—	—
Distrib'ns, Cap Gain ($)	0.20	0.08	0.03	0.01	—	—	—	—	—	—
Net Asset Value ($)	9.06	11.42	11.13	10.46	—	—	—	—	—	—
Expense Ratio (%)	0.00	0.00	0.00	0.00	—	—	—	—	—	—
Yield (%)	3.81	3.57	3.03	2.88	—	—	—	—	—	—
Portfolio Turnover (%)	18	7	8	12	—	—	—	—	—	—
Total Assets (Millions $)	234	262	168	65	—	—	—	—	—	—

PORTFOLIO (as of 9/30/08)

Portfolio Manager: Tyler/Torelli - 2004

Investment Style

Large Cap	Growth
Mid Cap	Grth/Val
Small Cap	Value

Portfolio

53.4%	U.S. stock	0.0%	conv't
11.5%	int'l stock	0.0%	preferred
0.9%	U.S. bonds	0.1%	other
12.8%	int'l bonds	21.3%	cash

Number of Investments: 8

Percent of Portfolio in Top 10 Investments: 100%

SHAREHOLDER INFORMATION

Minimum Investment

Initial: $2,500 Subsequent: $50

Minimum IRA Investment

Initial: $2,500 Subsequent: $50

Maximum Fees

Load: none 12b-1: none

Other: none

Services

✔ IRA

✔ Keogh

✔ Telephone Exchange

American Century One Choice: Very Con (AONIX)

800-345-2021
www.americancentury.com

Balanced: Domestic

PERFORMANCE — fund inception date: 9/30/04

	3yr Annual	5yr Annual	10yr Annual	Bull	Bear
Return (%)	2.0	na	na	na	-6.7
Differ From Category (+/-)	5.2 high	na	na	na	18.3 high

Standard Deviation	Category Risk Index	Beta
4.8%—low	0.44—low	0.28

	2008	2007	2006	2005	2004	2003	2002	2001	2000	1999
Return (%)	-6.7	5.7	7.5	2.4	—	—	—	—	—	—
Differ From Category (+/-)	16.7	-1.3	-3.4	-3.2	—	—	—	—	—	—
Return, Tax-Adjusted (%)	-8.0	4.2	6.1	1.3	—	—	—	—	—	—

PER SHARE DATA

	2008	2007	2006	2005	2004	2003	2002	2001	2000	1999
Dividends, Net Income ($)	0.35	0.44	0.37	0.31	—	—	—	—	—	—
Distrib'ns, Cap Gain ($)	0.06	0.04	0.02	0.01	—	—	—	—	—	—
Net Asset Value ($)	9.45	10.55	10.44	10.09	—	—	—	—	—	—
Expense Ratio (%)	0.00	0.00	0.00	0.00	—	—	—	—	—	—
Yield (%)	3.71	4.19	3.57	3.09	—	—	—	—	—	—
Portfolio Turnover (%)	17	17	34	38	—	—	—	—	—	—
Total Assets (Millions $)	92	52	31	12	—	—	—	—	—	—

PORTFOLIO (as of 9/30/08)

Portfolio Manager: Tyler/Torelli - 2004

Investment Style

Large Cap	Growth
Mid Cap	Grth/Val
Small Cap	Value

Portfolio

34.3%	U.S. stock	0.0%	conv't
1.2%	int'l stock	0.0%	preferred
1.1%	U.S. bonds	0.1%	other
15.2%	int'l bonds	48.1%	cash

Number of Investments: 7

Percent of Portfolio in Top 10 Investments: 100%

SHAREHOLDER INFORMATION

Minimum Investment
Initial: $2,500 Subsequent: $50

Minimum IRA Investment
Initial: $2,500 Subsequent: $50

Maximum Fees
Load: none 12b-1: none
Other: none

Services
✔ IRA
✔ Keogh
✔ Telephone Exchange

Berwyn Income
(BERIX)

800-992-6757
www.berwynfunds.com

Balanced: Domestic

PERFORMANCE — fund inception date: 9/3/87

	3yr Annual	5yr Annual	10yr Annual	Bull	Bear
Return (%)	1.4	2.7	5.9	46.2	-9.8
Differ From Category (+/-)	4.6 high	1.8 abv av	2.8 high	-31.1 low	15.2 high

Standard Deviation	Category Risk Index	Beta
6.7%—low	0.61—low	0.39

	2008	2007	2006	2005	2004	2003	2002	2001	2000	1999
Return (%)	-10.2	6.8	8.6	1.9	7.9	16.2	9.3	14.1	6.0	0.8
Differ From Category (+/-)	13.2	-0.2	-2.3	-3.7	-2.1	-5.8	17.4	15.0	1.0	-10.8
Return, Tax-Adjusted (%)	-12.0	4.6	6.9	0.4	6.3	14.2	7.0	10.9	2.8	-2.2

PER SHARE DATA

	2008	2007	2006	2005	2004	2003	2002	2001	2000	1999
Dividends, Net Income ($)	0.60	0.59	0.57	0.51	0.52	0.59	0.63	0.78	0.82	0.82
Distrib'ns, Cap Gain ($)	0.00	0.42	0.00	0.00	0.00	0.00	0.00	0.00	0.00	0.00
Net Asset Value ($)	10.30	12.10	12.28	11.85	12.13	11.74	10.64	10.32	9.76	10.00
Expense Ratio (%)	na	0.70	0.73	0.72	0.64	0.67	0.71	0.69	0.94	0.77
Yield (%)	5.85	4.70	4.65	4.30	4.32	5.00	5.92	7.57	8.40	8.19
Portfolio Turnover (%)	na	37	31	49	48	54	39	50	12	7
Total Assets (Millions $)	235	243	229	235	205	135	79	48	42	57

PORTFOLIO (as of 10/31/08)

Portfolio Manager: Killen/Grout/Killen/Cipolloni - 1994

Investment Style

Large Cap	Growth
Mid Cap	Grth/Val
Small Cap	Value

Portfolio

21.3%	U.S. stock	7.7%	conv't
3.0%	int'l stock	1.6%	preferred
58.0%	U.S. bonds	0.0%	other
0.0%	int'l bonds	8.4%	cash

Number of Investments: 94

Percent of Portfolio in Top 10 Investments: 26%

SHAREHOLDER INFORMATION

Minimum Investment

Initial: $3,000 Subsequent: $250

Minimum IRA Investment

Initial: $1,000 Subsequent: $250

Maximum Fees

Load: 1.00% redemption 12b-1: none

Other: redemption fee applies for 6 months

Services

✔ IRA

Keogh

✔ Telephone Exchange

Fidelity Asset Manager 20% (FASIX)

800-544-8544
www.fidelity.com

Balanced: Domestic

PERFORMANCE — fund inception date: 10/1/92

	3yr Annual	5yr Annual	10yr Annual	Bull	Bear
Return (%)	-1.2	1.7	3.2	45.1	-14.7
Differ From Category (+/-)	2.0 abv av	0.8 abv av	0.1 av	-32.2 low	10.3 high

Standard Deviation	Category Risk Index	Beta
6.2%—low	0.56—low	0.38

	2008	2007	2006	2005	2004	2003	2002	2001	2000	1999
Return (%)	-14.2	4.7	7.3	6.1	6.4	14.4	-0.5	1.3	3.6	5.7
Differ From Category (+/-)	9.2	-2.3	-3.6	0.5	-3.6	-7.6	7.6	2.2	-1.4	-5.9
Return, Tax-Adjusted (%)	-15.4	3.0	5.2	4.9	5.6	13.5	-1.9	-0.6	1.1	3.4

PER SHARE DATA

	2008	2007	2006	2005	2004	2003	2002	2001	2000	1999
Dividends, Net Income ($)	0.42	0.52	0.51	0.33	0.25	0.26	0.41	0.55	0.66	0.61
Distrib'ns, Cap Gain ($)	0.00	0.25	0.59	0.28	0.00	0.00	0.00	0.00	0.22	0.21
Net Asset Value ($)	10.32	12.47	12.65	12.83	12.67	12.15	10.86	11.33	11.73	12.18
Expense Ratio (%)	0.56	0.57	0.57	0.58	0.61	0.61	0.63	0.62	0.65	0.67
Yield (%)	4.05	4.12	3.88	2.51	1.97	2.13	3.77	4.85	5.52	4.92
Portfolio Turnover (%)	5	6	81	81	232	276	164	164	140	121
Total Assets (Millions $)	1,851	2,520	2,207	1,841	1,511	1,097	885	930	1,001	889

PORTFOLIO (as of 11/30/08)

Portfolio Manager: Young - 2007

Investment Style

Large Cap	Growth
Mid Cap	Grth/Val
Small Cap	Value

Portfolio

16.7%	U.S. Stock	0.0%	conv't
1.8%	int'l stock	0.0%	preferred
48.5%	U.S. bonds	6.2%	other
0.8%	int'l bonds	26.0%	cash

Number of Investments: 1,955

Percent of Portfolio in Top 10 Investments: 44%

SHAREHOLDER INFORMATION

Minimum Investment

Initial: $2,500 Subsequent: $250

Minimum IRA Investment

Initial: $500 Subsequent: $250

Maximum Fees

Load: none 12b-1: none

Other: none

Services

✔ IRA

Keogh

✔ Telephone Exchange

FPA Crescent (FPACX)

800-982-4372
www.fpafunds.com

Balanced: Domestic

PERFORMANCE — fund inception date: 6/2/93

	3yr Annual	5yr Annual	10yr Annual	Bull	Bear
Return (%)	-1.6	3.1	7.2	93.6	-21.3
Differ From Category (+/-)	1.6 abv av	2.2 high	4.1 high	16.3 high	3.7 abv av

Standard Deviation	Category Risk Index	Beta
11.3%—blw av	1.03—av	0.67

	2008	2007	2006	2005	2004	2003	2002	2001	2000	1999
Return (%)	-20.6	6.8	12.4	10.8	10.2	26.1	3.7	36.1	3.5	-6.3
Differ From Category (+/-)	2.8	-0.2	1.5	5.2	0.2	4.1	11.8	37.0	-1.5	-17.9
Return, Tax-Adjusted (%)	-21.2	4.6	10.8	9.9	9.8	25.8	2.7	35.3	1.8	-8.1

PER SHARE DATA

	2008	2007	2006	2005	2004	2003	2002	2001	2000	1999
Dividends, Net Income ($)	0.37	0.75	0.53	0.34	0.08	0.15	0.43	0.25	0.56	0.35
Distrib'ns, Cap Gain ($)	0.23	2.16	1.34	0.58	0.37	0.00	0.00	0.00	0.00	0.64
Net Asset Value ($)	19.59	25.29	26.40	25.17	23.55	21.79	17.40	17.19	12.82	12.95
Expense Ratio (%)	1.34	1.25	1.39	1.40	1.41	1.54	1.50	1.87	1.49	1.42
Yield (%)	1.86	2.73	1.91	1.30	0.33	0.68	2.47	1.44	4.38	2.60
Portfolio Turnover (%)	29	29	24	17	20	39	34	37	10	36
Total Assets (Millions $)	1,120	1,318	1,411	1,280	915	381	209	204	33	84

PORTFOLIO (as of 9/30/08)

Portfolio Manager: Romick - 1993

Investment Style

Large Cap	Growth
Mid Cap	Grth/Val
Small Cap	Value

Portfolio

41.3%	U.S. stock	0.2%	conv't
4.4%	int'l stock	0.4%	preferred
9.7%	U.S. bonds	1.3%	other
0.0%	int'l bonds	42.7%	cash

Number of Investments: 58

Percent of Portfolio in Top 10 Investments: 70%

SHAREHOLDER INFORMATION

Minimum Investment

Initial: $100 Subsequent: $100

Minimum IRA Investment

Initial: $100 Subsequent: $100

Maximum Fees

Load: 2.00% redemption 12b-1: none

Other: redemption fee applies for 90 days

Services

✔ IRA

Keogh

✔ Telephone Exchange

FundX Flexible Income (INCMX)

866-455-3863
www.fundxfund.com

Balanced: Domestic

PERFORMANCE — fund inception date: 7/1/02

	3yr Annual	5yr Annual	10yr Annual	Bull	Bear
Return (%)	4.3	4.0	na	40.3	-1.0
Differ From Category (+/-)	7.5 high	3.1 high	na	-37.0 low	24.0 high

Standard Deviation	Category Risk Index	Beta
3.5%—low	0.32—low	0.12

	2008	2007	2006	2005	2004	2003	2002	2001	2000	1999
Return (%)	-0.3	4.9	8.5	1.9	4.9	15.7	—	—	—	—
Differ From Category (+/-)	23.1	-2.1	-2.4	-3.7	-5.1	-6.3	—	—	—	—
Return, Tax-Adjusted (%)	-1.1	3.8	7.2	0.6	3.9	15.0	—	—	—	—

PER SHARE DATA

	2008	2007	2006	2005	2004	2003	2002	2001	2000	1999
Dividends, Net Income ($)	0.38	0.96	1.09	1.09	0.70	0.52	—	—	—	—
Distrib'ns, Cap Gain ($)	0.86	0.00	0.00	0.06	0.22	0.00	—	—	—	—
Net Asset Value ($)	29.38	30.68	30.18	28.89	29.48	29.02	—	—	—	—
Expense Ratio (%)	na	0.93	0.93	0.99	0.99	0.99	—	—	—	—
Yield (%)	1.26	3.12	3.61	3.75	2.35	1.77	—	—	—	—
Portfolio Turnover (%)	na	51	76	83	192	173	—	—	—	—
Total Assets (Millions $)	124	136	96	39	24	13	—	—	—	—

PORTFOLIO (as of 9/30/08)

Portfolio Manager: Brown/Browne/Burke/DeVault - 2002

Investment Style

Large Cap	Growth
Mid Cap	Grth/Val
Small Cap	Value

Portfolio

4.7%	U.S. stock	0.0%	conv't
0.4%	int'l stock	0.1%	preferred
33.9%	U.S. bonds	4.6%	other
1.0%	int'l bonds	55.3%	cash

Number of Investments: 19
Percent of Portfolio in Top 10 Investments: 89%

SHAREHOLDER INFORMATION

Minimum Investment
Initial: $2,500 Subsequent: $100

Minimum IRA Investment
Initial: $1,000 Subsequent: $100

Maximum Fees
Load: 2.00% redemption 12b-1: none
Other: redemption fee applies for 30 days

Services
✔ IRA
✔ Keogh
✔ Telephone Exchange

Greenspring
(GRSPX)

800-576-7498
www.greenspringfund.com

Balanced: Domestic

PERFORMANCE — fund inception date: 7/1/83

	3yr Annual	5yr Annual	10yr Annual	Bull	Bear
Return (%)	1.4	3.8	6.9	82.3	-14.1
Differ From Category (+/-)	4.6 high	2.9 high	3.8 high	5.0 abv av	10.9 high

Standard Deviation	Category Risk Index	Beta
11.0%—blw av	1.00—av	0.61

	2008	2007	2006	2005	2004	2003	2002	2001	2000	1999
Return (%)	-11.8	5.3	12.2	6.5	8.6	31.3	-6.0	10.2	15.6	2.6
Differ From Category (+/-)	11.6	-1.7	1.3	0.9	-1.4	9.3	2.1	11.1	10.6	-9.0
Return, Tax-Adjusted (%)	-12.4	4.1	11.2	5.6	7.4	29.9	-8.1	8.0	13.6	-0.2

PER SHARE DATA

	2008	2007	2006	2005	2004	2003	2002	2001	2000	1999
Dividends, Net Income ($)	0.35	0.56	0.58	0.44	0.65	0.61	0.94	0.96	0.79	1.12
Distrib'ns, Cap Gain ($)	0.16	0.53	0.19	0.25	0.10	0.00	0.00	0.00	0.00	0.00
Net Asset Value ($)	20.36	23.59	23.43	21.57	20.91	19.96	15.70	17.74	16.98	15.41
Expense Ratio (%)	na	1.03	1.07	1.16	1.06	1.14	1.19	1.19	1.24	1.08
Yield (%)	1.68	2.32	2.46	2.01	3.09	3.05	5.98	5.41	4.65	7.26
Portfolio Turnover (%)	na	54	39	36	35	102	78	89	100	91
Total Assets (Millions $)	307	258	244	157	132	109	51	50	47	61

PORTFOLIO (as of 11/30/08)

Portfolio Manager: Carlson - 1987

Investment Style

Large Cap	Growth
Mid Cap	Grth/Val
Small Cap	Value

Portfolio

38.7%	U.S. stock	16.9%	conv't
1.5%	int'l stock	0.0%	preferred
26.9%	U.S. bonds	0.0%	other
0.6%	int'l bonds	15.3%	cash

Number of Investments: 109
Percent of Portfolio in Top 10 Investments: 37%

SHAREHOLDER INFORMATION

Minimum Investment
Initial: $2,000 Subsequent: $100

Minimum IRA Investment
Initial: $1,000 Subsequent: $100

Maximum Fees
Load: 2.00% redemption 12b-1: none
Other: redemption fee applies for 60 days

Services
✔ IRA
✔ Keogh
✔ Telephone Exchange

Hussman Strategic Total Return (HSTRX)

800-487-7626
www.hussmanfunds.com

Balanced: Domestic

PERFORMANCE — fund inception date: 9/12/02

	3yr Annual	5yr Annual	10yr Annual	Bull	Bear
Return (%)	8.1	7.3	na	43.6	8.7
Differ From Category (+/-)	11.3 high	6.4 high	na	-33.7 low	33.7 high

Standard Deviation	Category Risk Index	Beta
7.5%—low	0.68—low	0.12

	2008	2007	2006	2005	2004	2003	2002	2001	2000	1999
Return (%)	6.3	12.6	5.6	6.0	6.5	9.8	—	—	—	—
Differ From Category (+/-)	29.7	5.6	-5.3	0.4	-3.5	-12.2	—	—	—	—
Return, Tax-Adjusted (%)	5.2	10.7	4.3	4.6	5.7	8.5	—	—	—	—

PER SHARE DATA

	2008	2007	2006	2005	2004	2003	2002	2001	2000	1999
Dividends, Net Income ($)	0.14	0.37	0.25	0.29	0.21	0.20	—	—	—	—
Distrib'ns, Cap Gain ($)	0.49	0.54	0.43	0.29	0.02	0.37	—	—	—	—
Net Asset Value ($)	11.56	11.50	11.05	11.11	11.05	10.60	—	—	—	—
Expense Ratio (%)	0.90	0.90	0.90	0.90	0.90	0.90	—	—	—	—
Yield (%)	1.16	3.07	2.16	2.56	1.90	1.86	—	—	—	—
Portfolio Turnover (%)	212	41	55	64	174	151	—	—	—	—
Total Assets (Millions $)	577	206	188	127	121	39	—	—	—	—

PORTFOLIO (as of 9/30/08)

Portfolio Manager: Hussman - 2002

Investment Style

Large Cap	Growth
Mid Cap	Grth/Val
Small Cap	Value

Portfolio

6.3%	U.S. stock	0.0%	conv't
7.6%	int'l stock	0.0%	preferred
28.6%	U.S. bonds	0.0%	other
0.0%	int'l bonds	57.5%	cash

Number of Investments: 28
Percent of Portfolio in Top 10 Investments: 84%

SHAREHOLDER INFORMATION

Minimum Investment
Initial: $1,000 Subsequent: $100

Minimum IRA Investment
Initial: $500 Subsequent: $50

Maximum Fees
Load: 1.50% redemption 12b-1: none
Other: redemption fee applies for 60 days

Services
✔ IRA
✔ Keogh
✔ Telephone Exchange

Janus Balanced
(JABAX)

800-525-3713
www.janus.com

Balanced: Domestic

PERFORMANCE — fund inception date: 9/1/92

	3yr Annual	5yr Annual	10yr Annual	Bull	Bear
Return (%)	1.0	3.8	3.9	68.3	-17.0
Differ From Category (+/-)	4.2 high	2.9 high	0.8 abv av	-9.0 av	8.0 high

Standard Deviation	Category Risk Index	Beta
9.2%—blw av	0.84—blw av	0.54

	2008	2007	2006	2005	2004	2003	2002	2001	2000	1999
Return (%)	-15.3	10.1	10.5	7.7	8.7	13.7	-6.6	-5.1	-2.2	23.5
Differ From Category (+/-)	-8.1	3.1	-0.4	2.1	-1.3	-8.3	1.5	-4.2	-7.2	11.9
Return, Tax-Adjusted (%)	-16.6	8.7	9.8	7.0	7.9	13.0	-7.5	-6.1	-4.4	22.2

PER SHARE DATA

	2008	2007	2006	2005	2004	2003	2002	2001	2000	1999
Dividends, Net Income ($)	0.59	0.61	0.43	0.40	0.41	0.37	0.47	0.53	0.96	0.46
Distrib'ns, Cap Gain ($)	0.93	0.84	0.00	0.00	0.00	0.00	0.00	0.00	0.69	0.32
Net Asset Value ($)	20.02	25.41	24.41	22.48	21.25	19.94	17.88	19.63	21.24	23.39
Expense Ratio (%)	na	0.79	0.81	0.80	0.87	0.88	0.84	0.83	0.85	0.91
Yield (%)	2.81	2.33	1.74	1.78	1.92	1.85	2.62	2.69	4.39	1.92
Portfolio Turnover (%)	na	60	50	47	45	73	88	117	87	64
Total Assets (Millions $)	2,303	2,751	2,499	2,569	2,901	3,750	3,902	4,472	4,739	3,420

PORTFOLIO (as of 9/30/08)

Portfolio Manager: Pinto/Smith - 2005

Investment Style

Large Cap	Growth
Mid Cap	Grth/Val
Small Cap	Value

Portfolio

28.9%	U.S. stock	0.0%	conv't
16.4%	int'l stock	0.1%	preferred
38.3%	U.S. bonds	4.2%	other
1.2%	int'l bonds	11.1%	cash

Number of Investments: 241
Percent of Portfolio in Top 10 Investments: 23%

SHAREHOLDER INFORMATION

Minimum Investment
Initial: $2,500 Subsequent: $100

Minimum IRA Investment
Initial: $1,000 Subsequent: $100

Maximum Fees
Load: none 12b-1: none
Other: none

Services
✔ IRA
✔ Keogh
✔ Telephone Exchange

Leuthold Core Investment (LCORX)

800-273-6886
www.leutholdfunds.com

Balanced: Domestic

PERFORMANCE — fund inception date: 11/20/95

	3yr Annual	5yr Annual	10yr Annual	Bull	Bear
Return (%)	-1.1	3.7	7.4	138.1	-26.2
Differ From Category (+/-)	2.1 abv av	2.8 high	4.3 high	60.8 high	-1.2 av

Standard Deviation	Category Risk Index	Beta
14.2%—blw av	1.29—high	0.81

	2008	2007	2006	2005	2004	2003	2002	2001	2000	1999
Return (%)	-27.5	19.0	12.2	14.5	8.2	47.6	-10.1	-4.9	22.7	9.5
Differ From Category (+/-)	-4.1	12.0	1.3	8.9	-1.8	25.6	-2.0	-4.0	17.7	-2.1
Return, Tax-Adjusted (%)	-28.0	15.2	11.1	13.4	7.5	47.2	-10.7	-5.8	19.4	7.8

PER SHARE DATA

	2008	2007	2006	2005	2004	2003	2002	2001	2000	1999
Dividends, Net Income ($)	0.27	0.37	0.46	0.18	0.05	0.10	0.17	0.31	0.57	0.41
Distrib'ns, Cap Gain ($)	0.00	3.75	0.09	0.74	0.64	0.00	0.00	0.00	0.73	0.14
Net Asset Value ($)	12.87	18.06	18.74	17.22	15.86	15.30	10.44	11.79	12.71	11.51
Expense Ratio (%)	1.11	1.15	1.08	1.19	1.21	1.21	1.21	1.24	1.24	1.25
Yield (%)	2.13	1.71	2.46	1.02	0.28	0.62	1.62	2.61	4.25	3.48
Portfolio Turnover (%)	238	144	86	164	133	90	133	122	130	159
Total Assets (Millions $)	803	1,549	1,504	1,357	592	453	126	134	109	61

PORTFOLIO (as of 9/30/08)

Portfolio Manager: Leuthold/Engel/Bjorgen - 1995

Investment Style

Large Cap	Growth
Mid Cap	Grth/Val
Small Cap	Value

Portfolio

49.6%	U.S. stock	0.0%	conv't
12.5%	int'l stock	0.0%	preferred
11.8%	U.S. bonds	5.9%	other
7.3%	int'l bonds	13.0%	cash

Number of Investments: 110
Percent of Portfolio in Top 10 Investments: 42%

SHAREHOLDER INFORMATION

Minimum Investment
Initial: $10,000 Subsequent: $100

Minimum IRA Investment
Initial: $1,000 Subsequent: $100

Maximum Fees
Load: 2.00% redemption 12b-1: none
Other: redemption fee applies for 5 months

Services
✔ IRA
Keogh
✔ Telephone Exchange

Manning & Napier Pro-Blend Cnsrv Term S (EXDAX)

800-466-3863
www.manningnapieradvisors.com

Balanced: Domestic

PERFORMANCE — fund inception date: 11/1/95

	3yr Annual	5yr Annual	10yr Annual	Bull	Bear
Return (%)	3.1	3.9	5.2	37.0	-5.0
Differ From Category (+/-)	6.3 high	3.0 high	2.1 high	-40.3 low	20.0 high

Standard Deviation	Category Risk Index	Beta
4.7%—low	0.43—low	0.25

	2008	2007	2006	2005	2004	2003	2002	2001	2000	1999
Return (%)	-5.1	6.4	8.5	4.2	6.2	7.0	4.2	6.0	13.3	2.0
Differ From Category (+/-)	18.3	-0.6	-2.4	-1.4	-3.8	-15.0	12.3	6.9	8.3	-9.6
Return, Tax-Adjusted (%)	-5.8	5.0	7.3	3.2	5.5	6.1	3.3	3.5	11.0	0.0

PER SHARE DATA

	2008	2007	2006	2005	2004	2003	2002	2001	2000	1999
Dividends, Net Income ($)	0.23	0.29	0.29	0.20	0.18	0.17	0.24	0.47	0.44	0.48
Distrib'ns, Cap Gain ($)	0.00	0.43	0.25	0.32	0.09	0.27	0.04	0.43	0.31	0.10
Net Asset Value ($)	11.24	12.08	12.03	11.58	11.61	11.18	10.85	10.68	10.94	10.33
Expense Ratio (%)	na	0.99	1.00	1.00	1.00	1.00	1.00	1.00	1.00	1.00
Yield (%)	2.04	2.31	2.36	1.67	1.49	1.45	2.17	4.27	3.89	4.61
Portfolio Turnover (%)	na	49	48	60	25	40	0	42	33	33
Total Assets (Millions $)	150	119	78	49	31	21	13	6	5	5

PORTFOLIO (as of 11/30/08)

Portfolio Manager: Coons/Herrmann/Magiera/Tommasi - 1995

Investment Style

Large Cap	Growth
Mid Cap	Grth/Val
Small Cap	Value

Portfolio

21.5%	U.S. stock	0.2%	conv't
4.3%	int'l stock	0.0%	preferred
62.6%	U.S. bonds	0.1%	other
0.0%	int'l bonds	11.4%	cash

Number of Investments: 369
Percent of Portfolio in Top 10 Investments: 58%

SHAREHOLDER INFORMATION

Minimum Investment
Initial: $2,000 Subsequent: $0

Minimum IRA Investment
Initial: $2,000 Subsequent: $0

Maximum Fees
Load: none 12b-1: none
Other: none

Services
✔ IRA
✔ Keogh
✔ Telephone Exchange

Manning & Napier Pro-Blend Extnd Term S (MNBAX)

800-466-3863
www.manningnapieradvisors.com

Balanced: Domestic

PERFORMANCE — fund inception date: 10/12/93

	3yr Annual	5yr Annual	10yr Annual	Bull	Bear
Return (%)	-2.2	2.6	5.1	89.3	-27.3
Differ From Category (+/-)	1.0 abv av	1.7 abv av	2.0 high	12.0 abv av	-2.3 av

Standard Deviation	Category Risk Index	Beta
12.1%—blw av	1.10—abv av	0.76

	2008	2007	2006	2005	2004	2003	2002	2001	2000	1999
Return (%)	-25.4	6.9	17.1	7.5	13.1	19.7	-10.0	3.9	16.3	11.0
Differ From Category (+/-)	-2.0	-0.1	6.2	1.9	3.1	-2.3	-1.9	4.8	11.3	-0.6
Return, Tax-Adjusted (%)	-25.9	4.9	15.4	6.3	12.4	19.2	-10.6	2.1	14.1	8.8

PER SHARE DATA

	2008	2007	2006	2005	2004	2003	2002	2001	2000	1999
Dividends, Net Income ($)	0.24	0.21	0.23	0.14	0.11	0.10	0.19	0.31	0.31	0.33
Distrib'ns, Cap Gain ($)	0.00	1.72	1.15	0.95	0.36	0.09	0.00	0.62	0.78	0.69
Net Asset Value ($)	11.30	15.44	16.26	15.05	15.00	13.68	11.59	13.08	13.50	12.57
Expense Ratio (%)	na	1.11	1.14	1.17	1.17	1.17	1.19	1.20	1.20	1.15
Yield (%)	2.10	1.20	1.29	0.84	0.72	0.75	1.59	2.26	2.17	2.48
Portfolio Turnover (%)	na	82	82	71	50	67	82	75	95	78
Total Assets (Millions $)	415	588	510	377	302	225	162	153	92	65

PORTFOLIO (as of 11/30/08)

Portfolio Manager: Coons/Herrmann/Magiera/Tommasi - 1995

Investment Style

Large Cap	Growth
Mid Cap	Grth/Val
Small Cap	Value

Portfolio

55.3%	U.S. stock	0.3%	conv't
13.1%	int'l stock	0.1%	preferred
29.2%	U.S. bonds	0.2%	other
0.0%	int'l bonds	1.8%	cash

Number of Investments: 360
Percent of Portfolio in Top 10 Investments: 31%

SHAREHOLDER INFORMATION

Minimum Investment
Initial: $2,000 Subsequent: $0

Minimum IRA Investment
Initial: $2,000 Subsequent: $0

Maximum Fees
Load: none 12b-1: none
Other: none

Services
✔ IRA
✔ Keogh
✔ Telephone Exchange

Manning & Napier Pro-Blend Mod Term S (EXBAX)

800-466-3863
www.manningnapieradvisors.com

Balanced: Domestic

PERFORMANCE — fund inception date: 9/15/93

	3yr Annual	5yr Annual	10yr Annual	Bull	Bear
Return (%)	-0.4	3.0	4.7	68.3	-19.9
Differ From Category (+/-)	2.8 abv av	2.1 high	1.6 abv av	-9.0 av	5.1 abv av

Standard Deviation	Category Risk Index	Beta
9.3%—blw av	0.85—blw av	0.58

	2008	2007	2006	2005	2004	2003	2002	2001	2000	1999
Return (%)	-18.5	6.3	13.9	6.4	10.5	15.0	-6.7	3.4	16.6	5.4
Differ From Category (+/-)	4.9	-0.7	3.0	0.8	0.5	-7.0	1.4	4.3	11.6	-6.2
Return, Tax-Adjusted (%)	-19.1	4.5	12.6	5.3	9.8	14.5	-7.3	1.5	13.2	3.6

PER SHARE DATA

	2008	2007	2006	2005	2004	2003	2002	2001	2000	1999
Dividends, Net Income ($)	0.21	0.23	0.22	0.13	0.11	0.10	0.17	0.33	0.35	0.39
Distrib'ns, Cap Gain ($)	0.00	1.02	0.56	0.62	0.22	0.12	0.00	0.43	1.16	0.25
Net Asset Value ($)	10.15	12.70	13.13	12.21	12.17	11.32	10.03	10.93	11.31	11.03
Expense Ratio (%)	na	1.11	1.16	1.20	1.20	1.20	1.20	1.20	0.00	1.20
Yield (%)	2.10	1.67	1.57	0.97	0.89	0.88	1.68	2.87	2.78	3.44
Portfolio Turnover (%)	na	78	72	77	42	60	0	77	0	45
Total Assets (Millions $)	243	381	309	196	103	69	49	38	18	25

PORTFOLIO (as of 11/30/08)

Portfolio Manager: Coons/Herrmann/Magiera/Tommasi - 1995

Investment Style

Large Cap	Growth
Mid Cap	Grth/Val
Small Cap	Value

Portfolio

39.9%	U.S. stock	0.4%	conv't
8.7%	int'l stock	0.1%	preferred
43.5%	U.S. bonds	0.1%	other
0.0%	int'l bonds	7.3%	cash

Number of Investments: 363
Percent of Portfolio in Top 10 Investments: 37%

SHAREHOLDER INFORMATION

Minimum Investment
Initial: $2,000 Subsequent: $0

Minimum IRA Investment
Initial: $2,000 Subsequent: $0

Maximum Fees
Load: none 12b-1: none
Other: none

Services
✔ IRA
✔ Keogh
✔ Telephone Exchange

Oakmark Equity & Income I (OAKBX)

800-625-6275
www.oakmark.com

Balanced: Domestic

PERFORMANCE

fund inception date: 11/1/95

	3yr Annual	5yr Annual	10yr Annual	Bull	Bear
Return (%)	1.3	4.5	8.6	89.8	-17.3
Differ From Category (+/-)	4.5 high	3.6 high	5.5 high	12.5 abv av	7.7 high

Standard Deviation	Category Risk Index	Beta
8.7%—blw av	0.79—blw av	0.50

	2008	2007	2006	2005	2004	2003	2002	2001	2000	1999
Return (%)	-16.2	11.9	10.8	8.6	10.3	23.2	-2.2	18.0	19.8	7.9
Differ From Category (+/-)	7.2	4.9	-0.1	3.0	0.3	1.2	5.9	18.9	14.8	-3.7
Return, Tax-Adjusted (%)	-17.1	10.2	9.3	7.9	9.6	22.9	-2.7	17.5	17.8	4.8

PER SHARE DATA

	2008	2007	2006	2005	2004	2003	2002	2001	2000	1999
Dividends, Net Income ($)	0.39	0.60	0.50	0.34	0.20	0.14	0.24	0.15	0.24	0.45
Distrib'ns, Cap Gain ($)	0.57	1.51	1.31	0.20	0.59	0.00	0.00	0.04	1.00	1.36
Net Asset Value ($)	21.56	26.88	25.88	24.98	23.50	22.02	17.99	18.63	15.96	14.40
Expense Ratio (%)	0.81	0.83	0.86	0.92	0.92	0.93	0.96	0.98	1.24	1.18
Yield (%)	1.74	2.13	1.84	1.35	0.83	0.62	1.34	0.82	1.43	2.86
Portfolio Turnover (%)	65	67	81	112	72	48	73	124	87	81
Total Assets (Millions $)	11,538	12,830	10,851	9,513	8,129	5,172	2,748	1,099	75	58

PORTFOLIO (as of 9/30/08)

Portfolio Manager: McGregor/Studzinski - 1995

Investment Style

Large Cap	Growth
Mid Cap	Grth/Val
Small Cap	Value

Portfolio

43.5%	U.S. stock	0.0%	conv't
7.6%	int'l stock	0.0%	preferred
33.0%	U.S. bonds	0.1%	other
0.3%	int'l bonds	15.4%	cash

Number of Investments: 99

Percent of Portfolio in Top 10 Investments: 35%

SHAREHOLDER INFORMATION

Minimum Investment

Initial: $1,000 Subsequent: $100

Minimum IRA Investment

Initial: $1,000 Subsequent: $100

Maximum Fees

Load: none 12b-1: none

Other: none

Services

✔ IRA

✔ Keogh

✔ Telephone Exchange

Permanent Portfolio (PRPFX)

800-531-5142
www.permanentportfolio funds.com

Balanced: Domestic

PERFORMANCE — fund inception date: 12/1/82

	3yr Annual	5yr Annual	10yr Annual	Bull	Bear
Return (%)	5.4	7.1	8.0	85.2	-8.8
Differ From Category (+/-)	8.6 high	6.2 high	4.9 high	7.9 abv av	16.2 high

Standard Deviation	Category Risk Index	Beta
11.3%—blw av	1.03—av	0.48

	2008	2007	2006	2005	2004	2003	2002	2001	2000	1999
Return (%)	-8.4	12.4	13.8	7.6	12.0	20.4	14.3	3.8	5.8	1.1
Differ From Category (+/-)	15.0	5.4	2.9	2.0	2.0	-1.6	22.4	4.7	0.8	-10.5
Return, Tax-Adjusted (%)	-8.7	12.1	13.6	7.3	11.5	20.0	13.6	3.0	4.9	-0.3

PER SHARE DATA

	2008	2007	2006	2005	2004	2003	2002	2001	2000	1999
Dividends, Net Income ($)	0.25	0.16	0.06	0.20	0.15	0.22	0.19	0.27	0.16	0.29
Distrib'ns, Cap Gain ($)	0.04	0.18	0.25	0.05	0.39	0.08	0.26	0.17	0.52	0.77
Net Asset Value ($)	32.71	36.04	32.36	28.70	26.90	24.49	20.59	18.41	18.16	17.81
Expense Ratio (%)	0.95	1.11	1.35	1.38	1.58	1.34	1.46	1.41	1.47	1.43
Yield (%)	0.76	0.44	0.18	0.69	0.54	0.89	0.91	1.45	0.85	1.56
Portfolio Turnover (%)	37	7	1	6	23	1	1	7	23	14
Total Assets (Millions $)	3,390	1,460	761	333	238	113	72	52	54	59

PORTFOLIO (as of 11/30/08)

Portfolio Manager: Cuggino - 1991

Investment Style

Large Cap	Growth
Mid Cap	Grth/Val
Small Cap	Value

Portfolio

33.5%	U.S. stock	0.0%	conv't
2.7%	int'l stock	0.0%	preferred
26.9%	U.S. bonds	20.1%	other
8.9%	int'l bonds	8.0%	cash

Number of Investments: 129
Percent of Portfolio in Top 10 Investments: 46%

SHAREHOLDER INFORMATION

Minimum Investment
Initial: $1,000 Subsequent: $100

Minimum IRA Investment
Initial: $1,000 Subsequent: $100

Maximum Fees
Load: none 12b-1: none
Other: none

Services
✔ IRA
✔ Keogh
✔ Telephone Exchange

Schwab MarketTrack Conservative (SWCGX)

800-435-4000
www.schwab.com

Balanced: Domestic

PERFORMANCE — fund inception date: 11/20/95

	3yr Annual	5yr Annual	10yr Annual	Bull	Bear
Return (%)	-2.2	1.0	2.5	53.3	-19.9
Differ From Category (+/-)	1.0 abv av	0.1 av	-0.6 av	-24.0 low	5.1 abv av

Standard Deviation	Category Risk Index	Beta
8.0%—low	0.73—low	0.50

	2008	2007	2006	2005	2004	2003	2002	2001	2000	1999
Return (%)	-18.4	4.9	9.5	3.9	7.8	15.0	-4.1	-0.4	2.7	8.6
Differ From Category (+/-)	5.0	-2.1	-1.4	-1.7	-2.2	-7.0	4.0	0.5	-2.3	-2.9
Return, Tax-Adjusted (%)	-19.6	3.5	8.0	3.0	6.9	13.9	-5.1	-2.0	0.9	7.4

PER SHARE DATA

	2008	2007	2006	2005	2004	2003	2002	2001	2000	1999
Dividends, Net Income ($)	0.43	0.48	0.49	0.36	0.30	0.35	0.34	0.51	0.55	0.37
Distrib'ns, Cap Gain ($)	0.09	0.13	0.19	0.01	0.00	0.00	0.00	0.06	0.09	0.03
Net Asset Value ($)	11.14	14.25	14.17	13.57	13.41	12.73	11.38	12.21	12.83	13.12
Expense Ratio (%)	na	0.50	0.50	0.50	0.50	0.50	0.50	0.50	0.56	0.57
Yield (%)	3.83	3.35	3.37	2.64	2.26	2.74	2.98	4.12	4.28	2.78
Portfolio Turnover (%)	na	4	11	9	10	17	32	15	16	8
Total Assets (Millions $)	177	243	235	313	306	298	267	219	197	178

PORTFOLIO (as of 7/31/08)

Portfolio Manager: Hung/Hastings/Mano/Lee/Kern - 2005

Investment Style

Large Cap	Growth
Mid Cap	Grth/Val
Small Cap	Value

Portfolio

27.4%	U.S. stock	0.0%	conv't
8.7%	int'l stock	0.3%	preferred
47.7%	U.S. bonds	1.6%	other
0.5%	int'l bonds	13.9%	cash

Number of Investments: 508

Percent of Portfolio in Top 10 Investments: 95%

SHAREHOLDER INFORMATION

Minimum Investment

Initial: $100 Subsequent: $0

Minimum IRA Investment

Initial: $0 Subsequent: $0

Maximum Fees

Load: 2.00% redemption 12b-1: none

Other: redemption fee applies for 30 days

Services

✔ IRA

✔ Keogh

✔ Telephone Exchange

T. Rowe Price Personal Strat Income (PRSIX)

800-638-5660
www.troweprice.com

Balanced: Domestic

PERFORMANCE — fund inception date: 7/29/94

	3yr Annual	5yr Annual	10yr Annual	Bull	Bear
Return (%)	-2.2	1.6	3.4	65.8	-21.7
Differ From Category (+/-)	1.0 abv av	0.7 abv av	0.3 abv av	-11.5 blw av	3.3 abv av

Standard Deviation	Category Risk Index	Beta
9.3%—blw av	0.85—blw av	0.59

	2008	2007	2006	2005	2004	2003	2002	2001	2000	1999
Return (%)	-20.4	7.2	9.6	5.1	9.9	18.5	-3.4	0.9	6.5	5.1
Differ From Category (+/-)	3.0	0.2	-1.3	-0.5	-0.1	-3.5	4.7	1.8	1.5	-6.5
Return, Tax-Adjusted (%)	-21.4	5.4	8.3	4.1	9.0	17.6	-4.6	-0.5	4.7	3.0

PER SHARE DATA

	2008	2007	2006	2005	2004	2003	2002	2001	2000	1999
Dividends, Net Income ($)	0.45	0.51	0.46	0.35	0.35	0.32	0.38	0.48	0.53	0.53
Distrib'ns, Cap Gain ($)	0.01	0.77	0.20	0.18	0.04	0.01	0.00	0.00	0.16	0.37
Net Asset Value ($)	12.08	15.69	15.84	15.07	14.84	13.87	12.00	12.81	13.18	13.03
Expense Ratio (%)	0.62	0.71	0.78	0.76	0.75	0.80	0.90	0.90	0.90	0.90
Yield (%)	3.72	3.09	2.86	2.29	2.35	2.30	3.16	3.74	3.97	3.95
Portfolio Turnover (%)	81	70	53	84	98	108	116	79	45	48
Total Assets (Millions $)	627	772	603	483	371	344	259	252	228	206

PORTFOLIO (as of 9/30/08)

Portfolio Manager: Notzon III - 1998

Investment Style

Large Cap	Growth
Mid Cap	Grth/Val
Small Cap	Value

Portfolio

32.1%	U.S. stock	0.0%	conv't
9.6%	int'l stock	0.2%	preferred
38.2%	U.S. bonds	1.0%	other
2.8%	int'l bonds	16.0%	cash

Number of Investments: 1,315

Percent of Portfolio in Top 10 Investments: 27%

SHAREHOLDER INFORMATION

Minimum Investment

Initial: $2,500 Subsequent: $100

Minimum IRA Investment

Initial: $1,000 Subsequent: $50

Maximum Fees

Load: none 12b-1: none

Other: none

Services

✔ IRA

✔ Keogh

✔ Telephone Exchange

Value Line Income & Growth (VALIX)

800-243-2729
www.valueline.com

Balanced: Domestic

PERFORMANCE — fund inception date: 10/1/52

	3yr Annual	5yr Annual	10yr Annual	Bull	Bear
Return (%)	-2.1	3.4	4.2	96.9	-23.2
Differ From Category (+/-)	1.1 abv av	2.5 high	1.1 abv av	19.6 high	1.8 abv av

Standard Deviation	Category Risk Index	Beta
10.7%—blw av	0.97—av	0.67

	2008	2007	2006	2005	2004	2003	2002	2001	2000	1999
Return (%)	-21.6	7.8	11.0	9.9	14.3	24.4	-12.1	-5.2	-1.7	25.3
Differ From Category (+/-)	-1.8	0.8	0.1	4.3	4.3	2.4	-4.0	-4.3	-6.7	13.7
Return, Tax-Adjusted (%)	-22.6	6.0	9.3	8.1	12.2	23.1	-12.8	-6.3	-3.8	21.3

PER SHARE DATA

	2008	2007	2006	2005	2004	2003	2002	2001	2000	1999
Dividends, Net Income ($)	0.23	0.19	0.17	0.15	0.11	0.10	0.11	0.12	0.13	0.11
Distrib'ns, Cap Gain ($)	0.03	0.60	0.54	0.66	0.94	0.36	0.08	0.24	0.81	1.67
Net Asset Value ($)	6.39	8.45	8.57	8.37	8.35	8.23	7.00	8.17	9.00	10.10
Expense Ratio (%)	na	1.04	1.06	1.09	1.11	1.15	1.15	1.08	0.95	0.83
Yield (%)	3.66	2.04	1.86	1.66	1.15	1.22	1.51	1.36	1.32	0.93
Portfolio Turnover (%)	na	56	62	71	103	106	155	88	41	64
Total Assets (Millions $)	308	386	358	277	231	208	189	198	218	229

PORTFOLIO (as of 9/30/08)

Portfolio Manager: Brooks - 2002

Investment Style

Large Cap	Growth
Mid Cap	Grth/Val
Small Cap	Value

Portfolio

45.5%	U.S. stock	4.4%	conv't
7.8%	int'l stock	0.5%	preferred
23.2%	U.S. bonds	0.0%	other
0.0%	int'l bonds	18.6%	cash

Number of Investments: 403

Percent of Portfolio in Top 10 Investments: 23%

SHAREHOLDER INFORMATION

Minimum Investment

Initial: $1,000 Subsequent: $100

Minimum IRA Investment

Initial: $1,000 Subsequent: $100

Maximum Fees

Load: none 12b-1: 0.25%

Other: none

Services

✔ IRA

✔ Keogh

✔ Telephone Exchange

Vanguard Balanced Index (VBINX)

800-997-2798
www.vanguard.com

Balanced: Domestic

PERFORMANCE **fund inception date: 11/9/92**

	3yr Annual	5yr Annual	10yr Annual	Bull	Bear
Return (%)	-2.9	0.9	2.0	68.4	-23.9
Differ From Category (+/-)	0.3 av	0.0 av	-1.1 av	-8.9 av	1.1 abv av

Standard Deviation	Category Risk Index	Beta
9.9%—blw av	0.90—blw av	0.64

	2008	2007	2006	2005	2004	2003	2002	2001	2000	1999
Return (%)	-22.3	6.1	11.0	4.6	9.3	19.8	-9.6	-3.1	-2.1	13.6
Differ From Category (+/-)	1.1	-0.9	0.1	-1.0	-0.7	-2.2	-1.5	-2.2	-7.1	2.0
Return, Tax-Adjusted (%)	-23.2	5.0	9.9	3.6	8.3	18.8	-10.7	-4.3	-3.5	12.2

PER SHARE DATA

	2008	2007	2006	2005	2004	2003	2002	2001	2000	1999
Dividends, Net Income ($)	0.60	0.66	0.60	0.53	0.50	0.45	0.52	0.60	0.65	0.58
Distrib'ns, Cap Gain ($)	0.00	0.00	0.00	0.00	0.00	0.00	0.00	0.03	0.10	0.14
Net Asset Value ($)	16.59	22.01	21.36	19.81	19.45	18.27	15.65	17.86	19.08	20.22
Expense Ratio (%)	na	0.19	0.20	0.20	0.20	0.22	0.22	0.22	0.22	0.20
Yield (%)	3.63	2.99	2.80	2.67	2.57	2.46	3.32	3.33	3.37	2.84
Portfolio Turnover (%)	na	26	33	31	26	27	40	33	28	29
Total Assets (Millions $)	2,731	3,717	3,926	4,098	4,674	3,895	2,990	3,117	3,586	3,128

PORTFOLIO (as of 9/30/08)

Portfolio Manager: Perre/Davis - 2000

Investment Style

Large Cap	Growth
Mid Cap	Grth/Val
Small Cap	Value

Portfolio

59.7% U.S. stock	0.0% conv't
0.2% int'l stock	0.0% preferred
38.3% U.S. bonds	0.1% other
1.0% int'l bonds	0.8% cash

Number of Investments: 7,449
Percent of Portfolio in Top 10 Investments: 10%

SHAREHOLDER INFORMATION

Minimum Investment
Initial: $3,000 Subsequent: $100

Minimum IRA Investment
Initial: $3,000 Subsequent: $100

Maximum Fees
Load: none 12b-1: none
Other: none

Services
✔ IRA
✔ Keogh
✔ Telephone Exchange

Vanguard LifeStrategy Conservative Gr (VSCGX)

800-997-2798
www.vanguard.com

Balanced: Domestic

PERFORMANCE

fund inception date: 9/30/94

	3yr Annual	5yr Annual	10yr Annual	Bull	Bear
Return (%)	-1.7	1.4	2.8	60.1	-20.6
Differ From Category (+/-)	1.5 abv av	0.5 abv av	-0.3 av	-17.2 blw av	4.4 abv av

Standard Deviation	Category Risk Index	Beta
8.5%—blw av	0.77—low	0.54

	2008	2007	2006	2005	2004	2003	2002	2001	2000	1999
Return (%)	-19.6	6.9	10.6	4.4	8.0	16.5	-5.4	-0.1	3.1	7.8
Differ From Category (+/-)	3.8	-0.1	-0.3	-1.2	-2.0	-5.5	2.7	0.8	-1.9	-3.8
Return, Tax-Adjusted (%)	-20.7	5.7	9.4	3.4	6.9	15.5	-6.8	-1.7	1.0	6.0

PER SHARE DATA

	2008	2007	2006	2005	2004	2003	2002	2001	2000	1999
Dividends, Net Income ($)	0.55	0.59	0.52	0.44	0.43	0.38	0.49	0.58	0.70	0.63
Distrib'ns, Cap Gain ($)	0.00	0.01	0.00	0.00	0.00	0.00	0.00	0.04	0.16	0.11
Net Asset Value ($)	13.30	17.14	16.59	15.49	15.26	14.54	12.82	14.06	14.71	15.10
Expense Ratio (%)	na	0.00	0.00	0.00	0.00	0.00	0.00	0.00	0.00	0.00
Yield (%)	4.11	3.44	3.13	2.84	2.81	2.61	3.82	4.11	4.70	4.14
Portfolio Turnover (%)	na	10	4	7	5	5	12	14	9	5
Total Assets (Millions $)	4,806	6,921	5,567	4,324	3,650	2,924	2,193	2,026	1,897	1,748

PORTFOLIO (as of 9/30/08)

Portfolio Manager: No Manager - 1994

Investment Style

Large Cap	Growth
Mid Cap	Grth/Val
Small Cap	Value

Portfolio

39.2%	U.S. stock	0.0%	conv't
4.7%	int'l stock	0.2%	preferred
45.2%	U.S. bonds	1.6%	other
1.0%	int'l bonds	8.1%	cash

Number of Investments: 6

Percent of Portfolio in Top 10 Investments: 100%

SHAREHOLDER INFORMATION

Minimum Investment

Initial: $3,000 Subsequent: $100

Minimum IRA Investment

Initial: $3,000 Subsequent: $100

Maximum Fees

Load: none 12b-1: none

Other: none

Services

✔ IRA

✔ Keogh

✔ Telephone Exchange

Vanguard LifeStrategy Growth (VASGX)

800-997-2798
www.vanguard.com

Balanced: Domestic

PERFORMANCE — fund inception date: 9/30/94

	3yr Annual	5yr Annual	10yr Annual	Bull	Bear
Return (%)	-6.5	-0.3	0.7	109.5	-37.1
Differ From Category (+/-)	-3.3 low	-1.2 blw av	-2.4 low	32.2 high	-12.1 low

Standard Deviation	Category Risk Index	Beta
14.6%—blw av	1.33—high	0.95

	2008	2007	2006	2005	2004	2003	2002	2001	2000	1999
Return (%)	-34.4	7.4	16.1	6.8	12.5	28.5	-15.9	-8.9	-5.5	17.3
Differ From Category (+/-)	-11.0	0.4	5.2	1.2	2.5	6.5	-7.8	-8.0	-10.5	5.7
Return, Tax-Adjusted (%)	-35.1	6.6	15.3	6.1	11.8	27.8	-16.6	-9.7	-6.6	16.2

PER SHARE DATA

	2008	2007	2006	2005	2004	2003	2002	2001	2000	1999
Dividends, Net Income ($)	0.50	0.58	0.49	0.41	0.39	0.28	0.32	0.37	0.51	0.45
Distrib'ns, Cap Gain ($)	0.00	0.00	0.00	0.00	0.00	0.00	0.00	0.06	0.17	0.16
Net Asset Value ($)	16.00	25.07	23.87	21.00	20.04	18.16	14.36	17.43	19.59	21.41
Expense Ratio (%)	na	0.00	0.00	0.00	0.00	0.00	0.00	0.00	0.00	0.00
Yield (%)	3.14	2.31	2.05	1.95	1.94	1.54	2.22	2.11	2.58	2.08
Portfolio Turnover (%)	na	4	3	4	5	2	7	7	9	1
Total Assets (Millions $)	6,016	9,860	8,783	7,001	6,040	4,754	3,281	3,726	3,738	3,177

PORTFOLIO (as of 9/30/08)

Portfolio Manager: No Manager - 1994

Investment Style

Large Cap	Growth
Mid Cap	Grth/Val
Small Cap	Value

Portfolio

69.0%	U.S. stock	0.0%	conv't
14.2%	int'l stock	0.0%	preferred
9.6%	U.S. bonds	1.2%	other
0.2%	int'l bonds	5.7%	cash

Number of Investments: 5

Percent of Portfolio in Top 10 Investments: 100%

SHAREHOLDER INFORMATION

Minimum Investment

Initial: $3,000 Subsequent: $100

Minimum IRA Investment

Initial: $3,000 Subsequent: $100

Maximum Fees

Load: none 12b-1: none

Other: none

Services

✔ IRA

✔ Keogh

✔ Telephone Exchange

Vanguard LifeStrategy Income (VASIX)

800-997-2798
www.vanguard.com

Balanced: Domestic

PERFORMANCE — fund inception date: 9/30/94

	3yr Annual	5yr Annual	10yr Annual	Bull	Bear
Return (%)	1.0	2.4	3.7	39.7	-10.4
Differ From Category (+/-)	4.2 high	1.5 abv av	0.6 abv av	-37.6 low	14.6 high

Standard Deviation	Category Risk Index	Beta
5.7%—low	0.52—low	0.34

	2008	2007	2006	2005	2004	2003	2002	2001	2000	1999
Return (%)	-10.6	6.6	7.9	3.2	6.0	10.7	0.1	4.0	8.0	2.8
Differ From Category (+/-)	12.8	-0.3	-3.0	-2.4	-4.0	-11.3	8.2	4.9	3.0	-8.8
Return, Tax-Adjusted (%)	-11.9	5.2	6.4	2.0	4.8	9.5	-1.6	2.0	5.6	0.6

PER SHARE DATA

	2008	2007	2006	2005	2004	2003	2002	2001	2000	1999
Dividends, Net Income ($)	0.54	0.58	0.54	0.47	0.45	0.43	0.55	0.64	0.74	0.69
Distrib'ns, Cap Gain ($)	0.00	0.03	0.07	0.00	0.00	0.00	0.00	0.01	0.08	0.07
Net Asset Value ($)	12.23	14.24	13.93	13.49	13.53	13.20	12.32	12.86	13.01	12.82
Expense Ratio (%)	na	0.00	0.00	0.00	0.00	0.00	0.00	0.00	0.00	0.00
Yield (%)	4.41	4.06	3.85	3.48	3.32	3.25	4.46	5.00	5.65	5.35
Portfolio Turnover (%)	na	8	14	6	4	4	10	4	17	11
Total Assets (Millions $)	1,639	1,887	1,690	1,708	1,654	1,404	1,028	809	632	555

PORTFOLIO (as of 9/30/08)

Portfolio Manager: No Manager - 1994

Investment Style

Large Cap	Growth
Mid Cap	Grth/Val
Small Cap	Value

Portfolio

24.1%	U.S. stock	0.0%	conv't
0.0%	int'l stock	0.2%	preferred
64.5%	U.S. bonds	1.6%	other
1.4%	int'l bonds	8.1%	cash

Number of Investments: 5

Percent of Portfolio in Top 10 Investments: 100%

SHAREHOLDER INFORMATION

Minimum Investment

Initial: $3,000 Subsequent: $100

Minimum IRA Investment

Initial: $3,000 Subsequent: $100

Maximum Fees

Load: none 12b-1: none

Other: none

Services

✔ IRA
✔ Keogh
✔ Telephone Exchange

Vanguard LifeStrategy Moderate Growth (VSMGX)

800-997-2798
www.vanguard.com

Balanced: Domestic

PERFORMANCE — fund inception date: 9/30/94

	3yr Annual	5yr Annual	10yr Annual	Bull	Bear
Return (%)	-3.7	0.8	1.9	83.7	-28.5
Differ From Category (+/-)	-0.5 av	-0.1 av	-1.2 blw av	6.4 abv av	-3.5 blw av

Standard Deviation	Category Risk Index	Beta
11.4%—blw av	1.04—av	0.74

	2008	2007	2006	2005	2004	2003	2002	2001	2000	1999
Return (%)	-26.5	7.3	13.3	5.6	10.5	22.3	-10.4	-4.5	-0.9	12.0
Differ From Category (+/-)	-3.1	0.3	2.4	0.0	0.5	0.4	-2.3	-3.6	-5.9	0.4
Return, Tax-Adjusted (%)	-27.5	6.2	12.2	4.8	9.6	21.5	-11.4	-5.7	-2.5	10.5

PER SHARE DATA

	2008	2007	2006	2005	2004	2003	2002	2001	2000	1999
Dividends, Net Income ($)	0.56	0.62	0.54	0.45	0.44	0.35	0.43	0.49	0.64	0.55
Distrib'ns, Cap Gain ($)	0.00	0.02	0.00	0.00	0.00	0.00	0.00	0.06	0.14	0.13
Net Asset Value ($)	15.08	21.21	20.36	18.47	17.91	16.61	13.87	15.93	17.25	18.18
Expense Ratio (%)	na	0.00	0.00	0.00	0.00	0.00	0.00	0.00	0.00	0.00
Yield (%)	3.71	2.91	2.65	2.43	2.45	2.10	3.06	3.06	3.68	3.00
Portfolio Turnover (%)	na	7	8	8	6	5	15	16	12	3
Total Assets (Millions $)	7,202	10,901	9,802	8,023	7,002	5,649	3,985	4,243	3,911	3,441

PORTFOLIO (as of 9/30/08)

Portfolio Manager: No Manager - 1994

Investment Style

Large Cap	Growth
Mid Cap	Grth/Val
Small Cap	Value

Portfolio

54.9%	U.S. stock	0.0%	conv't
9.6%	int'l stock	0.0%	preferred
28.8%	U.S. bonds	1.2%	other
0.7%	int'l bonds	4.9%	cash

Number of Investments: 5

Percent of Portfolio in Top 10 Investments: 100%

SHAREHOLDER INFORMATION

Minimum Investment

Initial: $3,000 Subsequent: $100

Minimum IRA Investment

Initial: $3,000 Subsequent: $100

Maximum Fees

Load: none 12b-1: none

Other: none

Services

✔ IRA

✔ Keogh

✔ Telephone Exchange

Vanguard Wellesley Income (VWINX)

800-662-6273
www.vanguard.com

Balanced: Domestic

PERFORMANCE — fund inception date: 7/1/70

	3yr Annual	5yr Annual	10yr Annual	Bull	Bear
Return (%)	1.9	3.3	4.9	46.5	-10.4
Differ From Category (+/-)	5.1 high	2.4 high	1.8 high	-30.8 low	14.6 high

Standard Deviation	Category Risk Index	Beta
6.5%—low	0.59—low	0.36

	2008	2007	2006	2005	2004	2003	2002	2001	2000	1999
Return (%)	-9.9	5.6	11.2	3.4	7.5	9.6	4.6	7.3	16.1	-4.2
Differ From Category (+/-)	13.5	-1.4	0.3	-2.2	-2.5	-12.4	12.7	8.2	11.1	-15.8
Return, Tax-Adjusted (%)	-11.7	3.9	9.2	1.8	6.1	8.1	2.8	4.6	13.5	-7.3

PER SHARE DATA

	2008	2007	2006	2005	2004	2003	2002	2001	2000	1999
Dividends, Net Income ($)	0.99	0.94	0.92	0.87	0.84	0.87	0.91	1.00	1.06	1.12
Distrib'ns, Cap Gain ($)	0.32	0.26	0.67	0.38	0.04	0.00	0.00	0.86	0.40	1.25
Net Asset Value ($)	18.40	21.82	21.81	21.07	21.58	20.91	19.90	19.91	20.34	18.85
Expense Ratio (%)	0.25	0.25	0.25	0.24	0.26	0.31	0.30	0.33	0.31	0.30
Yield (%)	5.26	4.25	4.07	4.04	3.88	4.16	4.57	4.83	5.11	5.57
Portfolio Turnover (%)	27	21	19	18	23	28	43	24	28	20
Total Assets (Millions $)	6,876	7,941	7,743	7,614	9,268	8,439	7,484	6,495	6,558	6,976

PORTFOLIO (as of 9/30/08)

Portfolio Manager: Keogh/Reckmeyer III - 2008

Investment Style

Large Cap	Growth
Mid Cap	Grth/Val
Small Cap	Value

Portfolio

34.0%	U.S. stock	0.1%	conv't
4.1%	int'l stock	0.0%	preferred
51.3%	U.S. bonds	0.0%	other
6.2%	int'l bonds	4.3%	cash

Number of Investments: 731

Percent of Portfolio in Top 10 Investments: 15%

SHAREHOLDER INFORMATION

Minimum Investment
Initial: $3,000 Subsequent: $100

Minimum IRA Investment
Initial: $3,000 Subsequent: $0

Maximum Fees
Load: none 12b-1: none
Other: none

Services
✔ IRA
✔ Keogh
✔ Telephone Exchange

Vanguard Wellington (VWELX)

800-662-6273
www.vanguard.com

Balanced: Domestic

PERFORMANCE — fund inception date: 7/1/29

	3yr Annual	5yr Annual	10yr Annual	Bull	Bear
Return (%)	-1.1	2.8	4.4	88.1	-23.7
Differ From Category (+/-)	2.1 abv av	1.9 abv av	1.3 abv av	10.8 abv av	1.3 abv av

Standard Deviation	Category Risk Index	Beta
10.7%—blw av	0.97—av	0.67

	2008	2007	2006	2005	2004	2003	2002	2001	2000	1999
Return (%)	-22.3	8.3	14.9	6.8	11.1	20.7	-7.0	4.1	10.3	4.4
Differ From Category (+/-)	1.1	1.3	4.0	1.2	1.1	-1.3	1.2	5.0	5.4	-7.2
Return, Tax-Adjusted (%)	-23.5	6.5	13.1	5.2	9.6	19.6	-8.1	2.0	7.8	1.8

PER SHARE DATA

	2008	2007	2006	2005	2004	2003	2002	2001	2000	1999
Dividends, Net Income ($)	1.04	1.08	0.98	0.90	0.88	0.76	0.84	0.95	1.07	1.14
Distrib'ns, Cap Gain ($)	0.00	1.42	1.40	0.97	0.91	0.00	0.00	1.12	1.48	1.50
Net Asset Value ($)	24.43	32.62	32.44	30.35	30.19	28.81	24.56	27.26	28.21	27.96
Expense Ratio (%)	na	0.27	0.30	0.29	0.31	0.36	0.36	0.36	0.31	0.30
Yield (%)	4.24	3.17	2.89	2.87	2.81	2.65	3.42	3.34	3.60	3.86
Portfolio Turnover (%)	na	23	25	24	24	28	25	33	33	22
Total Assets (Millions $)	23,233	30,979	29,675	26,251	28,328	24,326	19,495	21,724	22,799	25,529

PORTFOLIO (as of 9/30/08)

Portfolio Manager: Bousa/Keogh - 2002

Investment Style

Large Cap	Growth
Mid Cap	Grth/Val
Small Cap	Value

Portfolio

51.8%	U.S. stock	0.0%	conv't
12.7%	int'l stock	0.1%	preferred
31.9%	U.S. bonds	0.2%	other
1.6%	int'l bonds	1.8%	cash

Number of Investments: 2,366

Percent of Portfolio in Top 10 Investments: 16%

SHAREHOLDER INFORMATION

Minimum Investment

Initial: $10,000 Subsequent: $100

Minimum IRA Investment

Initial: $10,000 Subsequent: $100

Maximum Fees

Load: none 12b-1: none

Other: none

Services

✔ IRA
✔ Keogh
✔ Telephone Exchange

Balanced: Global Funds
Category Performance Ranked by 2008 Returns

Fund (Ticker)	Annual Return (%) 2008	3Yr	5Yr	10Yr	Category Risk	Total Risk
Fidelity Global Balanced (FGBLX)	-23.3	-0.3	4.2	4.7	blw av	blw av
American Century One Choice: Mod (AOMIX)	-26.0	-2.8	na	na	blw av	blw av
USAA Cornerstone Strategy (USCRX)	-34.5	-7.6	-1.5	1.3	av	blw av
Janus Smart Portfolio Growth (JSPGX)	-35.0	-3.8	na	na	abv av	av
Balanced: Global Category Average	**-27.8**	**-4.8**	**0.7**	**2.0**	**av**	**blw av**

American Century One Choice: Mod (AOMIX)

800-345-2021
www.americancentury.com

Balanced: Global

PERFORMANCE — fund inception date: 9/30/04

	3yr Annual	5yr Annual	10yr Annual	Bull	Bear
Return (%)	-2.8	na	na	na	-27.6
Differ From Category (+/-)	2.0 abv av	na	na	na	2.0 abv av

Standard Deviation	Category Risk Index	Beta
11.3%—blw av	0.80—blw av	0.72

	2008	2007	2006	2005	2004	2003	2002	2001	2000	1999
Return (%)	-26.0	9.8	12.8	6.5	—	—	—	—	—	—
Differ From Category (+/-)	1.8	1.1	2.0	0.7	—	—	—	—	—	—
Return, Tax-Adjusted (%)	-27.2	8.4	11.7	5.5	—	—	—	—	—	—

PER SHARE DATA

	2008	2007	2006	2005	2004	2003	2002	2001	2000	1999
Dividends, Net Income ($)	0.29	0.41	0.34	0.32	—	—	—	—	—	—
Distrib'ns, Cap Gain ($)	0.36	0.14	0.05	0.01	—	—	—	—	—	—
Net Asset Value ($)	8.77	12.68	12.06	11.03	—	—	—	—	—	—
Expense Ratio (%)	0.00	0.00	0.00	0.00	—	—	—	—	—	—
Yield (%)	3.22	3.21	2.77	2.91	—	—	—	—	—	—
Portfolio Turnover (%)	18	7	7	3	—	—	—	—	—	—
Total Assets (Millions $)	490	658	415	142	—	—	—	—	—	—

PORTFOLIO (as of 9/30/08)

Portfolio Manager: Tyler/Torelli - 2004

Investment Style

Large Cap	Growth
Mid Cap	Grth/Val
Small Cap	Value

Portfolio

59.4%	U.S. stock	0.0%	conv't
22.5%	int'l stock	0.0%	preferred
0.3%	U.S. bonds	0.1%	other
4.6%	int'l bonds	13.1%	cash

Number of Investments: 9

Percent of Portfolio in Top 10 Investments: 100%

SHAREHOLDER INFORMATION

Minimum Investment

Initial: $2,500 Subsequent: $50

Minimum IRA Investment

Initial: $2,500 Subsequent: $50

Maximum Fees

Load: none 12b-1: none

Other: none

Services

✔ IRA

✔ Keogh

✔ Telephone Exchange

Fidelity Global Balanced (FGBLX)

800-544-9797
www.fidelity.com

Balanced: Global

PERFORMANCE — fund inception date: 2/1/93

	3yr Annual	5yr Annual	10yr Annual	Bull	Bear
Return (%)	-0.3	4.2	4.7	121.6	-25.6
Differ From Category (+/-)	4.5 high	3.5 high	2.7 high	34.5 high	4.0 abv av

Standard Deviation	Category Risk Index	Beta
11.8%—blw av	0.83—blw av	0.68

	2008	2007	2006	2005	2004	2003	2002	2001	2000	1999
Return (%)	-23.3	13.7	13.6	9.0	13.6	29.8	-6.2	-8.2	-6.0	23.0
Differ From Category (+/-)	4.5	5.0	2.8	3.2	3.4	5.2	-1.0	-3.5	-2.7	5.2
Return, Tax-Adjusted (%)	-24.0	11.9	11.8	7.5	13.1	29.1	-6.7	-8.3	-7.9	21.9

PER SHARE DATA

	2008	2007	2006	2005	2004	2003	2002	2001	2000	1999
Dividends, Net Income ($)	0.38	0.33	0.20	0.14	0.13	0.32	0.22	0.03	0.32	0.32
Distrib'ns, Cap Gain ($)	0.17	1.83	2.10	1.67	0.32	0.00	0.00	0.00	1.24	0.25
Net Asset Value ($)	16.66	22.47	21.63	21.06	20.99	18.87	14.78	15.98	17.43	20.20
Expense Ratio (%)	na	1.12	1.14	1.15	1.19	1.28	1.27	1.27	1.25	1.19
Yield (%)	2.25	1.35	0.84	0.61	0.61	1.69	1.48	0.18	1.71	1.56
Portfolio Turnover (%)	na	169	208	94	94	113	126	102	62	80
Total Assets (Millions $)	351	382	275	205	161	125	88	92	102	106

PORTFOLIO (as of 11/30/08)

Portfolio Manager: Young/Weir/Calderon/Lo/Tucker - 2006

Investment Style

Large Cap	Growth
Mid Cap	Grth/Val
Small Cap	Value

Portfolio

22.5%	U.S. stock	0.0%	conv't
22.0%	int'l stock	0.0%	preferred
8.3%	U.S. bonds	1.2%	other
30.5%	int'l bonds	15.4%	cash

Number of Investments: 542
Percent of Portfolio in Top 10 Investments: 32%

SHAREHOLDER INFORMATION

Minimum Investment
Initial: $2,500 Subsequent: $250

Minimum IRA Investment
Initial: $500 Subsequent: $100

Maximum Fees
Load: 1.00% redemption 12b-1: none
Other: redemption fee applies for 30 days; maint fee for low bal

Services
✔ IRA
✔ Keogh
✔ Telephone Exchange

Janus Smart Portfolio Growth (JSPGX)

800-525-3713
www.janus.com

Balanced: Global

PERFORMANCE — fund inception date: 12/30/05

	3yr Annual	5yr Annual	10yr Annual	Bull	Bear
Return (%)	-3.8	na	na	na	-36.9
Differ From Category (+/-)	1.0 abv av	na	na	na	-7.3 av

Standard Deviation	Category Risk Index	Beta
16.2%—av	1.14—abv av	1.01

	2008	2007	2006	2005	2004	2003	2002	2001	2000	1999
Return (%)	-35.0	15.7	18.5	—	—	—	—	—	—	—
Differ From Category (+/-)	-7.2	7.0	7.6	—	—	—	—	—	—	—
Return, Tax-Adjusted (%)	-35.5	14.3	17.9	—	—	—	—	—	—	—

PER SHARE DATA

	2008	2007	2006	2005	2004	2003	2002	2001	2000	1999
Dividends, Net Income ($)	0.21	0.34	0.17	—	—	—	—	—	—	—
Distrib'ns, Cap Gain ($)	0.00	0.30	0.00	—	—	—	—	—	—	—
Net Asset Value ($)	8.17	12.88	11.68	—	—	—	—	—	—	—
Expense Ratio (%)	0.20	0.20	0.24	—	—	—	—	—	—	—
Yield (%)	2.54	2.58	1.46	—	—	—	—	—	—	—
Portfolio Turnover (%)	71	19	24	—	—	—	—	—	—	—
Total Assets (Millions $)	133	179	84	—	—	—	—	—	—	—

PORTFOLIO (as of 9/30/08)

Portfolio Manager: Scherman - 2005

Investment Style

Large Cap	Growth
Mid Cap	Grth/Val
Small Cap	Value

Portfolio

47.4%	U.S. stock	0.0%	conv't
25.5%	int'l stock	0.1%	preferred
19.7%	U.S. bonds	1.4%	other
0.7%	int'l bonds	5.3%	cash

Number of Investments: 12

Percent of Portfolio in Top 10 Investments: 94%

SHAREHOLDER INFORMATION

Minimum Investment

Initial: $2,500 Subsequent: $100

Minimum IRA Investment

Initial: $1,000 Subsequent: $100

Maximum Fees

Load: none 12b-1: none

Other: none

Services

✔ IRA

✔ Keogh

✔ Telephone Exchange

USAA Cornerstone Strategy (USCRX)

800-531-8181
www.usaa.com

Balanced: Global

PERFORMANCE — fund inception date: 8/15/84

	3yr Annual	5yr Annual	10yr Annual	Bull	Bear
Return (%)	-7.6	-1.5	1.3	92.0	-37.4
Differ From Category (+/-)	-2.8 blw av	-2.2 blw av	-0.7 abv av	4.9 abv av	-7.8 blw av

Standard Deviation	Category Risk Index	Beta
14.3%—blw av	1.01—av	0.90

	2008	2007	2006	2005	2004	2003	2002	2001	2000	1999
Return (%)	-34.5	6.0	13.8	5.5	11.5	23.7	-8.3	-3.1	2.7	8.1
Differ From Category (+/-)	-6.7	-2.7	2.9	-0.3	1.3	-1.0	-3.1	1.6	6.0	-9.7
Return, Tax-Adjusted (%)	-35.2	3.6	11.7	4.0	10.3	23.3	-9.1	-4.9	1.4	5.6

PER SHARE DATA

	2008	2007	2006	2005	2004	2003	2002	2001	2000	1999
Dividends, Net Income ($)	0.51	0.44	0.53	0.22	0.26	0.21	0.27	1.00	0.48	0.78
Distrib'ns, Cap Gain ($)	0.00	3.20	2.24	2.05	1.44	0.00	0.43	0.35	0.71	1.67
Net Asset Value ($)	15.64	24.67	26.68	25.89	26.69	25.47	20.76	23.38	25.53	25.98
Expense Ratio (%)	1.19	1.19	1.17	1.16	1.19	1.19	1.16	1.07	1.09	1.05
Yield (%)	3.27	1.58	1.83	0.80	0.92	0.83	1.25	4.21	1.82	2.83
Portfolio Turnover (%)	151	127	151	65	91	131	31	54	37	46
Total Assets (Millions $)	1,466	2,242	1,929	1,646	1,501	1,315	1,058	955	1,057	1,193

PORTFOLIO (as of 8/31/08)

Portfolio Manager: Johnson/Espe/Linkas/ Lovejoy - 1994

Investment Style

Large Cap	Growth
Mid Cap	Grth/Val
Small Cap	Value

Portfolio

50.1%	U.S. stock	0.0%	conv't
24.8%	int'l stock	0.8%	preferred
20.2%	U.S. bonds	0.7%	other
0.8%	int'l bonds	2.7%	cash

Number of Investments: 2,994
Percent of Portfolio in Top 10 Investments: 14%

SHAREHOLDER INFORMATION

Minimum Investment
Initial: $3,000 Subsequent: $50

Minimum IRA Investment
Initial: $250 Subsequent: $50

Maximum Fees
Load: none 12b-1: none
Other: none

Services
✔ IRA
✔ Keogh
✔ Telephone Exchange

Target Date: 2000–2014 Funds
Category Performance Ranked by 2008 Returns

Fund (Ticker)	Annual Return (%) 2008	3Yr	5Yr	10Yr	Category Risk	Total Risk
Vanguard Target Retirement Income (VTINX)	-11.0	0.8	2.5	na	blw av	low
Fidelity Freedom Income (FFFAX)	-12.2	-0.7	1.1	2.7	low	low
Fidelity Freedom 2000 (FFFBX)	-14.0	-1.2	1.0	2.7	low	low
Vanguard Target Retirement 2005 (VTOVX)	-15.9	-0.5	1.9	na	blw av	low
T. Rowe Price Retirement Income (TRRIX)	-18.4	-1.7	1.4	na	av	blw av
Target Date: 2000–2014 Category Average	**-19.5**	**-2.2**	**1.0**	**2.5**	**av**	**blw av**

Fidelity Freedom 2000 (FFFBX)

800-544-9797
www.fidelity.com

Target Date: 2000-2014

PERFORMANCE — fund inception date: 10/17/96

	3yr Annual	5yr Annual	10yr Annual	Bull	Bear
Return (%)	-1.2	1.0	2.7	35.3	-14.9
Differ From Category (+/-)	1.0 abv av	0.0 av	0.2 abv av	-18.6 av	6.1 high

Standard Deviation	Category Risk Index	Beta
6.0%—low	0.68—low	0.38

	2008	2007	2006	2005	2004	2003	2002	2001	2000	1999
Return (%)	-14.0	5.3	6.7	4.0	4.5	9.2	-1.9	-0.1	3.9	12.1
Differ From Category (+/-)	5.5	-1.2	-2.6	-0.7	-2.4	-5.5	1.1	0.7	0.3	-0.6
Return, Tax-Adjusted (%)	-15.5	3.6	5.3	3.0	3.8	8.4	-2.9	-1.1	0.2	10.0

PER SHARE DATA

	2008	2007	2006	2005	2004	2003	2002	2001	2000	1999
Dividends, Net Income ($)	0.41	0.48	0.43	0.33	0.23	0.24	0.30	0.28	0.75	0.52
Distrib'ns, Cap Gain ($)	0.21	0.27	0.14	0.02	0.00	0.00	0.00	0.00	0.93	0.29
Net Asset Value ($)	10.05	12.37	12.46	12.21	12.08	11.78	11.01	11.52	11.81	12.99
Expense Ratio (%)	0.00	0.00	0.01	0.58	0.08	0.08	0.07	0.06	0.08	0.07
Yield (%)	3.99	3.79	3.41	2.69	1.90	2.03	2.72	2.43	5.88	3.91
Portfolio Turnover (%)	36	34	20	11	7	7	13	51	37	27
Total Assets (Millions $)	1,493	1,790	1,648	1,575	1,613	1,517	1,195	1,046	648	715

PORTFOLIO (as of 11/30/08)

Portfolio Manager: Shelon/Sharpe - 2005

Investment Style

Large Cap	Growth
Mid Cap	Grth/Val
Small Cap	Value

Portfolio

20.6%	U.S. stock	0.0%	conv't
1.3%	int'l stock	0.2%	preferred
41.3%	U.S. bonds	7.1%	other
0.6%	int'l bonds	29.1%	cash

Number of Investments: 27

Percent of Portfolio in Top 10 Investments: 82%

SHAREHOLDER INFORMATION

Minimum Investment

Initial: $2,500 Subsequent: $250

Minimum IRA Investment

Initial: $500 Subsequent: $250

Maximum Fees

Load: none 12b-1: none

Other: maint fee for low bal

Services

✔ IRA
✔ Keogh
✔ Telephone Exchange

Fidelity Freedom Income (FFFAX)

800-544-9797
www.fidelity.com

Target Date: 2000-2014

PERFORMANCE — fund inception date: 10/17/96

	3yr Annual	5yr Annual	10yr Annual	Bull	Bear
Return (%)	-0.7	1.1	2.7	30.0	-12.7
Differ From Category (+/-)	1.5 high	0.1 abv av	0.2 high	-23.9 blw av	8.3 high

Standard Deviation	Category Risk Index	Beta
5.4%—low	0.61—low	0.33

	2008	2007	2006	2005	2004	2003	2002	2001	2000	1999
Return (%)	-12.2	4.8	6.3	3.7	3.8	7.3	-0.3	2.2	6.2	7.1
Differ From Category (+/-)	7.3	-1.7	-3.0	-1.0	-3.1	-7.4	2.7	3.0	2.6	-5.6
Return, Tax-Adjusted (%)	-13.6	3.1	4.9	2.8	3.1	6.5	-1.4	0.6	3.7	5.1

PER SHARE DATA

	2008	2007	2006	2005	2004	2003	2002	2001	2000	1999
Dividends, Net Income ($)	0.39	0.47	0.42	0.29	0.23	0.22	0.30	0.41	0.59	0.51
Distrib'ns, Cap Gain ($)	0.15	0.17	0.12	0.03	0.02	0.06	0.00	0.07	0.26	0.12
Net Asset Value ($)	9.56	11.45	11.54	11.37	11.27	11.09	10.60	10.93	11.17	11.33
Expense Ratio (%)	0.00	0.17	0.01	0.08	0.08	0.08	0.07	0.06	0.08	0.07
Yield (%)	4.01	4.04	3.60	2.54	2.03	1.97	2.83	3.72	5.16	4.45
Portfolio Turnover (%)	33	26	18	7	6	7	9	40	37	29
Total Assets (Millions $)	2,221	2,558	2,284	2,076	1,900	1,622	1,097	862	448	292

PORTFOLIO (as of 11/30/08)

Portfolio Manager: Shelon/Sharpe - 2005

Investment Style

Large Cap	Growth
Mid Cap	Grth/Val
Small Cap	Value

Portfolio

18.0%	U.S. stock	0.0%	conv't
0.8%	int'l stock	0.2%	preferred
43.6%	U.S. bonds	7.0%	other
0.6%	int'l bonds	29.7%	cash

Number of Investments: 21

Percent of Portfolio in Top 10 Investments: 84%

SHAREHOLDER INFORMATION

Minimum Investment

Initial: $2,500 Subsequent: $250

Minimum IRA Investment

Initial: $500 Subsequent: $250

Maximum Fees

Load: none 12b-1: none

Other: maint fee for low bal

Services

✔ IRA
✔ Keogh
✔ Telephone Exchange

T. Rowe Price Retirement Income (TRRIX)

800-492-7670
www.troweprice.com

Target Date: 2000-2014

PERFORMANCE — fund inception date: 9/30/02

	3yr Annual	5yr Annual	10yr Annual	Bull	Bear
Return (%)	-1.7	1.4	na	56.6	-19.5
Differ From Category (+/-)	0.5 abv av	0.4 abv av	na	2.7 abv av	1.5 abv av

Standard Deviation	Category Risk Index	Beta
8.2%—blw av	0.93—av	0.52

	2008	2007	2006	2005	2004	2003	2002	2001	2000	1999
Return (%)	-18.4	6.0	9.9	4.8	7.6	16.2	—	—	—	—
Differ From Category (+/-)	1.1	-0.4	0.6	0.1	0.7	1.5	—	—	—	—
Return, Tax-Adjusted (%)	-19.7	4.6	8.6	3.8	6.7	15.2	—	—	—	—

PER SHARE DATA

	2008	2007	2006	2005	2004	2003	2002	2001	2000	1999
Dividends, Net Income ($)	0.44	0.47	0.43	0.34	0.29	0.31	—	—	—	—
Distrib'ns, Cap Gain ($)	0.14	0.15	0.12	0.05	0.03	0.01	—	—	—	—
Net Asset Value ($)	10.32	13.30	13.13	12.46	12.26	11.70	—	—	—	—
Expense Ratio (%)	0.00	0.00	0.00	0.00	0.00	0.00	—	—	—	—
Yield (%)	4.19	3.49	3.25	2.68	2.37	2.62	—	—	—	—
Portfolio Turnover (%)	8	36	10	21	4	6	—	—	—	—
Total Assets (Millions $)	973	1,207	869	512	289	71	—	—	—	—

PORTFOLIO (as of 9/30/08)

Portfolio Manager: Clark/Notzon III - 2002

Investment Style

Large Cap	Growth
Mid Cap	Grth/Val
Small Cap	Value

Portfolio

30.5%	U.S. stock	0.0%	conv't
7.0%	int'l stock	0.2%	preferred
45.1%	U.S. bonds	2.0%	other
2.4%	int'l bonds	12.8%	cash

Number of Investments: 16

Percent of Portfolio in Top 10 Investments: 97%

SHAREHOLDER INFORMATION

Minimum Investment

Initial: $2,500 Subsequent: $100

Minimum IRA Investment

Initial: $1,000 Subsequent: $50

Maximum Fees

Load: none 12b-1: none

Other: none

Services

✔ IRA

✔ Keogh

✔ Telephone Exchange

Vanguard Target Retirement 2005 (VTOVX)

800-662-6273
www.vanguard.com

Target Date: 2000-2014

PERFORMANCE — fund inception date: 10/27/03

	3yr Annual	5yr Annual	10yr Annual	Bull	Bear
Return (%)	-0.5	1.9	na	na	-16.6
Differ From Category (+/-)	1.7 high	0.9 high	na	na	4.4 abv av

Standard Deviation	Category Risk Index	Beta
8.0%—low	0.91—blw av	0.49

	2008	2007	2006	2005	2004	2003	2002	2001	2000	1999
Return (%)	-15.9	8.1	8.2	3.5	7.7	—	—	—	—	—
Differ From Category (+/-)	3.6	1.6	-1.1	-1.2	0.8	—	—	—	—	—
Return, Tax-Adjusted (%)	-17.1	6.9	7.0	2.5	6.8	—	—	—	—	—

PER SHARE DATA

	2008	2007	2006	2005	2004	2003	2002	2001	2000	1999
Dividends, Net Income ($)	0.43	0.38	0.36	0.31	0.24	—	—	—	—	—
Distrib'ns, Cap Gain ($)	0.00	0.00	0.00	0.01	0.00	—	—	—	—	—
Net Asset Value ($)	9.69	12.02	11.47	10.93	10.86	—	—	—	—	—
Expense Ratio (%)	0.00	0.00	0.00	0.00	0.00	—	—	—	—	—
Yield (%)	4.40	3.16	3.13	2.83	2.20	—	—	—	—	—
Portfolio Turnover (%)	21	6	19	4	2	—	—	—	—	—
Total Assets (Millions $)	1,556	1,648	1,062	760	313	—	—	—	—	—

PORTFOLIO (as of 9/30/08)

Portfolio Manager: Kelly - 2003

Investment Style

Large Cap	Growth
Mid Cap	Grth/Val
Small Cap	Value

Portfolio

33.2%	U.S. stock	0.0%	conv't
8.0%	int'l stock	0.0%	preferred
54.5%	U.S. bonds	0.3%	other
0.9%	int'l bonds	3.1%	cash

Number of Investments: 9

Percent of Portfolio in Top 10 Investments: 100%

SHAREHOLDER INFORMATION

Minimum Investment

Initial: $3,000 Subsequent: $100

Minimum IRA Investment

Initial: $3,000 Subsequent: $100

Maximum Fees

Load: none 12b-1: none

Other: none

Services

✔ IRA
✔ Keogh
✔ Telephone Exchange

Vanguard Target Retirement Income (VTINX)

800-662-6273
www.vanguard.com

Target Date: 2000-2014

PERFORMANCE — fund inception date: 10/27/03

	3yr Annual	5yr Annual	10yr Annual	Bull	Bear
Return (%)	0.8	2.5	na	na	-10.8
Differ From Category (+/-)	3.0 high	1.5 high	na	na	10.2 high

Standard Deviation	Category Risk Index	Beta
6.6%—low	0.75—blw av	0.37

	2008	2007	2006	2005	2004	2003	2002	2001	2000	1999
Return (%)	-11.0	8.1	6.3	3.3	6.8	—	—	—	—	—
Differ From Category (+/-)	8.5	1.6	-3.0	-1.4	-0.1	—	—	—	—	—
Return, Tax-Adjusted (%)	-12.3	6.7	5.0	1.9	5.6	—	—	—	—	—

PER SHARE DATA

	2008	2007	2006	2005	2004	2003	2002	2001	2000	1999
Dividends, Net Income ($)	0.42	0.43	0.39	0.41	0.34	—	—	—	—	—
Distrib'ns, Cap Gain ($)	0.00	0.00	0.00	0.01	0.00	—	—	—	—	—
Net Asset Value ($)	9.52	11.13	10.70	10.44	10.52	—	—	—	—	—
Expense Ratio (%)	0.00	0.00	0.00	0.00	0.00	—	—	—	—	—
Yield (%)	4.42	3.86	3.64	3.92	3.23	—	—	—	—	—
Portfolio Turnover (%)	14	3	22	0	1	—	—	—	—	—
Total Assets (Millions $)	1,864	1,555	897	734	407	—	—	—	—	—

PORTFOLIO (as of 9/30/08)

Portfolio Manager: Kelly - 2003

Investment Style

Large Cap	Growth
Mid Cap	Grth/Val
Small Cap	Value

Portfolio

24.1%	U.S. stock	0.0%	conv't
5.6%	int'l stock	0.0%	preferred
63.2%	U.S. bonds	0.2%	other
1.0%	int'l bonds	6.0%	cash

Number of Investments: 8
Percent of Portfolio in Top 10 Investments: 100%

SHAREHOLDER INFORMATION

Minimum Investment
Initial: $3,000 Subsequent: $100

Minimum IRA Investment
Initial: $3,000 Subsequent: $100

Maximum Fees
Load: none 12b-1: none
Other: none

Services
✔ IRA
✔ Keogh
✔ Telephone Exchange

Target Date: 2015–2029 Funds
Category Performance Ranked by 2008 Returns

Fund (Ticker)	Annual Return (%) 2008	3Yr	5Yr	10Yr	Category Risk	Total Risk
Vanguard Target Retirement 2015 (VTXVX)	-24.1	-3.1	0.8	na	low	blw av
Fidelity Freedom 2015 (FFVFX)	-27.2	-4.7	0.1	na	blw av	blw av
T. Rowe Price Retirement 2015 (TRRGX)	-30.3	-5.4	na	na	abv av	blw av
Fidelity Freedom 2020 (FFFDX)	-32.2	-6.4	-0.6	1.4	abv av	blw av
T. Rowe Price Retirement 2020 (TRRBX)	-33.5	-6.7	-0.4	na	high	blw av
Target Date: 2015–2029 Category Average	**-29.2**	**-5.3**	**-0.5**	**0.6**	**av**	**blw av**

Fidelity Freedom 2015 (FFVFX)

800-544-9797
www.fidelity.com

Target Date: 2015-2029

PERFORMANCE — fund inception date: 11/6/03

	3yr Annual	5yr Annual	10yr Annual	Bull	Bear
Return (%)	-4.7	0.1	na	na	-29.3
Differ From Category (+/-)	0.6 abv av	0.6 high	na	na	2.4 abv av

Standard Deviation	Category Risk Index	Beta
11.4%—blw av	0.90—blw av	0.72

	2008	2007	2006	2005	2004	2003	2002	2001	2000	1999
Return (%)	-27.2	7.8	10.3	7.0	8.4	—	—	—	—	—
Differ From Category (+/-)	2.0	0.8	-2.2	0.6	-1.5	—	—	—	—	—
Return, Tax-Adjusted (%)	-28.4	6.4	9.2	6.2	7.9	—	—	—	—	—

PER SHARE DATA

	2008	2007	2006	2005	2004	2003	2002	2001	2000	1999
Dividends, Net Income ($)	0.30	0.30	0.23	0.19	0.14	—	—	—	—	—
Distrib'ns, Cap Gain ($)	0.29	0.38	0.31	0.08	0.01	—	—	—	—	—
Net Asset Value ($)	8.56	12.47	12.20	11.55	11.05	—	—	—	—	—
Expense Ratio (%)	0.00	0.00	0.00	0.08	0.08	—	—	—	—	—
Yield (%)	3.38	2.33	1.83	1.63	1.26	—	—	—	—	—
Portfolio Turnover (%)	24	4	1	0	2	—	—	—	—	—
Total Assets (Millions $)	6,213	6,996	4,276	1,857	564	—	—	—	—	—

PORTFOLIO (as of 11/30/08)

Portfolio Manager: Shelon/Sharpe - 2005

Investment Style

Large Cap	Growth
Mid Cap	Grth/Val
Small Cap	Value

Portfolio

37.1%	U.S. stock	0.1%	conv't
11.2%	int'l stock	0.2%	preferred
31.5%	U.S. bonds	8.9%	other
0.5%	int'l bonds	10.4%	cash

Number of Investments: 26

Percent of Portfolio in Top 10 Investments: 65%

SHAREHOLDER INFORMATION

Minimum Investment

Initial: $2,500 Subsequent: $250

Minimum IRA Investment

Initial: $500 Subsequent: $250

Maximum Fees

Load: none 12b-1: none

Other: maint fee for low bal

Services

✔ IRA

✔ Keogh

✔ Telephone Exchange

Fidelity Freedom 2020 (FFFDX)

800-544-9797
www.fidelity.com

Target Date: 2015-2029

PERFORMANCE

fund inception date: 10/17/96

	3yr Annual	5yr Annual	10yr Annual	Bull	Bear
Return (%)	-6.4	-0.6	1.4	89.5	-34.6
Differ From Category (+/-)	-1.1 av	-0.1 av	0.8 high	1.9 abv av	-2.9 blw av

Standard Deviation	Category Risk Index	Beta
13.5%—blw av	1.07—abv av	0.86

	2008	2007	2006	2005	2004	2003	2002	2001	2000	1999
Return (%)	-32.2	8.5	11.6	7.7	9.6	24.8	-13.8	-9.1	-3.1	25.3
Differ From Category (+/-)	-3.0	1.5	-0.9	1.3	-0.3	0.7	1.1	1.5	0.9	-0.4
Return, Tax-Adjusted (%)	-33.3	7.0	10.3	7.0	8.8	24.1	-14.4	-10.4	-5.2	23.2

PER SHARE DATA

	2008	2007	2006	2005	2004	2003	2002	2001	2000	1999
Dividends, Net Income ($)	0.31	0.37	0.28	0.23	0.26	0.22	0.22	0.26	0.39	0.45
Distrib'ns, Cap Gain ($)	0.51	0.67	0.59	0.09	0.04	0.04	0.00	0.43	0.96	0.57
Net Asset Value ($)	10.05	15.81	15.53	14.71	13.96	13.02	10.64	12.58	14.56	16.38
Expense Ratio (%)	0.00	0.00	0.01	0.08	0.08	0.08	0.07	0.06	0.08	0.07
Yield (%)	2.93	2.24	1.73	1.55	1.85	1.68	2.06	1.99	2.51	2.65
Portfolio Turnover (%)	35	7	4	0	3	6	10	50	28	18
Total Assets (Millions $)	15,117	21,276	16,889	12,265	9,338	6,736	3,735	2,796	1,893	1,560

PORTFOLIO (as of 11/30/08)

Portfolio Manager: Shelon/Sharpe - 2005

Investment Style

Large Cap	Growth
Mid Cap	Grth/Val
Small Cap	Value

Portfolio

45.6%	U.S. stock	0.1%	conv't
13.6%	int'l stock	0.3%	preferred
25.6%	U.S. bonds	8.2%	other
0.5%	int'l bonds	6.3%	cash

Number of Investments: 26

Percent of Portfolio in Top 10 Investments: 68%

SHAREHOLDER INFORMATION

Minimum Investment

Initial: $2,500 Subsequent: $250

Minimum IRA Investment

Initial: $500 Subsequent: $250

Maximum Fees

Load: none 12b-1: none

Other: maint fee for low bal

Services

✔ IRA

✔ Keogh

✔ Telephone Exchange

T. Rowe Price Retirement 2015 (TRRGX)

800-492-7670
www.troweprice.com

Target Date: 2015-2029

PERFORMANCE — fund inception date: 2/27/04

	3yr Annual	5yr Annual	10yr Annual	Bull	Bear
Return (%)	-5.4	na	na	na	-32.5
Differ From Category (+/-)	-0.1 av	na	na	na	-0.8 av

Standard Deviation	Category Risk Index	Beta
13.0%—blw av	1.03—abv av	0.84

	2008	2007	2006	2005	2004	2003	2002	2001	2000	1999
Return (%)	-30.3	6.7	13.7	6.6	—	—	—	—	—	—
Differ From Category (+/-)	-1.1	-0.3	1.2	0.2	—	—	—	—	—	—
Return, Tax-Adjusted (%)	-31.3	5.6	12.7	6.0	—	—	—	—	—	—

PER SHARE DATA

	2008	2007	2006	2005	2004	2003	2002	2001	2000	1999
Dividends, Net Income ($)	0.28	0.28	0.23	0.17	—	—	—	—	—	—
Distrib'ns, Cap Gain ($)	0.24	0.27	0.16	0.07	—	—	—	—	—	—
Net Asset Value ($)	8.30	12.65	12.37	11.22	—	—	—	—	—	—
Expense Ratio (%)	0.00	0.00	0.00	0.00	—	—	—	—	—	—
Yield (%)	3.27	2.16	1.83	1.50	—	—	—	—	—	—
Portfolio Turnover (%)	8	10	11	2	—	—	—	—	—	—
Total Assets (Millions $)	2,637	3,472	2,027	920	—	—	—	—	—	—

PORTFOLIO (as of 9/30/08)

Portfolio Manager: Clark/Notzon III - 2004

Investment Style

Large Cap	Growth
Mid Cap	Grth/Val
Small Cap	Value

Portfolio

49.5%	U.S. stock	0.1%	conv't
13.7%	int'l stock	0.3%	preferred
26.4%	U.S. bonds	1.2%	other
1.7%	int'l bonds	7.2%	cash

Number of Investments: 18

Percent of Portfolio in Top 10 Investments: 91%

SHAREHOLDER INFORMATION

Minimum Investment

Initial: $2,500 Subsequent: $100

Minimum IRA Investment

Initial: $1,000 Subsequent: $50

Maximum Fees

Load: none 12b-1: none

Other: none

Services

✔ IRA

✔ Keogh

✔ Telephone Exchange

T. Rowe Price Retirement 2020 (TRRBX)

800-492-7670
www.troweprice.com

Target Date: 2015-2029

PERFORMANCE — fund inception date: 9/30/02

	3yr Annual	5yr Annual	10yr Annual	Bull	Bear
Return (%)	-6.7	-0.4	na	103.6	-36.1
Differ From Category (+/-)	-1.4 blw av	0.1 abv av	na	16.0 high	-4.4 blw av

Standard Deviation	Category Risk Index	Beta
14.4%—blw av	1.14—high	0.93

	2008	2007	2006	2005	2004	2003	2002	2001	2000	1999
Return (%)	-33.5	6.7	14.6	7.1	12.8	27.4	—	—	—	—
Differ From Category (+/-)	-4.3	-0.3	2.1	0.7	2.9	3.2	—	—	—	—
Return, Tax-Adjusted (%)	-34.5	5.6	13.7	6.5	12.2	26.9	—	—	—	—

PER SHARE DATA

	2008	2007	2006	2005	2004	2003	2002	2001	2000	1999
Dividends, Net Income ($)	0.31	0.35	0.29	0.22	0.18	0.12	—	—	—	—
Distrib'ns, Cap Gain ($)	0.37	0.42	0.28	0.11	0.10	0.02	—	—	—	—
Net Asset Value ($)	11.11	17.74	17.35	15.63	14.89	13.45	—	—	—	—
Expense Ratio (%)	0.00	0.00	0.00	0.00	0.00	0.00	—	—	—	—
Yield (%)	2.70	1.92	1.64	1.39	1.20	0.89	—	—	—	—
Portfolio Turnover (%)	7	8	12	1	0	4	—	—	—	—
Total Assets (Millions $)	4,499	6,111	3,682	1,848	907	177	—	—	—	—

PORTFOLIO (as of 9/30/08)

Portfolio Manager: Clark/Notzon III - 2002

Investment Style

Large Cap	Growth
Mid Cap	Grth/Val
Small Cap	Value

Portfolio

54.8%	U.S. stock	0.1%	conv't
16.0%	int'l stock	0.3%	preferred
20.3%	U.S. bonds	1.0%	other
1.3%	int'l bonds	6.4%	cash

Number of Investments: 18

Percent of Portfolio in Top 10 Investments: 90%

SHAREHOLDER INFORMATION

Minimum Investment

Initial: $2,500 Subsequent: $100

Minimum IRA Investment

Initial: $1,000 Subsequent: $50

Maximum Fees

Load: none 12b-1: none

Other: none

Services

✔ IRA

✔ Keogh

✔ Telephone Exchange

Vanguard Target Retirement 2015 (VTXVX)

800-662-6273
www.vanguard.com

Target Date: 2015-2029

PERFORMANCE — fund inception date: 10/27/03

	3yr Annual	5yr Annual	10yr Annual	Bull	Bear
Return (%)	-3.1	0.8	na	na	-26.0
Differ From Category (+/-)	2.2 high	1.3 high	na	na	5.7 high

Standard Deviation	Category Risk Index	Beta
10.7%—blw av	0.85—low	0.69

	2008	2007	2006	2005	2004	2003	2002	2001	2000	1999
Return (%)	-24.1	7.5	11.4	4.9	9.0	—	—	—	—	—
Differ From Category (+/-)	5.1	0.5	-1.1	-1.5	-0.9	—	—	—	—	—
Return, Tax-Adjusted (%)	-25.1	6.5	10.4	4.1	8.3	—	—	—	—	—

PER SHARE DATA

	2008	2007	2006	2005	2004	2003	2002	2001	2000	1999
Dividends, Net Income ($)	0.36	0.34	0.31	0.26	0.20	—	—	—	—	—
Distrib'ns, Cap Gain ($)	0.00	0.00	0.00	0.00	0.00	—	—	—	—	—
Net Asset Value ($)	9.55	13.06	12.46	11.46	11.17	—	—	—	—	—
Expense Ratio (%)	0.00	0.00	0.00	0.00	0.00	—	—	—	—	—
Yield (%)	3.82	2.60	2.48	2.26	1.79	—	—	—	—	—
Portfolio Turnover (%)	24	5	15	1	1	—	—	—	—	—
Total Assets (Millions $)	7,051	7,273	4,355	2,293	707	—	—	—	—	—

PORTFOLIO (as of 9/30/08)

Portfolio Manager: Kelly - 2003

Investment Style

Large Cap	Growth
Mid Cap	Grth/Val
Small Cap	Value

Portfolio

50.2%	U.S. stock	0.0%	conv't
12.2%	int'l stock	0.0%	preferred
35.7%	U.S. bonds	0.3%	other
0.8%	int'l bonds	0.8%	cash

Number of Investments: 7
Percent of Portfolio in Top 10 Investments: 100%

SHAREHOLDER INFORMATION

Minimum Investment
Initial: $3,000 Subsequent: $100

Minimum IRA Investment
Initial: $3,000 Subsequent: $100

Maximum Fees
Load: none 12b-1: none
Other: none

Services
✔ IRA
✔ Keogh
✔ Telephone Exchange

Target Date: 2030+ Funds
Category Performance Ranked by 2008 Returns

Fund (Ticker)	Annual Return (%) 2008	3Yr	5Yr	10Yr	Category Risk	Total Risk
Vanguard Target Retirement 2045 (VTIVX)	-34.6	-6.6	-0.4	na	blw av	blw av
Vanguard Target Retirement 2035 (VTTHX)	-34.7	-6.9	-0.8	na	blw av	blw av
Fidelity Freedom 2030 (FFFEX)	-37.0	-8.1	-1.4	0.6	blw av	av
Fidelity Freedom 2035 (FFTHX)	-37.8	-8.5	-1.5	na	av	av
T. Rowe Price Retirement 2030 (TRRCX)	-37.8	-8.3	-1.0	na	abv av	av
Target Date: 2030+ Category Average	**-36.1**	**-7.4**	**-1.2**	**0.6**	**av**	**av**

Fidelity Freedom 2030

800-544-9797
www.fidelity.com

(FFFEX)

Target Date: 2030+

PERFORMANCE **fund inception date: 10/17/96**

	3yr Annual	5yr Annual	10yr Annual	Bull	Bear
Return (%)	-8.1	-1.4	0.6	105.6	-39.8
Differ From Category (+/-)	-0.7 av	-0.2 av	0.0 high	-9.1 blw av	-0.6 av

Standard Deviation	Category Risk Index	Beta
15.6%—av	0.95—blw av	1.00

	2008	2007	2006	2005	2004	2003	2002	2001	2000	1999
Return (%)	-37.0	9.2	12.8	8.8	10.4	28.4	-17.4	-11.7	-5.1	28.5
Differ From Category (+/-)	-0.9	1.6	-1.9	0.9	-1.8	-1.4	1.1	0.9	0.0	0.0
Return, Tax-Adjusted (%)	-38.1	8.0	11.7	8.2	9.8	27.7	-17.8	-13.0	-6.8	26.6

PER SHARE DATA

	2008	2007	2006	2005	2004	2003	2002	2001	2000	1999
Dividends, Net Income ($)	0.27	0.27	0.21	0.19	0.22	0.19	0.15	0.20	0.34	0.41
Distrib'ns, Cap Gain ($)	0.59	0.72	0.70	0.11	0.00	0.00	0.00	0.53	0.71	0.48
Net Asset Value ($)	9.76	16.52	16.03	15.02	14.08	12.95	10.24	12.56	15.00	16.88
Expense Ratio (%)	0.00	0.00	0.01	0.08	0.08	0.08	0.07	0.06	0.08	0.07
Yield (%)	2.60	1.56	1.25	1.25	1.56	1.46	1.46	1.52	2.16	2.36
Portfolio Turnover (%)	36	6	5	0	2	4	5	37	26	16
Total Assets (Millions $)	10,077	14,352	10,720	7,400	5,500	3,899	2,091	1,708	1,273	788

PORTFOLIO (as of 11/30/08)

Portfolio Manager: Shelon/Sharpe - 2005

Investment Style

Large Cap	Growth
Mid Cap	Grth/Val
Small Cap	Value

Portfolio

55.5%	U.S. stock	0.1%	conv't
16.5%	int'l stock	0.3%	preferred
15.4%	U.S. bonds	7.3%	other
0.4%	int'l bonds	4.5%	cash

Number of Investments: 24

Percent of Portfolio in Top 10 Investments: 73%

SHAREHOLDER INFORMATION

Minimum Investment

Initial: $2,500 Subsequent: $250

Minimum IRA Investment

Initial: $500 Subsequent: $250

Maximum Fees

Load: none 12b-1: none

Other: maint fee for low bal

Services

✔ IRA

✔ Keogh

✔ Telephone Exchange

Fidelity Freedom 2035 (FFTHX)

800-544-9797
www.fidelity.com

Target Date: 2030+

PERFORMANCE — fund inception date: 11/6/03

	3yr Annual	5yr Annual	10yr Annual	Bull	Bear
Return (%)	-8.5	-1.5	na	na	-40.7
Differ From Category (+/-)	-1.1 blw av	-0.3 blw av	na	na	-1.5 av

Standard Deviation	Category Risk Index	Beta
15.9%—av	0.97—av	1.02

	2008	2007	2006	2005	2004	2003	2002	2001	2000	1999
Return (%)	-37.8	9.2	12.9	9.0	10.8	—	—	—	—	—
Differ From Category (+/-)	-1.7	1.6	-1.9	1.1	-1.3	—	—	—	—	—
Return, Tax-Adjusted (%)	-38.8	8.1	11.9	8.4	10.4	—	—	—	—	—

PER SHARE DATA

	2008	2007	2006	2005	2004	2003	2002	2001	2000	1999
Dividends, Net Income ($)	0.20	0.21	0.17	0.13	0.13	—	—	—	—	—
Distrib'ns, Cap Gain ($)	0.44	0.52	0.44	0.11	0.00	—	—	—	—	—
Net Asset Value ($)	8.03	13.68	13.19	12.23	11.44	—	—	—	—	—
Expense Ratio (%)	0.00	0.00	0.00	0.08	0.08	—	—	—	—	—
Yield (%)	2.36	1.47	1.24	1.05	1.09	—	—	—	—	—
Portfolio Turnover (%)	28	3	1	0	18	—	—	—	—	—
Total Assets (Millions $)	3,476	3,779	1,994	800	191	—	—	—	—	—

PORTFOLIO (as of 11/30/08)

Portfolio Manager: Shelon/Sharpe - 2005

Investment Style

Large Cap Growth
Mid Cap Grth/Val
Small Cap Value

Portfolio

56.7%	U.S. stock	0.1%	conv't
17.3%	int'l stock	0.3%	preferred
13.4%	U.S. bonds	7.8%	other
0.4%	int'l bonds	4.1%	cash

Number of Investments: 24

Percent of Portfolio in Top 10 Investments: 76%

SHAREHOLDER INFORMATION

Minimum Investment

Initial: $2,500 Subsequent: $250

Minimum IRA Investment

Initial: $500 Subsequent: $250

Maximum Fees

Load: none 12b-1: none

Other: maint fee for low bal

Services

✔ IRA
✔ Keogh
✔ Telephone Exchange

T. Rowe Price Retirement 2030 (TRRCX)

800-492-7670
www.troweprice.com

Target Date: 2030+

PERFORMANCE — fund inception date: 9/30/02

	3yr Annual	5yr Annual	10yr Annual	Bull	Bear
Return (%)	-8.3	-1.0	na	119.0	-40.7
Differ From Category (+/-)	-0.9 av	0.2 abv av	na	4.3 abv av	-1.5 av

Standard Deviation	Category Risk Index	Beta
16.4%—av	1.00—abv av	1.06

	2008	2007	2006	2005	2004	2003	2002	2001	2000	1999
Return (%)	-37.8	6.8	16.1	8.1	14.1	29.9	—	—	—	—
Differ From Category (+/-)	-1.7	-0.8	1.3	0.2	1.9	0.1	—	—	—	—
Return, Tax-Adjusted (%)	-38.6	5.8	15.3	7.6	13.6	29.6	—	—	—	—

PER SHARE DATA

	2008	2007	2006	2005	2004	2003	2002	2001	2000	1999
Dividends, Net Income ($)	0.25	0.30	0.22	0.16	0.14	0.10	—	—	—	—
Distrib'ns, Cap Gain ($)	0.43	0.50	0.34	0.11	0.12	0.02	—	—	—	—
Net Asset Value ($)	11.16	19.05	18.59	16.49	15.50	13.81	—	—	—	—
Expense Ratio (%)	0.00	0.00	0.00	0.00	0.00	0.00	—	—	—	—
Yield (%)	2.15	1.53	1.16	0.96	0.89	0.72	—	—	—	—
Portfolio Turnover (%)	6	8	12	1	9	3	—	—	—	—
Total Assets (Millions $)	3,073	4,126	2,387	1,164	498	104	—	—	—	—

PORTFOLIO (as of 9/30/08)

Portfolio Manager: Clark/Notzon III - 2002

Investment Style

Large Cap	Growth
Mid Cap	Grth/Val
Small Cap	Value

Portfolio

63.2%	U.S. stock	0.1%	conv't
19.7%	int'l stock	0.3%	preferred
10.0%	U.S. bonds	0.6%	other
0.7%	int'l bonds	5.4%	cash

Number of Investments: 17

Percent of Portfolio in Top 10 Investments: 91%

SHAREHOLDER INFORMATION

Minimum Investment
Initial: $2,500 Subsequent: $100

Minimum IRA Investment
Initial: $1,000 Subsequent: $50

Maximum Fees
Load: none 12b-1: none
Other: none

Services
✔ IRA
✔ Keogh
✔ Telephone Exchange

Vanguard Target Retirement 2035 (VTTHX)

800-662-6273
www.vanguard.com

Target Date: 2030+

PERFORMANCE — fund inception date: 10/27/03

	3yr Annual	5yr Annual	10yr Annual	Bull	Bear
Return (%)	-6.9	-0.8	na	na	-37.6
Differ From Category (+/-)	0.5 abv av	0.4 high	na	na	1.6 abv av

Standard Deviation	Category Risk Index	Beta
14.9%—blw av	0.91—blw av	0.97

	2008	2007	2006	2005	2004	2003	2002	2001	2000	1999
Return (%)	-34.7	7.4	15.2	6.3	11.9	—	—	—	—	—
Differ From Category (+/-)	1.4	-0.2	0.4	-1.6	-0.3	—	—	—	—	—
Return, Tax-Adjusted (%)	-35.4	6.7	14.4	5.6	11.3	—	—	—	—	—

PER SHARE DATA

	2008	2007	2006	2005	2004	2003	2002	2001	2000	1999
Dividends, Net Income ($)	0.30	0.29	0.26	0.21	0.17	—	—	—	—	—
Distrib'ns, Cap Gain ($)	0.00	0.00	0.00	0.00	0.00	—	—	—	—	—
Net Asset Value ($)	9.25	14.62	13.87	12.26	11.73	—	—	—	—	—
Expense Ratio (%)	0.00	0.00	0.00	0.00	0.00	—	—	—	—	—
Yield (%)	3.23	1.98	1.87	1.71	1.44	—	—	—	—	—
Portfolio Turnover (%)	10	1	14	0	2	—	—	—	—	—
Total Assets (Millions $)	4,351	4,860	3,050	1,402	373	—	—	—	—	—

PORTFOLIO (as of 9/30/08)

Portfolio Manager: Kelly - 2003

Investment Style

Large Cap	Growth
Mid Cap	Grth/Val
Small Cap	Value

Portfolio

71.7%	U.S. stock	0.0%	conv't
17.5%	int'l stock	0.1%	preferred
9.7%	U.S. bonds	0.4%	other
0.2%	int'l bonds	0.5%	cash

Number of Investments: 7

Percent of Portfolio in Top 10 Investments: 100%

SHAREHOLDER INFORMATION

Minimum Investment

Initial: $3,000 Subsequent: $100

Minimum IRA Investment

Initial: $3,000 Subsequent: $100

Maximum Fees

Load: none 12b-1: none

Other: none

Services

✔ IRA

✔ Keogh

✔ Telephone Exchange

Vanguard Target Retirement 2045 (VTIVX)

800-662-6273
www.vanguard.com

Target Date: 2030+

PERFORMANCE

fund inception date: 10/27/03

	3yr Annual	5yr Annual	10yr Annual	Bull	Bear
Return (%)	-6.6	-0.4	na	na	-37.6
Differ From Category (+/-)	0.8 abv av	0.8 high	na	na	1.6 abv av

Standard Deviation	Category Risk Index	Beta
14.9%—blw av	0.91—blw av	0.97

	2008	2007	2006	2005	2004	2003	2002	2001	2000	1999
Return (%)	-34.6	7.4	15.9	6.9	12.8	—	—	—	—	—
Differ From Category (+/-)	1.5	-0.2	1.1	-1.0	0.6	—	—	—	—	—
Return, Tax-Adjusted (%)	-35.3	6.7	15.2	6.3	12.3	—	—	—	—	—

PER SHARE DATA

	2008	2007	2006	2005	2004	2003	2002	2001	2000	1999
Dividends, Net Income ($)	0.30	0.30	0.25	0.19	0.16	—	—	—	—	—
Distrib'ns, Cap Gain ($)	0.00	0.00	0.01	0.00	0.00	—	—	—	—	—
Net Asset Value ($)	9.57	15.09	14.32	12.57	11.93	—	—	—	—	—
Expense Ratio (%)	0.00	0.00	0.00	0.00	0.00	—	—	—	—	—
Yield (%)	3.14	1.98	1.74	1.51	1.34	—	—	—	—	—
Portfolio Turnover (%)	9	1	3	7	7	—	—	—	—	—
Total Assets (Millions $)	2,192	2,374	1,446	626	142	—	—	—	—	—

PORTFOLIO (as of 9/30/08)

Portfolio Manager: Kelly - 2003

Investment Style

Large Cap	Growth
Mid Cap	Grth/Val
Small Cap	Value

Portfolio

71.7%	U.S. stock	0.0%	conv't
17.4%	int'l stock	0.1%	preferred
9.8%	U.S. bonds	0.4%	other
0.2%	int'l bonds	0.5%	cash

Number of Investments: 7

Percent of Portfolio in Top 10 Investments: 100%

SHAREHOLDER INFORMATION

Minimum Investment

Initial: $3,000 Subsequent: $100

Minimum IRA Investment

Initial: $3,000 Subsequent: $100

Maximum Fees

Load: none 12b-1: none

Other: none

Services

✔ IRA

✔ Keogh

✔ Telephone Exchange

TAXABLE BOND FUNDS

Corporate High-Yield Bond Funds
Category Performance Ranked by 2008 Returns

Fund (Ticker)	Annual Return (%) 2008	3Yr	5Yr	10Yr	Category Risk	Total Risk
Fidelity Floating Rate High Income (FFRHX)	-16.5	-3.1	-0.2	na	low	low
Northern High Yield Fixed Income (NHFIX)	-19.4	-3.5	-0.1	2.6	blw av	blw av
Janus High-Yield (JAHYX)	-19.4	-3.2	0.4	3.2	blw av	blw av
Payden High Income (PYHRX)	-20.4	-3.9	-0.3	2.3	abv av	blw av
Fidelity Focused High Income (FHIFX)	-20.5	-3.9	na	na	av	blw av
Vanguard High-Yield Corporate (VWEHX)	-21.3	-4.6	-0.7	1.9	high	blw av
Fidelity High Income (SPHIX)	-23.8	-4.8	-0.4	1.1	abv av	blw av
T. Rowe Price High-Yield (PRHYX)	-24.5	-5.1	-0.5	2.8	abv av	blw av
Corporate High-Yield Bond Category Average	**-21.5**	**-4.6**	**-0.7**	**1.9**	**av**	**blw av**

Fidelity Floating Rate High Income (FFRHX)

800-544-4774
www.fidelity.com

Corporate High-Yield Bond

PERFORMANCE AND PER SHARE DATA **fund inception date: 9/19/02**

	3yr Annual	5yr Annual	10yr Annual	Category Risk Index
Return (%)	-3.1	-0.2	na	0.72—low
Differ From Category (+/-)	1.5 high	0.5 abv av	na	Avg Mat 4.1 yrs

	2008	2007	2006	2005	2004	2003	2002	2001	2000	1999
Return (%)	-16.5	2.6	6.3	4.2	4.4	6.4	—	—	—	—
Differ From Category (+/-)	5.0	0.2	-3.4	2.1	-5.0	-14.6	—	—	—	—
Return, Tax-Adjusted (%)	-18.2	0.4	4.2	2.6	3.3	5.2	—	—	—	—
Dividends, Net Income ($)	0.47	0.64	0.61	0.44	0.31	0.32	—	—	—	—
Expense Ratio (%)	na	0.72	0.81	0.82	0.84	0.86	—	—	—	—
Yield (%)	6.14	6.70	6.16	4.45	3.14	3.25	—	—	—	—
Total Assets (Millions $)	1,235	2,271	3,048	2,517	2,162	956	—	—	—	—

SHAREHOLDER INFORMATION

Minimum Investment
Initial: $2,500 IRA: $2,500
Subsequent: $250 IRA: $250

Maximum Fees
Load: 1.00% redemption 12b-1: none
Other: redemp fee applies for 60 days; maint fee for low bal

Fidelity Focused High Income (FHIFX)

800-544-6666
www.fidelity.com

Corporate High-Yield Bond

PERFORMANCE AND PER SHARE DATA **fund inception date: 9/8/04**

	3yr Annual	5yr Annual	10yr Annual	Category Risk Index
Return (%)	-3.9	na	na	1.01—av
Differ From Category (+/-)	0.7 abv av	na	na	Avg Mat 7.0 yrs

	2008	2007	2006	2005	2004	2003	2002	2001	2000	1999
Return (%)	-20.5	3.0	8.5	2.8	—	—	—	—	—	—
Differ From Category (+/-)	1.0	0.6	-1.2	0.7	—	—	—	—	—	—
Return, Tax-Adjusted (%)	-22.7	0.9	6.3	0.9	—	—	—	—	—	—
Dividends, Net Income ($)	0.61	0.64	0.60	0.54	—	—	—	—	—	—
Expense Ratio (%)	0.85	0.85	0.85	0.84	—	—	—	—	—	—
Yield (%)	8.30	6.45	5.87	5.37	—	—	—	—	—	—
Total Assets (Millions $)	77	54	52	39	—	—	—	—	—	—

SHAREHOLDER INFORMATION

Minimum Investment
Initial: $2,500 IRA: $500
Subsequent: $250 IRA: $250

Maximum Fees
Load: 1.00% redemption 12b-1: none
Other: redemp fee applies for 90 days; maint fee for low bal

Fidelity High Income (SPHIX)

800-544-6666
www.fidelity.com

Corporate High-Yield Bond

PERFORMANCE AND PER SHARE DATA **fund inception date: 8/29/90**

	3yr Annual	5yr Annual	10yr Annual	Category Risk Index	
Return (%)	-4.8	-0.4	1.1	1.13—abv av	
Differ From Category (+/-)	-0.2 av	0.3 av	-0.8 blw av	**Avg Mat**	5.8 yrs

	2008	2007	2006	2005	2004	2003	2002	2001	2000	1999
Return (%)	-23.8	2.3	10.7	3.4	9.6	27.2	1.4	-4.9	-14.2	8.9
Differ From Category (+/-)	-2.3	-0.1	1.0	1.3	0.2	6.2	0.4	-8.6	-9.9	4.5
Return, Tax-Adjusted (%)	-26.3	-0.2	8.2	1.1	7.0	24.0	-1.6	-8.6	-17.2	5.2
Dividends, Net Income ($)	0.63	0.66	0.63	0.61	0.68	0.69	0.63	0.89	0.84	1.04
Expense Ratio (%)	0.74	0.75	0.76	0.77	0.77	0.79	0.76	0.74	0.74	0.80
Yield (%)	10.45	7.69	6.94	6.92	7.48	7.68	8.28	10.99	8.78	8.56
Total Assets (Millions $)	4,113	5,200	4,509	3,355	3,114	2,902	1,741	1,551	2,131	3,262

SHAREHOLDER INFORMATION

Minimum Investment
Initial: $2,500 IRA: $500
Subsequent: $250 IRA: $250

Maximum Fees
Load: 1.00% redemption 12b-1: none
Other: redemp fee applies for 90 days; maint fee for low bal

Janus High-Yield (JAHYX)

800-525-3713
www.janus.com

Corporate High-Yield Bond

PERFORMANCE AND PER SHARE DATA **fund inception date: 12/29/95**

	3yr Annual	5yr Annual	10yr Annual	Category Risk Index	
Return (%)	-3.2	0.4	3.2	0.95—blw av	
Differ From Category (+/-)	1.4 abv av	1.1 high	1.3 high	**Avg Mat**	5.6 yrs

	2008	2007	2006	2005	2004	2003	2002	2001	2000	1999
Return (%)	-19.4	1.3	11.1	2.7	9.4	16.0	2.5	4.5	2.4	5.5
Differ From Category (+/-)	2.1	-1.1	1.4	0.6	0.0	-5.0	2.3	0.8	6.7	1.1
Return, Tax-Adjusted (%)	-22.2	-1.3	8.4	0.4	7.0	13.5	-0.1	1.5	-0.8	2.2
Dividends, Net Income ($)	0.75	0.73	0.72	0.65	0.67	0.65	0.63	0.76	0.85	0.89
Expense Ratio (%)	na	0.86	0.90	0.87	0.96	0.96	0.96	0.99	1.00	1.00
Yield (%)	11.11	7.86	7.28	6.84	6.71	6.71	7.03	8.06	8.74	8.69
Total Assets (Millions $)	358	553	532	509	563	666	668	433	301	275

SHAREHOLDER INFORMATION

Minimum Investment
Initial: $2,500 IRA: $1,000
Subsequent: $100 IRA: $100

Maximum Fees
Load: 2.00% redemption 12b-1: none
Other: redemption fee applies for 3 months

Northern High Yield Fixed Income (NHFIX)

800-595-9111
www.northernfunds.com

Corporate High-Yield Bond

PERFORMANCE AND PER SHARE DATA **fund inception date: 12/31/98**

	3yr Annual	5yr Annual	10yr Annual	Category Risk Index	
Return (%)	-3.5	-0.1	2.6	0.97—blw av	
Differ From Category (+/-)	1.1 abv av	0.6 abv av	0.7 abv av	**Avg Mat**	6.4 yrs

	2008	2007	2006	2005	2004	2003	2002	2001	2000	1999
Return (%)	-19.4	1.3	10.0	1.7	8.5	23.6	1.3	7.0	-6.9	4.8
Differ From Category (+/-)	2.2	-1.1	0.3	-0.4	-0.7	2.2	1.3	3.4	-2.6	0.4
Return, Tax-Adjusted (%)	-21.8	-1.3	7.5	-0.6	5.9	20.4	-1.9	3.1	-10.7	1.8
Dividends, Net Income ($)	0.55	0.60	0.58	0.57	0.62	0.67	0.65	0.81	0.93	0.75
Expense Ratio (%)	0.90	0.90	0.90	0.90	0.90	0.90	0.90	0.90	0.90	0.90
Yield (%)	9.55	7.83	7.09	7.11	7.29	7.99	8.84	10.24	11.39	7.70
Total Assets (Millions $)	1,161	1,803	1,726	1,060	943	711	330	248	177	127

SHAREHOLDER INFORMATION

Minimum Investment
Initial: $2,500 IRA: $500
Subsequent: $50 IRA: $50

Maximum Fees
Load: 2.00% redemption 12b-1: none
Other: redemption fee applies for 30 days

Payden High Income (PYHRX)

800-572-9336
www.payden.com

Corporate High-Yield Bond

PERFORMANCE AND PER SHARE DATA **fund inception date: 12/30/97**

	3yr Annual	5yr Annual	10yr Annual	Category Risk Index	
Return (%)	-3.9	-0.3	2.3	1.05—abv av	
Differ From Category (+/-)	0.7 abv av	0.4 abv av	0.4 abv av	**Avg Mat**	6.8 yrs

	2008	2007	2006	2005	2004	2003	2002	2001	2000	1999
Return (%)	-20.4	2.6	8.8	2.3	8.2	18.6	2.1	4.6	-1.8	3.1
Differ From Category (+/-)	1.1	0.2	-0.9	0.2	-1.2	-2.4	1.9	0.9	2.5	-1.3
Return, Tax-Adjusted (%)	-23.1	0.1	6.2	-0.2	5.8	15.8	-1.0	1.7	-5.3	-0.1
Dividends, Net Income ($)	0.60	0.60	0.60	0.61	0.60	0.62	0.67	0.63	0.84	0.80
Expense Ratio (%)	na	0.61	0.59	0.53	0.52	0.55	0.52	0.57	0.57	0.55
Yield (%)	10.45	7.56	7.28	7.48	7.01	7.29	8.60	7.60	9.85	8.40
Total Assets (Millions $)	242	209	284	242	494	317	254	231	144	105

SHAREHOLDER INFORMATION

Minimum Investment
Initial: $5,000 IRA: $2,000
Subsequent: $250 IRA: $250

Maximum Fees
Load: 2.00% redemption 12b-1: none
Other: redemption fee applies for 30 days

T. Rowe Price High-Yield (PRHYX)

800-638-5660
www.troweprice.com

Corporate High-Yield Bond

PERFORMANCE AND PER SHARE DATA **fund inception date: 12/31/84**

	3yr Annual	5yr Annual	10yr Annual	Category Risk Index	
Return (%)	-5.1	-0.5	2.8	1.07—abv av	
Differ From Category (+/-)	-0.5 blw av	0.2 av	0.9 abv av	**Avg Mat**	6.2 yrs

	2008	2007	2006	2005	2004	2003	2002	2001	2000	1999
Return (%)	-24.5	3.1	9.7	3.4	10.3	22.5	3.0	6.0	-3.3	4.1
Differ From Category (+/-)	-3.0	0.7	0.0	1.3	0.9	1.5	2.8	2.4	1.0	-0.3
Return, Tax-Adjusted (%)	-27.0	0.5	7.1	0.8	7.6	19.3	-0.4	2.2	-7.1	0.5
Dividends, Net Income ($)	0.48	0.52	0.52	0.52	0.54	0.57	0.59	0.69	0.76	0.76
Expense Ratio (%)	0.76	0.77	0.77	0.77	0.78	0.81	0.83	0.82	0.83	0.82
Yield (%)	10.31	7.74	7.33	7.57	7.55	8.05	9.43	10.27	10.96	9.55
Total Assets (Millions $)	3,124	4,033	3,943	3,175	3,517	3,216	1,940	1,577	1,447	1,682

SHAREHOLDER INFORMATION

Minimum Investment
Initial: $2,500 IRA: $1,000
Subsequent: $100 IRA: $50

Maximum Fees
Load: 1.00% redemption 12b-1: none
Other: redemption fee applies for 90 days

Vanguard High-Yield Corporate (VWEHX)

800-662-2739
www.vanguard.com

Corporate High-Yield Bond

PERFORMANCE AND PER SHARE DATA **fund inception date: 12/27/78**

	3yr Annual	5yr Annual	10yr Annual	Category Risk Index	
Return (%)	-4.6	-0.7	1.9	1.15—high	
Differ From Category (+/-)	0.0 av	0.0 blw av	0.0 av	**Avg Mat**	6.7 yrs

	2008	2007	2006	2005	2004	2003	2002	2001	2000	1999
Return (%)	-21.3	2.0	8.2	2.7	8.5	17.2	1.7	2.9	-0.9	2.4
Differ From Category (+/-)	0.2	-0.4	-1.5	0.6	-0.9	-3.8	1.5	-0.8	3.4	-2.0
Return, Tax-Adjusted (%)	-23.9	-0.5	5.7	0.3	5.9	14.3	-1.4	-0.6	-4.4	-0.7
Dividends, Net Income ($)	0.43	0.45	0.44	0.44	0.46	0.48	0.51	0.60	0.64	0.63
Expense Ratio (%)	0.25	0.26	0.25	0.22	0.23	0.26	0.27	0.27	0.28	0.29
Yield (%)	10.17	7.56	7.02	7.11	7.14	7.45	8.63	9.47	9.55	8.49
Total Assets (Millions $)	3,546	4,679	5,112	5,212	7,317	7,095	5,433	5,160	5,270	5,699

SHAREHOLDER INFORMATION

Minimum Investment
Initial: $3,000 IRA: $0
Subsequent: $100 IRA: $0

Maximum Fees
Load: 1.00% redemption 12b-1: none
Other: redemption fee applies for 1 year

Mortgage-Backed Bond Funds
Category Performance Ranked by 2008 Returns

Fund (Ticker)	Annual Return (%) 2008	3Yr	5Yr	10Yr	Category Risk	Total Risk
Payden GNMA (PYGNX)	7.6	6.1	5.0	na	high	low
USAA GNMA (USGNX)	7.2	5.8	4.7	5.0	av	low
Vanguard GNMA (VFIIX)	7.2	6.1	5.1	5.7	abv av	low
Fidelity Ginnie Mae (FGMNX)	7.1	5.9	4.9	5.4	abv av	low
American Century Ginnie Mae Inv (BGNMX)	7.0	5.8	4.6	5.0	abv av	low
T. Rowe Price GNMA (PRGMX)	5.6	5.3	4.5	5.2	blw av	low
Mortgage-Backed Bond Category Average	**1.0**	**3.5**	**3.3**	**4.4**	**av**	**low**

American Century Ginnie Mae Inv (BGNMX)

800-345-2021
www.americancentury.com

Mortgage-Backed Bond

PERFORMANCE AND PER SHARE DATA **fund inception date: 9/23/85**

	3yr Annual	5yr Annual	10yr Annual	Category Risk Index
Return (%)	5.8	4.6	5.0	1.00—abv av
Differ From Category (+/-)	2.3 high	1.3 high	0.6 abv av	**Avg Mat** 6.7 yrs

	2008	2007	2006	2005	2004	2003	2002	2001	2000	1999
Return (%)	7.0	6.4	4.0	2.8	3.1	2.0	8.3	7.4	10.4	0.9
Differ From Category (+/-)	6.0	0.6	-0.2	0.4	-0.3	-0.3	0.3	-0.2	-1.3	-0.7
Return, Tax-Adjusted (%)	5.5	4.7	2.3	1.2	1.5	0.4	6.1	5.0	7.8	-1.5
Dividends, Net Income ($)	0.46	0.50	0.50	0.48	0.48	0.50	0.58	0.63	0.67	0.65
Expense Ratio (%)	0.57	0.57	0.57	0.58	0.59	0.59	0.59	0.59	0.59	0.59
Yield (%)	4.34	4.89	4.91	4.66	4.60	4.74	5.32	5.96	6.42	6.41
Total Assets (Millions $)	1,255	1,165	1,238	1,400	1,517	1,732	2,069	1,646	1,288	1,298

SHAREHOLDER INFORMATION

Minimum Investment
Initial: $2,500 IRA: $2,500
Subsequent: $50 IRA: $50

Maximum Fees
Load: none 12b-1: none
Other: none

Fidelity Ginnie Mae (FGMNX)

800-544-6666
www.fidelity.com

Mortgage-Backed Bond

PERFORMANCE AND PER SHARE DATA **fund inception date: 11/8/85**

	3yr Annual	5yr Annual	10yr Annual	Category Risk Index
Return (%)	5.9	4.9	5.4	0.94—abv av
Differ From Category (+/-)	2.4 high	1.6 high	1.0 high	**Avg Mat** 5.2 yrs

	2008	2007	2006	2005	2004	2003	2002	2001	2000	1999
Return (%)	7.1	6.7	4.1	2.6	4.1	2.2	8.6	7.2	10.7	1.2
Differ From Category (+/-)	6.1	0.9	-0.1	0.2	0.8	-0.1	0.6	-0.4	0.4	0.1
Return, Tax-Adjusted (%)	5.4	4.9	2.4	1.0	2.7	1.1	6.7	4.9	8.0	-1.2
Dividends, Net Income ($)	0.54	0.55	0.51	0.50	0.46	0.31	0.54	0.63	0.70	0.66
Expense Ratio (%)	0.45	0.45	0.45	0.45	0.60	0.57	0.60	0.62	0.63	0.64
Yield (%)	4.81	5.00	4.76	4.60	4.11	2.81	4.80	5.81	6.53	6.38
Total Assets (Millions $)	4,245	3,212	3,332	3,789	4,036	4,505	6,808	3,901	1,890	1,758

SHAREHOLDER INFORMATION

Minimum Investment
Initial: $2,500 IRA: $500
Subsequent: $250 IRA: $250

Maximum Fees
Load: none 12b-1: none
Other: maint fee for low bal

Payden GNMA (PYGNX)

800-572-9336
www.payden.com

Mortgage-Backed Bond

PERFORMANCE AND PER SHARE DATA **fund inception date: 8/27/99**

	3yr Annual	5yr Annual	10yr Annual	Category Risk Index	
Return (%)	6.1	5.0	na	1.00—high	
Differ From Category (+/-)	2.6 high	1.7 high	na	**Avg Mat**	6.5 yrs

	2008	2007	2006	2005	2004	2003	2002	2001	2000	1999
Return (%)	7.6	6.2	4.4	2.9	4.1	3.0	9.8	7.6	11.2	—
Differ From Category (+/-)	6.6	0.4	0.2	0.5	0.7	0.7	1.9	0.1	0.9	—
Return, Tax-Adjusted (%)	5.8	4.4	2.6	1.1	2.1	1.0	7.4	4.8	8.4	—
Dividends, Net Income ($)	0.50	0.50	0.51	0.52	0.59	0.59	0.62	0.64	0.69	—
Expense Ratio (%)	na	0.50	0.50	0.50	0.50	0.50	0.35	0.35	0.35	—
Yield (%)	4.99	5.05	5.21	5.28	5.87	5.78	5.86	6.11	6.65	—
Total Assets (Millions $)	414	168	147	114	113	147	169	152	126	—

SHAREHOLDER INFORMATION

Minimum Investment
Initial: $5,000 IRA: $2,000
Subsequent: $250 IRA: $250

Maximum Fees
Load: none 12b-1: none
Other: none

T. Rowe Price GNMA (PRGMX)

800-638-5660
www.troweprice.com

Mortgage-Backed Bond

PERFORMANCE AND PER SHARE DATA **fund inception date: 11/26/85**

	3yr Annual	5yr Annual	10yr Annual	Category Risk Index	
Return (%)	5.3	4.5	5.2	0.91—blw av	
Differ From Category (+/-)	1.8 abv av	1.2 abv av	0.8 abv av	**Avg Mat**	5.8 yrs

	2008	2007	2006	2005	2004	2003	2002	2001	2000	1999
Return (%)	5.6	6.5	3.8	2.7	3.7	2.3	9.0	7.6	10.9	0.2
Differ From Category (+/-)	4.6	0.7	-0.4	0.3	0.4	0.0	1.0	0.0	0.6	-0.9
Return, Tax-Adjusted (%)	3.9	4.8	2.1	1.1	2.2	0.9	7.2	5.3	8.3	-2.3
Dividends, Net Income ($)	0.45	0.47	0.46	0.44	0.43	0.39	0.43	0.56	0.60	0.60
Expense Ratio (%)	0.62	0.65	0.66	0.67	0.69	0.70	0.69	0.70	0.71	0.71
Yield (%)	4.68	4.89	4.94	4.62	4.46	3.99	4.32	5.94	6.37	6.66
Total Assets (Millions $)	1,327	1,346	1,264	1,262	1,356	1,315	1,408	1,139	1,091	1,089

SHAREHOLDER INFORMATION

Minimum Investment
Initial: $2,500 IRA: $1,000
Subsequent: $100 IRA: $50

Maximum Fees
Load: none 12b-1: none
Other: none

USAA GNMA
(USGNX)

800-531-8181
www.usaa.com

Mortgage-Backed Bond

PERFORMANCE AND PER SHARE DATA **fund inception date: 2/1/91**

	3yr Annual	5yr Annual	10yr Annual	Category Risk Index	
Return (%)	5.8	4.7	5.0	0.91—av	
Differ From Category (+/-)	2.3 high	1.4 high	0.6 av	**Avg Mat**	5.3 yrs

	2008	2007	2006	2005	2004	2003	2002	2001	2000	1999
Return (%)	7.2	6.2	4.1	2.7	3.4	2.0	9.2	7.1	12.1	-3.6
Differ From Category (+/-)	6.2	0.4	-0.1	0.3	0.0	-0.3	1.2	-0.5	1.8	-4.7
Return, Tax-Adjusted (%)	5.6	4.6	2.5	1.0	1.7	0.3	7.0	4.7	9.3	-6.0
Dividends, Net Income ($)	0.44	0.45	0.46	0.48	0.47	0.49	0.57	0.61	0.66	0.64
Expense Ratio (%)	0.51	0.52	0.49	0.48	0.47	0.46	0.41	0.32	0.32	0.31
Yield (%)	4.45	4.68	4.79	4.99	4.83	4.92	5.61	6.14	6.70	6.80
Total Assets (Millions $)	552	499	513	563	610	649	727	533	439	449

SHAREHOLDER INFORMATION

Minimum Investment
Initial: $3,000 IRA: $250
Subsequent: $50 IRA: $50

Maximum Fees
Load: none 12b-1: none
Other: none

Vanguard GNMA
(VFIIX)

800-662-2739
www.vanguard.com

Mortgage-Backed Bond

PERFORMANCE AND PER SHARE DATA **fund inception date: 6/27/80**

	3yr Annual	5yr Annual	10yr Annual	Category Risk Index	
Return (%)	6.1	5.1	5.7	1.00—abv av	
Differ From Category (+/-)	2.6 high	1.8 high	1.3 high	**Avg Mat**	5.8 yrs

	2008	2007	2006	2005	2004	2003	2002	2001	2000	1999
Return (%)	7.2	7.0	4.3	3.3	4.1	2.4	9.6	7.9	11.2	0.7
Differ From Category (+/-)	6.2	1.2	0.1	0.9	0.7	0.1	1.6	0.3	0.9	-0.4
Return, Tax-Adjusted (%)	5.4	5.1	2.5	1.7	2.5	0.8	7.4	5.4	8.4	-1.8
Dividends, Net Income ($)	0.52	0.53	0.52	0.48	0.48	0.51	0.59	0.66	0.68	0.67
Expense Ratio (%)	0.21	0.21	0.21	0.20	0.20	0.22	0.27	0.27	0.27	0.30
Yield (%)	4.86	5.13	5.09	4.66	4.62	4.86	5.46	6.31	6.67	6.77
Total Assets (Millions $)	14,725	12,776	12,869	13,890	18,858	19,408	21,792	15,531	13,911	12,548

SHAREHOLDER INFORMATION

Minimum Investment
Initial: $3,000 IRA: $3,000
Subsequent: $100 IRA: $0

Maximum Fees
Load: none 12b-1: none
Other: none

Government: Short-Term Bond Funds
Category Performance Ranked by 2008 Returns

Fund (Ticker)	Annual Return (%) 2008	3Yr	5Yr	10Yr	Category Risk	Total Risk
Fidelity Spartan S/T Tr Bd Idx Inv (FSBIX)	8.7	6.6	na	na	high	low
Vanguard Short-Term Federal (VSGBX)	7.0	6.2	4.3	5.1	abv av	low
American Century Target Mat 2010 Inv (BTTNX)	6.9	6.0	4.6	5.6	high	low
Vanguard Short-Term Treasury (VFISX)	6.6	6.1	4.1	4.9	av	low
Dreyfus Short-Intermediate Government (DSIGX)	6.5	5.2	3.5	4.1	blw av	low
American Century Short-Term Govt Inv (TWUSX)	4.7	5.0	3.4	3.9	av	low
Gov't: Short-Term Bond Category Average	**4.9**	**5.0**	**3.4**	**4.2**	**av**	**low**

American Century Short-Term Govt Inv (TWUSX)

800-345-2021
www.americancentury.com

Government: Short-Term Bond

PERFORMANCE AND PER SHARE DATA **fund inception date: 12/15/82**

	3yr Annual	5yr Annual	10yr Annual	Category Risk Index
Return (%)	5.0	3.4	3.9	0.83—av
Differ From Category (+/-)	0.0 av	0.0 av	-0.3 blw av	**Avg Mat** na

	2008	2007	2006	2005	2004	2003	2002	2001	2000	1999
Return (%)	4.7	6.3	3.9	1.6	0.6	1.1	5.2	7.0	7.6	1.8
Differ From Category (+/-)	-0.2	0.0	0.1	0.0	-0.5	-0.5	-1.3	0.4	-1.9	0.4
Return, Tax-Adjusted (%)	3.4	4.7	2.5	0.5	-0.1	0.4	3.9	5.0	5.3	-0.2
Dividends, Net Income ($)	0.33	0.42	0.40	0.30	0.18	0.19	0.32	0.48	0.53	0.49
Expense Ratio (%)	0.57	0.57	0.57	0.58	0.59	0.59	0.59	0.59	0.59	0.59
Yield (%)	3.44	4.41	4.23	3.16	1.91	1.93	3.33	5.05	5.69	5.36
Total Assets (Millions $)	1,016	1,138	899	869	923	1,006	944	823	768	773

SHAREHOLDER INFORMATION

Minimum Investment
Initial: $2,500 IRA: $2,500
Subsequent: $50 IRA: $50

Maximum Fees
Load: none 12b-1: none
Other: none

American Century Target Mat 2010 Inv (BTTNX)

800-345-2021
www.americancentury.com

Government: Short-Term Bond

PERFORMANCE AND PER SHARE DATA **fund inception date: 3/25/85**

	3yr Annual	5yr Annual	10yr Annual	Category Risk Index
Return (%)	6.0	4.6	5.6	1.61—high
Differ From Category (+/-)	1.0 abv av	1.2 high	1.4 high	**Avg Mat** 2.0 yrs

	2008	2007	2006	2005	2004	2003	2002	2001	2000	1999
Return (%)	6.9	8.3	2.8	1.3	4.0	3.1	18.2	4.2	22.5	-11.8
Differ From Category (+/-)	2.0	2.0	-1.0	-0.3	2.9	1.5	11.7	-2.5	13.5	-12.9
Return, Tax-Adjusted (%)	5.4	6.6	1.1	-0.3	2.3	0.9	15.8	2.0	20.2	-13.8
Dividends, Net Income ($)	3.52	4.40	4.75	4.48	4.72	5.14	5.03	5.77	5.46	5.64
Expense Ratio (%)	0.57	0.57	0.57	0.58	0.59	0.59	0.59	0.59	0.59	0.59
Yield (%)	3.30	4.20	4.71	4.34	4.35	4.47	4.16	5.34	4.98	5.98
Total Assets (Millions $)	271	240	208	218	212	236	305	252	270	219

SHAREHOLDER INFORMATION

Minimum Investment
Initial: $2,500 IRA: $2,500
Subsequent: $50 IRA: $0

Maximum Fees
Load: none 12b-1: none
Other: none

Dreyfus Short-Intermediate Government (DSIGX)

800-645-6561
www.dreyfus.com

Government: Short-Term Bond

PERFORMANCE AND PER SHARE DATA **fund inception date: 4/6/87**

	3yr Annual	5yr Annual	10yr Annual	Category Risk Index	
Return (%)	5.2	3.5	4.1	0.78—blw av	
Differ From Category (+/-)	0.2 av	0.1 av	-0.1 abv av	**Avg Mat**	1.9 yrs

	2008	2007	2006	2005	2004	2003	2002	2001	2000	1999
Return (%)	6.5	5.6	3.5	1.6	0.3	2.2	5.2	6.0	8.9	1.8
Differ From Category (+/-)	1.6	-0.7	-0.3	0.0	-0.8	0.6	-1.3	-0.7	-0.1	0.7
Return, Tax-Adjusted (%)	5.3	4.1	2.2	0.5	-0.7	0.9	3.8	4.2	6.6	-0.4
Dividends, Net Income ($)	0.36	0.43	0.39	0.33	0.31	0.40	0.39	0.47	0.61	0.62
Expense Ratio (%)	na	0.76	0.76	0.73	0.71	0.76	0.74	0.73	0.71	0.71
Yield (%)	3.31	4.09	3.78	3.14	2.92	3.65	3.52	4.38	5.71	5.94
Total Assets (Millions $)	218	180	213	265	323	434	477	473	372	422

SHAREHOLDER INFORMATION

Minimum Investment
Initial: $2,500 IRA: $750
Subsequent: $100 IRA: $0

Maximum Fees
Load: none 12b-1: none
Other: none

Fidelity Spartan S/T Tr Bd Idx Inv (FSBIX)

800-544-6666
www.fidelity.com

Government: Short-Term Bond

PERFORMANCE AND PER SHARE DATA **fund inception date: 12/20/05**

	3yr Annual	5yr Annual	10yr Annual	Category Risk Index	
Return (%)	6.6	na	na	1.39—high	
Differ From Category (+/-)	1.6 high	na	na	**Avg Mat**	2.5 yrs

	2008	2007	2006	2005	2004	2003	2002	2001	2000	1999
Return (%)	8.7	7.8	3.5	—	—	—	—	—	—	—
Differ From Category (+/-)	3.8	1.5	-0.3	—	—	—	—	—	—	—
Return, Tax-Adjusted (%)	7.4	6.4	2.2	—	—	—	—	—	—	—
Dividends, Net Income ($)	0.33	0.41	0.38	—	—	—	—	—	—	—
Expense Ratio (%)	0.20	0.20	0.20	—	—	—	—	—	—	—
Yield (%)	2.99	4.00	3.77	—	—	—	—	—	—	—
Total Assets (Millions $)	229	90	21	—	—	—	—	—	—	—

SHAREHOLDER INFORMATION

Minimum Investment
Initial: $10,000 IRA: $0
Subsequent: $1,000 IRA: $0

Maximum Fees
Load: none 12b-1: none
Other: maint fee for low bal

Vanguard Short-Term Federal (VSGBX)

800-662-2739
www.vanguard.com

Government: Short-Term Bond

PERFORMANCE AND PER SHARE DATA **fund inception date: 12/31/87**

	3yr Annual	5yr Annual	10yr Annual	Category Risk Index	
Return (%)	6.2	4.3	5.1	1.17—abv av	
Differ From Category (+/-)	1.2 high	0.9 high	0.9 high	**Avg Mat**	2.7 yrs

	2008	2007	2006	2005	2004	2003	2002	2001	2000	1999
Return (%)	7.0	7.4	4.3	1.7	1.3	1.9	7.6	8.6	9.1	2.0
Differ From Category (+/-)	2.1	1.1	0.5	0.2	0.2	0.3	1.1	1.9	0.1	0.9
Return, Tax-Adjusted (%)	5.6	5.8	2.9	0.6	0.3	0.9	5.7	6.5	6.7	-0.2
Dividends, Net Income ($)	0.42	0.46	0.41	0.33	0.29	0.31	0.43	0.55	0.61	0.57
Expense Ratio (%)	0.20	0.20	0.20	0.20	0.22	0.26	0.31	0.28	0.27	0.27
Yield (%)	3.83	4.39	4.02	3.25	2.78	2.95	3.97	5.22	5.96	5.71
Total Assets (Millions $)	2,104	1,581	1,513	1,698	2,432	2,673	2,851	1,783	1,502	1,521

SHAREHOLDER INFORMATION

Minimum Investment
Initial: $3,000 IRA: $3,000
Subsequent: $100 IRA: $0

Maximum Fees
Load: none 12b-1: none
Other: none

Vanguard Short-Term Treasury (VFISX)

800-662-2739
www.vanguard.com

Government: Short-Term Bond

PERFORMANCE AND PER SHARE DATA **fund inception date: 10/28/91**

	3yr Annual	5yr Annual	10yr Annual	Category Risk Index	
Return (%)	6.1	4.1	4.9	1.17—av	
Differ From Category (+/-)	1.1 abv av	0.7 abv av	0.7 high	**Avg Mat**	2.4 yrs

	2008	2007	2006	2005	2004	2003	2002	2001	2000	1999
Return (%)	6.6	7.8	3.7	1.7	1.0	2.3	8.0	7.8	8.8	1.8
Differ From Category (+/-)	1.7	1.5	-0.1	0.1	-0.1	0.7	1.5	1.1	-0.2	0.7
Return, Tax-Adjusted (%)	5.5	6.3	2.3	0.6	0.1	1.2	6.2	5.8	6.4	-0.3
Dividends, Net Income ($)	0.30	0.45	0.43	0.32	0.28	0.27	0.42	0.52	0.59	0.53
Expense Ratio (%)	0.22	0.26	0.26	0.24	0.26	0.28	0.29	0.27	0.27	0.27
Yield (%)	2.68	4.24	4.18	3.11	2.65	2.53	3.79	4.94	5.78	5.27
Total Assets (Millions $)	2,935	1,594	1,331	1,383	1,886	2,086	2,211	1,394	1,200	1,235

SHAREHOLDER INFORMATION

Minimum Investment
Initial: $3,000 IRA: $3,000
Subsequent: $100 IRA: $0

Maximum Fees
Load: none 12b-1: none
Other: none

Government: Intermediate-Term Bond Funds
Category Performance Ranked by 2008 Returns

Fund (Ticker)	Annual Return (%) 2008	3Yr	5Yr	10Yr	Category Risk	Total Risk
Fidelity Spartan Interm Tr Bd Idx Inv (FIBIX)	16.3	9.5	na	na	high	low
T. Rowe Price U.S. Treasury Interm (PRTIX)	14.1	8.7	5.7	5.8	high	low
Vanguard Interm-Term Treasury (VFITX)	13.3	8.7	6.3	6.5	high	low
American Century Target Mat 2015 Inv (BTFTX)	12.7	8.2	7.7	7.1	high	low
Dreyfus U.S. Treasury Intermediate Term (DRGIX)	11.1	7.4	5.0	5.3	av	low
Fidelity Government Income (FGOVX)	11.0	7.4	5.6	5.7	abv av	low
Fidelity Intermediate Government (FSTGX)	10.0	7.1	5.0	5.5	low	low
American Century Government Bond Inv (CPTNX)	9.5	7.0	5.2	5.4	av	low
Gov't: Intermediate-Term Bond Category Average	**9.6**	**6.9**	**5.1**	**5.4**	**av**	**low**

American Century Government Bond Inv (CPTNX)

800-345-2021
www.americancentury.com

Government: Intermediate-Term Bond

PERFORMANCE AND PER SHARE DATA **fund inception date: 5/16/80**

	3yr Annual	5yr Annual	10yr Annual	Category Risk Index	
Return (%)	7.0	5.2	5.4	0.93—av	
Differ From Category (+/-)	0.1 av	0.1 abv av	0.0 av	**Avg Mat**	5.7 yrs

	2008	2007	2006	2005	2004	2003	2002	2001	2000	1999
Return (%)	9.5	7.8	3.9	2.4	2.4	1.9	10.9	6.7	12.4	-2.1
Differ From Category (+/-)	-0.1	0.0	0.5	0.3	-0.8	-0.5	0.2	0.0	-0.7	0.4
Return, Tax-Adjusted (%)	7.9	6.2	2.3	1.1	1.3	0.5	8.8	4.8	10.3	-4.1
Dividends, Net Income ($)	0.44	0.48	0.47	0.39	0.28	0.30	0.41	0.50	0.54	0.51
Expense Ratio (%)	0.49	0.49	0.49	0.50	0.51	0.51	0.51	0.51	0.51	0.51
Yield (%)	3.85	4.49	4.52	3.74	2.57	2.73	3.56	4.66	5.10	5.07
Total Assets (Millions $)	858	582	478	521	436	486	588	440	352	352

SHAREHOLDER INFORMATION

Minimum Investment
Initial: $2,500 IRA: $2,500
Subsequent: $50 IRA: $50

Maximum Fees
Load: none 12b-1: none
Other: none

American Century Target Mat 2015 Inv (BTFTX)

800-345-2021
www.americancentury.com

Government: Intermediate-Term Bond

PERFORMANCE AND PER SHARE DATA **fund inception date: 9/2/86**

	3yr Annual	5yr Annual	10yr Annual	Category Risk Index	
Return (%)	8.2	7.7	7.1	1.85—high	
Differ From Category (+/-)	1.3 abv av	2.6 high	1.7 high	**Avg Mat**	6.7 yrs

	2008	2007	2006	2005	2004	2003	2002	2001	2000	1999
Return (%)	12.7	10.0	2.0	4.9	9.0	3.9	21.2	0.6	26.5	-14.6
Differ From Category (+/-)	3.1	2.2	-1.4	2.8	5.8	1.5	10.5	-6.1	13.8	-11.8
Return, Tax-Adjusted (%)	11.1	8.4	0.3	3.3	7.2	1.6	19.2	-1.6	24.0	-16.5
Dividends, Net Income ($)	3.62	3.98	4.20	3.89	3.90	4.73	4.03	4.53	4.45	4.12
Expense Ratio (%)	0.57	0.57	0.57	0.58	0.59	0.59	0.59	0.59	0.59	0.59
Yield (%)	3.68	4.39	4.89	4.36	4.31	5.27	4.40	5.71	5.32	5.89
Total Assets (Millions $)	329	248	198	204	162	144	164	130	159	200

SHAREHOLDER INFORMATION

Minimum Investment
Initial: $2,500 IRA: $2,500
Subsequent: $50 IRA: $0

Maximum Fees
Load: none 12b-1: none
Other: none

Dreyfus U.S. Treasury Intermediate Term (DRGIX)

800-645-6561
www.dreyfus.com

Government: Intermediate-Term Bond

PERFORMANCE AND PER SHARE DATA **fund inception date: 3/27/87**

	3yr Annual	5yr Annual	10yr Annual	Category Risk Index	
Return (%)	7.4	5.0	5.3	0.88—av	
Differ From Category (+/-)	0.5 abv av	-0.1 av	-0.1 av	**Avg Mat**	3.8 yrs

	2008	2007	2006	2005	2004	2003	2002	2001	2000	1999
Return (%)	11.1	8.2	3.0	2.3	0.8	3.1	8.5	7.8	12.8	-3.5
Differ From Category (+/-)	1.5	0.4	-0.4	0.2	-2.4	0.7	-2.2	1.1	0.1	-0.7
Return, Tax-Adjusted (%)	9.6	6.7	1.7	1.1	-0.5	1.9	6.8	5.6	10.2	-5.9
Dividends, Net Income ($)	0.54	0.52	0.47	0.44	0.49	0.46	0.56	0.69	0.78	0.75
Expense Ratio (%)	na	0.65	0.65	0.65	0.66	0.80	0.80	0.80	0.80	0.80
Yield (%)	3.90	4.07	3.75	3.51	3.84	3.54	4.26	5.44	6.30	6.46
Total Assets (Millions $)	243	194	191	177	195	191	144	141	132	160

SHAREHOLDER INFORMATION

Minimum Investment
Initial: $2,500 IRA: $750
Subsequent: $100 IRA: $0

Maximum Fees
Load: none 12b-1: none
Other: none

Fidelity Government Income (FGOVX)

800-544-6666
www.fidelity.com

Government: Intermediate-Term Bond

PERFORMANCE AND PER SHARE DATA **fund inception date: 4/4/79**

	3yr Annual	5yr Annual	10yr Annual	Category Risk Index	
Return (%)	7.4	5.6	5.7	0.98—abv av	
Differ From Category (+/-)	0.5 abv av	0.5 abv av	0.3 abv av	**Avg Mat**	5.2 yrs

	2008	2007	2006	2005	2004	2003	2002	2001	2000	1999
Return (%)	11.0	7.9	3.5	2.4	3.5	2.2	10.9	6.7	12.6	-2.3
Differ From Category (+/-)	1.4	0.1	0.1	0.3	0.4	-0.2	0.2	0.0	-0.1	0.5
Return, Tax-Adjusted (%)	9.4	6.3	2.0	1.1	2.4	0.9	9.0	4.5	10.0	-4.5
Dividends, Net Income ($)	0.42	0.45	0.42	0.36	0.31	0.33	0.43	0.55	0.62	0.56
Expense Ratio (%)	0.45	0.44	0.44	0.58	0.63	0.65	0.68	0.60	0.66	0.67
Yield (%)	3.78	4.37	4.20	3.59	2.99	3.14	4.01	5.51	6.27	6.03
Total Assets (Millions $)	6,338	6,440	5,975	5,590	4,478	3,886	3,381	2,402	1,699	1,589

SHAREHOLDER INFORMATION

Minimum Investment
Initial: $2,500 IRA: $500
Subsequent: $250 IRA: $250

Maximum Fees
Load: none 12b-1: none
Other: maint fee for low bal

Fidelity Intermediate Government (FSTGX)

800-544-6666
www.fidelity.com

Government: Intermediate-Term Bond

PERFORMANCE AND PER SHARE DATA **fund inception date: 5/2/88**

	3yr Annual	5yr Annual	10yr Annual	Category Risk Index	
Return (%)	7.1	5.0	5.5	0.76—low	
Differ From Category (+/-)	0.2 av	-0.1 av	0.1 abv av	**Avg Mat**	4.6 yrs

	2008	2007	2006	2005	2004	2003	2002	2001	2000	1999
Return (%)	10.0	7.9	3.6	1.4	2.4	1.9	10.2	7.9	10.3	0.6
Differ From Category (+/-)	0.4	0.1	0.2	-0.7	-0.8	-0.5	-0.5	1.2	-2.4	3.4
Return, Tax-Adjusted (%)	8.9	6.2	2.1	0.2	1.3	0.9	8.6	5.6	7.7	-1.8
Dividends, Net Income ($)	0.35	0.46	0.42	0.36	0.29	0.29	0.41	0.56	0.62	0.60
Expense Ratio (%)	0.45	0.45	0.45	0.57	0.60	0.60	0.59	0.60	0.61	0.53
Yield (%)	3.15	4.46	4.18	3.54	2.87	2.79	3.96	5.67	6.39	6.44
Total Assets (Millions $)	1,610	755	724	831	941	1,116	1,367	918	766	820

SHAREHOLDER INFORMATION

Minimum Investment
Initial: $2,500 IRA: $500
Subsequent: $250 IRA: $250

Maximum Fees
Load: none 12b-1: none
Other: maint fee for low bal

Fidelity Spartan Interm Tr Bd Idx Inv (FIBIX)

800-544-6666
www.fidelity.com

Government: Intermediate-Term Bond

PERFORMANCE AND PER SHARE DATA **fund inception date: 12/20/05**

	3yr Annual	5yr Annual	10yr Annual	Category Risk Index	
Return (%)	9.5	na	na	1.49—high	
Differ From Category (+/-)	2.6 high	na	na	**Avg Mat**	6.8 yrs

	2008	2007	2006	2005	2004	2003	2002	2001	2000	1999
Return (%)	16.3	10.0	2.6	—	—	—	—	—	—	—
Differ From Category (+/-)	6.7	2.2	-0.8	—	—	—	—	—	—	—
Return, Tax-Adjusted (%)	14.8	8.5	1.1	—	—	—	—	—	—	—
Dividends, Net Income ($)	0.39	0.42	0.41	—	—	—	—	—	—	—
Expense Ratio (%)	0.20	0.20	0.00	—	—	—	—	—	—	—
Yield (%)	3.32	4.02	4.17	—	—	—	—	—	—	—
Total Assets (Millions $)	1,193	824	554	—	—	—	—	—	—	—

SHAREHOLDER INFORMATION

Minimum Investment
Initial: $10,000 IRA: $0
Subsequent: $1,000 IRA: $0

Maximum Fees
Load: none 12b-1: none
Other: maint fee for low bal

T. Rowe Price U.S. Treasury Interm (PRTIX)

800-638-5660
www.troweprice.com

Government: Intermediate-Term Bond

PERFORMANCE AND PER SHARE DATA **fund inception date: 9/29/89**

	3yr Annual	5yr Annual	10yr Annual	Category Risk Index	
Return (%)	8.7	5.7	5.8	1.34—high	
Differ From Category (+/-)	1.8 high	0.6 high	0.4 high	**Avg Mat**	6.6 yrs

	2008	2007	2006	2005	2004	2003	2002	2001	2000	1999
Return (%)	14.1	9.9	2.5	1.5	1.1	1.8	12.0	7.5	12.1	-3.3
Differ From Category (+/-)	4.5	2.1	-0.9	-0.6	-2.1	-0.6	1.3	0.8	-0.6	-0.5
Return, Tax-Adjusted (%)	12.8	8.4	1.2	0.1	-0.1	0.5	10.1	5.5	9.9	-5.4
Dividends, Net Income ($)	0.19	0.22	0.20	0.20	0.18	0.19	0.23	0.26	0.28	0.27
Expense Ratio (%)	0.54	0.57	0.62	0.65	0.65	0.64	0.64	0.65	0.64	0.62
Yield (%)	3.17	3.91	3.79	3.76	3.36	3.42	4.01	4.80	5.38	5.32
Total Assets (Millions $)	661	274	232	262	291	348	398	280	225	244

SHAREHOLDER INFORMATION

Minimum Investment
Initial: $2,500 IRA: $1,000
Subsequent: $100 IRA: $50

Maximum Fees
Load: none 12b-1: none
Other: none

Vanguard Interm-Term Treasury (VFITX)

800-662-2739
www.vanguard.com

Government: Intermediate-Term Bond

PERFORMANCE AND PER SHARE DATA **fund inception date: 10/28/91**

	3yr Annual	5yr Annual	10yr Annual	Category Risk Index	
Return (%)	8.7	6.3	6.5	1.29—high	
Differ From Category (+/-)	1.8 high	1.2 high	1.1 high	**Avg Mat**	6.6 yrs

	2008	2007	2006	2005	2004	2003	2002	2001	2000	1999
Return (%)	13.3	9.9	3.1	2.3	3.4	2.3	14.1	7.5	14.0	-3.6
Differ From Category (+/-)	3.7	2.1	-0.3	0.2	0.2	-0.1	3.4	0.8	1.3	-0.8
Return, Tax-Adjusted (%)	11.6	8.3	1.5	0.6	1.8	0.7	11.7	5.3	11.4	-5.8
Dividends, Net Income ($)	0.44	0.49	0.50	0.51	0.50	0.48	0.58	0.62	0.65	0.62
Expense Ratio (%)	0.36	0.26	0.26	0.24	0.26	0.28	0.29	0.28	0.27	0.27
Yield (%)	3.54	4.36	4.64	4.61	4.46	4.15	4.84	5.65	5.97	6.16
Total Assets (Millions $)	3,265	2,076	1,696	1,761	2,160	2,296	2,685	1,971	1,761	1,705

SHAREHOLDER INFORMATION

Minimum Investment
Initial: $3,000 IRA: $3,000
Subsequent: $100 IRA: $0

Maximum Fees
Load: none 12b-1: none
Other: none

Government: Long-Term Bond Funds
Category Performance Ranked by 2008 Returns

Fund (Ticker)	Annual Return (%) 2008	3Yr	5Yr	10Yr	Category Risk	Total Risk
Wasatch-Hoisington U.S. Treasury (WHOSX)	37.7	14.7	13.0	9.1	abv av	av
American Century Target Mat 2025 Inv (BTTRX)	26.5	10.9	12.7	8.6	abv av	av
Fidelity Spartan L/T Tr Bd Idx Inv (FLBIX)	24.1	11.4	na	na	low	blw av
T. Rowe Price U.S. Treasury Long-Term (PRULX)	23.2	11.0	8.8	7.2	blw av	blw av
Vanguard Long-Term U.S. Treasury (VUSTX)	22.5	10.8	9.2	7.8	low	blw av
Dreyfus U.S. Treasury Long-Term (DRGBX)	21.5	10.7	8.3	6.7	blw av	blw av
Gov't: Long-Term Bond Category Average	**30.7**	**12.9**	**10.8**	**7.8**	**av**	**blw av**

American Century Target Mat 2025 Inv (BTTRX)

800-345-2021
www.americancentury.com

Government: Long-Term Bond

PERFORMANCE AND PER SHARE DATA **fund inception date: 2/15/96**

	3yr Annual	5yr Annual	10yr Annual	Category Risk Index
Return (%)	10.9	12.7	8.6	1.20—abv av
Differ From Category (+/-)	-2.0 av	1.9 abv av	0.8 high	**Avg Mat** 16.5 yrs

	2008	2007	2006	2005	2004	2003	2002	2001	2000	1999
Return (%)	26.5	9.4	-1.4	14.6	16.3	2.0	20.5	-2.7	32.6	-20.8
Differ From Category (+/-)	-4.2	-1.0	-1.3	6.1	7.4	0.6	3.4	-4.4	9.8	-7.6
Return, Tax-Adjusted (%)	24.7	7.4	-2.9	13.5	12.6	-0.5	17.0	-5.6	29.3	-22.1
Dividends, Net Income ($)	2.97	3.19	2.49	1.64	3.03	3.06	3.39	4.23	4.13	2.48
Expense Ratio (%)	0.57	0.57	0.57	0.58	0.59	0.59	0.59	0.59	0.59	0.59
Yield (%)	4.16	5.41	4.38	2.70	4.92	5.03	5.05	6.92	6.02	4.50
Total Assets (Millions $)	241	229	280	239	86	125	187	244	593	696

SHAREHOLDER INFORMATION

Minimum Investment
Initial: $2,500 IRA: $2,500
Subsequent: $50 IRA: $0

Maximum Fees
Load: none 12b-1: none
Other: none

Dreyfus U.S. Treasury Long-Term (DRGBX)

800-645-6561
www.dreyfus.com

Government: Long-Term Bond

PERFORMANCE AND PER SHARE DATA **fund inception date: 3/27/87**

	3yr Annual	5yr Annual	10yr Annual	Category Risk Index
Return (%)	10.7	8.3	6.7	0.75—blw av
Differ From Category (+/-)	-2.2 blw av	-2.5 low	-1.1 low	**Avg Mat** 15.6 yrs

	2008	2007	2006	2005	2004	2003	2002	2001	2000	1999
Return (%)	21.5	10.3	1.2	5.6	3.8	4.4	11.4	2.5	17.7	-8.2
Differ From Category (+/-)	-9.2	-0.1	1.3	-2.9	-5.2	3.0	-5.7	0.8	-5.1	4.9
Return, Tax-Adjusted (%)	19.9	8.7	-0.3	4.0	2.3	3.0	9.6	0.5	15.4	-10.2
Dividends, Net Income ($)	0.77	0.74	0.70	0.71	0.71	0.66	0.72	0.79	0.82	0.82
Expense Ratio (%)	na	0.65	0.65	0.65	0.66	0.80	0.80	0.80	0.80	0.80
Yield (%)	4.00	4.42	4.42	4.32	4.43	4.05	4.43	5.17	5.23	5.83
Total Assets (Millions $)	115	83	77	83	82	100	101	109	116	121

SHAREHOLDER INFORMATION

Minimum Investment
Initial: $2,500 IRA: $750
Subsequent: $100 IRA: $0

Maximum Fees
Load: none 12b-1: none
Other: none

Fidelity Spartan L/T Tr Bd Idx Inv (FLBIX)

800-544-6666
www.fidelity.com

Government: Long-Term Bond

PERFORMANCE AND PER SHARE DATA **fund inception date: 12/20/05**

	3yr Annual	5yr Annual	10yr Annual	Category Risk Index
Return (%)	11.4	na	na	0.75—low
Differ From Category (+/-)	-1.5 abv av	na	na	**Avg Mat** 17.8 yrs

	2008	2007	2006	2005	2004	2003	2002	2001	2000	1999
Return (%)	24.1	9.5	1.6	—	—	—	—	—	—	—
Differ From Category (+/-)	-6.6	-0.9	1.7	—	—	—	—	—	—	—
Return, Tax-Adjusted (%)	22.6	7.8	0.0	—	—	—	—	—	—	—
Dividends, Net Income ($)	0.43	0.45	0.46	—	—	—	—	—	—	—
Expense Ratio (%)	0.20	0.20	0.20	—	—	—	—	—	—	—
Yield (%)	3.53	4.42	4.64	—	—	—	—	—	—	—
Total Assets (Millions $)	188	36	8	—	—	—	—	—	—	—

SHAREHOLDER INFORMATION

Minimum Investment
Initial: $10,000 IRA: $0
Subsequent: $1,000 IRA: $0

Maximum Fees
Load: none 12b-1: none
Other: maint fee for low bal

T. Rowe Price U.S. Treasury Long-Term (PRULX)

800-638-5660
www.troweprice.com

Government: Long-Term Bond

PERFORMANCE AND PER SHARE DATA **fund inception date: 9/29/89**

	3yr Annual	5yr Annual	10yr Annual	Category Risk Index
Return (%)	11.0	8.8	7.2	0.75—blw av
Differ From Category (+/-)	-1.9 av	-2.0 blw av	-0.6 blw av	**Avg Mat** 17.1 yrs

	2008	2007	2006	2005	2004	2003	2002	2001	2000	1999
Return (%)	23.2	9.9	1.0	5.4	5.7	2.0	15.1	3.3	19.1	-8.8
Differ From Category (+/-)	-7.5	-0.5	1.1	-3.1	-3.3	0.7	-2.0	1.6	-3.7	4.3
Return, Tax-Adjusted (%)	21.3	8.3	-0.6	3.7	4.2	0.2	13.0	1.3	16.7	-11.0
Dividends, Net Income ($)	0.50	0.52	0.51	0.53	0.51	0.53	0.57	0.60	0.62	0.62
Expense Ratio (%)	0.53	0.55	0.63	0.67	0.67	0.68	0.66	0.63	0.64	0.66
Yield (%)	3.53	4.34	4.47	4.45	4.32	4.45	4.59	5.27	5.37	6.02
Total Assets (Millions $)	399	466	292	225	232	245	297	306	315	324

SHAREHOLDER INFORMATION

Minimum Investment
Initial: $2,500 IRA: $1,000
Subsequent: $100 IRA: $50

Maximum Fees
Load: none 12b-1: none
Other: none

Vanguard Long-Term U.S. Treasury (VUSTX)

800-662-2739
www.vanguard.com

Government: Long-Term Bond

PERFORMANCE AND PER SHARE DATA **fund inception date: 5/19/86**

	3yr Annual	5yr Annual	10yr Annual	Category Risk Index
Return (%)	10.8	9.2	7.8	0.74—low
Differ From Category (+/-)	-2.1 blw av	-1.6 av	0.0 abv av	**Avg Mat** 16.4 yrs

	2008	2007	2006	2005	2004	2003	2002	2001	2000	1999
Return (%)	22.5	9.2	1.7	6.6	7.1	2.6	16.6	4.3	19.7	-8.7
Differ From Category (+/-)	-8.2	-1.2	1.8	-1.9	-1.9	1.2	-0.5	2.6	-3.1	4.4
Return, Tax-Adjusted (%)	20.8	7.4	0.0	4.7	5.2	0.8	14.2	2.1	17.1	-11.1
Dividends, Net Income ($)	0.51	0.54	0.55	0.57	0.57	0.56	0.59	0.60	0.62	0.61
Expense Ratio (%)	0.26	0.26	0.26	0.24	0.26	0.28	0.29	0.29	0.28	0.27
Yield (%)	3.77	4.62	4.89	4.83	4.95	4.87	4.92	5.60	5.69	6.24
Total Assets (Millions $)	2,204	1,364	1,293	1,422	1,444	1,489	1,682	1,373	1,358	1,224

SHAREHOLDER INFORMATION

Minimum Investment
Initial: $3,000 IRA: $3,000
Subsequent: $100 IRA: $0

Maximum Fees
Load: none 12b-1: none
Other: none

Wasatch-Hoisington U.S. Treasury (WHOSX)

800-551-1700
www.wasatchfunds.com

Government: Long-Term Bond

PERFORMANCE AND PER SHARE DATA **fund inception date: 12/8/86**

	3yr Annual	5yr Annual	10yr Annual	Category Risk Index
Return (%)	14.7	13.0	9.1	1.10—abv av
Differ From Category (+/-)	1.8 abv av	2.2 abv av	1.3 high	**Avg Mat** 23.0 yrs

	2008	2007	2006	2005	2004	2003	2002	2001	2000	1999
Return (%)	37.7	10.0	-0.2	10.4	10.2	1.2	16.8	2.8	21.9	-12.4
Differ From Category (+/-)	7.0	-0.4	-0.1	1.9	1.2	-0.2	-0.3	1.1	-0.9	0.7
Return, Tax-Adjusted (%)	36.4	8.4	-1.6	9.7	8.5	-0.7	14.8	0.4	19.9	-14.6
Dividends, Net Income ($)	0.56	0.64	0.57	0.29	0.60	0.73	0.63	0.77	0.56	0.73
Expense Ratio (%)	0.74	0.71	0.72	0.75	0.75	0.75	0.75	0.75	0.75	0.75
Yield (%)	2.88	4.34	4.09	2.00	4.48	5.67	4.73	6.46	4.48	6.86
Total Assets (Millions $)	191	118	200	159	47	57	77	59	63	65

SHAREHOLDER INFORMATION

Minimum Investment
Initial: $2,000 IRA: $1,000
Subsequent: $100 IRA: $100

Maximum Fees
Load: 2.00% redemption 12b-1: none
Other: redemption fee applies for 2 months

Inflation-Protected Bond Funds
Category Performance Ranked by 2008 Returns

Fund (Ticker)	Annual Return (%) 2008	3Yr	5Yr	10Yr	Category Risk	Total Risk
American Century Infl-Adjusted Bond Inv (ACITX)	-1.1	3.1	3.9	6.3	blw av	low
T. Rowe Price Inflation Protected Bd (PRIPX)	-1.9	2.9	3.7	na	low	low
Fidelity Inflation-Protected Bond (FINPX)	-2.4	2.2	3.3	na	av	low
Vanguard Inflation-Protected Secs (VIPSX)	-2.9	2.8	3.8	na	abv av	blw av
Inflation-Protected Bond Category Average	**-2.7**	**2.5**	**3.6**	**6.3**	**av**	**blw av**

American Century Infl-Adjusted Bond Inv (ACITX)

800-345-2021
www.americancentury.com

Inflation-Protected Bond

PERFORMANCE AND PER SHARE DATA **fund inception date: 2/10/97**

	3yr Annual	5yr Annual	10yr Annual	Category Risk Index	
Return (%)	3.1	3.9	6.3	0.96—blw av	
Differ From Category (+/-)	0.6 high	0.3 high	0.0 av	**Avg Mat**	9.5 yrs

	2008	2007	2006	2005	2004	2003	2002	2001	2000	1999
Return (%)	-1.1	10.9	0.0	2.4	7.9	7.3	15.1	7.6	12.0	1.6
Differ From Category (+/-)	1.6	0.2	-0.1	0.1	-0.2	-0.3	-0.9	-0.2	-0.5	-1.8
Return, Tax-Adjusted (%)	-2.9	9.4	-1.2	0.5	6.3	5.9	13.1	5.6	9.2	-0.7
Dividends, Net Income ($)	0.59	0.47	0.39	0.59	0.48	0.40	0.43	0.50	0.64	0.56
Expense Ratio (%)	0.49	0.49	0.49	0.50	0.50	0.51	0.59	0.51	0.51	0.49
Yield (%)	5.62	4.14	3.71	5.34	4.23	3.60	3.94	5.04	6.70	6.12
Total Assets (Millions $)	973	647	621	721	585	365	328	167	37	18

SHAREHOLDER INFORMATION

Minimum Investment
Initial: $2,500 IRA: $2,500
Subsequent: $50 IRA: $50

Maximum Fees
Load: none 12b-1: none
Other: none

Fidelity Inflation-Protected Bond (FINPX)

800-544-9797
www.fidelity.com

Inflation-Protected Bond

PERFORMANCE AND PER SHARE DATA **fund inception date: 6/26/02**

	3yr Annual	5yr Annual	10yr Annual	Category Risk Index	
Return (%)	2.2	3.3	na	0.98—av	
Differ From Category (+/-)	-0.3 blw av	-0.3 blw av	na	**Avg Mat**	9.1 yrs

	2008	2007	2006	2005	2004	2003	2002	2001	2000	1999
Return (%)	-2.4	9.0	0.2	2.1	8.2	7.7	—	—	—	—
Differ From Category (+/-)	0.3	-1.7	0.1	-0.2	0.1	0.1	—	—	—	—
Return, Tax-Adjusted (%)	-3.1	7.8	-0.7	1.0	7.2	6.8	—	—	—	—
Dividends, Net Income ($)	0.16	0.23	0.24	0.15	0.16	0.18	—	—	—	—
Expense Ratio (%)	0.45	0.45	0.45	0.45	0.50	0.50	—	—	—	—
Yield (%)	1.48	2.00	2.24	1.30	1.32	1.57	—	—	—	—
Total Assets (Millions $)	1,710	1,380	1,344	1,619	1,317	724	—	—	—	—

SHAREHOLDER INFORMATION

Minimum Investment
Initial: $2,500 IRA: $500
Subsequent: $250 IRA: $100

Maximum Fees
Load: none 12b-1: none
Other: maint fee for low bal

T. Rowe Price Inflation Protected Bd (PRIPX)

800-638-5660
www.troweprice.com

Inflation-Protected Bond

PERFORMANCE AND PER SHARE DATA **fund inception date: 10/31/02**

	3yr Annual	5yr Annual	10yr Annual	Category Risk Index	
Return (%)	2.9	3.7	na	0.95—low	
Differ From Category (+/-)	0.4 abv av	0.1 av	na	**Avg Mat**	8.8 yrs

	2008	2007	2006	2005	2004	2003	2002	2001	2000	1999
Return (%)	-1.9	11.1	0.0	2.3	7.4	7.0	—	—	—	—
Differ From Category (+/-)	0.8	0.4	-0.1	0.0	-0.7	-0.6	—	—	—	—
Return, Tax-Adjusted (%)	-2.6	10.1	-0.7	1.3	6.6	6.4	—	—	—	—
Dividends, Net Income ($)	0.15	0.17	0.15	0.14	0.15	0.11	—	—	—	—
Expense Ratio (%)	0.50	0.50	0.50	0.50	0.50	0.50	—	—	—	—
Yield (%)	1.36	1.48	1.42	1.27	1.34	0.99	—	—	—	—
Total Assets (Millions $)	216	125	102	108	75	34	—	—	—	—

SHAREHOLDER INFORMATION

Minimum Investment
Initial: $2,500 IRA: $1,000
Subsequent: $100 IRA: $50

Maximum Fees
Load: none 12b-1: none
Other: none

Vanguard Inflation-Protected Secs (VIPSX)

800-662-7447
www.vanguard.com

Inflation-Protected Bond

PERFORMANCE AND PER SHARE DATA **fund inception date: 6/29/00**

	3yr Annual	5yr Annual	10yr Annual	Category Risk Index	
Return (%)	2.8	3.8	na	0.98—abv av	
Differ From Category (+/-)	0.3 av	0.2 abv av	na	**Avg Mat**	8.8 yrs

	2008	2007	2006	2005	2004	2003	2002	2001	2000	1999
Return (%)	-2.9	11.5	0.4	2.5	8.2	8.0	16.6	7.6	—	—
Differ From Category (+/-)	-0.2	0.8	0.3	0.2	0.1	0.4	0.6	-0.2	—	—
Return, Tax-Adjusted (%)	-4.6	9.6	-0.8	0.6	6.5	6.5	14.8	5.7	—	—
Dividends, Net Income ($)	0.61	0.65	0.43	0.68	0.56	0.45	0.46	0.44	—	—
Expense Ratio (%)	na	0.20	0.20	0.17	0.18	0.22	0.25	0.25	—	—
Yield (%)	5.32	5.19	3.61	5.57	4.47	3.64	3.86	4.16	—	—
Total Assets (Millions $)	8,593	6,662	5,440	6,332	7,182	4,746	2,988	772	—	—

SHAREHOLDER INFORMATION

Minimum Investment
Initial: $3,000 IRA: $3,000
Subsequent: $100 IRA: $0

Maximum Fees
Load: none 12b-1: none
Other: none

General Bond: Short-Term
Category Performance Ranked by 2008 Returns

Fund (Ticker)	Annual Return (%) 2008	3Yr	5Yr	10Yr	Category Risk	Total Risk
Vanguard Short-Term Bond Index (VBISX)	5.4	5.5	3.9	4.8	av	low
Janus Short-Term Bond (JASBX)	4.6	4.6	3.4	4.2	low	low
Weitz Short-Intermediate Income (WEFIX)	2.2	4.1	3.3	4.5	av	low
T. Rowe Price Short-Term Bond (PRWBX)	1.2	3.6	2.8	4.2	blw av	low
Payden Short Bond (PYSBX)	1.1	3.7	2.7	4.2	low	low
Wells Fargo Advantage Short-Term Bd Inv (SSTBX)	-0.6	2.7	2.4	3.2	low	low
USAA Short-Term Bond (USSBX)	-2.6	2.5	2.3	3.1	blw av	low
Fidelity Short-Term Bond (FSHBX)	-3.7	0.8	1.2	3.5	blw av	low
Vanguard Short-Term Investment-Grade (VFSTX)	-4.8	1.9	2.0	3.8	abv av	low
Schwab Short-Term Bond Market (SWBDX)	-5.5	1.1	1.4	3.4	abv av	low
General Bond: Short-Term Category Average	**-7.1**	**0.0**	**0.8**	**3.4**	**av**	**low**

Fidelity Short-Term Bond (FSHBX)

800-544-9797
www.fidelity.com

General Bond: Short-Term

PERFORMANCE AND PER SHARE DATA **fund inception date: 9/15/86**

	3yr Annual	5yr Annual	10yr Annual	Category Risk Index	
Return (%)	0.8	1.2	3.5	0.57—blw av	
Differ From Category (+/-)	0.8 blw av	0.4 blw av	0.1 av	**Avg Mat**	2.0 yrs

	2008	2007	2006	2005	2004	2003	2002	2001	2000	1999
Return (%)	-3.7	1.6	4.5	2.1	1.8	3.5	6.7	7.6	7.8	3.2
Differ From Category (+/-)	3.4	-2.3	-0.1	0.0	-0.3	0.4	2.8	0.6	0.2	-0.2
Return, Tax-Adjusted (%)	-5.1	0.0	3.0	0.9	0.9	2.5	5.0	5.5	5.4	1.0
Dividends, Net Income ($)	0.33	0.41	0.39	0.31	0.23	0.27	0.39	0.46	0.52	0.49
Expense Ratio (%)	0.45	0.45	0.44	0.56	0.57	0.57	0.58	0.58	0.63	0.65
Yield (%)	4.18	4.82	4.35	3.50	2.51	2.94	4.28	5.28	6.09	5.75
Total Assets (Millions $)	5,418	7,124	6,929	5,244	5,050	5,406	5,195	3,339	1,773	1,333

SHAREHOLDER INFORMATION

Minimum Investment
Initial: $2,500 IRA: $500
Subsequent: $250 IRA: $250

Maximum Fees
Load: none 12b-1: none
Other: maint fee for low bal

Janus Short-Term Bond (JASBX)

800-525-3713
www.janus.com

General Bond: Short-Term

PERFORMANCE AND PER SHARE DATA **fund inception date: 9/1/92**

	3yr Annual	5yr Annual	10yr Annual	Category Risk Index	
Return (%)	4.6	3.4	4.2	0.38—low	
Differ From Category (+/-)	4.6 high	2.6 high	0.8 high	**Avg Mat**	1.7 yrs

	2008	2007	2006	2005	2004	2003	2002	2001	2000	1999
Return (%)	4.6	5.2	4.2	1.5	1.9	3.9	3.5	6.8	7.7	2.9
Differ From Category (+/-)	11.7	1.3	-0.4	-0.6	-0.2	0.8	-0.4	-0.2	0.1	-0.5
Return, Tax-Adjusted (%)	3.5	3.5	2.8	0.5	0.9	2.8	2.2	5.0	5.4	0.7
Dividends, Net Income ($)	0.09	0.14	0.11	0.08	0.08	0.08	0.10	0.13	0.16	0.16
Expense Ratio (%)	na	0.64	0.64	0.64	0.64	0.65	0.65	0.65	0.65	0.65
Yield (%)	3.11	4.72	3.76	2.90	2.69	2.53	3.49	4.53	5.62	5.72
Total Assets (Millions $)	250	176	172	192	254	334	480	497	173	136

SHAREHOLDER INFORMATION

Minimum Investment
Initial: $2,500 IRA: $1,000
Subsequent: $100 IRA: $100

Maximum Fees
Load: none 12b-1: none
Other: none

Payden Short Bond (PYSBX)

800-572-9336
www.payden.com

General Bond: Short-Term

PERFORMANCE AND PER SHARE DATA **fund inception date: 12/31/93**

	3yr Annual	5yr Annual	10yr Annual	Category Risk Index	
Return (%)	3.7	2.7	4.2	0.49—low	
Differ From Category (+/-)	3.7 high	1.9 high	0.8 high	**Avg Mat**	3.5 yrs

	2008	2007	2006	2005	2004	2003	2002	2001	2000	1999
Return (%)	1.1	5.9	4.2	1.3	1.2	2.3	6.2	8.7	8.5	2.6
Differ From Category (+/-)	8.2	2.0	-0.4	-0.9	-0.9	-0.8	2.3	1.7	0.9	-0.8
Return, Tax-Adjusted (%)	-0.1	4.3	2.7	0.0	0.4	1.5	4.7	6.7	6.0	0.4
Dividends, Net Income ($)	0.35	0.45	0.42	0.36	0.22	0.21	0.34	0.51	0.59	0.56
Expense Ratio (%)	na	0.47	0.45	0.45	0.45	0.50	0.50	0.40	0.40	0.40
Yield (%)	3.61	4.49	4.24	3.62	2.19	2.05	3.30	5.04	6.03	5.79
Total Assets (Millions $)	353	351	313	300	358	320	215	108	67	57

SHAREHOLDER INFORMATION

Minimum Investment
Initial: $5,000 IRA: $2,000
Subsequent: $250 IRA: $250

Maximum Fees
Load: none 12b-1: none
Other: none

Schwab Short-Term Bond Market (SWBDX)

800-407-0256
www.schwab.com

General Bond: Short-Term

PERFORMANCE AND PER SHARE DATA **fund inception date: 11/5/91**

	3yr Annual	5yr Annual	10yr Annual	Category Risk Index	
Return (%)	1.1	1.4	3.4	0.84—abv av	
Differ From Category (+/-)	1.1 av	0.6 av	0.0 av	**Avg Mat**	2.7 yrs

	2008	2007	2006	2005	2004	2003	2002	2001	2000	1999
Return (%)	-5.5	4.6	4.5	1.5	2.0	3.4	6.6	7.3	9.0	1.6
Differ From Category (+/-)	1.6	0.7	-0.1	-0.6	-0.1	0.3	2.7	0.4	1.5	-1.8
Return, Tax-Adjusted (%)	-6.8	2.8	2.9	0.3	1.0	2.3	4.8	5.1	6.6	-0.5
Dividends, Net Income ($)	0.38	0.51	0.45	0.35	0.27	0.32	0.45	0.56	0.59	0.51
Expense Ratio (%)	0.55	0.56	0.55	0.55	0.53	0.43	0.35	0.35	0.35	0.35
Yield (%)	4.19	5.14	4.55	3.47	2.64	3.11	4.45	5.58	6.00	5.35
Total Assets (Millions $)	287	584	601	619	723	690	564	389	257	216

SHAREHOLDER INFORMATION

Minimum Investment
Initial: $100 IRA: $0
Subsequent: $0 IRA: $0

Maximum Fees
Load: none 12b-1: none
Other: none

T. Rowe Price Short-Term Bond (PRWBX)

800-492-7670
www.troweprice.com

General Bond: Short-Term

PERFORMANCE AND PER SHARE DATA **fund inception date: 3/2/84**

	3yr Annual	5yr Annual	10yr Annual	Category Risk Index
Return (%)	3.6	2.8	4.2	0.57—blw av
Differ From Category (+/-)	3.6 high	2.0 high	0.8 high	**Avg Mat** 2.8 yrs

	2008	2007	2006	2005	2004	2003	2002	2001	2000	1999
Return (%)	1.2	5.4	4.3	1.7	1.4	3.7	5.3	8.4	8.4	2.2
Differ From Category (+/-)	8.3	1.5	-0.3	-0.4	-0.7	0.6	1.4	1.4	0.8	-1.2
Return, Tax-Adjusted (%)	-0.3	3.9	2.9	0.5	0.5	2.5	3.5	6.2	6.1	0.1
Dividends, Net Income ($)	0.20	0.21	0.19	0.16	0.13	0.16	0.22	0.27	0.27	0.25
Expense Ratio (%)	0.55	0.55	0.55	0.55	0.55	0.55	0.55	0.59	0.72	0.73
Yield (%)	4.32	4.46	4.06	3.44	2.75	3.24	4.52	5.56	5.87	5.59
Total Assets (Millions $)	1,831	1,561	1,439	1,262	1,516	1,288	904	599	467	305

SHAREHOLDER INFORMATION

Minimum Investment
Initial: $2,500 IRA: $1,000
Subsequent: $100 IRA: $50

Maximum Fees
Load: none 12b-1: none
Other: none

USAA Short-Term Bond (USSBX)

800-531-8181
www.usaa.com

General Bond: Short-Term

PERFORMANCE AND PER SHARE DATA **fund inception date: 6/1/93**

	3yr Annual	5yr Annual	10yr Annual	Category Risk Index
Return (%)	2.5	2.3	3.1	0.57—blw av
Differ From Category (+/-)	2.5 abv av	1.5 abv av	-0.3 blw av	**Avg Mat** 2.4 yrs

	2008	2007	2006	2005	2004	2003	2002	2001	2000	1999
Return (%)	-2.6	5.7	4.7	2.2	1.8	4.2	-0.2	4.8	7.1	3.9
Differ From Category (+/-)	4.5	1.8	0.1	0.1	-0.3	1.1	-4.1	-2.2	-0.5	0.5
Return, Tax-Adjusted (%)	-4.2	4.1	3.1	1.0	0.7	2.9	-2.1	2.4	4.4	1.5
Dividends, Net Income ($)	0.41	0.41	0.39	0.32	0.29	0.34	0.49	0.61	0.65	0.58
Expense Ratio (%)	0.69	0.69	0.69	0.56	0.55	0.55	0.58	0.46	0.48	0.50
Yield (%)	4.93	4.57	4.36	3.63	3.22	3.70	5.37	6.43	6.66	5.95
Total Assets (Millions $)	621	557	457	427	416	394	364	443	311	250

SHAREHOLDER INFORMATION

Minimum Investment
Initial: $3,000 IRA: $250
Subsequent: $50 IRA: $50

Maximum Fees
Load: none 12b-1: none
Other: none

Vanguard Short-Term Bond Index (VBISX)

800-662-6273
www.vanguard.com

General Bond: Short-Term

PERFORMANCE AND PER SHARE DATA **fund inception date: 3/1/94**

	3yr Annual	5yr Annual	10yr Annual	Category Risk Index	
Return (%)	5.5	3.9	4.8	0.65—av	
Differ From Category (+/-)	5.5 high	3.1 high	1.4 high	**Avg Mat**	2.8 yrs

	2008	2007	2006	2005	2004	2003	2002	2001	2000	1999
Return (%)	5.4	7.2	4.0	1.3	1.7	3.3	6.0	8.8	8.8	2.0
Differ From Category (+/-)	12.5	3.3	-0.6	-0.8	-0.4	0.2	2.2	1.8	1.2	-1.4
Return, Tax-Adjusted (%)	4.0	5.6	2.5	0.1	0.6	2.1	4.3	6.5	6.3	-0.2
Dividends, Net Income ($)	0.39	0.46	0.43	0.35	0.30	0.33	0.45	0.57	0.60	0.54
Expense Ratio (%)	na	0.18	0.18	0.18	0.18	0.20	0.21	0.21	0.21	0.20
Yield (%)	3.78	4.50	4.30	3.52	2.98	3.17	4.36	5.53	6.03	5.52
Total Assets (Millions $)	3,680	2,773	2,731	2,951	3,795	3,041	2,553	1,680	1,287	1,156

SHAREHOLDER INFORMATION

Minimum Investment
Initial: $3,000 IRA: $3,000
Subsequent: $100 IRA: $100

Maximum Fees
Load: none 12b-1: none
Other: none

Vanguard Short-Term Investment-Grade (VFSTX)

800-662-2739
www.vanguard.com

General Bond: Short-Term

PERFORMANCE AND PER SHARE DATA **fund inception date: 10/29/82**

	3yr Annual	5yr Annual	10yr Annual	Category Risk Index	
Return (%)	1.9	2.0	3.8	0.89—abv av	
Differ From Category (+/-)	1.9 abv av	1.2 av	0.4 abv av	**Avg Mat**	2.9 yrs

	2008	2007	2006	2005	2004	2003	2002	2001	2000	1999
Return (%)	-4.8	5.8	4.9	2.2	2.1	4.1	5.2	8.1	8.1	3.3
Differ From Category (+/-)	2.3	1.9	0.3	0.1	0.0	1.1	1.3	1.1	0.5	-0.1
Return, Tax-Adjusted (%)	-6.4	4.1	3.4	0.9	0.9	2.7	3.1	5.6	5.5	0.9
Dividends, Net Income ($)	0.49	0.51	0.46	0.38	0.36	0.44	0.58	0.68	0.71	0.66
Expense Ratio (%)	0.21	0.21	0.21	0.18	0.21	0.23	0.24	0.24	0.25	0.27
Yield (%)	5.11	4.82	4.38	3.61	3.41	4.03	5.34	6.26	6.64	6.24
Total Assets (Millions $)	9,179	11,155	10,377	10,409	13,122	11,120	8,668	7,383	7,341	6,799

SHAREHOLDER INFORMATION

Minimum Investment
Initial: $3,000 IRA: $3,000
Subsequent: $100 IRA: $0

Maximum Fees
Load: none 12b-1: none
Other: none

Weitz Short-Intermediate Income (WEFIX)

800-304-9745
www.weitzfunds.com

General Bond: Short-Term

PERFORMANCE AND PER SHARE DATA **fund inception date: 12/23/88**

	3yr Annual	5yr Annual	10yr Annual	Category Risk Index
Return (%)	4.1	3.3	4.5	0.68—av
Differ From Category (+/-)	4.1 high	2.5 high	1.1 high	**Avg Mat** 3.3 yrs

	2008	2007	2006	2005	2004	2003	2002	2001	2000	1999
Return (%)	2.2	6.0	4.0	1.6	2.6	6.3	4.1	8.4	9.6	0.8
Differ From Category (+/-)	9.3	2.2	-0.6	-0.5	0.5	3.2	0.2	1.4	2.0	-2.6
Return, Tax-Adjusted (%)	0.8	4.5	2.6	0.4	1.8	5.2	2.5	6.4	6.9	-1.5
Dividends, Net Income ($)	0.43	0.49	0.44	0.36	0.25	0.33	0.49	0.56	0.73	0.67
Expense Ratio (%)	0.70	0.71	0.74	0.76	0.75	0.75	0.75	0.75	0.75	0.75
Yield (%)	3.77	4.23	3.86	3.15	2.17	2.82	4.34	4.96	6.71	6.29
Total Assets (Millions $)	150	118	127	167	154	68	52	49	31	32

SHAREHOLDER INFORMATION

Minimum Investment
Initial: $2,500 IRA: $0
Subsequent: $0 IRA: $0

Maximum Fees
Load: none 12b-1: none
Other: none

Wells Fargo Advantage Short-Term Bd Inv (SSTBX)

800-222-8222
www.wellsfargofunds.com

General Bond: Short-Term

PERFORMANCE AND PER SHARE DATA **fund inception date: 8/31/87**

	3yr Annual	5yr Annual	10yr Annual	Category Risk Index
Return (%)	2.7	2.4	3.2	0.51—low
Differ From Category (+/-)	2.7 abv av	1.6 abv av	-0.2 blw av	**Avg Mat** 2.7 yrs

	2008	2007	2006	2005	2004	2003	2002	2001	2000	1999
Return (%)	-0.6	4.4	4.3	1.9	2.1	3.7	0.6	4.5	7.2	4.2
Differ From Category (+/-)	6.5	0.5	-0.3	-0.2	0.0	0.6	-3.3	-2.5	-0.4	0.8
Return, Tax-Adjusted (%)	-2.1	2.7	2.7	0.5	0.9	2.4	-1.3	2.0	4.5	1.7
Dividends, Net Income ($)	0.36	0.41	0.39	0.35	0.31	0.34	0.44	0.58	0.63	0.61
Expense Ratio (%)	0.87	0.90	0.90	0.90	1.00	0.90	0.90	0.90	0.90	0.80
Yield (%)	4.39	4.88	4.62	4.07	3.52	3.82	4.96	6.28	6.72	6.46
Total Assets (Millions $)	242	278	362	438	494	652	852	1,281	1,146	1,225

SHAREHOLDER INFORMATION

Minimum Investment
Initial: $2,500 IRA: $1,000
Subsequent: $100 IRA: $100

Maximum Fees
Load: none 12b-1: none
Other: none

General Bond: Intermediate-Term
Category Performance Ranked by 2008 Returns

Fund (Ticker)	Annual Return (%) 2008	3Yr	5Yr	10Yr	Category Risk	Total Risk
Dreyfus Bond Market Index Basic (DBIRX)	5.8	5.6	4.6	5.4	blw av	low
T. Rowe Price U.S. Bond Index (PBDIX)	5.4	5.3	4.4	na	blw av	low
Vanguard Total Bond Market Index (VBMFX)	5.0	5.4	4.5	5.3	blw av	low
Vanguard Interm-Term Bond Index (VBIIX)	4.9	5.4	4.6	5.8	high	low
PIMCO Total Return D (PTTDX)	4.4	5.6	4.8	5.8	av	low
Fidelity U.S. Bond Index (FBIDX)	3.7	4.4	4.0	5.3	low	low
T. Rowe Price New Income (PRCIX)	1.4	3.9	3.8	4.9	blw av	low
Managers Fremont Bond (MBDFX)	4.1	3.9	4.0	5.5	abv av	low
Dodge & Cox Income (DODIX)	-0.3	3.2	3.0	5.1	abv av	low
Metropolitan West Total Return Bond M (MWTRX)	-1.5	3.8	3.9	5.2	low	low
Westcore Plus Bond (WTIBX)	-1.9	3.0	3.5	5.3	blw av	low
Vanguard Interm-Term Investment-Grade (VFICX)	-6.2	1.3	2.1	4.5	high	low
General Bond: Intermediate-Term Category Average	**-2.4**	**2.2**	**2.6**	**4.5**	**av**	**low**

Dodge & Cox Income (DODIX)

800-621-3979
www.dodgeandcox.com

General Bond: Intermediate-Term

PERFORMANCE AND PER SHARE DATA **fund inception date: 1/3/89**

	3yr Annual	5yr Annual	10yr Annual	Category Risk Index	
Return (%)	3.2	3.0	5.1	1.00—abv av	
Differ From Category (+/-)	1.0 av	0.4 av	0.6 abv av	**Avg Mat**	6.3 yrs

	2008	2007	2006	2005	2004	2003	2002	2001	2000	1999
Return (%)	-0.3	4.6	5.3	1.9	3.6	5.9	10.7	10.3	10.6	-0.9
Differ From Category (+/-)	2.1	-0.6	0.8	-0.2	-0.7	-0.2	2.0	2.5	1.0	0.0
Return, Tax-Adjusted (%)	-2.2	2.9	3.5	0.4	2.1	4.3	8.5	7.7	7.9	-3.2
Dividends, Net Income ($)	0.68	0.63	0.62	0.55	0.54	0.60	0.66	0.74	0.78	0.71
Expense Ratio (%)	na	0.44	0.44	0.44	0.44	0.45	0.45	0.45	0.46	0.46
Yield (%)	5.72	5.07	4.90	4.38	4.20	4.64	5.14	6.03	6.61	6.20
Total Assets (Millions $)	13,796	15,895	11,972	9,610	7,870	5,697	3,405	1,512	1,021	974

SHAREHOLDER INFORMATION

Minimum Investment
Initial: $2,500 IRA: $1,000
Subsequent: $100 IRA: $100

Maximum Fees
Load: none 12b-1: none
Other: none

Dreyfus Bond Market Index Basic (DBIRX)

800-645-6561
www.dreyfus.com

General Bond: Intermediate-Term

PERFORMANCE AND PER SHARE DATA **fund inception date: 11/30/93**

	3yr Annual	5yr Annual	10yr Annual	Category Risk Index	
Return (%)	5.6	4.6	5.4	0.80—blw av	
Differ From Category (+/-)	3.4 high	2.0 high	0.9 high	**Avg Mat**	7.0 yrs

	2008	2007	2006	2005	2004	2003	2002	2001	2000	1999
Return (%)	5.8	7.0	4.1	2.1	4.1	3.7	10.0	8.0	11.0	-1.1
Differ From Category (+/-)	8.2	1.8	-0.4	0.0	-0.2	-2.4	1.3	0.2	1.3	-0.2
Return, Tax-Adjusted (%)	4.1	5.2	2.4	0.6	2.5	2.1	7.9	5.6	8.3	-3.4
Dividends, Net Income ($)	0.49	0.50	0.49	0.46	0.46	0.47	0.54	0.60	0.62	0.59
Expense Ratio (%)	na	0.15	0.15	0.15	0.15	0.15	0.15	0.15	0.15	0.15
Yield (%)	4.82	4.96	4.86	4.57	4.43	4.51	5.15	5.94	6.32	6.24
Total Assets (Millions $)	474	238	195	194	192	158	117	83	73	72

SHAREHOLDER INFORMATION

Minimum Investment
Initial: $10,000 IRA: $5,000
Subsequent: $1,000 IRA: $1,000

Maximum Fees
Load: none 12b-1: none
Other: none

Fidelity U.S. Bond Index (FBIDX)

800-544-5555
www.fidelity.com

General Bond: Intermediate-Term

PERFORMANCE AND PER SHARE DATA **fund inception date: 3/8/90**

	3yr Annual	5yr Annual	10yr Annual	Category Risk Index
Return (%)	4.4	4.0	5.3	0.74—low
Differ From Category (+/-)	2.2 high	1.4 high	0.8 high	**Avg Mat** 5.8 yrs

	2008	2007	2006	2005	2004	2003	2002	2001	2000	1999
Return (%)	3.7	5.4	4.3	2.2	4.3	4.9	10.2	8.0	11.4	-1.0
Differ From Category (+/-)	6.1	0.2	-0.2	0.1	0.0	-1.2	1.5	0.2	1.7	-0.1
Return, Tax-Adjusted (%)	2.1	3.6	2.7	0.8	2.8	3.3	8.1	5.7	8.6	-3.5
Dividends, Net Income ($)	0.50	0.54	0.50	0.45	0.43	0.41	0.51	0.63	0.72	0.67
Expense Ratio (%)	0.32	0.31	0.31	0.32	0.32	0.32	0.31	0.31	0.31	0.31
Yield (%)	4.60	4.96	4.58	4.07	3.79	3.62	4.52	5.81	6.78	6.50
Total Assets (Millions $)	9,172	8,179	6,479	5,842	5,263	4,765	4,405	2,954	1,785	1,533

SHAREHOLDER INFORMATION

Minimum Investment		**Maximum Fees**	
Initial: $10,000	IRA: $2,500	Load: none	12b-1: none
Subsequent: $1,000	IRA: $1,000	Other: none	

Managers Fremont Bond (MBDFX)

800-548-4539
www.managersfunds.com

General Bond: Intermediate-Term

PERFORMANCE AND PER SHARE DATA **fund inception date: 4/30/93**

	3yr Annual	5yr Annual	10yr Annual	Category Risk Index
Return (%)	3.9	4.0	5.5	0.98—abv av
Differ From Category (+/-)	1.7 abv av	1.4 high	1.0 high	**Avg Mat** 6.4 yrs

	2008	2007	2006	2005	2004	2003	2002	2001	2000	1999
Return (%)	4.1	8.8	3.4	2.9	5.3	5.3	9.7	9.7	12.7	-1.3
Differ From Category (+/-)	2.2	3.6	-1.1	0.7	1.0	-0.8	1.0	1.9	3.0	-0.4
Return, Tax-Adjusted (%)	0.2	6.9	1.8	1.7	4.0	3.9	7.7	7.0	9.8	-3.6
Dividends, Net Income ($)	0.90	0.55	0.48	0.37	0.25	0.35	0.39	0.57	0.71	0.58
Expense Ratio (%)	na	0.60	0.60	0.60	0.60	0.61	0.59	0.57	1.83	0.60
Yield (%)	8.94	5.16	4.72	3.56	2.35	3.29	3.62	5.54	7.11	6.13
Total Assets (Millions $)	1,026	1,256	1,166	1,007	879	851	1,228	783	298	175

SHAREHOLDER INFORMATION

Minimum Investment		**Maximum Fees**	
Initial: $2,000	IRA: $1,000	Load: none	12b-1: none
Subsequent: $100	IRA: $100	Other: none	

Metropolitan West Total Return Bond M (MWTRX)

800-241-4671
www.mwamllc.com

General Bond: Intermediate-Term

PERFORMANCE AND PER SHARE DATA **fund inception date: 3/31/97**

	3yr Annual	5yr Annual	10yr Annual	Category Risk Index	
Return (%)	3.8	3.9	5.2	0.78—low	
Differ From Category (+/-)	1.6 abv av	1.3 abv av	0.7 high	**Avg Mat**	5.0 yrs

	2008	2007	2006	2005	2004	2003	2002	2001	2000	1999
Return (%)	-1.5	6.2	6.9	3.0	5.1	13.8	-1.0	9.1	10.1	1.7
Differ From Category (+/-)	0.9	1.0	2.4	1.0	0.8	7.7	-9.7	1.3	0.4	2.5
Return, Tax-Adjusted (%)	-3.6	4.5	5.2	1.1	3.0	11.5	-3.8	6.0	6.5	-1.2
Dividends, Net Income ($)	0.51	0.48	0.49	0.55	0.59	0.63	0.70	0.76	0.91	0.76
Expense Ratio (%)	0.65	0.65	0.65	0.65	0.65	0.65	0.65	0.65	0.65	0.65
Yield (%)	5.59	4.91	5.00	5.72	6.03	6.32	7.53	7.44	9.03	7.59
Total Assets (Millions $)	3,369	2,708	882	503	453	499	568	621	278	187

SHAREHOLDER INFORMATION

Minimum Investment
Initial: $5,000 IRA: $1,000
Subsequent: $0 IRA: $0

Maximum Fees
Load: none 12b-1: 0.21%
Other: none

PIMCO Total Return D (PTTDX)

800-426-0107
www.pimco.com

General Bond: Intermediate-Term

PERFORMANCE AND PER SHARE DATA **fund inception date: 4/8/98**

	3yr Annual	5yr Annual	10yr Annual	Category Risk Index	
Return (%)	5.6	4.8	5.8	0.92—av	
Differ From Category (+/-)	3.4 high	2.2 high	1.3 high	**Avg Mat**	6.1 yrs

	2008	2007	2006	2005	2004	2003	2002	2001	2000	1999
Return (%)	4.4	8.7	3.6	2.5	4.8	5.1	9.8	9.1	11.7	-0.7
Differ From Category (+/-)	6.8	3.5	-0.9	0.4	0.5	-1.0	1.1	1.3	2.0	0.2
Return, Tax-Adjusted (%)	2.1	6.9	2.0	1.2	3.6	3.8	7.5	6.4	9.2	-2.8
Dividends, Net Income ($)	0.51	0.50	0.46	0.36	0.22	0.33	0.44	0.56	0.63	0.57
Expense Ratio (%)	0.75	0.75	0.75	0.75	0.75	0.75	0.75	0.75	0.75	0.75
Yield (%)	4.81	4.64	4.37	3.36	2.01	2.99	4.03	5.20	6.05	5.80
Total Assets (Millions $)	14,443	4,410	3,748	3,106	2,208	1,703	1,323	530	174	64

SHAREHOLDER INFORMATION

Minimum Investment
Initial: $1,000 IRA: $1,000
Subsequent: $50 IRA: $50

Maximum Fees
Load: none 12b-1: 0.25%
Other: none

T. Rowe Price New Income (PRCIX)

800-225-5132
www.troweprice.com

General Bond: Intermediate-Term

PERFORMANCE AND PER SHARE DATA **fund inception date: 10/15/73**

	3yr Annual	5yr Annual	10yr Annual	Category Risk Index
Return (%)	3.9	3.8	4.9	0.84—blw av
Differ From Category (+/-)	1.7 abv av	1.2 abv av	0.4 abv av	**Avg Mat** 7.0 yrs

	2008	2007	2006	2005	2004	2003	2002	2001	2000	1999
Return (%)	1.4	6.3	4.1	2.8	4.5	5.6	7.4	8.1	11.1	-1.6
Differ From Category (+/-)	3.8	1.1	-0.4	0.7	0.3	-0.5	-1.3	0.3	1.4	-0.7
Return, Tax-Adjusted (%)	-0.5	4.6	2.5	1.3	3.2	4.3	5.6	5.8	8.5	-3.9
Dividends, Net Income ($)	0.42	0.43	0.41	0.38	0.34	0.33	0.42	0.50	0.53	0.51
Expense Ratio (%)	0.64	0.66	0.67	0.69	0.71	0.74	0.72	0.73	0.73	0.72
Yield (%)	4.82	4.74	4.57	4.17	3.69	3.66	4.74	5.74	6.27	6.28
Total Assets (Millions $)	6,757	7,614	4,696	3,519	2,866	2,297	2,018	1,803	1,715	1,795

SHAREHOLDER INFORMATION

Minimum Investment
Initial: $2,500 IRA: $1,000
Subsequent: $100 IRA: $50

Maximum Fees
Load: none 12b-1: none
Other: none

T. Rowe Price U.S. Bond Index (PBDIX)

800-638-5660
www.troweprice.com

General Bond: Intermediate-Term

PERFORMANCE AND PER SHARE DATA **fund inception date: 11/30/00**

	3yr Annual	5yr Annual	10yr Annual	Category Risk Index
Return (%)	5.3	4.4	na	0.80—blw av
Differ From Category (+/-)	3.1 high	1.8 high	na	**Avg Mat** 6.9 yrs

	2008	2007	2006	2005	2004	2003	2002	2001	2000	1999
Return (%)	5.4	6.7	3.8	2.1	3.8	4.1	9.3	7.8	—	—
Differ From Category (+/-)	7.8	1.5	-0.7	0.0	-0.5	-2.0	0.6	0.0	—	—
Return, Tax-Adjusted (%)	3.7	5.0	2.2	0.6	2.4	2.6	7.4	5.5	—	—
Dividends, Net Income ($)	0.50	0.50	0.49	0.46	0.44	0.45	0.50	0.59	—	—
Expense Ratio (%)	na	0.30	0.30	0.30	0.30	0.30	0.30	0.30	—	—
Yield (%)	4.67	4.76	4.73	4.38	4.06	4.16	4.67	5.72	—	—
Total Assets (Millions $)	307	267	190	175	139	72	88	52	—	—

SHAREHOLDER INFORMATION

Minimum Investment
Initial: $2,500 IRA: $1,000
Subsequent: $100 IRA: $50

Maximum Fees
Load: 0.50% redemption 12b-1: none
Other: redemption fee applies for 90 days

Vanguard Interm-Term Bond Index (VBIIX)

800-662-6273
www.vanguard.com

General Bond: Intermediate-Term

PERFORMANCE AND PER SHARE DATA **fund inception date: 3/1/94**

	3yr Annual	5yr Annual	10yr Annual	Category Risk Index	
Return (%)	5.4	4.6	5.8	1.30—high	
Differ From Category (+/-)	3.2 high	2.0 high	1.3 high	**Avg Mat**	7.6 yrs

	2008	2007	2006	2005	2004	2003	2002	2001	2000	1999
Return (%)	4.9	7.6	3.9	1.7	5.2	5.6	10.8	9.2	12.7	-3.0
Differ From Category (+/-)	7.3	2.4	-0.6	-0.4	0.9	-0.5	2.1	1.4	3.0	-2.1
Return, Tax-Adjusted (%)	3.2	5.8	2.2	0.1	3.4	3.7	8.5	6.7	10.0	-5.5
Dividends, Net Income ($)	0.50	0.51	0.50	0.49	0.51	0.53	0.60	0.65	0.65	0.63
Expense Ratio (%)	na	0.18	0.18	0.18	0.18	0.20	0.21	0.21	0.21	0.20
Yield (%)	4.74	4.83	4.86	4.74	4.72	4.91	5.55	6.33	6.52	6.57
Total Assets (Millions $)	3,318	3,020	2,929	3,009	3,501	2,749	2,415	2,096	1,642	1,449

SHAREHOLDER INFORMATION

Minimum Investment
Initial: $3,000 IRA: $3,000
Subsequent: $100 IRA: $100

Maximum Fees
Load: none 12b-1: none
Other: none

Vanguard Interm-Term Investment-Grade (VFICX)

800-662-2739
www.vanguard.com

General Bond: Intermediate-Term

PERFORMANCE AND PER SHARE DATA **fund inception date: 11/1/93**

	3yr Annual	5yr Annual	10yr Annual	Category Risk Index	
Return (%)	1.3	2.1	4.5	1.34—high	
Differ From Category (+/-)	-0.9 blw av	-0.5 blw av	0.0 av	**Avg Mat**	6.1 yrs

	2008	2007	2006	2005	2004	2003	2002	2001	2000	1999
Return (%)	-6.2	6.1	4.4	1.9	4.7	6.2	10.2	9.4	10.6	-1.6
Differ From Category (+/-)	-3.8	0.9	-0.1	-0.2	0.4	0.1	1.5	1.6	1.0	-0.7
Return, Tax-Adjusted (%)	-8.1	4.3	2.6	0.3	3.0	4.3	7.9	6.8	7.8	-4.1
Dividends, Net Income ($)	0.51	0.50	0.49	0.47	0.47	0.52	0.59	0.63	0.66	0.62
Expense Ratio (%)	0.21	0.21	0.21	0.20	0.20	0.20	0.21	0.22	0.25	0.27
Yield (%)	5.85	5.10	5.01	4.75	4.67	5.13	5.79	6.51	6.96	6.71
Total Assets (Millions $)	3,060	2,549	2,432	2,451	3,145	2,747	2,498	2,015	1,920	1,457

SHAREHOLDER INFORMATION

Minimum Investment
Initial: $3,000 IRA: $3,000
Subsequent: $100 IRA: $0

Maximum Fees
Load: none 12b-1: none
Other: none

Vanguard Total Bond Market Index (VBMFX)

800-662-6273
www.vanguard.com

General Bond: Intermediate-Term

PERFORMANCE AND PER SHARE DATA **fund inception date: 12/11/86**

	3yr Annual	5yr Annual	10yr Annual	Category Risk Index	
Return (%)	5.4	4.5	5.3	0.80—blw av	
Differ From Category (+/-)	3.2 high	1.9 high	0.8 high	**Avg Mat**	7.1 yrs

	2008	2007	2006	2005	2004	2003	2002	2001	2000	1999
Return (%)	5.0	6.9	4.2	2.4	4.2	3.9	8.2	8.4	11.3	-0.8
Differ From Category (+/-)	7.4	1.7	-0.3	0.3	-0.1	-2.2	-0.5	0.6	1.6	0.1
Return, Tax-Adjusted (%)	3.4	5.1	2.5	0.8	2.6	2.3	6.0	5.9	8.7	-3.2
Dividends, Net Income ($)	0.48	0.50	0.48	0.45	0.45	0.47	0.57	0.63	0.65	0.62
Expense Ratio (%)	na	0.19	0.20	0.20	0.20	0.22	0.22	0.22	0.22	0.20
Yield (%)	4.68	4.93	4.85	4.46	4.33	4.60	5.49	6.22	6.50	6.44
Total Assets (Millions $)	29,687	29,532	23,769	21,643	19,479	17,032	16,676	14,116	11,180	9,477

SHAREHOLDER INFORMATION

Minimum Investment
Initial: $3,000 IRA: $3,000
Subsequent: $100 IRA: $100

Maximum Fees
Load: none 12b-1: none
Other: none

Westcore Plus Bond (WTIBX)

800-392-2673
www.westcore.com

General Bond: Intermediate-Term

PERFORMANCE AND PER SHARE DATA **fund inception date: 6/1/88**

	3yr Annual	5yr Annual	10yr Annual	Category Risk Index	
Return (%)	3.0	3.5	5.3	0.80—blw av	
Differ From Category (+/-)	0.8 av	0.9 abv av	0.8 high	**Avg Mat**	7.9 yrs

	2008	2007	2006	2005	2004	2003	2002	2001	2000	1999
Return (%)	-1.9	5.4	5.8	2.0	6.3	11.6	7.1	6.7	10.3	0.4
Differ From Category (+/-)	0.5	0.2	1.3	-0.1	2.0	5.5	-1.6	-1.1	0.6	1.3
Return, Tax-Adjusted (%)	-3.6	3.6	4.0	0.2	4.4	9.4	4.5	4.2	7.7	-1.9
Dividends, Net Income ($)	0.51	0.55	0.55	0.58	0.59	0.64	0.70	0.67	0.64	0.61
Expense Ratio (%)	na	0.55	0.55	0.55	0.55	0.55	0.55	0.62	0.85	0.85
Yield (%)	5.15	5.16	5.25	5.47	5.35	5.87	6.72	6.53	6.20	6.15
Total Assets (Millions $)	1,067	1,101	730	379	164	60	51	55	54	37

SHAREHOLDER INFORMATION

Minimum Investment
Initial: $2,500 IRA: $1,000
Subsequent: $100 IRA: $100

Maximum Fees
Load: 2.00% redemption 12b-1: none
Other: redemption fee applies for 90 days

General Bond: Long-Term
Category Performance Ranked by 2008 Returns

Fund (Ticker)	Annual Return (%) 2008	3Yr	5Yr	10Yr	Category Risk	Total Risk
Vanguard Long-Term Bond Index (VBLTX)	8.6	5.9	6.3	6.6	high	blw av
TCW Core Fixed-Income N (TGFNX)	3.6	4.7	3.8	na	low	low
Vanguard Long-Term Investment-Grade (VWESX)	2.2	2.9	4.5	5.6	high	blw av
T. Rowe Price Corporate Income (PRPIX)	-10.0	-0.7	1.4	4.0	av	low
General Bond: Long-Term Category Average	**-3.7**	**1.7**	**2.8**	**4.9**	**av**	**low**

T. Rowe Price Corporate Income (PRPIX)

800-638-5660
www.troweprice.com

General Bond: Long-Term

PERFORMANCE AND PER SHARE DATA **fund inception date: 10/31/95**

	3yr Annual	5yr Annual	10yr Annual	Category Risk Index
Return (%)	-0.7	1.4	4.0	0.99—av
Differ From Category (+/-)	-2.4 av	-1.4 av	-0.9 av	**Avg Mat** 10.8 yrs

	2008	2007	2006	2005	2004	2003	2002	2001	2000	1999
Return (%)	-10.0	3.7	4.9	2.5	7.0	13.0	4.2	9.7	7.9	-0.9
Differ From Category (+/-)	-6.3	-1.4	0.6	0.0	0.7	3.8	-6.0	1.3	-2.3	1.6
Return, Tax-Adjusted (%)	-11.9	1.8	3.1	0.8	5.3	11.0	1.6	6.9	5.0	-3.6
Dividends, Net Income ($)	0.50	0.50	0.49	0.46	0.49	0.53	0.62	0.65	0.68	0.67
Expense Ratio (%)	0.74	0.73	0.78	0.78	0.75	0.80	0.80	0.80	0.80	0.80
Yield (%)	6.15	5.25	5.06	4.78	4.91	5.46	6.87	7.00	7.49	7.33
Total Assets (Millions $)	242	221	205	210	215	101	84	73	50	52

SHAREHOLDER INFORMATION

Minimum Investment
Initial: $2,500 IRA: $1,000
Subsequent: $100 IRA: $50

Maximum Fees
Load: none 12b-1: none
Other: none

TCW Core Fixed-Income N (TGFNX)

800-386-3829
www.tcw.com

General Bond: Long-Term

PERFORMANCE AND PER SHARE DATA **fund inception date: 3/1/99**

	3yr Annual	5yr Annual	10yr Annual	Category Risk Index
Return (%)	4.7	3.8	na	0.46—low
Differ From Category (+/-)	3.0 high	1.0 abv av	na	**Avg Mat** 16.2 yrs

	2008	2007	2006	2005	2004	2003	2002	2001	2000	1999
Return (%)	3.6	6.9	3.6	0.3	4.9	7.3	10.9	5.5	7.5	—
Differ From Category (+/-)	7.3	1.8	-0.7	-2.2	-1.4	-1.9	0.7	-2.9	-2.7	—
Return, Tax-Adjusted (%)	1.7	5.3	2.2	-1.4	3.4	5.6	8.9	3.1	5.0	—
Dividends, Net Income ($)	0.52	0.43	0.39	0.50	0.43	0.48	0.49	0.56	0.59	—
Expense Ratio (%)	na	0.76	1.08	1.10	1.10	1.06	1.00	1.00	1.13	—
Yield (%)	5.26	4.28	3.99	5.10	4.18	4.67	4.86	5.95	6.21	—
Total Assets (Millions $)	94	109	68	17	17	16	5	12	0	—

SHAREHOLDER INFORMATION

Minimum Investment
Initial: $2,000 IRA: $500
Subsequent: $250 IRA: $250

Maximum Fees
Load: none 12b-1: 0.25%
Other: none

Vanguard Long-Term Bond Index (VBLTX)

800-662-6273
www.vanguard.com

General Bond: Long-Term

PERFORMANCE AND PER SHARE DATA **fund inception date: 3/1/94**

	3yr Annual	5yr Annual	10yr Annual	Category Risk Index
Return (%)	5.9	6.3	6.6	1.39—high
Differ From Category (+/-)	4.2 high	3.5 high	1.7 high	**Avg Mat** 20.8 yrs

	2008	2007	2006	2005	2004	2003	2002	2001	2000	1999
Return (%)	8.6	6.5	2.6	5.3	8.3	5.5	14.3	8.1	16.6	-7.9
Differ From Category (+/-)	12.3	1.4	-1.7	2.8	2.1	-3.7	4.1	-0.3	6.4	-5.4
Return, Tax-Adjusted (%)	6.7	4.7	0.8	3.5	6.5	3.3	12.0	5.6	13.8	-10.2
Dividends, Net Income ($)	0.62	0.61	0.60	0.60	0.62	0.63	0.66	0.68	0.68	0.66
Expense Ratio (%)	na	0.18	0.18	0.18	0.18	0.20	0.21	0.21	0.21	0.20
Yield (%)	5.15	5.26	5.23	5.07	5.21	5.36	5.64	6.30	6.36	6.76
Total Assets (Millions $)	2,518	2,277	1,898	1,893	1,310	951	794	542	417	313

SHAREHOLDER INFORMATION

Minimum Investment
Initial: $3,000 IRA: $3,000
Subsequent: $100 IRA: $100

Maximum Fees
Load: none 12b-1: none
Other: none

Vanguard Long-Term Investment-Grade (VWESX)

800-662-2739
www.vanguard.com

General Bond: Long-Term

PERFORMANCE AND PER SHARE DATA **fund inception date: 7/9/73**

	3yr Annual	5yr Annual	10yr Annual	Category Risk Index
Return (%)	2.9	4.5	5.6	1.54—high
Differ From Category (+/-)	1.2 abv av	1.7 high	0.7 high	**Avg Mat** 22.3 yrs

	2008	2007	2006	2005	2004	2003	2002	2001	2000	1999
Return (%)	2.2	3.7	2.8	5.1	8.9	6.2	13.2	9.5	11.7	-6.3
Differ From Category (+/-)	5.9	-1.4	-1.5	2.6	2.6	-3.0	3.0	1.1	1.5	-3.8
Return, Tax-Adjusted (%)	0.3	1.7	0.9	3.2	6.9	4.2	10.7	6.9	8.9	-8.8
Dividends, Net Income ($)	0.51	0.52	0.52	0.52	0.52	0.53	0.56	0.56	0.57	0.56
Expense Ratio (%)	0.22	0.25	0.25	0.25	0.28	0.31	0.32	0.30	0.30	0.30
Yield (%)	5.90	5.77	5.62	5.41	5.46	5.67	6.02	6.47	6.78	6.87
Total Assets (Millions $)	3,658	4,273	4,187	4,224	4,213	3,851	3,753	3,550	3,704	3,724

SHAREHOLDER INFORMATION

Minimum Investment
Initial: $3,000 IRA: $3,000
Subsequent: $100 IRA: $0

Maximum Fees
Load: none 12b-1: none
Other: none

MUNICIPAL BOND FUNDS

National Muni: Short-Term Bond Funds
Category Performance Ranked by 2008 Returns

Fund (Ticker)	Annual Return (%) 2008	3Yr	5Yr	10Yr	Category Risk	Total Risk
Vanguard Short-Term Tax-Ex (VWSTX)	3.7	3.7	2.7	3.1	blw av	low
T. Rowe Price Tax-Free Short-Interm (PRFSX)	3.0	3.3	2.5	3.5	high	low
Vanguard Ltd-Term Tax-Ex (VMLTX)	2.9	3.5	2.6	3.5	abv av	low
USAA Tax Exempt Short-Term (USSTX)	1.3	2.7	2.2	3.2	av	low
Nat'l Muni: Short-Term Bond Category Average	**1.1**	**2.4**	**2.3**	**3.0**	**av**	**low**

T. Rowe Price Tax-Free Short-Interm (PRFSX)

800-225-5132
www.troweprice.com

National Muni: Short-Term Bond

PERFORMANCE AND PER SHARE DATA **fund inception date: 12/23/83**

	3yr Annual	5yr Annual	10yr Annual	Category Risk Index	
Return (%)	3.3	2.5	3.5	1.50—high	
Differ From Category (+/-)	0.9 abv av	0.2 abv av	0.5 high	**Avg Mat**	3.5 yrs

	2008	2007	2006	2005	2004	2003	2002	2001	2000	1999
Return (%)	3.0	3.8	3.2	0.9	1.6	2.7	6.1	5.8	6.7	0.9
Differ From Category (+/-)	1.9	0.7	0.1	-0.8	0.2	0.1	1.8	0.9	1.5	-1.1
Return, Tax-Adjusted (%)	3.0	3.8	3.2	0.9	1.6	2.7	6.0	5.8	6.7	0.9
Dividends, Net Income ($)	0.18	0.18	0.17	0.15	0.15	0.17	0.20	0.22	0.22	0.21
Expense Ratio (%)	0.51	0.51	0.51	0.51	0.51	0.52	0.52	0.53	0.53	0.53
Yield (%)	3.34	3.39	3.20	2.83	2.68	3.10	3.55	3.97	4.19	4.08
Total Assets (Millions $)	579	526	490	513	571	582	560	447	405	417

SHAREHOLDER INFORMATION

Minimum Investment
Initial: $2,500 IRA: $1,000
Subsequent: $100 IRA: $50

Maximum Fees
Load: none 12b-1: none
Other: none

USAA Tax Exempt Short-Term (USSTX)

800-531-8722
www.usaa.com

National Muni: Short-Term Bond

PERFORMANCE AND PER SHARE DATA **fund inception date: 3/19/82**

	3yr Annual	5yr Annual	10yr Annual	Category Risk Index	
Return (%)	2.7	2.2	3.2	1.00—av	
Differ From Category (+/-)	0.3 av	-0.1 blw av	0.2 abv av	**Avg Mat**	2.9 yrs

	2008	2007	2006	2005	2004	2003	2002	2001	2000	1999
Return (%)	1.3	3.3	3.5	1.7	1.5	2.9	4.9	5.0	6.0	1.7
Differ From Category (+/-)	0.2	0.2	0.4	0.0	0.1	0.3	0.6	0.2	0.8	-0.3
Return, Tax-Adjusted (%)	1.3	3.3	3.5	1.7	1.5	2.9	4.9	5.0	6.0	1.7
Dividends, Net Income ($)	0.45	0.40	0.38	0.33	0.27	0.30	0.36	0.44	0.49	0.49
Expense Ratio (%)	0.55	0.55	0.56	0.55	0.56	0.54	0.48	0.38	0.38	0.38
Yield (%)	4.40	3.74	3.57	3.08	2.53	2.74	3.34	4.13	4.58	4.66
Total Assets (Millions $)	1,108	1,006	1,086	1,177	1,319	1,367	1,226	1,122	1,003	988

SHAREHOLDER INFORMATION

Minimum Investment
Initial: $3,000 IRA: na
Subsequent: $50 IRA: na

Maximum Fees
Load: none 12b-1: none
Other: none

Vanguard Ltd-Term Tax-Ex (VMLTX)

800-997-2798
www.vanguard.com

National Muni: Short-Term Bond

PERFORMANCE AND PER SHARE DATA **fund inception date: 8/31/87**

	3yr Annual	5yr Annual	10yr Annual	Category Risk Index	
Return (%)	3.5	2.6	3.5	1.25—abv av	
Differ From Category (+/-)	1.1 high	0.3 high	0.5 high	**Avg Mat**	2.6 yrs

	2008	2007	2006	2005	2004	2003	2002	2001	2000	1999
Return (%)	2.9	4.3	3.3	1.1	1.5	2.7	6.3	5.5	6.3	1.4
Differ From Category (+/-)	1.8	1.2	0.2	-0.6	0.1	0.1	2.0	0.6	1.1	-0.6
Return, Tax-Adjusted (%)	2.9	4.3	3.3	1.1	1.5	2.7	6.3	5.5	6.3	1.4
Dividends, Net Income ($)	0.36	0.37	0.35	0.33	0.32	0.35	0.41	0.47	0.47	0.46
Expense Ratio (%)	na	0.15	0.16	0.16	0.14	0.17	0.17	0.19	0.18	0.18
Yield (%)	3.34	3.45	3.27	3.06	2.89	3.11	3.71	4.34	4.40	4.33
Total Assets (Millions $)	2,192	1,822	1,930	2,169	3,494	3,256	2,773	2,104	2,932	2,569

SHAREHOLDER INFORMATION

Minimum Investment		**Maximum Fees**	
Initial: $3,000	IRA: na	Load: none	12b-1: none
Subsequent: $100	IRA: na	Other: none	

Vanguard Short-Term Tax-Ex (VWSTX)

800-997-2798
www.vanguard.com

National Muni: Short-Term Bond

PERFORMANCE AND PER SHARE DATA **fund inception date: 9/1/77**

	3yr Annual	5yr Annual	10yr Annual	Category Risk Index	
Return (%)	3.7	2.7	3.1	0.56—blw av	
Differ From Category (+/-)	1.3 high	0.4 high	0.1 av	**Avg Mat**	1.2 yrs

	2008	2007	2006	2005	2004	2003	2002	2001	2000	1999
Return (%)	3.7	4.1	3.2	1.6	1.1	1.6	3.4	4.7	4.9	2.5
Differ From Category (+/-)	2.6	1.0	0.1	-0.1	-0.3	-1.0	-0.9	-0.2	-0.3	0.5
Return, Tax-Adjusted (%)	3.7	4.1	3.2	1.6	1.1	1.6	3.4	4.7	4.9	2.5
Dividends, Net Income ($)	0.50	0.53	0.46	0.35	0.29	0.31	0.42	0.61	0.63	0.58
Expense Ratio (%)	na	0.15	0.16	0.16	0.14	0.17	0.17	0.19	0.18	0.18
Yield (%)	3.16	3.38	2.95	2.28	1.88	1.94	2.65	3.87	4.06	3.73
Total Assets (Millions $)	1,474	1,081	1,110	1,305	2,164	2,153	2,022	1,359	2,117	1,917

SHAREHOLDER INFORMATION

Minimum Investment		**Maximum Fees**	
Initial: $3,000	IRA: na	Load: none	12b-1: none
Subsequent: $100	IRA: na	Other: none	

National Muni: Intermediate-Term Bond Funds
Category Performance Ranked by 2008 Returns

Fund (Ticker)	Annual Return (%) 2008	3Yr	5Yr	10Yr	Category Risk	Total Risk
Fidelity Short-Intermediate Muni Income (FSTFX)	3.5	3.6	2.7	3.6	low	low
Bernstein Diversified Municipal (SNDPX)	2.4	3.2	2.7	3.9	low	low
Fidelity Intermediate Municipal Income (FLTMX)	0.9	2.9	3.0	4.2	low	low
Northern Intermediate Tax-Exempt (NOITX)	0.4	2.5	2.5	3.8	abv av	low
T. Rowe Price Summit Municipal Interm (PRSMX)	0.1	2.6	2.6	3.9	blw av	low
Vanguard Interm-Term Tax-Ex (VWITX)	-0.2	2.5	2.6	3.8	abv av	low
American Century Tax-Free Bond Inv (TWTIX)	-0.3	2.4	2.4	3.8	blw av	low
Dreyfus Intermediate Municipal Bond (DITEX)	-1.5	1.6	2.0	3.1	av	low
Nat'l Muni: Interm-Term Bond Category Average	**-1.7**	**1.7**	**2.0**	**3.4**	**av**	**low**

American Century Tax-Free Bond Inv (TWTIX)

877-256-6083
www.americancentury.com

National Muni: Intermediate-Term Bond

PERFORMANCE AND PER SHARE DATA **fund inception date: 3/2/87**

	3yr Annual	5yr Annual	10yr Annual	Category Risk Index	
Return (%)	2.4	2.4	3.8	0.95—blw av	
Differ From Category (+/-)	0.7 av	0.4 av	0.4 abv av	**Avg Mat**	6.3 yrs

	2008	2007	2006	2005	2004	2003	2002	2001	2000	1999
Return (%)	-0.3	3.4	4.0	2.4	2.6	4.0	9.1	5.2	9.7	-1.0
Differ From Category (+/-)	1.4	0.2	0.4	0.5	-0.3	-0.2	0.8	0.3	0.5	0.0
Return, Tax-Adjusted (%)	-0.3	3.4	4.0	2.4	2.6	4.0	9.0	5.0	9.7	-1.0
Dividends, Net Income ($)	0.41	0.43	0.41	0.39	0.36	0.38	0.41	0.46	0.48	0.47
Expense Ratio (%)	0.49	0.49	0.49	0.50	0.51	0.51	0.51	0.51	0.91	0.51
Yield (%)	4.01	3.96	3.81	3.64	3.34	3.42	3.73	4.38	4.59	4.71
Total Assets (Millions $)	1,010	857	632	639	590	605	556	316	163	161

SHAREHOLDER INFORMATION

Minimum Investment		Maximum Fees	
Initial: $5,000	IRA: na	Load: none	12b-1: none
Subsequent: $50	IRA: na	Other: none	

Bernstein Diversified Municipal (SNDPX)

800-221-5672
www.bernstein.com

National Muni: Intermediate-Term Bond

PERFORMANCE AND PER SHARE DATA **fund inception date: 1/9/89**

	3yr Annual	5yr Annual	10yr Annual	Category Risk Index	
Return (%)	3.2	2.7	3.9	0.80—low	
Differ From Category (+/-)	1.5 high	0.7 high	0.5 high	**Avg Mat**	4.9 yrs

	2008	2007	2006	2005	2004	2003	2002	2001	2000	1999
Return (%)	2.4	4.0	3.1	1.4	2.5	4.0	6.8	5.4	7.8	0.5
Differ From Category (+/-)	4.2	0.8	-0.6	-0.5	-0.4	-0.1	-1.4	0.8	-0.6	2.1
Return, Tax-Adjusted (%)	2.4	4.0	3.1	1.4	2.5	4.0	6.8	5.4	7.8	0.4
Dividends, Net Income ($)	0.48	0.47	0.46	0.45	0.45	0.50	0.55	0.59	0.58	0.56
Expense Ratio (%)	0.57	0.57	0.59	0.61	0.61	0.64	0.64	0.63	0.63	0.63
Yield (%)	3.46	3.30	3.26	3.18	3.12	3.46	3.83	4.26	4.24	4.20
Total Assets (Millions $)	4,638	4,924	3,882	3,098	2,623	2,132	1,976	1,433	1,217	1,417

SHAREHOLDER INFORMATION

Minimum Investment		Maximum Fees	
Initial: $25,000	IRA: na	Load: none	12b-1: none
Subsequent: $0	IRA: na	Other: none	

Dreyfus Intermediate Municipal Bond (DITEX)

800-645-6561
www.dreyfus.com

National Muni: Intermediate-Term Bond

PERFORMANCE AND PER SHARE DATA **fund inception date: 8/11/83**

	3yr Annual	5yr Annual	10yr Annual	Category Risk Index	
Return (%)	1.6	2.0	3.1	0.98—av	
Differ From Category (+/-)	-0.1 blw av	0.0 av	-0.3 low	**Avg Mat**	8.8 yrs

	2008	2007	2006	2005	2004	2003	2002	2001	2000	1999
Return (%)	-1.5	2.7	3.7	2.0	3.3	3.8	6.9	3.9	7.7	-1.6
Differ From Category (+/-)	0.2	-0.5	0.0	0.1	0.4	-0.4	-1.4	-1.0	-1.1	-0.2
Return, Tax-Adjusted (%)	-1.5	2.7	3.7	2.0	3.3	3.8	6.9	3.9	7.7	-1.7
Dividends, Net Income ($)	0.50	0.50	0.49	0.50	0.50	0.54	0.61	0.65	0.65	0.66
Expense Ratio (%)	0.79	0.80	0.74	0.73	0.74	0.74	0.74	1.01	0.75	0.75
Yield (%)	4.03	3.77	3.68	3.72	3.69	3.93	4.45	4.88	4.80	5.01
Total Assets (Millions $)	753	855	764	828	895	967	1,059	1,057	1,066	1,133

SHAREHOLDER INFORMATION

Minimum Investment
Initial: $2,500 IRA: na
Subsequent: $100 IRA: na

Maximum Fees
Load: none 12b-1: none
Other: none

Fidelity Intermediate Municipal Income (FLTMX)

877-208-0098
www.fidelity.com

National Muni: Intermediate-Term Bond

PERFORMANCE AND PER SHARE DATA **fund inception date: 4/15/77**

	3yr Annual	5yr Annual	10yr Annual	Category Risk Index	
Return (%)	2.9	3.0	4.2	0.83—low	
Differ From Category (+/-)	1.2 high	1.0 high	0.8 high	**Avg Mat**	7.8 yrs

	2008	2007	2006	2005	2004	2003	2002	2001	2000	1999
Return (%)	0.9	3.9	3.9	2.5	3.7	5.3	9.0	5.4	9.2	-1.1
Differ From Category (+/-)	2.6	0.7	0.2	0.6	0.8	1.1	0.7	0.5	0.4	0.3
Return, Tax-Adjusted (%)	0.9	3.9	3.9	2.4	3.6	5.0	8.8	5.4	9.2	-1.1
Dividends, Net Income ($)	0.37	0.38	0.38	0.38	0.39	0.41	0.43	0.46	0.48	0.47
Expense Ratio (%)	na	0.37	0.34	0.36	0.43	0.43	0.42	0.39	0.49	0.48
Yield (%)	3.84	3.82	3.85	3.83	3.87	3.95	4.18	4.65	4.87	4.95
Total Assets (Millions $)	2,688	2,006	2,023	1,936	1,809	1,797	1,752	1,487	1,210	1,061

SHAREHOLDER INFORMATION

Minimum Investment
Initial: $10,000 IRA: na
Subsequent: $1,000 IRA: na

Maximum Fees
Load: 0.50% redemption 12b-1: none
Other: redemption fee applies for 30 days

Fidelity Short-Intermediate Muni Income (FSTFX)

800-544-6666
www.fidelity.com

National Muni: Intermediate-Term Bond

PERFORMANCE AND PER SHARE DATA **fund inception date: 12/24/86**

	3yr Annual	5yr Annual	10yr Annual	Category Risk Index	
Return (%)	3.6	2.7	3.6	0.58—low	
Differ From Category (+/-)	1.9 high	0.7 high	0.2 av	**Avg Mat**	3.7 yrs

	2008	2007	2006	2005	2004	2003	2002	2001	2000	1999
Return (%)	3.5	4.4	2.9	1.0	1.8	3.0	6.4	5.6	6.1	1.6
Differ From Category (+/-)	5.2	1.2	-0.8	-0.9	-1.1	-1.2	-1.9	0.8	-2.6	3.0
Return, Tax-Adjusted (%)	3.5	4.4	2.9	1.0	1.7	2.9	6.3	5.6	6.1	1.6
Dividends, Net Income ($)	0.33	0.32	0.31	0.28	0.27	0.28	0.34	0.40	0.41	0.39
Expense Ratio (%)	na	0.49	0.41	0.42	0.47	0.47	0.45	0.41	0.45	0.55
Yield (%)	3.15	3.13	3.00	2.78	2.58	2.67	3.20	3.84	4.05	3.91
Total Assets (Millions $)	1,866	1,648	1,484	1,666	1,840	1,839	1,683	1,189	958	765

SHAREHOLDER INFORMATION

Minimum Investment
Initial: $10,000 IRA: na
Subsequent: $1,000 IRA: na

Maximum Fees
Load: 0.50% redemption 12b-1: none
Other: redemp fee applies for 30 days; maint fee for low bal

Northern Intermediate Tax-Exempt (NOITX)

800-595-9111
www.northernfunds.com

National Muni: Intermediate-Term Bond

PERFORMANCE AND PER SHARE DATA **fund inception date: 3/31/94**

	3yr Annual	5yr Annual	10yr Annual	Category Risk Index	
Return (%)	2.5	2.5	3.8	1.02—abv av	
Differ From Category (+/-)	0.8 av	0.5 abv av	0.4 abv av	**Avg Mat**	10.3 yrs

	2008	2007	2006	2005	2004	2003	2002	2001	2000	1999
Return (%)	0.4	3.4	3.8	2.0	3.1	4.6	9.0	4.9	8.0	-0.9
Differ From Category (+/-)	2.1	0.2	0.1	0.1	0.2	0.3	0.8	0.0	-0.9	0.4
Return, Tax-Adjusted (%)	0.4	3.4	3.6	1.9	3.0	4.3	8.6	4.7	8.0	-0.9
Dividends, Net Income ($)	0.34	0.38	0.36	0.34	0.34	0.33	0.36	0.40	0.41	0.39
Expense Ratio (%)	0.75	0.75	0.85	0.85	0.85	0.85	0.85	0.85	0.85	0.85
Yield (%)	3.44	3.69	3.52	3.27	3.22	3.08	3.35	3.90	4.03	3.92
Total Assets (Millions $)	971	698	604	572	587	629	677	690	664	682

SHAREHOLDER INFORMATION

Minimum Investment
Initial: $2,500 IRA: $500
Subsequent: $50 IRA: $50

Maximum Fees
Load: none 12b-1: none
Other: none

T. Rowe Price Summit Municipal Interm (PRSMX)

800-638-5660
www.troweprice.com

National Muni: Intermediate-Term Bond

PERFORMANCE AND PER SHARE DATA **fund inception date: 10/29/93**

	3yr Annual	5yr Annual	10yr Annual	Category Risk Index
Return (%)	2.6	2.6	3.9	0.90—blw av
Differ From Category (+/-)	0.9 abv av	0.6 abv av	0.5 high	**Avg Mat** 8.5 yrs

	2008	2007	2006	2005	2004	2003	2002	2001	2000	1999
Return (%)	0.1	3.7	4.1	2.2	3.0	4.4	8.6	5.6	8.7	-1.3
Differ From Category (+/-)	1.8	0.5	0.4	0.3	0.1	0.2	0.3	0.7	-0.1	0.1
Return, Tax-Adjusted (%)	0.1	3.7	4.1	2.2	3.0	4.4	8.6	5.6	8.7	-1.3
Dividends, Net Income ($)	0.42	0.42	0.40	0.38	0.38	0.43	0.46	0.47	0.48	0.46
Expense Ratio (%)	na	0.50	0.50	0.50	0.50	0.50	0.50	0.50	0.50	0.50
Yield (%)	3.98	3.81	3.69	3.53	3.41	3.90	4.15	4.48	4.58	4.60
Total Assets (Millions $)	782	630	558	226	168	119	110	94	82	79

SHAREHOLDER INFORMATION

Minimum Investment
Initial: $25,000 IRA: $25,000
Subsequent: $1,000 IRA: $1,000

Maximum Fees
Load: none 12b-1: none
Other: none

Vanguard Interm-Term Tax-Ex (VWITX)

800-997-2798
www.vanguard.com

National Muni: Intermediate-Term Bond

PERFORMANCE AND PER SHARE DATA **fund inception date: 9/1/77**

	3yr Annual	5yr Annual	10yr Annual	Category Risk Index
Return (%)	2.5	2.6	3.8	1.08—abv av
Differ From Category (+/-)	0.8 abv av	0.6 abv av	0.4 high	**Avg Mat** 7.6 yrs

	2008	2007	2006	2005	2004	2003	2002	2001	2000	1999
Return (%)	-0.2	3.4	4.4	2.2	3.2	4.4	7.9	5.0	9.2	-0.5
Differ From Category (+/-)	1.5	0.2	0.7	0.3	0.3	0.2	-0.4	0.1	0.4	0.9
Return, Tax-Adjusted (%)	-0.2	3.4	4.4	2.2	3.2	4.4	7.8	5.0	9.2	-0.5
Dividends, Net Income ($)	0.53	0.55	0.56	0.55	0.55	0.56	0.60	0.63	0.65	0.64
Expense Ratio (%)	na	0.15	0.17	0.16	0.14	0.17	0.17	0.19	0.18	0.18
Yield (%)	4.19	4.11	4.16	4.11	4.05	4.05	4.38	4.75	4.87	5.05
Total Assets (Millions $)	5,714	4,956	4,901	4,682	6,897	6,970	7,338	6,653	8,925	7,920

SHAREHOLDER INFORMATION

Minimum Investment
Initial: $3,000 IRA: na
Subsequent: $100 IRA: na

Maximum Fees
Load: none 12b-1: none
Other: none

National Muni: Long-Term Bond Funds
Category Performance Ranked by 2008 Returns

Fund (Ticker)	Annual Return (%) 2008	3Yr	5Yr	10Yr	Category Risk	Total Risk
Schwab Tax-Free Bond (SWNTX)	0.3	1.9	2.3	3.9	low	low
Northern Tax-Exempt (NOTEX)	-1.9	1.8	2.5	4.0	blw av	low
Fidelity Tax-Free Bond (FTABX)	-3.4	1.4	2.6	na	av	low
Fidelity Municipal Income (FHIGX)	-4.7	1.0	2.2	4.1	blw av	low
Vanguard Long-Term Tax-Exempt (VWLTX)	-4.9	0.8	1.9	3.8	high	low
T. Rowe Price Tax-Free Income (PRTAX)	-5.9	0.4	1.8	3.5	av	low
T. Rowe Price Summit Municipal Income (PRINX)	-8.1	-0.5	1.5	3.5	abv av	low
Dreyfus Municipal Bond (DRTAX)	-8.5	-0.9	1.0	2.4	blw av	low
Nat'l Muni: Long-Term Bond Category Average	**-5.4**	**0.3**	**1.7**	**3.3**	**av**	**low**

Dreyfus Municipal Bond (DRTAX)

800-645-6561
www.dreyfus.com

National Muni: Long-Term Bond

PERFORMANCE AND PER SHARE DATA **fund inception date: 10/4/76**

	3yr Annual	5yr Annual	10yr Annual	Category Risk Index
Return (%)	-0.9	1.0	2.4	0.96—blw av
Differ From Category (+/-)	-1.2 blw av	-0.7 blw av	-0.9 low	**Avg Mat** 18.3 yrs

	2008	2007	2006	2005	2004	2003	2002	2001	2000	1999
Return (%)	-8.5	1.1	5.1	3.9	4.2	4.6	7.1	2.7	11.9	-6.0
Differ From Category (+/-)	-3.1	-1.2	0.4	0.5	-0.3	-0.7	-2.2	-1.5	0.2	-1.5
Return, Tax-Adjusted (%)	-8.5	1.1	5.1	3.9	4.2	4.6	7.1	2.7	11.9	-6.0
Dividends, Net Income ($)	0.53	0.51	0.51	0.52	0.49	0.50	0.60	0.62	0.60	0.61
Expense Ratio (%)	0.80	0.89	0.86	0.68	0.68	0.72	0.71	0.72	0.76	0.73
Yield (%)	5.22	4.43	4.25	4.38	4.15	4.23	5.02	5.31	5.01	5.47
Total Assets (Millions $)	1,611	1,928	1,967	2,024	2,109	2,280	2,467	2,489	2,611	2,606

SHAREHOLDER INFORMATION

Minimum Investment
Initial: $2,500 IRA: na
Subsequent: $100 IRA: na

Maximum Fees
Load: none 12b-1: none
Other: none

Fidelity Municipal Income (FHIGX)

800-544-9797
www.fidelity.com

National Muni: Long-Term Bond

PERFORMANCE AND PER SHARE DATA **fund inception date: 12/1/77**

	3yr Annual	5yr Annual	10yr Annual	Category Risk Index
Return (%)	1.0	2.2	4.1	0.92—blw av
Differ From Category (+/-)	0.7 abv av	0.5 abv av	0.8 high	**Avg Mat** 14.2 yrs

	2008	2007	2006	2005	2004	2003	2002	2001	2000	1999
Return (%)	-4.7	3.1	4.7	3.6	4.7	5.8	10.4	5.0	12.3	-2.5
Differ From Category (+/-)	0.7	0.8	0.0	0.2	0.2	0.5	1.1	0.8	0.6	2.0
Return, Tax-Adjusted (%)	-4.7	3.0	4.6	3.4	4.5	5.5	10.2	4.9	12.2	-2.5
Dividends, Net Income ($)	0.51	0.51	0.53	0.55	0.57	0.59	0.60	0.61	0.63	0.60
Expense Ratio (%)	na	0.44	0.45	0.45	0.47	0.47	0.46	0.43	0.48	0.49
Yield (%)	4.46	4.06	4.08	4.20	4.31	4.37	4.48	4.82	4.95	5.00
Total Assets (Millions $)	4,531	5,135	4,679	4,670	4,619	4,775	4,801	4,514	4,452	4,063

SHAREHOLDER INFORMATION

Minimum Investment
Initial: $10,000 IRA: na
Subsequent: $1,000 IRA: na

Maximum Fees
Load: 0.50% redemption 12b-1: none
Other: redemp fee applies for 30 days; maint fee for low bal

Fidelity Tax-Free Bond (FTABX)

800-544-6666
www.fidelity.com

National Muni: Long-Term Bond

PERFORMANCE AND PER SHARE DATA **fund inception date: 4/10/01**

	3yr Annual	5yr Annual	10yr Annual	Category Risk Index
Return (%)	1.4	2.6	na	0.96—av
Differ From Category (+/-)	1.1 abv av	0.9 high	na	**Avg Mat** 13.5 yrs

	2008	2007	2006	2005	2004	2003	2002	2001	2000	1999
Return (%)	-3.4	3.2	4.8	3.7	4.8	6.1	10.6	—	—	—
Differ From Category (+/-)	2.0	0.9	0.1	0.3	0.3	0.8	1.3	—	—	—
Return, Tax-Adjusted (%)	-3.4	3.2	4.7	3.7	4.7	6.0	10.6	—	—	—
Dividends, Net Income ($)	0.43	0.42	0.43	0.42	0.44	0.44	0.43	—	—	—
Expense Ratio (%)	0.18	0.17	0.17	0.22	0.23	0.14	0.06	—	—	—
Yield (%)	4.38	3.96	3.93	3.94	4.03	4.07	4.05	—	—	—
Total Assets (Millions $)	1,130	867	504	365	253	220	257	—	—	—

SHAREHOLDER INFORMATION

Minimum Investment
Initial: $25,000 IRA: na
Subsequent: $1,000 IRA: na

Maximum Fees
Load: 0.50% redemption 12b-1: none
Other: redemp fee applies for 30 days; maint fee for low bal

Northern Tax-Exempt (NOTEX)

800-595-9111
www.northernfunds.com

National Muni: Long-Term Bond

PERFORMANCE AND PER SHARE DATA **fund inception date: 3/31/94**

	3yr Annual	5yr Annual	10yr Annual	Category Risk Index
Return (%)	1.8	2.5	4.0	0.92—blw av
Differ From Category (+/-)	1.5 high	0.8 high	0.7 high	**Avg Mat** 13.6 yrs

	2008	2007	2006	2005	2004	2003	2002	2001	2000	1999
Return (%)	-1.9	2.9	4.2	3.1	4.0	5.3	9.8	4.7	12.4	-4.1
Differ From Category (+/-)	3.6	0.8	-0.5	-0.3	-0.5	-0.2	0.6	0.5	0.6	0.4
Return, Tax-Adjusted (%)	-1.9	2.9	4.0	3.0	3.8	5.1	9.4	4.7	12.4	-4.1
Dividends, Net Income ($)	0.38	0.42	0.42	0.43	0.45	0.43	0.46	0.47	0.48	0.44
Expense Ratio (%)	0.75	0.75	0.85	0.85	0.85	0.85	0.85	0.85	0.85	0.85
Yield (%)	3.93	4.01	3.96	4.08	4.10	3.94	4.16	4.45	4.58	4.44
Total Assets (Millions $)	833	689	542	470	489	525	556	538	535	515

SHAREHOLDER INFORMATION

Minimum Investment
Initial: $2,500 IRA: $500
Subsequent: $50 IRA: $50

Maximum Fees
Load: none 12b-1: none
Other: none

Schwab Tax-Free Bond (SWNTX)

800-407-0256
www.schwab.com

National Muni: Long-Term Bond

PERFORMANCE AND PER SHARE DATA **fund inception date: 9/11/92**

	3yr Annual	5yr Annual	10yr Annual	Category Risk Index
Return (%)	1.9	2.3	3.9	0.77—low
Differ From Category (+/-)	1.6 high	0.6 high	0.6 high	**Avg Mat** 7.5 yrs

	2008	2007	2006	2005	2004	2003	2002	2001	2000	1999
Return (%)	0.3	1.6	3.9	2.0	4.0	5.4	10.9	3.8	15.5	-7.4
Differ From Category (+/-)	5.7	-0.7	-0.8	-1.4	-0.5	0.1	1.6	-0.3	3.9	-2.8
Return, Tax-Adjusted (%)	0.3	1.6	3.9	2.0	4.0	5.4	10.9	3.8	15.5	-7.4
Dividends, Net Income ($)	0.45	0.45	0.45	0.44	0.44	0.45	0.48	0.49	0.50	0.50
Expense Ratio (%)	0.48	0.59	0.65	0.65	0.65	0.62	0.49	0.49	0.49	0.49
Yield (%)	4.28	4.12	4.01	3.95	3.90	3.96	4.28	4.65	4.73	5.19
Total Assets (Millions $)	127	98	93	92	86	81	84	81	83	81

SHAREHOLDER INFORMATION

Minimum Investment
Initial: $100 IRA: na
Subsequent: $0 IRA: na

Maximum Fees
Load: none 12b-1: none
Other: none

T. Rowe Price Summit Municipal Income (PRINX)

800-638-5660
www.troweprice.com

National Muni: Long-Term Bond

PERFORMANCE AND PER SHARE DATA **fund inception date: 10/29/93**

	3yr Annual	5yr Annual	10yr Annual	Category Risk Index
Return (%)	-0.5	1.5	3.5	0.98—abv av
Differ From Category (+/-)	-0.8 blw av	-0.2 blw av	0.2 av	**Avg Mat** 13.7 yrs

	2008	2007	2006	2005	2004	2003	2002	2001	2000	1999
Return (%)	-8.1	1.6	5.4	4.2	5.1	6.0	9.1	5.2	11.9	-4.1
Differ From Category (+/-)	-2.7	-0.7	0.7	0.8	0.6	0.7	-0.2	1.0	0.2	0.4
Return, Tax-Adjusted (%)	-8.1	1.6	5.4	4.2	5.1	6.0	9.1	5.2	11.9	-4.1
Dividends, Net Income ($)	0.46	0.44	0.45	0.48	0.49	0.50	0.50	0.52	0.52	0.49
Expense Ratio (%)	na	0.50	0.50	0.50	0.50	0.50	0.50	0.50	0.50	0.50
Yield (%)	4.74	4.02	4.04	4.31	4.44	4.51	4.64	4.94	5.01	5.02
Total Assets (Millions $)	338	443	426	160	105	94	91	81	71	70

SHAREHOLDER INFORMATION

Minimum Investment
Initial: $25,000 IRA: $25,000
Subsequent: $1,000 IRA: $1,000

Maximum Fees
Load: none 12b-1: none
Other: none

T. Rowe Price Tax-Free Income (PRTAX)

800-225-5132
www.troweprice.com

National Muni: Long-Term Bond

PERFORMANCE AND PER SHARE DATA **fund inception date: 10/26/76**

	3yr Annual	5yr Annual	10yr Annual	Category Risk Index
Return (%)	0.4	1.8	3.5	0.96—av
Differ From Category (+/-)	0.1 av	0.1 av	0.2 av	**Avg Mat** 14.5 yrs

	2008	2007	2006	2005	2004	2003	2002	2001	2000	1999
Return (%)	-5.9	2.2	5.1	3.7	4.3	5.1	9.2	4.3	12.2	-4.0
Differ From Category (+/-)	-0.5	-0.1	0.4	0.3	-0.2	-0.2	-0.1	0.1	0.5	0.5
Return, Tax-Adjusted (%)	-5.9	2.2	5.1	3.7	4.3	5.1	9.2	4.3	12.2	-4.0
Dividends, Net Income ($)	0.44	0.44	0.44	0.44	0.43	0.45	0.47	0.48	0.49	0.49
Expense Ratio (%)	0.52	0.52	0.53	0.54	0.54	0.55	0.54	0.54	0.55	0.55
Yield (%)	4.94	4.43	4.38	4.35	4.30	4.46	4.67	4.98	5.10	5.41
Total Assets (Millions $)	1,372	1,529	1,486	1,467	1,451	1,488	1,401	1,416	1,396	1,328

SHAREHOLDER INFORMATION

Minimum Investment
Initial: $2,500 IRA: $1,000
Subsequent: $100 IRA: $50

Maximum Fees
Load: none 12b-1: none
Other: none

Vanguard Long-Term Tax-Exempt (VWLTX)

800-997-2798
www.vanguard.com

National Muni: Long-Term Bond

PERFORMANCE AND PER SHARE DATA **fund inception date: 9/1/77**

	3yr Annual	5yr Annual	10yr Annual	Category Risk Index
Return (%)	0.8	1.9	3.8	1.06—high
Differ From Category (+/-)	0.5 abv av	0.2 av	0.5 abv av	**Avg Mat** 12.4 yrs

	2008	2007	2006	2005	2004	2003	2002	2001	2000	1999
Return (%)	-4.9	2.5	5.1	3.0	4.1	5.2	10.1	4.5	13.3	-3.6
Differ From Category (+/-)	0.5	0.2	0.4	-0.4	-0.4	-0.1	0.8	0.3	1.6	0.9
Return, Tax-Adjusted (%)	-4.9	2.5	5.1	3.0	4.1	5.2	10.0	4.4	13.3	-3.6
Dividends, Net Income ($)	0.49	0.51	0.52	0.51	0.52	0.52	0.54	0.56	0.57	0.57
Expense Ratio (%)	na	0.15	0.16	0.15	0.15	0.17	0.17	0.19	0.19	0.18
Yield (%)	4.91	4.59	4.55	4.52	4.53	4.53	4.64	5.06	5.15	5.48
Total Assets (Millions $)	1,519	643	638	641	1,127	1,146	1,248	1,187	1,746	1,487

SHAREHOLDER INFORMATION

Minimum Investment
Initial: $3,000 IRA: na
Subsequent: $100 IRA: na

Maximum Fees
Load: none 12b-1: none
Other: none

National Muni: High-Yield Bond Funds
Category Performance Ranked by 2008 Returns

Fund (Ticker)	Annual Return (%) 2008	3Yr	5Yr	10Yr	Category Risk	Total Risk
Vanguard High-Yield Tax-Exempt (VWAHX)	-10.5	-1.4	1.0	3.0	low	low
Northern High Yield Muni (NHYMX)	-21.4	-7.0	-2.1	0.8	blw av	low
T. Rowe Price Tax-Free High-Yield (PRFHX)	-21.5	-6.1	-1.3	1.4	av	blw av
Nat'l Muni: High-Yield Bond Category Average	**-20.5**	**-5.6**	**-1.3**	**1.6**	**av**	**low**

Northern High Yield Muni (NHYMX)

800-595-9111
www.northernfunds.com

National Muni: High-Yield Bond

PERFORMANCE AND PER SHARE DATA **fund inception date: 12/31/98**

	3yr Annual	5yr Annual	10yr Annual	Category Risk Index	
Return (%)	-7.0	-2.1	0.8	1.01—blw av	
Differ From Category (+/-)	-1.4 low	-0.8 blw av	-0.8 low	**Avg Mat**	17.6 yrs

	2008	2007	2006	2005	2004	2003	2002	2001	2000	1999
Return (%)	-21.4	-3.6	6.3	4.8	6.5	6.4	7.3	6.3	6.3	-6.2
Differ From Category (+/-)	-0.9	-2.6	-0.7	-0.7	0.7	-0.1	-0.2	1.0	-1.7	-2.6
Return, Tax-Adjusted (%)	-21.4	-3.6	6.3	4.8	6.5	6.4	7.3	6.3	6.3	-6.2
Dividends, Net Income ($)	0.41	0.44	0.42	0.42	0.43	0.45	0.46	0.49	0.48	0.39
Expense Ratio (%)	0.85	0.85	0.85	0.85	0.85	0.85	0.85	0.85	0.85	0.85
Yield (%)	6.02	4.78	4.21	4.31	4.43	4.68	4.89	5.29	5.25	4.28
Total Assets (Millions $)	266	363	293	185	122	84	47	34	28	19

SHAREHOLDER INFORMATION

Minimum Investment
Initial: $2,500 IRA: $500
Subsequent: $50 IRA: $50

Maximum Fees
Load: none 12b-1: none
Other: none

T. Rowe Price Tax-Free High-Yield (PRFHX)

800-225-5132
www.troweprice.com

National Muni: High-Yield Bond

PERFORMANCE AND PER SHARE DATA **fund inception date: 3/1/85**

	3yr Annual	5yr Annual	10yr Annual	Category Risk Index	
Return (%)	-6.1	-1.3	1.4	1.03—av	
Differ From Category (+/-)	-0.5 av	0.0 abv av	-0.2 av	**Avg Mat**	18.0 yrs

	2008	2007	2006	2005	2004	2003	2002	2001	2000	1999
Return (%)	-21.5	-1.2	6.8	6.2	6.6	7.0	6.3	4.6	8.1	-5.1
Differ From Category (+/-)	-1.0	-0.2	-0.1	0.7	0.8	0.8	-1.3	-0.8	0.1	-1.5
Return, Tax-Adjusted (%)	-21.5	-1.2	6.8	6.2	6.6	7.0	6.3	4.6	8.1	-5.1
Dividends, Net Income ($)	0.57	0.57	0.58	0.58	0.60	0.61	0.64	0.66	0.67	0.65
Expense Ratio (%)	0.72	0.72	0.70	0.70	0.71	0.71	0.71	0.72	0.71	0.71
Yield (%)	6.75	4.96	4.77	4.89	5.10	5.24	5.57	5.80	5.81	5.77
Total Assets (Millions $)	1,204	1,441	1,570	1,380	1,218	1,136	1,119	1,089	1,084	1,132

SHAREHOLDER INFORMATION

Minimum Investment
Initial: $2,500 IRA: $1,000
Subsequent: $100 IRA: $50

Maximum Fees
Load: none 12b-1: none
Other: none

Vanguard High-Yield Tax-Exempt (VWAHX)

800-997-2798
www.vanguard.com

National Muni: High-Yield Bond

PERFORMANCE AND PER SHARE DATA **fund inception date: 12/27/78**

	3yr Annual	5yr Annual	10yr Annual	Category Risk Index
Return (%)	-1.4	1.0	3.0	0.72—low
Differ From Category (+/-)	4.2 high	2.3 high	1.4 high	**Avg Mat** 14.5 yrs

	2008	2007	2006	2005	2004	2003	2002	2001	2000	1999
Return (%)	-10.5	1.5	5.5	4.3	4.9	6.3	7.3	5.3	10.7	-3.4
Differ From Category (+/-)	10.0	2.5	-1.4	-1.2	-0.9	0.0	-0.3	-0.1	2.7	0.2
Return, Tax-Adjusted (%)	-10.5	1.5	5.5	4.3	4.9	6.3	7.3	5.3	10.7	-3.4
Dividends, Net Income ($)	0.49	0.50	0.49	0.49	0.50	0.52	0.56	0.58	0.58	0.57
Expense Ratio (%)	na	0.15	0.17	0.15	0.15	0.17	0.17	0.19	0.19	0.18
Yield (%)	5.47	4.70	4.52	4.54	4.64	4.81	5.23	5.48	5.54	5.71
Total Assets (Millions $)	1,540	1,914	1,845	1,745	2,764	2,668	2,669	2,650	3,143	2,753

SHAREHOLDER INFORMATION

Minimum Investment
Initial: $3,000 IRA: na
Subsequent: $100 IRA: na

Maximum Fees
Load: none 12b-1: none
Other: none

STATE-SPECIFIC BOND FUNDS

Category Performance Ranked by 2008 Returns

Fund (Ticker)	Annual Return (%) 2008	3Yr	5Yr	10Yr	Category Risk	Total Risk
T. Rowe Price MD Short-Term Tax-Free (PRMDX)	3.3	3.3	2.3	3.0	blw av	low
Dupree KY Tax-Free Short-to-Medium (KYSMX)	3.1	3.2	2.4	3.3	av	low
Bernstein Short Duration CA Municipal (SDCMX)	3.0	3.1	2.2	2.8	low	low
Bernstein Short Duration NY Municipal (SDNYX)	2.8	3.0	2.3	2.9	low	low
Bernstein CA Municipal (SNCAX)	1.5	2.9	2.5	3.6	low	low
Bernstein NY Municipal (SNNYX)	1.3	2.8	2.5	3.7	blw av	low
Dupree KY Tax-Free Income (KYTFX)	0.9	2.9	3.1	3.9	high	low
Empire Builder Tax-Free Bond Prem (EMTPX)	0.8	2.5	2.3	3.5	blw av	low
Fidelity Michigan Municipal Income (FMHTX)	-0.1	2.6	2.9	4.2	high	low
Fidelity Minnesota Municipal Income (FIMIX)	-0.3	2.3	2.7	3.9	av	low
American Century CA Tax-Free Bond (BCITX)	-0.7	2.0	2.2	3.5	blw av	low
Fidelity Pennsylvania Municipal Income (FPXTX)	-0.8	2.3	2.8	4.1	av	low
Schwab CA Tax-Free Bond (SWCAX)	-1.1	1.8	2.7	3.9	blw av	low
Fidelity Connecticut Municipal Income (FICNX)	-1.2	2.1	2.4	4.0	high	low
Northern CA Intermediate Tax-Exempt (NCITX)	-1.3	1.5	1.9	na	blw av	low
Vanguard MA Tax-Exempt (VMATX)	-1.3	2.1	2.7	4.0	high	low
Westcore CO Tax-Exempt (WTCOX)	-1.4	1.8	1.9	3.2	high	low
Northern AZ Tax-Exempt (NOAZX)	-1.5	1.8	2.2	na	av	low
Dupree NC Tax-Free Income (NTFIX)	-1.5	1.8	2.4	3.6	high	low
Fidelity Ohio Municipal Income (FOHFX)	-1.7	2.1	2.7	4.1	high	low
Wells Fargo Advantage WI Tax-Free Inv (SWFRX)	-1.8	1.9	2.7	na	high	low
Vanguard CA Interm-Term Tax-Exempt (VCAIX)	-2.2	1.6	1.9	3.7	av	low
Dupree TN Tax-Free Income (TNTIX)	-2.4	1.5	2.2	3.5	high	low
Fidelity New York Municipal Income (FTFMX)	-2.5	1.7	2.5	4.2	av	low
Vanguard OH Long-Term Tax-Exempt (VOHIX)	-2.8	1.7	2.3	4.1	av	low
Fidelity New Jersey Municipal Income (FNJHX)	-3.0	1.7	2.4	4.1	blw av	low
Vanguard NJ Long-Term Tax-Exempt (VNJTX)	-3.1	1.6	2.3	4.0	high	low
WesMark WV Municipal Bond (WMKMX)	-3.1	0.8	1.4	3.0	high	low
Fidelity Massachusetts Municipal Income (FDMMX)	-3.6	1.4	2.4	4.0	av	low
Vanguard PA Long-Term Tax-Exempt (VPAIX)	-3.7	1.2	2.0	4.0	high	low
Vanguard NY Long-Term Tax-Exempt (VNYTX)	-3.7	1.1	2.0	3.9	high	low
T. Rowe Price VA Tax-Free Bond (PRVAX)	-3.9	0.9	2.0	3.7	abv av	low
Dreyfus NY Tax-Exempt Bond (DRNYX)	-4.2	0.9	1.8	3.2	abv av	low
Fidelity Arizona Municipal Income (FSAZX)	-4.3	0.8	1.7	3.7	high	low
Hawaii Municipal (SURFX)	-5.0	0.2	1.3	3.0	high	low
Vanguard FL Long-Term Tax-Exempt (VFLTX)	-5.1	0.8	1.8	3.9	av	low
T. Rowe Price NJ Tax-Free Bond (NJTFX)	-5.2	0.3	1.7	3.4	abv av	low
T. Rowe Price GA Tax-Free Bond (GTFBX)	-5.4	0.2	1.5	3.3	high	low
T. Rowe Price NY Tax-Free Bond (PRNYX)	-5.6	0.4	1.7	3.4	av	low

STATE-SPECIFIC BOND FUNDS (cont.)

Category Performance Ranked by 2008 Returns

Fund (Ticker)	Annual Return (%) 2008	3Yr	5Yr	10Yr	Category Risk	Total Risk
Fidelity California Municipal Income (FCTFX)	-5.7	0.5	2.0	3.7	av	low
General NY Municipal Bond (GNYMX)	-6.7	-0.2	1.0	2.8	abv av	low
T. Rowe Price MD Tax-Free Bond (MDXBX)	-6.7	-0.2	1.2	3.2	high	low
Vanguard CA Long-Term Tax-Exempt (VCITX)	-6.9	-0.2	1.4	3.6	high	low
USAA VA Bond (USVAX)	-7.5	-0.8	1.0	3.1	high	low
USAA FL Tax-Free Income (UFLTX)	-8.7	-1.2	0.9	3.0	high	low
Sit MN Tax-Free Income (SMTFX)	-10.9	-1.9	0.4	2.2	high	low

Fidelity Arizona Municipal Income (FSAZX)

800-544-5555
www.fidelity.com

Muni: Arizona Bond

PERFORMANCE AND PER SHARE DATA **fund inception date: 10/11/94**

	3yr Annual	5yr Annual	10yr Annual	Category Risk Index	
Return (%)	0.8	1.7	3.7	1.02—high	
Differ From Category (+/-)	-0.5 av	-0.3 av	0.0 high	**Avg Mat**	12.2 yrs

	2008	2007	2006	2005	2004	2003	2002	2001	2000	1999
Return (%)	-4.3	2.5	4.4	2.7	3.7	5.2	9.9	4.8	10.9	-1.9
Differ From Category (+/-)	-1.4	-0.4	0.4	0.4	0.1	0.7	0.0	0.1	-0.2	0.0
Return, Tax-Adjusted (%)	-4.3	2.5	4.3	2.6	3.6	5.1	9.7	4.8	10.9	-1.9
Dividends, Net Income ($)	0.42	0.42	0.42	0.42	0.43	0.43	0.44	0.46	0.49	0.46
Expense Ratio (%)	0.52	0.48	0.50	0.50	0.53	0.52	0.48	0.41	0.48	0.55
Yield (%)	4.08	3.71	3.64	3.63	3.67	3.70	3.79	4.18	4.49	4.47
Total Assets (Millions $)	120	136	115	99	86	76	73	54	40	27

SHAREHOLDER INFORMATION

Minimum Investment
Initial: $10,000 IRA: na
Subsequent: $1,000 IRA: na

Maximum Fees
Load: 0.50% redemption 12b-1: none
Other: redemp fee applies for 30 days; maint fee for low bal

Northern AZ Tax-Exempt (NOAZX)

800-595-9111
www.northernfunds.com

Muni: Arizona Bond

PERFORMANCE AND PER SHARE DATA **fund inception date: 10/1/99**

	3yr Annual	5yr Annual	10yr Annual	Category Risk Index	
Return (%)	1.8	2.2	na	0.98—av	
Differ From Category (+/-)	0.5 high	0.2 high	na	**Avg Mat**	12.2 yrs

	2008	2007	2006	2005	2004	2003	2002	2001	2000	1999
Return (%)	-1.5	3.3	3.7	2.0	3.5	3.9	9.9	4.6	11.2	—
Differ From Category (+/-)	1.4	0.4	-0.4	-0.3	-0.1	-0.7	0.1	-0.1	0.1	—
Return, Tax-Adjusted (%)	-1.5	3.2	3.6	1.9	3.3	3.8	9.5	4.3	11.2	—
Dividends, Net Income ($)	0.38	0.41	0.41	0.41	0.41	0.44	0.41	0.43	0.44	—
Expense Ratio (%)	0.75	0.75	0.85	0.85	0.85	0.85	0.85	0.85	0.85	—
Yield (%)	3.96	4.01	3.97	3.93	3.82	4.03	3.70	4.10	4.17	—
Total Assets (Millions $)	84	66	54	55	69	80	81	80	73	—

SHAREHOLDER INFORMATION

Minimum Investment
Initial: $2,500 IRA: $500
Subsequent: $50 IRA: $50

Maximum Fees
Load: none 12b-1: none
Other: none

American Century CA Tax-Free Bond (BCITX)

800-345-2021
www.americancentury.com

Muni: California Bond

PERFORMANCE AND PER SHARE DATA **fund inception date: 11/9/83**

	3yr Annual	5yr Annual	10yr Annual	Category Risk Index
Return (%)	2.0	2.2	3.5	0.80—blw av
Differ From Category (+/-)	1.4 high	0.4 abv av	0.1 av	**Avg Mat** 5.8 yrs

	2008	2007	2006	2005	2004	2003	2002	2001	2000	1999
Return (%)	-0.7	2.6	4.0	2.2	2.8	3.2	8.7	4.3	10.0	-1.1
Differ From Category (+/-)	3.6	0.4	-0.2	-0.7	-1.0	-1.0	0.7	0.2	-2.4	1.4
Return, Tax-Adjusted (%)	-0.7	2.6	4.0	2.2	2.8	3.2	8.6	4.1	10.0	-1.1
Dividends, Net Income ($)	0.43	0.45	0.46	0.46	0.45	0.44	0.46	0.49	0.49	0.49
Expense Ratio (%)	0.49	0.49	0.49	0.49	0.50	0.51	0.51	0.51	0.51	0.51
Yield (%)	4.07	4.05	4.11	4.10	3.90	3.85	3.90	4.34	4.38	4.61
Total Assets (Millions $)	556	580	443	439	418	450	479	440	445	439

SHAREHOLDER INFORMATION

Minimum Investment		**Maximum Fees**	
Initial: $5,000	IRA: na	Load: none	12b-1: none
Subsequent: $50	IRA: na	Other: none	

Bernstein CA Municipal (SNCAX)

800-221-5672
www.bernstein.com

Muni: California Bond

PERFORMANCE AND PER SHARE DATA **fund inception date: 8/6/90**

	3yr Annual	5yr Annual	10yr Annual	Category Risk Index
Return (%)	2.9	2.5	3.6	0.67—low
Differ From Category (+/-)	2.3 high	0.7 high	0.2 abv av	**Avg Mat** 5.0 yrs

	2008	2007	2006	2005	2004	2003	2002	2001	2000	1999
Return (%)	1.5	3.9	3.2	1.5	2.5	3.6	5.8	4.5	8.6	0.0
Differ From Category (+/-)	5.8	1.7	-0.9	-1.4	-1.3	-0.5	-2.1	0.6	-3.1	2.9
Return, Tax-Adjusted (%)	1.4	3.9	3.2	1.5	2.5	3.6	5.8	4.5	8.6	-0.1
Dividends, Net Income ($)	0.49	0.47	0.45	0.45	0.42	0.46	0.50	0.56	0.57	0.55
Expense Ratio (%)	0.62	0.62	0.63	0.65	0.64	0.65	0.66	0.65	0.64	0.64
Yield (%)	3.47	3.28	3.17	3.16	2.95	3.19	3.44	3.98	4.09	4.04
Total Assets (Millions $)	1,213	1,396	1,247	1,002	878	711	692	513	447	561

SHAREHOLDER INFORMATION

Minimum Investment		**Maximum Fees**	
Initial: $25,000	IRA: na	Load: none	12b-1: none
Subsequent: $0	IRA: na	Other: none	

Bernstein Short Duration CA Municipal (SDCMX)

800-221-5672
www.bernstein.com

Muni: California Bond

PERFORMANCE AND PER SHARE DATA **fund inception date: 10/3/94**

	3yr Annual	5yr Annual	10yr Annual	Category Risk Index	
Return (%)	3.1	2.2	2.8	0.27—low	
Differ From Category (+/-)	2.5 high	0.4 high	-0.6 low	**Avg Mat**	1.5 yrs

	2008	2007	2006	2005	2004	2003	2002	2001	2000	1999
Return (%)	3.0	3.5	2.7	1.1	0.7	1.5	2.6	4.4	4.9	2.4
Differ From Category (+/-)	7.3	1.3	-1.5	-1.8	-3.1	-2.7	-5.3	0.5	-6.8	5.3
Return, Tax-Adjusted (%)	3.0	3.5	2.7	1.1	0.7	1.5	2.6	4.4	4.9	2.3
Dividends, Net Income ($)	0.35	0.36	0.31	0.26	0.21	0.21	0.31	0.45	0.47	0.40
Expense Ratio (%)	0.69	0.73	0.81	0.81	0.78	0.80	0.79	0.79	0.73	0.73
Yield (%)	2.79	2.85	2.50	2.05	1.64	1.66	2.42	3.52	3.70	3.22
Total Assets (Millions $)	120	95	76	67	70	82	76	54	59	96

SHAREHOLDER INFORMATION

Minimum Investment
Initial: $25,000 IRA: na
Subsequent: $0 IRA: na

Maximum Fees
Load: none 12b-1: none
Other: none

Fidelity California Municipal Income (FCTFX)

800-544-6666
www.fidelity.com

Muni: California Bond

PERFORMANCE AND PER SHARE DATA **fund inception date: 7/9/84**

	3yr Annual	5yr Annual	10yr Annual	Category Risk Index	
Return (%)	0.5	2.0	3.7	1.09—av	
Differ From Category (+/-)	-0.1 av	0.2 abv av	0.3 high	**Avg Mat**	12.4 yrs

	2008	2007	2006	2005	2004	2003	2002	2001	2000	1999
Return (%)	-5.7	2.9	4.6	3.6	4.8	4.9	8.4	4.6	12.5	-2.8
Differ From Category (+/-)	-1.4	0.7	0.4	0.7	1.0	0.7	0.4	0.6	0.5	0.0
Return, Tax-Adjusted (%)	-5.7	2.8	4.5	3.5	4.6	4.7	8.3	4.6	12.5	-2.9
Dividends, Net Income ($)	0.49	0.49	0.51	0.51	0.53	0.54	0.54	0.56	0.57	0.55
Expense Ratio (%)	0.43	0.44	0.45	0.47	0.48	0.47	0.43	0.42	0.49	0.52
Yield (%)	4.47	4.01	4.06	4.10	4.16	4.21	4.23	4.50	4.63	4.78
Total Assets (Millions $)	1,363	1,584	1,573	1,566	1,470	1,520	1,686	1,603	1,430	1,224

SHAREHOLDER INFORMATION

Minimum Investment
Initial: $10,000 IRA: na
Subsequent: $1,000 IRA: na

Maximum Fees
Load: 0.50% redemption 12b-1: none
Other: redemp fee applies for 30 days; maint fee for low bal

Northern CA Intermediate Tax-Exempt (NCITX)

800-595-9111
www.northernfunds.com

Muni: California Bond

PERFORMANCE AND PER SHARE DATA **fund inception date: 10/1/99**

	3yr Annual	5yr Annual	10yr Annual	Category Risk Index
Return (%)	1.5	1.9	na	0.93—blw av
Differ From Category (+/-)	0.9 abv av	0.1 av	na	**Avg Mat** 10.0 yrs

	2008	2007	2006	2005	2004	2003	2002	2001	2000	1999
Return (%)	-1.3	2.4	3.6	2.1	3.1	3.5	8.6	3.9	10.2	—
Differ From Category (+/-)	3.0	0.2	-0.6	-0.8	-0.7	-0.8	0.7	-0.2	-1.7	—
Return, Tax-Adjusted (%)	-1.3	2.4	3.5	2.0	3.0	3.4	8.3	3.7	10.2	—
Dividends, Net Income ($)	0.32	0.38	0.38	0.39	0.38	0.36	0.38	0.43	0.44	—
Expense Ratio (%)	0.75	0.75	0.85	0.85	0.85	0.85	0.85	0.85	0.85	—
Yield (%)	3.36	3.77	3.74	3.77	3.58	3.39	3.48	4.13	4.22	—
Total Assets (Millions $)	175	130	95	72	69	74	87	90	93	—

SHAREHOLDER INFORMATION

Minimum Investment
Initial: $2,500 IRA: $500
Subsequent: $50 IRA: $50

Maximum Fees
Load: none 12b-1: none
Other: none

Schwab CA Tax-Free Bond (SWCAX)

800-407-0256
www.schwab.com

Muni: California Bond

PERFORMANCE AND PER SHARE DATA **fund inception date: 2/24/92**

	3yr Annual	5yr Annual	10yr Annual	Category Risk Index
Return (%)	1.8	2.7	3.9	0.78—blw av
Differ From Category (+/-)	1.2 abv av	0.9 high	0.5 high	**Avg Mat** 8.1 yrs

	2008	2007	2006	2005	2004	2003	2002	2001	2000	1999
Return (%)	-1.1	2.2	4.3	3.3	5.0	4.6	8.1	4.9	15.1	-6.1
Differ From Category (+/-)	3.2	0.0	0.1	0.4	1.2	0.4	0.2	0.9	3.2	-3.3
Return, Tax-Adjusted (%)	-1.1	2.2	4.2	3.2	4.9	4.6	8.1	4.9	15.1	-6.1
Dividends, Net Income ($)	0.47	0.48	0.48	0.49	0.50	0.49	0.52	0.54	0.55	0.55
Expense Ratio (%)	0.48	0.56	0.60	0.61	0.61	0.58	0.49	0.49	0.49	0.49
Yield (%)	4.29	4.20	4.12	4.21	4.21	4.18	4.43	4.75	4.83	5.29
Total Assets (Millions $)	295	231	207	197	185	190	233	216	190	166

SHAREHOLDER INFORMATION

Minimum Investment
Initial: $100 IRA: na
Subsequent: $0 IRA: na

Maximum Fees
Load: none 12b-1: none
Other: none

Vanguard CA Interm-Term Tax-Exempt (VCAIX)

800-662-6273
www.vanguard.com

Muni: California Bond

PERFORMANCE AND PER SHARE DATA **fund inception date: 3/4/94**

	3yr Annual	5yr Annual	10yr Annual	Category Risk Index
Return (%)	1.6	1.9	3.7	0.93—av
Differ From Category (+/-)	1.0 abv av	0.1 av	0.3 high	**Avg Mat** 8.0 yrs

	2008	2007	2006	2005	2004	2003	2002	2001	2000	1999
Return (%)	-2.2	3.0	4.2	1.8	2.8	4.1	9.1	4.4	10.9	-0.6
Differ From Category (+/-)	2.1	0.8	0.0	-1.1	-1.0	-0.1	1.1	0.3	-1.1	2.2
Return, Tax-Adjusted (%)	-2.2	3.0	4.2	1.8	2.8	3.9	9.0	4.4	10.9	-0.6
Dividends, Net Income ($)	0.42	0.43	0.44	0.43	0.44	0.45	0.47	0.49	0.50	0.48
Expense Ratio (%)	na	0.15	0.16	0.16	0.15	0.17	0.17	0.17	0.17	0.17
Yield (%)	4.12	3.98	3.97	3.94	3.90	3.95	4.08	4.47	4.53	4.63
Total Assets (Millions $)	1,279	1,266	1,084	1,003	1,523	1,494	1,655	1,499	1,783	1,262

SHAREHOLDER INFORMATION

Minimum Investment
Initial: $3,000 IRA: na
Subsequent: $100 IRA: na

Maximum Fees
Load: none 12b-1: none
Other: none

Vanguard CA Long-Term Tax-Exempt (VCITX)

800-662-6273
www.vanguard.com

Muni: California Bond

PERFORMANCE AND PER SHARE DATA **fund inception date: 4/7/86**

	3yr Annual	5yr Annual	10yr Annual	Category Risk Index
Return (%)	-0.2	1.4	3.6	1.20—high
Differ From Category (+/-)	-0.8 blw av	-0.4 low	0.2 abv av	**Avg Mat** 13.7 yrs

	2008	2007	2006	2005	2004	2003	2002	2001	2000	1999
Return (%)	-6.9	1.5	5.2	3.7	4.1	4.9	9.4	3.3	15.1	-3.1
Differ From Category (+/-)	-2.6	-0.7	1.0	0.8	0.3	0.7	1.4	-0.8	3.1	-0.3
Return, Tax-Adjusted (%)	-6.9	1.5	5.2	3.7	4.1	4.7	9.4	3.3	15.1	-3.1
Dividends, Net Income ($)	0.50	0.53	0.53	0.53	0.54	0.54	0.55	0.57	0.58	0.56
Expense Ratio (%)	na	0.15	0.16	0.16	0.15	0.17	0.18	0.18	0.18	0.18
Yield (%)	4.89	4.63	4.48	4.48	4.56	4.52	4.59	4.93	4.93	5.26
Total Assets (Millions $)	660	724	684	651	1,286	1,284	1,464	1,479	1,808	1,493

SHAREHOLDER INFORMATION

Minimum Investment
Initial: $3,000 IRA: na
Subsequent: $100 IRA: na

Maximum Fees
Load: none 12b-1: none
Other: none

Westcore CO Tax-Exempt (WTCOX)

800-392-2673
www.westcore.com

Muni: Colorado Bond

PERFORMANCE AND PER SHARE DATA **fund inception date: 5/31/91**

	3yr Annual	5yr Annual	10yr Annual	Category Risk Index	
Return (%)	1.8	1.9	3.2	1.00—high	
Differ From Category (+/-)	0.0 high	0.0 high	0.0 high	**Avg Mat**	5.9 yrs

	2008	2007	2006	2005	2004	2003	2002	2001	2000	1999
Return (%)	-1.4	2.8	4.0	1.5	2.5	4.4	7.9	4.3	9.0	-2.3
Differ From Category (+/-)	0.0	0.0	0.0	0.0	0.0	0.0	0.0	0.0	0.0	0.0
Return, Tax-Adjusted (%)	-1.4	2.8	4.0	1.5	2.5	4.4	7.9	4.3	9.0	-2.3
Dividends, Net Income ($)	0.42	0.43	0.43	0.42	0.42	0.41	0.43	0.44	0.45	0.46
Expense Ratio (%)	na	0.65	0.65	0.65	0.65	0.65	0.65	0.65	0.63	0.53
Yield (%)	3.96	3.88	3.84	3.76	3.65	3.59	3.76	4.03	4.13	4.34
Total Assets (Millions $)	67	57	56	58	62	52	50	47	43	37

SHAREHOLDER INFORMATION

Minimum Investment
Initial: $2,500 IRA: $1,000
Subsequent: $100 IRA: $100

Maximum Fees
Load: 2.00% redemption 12b-1: none
Other: redemption fee applies for 90 days

Fidelity Connecticut Municipal Income (FICNX)

800-544-9797
www.fidelity.com

Muni: Connecticut Bond

PERFORMANCE AND PER SHARE DATA **fund inception date: 10/29/87**

	3yr Annual	5yr Annual	10yr Annual	Category Risk Index	
Return (%)	2.1	2.4	4.0	1.02—high	
Differ From Category (+/-)	0.1 high	0.2 high	0.4 high	**Avg Mat**	11.2 yrs

	2008	2007	2006	2005	2004	2003	2002	2001	2000	1999
Return (%)	-1.2	3.7	3.9	2.2	3.4	5.0	10.0	4.9	10.9	-2.1
Differ From Category (+/-)	-0.3	0.3	0.3	0.4	0.4	0.8	0.7	0.3	0.4	0.4
Return, Tax-Adjusted (%)	-1.2	3.7	3.8	2.0	3.3	4.8	9.9	4.8	10.9	-2.1
Dividends, Net Income ($)	0.43	0.43	0.44	0.46	0.48	0.49	0.49	0.52	0.55	0.53
Expense Ratio (%)	na	0.44	0.42	0.47	0.49	0.49	0.46	0.41	0.42	0.49
Yield (%)	3.98	3.79	3.87	3.98	4.03	4.06	4.14	4.61	4.88	4.89
Total Assets (Millions $)	450	440	426	434	430	439	468	411	356	330

SHAREHOLDER INFORMATION

Minimum Investment
Initial: $10,000 IRA: na
Subsequent: $1,000 IRA: na

Maximum Fees
Load: 0.50% redemption 12b-1: none
Other: redemp fee applies for 30 days; maint fee for low bal

USAA FL Tax-Free Income (UFLTX)

800-531-8722
www.usaa.com

Muni: Florida Bond

PERFORMANCE AND PER SHARE DATA **fund inception date: 10/1/93**

	3yr Annual	5yr Annual	10yr Annual	Category Risk Index
Return (%)	-1.2	0.9	3.0	1.05—high
Differ From Category (+/-)	-1.0 av	-0.4 av	-0.4 av	**Avg Mat** 14.0 yrs

	2008	2007	2006	2005	2004	2003	2002	2001	2000	1999
Return (%)	-8.7	0.8	4.7	3.4	4.7	6.5	8.7	4.9	12.8	-6.4
Differ From Category (+/-)	-1.8	-1.3	0.1	0.4	0.3	0.5	-1.0	0.2	-0.2	-1.8
Return, Tax-Adjusted (%)	-8.8	0.8	4.7	3.4	4.7	6.5	8.7	4.9	12.8	-6.4
Dividends, Net Income ($)	0.46	0.45	0.43	0.42	0.43	0.45	0.45	0.48	0.49	0.49
Expense Ratio (%)	0.57	0.62	0.62	0.63	0.64	0.63	0.56	0.49	0.48	0.47
Yield (%)	5.37	4.55	4.24	4.19	4.19	4.38	4.53	5.02	5.09	5.48
Total Assets (Millions $)	154	205	253	285	267	240	228	202	187	170

SHAREHOLDER INFORMATION

Minimum Investment		**Maximum Fees**	
Initial: $3,000	IRA: na	Load: none	12b-1: none
Subsequent: $50	IRA: na	Other: none	

Vanguard FL Long-Term Tax-Exempt (VFLTX)

800-662-6273
www.vanguard.com

Muni: Florida Bond

PERFORMANCE AND PER SHARE DATA **fund inception date: 9/1/92**

	3yr Annual	5yr Annual	10yr Annual	Category Risk Index
Return (%)	0.8	1.8	3.9	0.95—av
Differ From Category (+/-)	1.0 high	0.5 high	0.5 high	**Avg Mat** 11.9 yrs

	2008	2007	2006	2005	2004	2003	2002	2001	2000	1999
Return (%)	-5.1	3.4	4.5	2.5	4.0	5.6	10.8	4.5	13.2	-2.8
Differ From Category (+/-)	1.8	1.3	-0.1	-0.5	-0.4	-0.4	1.1	-0.2	0.2	1.8
Return, Tax-Adjusted (%)	-5.1	3.3	4.4	2.5	4.0	5.4	10.6	4.4	13.2	-2.8
Dividends, Net Income ($)	0.51	0.51	0.51	0.51	0.51	0.51	0.53	0.55	0.56	0.54
Expense Ratio (%)	na	0.15	0.16	0.16	0.14	0.17	0.18	0.15	0.15	0.18
Yield (%)	4.87	4.48	4.41	4.36	4.25	4.18	4.39	4.83	4.90	5.13
Total Assets (Millions $)	213	260	298	326	694	735	793	805	994	885

SHAREHOLDER INFORMATION

Minimum Investment		**Maximum Fees**	
Initial: $3,000	IRA: $3,000	Load: none	12b-1: none
Subsequent: $100	IRA: $0	Other: none	

T. Rowe Price GA Tax-Free Bond (GTFBX)

800-638-5660
www.troweprice.com

Muni: Georgia Bond

PERFORMANCE AND PER SHARE DATA **fund inception date: 3/31/93**

	3yr Annual	5yr Annual	10yr Annual	Category Risk Index
Return (%)	0.2	1.5	3.3	1.00—high
Differ From Category (+/-)	0.0 high	0.0 high	0.0 high	**Avg Mat** 14.7 yrs

	2008	2007	2006	2005	2004	2003	2002	2001	2000	1999
Return (%)	-5.4	2.0	4.2	3.2	4.0	5.0	8.8	4.7	11.6	-3.7
Differ From Category (+/-)	0.0	0.0	0.0	0.0	0.0	0.0	0.0	0.0	0.0	0.0
Return, Tax-Adjusted (%)	-5.4	2.0	4.2	3.2	4.0	5.0	8.8	4.7	11.6	-3.7
Dividends, Net Income ($)	0.45	0.46	0.46	0.46	0.46	0.47	0.49	0.51	0.52	0.50
Expense Ratio (%)	0.61	0.60	0.62	0.64	0.65	0.65	0.65	0.65	0.65	0.65
Yield (%)	4.55	4.15	4.13	4.07	4.08	4.14	4.33	4.70	4.78	4.90
Total Assets (Millions $)	125	130	120	107	95	86	87	75	67	58

SHAREHOLDER INFORMATION

Minimum Investment
Initial: $2,500 IRA: $1,000
Subsequent: $100 IRA: $50

Maximum Fees
Load: none 12b-1: none
Other: none

Hawaii Municipal (SURFX)

808-988-8088
www.leehawaii.com

Muni: Hawaii Bond

PERFORMANCE AND PER SHARE DATA **fund inception date: 11/23/88**

	3yr Annual	5yr Annual	10yr Annual	Category Risk Index
Return (%)	0.2	1.3	3.0	1.00—high
Differ From Category (+/-)	0.0 high	0.0 high	0.0 high	**Avg Mat** 5.0 yrs

	2008	2007	2006	2005	2004	2003	2002	2001	2000	1999
Return (%)	-5.0	2.1	3.8	2.2	3.7	5.4	8.2	4.2	8.5	-2.0
Differ From Category (+/-)	0.0	0.0	0.0	0.0	0.0	0.0	0.0	0.0	0.0	0.0
Return, Tax-Adjusted (%)	-5.0	2.1	3.8	2.2	3.7	5.3	8.2	4.2	8.5	-2.0
Dividends, Net Income ($)	0.39	0.39	0.39	0.40	0.44	0.46	0.48	0.50	0.52	0.53
Expense Ratio (%)	1.02	0.96	0.90	0.94	0.98	1.01	1.02	1.03	0.98	0.94
Yield (%)	3.92	3.57	3.55	3.63	3.91	4.07	4.29	4.61	4.78	5.09
Total Assets (Millions $)	141	156	152	151	145	144	134	123	115	113

SHAREHOLDER INFORMATION

Minimum Investment
Initial: $10,000 IRA: na
Subsequent: $100 IRA: na

Maximum Fees
Load: none 12b-1: 0.15%
Other: none

Dupree KY Tax-Free Income (KYTFX)

800-866-0614
www.dupree-funds.com

Muni: Kentucky Bond

PERFORMANCE AND PER SHARE DATA **fund inception date: 7/3/79**

	3yr Annual	5yr Annual	10yr Annual	Category Risk Index
Return (%)	2.9	3.1	3.9	1.19—high
Differ From Category (+/-)	-0.2 av	0.4 high	0.3 high	**Avg Mat** 11.5 yrs

	2008	2007	2006	2005	2004	2003	2002	2001	2000	1999
Return (%)	0.9	3.5	4.4	2.6	4.0	5.5	7.1	5.0	8.0	-1.5
Differ From Category (+/-)	-1.1	-0.1	0.9	1.1	1.2	1.0	0.3	-0.1	1.3	-0.9
Return, Tax-Adjusted (%)	0.9	3.5	4.3	2.6	4.0	5.5	7.1	5.0	8.0	-1.5
Dividends, Net Income ($)	0.31	0.30	0.30	0.31	0.33	0.34	0.35	0.37	0.38	0.37
Expense Ratio (%)	0.58	0.58	0.58	0.60	0.58	0.58	0.59	0.60	0.61	0.61
Yield (%)	4.18	3.92	3.94	4.10	4.27	4.37	4.62	4.92	5.04	5.15
Total Assets (Millions $)	757	708	708	696	654	617	576	498	443	414

SHAREHOLDER INFORMATION

Minimum Investment		**Maximum Fees**	
Initial: $100	IRA: na	Load: none	12b-1: none
Subsequent: $0	IRA: na	Other: none	

Dupree KY Tax-Free Short-to-Medium (KYSMX)

800-866-0614
www.dupree-funds.com

Muni: Kentucky Bond

PERFORMANCE AND PER SHARE DATA **fund inception date: 9/15/87**

	3yr Annual	5yr Annual	10yr Annual	Category Risk Index
Return (%)	3.2	2.4	3.3	0.81—av
Differ From Category (+/-)	0.1 high	-0.3 av	-0.3 av	**Avg Mat** 5.0 yrs

	2008	2007	2006	2005	2004	2003	2002	2001	2000	1999
Return (%)	3.1	3.9	2.7	0.4	1.7	3.5	6.5	5.3	5.4	0.2
Differ From Category (+/-)	1.1	0.2	-0.8	-1.1	-1.2	-1.0	-0.3	0.2	-1.3	0.8
Return, Tax-Adjusted (%)	3.1	3.9	2.7	0.4	1.7	3.5	6.4	5.3	5.4	0.2
Dividends, Net Income ($)	0.17	0.17	0.16	0.15	0.16	0.17	0.19	0.21	0.22	0.20
Expense Ratio (%)	0.72	0.72	0.71	0.71	0.68	0.69	0.69	0.70	0.69	0.72
Yield (%)	3.26	3.25	3.08	2.90	2.92	3.15	3.62	4.07	4.33	3.99
Total Assets (Millions $)	57	57	66	90	101	104	93	78	50	58

SHAREHOLDER INFORMATION

Minimum Investment		**Maximum Fees**	
Initial: $100	IRA: na	Load: none	12b-1: none
Subsequent: $0	IRA: na	Other: none	

T. Rowe Price MD Short-Term Tax-Free (PRMDX)

800-638-5660
www.troweprice.com

Muni: Maryland Bond

PERFORMANCE AND PER SHARE DATA **fund inception date: 1/29/93**

	3yr Annual	5yr Annual	10yr Annual	Category Risk Index	
Return (%)	3.3	2.3	3.0	0.40—blw av	
Differ From Category (+/-)	2.1 high	0.5 high	-0.3 blw av	**Avg Mat**	2.0 yrs

	2008	2007	2006	2005	2004	2003	2002	2001	2000	1999
Return (%)	3.3	3.7	2.8	0.8	0.8	1.8	4.0	5.6	5.5	1.5
Differ From Category (+/-)	6.2	0.9	-1.1	-1.5	-2.1	-2.4	-3.4	0.7	-4.3	3.4
Return, Tax-Adjusted (%)	3.3	3.7	2.8	0.8	0.8	1.8	4.0	5.6	5.5	1.5
Dividends, Net Income ($)	0.15	0.16	0.15	0.11	0.11	0.12	0.15	0.19	0.19	0.19
Expense Ratio (%)	0.59	0.56	0.55	0.53	0.53	0.54	0.60	0.60	0.60	0.65
Yield (%)	2.91	3.08	2.83	2.23	2.03	2.37	2.85	3.56	3.78	3.71
Total Assets (Millions $)	171	146	151	172	212	243	217	148	118	129

SHAREHOLDER INFORMATION

Minimum Investment
Initial: $2,500 IRA: $1,000
Subsequent: $100 IRA: $50

Maximum Fees
Load: none 12b-1: none
Other: none

T. Rowe Price MD Tax-Free Bond (MDXBX)

800-638-5660
www.troweprice.com

Muni: Maryland Bond

PERFORMANCE AND PER SHARE DATA **fund inception date: 3/31/87**

	3yr Annual	5yr Annual	10yr Annual	Category Risk Index	
Return (%)	-0.2	1.2	3.2	1.23—high	
Differ From Category (+/-)	-1.4 blw av	-0.6 blw av	-0.1 av	**Avg Mat**	15.3 yrs

	2008	2007	2006	2005	2004	2003	2002	2001	2000	1999
Return (%)	-6.7	1.8	4.5	3.3	3.5	4.8	9.4	4.9	11.4	-3.2
Differ From Category (+/-)	-3.8	-0.9	0.6	1.0	0.6	0.6	1.9	0.0	1.6	-1.3
Return, Tax-Adjusted (%)	-6.7	1.8	4.5	3.3	3.4	4.8	9.4	4.9	11.4	-3.2
Dividends, Net Income ($)	0.47	0.47	0.47	0.47	0.47	0.48	0.50	0.51	0.53	0.53
Expense Ratio (%)	0.47	0.47	0.48	0.48	0.48	0.49	0.49	0.49	0.51	0.51
Yield (%)	5.10	4.49	4.43	4.40	4.35	4.36	4.56	4.92	5.10	5.38
Total Assets (Millions $)	1,374	1,441	1,432	1,354	1,285	1,315	1,334	1,186	1,083	990

SHAREHOLDER INFORMATION

Minimum Investment
Initial: $2,500 IRA: $1,000
Subsequent: $100 IRA: $50

Maximum Fees
Load: none 12b-1: none
Other: none

Fidelity Massachusetts Municipal Income (FDMMX)

800-544-8544
www.fidelity.com

Muni: Massachusetts Bond

PERFORMANCE AND PER SHARE DATA **fund inception date: 11/10/83**

	3yr Annual	5yr Annual	10yr Annual	Category Risk Index
Return (%)	1.4	2.4	4.0	0.94—av
Differ From Category (+/-)	-0.3 av	0.1 av	0.2 abv av	**Avg Mat** 12.2 yrs

	2008	2007	2006	2005	2004	2003	2002	2001	2000	1999
Return (%)	-3.6	3.2	4.6	3.6	4.5	5.3	9.6	4.4	11.8	-2.2
Differ From Category (+/-)	-1.4	-0.1	0.4	0.7	0.9	0.7	0.4	0.0	0.2	0.5
Return, Tax-Adjusted (%)	-3.6	3.2	4.6	3.4	4.3	5.1	9.5	4.3	11.8	-2.2
Dividends, Net Income ($)	0.46	0.47	0.48	0.50	0.52	0.53	0.53	0.55	0.57	0.56
Expense Ratio (%)	0.42	0.44	0.44	0.46	1.15	0.46	0.42	0.42	0.49	0.49
Yield (%)	4.25	4.00	4.00	4.14	4.25	4.23	4.30	4.66	4.80	5.02
Total Assets (Millions $)	1,832	1,876	1,843	1,843	1,754	1,841	1,999	1,885	1,614	1,278

SHAREHOLDER INFORMATION

Minimum Investment
Initial: $10,000 IRA: na
Subsequent: $1,000 IRA: na

Maximum Fees
Load: 0.50% redemption 12b-1: none
Other: redemption fee applies for 30 days

Vanguard MA Tax-Exempt (VMATX)

800-662-6237
www.vanguard.com

Muni: Massachusetts Bond

PERFORMANCE AND PER SHARE DATA **fund inception date: 12/9/98**

	3yr Annual	5yr Annual	10yr Annual	Category Risk Index
Return (%)	2.1	2.7	4.0	1.06—high
Differ From Category (+/-)	0.4 abv av	0.4 high	0.2 high	**Avg Mat** 11.4 yrs

	2008	2007	2006	2005	2004	2003	2002	2001	2000	1999
Return (%)	-1.3	2.8	4.9	3.2	4.0	5.0	9.0	4.3	13.7	-4.2
Differ From Category (+/-)	0.9	-0.5	0.6	0.3	0.4	0.5	-0.3	-0.1	2.1	-1.5
Return, Tax-Adjusted (%)	-1.3	2.8	4.9	3.2	4.0	5.0	9.0	4.3	13.7	-4.2
Dividends, Net Income ($)	0.41	0.42	0.43	0.42	0.42	0.44	0.46	0.47	0.48	0.44
Expense Ratio (%)	na	0.12	0.14	0.14	0.14	0.16	0.14	0.16	0.19	0.20
Yield (%)	4.31	4.18	4.16	4.10	4.04	4.27	4.53	4.82	4.87	4.77
Total Assets (Millions $)	728	695	573	505	456	409	386	290	196	117

SHAREHOLDER INFORMATION

Minimum Investment
Initial: $3,000 IRA: $3,000
Subsequent: $100 IRA: $0

Maximum Fees
Load: none 12b-1: none
Other: none

Fidelity Michigan Municipal Income (FMHTX)

800-544-5555
www.fidelity.com

Muni: Michigan Bond

PERFORMANCE AND PER SHARE DATA **fund inception date: 11/12/85**

	3yr Annual	5yr Annual	10yr Annual	Category Risk Index	
Return (%)	2.6	2.9	4.2	1.00—high	
Differ From Category (+/-)	0.0 high	0.0 high	0.0 high	**Avg Mat**	9.6 yrs

	2008	2007	2006	2005	2004	2003	2002	2001	2000	1999
Return (%)	-0.1	3.7	4.4	2.6	3.9	5.8	9.7	4.7	11.1	-2.7
Differ From Category (+/-)	0.0	0.0	0.0	0.0	0.0	0.0	0.0	0.0	0.0	0.0
Return, Tax-Adjusted (%)	-0.1	3.6	4.3	2.5	3.7	5.8	9.7	4.7	11.1	-2.7
Dividends, Net Income ($)	0.46	0.46	0.47	0.47	0.49	0.51	0.53	0.55	0.57	0.55
Expense Ratio (%)	na	0.44	0.44	0.45	0.49	0.55	0.48	0.44	0.45	0.52
Yield (%)	4.04	3.91	3.95	3.94	4.01	4.19	4.40	4.81	4.96	5.07
Total Assets (Millions $)	568	591	571	563	559	559	571	505	458	424

SHAREHOLDER INFORMATION

Minimum Investment
Initial: $10,000 IRA: na
Subsequent: $1,000 IRA: na

Maximum Fees
Load: 0.50% redemption 12b-1: none
Other: redemp fee applies for 30 days; maint fee for low bal

Fidelity Minnesota Municipal Income (FIMIX)

800-544-5555
www.fidelity.com

Muni: Minnesota Bond

PERFORMANCE AND PER SHARE DATA **fund inception date: 11/21/85**

	3yr Annual	5yr Annual	10yr Annual	Category Risk Index	
Return (%)	2.3	2.7	3.9	0.85—av	
Differ From Category (+/-)	2.1 high	1.2 high	0.8 high	**Avg Mat**	8.8 yrs

	2008	2007	2006	2005	2004	2003	2002	2001	2000	1999
Return (%)	-0.3	3.1	4.1	2.6	3.9	5.2	8.5	4.6	10.6	-2.5
Differ From Category (+/-)	5.3	1.0	-0.4	-0.9	0.2	0.4	0.8	-0.5	1.3	0.7
Return, Tax-Adjusted (%)	-0.4	3.1	4.0	2.5	3.8	5.1	8.5	4.6	10.6	-2.5
Dividends, Net Income ($)	0.43	0.44	0.46	0.46	0.46	0.46	0.51	0.52	0.53	0.51
Expense Ratio (%)	na	0.44	0.47	0.48	0.49	0.49	0.49	0.46	0.46	0.51
Yield (%)	3.99	3.93	4.00	4.01	3.93	3.94	4.38	4.67	4.70	4.80
Total Assets (Millions $)	372	349	336	343	355	343	344	315	293	284

SHAREHOLDER INFORMATION

Minimum Investment
Initial: $10,000 IRA: na
Subsequent: $1,000 IRA: na

Maximum Fees
Load: 0.50% redemption 12b-1: none
Other: redemp fee applies for 30 days; maint fee for low bal

Sit MN Tax-Free Income (SMTFX)

800-332-5580
www.sitfunds.com

Muni: Minnesota Bond

PERFORMANCE AND PER SHARE DATA **fund inception date: 12/1/93**

	3yr Annual	5yr Annual	10yr Annual	Category Risk Index	
Return (%)	-1.9	0.4	2.2	1.13—high	
Differ From Category (+/-)	-2.1 av	-1.1 av	-0.9 av	**Avg Mat**	6.1 yrs

	2008	2007	2006	2005	2004	2003	2002	2001	2000	1999
Return (%)	-10.9	1.0	4.8	4.4	3.5	4.4	6.9	5.7	8.0	-4.0
Differ From Category (+/-)	-5.3	-1.1	0.4	0.9	-0.2	-0.4	-0.8	0.6	-1.3	-0.8
Return, Tax-Adjusted (%)	-10.9	1.0	4.8	4.4	3.5	4.4	6.9	5.7	8.0	-4.0
Dividends, Net Income ($)	0.43	0.42	0.41	0.42	0.43	0.46	0.46	0.49	0.52	0.50
Expense Ratio (%)	0.80	0.80	0.80	0.80	0.80	0.80	0.80	0.80	0.80	0.80
Yield (%)	5.03	4.27	4.03	4.12	4.22	4.49	4.51	4.90	5.19	5.16
Total Assets (Millions $)	226	304	283	251	223	213	211	185	173	180

SHAREHOLDER INFORMATION

Minimum Investment
Initial: $5,000 IRA: $2,000
Subsequent: $100 IRA: $100

Maximum Fees
Load: none 12b-1: none
Other: none

Fidelity New Jersey Municipal Income (FNJHX)

800-544-9797
www.fidelity.com

Muni: New Jersey Bond

PERFORMANCE AND PER SHARE DATA **fund inception date: 12/31/87**

	3yr Annual	5yr Annual	10yr Annual	Category Risk Index	
Return (%)	1.7	2.4	4.1	0.96—blw av	
Differ From Category (+/-)	0.5 high	0.3 high	0.3 high	**Avg Mat**	11.2 yrs

	2008	2007	2006	2005	2004	2003	2002	2001	2000	1999
Return (%)	-3.0	3.6	4.6	3.3	3.9	5.4	9.7	4.2	11.3	-1.5
Differ From Category (+/-)	0.8	0.9	-0.2	0.2	-0.1	0.2	0.0	-0.3	-0.3	1.2
Return, Tax-Adjusted (%)	-3.1	3.6	4.5	3.1	3.7	5.2	9.6	4.1	11.3	-1.5
Dividends, Net Income ($)	0.44	0.44	0.45	0.46	0.47	0.49	0.49	0.53	0.56	0.53
Expense Ratio (%)	na	0.43	0.41	0.43	0.49	0.49	0.47	0.41	0.45	0.55
Yield (%)	4.10	3.83	3.85	3.92	3.98	4.06	4.14	4.66	4.91	4.89
Total Assets (Millions $)	538	581	580	555	535	549	580	495	400	366

SHAREHOLDER INFORMATION

Minimum Investment
Initial: $10,000 IRA: na
Subsequent: $1,000 IRA: na

Maximum Fees
Load: 0.50% redemption 12b-1: none
Other: redemp fee applies for 30 days; maint fee for low bal

T. Rowe Price NJ Tax-Free Bond (NJTFX)

800-638-5660
www.troweprice.com

Muni: New Jersey Bond

PERFORMANCE AND PER SHARE DATA **fund inception date: 4/30/91**

	3yr Annual	5yr Annual	10yr Annual	Category Risk Index
Return (%)	0.3	1.7	3.4	0.96—abv av
Differ From Category (+/-)	-0.9 blw av	-0.4 blw av	-0.4 blw av	**Avg Mat** 14.7 yrs

	2008	2007	2006	2005	2004	2003	2002	2001	2000	1999
Return (%)	-5.2	1.8	4.7	3.2	4.1	5.0	9.6	4.8	11.4	-4.2
Differ From Category (+/-)	-1.4	-0.9	-0.1	0.1	0.1	-0.1	-0.1	0.3	-0.3	-1.5
Return, Tax-Adjusted (%)	-5.2	1.8	4.7	3.2	4.1	5.0	9.6	4.8	11.4	-4.2
Dividends, Net Income ($)	0.48	0.49	0.50	0.50	0.51	0.52	0.54	0.55	0.55	0.53
Expense Ratio (%)	0.55	0.55	0.57	0.58	0.58	0.59	0.60	0.63	0.65	0.65
Yield (%)	4.61	4.25	4.21	4.24	4.32	4.35	4.56	4.85	4.87	5.00
Total Assets (Millions $)	206	217	199	177	161	155	145	128	117	108

SHAREHOLDER INFORMATION

Minimum Investment
Initial: $2,500 IRA: $1,000
Subsequent: $100 IRA: $50

Maximum Fees
Load: none 12b-1: none
Other: none

Vanguard NJ Long-Term Tax-Exempt (VNJTX)

800-662-6273
www.vanguard.com

Muni: New Jersey Bond

PERFORMANCE AND PER SHARE DATA **fund inception date: 2/3/88**

	3yr Annual	5yr Annual	10yr Annual	Category Risk Index
Return (%)	1.6	2.3	4.0	1.08—high
Differ From Category (+/-)	0.4 abv av	0.2 abv av	0.2 abv av	**Avg Mat** 10.1 yrs

	2008	2007	2006	2005	2004	2003	2002	2001	2000	1999
Return (%)	-3.1	2.8	5.2	2.8	3.9	5.1	9.9	4.5	12.4	-2.4
Differ From Category (+/-)	0.7	0.1	0.4	-0.3	-0.1	-0.1	0.2	0.0	0.7	0.3
Return, Tax-Adjusted (%)	-3.1	2.8	5.1	2.7	3.8	5.0	9.8	4.5	12.4	-2.4
Dividends, Net Income ($)	0.49	0.51	0.52	0.53	0.55	0.55	0.57	0.58	0.60	0.59
Expense Ratio (%)	na	0.15	0.16	0.16	0.14	0.17	0.18	0.20	0.19	0.19
Yield (%)	4.53	4.35	4.36	4.41	4.49	4.44	4.66	4.93	5.07	5.32
Total Assets (Millions $)	415	424	430	438	907	918	978	931	1,284	1,118

SHAREHOLDER INFORMATION

Minimum Investment
Initial: $3,000 IRA: na
Subsequent: $100 IRA: na

Maximum Fees
Load: none 12b-1: none
Other: none

Bernstein NY Municipal (SNNYX)

800-221-5672
www.bernstein.com

Muni: New York Bond

PERFORMANCE AND PER SHARE DATA **fund inception date: 1/9/89**

	3yr Annual	5yr Annual	10yr Annual	Category Risk Index	
Return (%)	2.8	2.5	3.7	0.70—blw av	
Differ From Category (+/-)	1.7 high	0.7 high	0.4 high	**Avg Mat**	5.1 yrs

	2008	2007	2006	2005	2004	2003	2002	2001	2000	1999
Return (%)	1.3	4.0	3.2	1.7	2.5	3.9	7.2	4.5	8.2	0.0
Differ From Category (+/-)	4.4	1.5	-1.0	-0.7	-0.7	-0.1	-1.4	0.7	-3.1	3.6
Return, Tax-Adjusted (%)	1.3	4.0	3.2	1.7	2.5	3.9	7.2	4.5	8.2	-0.1
Dividends, Net Income ($)	0.47	0.47	0.47	0.47	0.46	0.49	0.53	0.57	0.57	0.56
Expense Ratio (%)	0.61	0.61	0.62	0.63	0.63	0.65	0.66	0.64	0.64	0.64
Yield (%)	3.47	3.39	3.37	3.39	3.27	3.44	3.74	4.18	4.20	4.25
Total Assets (Millions $)	1,620	1,784	1,545	1,301	1,145	1,018	1,028	782	683	791

SHAREHOLDER INFORMATION

Minimum Investment
Initial: $25,000 IRA: na
Subsequent: $0 IRA: na

Maximum Fees
Load: none 12b-1: none
Other: none

Bernstein Short Duration NY Municipal (SDNYX)

800-221-5672
www.bernstein.com

Muni: New York Bond

PERFORMANCE AND PER SHARE DATA **fund inception date: 10/3/94**

	3yr Annual	5yr Annual	10yr Annual	Category Risk Index	
Return (%)	3.0	2.3	2.9	0.27—low	
Differ From Category (+/-)	1.9 high	0.5 high	-0.4 blw av	**Avg Mat**	1.6 yrs

	2008	2007	2006	2005	2004	2003	2002	2001	2000	1999
Return (%)	2.8	3.6	2.7	1.5	1.0	1.7	3.0	4.5	4.8	2.4
Differ From Category (+/-)	5.9	1.1	-1.5	-0.9	-2.2	-2.3	-5.6	0.7	-6.6	5.9
Return, Tax-Adjusted (%)	2.8	3.6	2.7	1.5	1.0	1.7	3.0	4.5	4.8	2.4
Dividends, Net Income ($)	0.37	0.38	0.33	0.27	0.23	0.24	0.33	0.43	0.48	0.45
Expense Ratio (%)	0.67	0.69	0.74	0.74	0.74	0.76	0.77	0.73	0.72	0.74
Yield (%)	2.97	3.09	2.67	2.16	1.80	1.94	2.63	3.44	3.83	3.68
Total Assets (Millions $)	160	122	109	120	119	127	117	96	92	112

SHAREHOLDER INFORMATION

Minimum Investment
Initial: $25,000 IRA: na
Subsequent: $0 IRA: na

Maximum Fees
Load: none 12b-1: none
Other: none

Dreyfus NY Tax-Exempt Bond (DRNYX)

800-645-6561
www.dreyfus.com

Muni: New York Bond

PERFORMANCE AND PER SHARE DATA **fund inception date: 7/26/83**

	3yr Annual	5yr Annual	10yr Annual	Category Risk Index
Return (%)	0.9	1.8	3.2	1.16—abv av
Differ From Category (+/-)	-0.2 av	0.0 av	-0.1 av	**Avg Mat** 15.6 yrs

	2008	2007	2006	2005	2004	2003	2002	2001	2000	1999
Return (%)	-4.2	2.3	4.7	3.1	3.4	3.5	9.0	4.5	11.1	-3.9
Differ From Category (+/-)	-1.1	-0.2	0.5	0.5	0.3	-0.5	0.2	0.5	-0.6	-0.5
Return, Tax-Adjusted (%)	-4.2	2.3	4.7	3.1	3.4	3.5	8.8	4.5	11.0	-4.0
Dividends, Net Income ($)	0.57	0.58	0.58	0.60	0.63	0.65	0.71	0.74	0.71	0.73
Expense Ratio (%)	0.78	0.80	0.74	0.72	0.71	0.71	0.70	0.73	0.75	0.75
Yield (%)	4.28	3.96	3.92	4.04	4.20	4.29	4.61	4.94	4.77	5.13
Total Assets (Millions $)	1,297	1,479	1,249	1,257	1,290	1,381	1,459	1,431	1,456	1,441

SHAREHOLDER INFORMATION

Minimum Investment
Initial: $2,500 IRA: na
Subsequent: $100 IRA: na

Maximum Fees
Load: none 12b-1: none
Other: none

Empire Builder Tax-Free Bond Prem (EMTPX)

800-847-5886
www.glickenhaus.com

Muni: New York Bond

PERFORMANCE AND PER SHARE DATA **fund inception date: 4/29/96**

	3yr Annual	5yr Annual	10yr Annual	Category Risk Index
Return (%)	2.5	2.3	3.5	0.70—blw av
Differ From Category (+/-)	1.4 high	0.5 abv av	0.2 abv av	**Avg Mat** na

	2008	2007	2006	2005	2004	2003	2002	2001	2000	1999
Return (%)	0.8	2.7	4.0	1.6	2.4	4.0	9.2	3.2	13.8	-4.6
Differ From Category (+/-)	3.9	0.2	-0.3	-0.8	-0.7	-0.2	0.1	-0.9	1.6	-1.6
Return, Tax-Adjusted (%)	0.8	2.6	3.9	1.6	2.3	3.8	8.9	3.0	13.8	-4.7
Dividends, Net Income ($)	0.53	0.63	0.64	0.48	0.45	0.58	0.68	0.76	0.80	0.80
Expense Ratio (%)	1.12	1.08	1.02	0.95	0.86	0.89	0.88	0.86	0.79	0.82
Yield (%)	3.09	3.61	3.62	2.70	2.53	3.17	3.72	4.34	4.50	4.92
Total Assets (Millions $)	45	47	50	54	57	60	61	58	60	57

SHAREHOLDER INFORMATION

Minimum Investment
Initial: $20,000 IRA: na
Subsequent: $100 IRA: na

Maximum Fees
Load: none 12b-1: none
Other: none

Fidelity New York Municipal Income (FTFMX)

877-208-0098
www.fidelity.com

Muni: New York Bond

PERFORMANCE AND PER SHARE DATA **fund inception date: 7/10/84**

	3yr Annual	5yr Annual	10yr Annual	Category Risk Index	
Return (%)	1.7	2.5	4.2	1.14—av	
Differ From Category (+/-)	0.6 abv av	0.7 high	0.9 high	**Avg Mat**	13.3 yrs

	2008	2007	2006	2005	2004	2003	2002	2001	2000	1999
Return (%)	-2.5	3.3	4.5	3.0	4.4	5.5	10.9	4.3	12.8	-3.3
Differ From Category (+/-)	0.6	0.8	0.3	0.6	1.3	1.4	2.1	0.3	1.1	0.1
Return, Tax-Adjusted (%)	-2.5	3.2	4.4	2.9	4.2	5.1	10.6	4.3	12.8	-3.4
Dividends, Net Income ($)	0.48	0.48	0.49	0.51	0.53	0.55	0.57	0.58	0.60	0.59
Expense Ratio (%)	0.44	0.45	0.45	0.48	0.48	0.47	0.44	0.42	0.49	0.53
Yield (%)	4.06	3.76	3.78	3.92	4.02	4.08	4.23	4.58	4.73	4.94
Total Assets (Millions $)	1,368	1,437	1,395	1,402	1,375	1,421	1,494	1,316	1,151	1,042

SHAREHOLDER INFORMATION

Minimum Investment
Initial: $10,000 IRA: na
Subsequent: $1,000 IRA: na

Maximum Fees
Load: 0.50% redemption 12b-1: none
Other: redemp fee applies for 30 days; maint fee for low bal

General NY Municipal Bond (GNYMX)

800-645-6561
www.dreyfus.com

Muni: New York Bond

PERFORMANCE AND PER SHARE DATA **fund inception date: 11/19/84**

	3yr Annual	5yr Annual	10yr Annual	Category Risk Index	
Return (%)	-0.2	1.0	2.8	1.23—abv av	
Differ From Category (+/-)	-1.3 blw av	-0.8 low	-0.5 low	**Avg Mat**	9.6 yrs

	2008	2007	2006	2005	2004	2003	2002	2001	2000	1999
Return (%)	-6.7	2.0	4.6	2.4	3.1	3.9	9.3	3.9	12.0	-4.7
Differ From Category (+/-)	-3.6	-0.5	0.4	-0.1	0.0	-0.2	0.5	-0.1	0.3	-1.3
Return, Tax-Adjusted (%)	-6.7	1.9	4.5	2.3	3.1	3.8	9.1	3.9	11.9	-4.8
Dividends, Net Income ($)	0.75	0.75	0.75	0.75	0.79	0.84	0.90	0.93	0.92	0.94
Expense Ratio (%)	0.86	0.88	0.85	0.89	0.89	0.88	0.89	0.89	0.91	0.92
Yield (%)	4.37	3.96	3.85	3.83	3.95	4.13	4.41	4.74	4.69	5.05
Total Assets (Millions $)	210	242	253	274	305	324	336	329	341	339

SHAREHOLDER INFORMATION

Minimum Investment
Initial: $2,500 IRA: na
Subsequent: $100 IRA: na

Maximum Fees
Load: none 12b-1: 0.20%
Other: none

T. Rowe Price NY Tax-Free Bond (PRNYX)

800-638-5660
www.troweprice.com

Muni: New York Bond

PERFORMANCE AND PER SHARE DATA **fund inception date: 8/28/86**

	3yr Annual	5yr Annual	10yr Annual	Category Risk Index
Return (%)	0.4	1.7	3.4	1.14—av
Differ From Category (+/-)	-0.7 blw av	-0.1 blw av	0.1 abv av	**Avg Mat** 15.2 yrs

	2008	2007	2006	2005	2004	2003	2002	2001	2000	1999
Return (%)	-5.6	2.5	4.7	3.4	3.8	4.9	9.6	4.0	12.8	-4.8
Differ From Category (+/-)	-2.5	0.0	0.5	1.0	0.7	0.8	0.8	0.1	1.1	-1.4
Return, Tax-Adjusted (%)	-5.6	2.5	4.7	3.4	3.8	4.9	9.6	4.0	12.8	-4.8
Dividends, Net Income ($)	0.47	0.47	0.48	0.47	0.47	0.48	0.50	0.51	0.53	0.52
Expense Ratio (%)	0.53	0.53	0.55	0.55	0.55	0.55	0.56	0.56	0.58	0.59
Yield (%)	4.66	4.24	4.24	4.16	4.11	4.19	4.38	4.73	4.86	5.11
Total Assets (Millions $)	274	285	268	247	238	241	229	208	201	188

SHAREHOLDER INFORMATION

Minimum Investment
Initial: $2,500 IRA: $1,000
Subsequent: $100 IRA: $50

Maximum Fees
Load: none 12b-1: none
Other: none

Vanguard NY Long-Term Tax-Exempt (VNYTX)

800-662-6273
www.vanguard.com

Muni: New York Bond

PERFORMANCE AND PER SHARE DATA **fund inception date: 4/7/86**

	3yr Annual	5yr Annual	10yr Annual	Category Risk Index
Return (%)	1.1	2.0	3.9	1.23—high
Differ From Category (+/-)	0.0 av	0.2 av	0.6 high	**Avg Mat** 12.4 yrs

	2008	2007	2006	2005	2004	2003	2002	2001	2000	1999
Return (%)	-3.7	2.4	4.8	2.8	3.9	5.3	10.7	4.1	13.7	-3.4
Differ From Category (+/-)	-0.6	-0.1	0.6	0.4	0.8	1.2	1.9	0.1	2.0	0.0
Return, Tax-Adjusted (%)	-3.7	2.4	4.7	2.7	3.9	5.3	10.5	4.0	13.7	-3.4
Dividends, Net Income ($)	0.46	0.49	0.49	0.49	0.49	0.48	0.50	0.52	0.55	0.55
Expense Ratio (%)	na	0.15	0.16	0.16	0.14	0.17	0.18	0.20	0.20	0.20
Yield (%)	4.51	4.38	4.29	4.27	4.22	4.16	4.32	4.72	4.99	5.31
Total Assets (Millions $)	645	678	668	689	1,317	1,325	1,367	1,296	1,725	1,426

SHAREHOLDER INFORMATION

Minimum Investment
Initial: $3,000 IRA: na
Subsequent: $100 IRA: na

Maximum Fees
Load: none 12b-1: none
Other: none

Dupree NC Tax-Free Income (NTFIX)

800-866-0614
www.dupree-funds.com

Muni: North Carolina Bond

PERFORMANCE AND PER SHARE DATA **fund inception date: 11/15/95**

	3yr Annual	5yr Annual	10yr Annual	Category Risk Index
Return (%)	1.8	2.4	3.6	1.00—high
Differ From Category (+/-)	0.0 high	0.0 high	0.0 high	**Avg Mat** 13.9 yrs

	2008	2007	2006	2005	2004	2003	2002	2001	2000	1999
Return (%)	-1.5	3.0	4.0	2.6	4.1	5.0	8.5	2.8	10.7	-2.8
Differ From Category (+/-)	0.0	0.0	0.0	0.0	0.0	0.0	0.0	0.0	0.0	0.0
Return, Tax-Adjusted (%)	-1.5	3.0	4.0	2.6	4.1	5.0	8.5	2.8	10.7	-2.8
Dividends, Net Income ($)	0.41	0.41	0.42	0.43	0.44	0.45	0.49	0.49	0.50	0.50
Expense Ratio (%)	0.71	0.73	0.74	0.72	0.69	0.68	0.57	0.55	0.55	0.45
Yield (%)	3.93	3.76	3.79	3.95	3.98	4.09	4.42	4.63	4.64	4.86
Total Assets (Millions $)	61	61	53	45	41	39	35	29	24	19

SHAREHOLDER INFORMATION

Minimum Investment
Initial: $100 IRA: na
Subsequent: $0 IRA: na

Maximum Fees
Load: none 12b-1: none
Other: none

Fidelity Ohio Municipal Income (FOHFX)

800-544-5555
www.fidelity.com

Muni: Ohio Bond

PERFORMANCE AND PER SHARE DATA **fund inception date: 11/15/85**

	3yr Annual	5yr Annual	10yr Annual	Category Risk Index
Return (%)	2.1	2.7	4.1	1.00—high
Differ From Category (+/-)	0.2 high	0.2 high	0.0 high	**Avg Mat** 12.0 yrs

	2008	2007	2006	2005	2004	2003	2002	2001	2000	1999
Return (%)	-1.7	3.5	4.4	2.9	4.4	5.7	9.6	4.7	11.6	-2.9
Differ From Category (+/-)	0.5	0.1	-0.2	0.2	0.2	0.2	-0.5	0.1	-0.6	0.1
Return, Tax-Adjusted (%)	-1.7	3.5	4.3	2.6	4.2	5.6	9.5	4.7	11.6	-2.9
Dividends, Net Income ($)	0.45	0.44	0.46	0.48	0.50	0.51	0.52	0.54	0.55	0.54
Expense Ratio (%)	na	0.45	0.45	0.47	0.50	0.50	0.49	0.46	0.46	0.51
Yield (%)	4.12	3.84	3.91	4.01	4.09	4.16	4.33	4.67	4.79	4.92
Total Assets (Millions $)	429	424	421	424	423	430	434	398	379	352

SHAREHOLDER INFORMATION

Minimum Investment
Initial: $10,000 IRA: na
Subsequent: $1,000 IRA: na

Maximum Fees
Load: 0.50% redemption 12b-1: none
Other: redemp fee applies for 30 days; maint fee for low bal

Vanguard OH Long-Term Tax-Exempt (VOHIX)

800-662-6273
www.vanguard.com

Muni: Ohio Bond

PERFORMANCE AND PER SHARE DATA **fund inception date: 6/18/90**

	3yr Annual	5yr Annual	10yr Annual	Category Risk Index	
Return (%)	1.7	2.3	4.1	0.98—av	
Differ From Category (+/-)	-0.2 av	-0.2 av	0.0 av	**Avg Mat**	12.3 yrs

	2008	2007	2006	2005	2004	2003	2002	2001	2000	1999
Return (%)	-2.8	3.2	4.8	2.6	4.0	5.3	10.7	4.6	12.8	-3.0
Differ From Category (+/-)	-0.6	-0.2	0.2	-0.1	-0.1	-0.2	0.6	0.0	0.7	0.0
Return, Tax-Adjusted (%)	-2.8	3.2	4.8	2.5	3.9	5.2	10.6	4.5	12.8	-3.0
Dividends, Net Income ($)	0.51	0.51	0.52	0.53	0.55	0.54	0.56	0.58	0.59	0.58
Expense Ratio (%)	na	0.13	0.14	0.14	0.14	0.15	0.14	0.17	0.19	0.19
Yield (%)	4.58	4.29	4.32	4.35	4.40	4.35	4.51	4.87	5.00	5.26
Total Assets (Millions $)	778	727	607	529	506	497	536	479	419	366

SHAREHOLDER INFORMATION

Minimum Investment
Initial: $3,000 IRA: na
Subsequent: $100 IRA: na

Maximum Fees
Load: none 12b-1: none
Other: none

Fidelity Pennsylvania Municipal Income (FPXTX)

800-544-5555
www.fidelity.com

Muni: Pennsylvania Bond

PERFORMANCE AND PER SHARE DATA **fund inception date: 8/6/86**

	3yr Annual	5yr Annual	10yr Annual	Category Risk Index	
Return (%)	2.3	2.8	4.1	0.91—av	
Differ From Category (+/-)	0.5 high	0.4 high	0.1 high	**Avg Mat**	9.7 yrs

	2008	2007	2006	2005	2004	2003	2002	2001	2000	1999
Return (%)	-0.8	3.9	4.0	2.7	4.2	5.1	9.1	4.9	10.9	-2.2
Differ From Category (+/-)	1.5	0.6	-0.4	0.0	0.2	-0.2	-0.5	0.1	-0.9	0.3
Return, Tax-Adjusted (%)	-0.9	3.8	4.0	2.6	4.2	4.9	9.0	4.9	10.9	-2.3
Dividends, Net Income ($)	0.42	0.42	0.43	0.44	0.45	0.46	0.48	0.49	0.50	0.48
Expense Ratio (%)	na	0.46	0.42	0.45	0.50	0.50	0.49	0.45	0.44	0.50
Yield (%)	4.06	3.88	4.01	4.03	4.08	4.13	4.33	4.61	4.65	4.76
Total Assets (Millions $)	326	316	305	306	298	291	299	268	243	241

SHAREHOLDER INFORMATION

Minimum Investment
Initial: $10,000 IRA: na
Subsequent: $1,000 IRA: na

Maximum Fees
Load: 0.50% redemption 12b-1: none
Other: redemp fee applies for 30 days; maint fee for low bal

Vanguard PA Long-Term Tax-Exempt (VPAIX)

800-662-6273
www.vanguard.com

Muni: Pennsylvania Bond

PERFORMANCE AND PER SHARE DATA **fund inception date: 4/7/86**

	3yr Annual	5yr Annual	10yr Annual	Category Risk Index
Return (%)	1.2	2.0	4.0	1.07—high
Differ From Category (+/-)	-0.6 av	-0.4 av	0.0 av	**Avg Mat** 10.5 yrs

	2008	2007	2006	2005	2004	2003	2002	2001	2000	1999
Return (%)	-3.7	2.7	4.8	2.7	3.8	5.5	10.0	4.7	12.7	-2.7
Differ From Category (+/-)	-1.4	-0.6	0.4	0.0	-0.2	0.3	0.4	-0.1	0.9	-0.2
Return, Tax-Adjusted (%)	-3.7	2.7	4.7	2.6	3.8	5.5	9.9	4.6	12.7	-2.7
Dividends, Net Income ($)	0.48	0.50	0.51	0.52	0.53	0.52	0.54	0.57	0.58	0.58
Expense Ratio (%)	na	0.15	0.16	0.16	0.14	0.17	0.18	0.20	0.19	0.19
Yield (%)	4.69	4.52	4.50	4.55	4.53	4.38	4.64	5.07	5.19	5.47
Total Assets (Millions $)	593	630	663	704	1,457	1,525	1,627	1,514	2,007	1,793

SHAREHOLDER INFORMATION

Minimum Investment		**Maximum Fees**	
Initial: $3,000	IRA: na	Load: none	12b-1: none
Subsequent: $100	IRA: na	Other: none	

Dupree TN Tax-Free Income (TNTIX)

800-866-0614
www.dupree-funds.com

Muni: Tennessee

PERFORMANCE AND PER SHARE DATA **fund inception date: 12/15/93**

	3yr Annual	5yr Annual	10yr Annual	Category Risk Index
Return (%)	1.5	2.2	3.5	1.00—high
Differ From Category (+/-)	0.0 high	0.0 high	0.0 high	**Avg Mat** 14.2 yrs

	2008	2007	2006	2005	2004	2003	2002	2001	2000	1999
Return (%)	-2.4	2.7	4.2	2.5	3.9	5.1	8.4	4.3	9.7	-2.8
Differ From Category (+/-)	0.0	0.0	0.0	0.0	0.0	0.0	0.0	0.0	0.0	0.0
Return, Tax-Adjusted (%)	-2.4	2.7	4.2	2.5	3.9	5.1	8.4	4.3	9.7	-2.8
Dividends, Net Income ($)	0.41	0.41	0.41	0.43	0.44	0.46	0.50	0.52	0.53	0.53
Expense Ratio (%)	0.71	0.72	0.71	0.69	0.67	0.65	0.54	0.54	0.54	0.48
Yield (%)	3.97	3.70	3.72	3.87	3.97	4.14	4.51	4.80	4.88	5.09
Total Assets (Millions $)	85	101	95	85	78	66	55	48	42	40

SHAREHOLDER INFORMATION

Minimum Investment		**Maximum Fees**	
Initial: $100	IRA: na	Load: none	12b-1: none
Subsequent: $0	IRA: na	Other: none	

T. Rowe Price VA Tax-Free Bond (PRVAX)

800-638-5660
www.troweprice.com

Muni: Virginia Bond

PERFORMANCE AND PER SHARE DATA **fund inception date: 4/30/91**

	3yr Annual	5yr Annual	10yr Annual	Category Risk Index
Return (%)	0.9	2.0	3.7	1.00—abv av
Differ From Category (+/-)	0.0 abv av	0.2 abv av	0.2 high	**Avg Mat** 15.9 yrs

	2008	2007	2006	2005	2004	2003	2002	2001	2000	1999
Return (%)	-3.9	2.2	4.5	3.2	4.0	5.0	9.7	4.8	11.9	-3.5
Differ From Category (+/-)	-0.6	0.1	0.4	0.6	0.2	-0.2	0.6	0.5	-0.2	0.7
Return, Tax-Adjusted (%)	-3.9	2.2	4.5	3.2	4.0	4.9	9.7	4.8	11.9	-3.5
Dividends, Net Income ($)	0.48	0.48	0.49	0.49	0.49	0.49	0.52	0.54	0.55	0.54
Expense Ratio (%)	0.49	0.50	0.51	0.51	0.52	0.52	0.53	0.54	0.55	0.57
Yield (%)	4.59	4.23	4.19	4.16	4.19	4.17	4.38	4.79	4.94	5.11
Total Assets (Millions $)	571	572	525	477	431	416	402	352	307	265

SHAREHOLDER INFORMATION

Minimum Investment
Initial: $2,500 IRA: $1,000
Subsequent: $100 IRA: $50

Maximum Fees
Load: none 12b-1: none
Other: none

USAA VA Bond (USVAX)

800-531-8722
www.usaa.com

Muni: Virginia Bond

PERFORMANCE AND PER SHARE DATA **fund inception date: 10/15/90**

	3yr Annual	5yr Annual	10yr Annual	Category Risk Index
Return (%)	-0.8	1.0	3.1	1.10—high
Differ From Category (+/-)	-1.7 blw av	-0.8 blw av	-0.4 blw av	**Avg Mat** 14.9 yrs

	2008	2007	2006	2005	2004	2003	2002	2001	2000	1999
Return (%)	-7.5	1.0	4.4	2.9	4.4	5.7	9.2	4.2	13.1	-4.6
Differ From Category (+/-)	-4.2	-1.1	0.3	0.3	0.6	0.5	0.1	-0.1	1.0	-0.4
Return, Tax-Adjusted (%)	-7.5	1.0	4.3	2.9	4.4	5.7	9.2	4.2	13.1	-4.6
Dividends, Net Income ($)	0.51	0.49	0.49	0.49	0.50	0.51	0.52	0.57	0.59	0.60
Expense Ratio (%)	0.54	0.58	0.58	0.60	0.61	0.59	0.52	0.43	0.43	0.43
Yield (%)	5.13	4.37	4.24	4.25	4.26	4.32	4.47	5.07	5.24	5.71
Total Assets (Millions $)	485	543	542	531	511	502	504	461	418	371

SHAREHOLDER INFORMATION

Minimum Investment
Initial: $3,000 IRA: na
Subsequent: $50 IRA: na

Maximum Fees
Load: none 12b-1: none
Other: none

WesMark WV Municipal Bond (WMKMX)

800-864-1013
www.wesmarkfunds.com

Muni: West Virginia

PERFORMANCE AND PER SHARE DATA **fund inception date: 4/14/97**

	3yr Annual	5yr Annual	10yr Annual	Category Risk Index	
Return (%)	0.8	1.4	3.0	1.00—high	
Differ From Category (+/-)	0.0 high	0.0 high	0.0 high	Avg Mat	7.9 yrs

	2008	2007	2006	2005	2004	2003	2002	2001	2000	1999
Return (%)	-3.1	2.5	3.2	1.6	2.7	3.5	8.0	4.3	9.9	-1.8
Differ From Category (+/-)	0.0	0.0	0.0	0.0	0.0	0.0	0.0	0.0	0.0	0.0
Return, Tax-Adjusted (%)	-3.1	2.5	3.2	1.6	2.7	3.5	8.0	4.3	9.9	-1.8
Dividends, Net Income ($)	0.35	0.34	0.34	0.32	0.31	0.33	0.40	0.45	0.45	0.44
Expense Ratio (%)	1.14	1.11	1.13	1.03	0.97	0.74	0.30	0.65	0.65	—
Yield (%)	3.61	3.33	3.27	3.05	2.96	3.07	3.75	4.38	4.40	4.48
Total Assets (Millions $)	73	69	71	73	74	75	71	64	63	64

SHAREHOLDER INFORMATION

Minimum Investment
Initial: $1,000 IRA: $500
Subsequent: $100 IRA: $100

Maximum Fees
Load: none 12b-1: none
Other: none

Wells Fargo Advantage WI Tax-Free Inv (SWFRX)

800-222-8222
www.wellsfargofunds.com

Muni: Wisconsin

PERFORMANCE AND PER SHARE DATA **fund inception date: 4/6/01**

	3yr Annual	5yr Annual	10yr Annual	Category Risk Index	
Return (%)	1.9	2.7	na	1.00—high	
Differ From Category (+/-)	0.0 high	0.0 high	na	Avg Mat	5.9 yrs

	2008	2007	2006	2005	2004	2003	2002	2001	2000	1999
Return (%)	-1.8	3.2	4.5	3.3	4.3	5.6	9.9	—	—	—
Differ From Category (+/-)	0.0	0.0	0.0	0.0	0.0	0.0	0.0	—	—	—
Return, Tax-Adjusted (%)	-1.8	3.2	4.4	3.3	4.0	5.5	9.9	—	—	—
Dividends, Net Income ($)	0.38	0.38	0.38	0.40	0.44	0.43	0.47	—	—	—
Expense Ratio (%)	0.75	0.75	0.75	0.51	0.40	0.10	0.10	—	—	—
Yield (%)	3.78	3.59	3.58	3.73	4.08	3.98	4.43	—	—	—
Total Assets (Millions $)	83	75	64	56	49	59	69	—	—	—

SHAREHOLDER INFORMATION

Minimum Investment
Initial: $2,500 IRA: $1,000
Subsequent: $100 IRA: $100

Maximum Fees
Load: none 12b-1: none
Other: none

International Bond: General
Category Performance Ranked by 2008 Returns

Fund (Ticker)	Annual Return (%) 2008	3Yr	5Yr	10Yr	Category Risk	Total Risk
Northern Global Fixed Income (NOIFX)	10.9	8.3	5.0	4.3	av	low
American Century International Bd Inv (BEGBX)	2.4	6.8	4.8	5.0	high	blw av
T. Rowe Price International Bond (RPIBX)	1.7	6.4	4.2	4.3	abv av	blw av
PIMCO Foreign Bond (Unhedged) D (PFBDX)	-4.5	3.7	na	na	high	blw av
International Bond: General Category Average	**-0.5**	**4.0**	**3.4**	**4.4**	**av**	**low**

American Century International Bd Inv (BEGBX)

800-345-2021
www.americancentury.com

International Bond: General

PERFORMANCE AND PER SHARE DATA — **fund inception date: 1/7/92**

	3yr Annual	5yr Annual	10yr Annual	Category Risk Index	
Return (%)	6.8	4.8	5.0	1.30—high	
Differ From Category (+/-)	2.8 high	1.4 abv av	0.6 abv av	**Avg Mat**	na

	2008	2007	2006	2005	2004	2003	2002	2001	2000	1999
Return (%)	2.4	9.8	8.2	-8.3	13.1	19.9	23.5	-1.7	-1.3	-10.4
Differ From Category (+/-)	2.9	2.5	2.7	-5.0	5.2	7.1	8.9	-4.0	-3.9	-6.5
Return, Tax-Adjusted (%)	0.8	8.3	7.4	-9.4	11.5	17.3	22.5	-1.7	-1.8	-12.1
Dividends, Net Income ($)	0.54	0.61	0.31	0.41	0.59	0.85	0.26	0.00	0.11	0.43
Expense Ratio (%)	0.82	0.83	0.82	0.82	0.83	0.84	0.85	0.86	0.87	0.85
Yield (%)	3.73	4.23	2.23	3.08	3.98	6.18	2.09	0.00	1.06	3.98
Total Assets (Millions $)	1,484	1,709	1,315	1,040	973	593	301	116	111	113

SHAREHOLDER INFORMATION

Minimum Investment
Initial: $2,500 IRA: $2,500
Subsequent: $50 IRA: $0

Maximum Fees
Load: none 12b-1: none
Other: none

Northern Global Fixed Income (NOIFX)

800-595-9111
www.northernfunds.com

International Bond: General

PERFORMANCE AND PER SHARE DATA — **fund inception date: 3/31/94**

	3yr Annual	5yr Annual	10yr Annual	Category Risk Index	
Return (%)	8.3	5.0	4.3	1.04—av	
Differ From Category (+/-)	4.3 high	1.6 high	-0.1 abv av	**Avg Mat**	6.3 yrs

	2008	2007	2006	2005	2004	2003	2002	2001	2000	1999
Return (%)	10.9	9.3	4.7	-8.0	9.2	14.5	11.8	2.0	0.3	-8.5
Differ From Category (+/-)	11.4	2.0	-0.8	-4.7	1.3	1.7	-2.8	-0.3	-2.4	-4.6
Return, Tax-Adjusted (%)	9.0	8.2	3.2	-8.7	7.4	12.6	11.0	0.0	0.0	-9.9
Dividends, Net Income ($)	0.60	0.33	0.47	0.24	0.56	0.55	0.21	0.48	0.09	0.41
Expense Ratio (%)	1.15	1.15	1.15	1.16	1.15	1.15	1.15	1.15	1.15	1.15
Yield (%)	5.09	2.94	4.41	2.29	4.82	4.94	2.04	5.10	0.89	4.23
Total Assets (Millions $)	94	45	29	38	39	45	26	28	19	20

SHAREHOLDER INFORMATION

Minimum Investment
Initial: $2,500 IRA: $500
Subsequent: $50 IRA: $50

Maximum Fees
Load: none 12b-1: none
Other: none

PIMCO Foreign Bond (Unhedged) D (PFBDX)

800-426-0107
www.pimco.com

International Bond: General

PERFORMANCE AND PER SHARE DATA **fund inception date: 4/30/04**

	3yr Annual	5yr Annual	10yr Annual	Category Risk Index	
Return (%)	3.7	na	na	1.49—high	
Differ From Category (+/-)	-0.3 abv av	na	na	**Avg Mat**	8.9 yrs

	2008	2007	2006	2005	2004	2003	2002	2001	2000	1999
Return (%)	-4.5	10.0	6.1	-9.5	—	—	—	—	—	—
Differ From Category (+/-)	-4.0	2.7	0.6	-6.2	—	—	—	—	—	—
Return, Tax-Adjusted (%)	-7.2	8.3	5.0	-10.3	—	—	—	—	—	—
Dividends, Net Income ($)	0.40	0.34	0.30	0.25	—	—	—	—	—	—
Expense Ratio (%)	0.95	0.95	0.95	0.95	—	—	—	—	—	—
Yield (%)	4.16	3.11	2.92	2.55	—	—	—	—	—	—
Total Assets (Millions $)	243	143	136	94	—	—	—	—	—	—

SHAREHOLDER INFORMATION

Minimum Investment
Initial: $1,000 IRA: $1,000
Subsequent: $50 IRA: $50

Maximum Fees
Load: 2.00% redemption 12b-1: 0.25%
Other: redemption fee applies for 30 days

T. Rowe Price International Bond (RPIBX)

800-225-5132
www.troweprice.com

International Bond: General

PERFORMANCE AND PER SHARE DATA **fund inception date: 9/10/86**

	3yr Annual	5yr Annual	10yr Annual	Category Risk Index	
Return (%)	6.4	4.2	4.3	1.30—abv av	
Differ From Category (+/-)	2.4 abv av	0.8 abv av	-0.1 av	**Avg Mat**	8.3 yrs

	2008	2007	2006	2005	2004	2003	2002	2001	2000	1999
Return (%)	1.7	10.0	7.5	-8.2	11.4	18.7	21.7	-3.5	-3.2	-7.9
Differ From Category (+/-)	2.2	2.7	2.0	-4.9	3.5	5.9	7.2	-5.8	-5.9	-4.0
Return, Tax-Adjusted (%)	0.0	8.4	6.2	-9.3	9.9	17.0	20.5	-5.0	-4.9	-9.6
Dividends, Net Income ($)	0.37	0.35	0.32	0.26	0.25	0.25	0.25	0.32	0.39	0.38
Expense Ratio (%)	na	0.82	0.84	0.86	0.88	0.91	0.93	0.95	1.15	0.90
Yield (%)	3.74	3.40	3.22	2.76	2.25	2.36	2.71	4.12	4.65	4.12
Total Assets (Millions $)	2,003	2,366	2,030	1,595	1,658	1,303	1,058	762	753	779

SHAREHOLDER INFORMATION

Minimum Investment
Initial: $2,500 IRA: $1,000
Subsequent: $100 IRA: $50

Maximum Fees
Load: 2.00% redemption 12b-1: none
Other: redemption fee applies for 90 days

International Bond: Emerging
Category Performance Ranked by 2008 Returns

Fund (Ticker)	Annual Return (%) 2008	3Yr	5Yr	10Yr	Category Risk	Total Risk
Payden Emerging Markets Bond (PYEMX)	-10.3	0.5	5.1	10.1	blw av	blw av
PIMCO Emerging Markets Bond D (PEMDX)	-14.4	-0.5	4.1	na	av	blw av
PIMCO Developing Local Markets D (PLMDX)	-14.9	2.2	na	na	low	blw av
T. Rowe Price Emerging Markets Bond (PREMX)	-17.8	-1.0	5.5	10.8	abv av	blw av
International Bond: Emerging Category Average	**-16.7**	**-0.6**	**4.3**	**10.5**	**av**	**blw av**

Payden Emerging Markets Bond (PYEMX)

800-572-9336
www.payden.com

International Bond: Emerging

PERFORMANCE AND PER SHARE DATA **fund inception date: 12/17/98**

	3yr Annual	5yr Annual	10yr Annual	Category Risk Index	
Return (%)	0.5	5.1	10.1	0.92—blw av	
Differ From Category (+/-)	1.1 high	0.8 high	-0.4 av	**Avg Mat**	11.8 yrs

	2008	2007	2006	2005	2004	2003	2002	2001	2000	1999
Return (%)	-10.3	2.8	10.0	11.7	13.1	18.3	9.7	13.8	12.4	23.5
Differ From Category (+/-)	6.4	-3.2	-1.4	-1.1	-0.1	-9.2	-1.6	0.2	-0.6	-2.9
Return, Tax-Adjusted (%)	-12.5	0.9	8.1	9.4	10.9	14.1	7.4	9.6	8.2	19.0
Dividends, Net Income ($)	0.80	0.72	0.69	0.78	0.71	0.81	0.68	1.17	1.07	1.01
Expense Ratio (%)	na	0.80	0.80	0.80	0.71	0.86	0.80	0.80	0.80	0.80
Yield (%)	7.24	5.54	5.12	6.06	5.81	6.28	5.85	10.41	9.60	9.05
Total Assets (Millions $)	83	137	88	126	34	58	91	30	55	12

SHAREHOLDER INFORMATION

Minimum Investment
Initial: $5,000 IRA: $2,000
Subsequent: $250 IRA: $250

Maximum Fees
Load: 2.00% redemption 12b-1: none
Other: redemption fee applies for 30 days

PIMCO Developing Local Markets D (PLMDX)

800-426-0107
www.pimco.com

International Bond: Emerging

PERFORMANCE AND PER SHARE DATA **fund inception date: 5/31/05**

	3yr Annual	5yr Annual	10yr Annual	Category Risk Index	
Return (%)	2.2	na	na	0.77—low	
Differ From Category (+/-)	2.8 high	na	na	**Avg Mat**	1.0 yrs

	2008	2007	2006	2005	2004	2003	2002	2001	2000	1999
Return (%)	-14.9	12.7	11.5	—	—	—	—	—	—	—
Differ From Category (+/-)	1.8	6.7	0.1	—	—	—	—	—	—	—
Return, Tax-Adjusted (%)	-16.5	9.7	9.7	—	—	—	—	—	—	—
Dividends, Net Income ($)	0.38	0.48	0.41	—	—	—	—	—	—	—
Expense Ratio (%)	1.25	1.25	1.25	—	—	—	—	—	—	—
Yield (%)	4.36	4.14	3.77	—	—	—	—	—	—	—
Total Assets (Millions $)	376	462	331	—	—	—	—	—	—	—

SHAREHOLDER INFORMATION

Minimum Investment
Initial: $1,000 IRA: $1,000
Subsequent: $50 IRA: $50

Maximum Fees
Load: 2.00% redemption 12b-1: 0.25%
Other: redemption fee applies for 30 days

PIMCO Emerging Markets Bond D (PEMDX)

800-426-0107
www.pimco.com

International Bond: Emerging

PERFORMANCE AND PER SHARE DATA **fund inception date: 3/31/00**

	3yr Annual	5yr Annual	10yr Annual	Category Risk Index
Return (%)	-0.5	4.1	na	0.95—av
Differ From Category (+/-)	0.1 abv av	-0.2 abv av	na	**Avg Mat** 11.4 yrs

	2008	2007	2006	2005	2004	2003	2002	2001	2000	1999
Return (%)	-14.4	5.2	9.3	11.2	11.7	32.0	12.3	27.7	—	—
Differ From Category (+/-)	2.3	-0.8	-2.1	-1.6	-1.5	4.5	1.1	14.1	—	—
Return, Tax-Adjusted (%)	-16.6	2.8	6.8	9.0	9.7	28.2	9.0	22.8	—	—
Dividends, Net Income ($)	0.63	0.60	0.58	0.55	0.44	0.54	0.66	0.78	—	—
Expense Ratio (%)	1.25	1.25	1.25	1.25	1.25	1.25	1.25	1.25	—	—
Yield (%)	7.38	5.42	5.02	4.73	3.91	4.68	6.99	8.14	—	—
Total Assets (Millions $)	232	174	215	245	190	161	33	5	—	—

SHAREHOLDER INFORMATION

Minimum Investment
Initial: $1,000 IRA: $1,000
Subsequent: $50 IRA: $50

Maximum Fees
Load: 2.00% redemption 12b-1: 0.25%
Other: redemption fee applies for 30 days

T. Rowe Price Emerging Markets Bond (PREMX)

800-225-5132
www.troweprice.com

International Bond: Emerging

PERFORMANCE AND PER SHARE DATA **fund inception date: 12/30/94**

	3yr Annual	5yr Annual	10yr Annual	Category Risk Index
Return (%)	-1.0	5.5	10.8	0.98—abv av
Differ From Category (+/-)	-0.4 av	1.2 high	0.3 abv av	**Avg Mat** 12.7 yrs

	2008	2007	2006	2005	2004	2003	2002	2001	2000	1999
Return (%)	-17.8	5.8	11.4	17.2	14.8	26.0	9.5	9.3	15.1	22.9
Differ From Category (+/-)	-1.1	-0.2	0.0	4.4	1.6	-1.5	-1.8	-4.3	2.2	-3.5
Return, Tax-Adjusted (%)	-20.5	3.0	8.6	13.7	12.5	23.5	6.3	5.0	11.1	18.3
Dividends, Net Income ($)	1.03	1.02	0.98	0.97	0.79	0.75	0.85	1.16	1.05	1.08
Expense Ratio (%)	na	0.96	0.98	1.03	1.08	1.10	1.14	1.16	1.21	1.25
Yield (%)	10.12	7.47	6.95	6.68	5.92	6.12	8.13	11.21	9.92	10.71
Total Assets (Millions $)	506	697	618	475	277	252	211	156	164	173

SHAREHOLDER INFORMATION

Minimum Investment
Initial: $2,500 IRA: $1,000
Subsequent: $100 IRA: $50

Maximum Fees
Load: 2.00% redemption 12b-1: none
Other: redemption fee applies for 90 days

Appendix: Index Funds

DOMESTIC STOCK INDEXES

MSCI US Broad Market
Vanguard Total Stock Mkt Idx (VTSMX)

DJ Wilshire 5000
Fidelity Spartan Total Market Index Inv (FSTMX)

DJ Wilshire 4500
Fidelity Spartan Extended Mkt Index Inv (FSEMX)
T. Rowe Price Extended Equity Market Idx (PEXMX)

S&P Completion
Vanguard Extended Market Idx (VEXMX)

S&P 500
Vanguard 500 Index (VFINX)

MSCI US Prime 750
Vanguard Large Cap Index (VLACX)

MSCI US Prime Market Growth
Vanguard Growth Index (VIGRX)

MSCI US Prime Market Value
Vanguard Value Index (VIVAX)

S&P MidCap 400
Dreyfus MidCap Index (PESPX)
Federated Mid-Cap Index (FMDCX)

MSCI US Midcap 450
Vanguard Mid Capitalization Index (VIMSX)

MSCI US Mid Cap Growth
Vanguard Mid-Cap Growth Index Inv (VMGIX)

MSCI US Mid Cap Value
Vanguard Mid-Cap Value Index Inv (VMVIX)

S&P SmallCap 600
Dreyfus Small Cap Stock Index (DISSX)

MSCI US SmallCap 1750
Vanguard Small Cap Index (NAESX)

MSCI US SmallCap Growth
Vanguard Small Cap Growth Index (VISGX)

MSCI US SmallCap Value
Vanguard Small Cap Value Index (VISVX)

Russell 2000
E*TRADE Russell 2000 Index (ETRUX)
Northern Small Cap Index (NSIDX)

CRSP 9-10 Decile
Bridgeway Ultra-Small Company Market (BRSIX)

NASDAQ 100
Rydex Nasdaq-100 Inv (RYOCX)

Morgan Stanley REIT
Vanguard REIT Index (VGSIX)

American Gas Association
FBR Gas Utility Index (GASFX)

FOREIGN STOCK INDEXES

MSCI EAFE / MSCI Emerging Markets Free
Vanguard Total Intl Stock Index (VGTSX)

MSCI EAFE
Fidelity Spartan International Index Inv (FSIIX)
Vanguard Developed Markets Index (VDMIX)

MSCI Europe
Vanguard European Stock Index (VEURX)

MSCI Pacific
Vanguard Pacific Stock Index (VPACX)

MSCI Emerging Markets
Vanguard Emerging Mkts Stock Idx (VEIEX)

BOND INDEXES

Barclays Capital Aggregate Bond
Dreyfus Bond Market Index Basic (DBIRX)
Fidelity U.S. Bond Index (FBIDX)
T. Rowe Price U.S. Bond Index (PBDIX)
Vanguard Total Bond Market Index (VBMFX)

Barclays Capital Short (1-5) Government/Corporate
Schwab Short-Term Bond Market (SWBDX)
Vanguard Short-Term Bond Index (VBISX)

Barclays Capital Intermediate (5-10) Government/Corporate
Vanguard Interm-Term Bond Index (VBIIX)

Barclays Capital Long (10+) Government/Corporate
Vanguard Long-Term Bond Index (VBLTX)

Barclays Capital 1-5 Year Treasury
Fidelity Spartan S/T Tr Bd Idx Inv (FSBIX)

Barclays Capital 5-10 Year Treasury
Fidelity Spartan Interm Tr Bd Idx Inv (FIBIX)

Barclays Capital Long Treasury Bond
Fidelity Spartan L/T Tr Bd Idx Inv (FLBIX)

BALANCED INDEXES

DJ Wilshire 5000 (60%)/Barclays Capital Aggregate Bond (40%)
Vanguard Balanced Index (VBINX)

Index

A

B

C

D

E

F

G

H

I

J

K

L

M

N

O

P

R

S

T

U

V

W